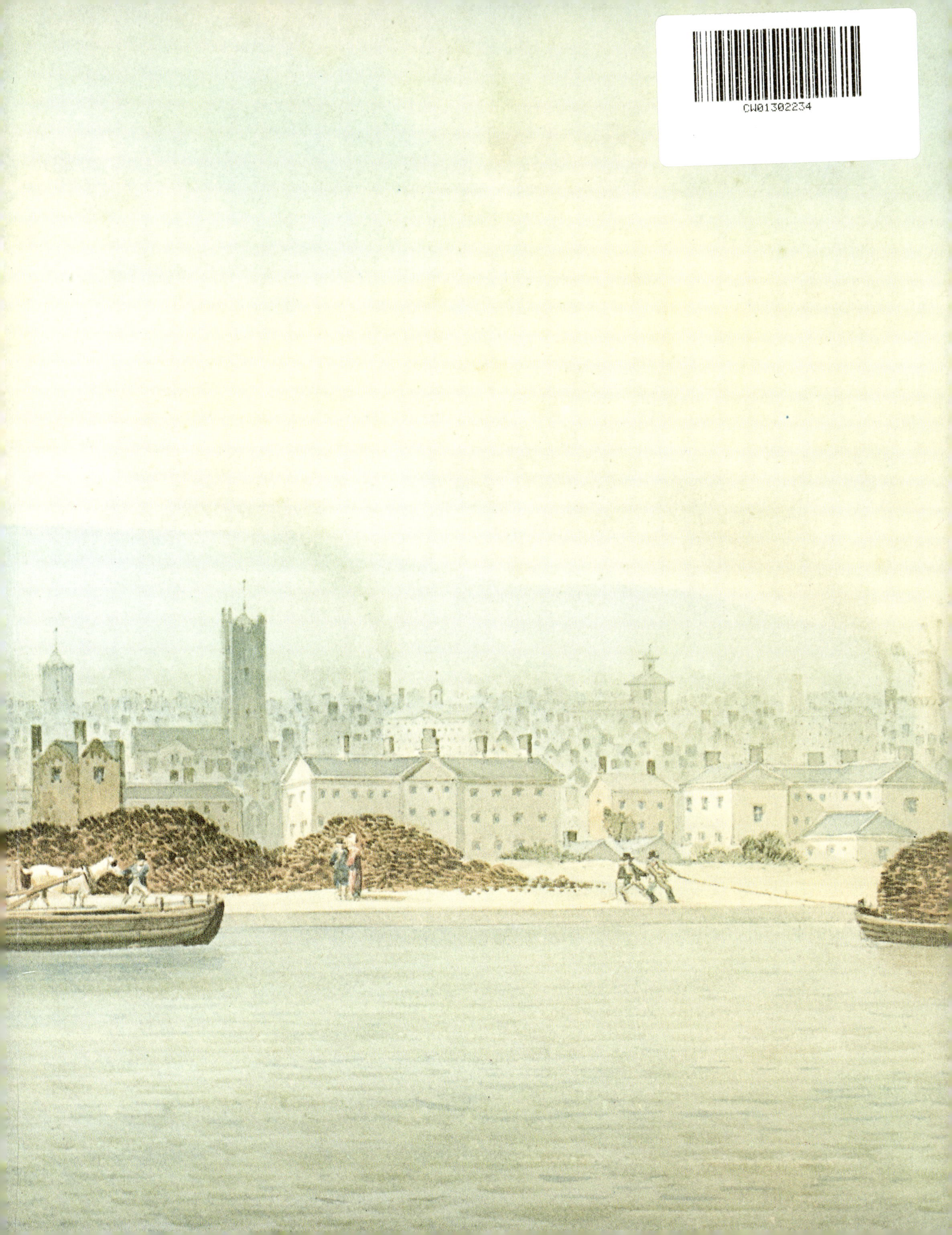

DUBLIN MOVING EAST, 1708–1844

Dublin Moving East, 1708–1844

How the city took over the sea

Michael Branagan

This book is dedicated to Thomas Pearson, who was appointed treasurer to the first committee of the directors of the Ballast Board in 1708. The works instigated by the board spanned 120 years and had a direct and immediate impact on the transformation of the city of Dublin.

First published in 2020
Wordwell Ltd
Unit 9, 78 Furze Road, Sandyford Industrial Estate, Dublin 18
www.wordwellbooks.com

© Copyright text: the author
© Copyright design and layout: Wordwell Ltd

Cover image—Essex Bridge at the beginning of the improvement of the city under the Wide Streets Commission (photo: Brian Matthews, with the kind permission of the NLI).

All rights reserved. No part of this book may be reprinted or reproduced or utilised in any electronic, mechanical or other means, now known or hereafter invented, including photocopying and recording, or otherwise without either the prior written consent of the publishers or a licence permitting restricted copying in Ireland issued by the Irish Copyright Licensing Agency Ltd, The Writers' Centre, 19 Parnell Square, Dublin 1.

ISBN 978-1-9164922-6-4

British Library Cataloguing-in-Publication Data.
A catalogue record for this book is available from the British Library.

Typeset in Ireland by Wordwell Ltd
Copy-editor: Emer Condit
Index: Geraldine Begley
Cover design and artwork: Wordwell Ltd
Printed by Gráficas Castuera, Pamplona

The author and publisher would like to acknowledge the generous financial contribution made by Dublin Port Company to the preparation and publication of this book.

Contents

Foreword	VI
Introduction	VIII
1. Geology and archaeology	1
2. Seventeenth-century context before the Ballast Board Act of 1707	6
3. Embanking of the Liffey and the construction of the Great South Bull Wall	20
4. Building the Grand Canal Docks and taming the Dodder	62
5. The Dublin to Kingstown Railway, including the building of Dunleary Harbour	96
6. North Dublin before the Ballast Act	126
7. Walling of the north bank of the Liffey to 1728 and beyond	129
8. Inside the new enclosure after 1728	136
9. Clustering structures along the north side of the Liffey	151
10. Churches, schools and hospitals on the north side of Dublin	193
11. Gas in Dublin in the nineteenth century	240
12. Howth Harbour	244
13. The Great North Bull Wall	259
14. The Drogheda Railway	277
Bibliography	297
Index	309

Foreword

We readily think of cities like Hamburg, Rotterdam and Antwerp as great port cities. Closer to home, we easily acknowledge the likes of London and Liverpool in a similar manner. When we think of Belfast, its history of shipbuilding immediately comes to mind, and Belfast without its port and docks is unthinkable. But Dublin? How many people think of Dublin as a port city, let alone a great port city?

Michael Branagan's *Dublin moving east: how the city took over the sea* is a welcome and timely reminder of the origins of the modern city of Dublin, and it expertly and lavishly charts the development of the city over some fourteen decades as it expanded eastwards.

As the city grew, more bridges were needed and the ships on which the growing city depended had to berth ever further to the east. As the population increased, trade grew to the point where the city's merchants demanded solutions to the problems of Dublin's poor harbour, with its shallow channel meandering through the sandy estuary of the Liffey and onwards into Dublin Bay.

The starting point for Michael Branagan is the creation of Dublin's first port authority, the Ballast Office, in 1708. The achievements of this authority and its successor in building the Great South Wall and, later, the North Bull Wall set the shape of the city we know today. These sea walls have a combined length of 7.5km and are achievements of marine engineering as impressive as you will find anywhere in Europe.

Unfortunately, the Liffey is not a very impressive river. It is a mere 130km long and, as the crow flies, enters Dublin Bay only 21km from where it rises in the Wicklow Mountains. Dublin's great sea walls made up for nature's shortcomings. They gave Dublin Port the protection that ships needed from the elemental forces of nature and, more particularly, they created the extra depth required to allow the port to support the needs of a growing city.

The eastward movement of the city up to 1844 within the embrace of the two sea walls was accomplished by the canalisation of the Liffey, the making of new land, the construction of the Royal and Grand canals and their docks and, in the early decades of the nineteenth century, the coming of urban gas networks, along with the construction of the Kingstown and Drogheda railways.

The challenges and achievements seen in the development and growth of Dublin City up to 1844 are a precursor to the urban-age challenges Dublin and most other cities around the world face today—problems of energy, transport and densification, with the added constraint of climate change but with digitalisation as a powerful enabler.

In the late nineteenth century and through the twentieth century the port continued its eastward journey to its present location on made land protruding into Dublin Bay. As this occurred, the port became nearly invisible to the city and the citizens it served. In recent years, the infilling of the industrial void between the city and the port has created the new docklands, a shining hub of multinational commerce and high tech, if not of dense residential settlement.

The development of Dublin over the period from 1708 to 1844 was, as this book expertly records, an achievement at least equal to, if not greater than, the more recent Celtic Tiger boom. The recording of this earlier period is important not just in academic terms but also as a reminder of where we have come from as we confront the urban challenges of today.

In 1985 Frank McDonald's *The destruction of Dublin* recounted the fate of much of Georgian Dublin in the 1960s and 1970s. The same forces that so changed Dublin 50 years ago are still there, and Dublin Port is today covetously eyed as the next Klondike for developers.

Michael Branagan has done us a great service by making the history of the eastward development of the city accessible, particularly through the illustrations of his expert text with charts, maps, paintings and drawings, alongside contemporary photographs of important remnants of Georgian and early Victorian Dublin. By understanding the past eastward development of Dublin over the formative decades to 1844, we can better plan the development of the city in the years ahead.

Although many port cities face similar challenges and share certain characteristics, each is unique. Dublin's solutions to its challenges are Dublin's alone, and Michael Branagan's book shows us how we rose to these challenges 200 years ago. It deserves to be read in detail to remind us of how Dublin's city and port developed to what they are today, so that as we plan the future of our great port city to meet the needs of future generations we do so in a way that might be just as lovingly recorded many years from now.

Eamonn O'Reilly
Chief Executive
Dublin Port Company

Introduction

St Patrick said this town will be prophetical; although small and miserable, it will be a large town in time to come. It will be told and spoken of far and near, and will be increasing until it is the chief town in the kingdom.

There is an idea current in Dublin that the city experienced massive change, expansion and a building boom like no other during the so-called 'Celtic Tiger' era, and the number of cranes on the skyline was often cited as a barometer of this growth. This is neither a true nor an accurate picture. In the thousand years of Dublin history no period of expansion comes anywhere near that of 1708–1844, when the city more than doubled in size. Our objective here is to evaluate that period in terms of what took place. All of this activity was triggered and driven by the actions of the port authorities known as the Ballast Board and later, after 1786, as the Corporation for Preserving and Improving the Port of Dublin.

The old walled town of Dublin was located upriver, mainly west of Capel Street Bridge on both sides of the river. The river walls outside the medieval town were completed in 1728, and over the following 120 years the city grew in the newly enclosed space and beyond to contain about 250,000 people. It would expand down the river for a distance of over 2km and occupy an area measuring 2–2.5km from north to south. It would also increase in size through the creation of a series of new suburbs along the edges (both interior and exterior) of the river walls on the Liffey, Dodder and Tolka. This book will look at what happened south of the Liffey in the strip 1.5km long by 400m wide after the walls were erected in 1728 downriver and round into the mouth of the Dodder. On the north side it will look at the growth towards the north and east after the Liffey and Tolka walls were built, originating around the Capel Street area. Much of the area to the east was tidal estuary, aside from some patches of higher ground; this large triangle of space was to be walled in and then reclaimed from the sea and built on. The ground as it sloped upwards was taken from greenfield terrain above the water-line, which was quite fluid. This area became the new, primarily Georgian city. The growth after 1800 became Victorian, reflecting all the changes that took place in the first four decades of the nineteenth century.

On the south side of the newly walled river the ground was drained and used in turn as farmland, oyster-beds, dwellings, streets, factories, yards, warehouses and stores. The old road up from Ringsend to Townsend Street became Great Brunswick Street (later Pearse Street). Subsequent to the river walls, the South Bull Wall (which took 100 years to complete) was erected, and this was followed by the digging out of the Grand Canal Docks and the embankment of the River Dodder. All this activity joined the Ringsend spit to the city and created 200 acres of new ground. As the eighteenth century drew to a close, the needs of the port of Dublin once more triggered great activity.

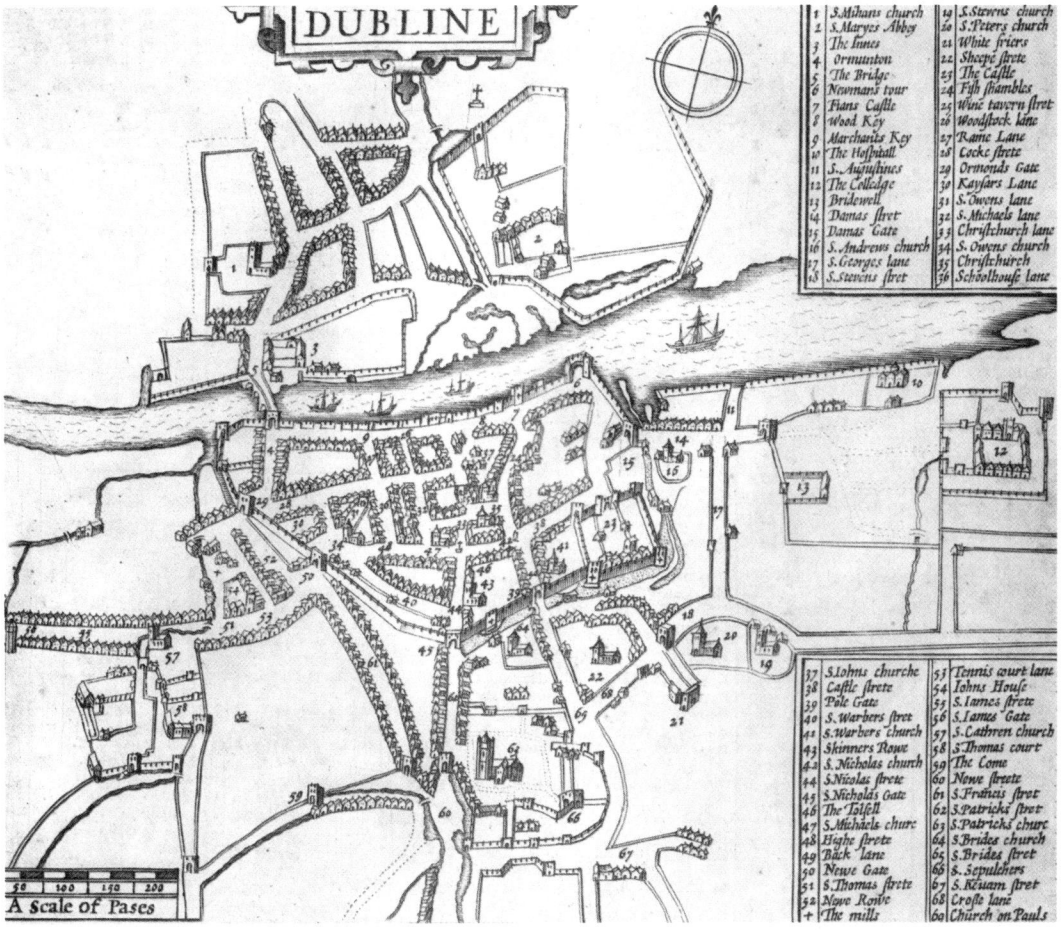

Fig. 1.1—John Speed's 1610 map of Dublin, before the construction of the river walls and the subsequent development (photo: Brian Matthews).

After Howth Harbour—considered a commercial and marine failure—lost the mail contract, emphasis moved across to Kingstown (Dún Laoghaire), where a new harbour was completed, along with the first Irish railway, from Kingstown to Dublin. Both of these works had an enormous impact on the city, entailing the creation of new suburbs from Sandymount and Ballsbridge all the way out to Kingstown, along the coastal strip at first. After the opening of the railway the strip along the Liffey underwent more change and development, as the city expanded eastwards along Pearse Street all the way to Ringsend and Irishtown.

Over on the north side, the enclosed area of the newly walled Liffey and along the Tolka to Ballybough Bridge offered great possibilities—a vast space, measured in square kilometres rather than metres, now claimed back from the tides. Immediately the space behind the walls began to be drained and built on in the Capel Street zone, and the walls were consistently reinforced and banked and faced with stone. Development crept up Capel Street and Bolton Street, out along Henry Street, Liffey Street, Moore Street and Parnell Street. Within 25 years occupation and building had moved past O'Connell Street in an easterly direction into Marlborough Street and its surrounds.

In the last quarter of the eighteenth century a series of large structures and complexes were built along the river-bank, creating a further inner border: the Four Courts, Carlisle Bridge, the

Custom House, Aldeborough House, Annesley Bridge and the Royal Canal, preceded by both the Rotunda Hospital and Tyrone House in being built in this new city space, mainly taken from the tide. These structures created social and commercial clusters which pioneered further development. The new century brought a move to Howth Harbour for the packet-boats because of military requirements based on security reasons. While the construction was under way, the Corporation for Preserving and Improving the Port of Dublin (which took over from the Ballast Board in 1786 as the authority for the port) began to build the North Bull Wall out at Clontarf; it was finished in 1824, at last enclosing the harbour while finally removing the dreaded bar at the mouth of the Liffey, combining dredging with the scouring effect of ebb tide and river outflow. The supply of water and, later, gas across this new city will be evaluated, along with the filling of the entire area with schools, hospitals and churches in response to the changes in politics, religion and technology. The story concludes with the building of the Drogheda Railway across the tidal strand north of Clontarf Island, enclosing even more space for human occupation out to and beyond Clontarf. Each of these major construction projects had an immediate and cumulative effect on the topography of this newly enclosed space and beyond, boosting the growth of new suburbs on both sides of the city.

It would be easy just to produce two maps—a 'before' and an 'after'—to illustrate the point, but that would not present any real understanding of what took place. The sources to document and prove the story will comprise three separate types. (i) Visual sources include paintings, sketches, diagrams and blueprints, estate maps, city and civilian surveyor maps, Wide Street Commission maps, road maps, railway maps, marine and harbour charts, nautical and hydrography charts, naval charts, old seventeenth-century maps of Dublin Bay, and technical drawings and plans from both architects and engineers. (ii) Documentary sources include the *Calendar of ancient records of Dublin*, travellers' and visitors' accounts of visits to Dublin from the 1600s to 1845, letters, diaries, parliamentary papers, minute-books of the Grand Canal Company, ledgers of the Dublin Port Company, almanacs and directories for the city in the period, newspapers, church records of major religions operating in Dublin, education records and medical records, estate papers and letters, records of deeds and leases, and many theses presented both at home and abroad as far back as the early twentieth century, as well as statistical information on a variety of subjects. (iii) Much information will come from the physical environment as it still exists today in the form of bridges, harbours, houses, quay walls, stores, military establishments, churches, railway embankments, docks, locks, ground levels, ramps, water storage basins, streets and public buildings, and the different levels to be seen in the topography of the city. All of these will contribute to the story as it unfolds. Madrid, Lisbon, Liverpool, London, Belfast, Amsterdam, Galway, Cork and Armagh were visited as part of the research. The story begins with the geology and the archaeology, both of which were vital ingredients in the development and had an important bearing on decisions taken along the way.

1. Geology and archaeology

Geology

The origins of the story lie in the geology, since it had a direct connection to the pace and spread of development on the ground as well as providing the raw material for so much of the infrastructure we still see today. The geology will continue to be relevant as matters unfold, along with the archaeological excavations which took place in the area. It comprises both the underlying rock and the sedimentary deposits on top of this rock. This stone has been used for building throughout the city, from railway bridges and embankments to houses and churches as far back as Christ Church Cathedral, for example, and the sedimentary deposits continue to be exposed in the archaeological activity today. Geological evidence is plentiful thanks to the extensive research carried out by the Geological Survey of Ireland (Fig. 1.2).

The world of commerce, too, is interested in geology and archaeology. The two go hand in hand because the height and size of buildings and the consequent weight of structures now require the drilling of boreholes for foundations supporting large structures. Ever since the contentious excavations at Wood Quay there has been a more welcoming attitude towards archaeology and its positive contribution is better appreciated. The geology also takes in the sedimentary deposits along the Liffey Basin and would have a bearing on works undertaken in the harbour in the early nineteenth century, specifically the North Bull Wall in the 1820s. The depth of sedimentary deposits played a crucial part in the choice of location for the North Bull Wall.

Dublin Bay is a very wide-mouthed bay, horseshoe-shaped, with the ends or headlands bent backwards, which can be problematic for ships in terms of weather. This was especially true for sailing-ships in the seventeenth and eighteenth centuries. It is also shallow and shelving, which meant that the tide went out literally for miles, exposing a vast area of sand and draining channels. Consequently, ships had to go even further out to reach water deep enough for safe anchorage. The lower estuary is fed by the Liffey, which is joined by the Tolka from the northern shore and the Dodder from the southern shore. The balance is geographically maintained by the existence of the Ringsend spit just below the exit of the Dodder into the estuary. The spit was a bar of gravel and sand formed from a raised beach, barely joined to the land opposite the Londonbridge Bridge over the Dodder and vulnerable to very high tides. Indeed, it was often overcome and cut off before the construction of a substantial stone bridge in the early nineteenth century. Over on the north side, near the present Port Tunnel exit, was Clontarf Island, which had been formed by the build-up of sand and sediment over millions of years. The gravel content was identified and confirmed in both the Tolka and Dodder rivers by Naylor in 1965.[1]

Farrell and Wall (see note 1) illustrated a contour line of 5m above sea level, corresponding to roughly the same track as the alluvial/sedimentary deposits in the area. The two exceptions are the

Dublin moving east, 1708–1844

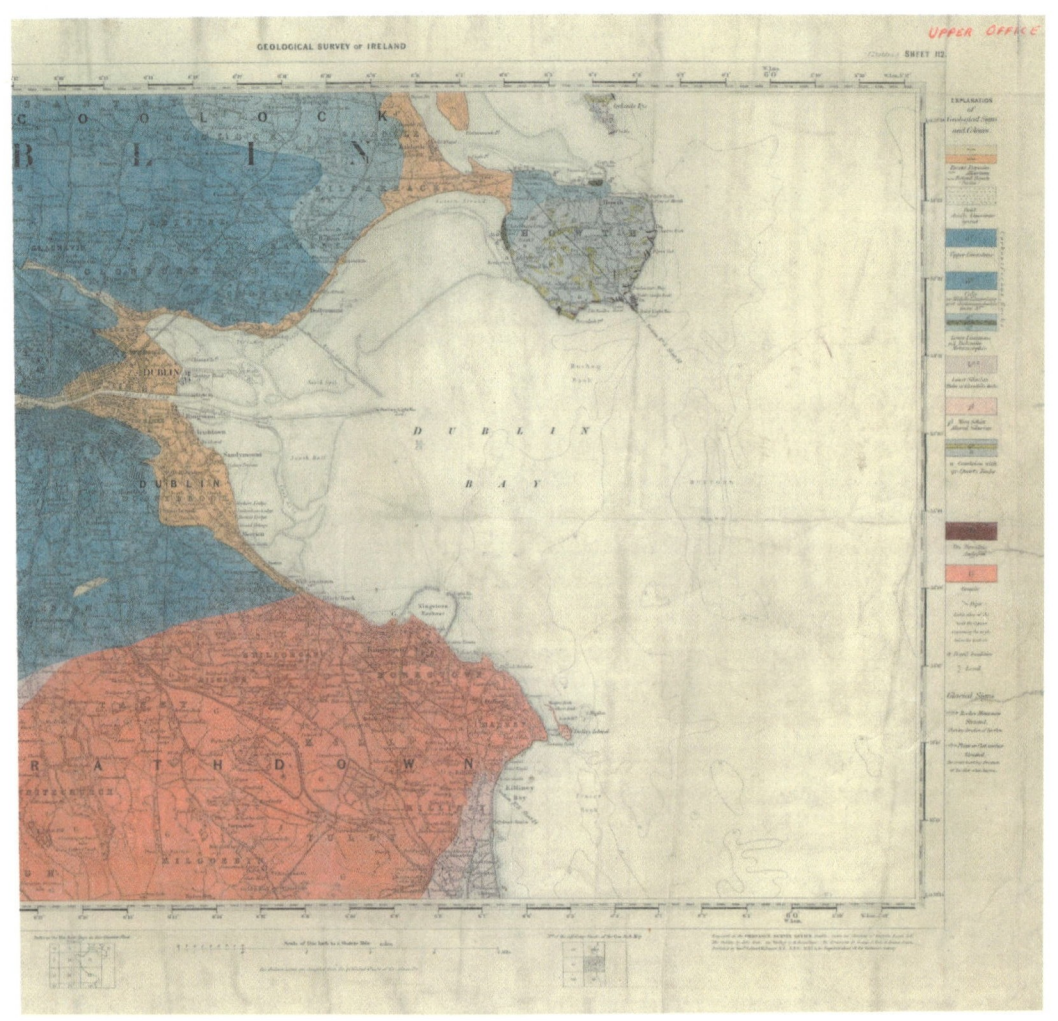

Fig. 1.2—Geological map of the city in the nineteenth century, showing the geological make-up of the city, mainly calp limestone (courtesy of Les Fox, Geological Survey of Ireland).

ground level around Connolly Station at Amiens Street, with the raised embankment along the railway to Clontarf including the raised land mass at Fairview Park, and the similar raised platform at Westland Row and its embankment out to Lansdowne Road. The contour lines show both the gradient and the higher ground in the city, where building first took place prior to the development that occurred on reclaimed land.

The bedrock of Dublin Bay is calp limestone. Formed as far back as 360 million years ago as Carboniferous limestone, calp is seen throughout the city today in a wide variety of structures. Its distinctive dark blue/black colour is particularly striking when wet, just as granite, too, takes on a striking appearance when wet as its silica particles glisten and sparkle. The term 'calp' was coined by Richard Kirwan in 1794 to describe the dark Carboniferous limestone of the Dublin district.[2] Calp has been quarried in Clontarf at Clontarf Golf Club, outside Skerries at Milverton quarry, in Howth at Corr Bridge and at Glasnevin, among several other sites.

When the foundations for the Jervis Street shopping centre were being dug in the 1980s, Long and Murphy reported on the difficulties of ground anchorages in hard rock.[3] The 443 boreholes

Geology and archaeology

that were drilled out gave valuable data about depths of material down to the limestone below. They showed that the first 2.6–3.7m below the surface consisted of made or reclaimed ground. Below the made ground was 1.7–3m of gravel, and in some cores boulder clay below that. This indicates why the walls were constructed to a height of 4–5m above the high-water mark along the river and agrees with the documentary evidence. During excavation of the Jervis Centre the tide seeped into the foundations, providing further proof that this area was tidal. To this day, some of the houses on the north quays east of Capel Street Bridge still absorb water in their cellars at high tide. Indeed, in the eighteenth century Edmund Burke himself alluded to the same problem. The tide also affected the basement of Jervis Street Hospital, according to one person who worked there,[4] and the cellar of the North Star Hotel in Amiens Street some 50 years ago suffered from tide seepage all of 250m inside the north wall of the Liffey.[5] The Jervis Centre site is especially relevant to this book because it was carried out on the edge of medieval Dublin, as evidenced by Speed's map of 1610 as well as other primary documentary sources.

Archaeology

The available archaeological evidence confirms the topography of Dublin Bay, thanks to the work of Melanie McQuade, among others. Archaeologists have been working up and down both sides of the Liffey in this area east of the Viking settlements for decades now. They have never unearthed anything earlier than the eighteenth century because there was nothing there except tidal sands. There is one important exception, however: when McQuade carried out three phases of excavation at Spencer Dock in 2004, she discovered a number of fish-traps inside and below the north wall of the Liffey, 7m below sea level, down in the phase 1 sediment. In phase 2, in the same reclaimed

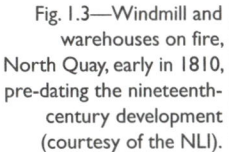

Fig. 1.3—Windmill and warehouses on fire, North Quay, early in 1810, pre-dating the nineteenth-century development (courtesy of the NLI).

Dublin moving east, 1708–1844

Fig. 1.4—View of the Convention Centre, North Quay, which was the site of the windmill and the fish-trap excavations (photo: Brian Matthews).

ground, she came across items dated to the eighteenth and nineteenth centuries but nothing earlier. In phase 3 she unearthed the remains of a circular masonry structure, and its location—again on reclaimed ground—corresponded to the site of a windmill that burned down in 1810. This windmill features in several sketches and drawings of the time (Figs 1.3 and 1.4).

It can therefore be assumed that sediment continued pouring down the river, along with the other deposits of material, and covered the trap to this depth. The depth of 7m gives a clear picture of the amount of sediment continually deposited by the river and tides. The fish-traps were radiocarbon-dated to 6070–5920 BC, or halfway back to the Ice Age. McQuade clearly states that there was no evidence of any settlement down here on the north wall quay. Her finds are conclusive that people were placing baskets and traps and using the ebb and flow of the tide to catch fish. This method of fishing continues to be used today across various parts of the world. The people who set the traps would have lived locally, more than likely at Summerhill, as can be seen in the 5m contour map from the Irish Geological Survey. McQuade discovered that a Mesolithic shoreline existed 30m north of the present quay wall. The fish-traps long pre-date Newgrange, a popular date benchmark here in Ireland.[6] McQuade also excavated on the other side of the Liffey at George's Quay and Sir John Rogerson's Quay and found nothing earlier than the eighteenth century.[7] The conclusion, therefore, is that there was nothing down here in this estuary until man began his activities in the early eighteenth century.

Notes

[1] Eric Farrell and Denis Wall, 'Soils of Dublin', a paper presented to a joint meeting of the Structures and Construction Section, the Geotechnical Society of Ireland and the Institution of Structural Engineers, Republic of Ireland branch, on 10 October 1990.
[2] T.R. Marchant and G.D. Sevastopulo, 'The calp of the Dublin district', *Irish Journal of Earth Sciences* **3** (2) (1980), 195.
[3] M. Long and B. Murphy, *Difficulty with ground anchorages in hard rock in Dublin* (http:dx.doi.org/10.1023/A:1023584813392; accessed 4/1/2016), p. 4.
[4] Joe Phelan, laboratory technician at Jervis Street Hospital, related his personal experience during the 1960s to the writer.
[5] Information from Captain Peter McKenna, a regular visitor to the hotel in the 1960s.
[6] Melanie McQuade, 'Archaeology at Spencer Dock, North Quays, Dublin, June to September 2004', licence no. 03E0654, excavation no. 2004:0565, 2007. Margaret Gowan and Co., Dublin Archaeological Archive, 25/9/2009.
[7] Melanie McQuade, 'George's Quay to Sir John Rogerson's Quay', *Excavations.ie*, site no. 2010:263.

2. Seventeenth-century context before the Ballast Board Act of 1707

The city in the seventeenth century
The primary stimulus to urban development during the first half of the seventeenth century was the location in Dublin of the central government. Significant administrative measures adopted early in the century increased the effectiveness of central government, which gradually imposed unity on the country and allowed for population growth. As the number of people involved in central government and administration increased, so did the demand for residential building in Dublin, influencing the morphological development of the city over the following two centuries. This is the argument proposed by Nuala Burke,[1] who maintained that another factor in the urbanisation of Dublin in the seventeenth century was the power and authority held by the various viceroys after Thomas Wentworth who were increasingly independent of the established administration in the Castle.

In 1600 there was only one parish on the north bank of the Liffey, whereas there were twelve to the south of it. Thomas Jordan maintained that seventeenth-century Dublin 'occupied the south bank of the river Liffey' and that the subsequent development of the area around St Michan's and Oxmantown and new quays opened up traffic and trade on that side.[2] The earl of Drogheda owned much of the land on the north side. After the restoration of Charles II the Drogheda estate planned much of the development.[3] In fig. 22 of her thesis Nuala Burke showed the extent of the Gardiner estate, the other major landowner in the area, whose border lay south of the Tolka, extending to the east just past Ballybough Bridge and running to the west almost as far as Glasnevin Road and west of Dorset Street. She maintained that Gardiner was the most extensive landholder on the North Lotts by 1734.

An indication of the development time-line of the city can be seen in the issuing by William Jervis of a lease on premises at Capel Street and the corner of Abbey Street to Thomas Plansante on 1 December 1682,[4] suggesting that by this stage this patch of ground outside the old town walls was sufficiently stabilised.

In their recent collection on the city, Gillian O'Brien and Finola O'Kane observe that 'The term landscape acknowledges the role of a topographical way of seeing a culturally configured nature and related paradigms in the history of ideas to advance a portrait of the city which tries to frame not only the physical place of the city but also the cultural, historic, artistic and intellectual landscape that the city itself redraws over and over again'.[5] They also maintain that 'visual sources are in the minority when compared with documentary sources, and the bias painter, client and subscriber have on point of view renders them frequently suspect'; nevertheless, 'landscape is a profoundly visual concept and the concept of historic urban landscape now current in conservation thought an intensely visual manner of assessment'. They further add that Dublin's awareness and knowledge of her own portrait is weak.[6] I would contend that there is in fact plenty of visual material; it is just not all conveniently in the form of paintings. Much is in the form of buildings, maps, charts, estate maps, diagrams, architectural drawings and sketch-books. This work will look at the present landscape to interpret the past, through the deployment of visual and documentary sources. As Patrick Duffy said, 'The study of landscape in many cases is the primary source of investigation either directly in the field or amplified by a wide range of documentary sources such as surveys and maps as well as artistic records'.[7] In addition, of course, some structures, such as bridges and houses, bear date-stones marked with the year of construction.

The seventeenth century was a period of turbulence in both England and Ireland, with constant political change, famine and general instability, and the ever-present fear of plague. There was almost continuous external war to contend with, mainly with the Dutch, as well as aggressive commercial activity involving privateers (in reality government-sanctioned pirates). Civil war in the reign of Charles I was followed by Cromwell's Protectorate, which gave way in turn to the settled period of the rule of Charles II, who died in 1685. His brother, James II, succeeded to the throne but his reign lasted only three years. James, a Catholic, favoured religious toleration but was overthrown by the Protestant 'Glorious Revolution' which invited Prince William of Orange to take the throne. William's victory brought stability to the kingdom at last, allowing decisions to be taken and plans to be carried out.

In Ireland there was not only the continuous encouragement of settlement of Protestant planters—adding to the constant tension between the Catholic and Protestant assemblymen in the corporation—but also the real military threat of an actual uprising, against a backdrop of land seizures. The rebellion of 1641 left a long and virulent legacy. The mid-century entrance of Cromwell on the scene added yet another stress factor. Politically, matters did settle somewhat after the restoration of Charles II and the arrival of his viceroy, the duke of Ormonde. Between them they brought 25 years of near calm from 1660 to 1685. The ascension of King James II and the activities of his lord deputy, the earl of Tyrconnell, upset that calm, bringing uncertainty to the Protestant population of Dublin. As Simms said, 'Flight and fear were to be their experience until deliverance arrived'.[8]

At the end of the century stability finally came to England with the arrival on the throne of Prince William of Orange and the establishment of Protestantism as the dominant and State religion in 1688. The moment in history is perfectly caught by a painting on display in the Rijksmuseum in Amsterdam, showing William's ship, the *Brielle*, flying an enormous flag on the stern bearing the words 'For freedom and religion'.[9] William followed the calming of England with the pacification of Ireland by 1691.

If we understand the continued impact of the Famine on the Irish psyche 170 years after the event, we can appreciate the psychological effect of the great seventeenth-century religious and political upheavals which framed attitudes and opinions for the next 200 years. In the seventeenth century the two great questions of politics and religion which affected Europe remained to be settled. Until that settlement was achieved matters remained turbulent, making many civic and political decisions too difficult to implement. We will examine the situation both in England and in Ireland and then more specifically in Dublin between 1603 and 1691.

War, invasion and rebellion

War was waged almost continuously during the seventeenth century, much of it between England and Holland, as England attempted to catch up with Dutch naval power. The Dutch reigned supreme in shipping, navigation and trade with the East Indies. English ships were constantly patrolling the seas off Ireland to bolster their claim of sovereignty. Merchant and fishing vessels suffered from the attentions of Spanish and French privateers, who used the Anglo-French and Anglo-Spanish wars of the 1620s as an excuse to plunder. In 1627 the French 'Dunkirkers', as they were called, invaded as far north as the Shetland Islands, 'putting people to the sword'.[10] In 1667 the Dutch invaded the Medway River off the Thames, within sight of London, and destroyed the greater part of the English fleet.[11] Yet only nine years after this event the Dutch city of Amsterdam presented King Charles II with a yacht, the *Mary*, which was subsequently wrecked off the Isle of Anglesey on its passage home from Ireland.

The English Civil War overlapped with the Irish rebellion of 1641 and both gave rise to much mythology. The rebellion had broken out in the southern half of Ireland in 1641, before the outbreak

Fig. 2.1—Persecution in Ireland *c.* 1651. The painting depicts savage butchery as being as universal in Ireland as everywhere else (courtesy of Louise Morgan and Brendan Maher, NGI).

of Civil War in England in 1642. The mass drowning by Catholics of Protestants at Lurgan became an infamous episode which was greatly propagandised by the Protestant side. At Silvermines, Co. Tipperary, Irish rebels stripped and beat to death a group of twenty Protestants. It did not matter whether the events were wildly exaggerated: they were believed to be true. There is no doubt that the 1642 Depositions (the subject of an exhibition in the Long Room at Trinity College Dublin in 2012) and accounts of the events published at the time had a frightening effect on the populace (Fig. 2.1).

In 1644, 70 men and two women were taken from their own ship, tied together and thrown overboard on the orders of Captain Swanley, an act for which he appeared before Parliament and was presented with a £200 gold chain.[12] Swanley acted in accordance with parliamentary law and with the approval of the contemporary press.[13] *Mercurius Britanicus* wrote: 'It was just to cast them in to the sea and wash them to death from the blood of Protestants that was upon them'. *The Spie* reported that 'Salt water was a very convenient drench to cur those barbarous wretches which had taken a surfeit of Protestant blood in Ireland'.[14] Cromwell, of course, is said to have left not one single person alive in the sack of Drogheda—this after he is supposed to have landed 15,000 troops with baggage train, supplies, cannon and horses at Ringsend just beforehand, an event which would have required all ships, men, horses and train to arrive at precisely the same time and carefully go ashore and assemble, tightly packed, on the sandbank. Propaganda reigned and accuracy certainly suffered, as in many cases rumour fuelled public opinion.

Into the political mix we must also add the lingering effects of Guy Fawkes and the 'gunpowder plot' to blow up Parliament, which would have terrified the populace of London. This was and still is viewed as a Catholic conspiracy, made worse by the perceived involvement of the Jesuits. The defeat of this plot is still celebrated today, 400 years later.

As the English strove to control matters on both sides of the Irish Sea with patrols, trade was much affected by boarding and seizures. Vessels from all over were chased down on suspicion of supporting the Irish rebels. The English had not forgotten the attempted Spanish invasion. Butchery became the norm everywhere. The London authorities lost control of the ports of Dublin, Kinsale, Youghal and Duncannon, leaving Milford Haven in Wales as the base for operations to guard the Irish coast.

Another important aspect of the situation in the 1600s was that the English ships possessed none of their own naval charts, leaving them open to sabotage through the use of captured or purchased charts, mainly Dutch. In 1681 Sir Samuel Pepys, then secretary to the Admiralty, appointed Captain Grenville Collins 'to make a survey of the coasts of the kingdom', which was complete by 1693. His pilot book on the coasts, a companion to his map, can be found in the Early Printed Books collection at TCD.[15]

Plague and natural disaster
Coming hard on the heels of the Great Plague of 1665, which decimated the population of London, the Great Fire of 1666 destroyed 400 acres of the city, leaving over 100,000 homeless. London suffered from plague several times during the 1600s.[16] John Gaunt wrote in 1665 that 'There have been in London within this age, four times of great mortality', that is to say the years 1592, 1593, 1603, 1625 and 1626.[17] Famine, too, was present in Scotland and in northern England in the last quarter of the century.

Word of each outbreak of plague in England spread to Dublin and beyond. As early as 1575 Sir

Fig. 2.2—Clontarf Island, showing its separation from the mainland, 1812 (photo: Brian Matthews, with the kind permission of the NLI).

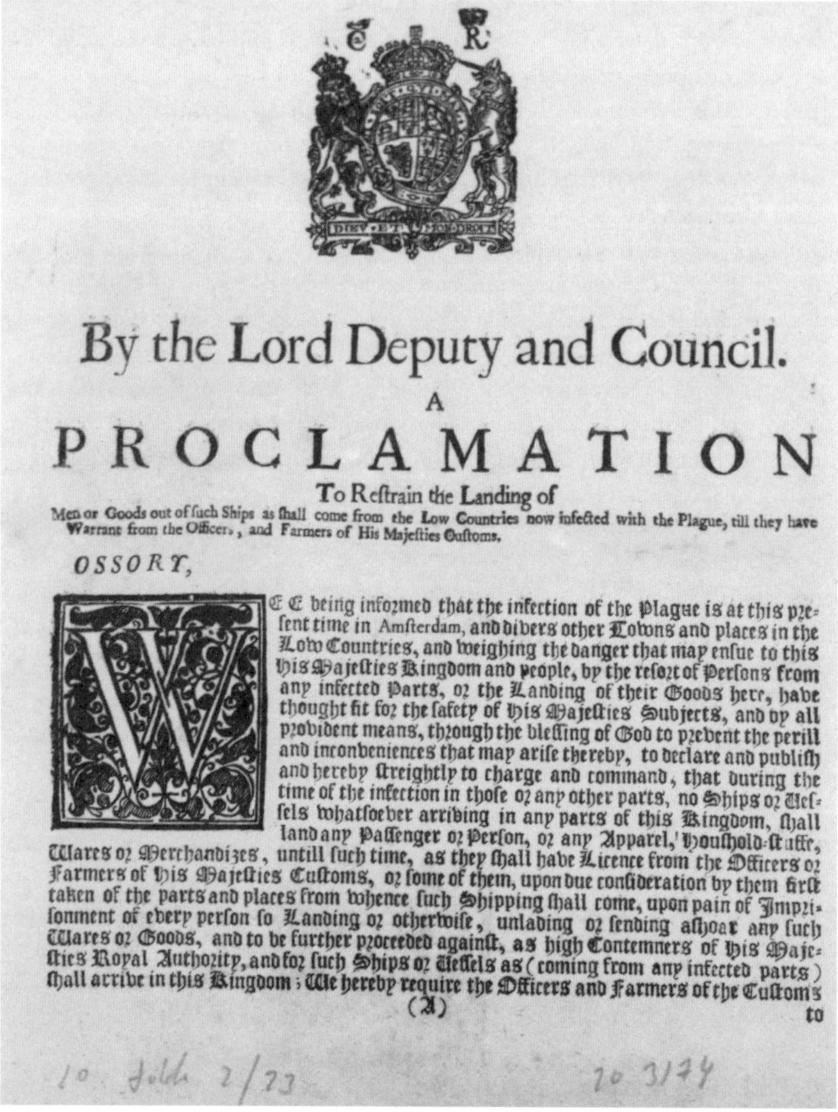

Fig. 2.3—Proclamation and warnings on shipping (photo: Brian Matthews, with the kind permission of the NLI).

Henry Sydney, sent as lord deputy by Queen Elizabeth I, landed at Skerries owing to plague in Dublin and held his court at Drogheda. A house in Georges Street was bought for use as an isolation hospital, and access was strictly controlled. The city also operated a quarantine station on Clontarf Island, then well outside the city in tidal waters, and both passengers and crew were only allowed ashore after a period of isolation (Figs 2.2 and 2.3).

Plague inspired such terror because of the speed of contagion, which owed much to dirt, bad living conditions, the close proximity of animals (including vermin), poor diet and filthy water. Smallpox—a disease always present in society in the period—was also a major killer. Peter Razzell claimed that 20% of all deaths were due to the disease. A form of inoculation was tried successfully on prisoners in Cork gaol. Elsewhere it was not always as successful: in Donegal 51 children out of 52 died after inoculation.

In 1650 a very serious famine wreaked havoc on the country, sending people *en masse* to the city and causing further disruption and alarm there.

Piracy and smuggling

Piracy and smuggling were major problems for the authorities. Sacking and kidnapping occurred, as evidenced in the sack of Baltimore by Algerians and cattle-rustling raids on the Saltee Islands by French privateers, besides the kidnapping of a man called Boxall.[18] Charles Cosslett, too, recorded cattle raids conducted from a French sloop of war in 1793 off the Antrim coast.[19] Smuggling was an ever-present headache for the government in terms of loss of revenue and legal compliance. Maighread Ni Mhurchadha said that the story of increased smuggling in the eighteenth century, principally involving the Isle of Man, led to bigger vessels and more revenue stations at Baldoyle, Malahide, Skerries, Howth, Sutton and Clontarf. Violence was often involved, with many attacks on the revenue men and cutters.[20] Isaac Butler, in his wanderings around County Dublin in 1744, described the men of Rush as being employed in both fishing and smuggling: 'the very time I came there when the officers of the revenue seized a quantity of brandy, tobacco, tea and Canary wine to the amount upwards of £250 which they drove in carts to Dublin'.[21] The problem of both piracy and smuggling would be finally dealt with thanks to the arrival of steam vessels, which gave the Revenue Service and the Coast Guard the upper hand.

Political instability

The automatic suspicion and distrust of Catholics aroused by the attempt to blow up Parliament in London were intensified in Ireland, where Catholics were in the majority, and native citizens became accustomed to slipping away from the city during times of higher tension.

Some of the soldiers who came to Ireland in the wake of England's Irish wars settled in Dublin. These included John Vernon, who received lands at Clontarf, and Sir Humphrey Jervis, who developed and built around Capel Street. The city received an influx of Huguenots in 1680–1, one of a number of such groups to boost the Protestant population of the city. J.G. Simms claimed that some 35,000 migrants arrived in Dublin between 1662 and 1687. Jordan wrote that in the latter decades of the 1600s Dublin had become a largely English and Anglican town. Another group that settled were Quakers from Yorkshire, who developed the woollen industry in the Coombe area of the south city.

Land ownership had already begun to change on a large scale after the 1641 rebellion; according to John Woodhouse, 'Two and a half million acres may be assigned, allotted, and divided amongst them after this proposition'.

Sir Paul Rycut, secretary to the lord lieutenant, wrote to London in 1686 that 'The great care of my Lord Lieutenant is to keep all the people in quietness'. Tension was high at the time; Rycut noted 'scuffles between new Irish soldiers and the rabble of the city', and 'meantime fears and rumours in these matters cause great disturbances in the minds of people so that all trade is at a stand'. He reported that 'The Irish talk of nothing but recovering their lands and bringing the English under their subjugation'. A Reverend Verdon confirmed the attitude towards the Irish that prevailed in 1699: 'They beg all summer, thousands of them are constantly in Dublin for they are naturally lazy and that cannot work and so roguish that nobody dare employ them'.

Ireland was seen as a colony that needed to be strictly controlled. The question was how to deal with a majority native Irish population that was regarded as Catholic, superstitious and inherently rebellious, always on the lookout for an opportunity to dispossess the colonisers. Ruthlessness was seen as the only way to control them. The words of the earl of Cork, Richard Boyle, would apply for many decades into the future: 'So long as the English and Irish Protestants and papists live here intermingled together we can never have firm and assured peace'.

The Ringsend spit

We now turn to look specifically at Dublin at the end of the seventeenth century. It could be done superficially using maps but that would not do the task justice. The maps of Bernard de Gomme (1673), Andrew Yarranton (1674), Thomas Phillips (1685) and Grenville Collins (1693) show no great evidence of change from the 1610 map of John Speed (Figs 2.4–2.8).

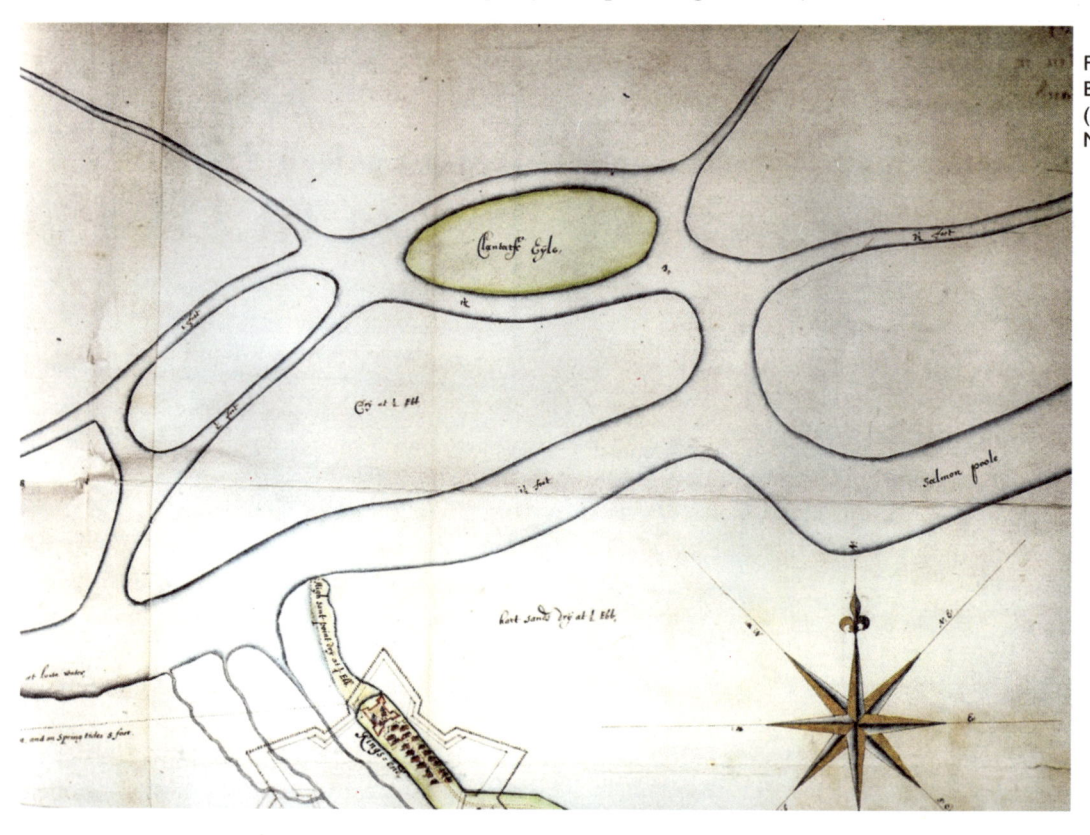

Fig. 2.4—Ringsend, from Bernard de Gomme's map (1673) (photo: Brian Matthews).

SEVENTEENTH-CENTURY CONTEXT BEFORE THE BALLAST BOARD ACT OF 1707

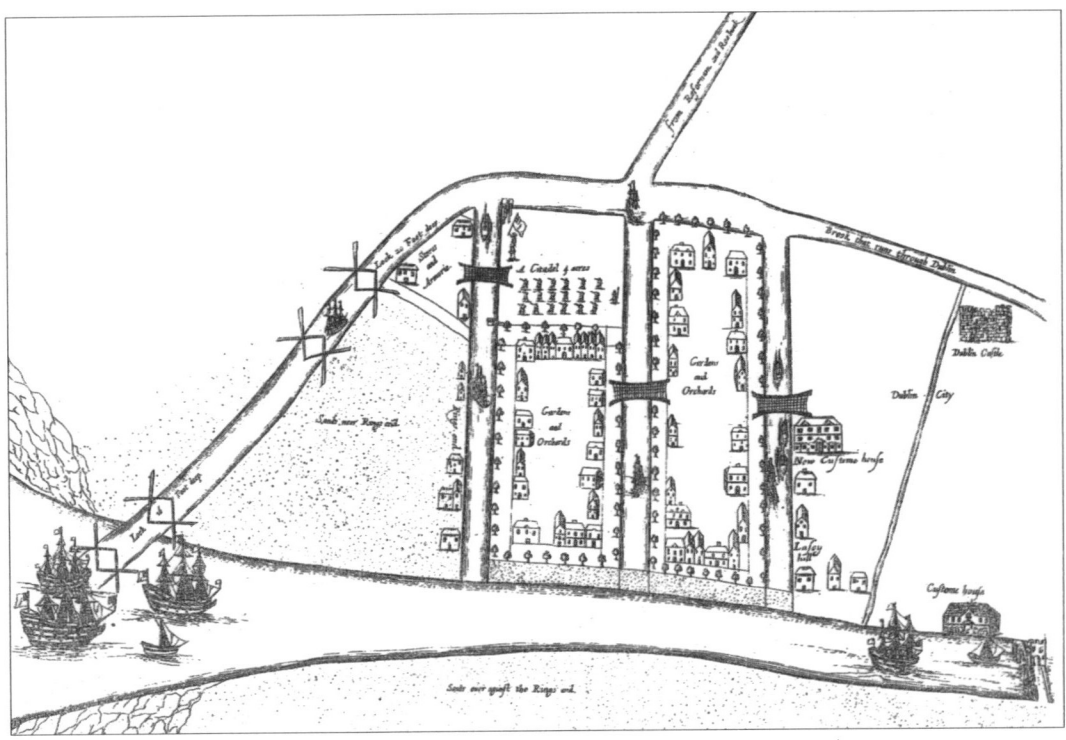

Fig. 2.5—Andrew Yarranton's map (1674), showing proposed harbour and canals (photo: Brian Matthews).

Fig. 2.6—Thomas Dinelly's map of 1681, showing little change since Speed's 1610 map.

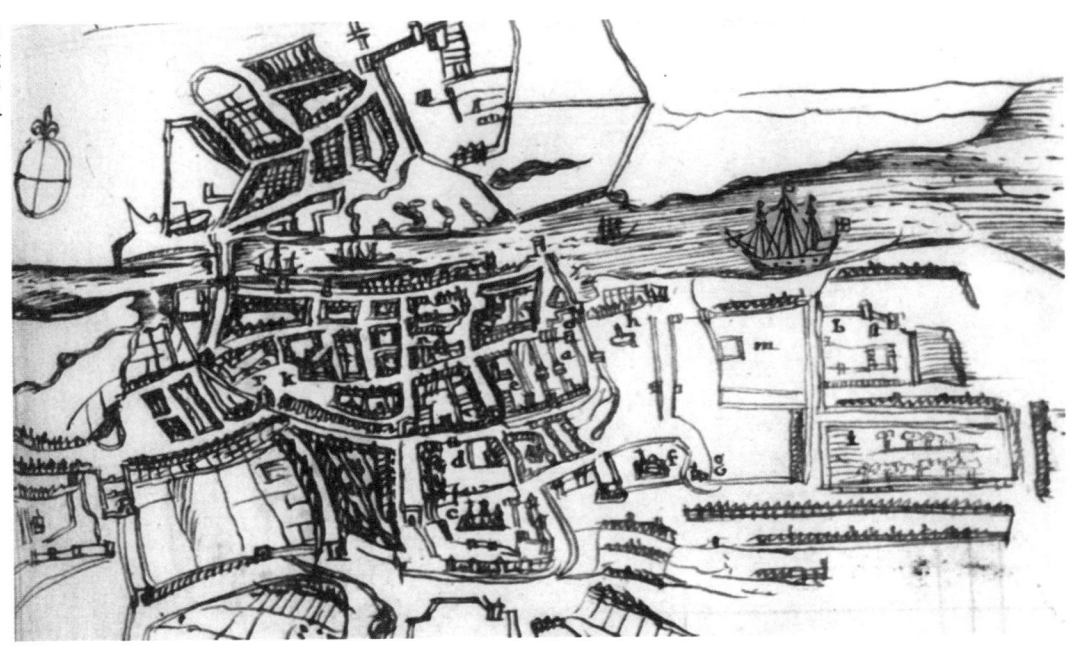

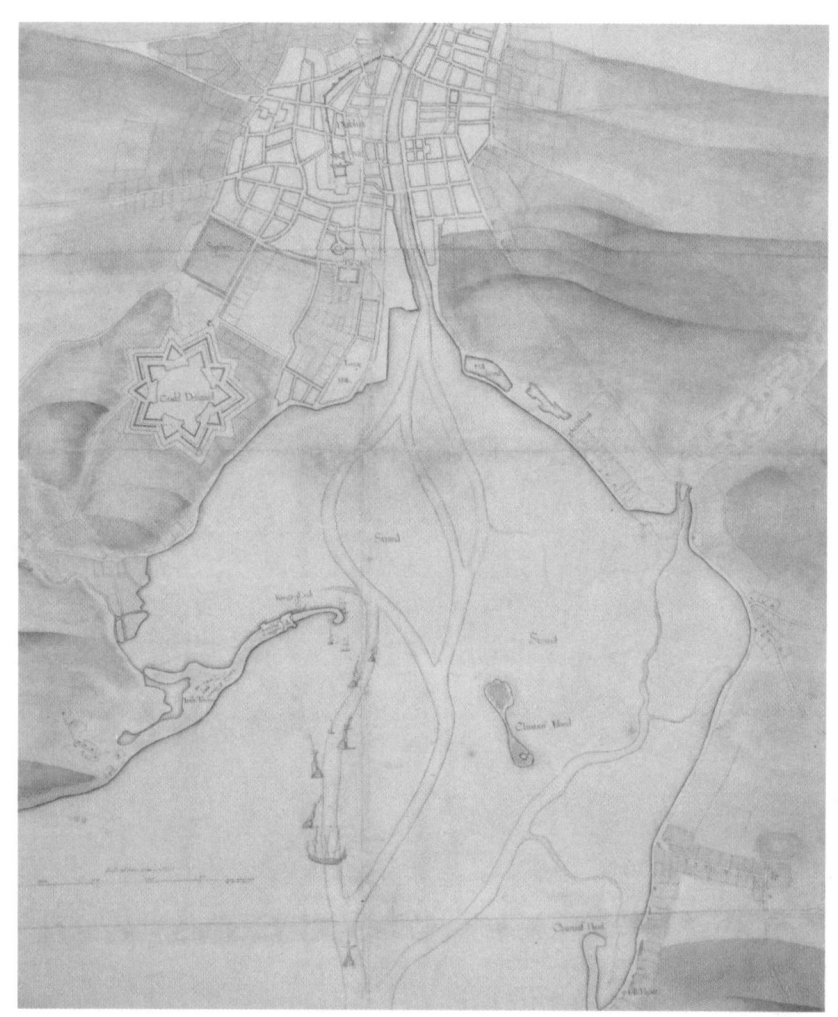

Fig. 2.7—Thomas Phillips's map of Dublin (1685), showing the estuary before construction of the Liffey walls, with more detail (photo: Brian Matthews).

By 1728, however, when the walls were completed, the maps of Charles Brooking (1728) and Charles Price (1730) confirm the fact that the Liffey had become one single channel. Down here at this time there existed tidal strands and a dog-leg spit of ground tenuously connected to the shore and often overrun by tides. The nearest dry ground was up at the corner of Trinity College, or over to the east at Beggar's Bush. The spit was about 400 yards long and perhaps 100 yards wide. The first record of occupation was in 1454, when the Irish were expelled from the city.[22] This ban even included friars, nuns, hermits and clerics.[23] Ringsend became established when two merchants, Edward Gough and James Sedgrove, began to use the spit for shipping, having moved there because of overcharging by King, who controlled the port, at the pool at Clontarf in the early seventeenth century. Nuala Burke said that it had become established by mid-century, with packet ships coming from Chester.[24] Francis Place, an English painter, recorded a scene of Ringsend in 1698; it depicts clusters of ships and shows the myriad channels in the estuary and the isolation of Clontarf Island for quarantine purposes, confirming the Phillips map. We must remind ourselves here that ships at the time could range from twenty to 70 tons, but the lower end of the scale was the norm. Larger ships could not access the port because of the lack of deep water. Fionnáin O Cionnaith wrote that 'the area was virtually devoid of

Fig. 2.8—Grenville Collins's map of Dublin, the estuary, the Ringsend spit and Clontarf Island in 1686, before construction of the Liffey walls (photo: Brian Matthews).

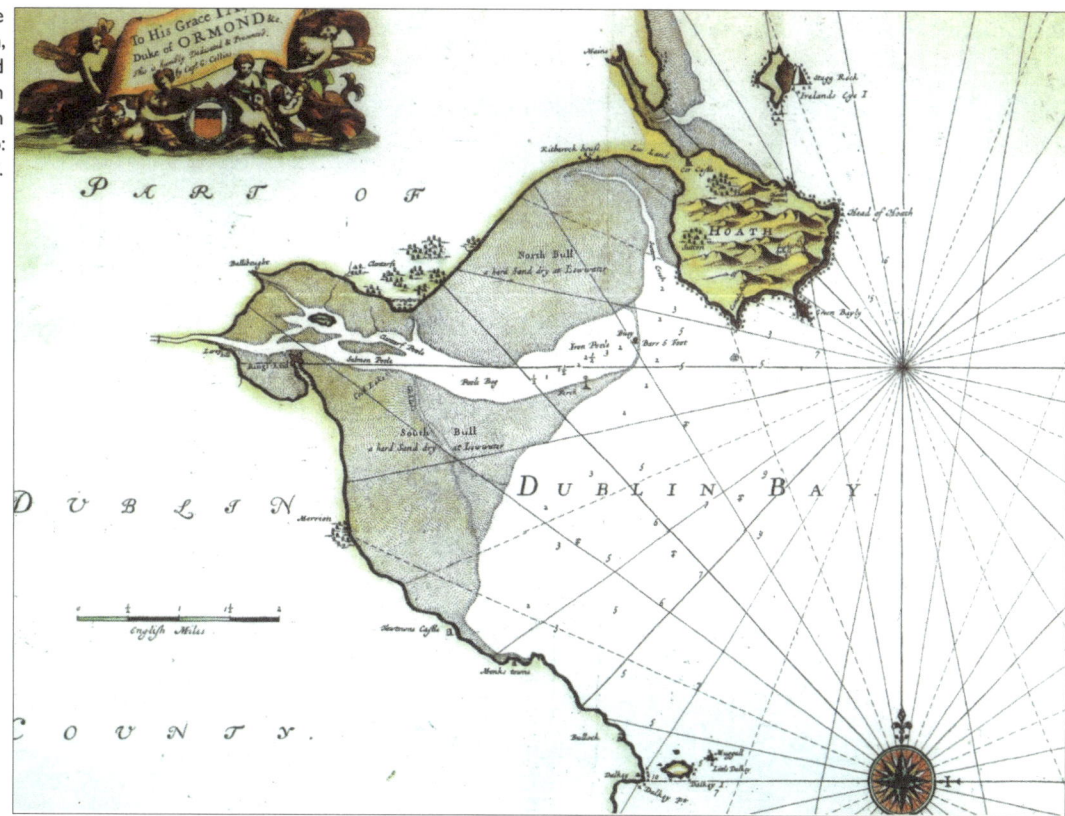

human interference', so small was the impact of 'the few down here'.[25] It has to be noted that in the period 1603–40 the government took no cognisance of the native Irish; moreover, 'it managed the municipality without reference to them whatsoever'.[26] In 1716 Isaac Butler went out to Clontarf, then far out from the city, and reported that on the sands there on the North Bull he found 42 dead porpoises, cut up for food. The area was overrun twice daily by tides.[27]

Shipping conditions in Dublin Bay

Dublin Bay was treacherous for ships because it was shallow and offered no shelter. Further, the tide went out across hard sands for miles. In a comment that could be applied perfectly to Dublin Bay, British historian Geoffrey Moorehouse described the Goodwin Sands on the coast outside London as 'a little more than four miles wide and just over ten miles deep, riddled with narrow channels and little creeks where perverse tidal currents swirled, and if you walked across them before the sand had dried out it felt as if you trod on a living creature, which would suck you into its depths if you stood still'.[28] An idea of the hazards is provided by John Stevens, who on 11 January 1689 boarded a Deale hooker at London to travel to France to enlist with the French Jacobites. The boat ran aground at Gravesend and he spent the following four days and nights bouncing on the sands, unable to walk ashore across the dangerous sands around Margate and Sandwich Bay. The physical situation in Dublin was almost identical.[29] Another example is given by Captain John Appleby, who reported that while on patrol he took shelter and anchored in Milford Haven, which has similar topography to Dublin Bay, and in the teeth of a violent storm laid out three anchors for fear of dragging.[30] The only other

Fig. 2.9—Ringsend Car, for accessing Dublin from Ringsend just before 1700 (photo: Brian Matthews, with the kind permission of the RSAI).

reference that this writer has come across of riding to three anchors was the case of Darwin's *Beagle* in the Gulf of Penas on the coast of southern Chile in June 1828.[31]

Sir William Brereton, a military engineer, wrote in 1635 in praise of Drogheda, where he landed. On Dublin he wrote that 'The river is no good channel but full of shelves and sands', adding that the Bar 'is a very vile barred haven'. He further describes the harbour as a 'Naked plain ... most ships ride by Ringsend which offered little or no shelter, a low point which runs out in to the sea'.[32] Two years later, in November 1637, as reported by Boate, between ten and twelve vessels were lost in one night, thanks to their anchors dragging.[33]

John Dunton, who came to Dublin in 1698, described Ringsend: 'the place of my landing, when the tide is in, it is a peninsula having but one avenue to it by land ... a small village with three or four tolerable brick houses with several other lesser ones ... no shelter ... a bleak place exposed to all winds and weather'[34]—a clear indication of what was involved in arriving in Dublin at the end of the seventeenth century (Fig. 2.9).

At this stage it was no foregone conclusion that Dublin would become the premier port on the east coast, as both Drogheda and Waterford offered stiff competition. Van der Hagen painted both of the latter ports and even now, 300 years later, the advantages that they enjoyed over Dublin are clearly obvious. His view of Drogheda was painted in 1718 (the original hangs in the hall of Beaulieu House, Drogheda), and that of Waterford, showing a protected port, safe and secure up the river from the sea, shortly after. In 1753 Ricciardelli too painted Drogheda, also depicting a protected and secure port town (Fig. 2.10).

Dublin faced competition from other ports as well. As late as 1797 it was noted that the Talbot family enjoyed many grants and prerogatives, such as importing coals and other merchandise duty-

Fig. 2.10—Ricciardelli's view of Drogheda (1753) (photo: Brian Matthews, with the kind permission of Highlanes Gallery, Drogheda).

free into Malahide, where there was a small harbour and a short pier at Robswall, allowing trade to bypass Dublin.[35]

Dublin's problems had been evident as far back as 1358, when its merchants petitioned Edward III regarding the lack of proper port facilities. They complained of large ships going to Dalkey and goods arriving in the city by barge.[36] Again, in 1437 the mayor of Dublin complained to Henry IV that the port of Dublin was being bypassed and that ships were calling to Howth, Baldoyle, Malahide, Portrane, Rogerstown, Rush and Skerries. These and other secondary ports were owned by local landlords and would continue to trade well into the end of the eighteenth century. Others would be added, such as Balbriggan (built by Baron Hampton of Balbriggan), and Balscadden, Cromwell Harbour and New Haven (all three just north of Balbriggan). Lord Gormanstown was in control of Balscadden and Cromwell Harbour. Carlingford was important, too; Butler reported in 1744 that it handled the shipping of turf and 'all manner of earthenware, pots, pitchers, vases, square tiles and pan tiles which are brought to Dublin by water …', and that 'oysters too were sent … by boat'.[37]

In 1678 the corporation began to take action at last, deciding to charge for ballast across a range of tonnages. Six of the ten categories were in the smaller ton range, confirming that the ships using Dublin were small (twenty tons was normal).[38]

Sir Bernard de Gomme, a Dutch military engineer, proposed that a citadel be built on the sands between Ringsend and Lazy Hill at Townsend Street on ground to be reclaimed. The tide at the time came to within 75 yards of the wall at Trinity College, and on one occasion the area was entirely flooded. The proposal shows the sense of a threat from the Dutch, illustrating the way that security went hand in hand with development.[39]

Andrew Yarranton, another military engineer, also had proposals for harbour development alongside security. In 1674 he argued that 'If there was a harbour at Ringsend as in the map [referring to his own proposal] advantage would be gained'. He confirmed that lack of facilities was hurting trade in Dublin, as discussed with Mayor Brewster of Liverpool.

In 1693 the Pembroke estate ordered a survey map of the area, which clearly shows 28 dwellings/buildings in Irishtown and seven in Ringsend. One bridge, described as wooden, is shown at the present Londonbridge Road location. It also depicts some shipping around the spit.[40] This estate map mirrors information presented in the Phillips map.

As the eighteenth century dawned, trade was increasing everywhere; the volume of shipping was growing, as was the size of individual ships. Dublin was coming under increasing pressure to do something. Loading and unloading up at the Essex Bridge entailed problems which would have to be dealt with at some stage. Louis Cullen noted that Dublin exported butter, woollen yarns and beef, but it was as a centre for imports that it thrived. By the end of the seventeenth century, as Ireland's largest town, it was importing vast quantities of coal.[41]

In the stability that followed the end of the Williamite wars, with new owners of the land, new laws and the military might to enforce them, money and political power became concentrated in the hands of the élite. The bulk of the population were left leaderless, as the Catholic officer corps and old ruling class left the country and became the mercenaries of Europe (referred to as the Wild Geese). The final arrival of the pacification of the colony of Ireland enabled plans to be made more easily. Those now in authority were the undisputed owners of the country and could make all decisions in full confidence. One of the most important ever taken about the affairs of Dublin was the Ballast Act of 1707.

Notes

[1] Nuala Burke, 'Dublin 1600–1800: a study in morphogenesis', unpublished Ph.D thesis, Trinity College Dublin (1972), p. 90.
[2] Thomas E. Jordan, 'Quality of life in seventeenth-century Dublin', *Dublin Historical Record* **61** (2) (2008), 136–54, at p. 136.
[3] Burke, 'Dublin 1600–1800', p. 139.
[4] Monck papers, part MSS 26813–269746, Accession no. 1478, Collection List no. 4, National Library of Ireland.
[5] Gillian O'Brien and Finola O'Kane (eds), *Portraits of the city: Dublin and the wider world* (Dublin, 2012), p. 18.
[6] *Ibid.*, p. 19.
[7] Patrick J. Duffy, *Exploring the history and heritage of Irish landscapes* (Dublin, 2007), p. 17.
[8] J.G. Simms, 'Dublin in 1685', *Irish Historical Studies* **14** (55) (1965), 212–26, at p. 226.
[9] *Attack on Chatham* by William Schellinks (Rijksmuseum, Amsterdam). Painted in 1668, it depicts the burning of much of the English fleet by a Dutch fleet under Michiel de Ruyter in June 1667.
[10] John C. Appleby, 'The defence of Ireland: a naval journal of 1627', *Analecta Hibernica* **37** (1998), 237–48, at p. 239.
[11] See note 9.
[12] Elaine Murphy, 'Atrocities at sea and the treatment of prisoners of war by the Parliamentary navy in Ireland 1641–1649', *Historical Journal* **53** (1) (2010), 21–37, at pp 21–2.
[13] *Ibid.* The Act was called *Two ordinances of the Lords and Commons assembled in Parliament one commanding that officer or soldier either by sea or land shall give any quarter to any Irishman, or to any papist borne in Ireland which shall be taken in armies against Parliament in England.*
[14] *Ibid.*
[15] Peter Kemp (ed.), *The Oxford companion to ships and the sea* (Oxford, 1976), p. 181.
[16] Tony Farmer, *Patients, potions and physicians: a social history of medicine in Ireland* (Dublin, 2004), p. 29.
[17] Captain John Gaunt, *Natural and political observations mentioned in the following index and made upon the Bills of Mortality* (London, 1665), p. 46.
[18] John Boxall, 'Raids on the Saltee Islands by French privateers: the petition of John Boxall', *The Wexford Independent*, 18 August 1849, p. 48 (sourced from the original State papers).

19. Diaries of Charles Cosslett (1793–4), Diary A, p. 4 (in the archive of St Malachy's College, Belfast).
20. Maighread Ní Mhurchadha, *The customs and excise of Fingal 1684–1765* (Dublin, 1999), pp 58–9.
21. Isaac Butler, 'Itinerary of a journey through the counties of Dublin, Meath and Louth, personal journal', p. 8 (Armagh Public Library).
22. John T. Gilbert (ed.), *Calendar of ancient records of Dublin* [hereafter *CARD*], vol. 1 (Dublin, 1889), p. 280.
23. *Ibid.*, p. 287.
24. Burke, 'Dublin 1600–1800', pp 98–9.
25. Fionnáin Ó Cionnaith, *Mapping, measurement and metropolis: how land surveyors changed eighteenth-century Dublin* (Dublin, 2012), p. 231.
26. Brendan Fitzpatrick, 'The municipal corporation of Dublin 1603–1640', unpublished Ph.D thesis, Trinity College Dublin (1985), p. 264.
27. Isaac Butler, 'Weather Diary 1716–1734', p. 4.
28. Geoffrey Moorhouse, *Great Harry's navy: how Henry VIII gave England sea power* (London, 2005), p. 1.
29. John Stevens (ed. R.H. Murray), *The journal of John Stevens, containing a brief account of the war in Ireland, 1689–1691* (Oxford, 1912), pp 14–16.
30. Appleby, 'The defence of Ireland', p. 247.
31. David Barrie, *Sextant: a voyage guided by the stars and the men who mapped the world* (London, 2014), p. 213.
32. Sir William Brereton's 'Travels in Ireland' (1635), in C. Litton Falkiner (ed.), *Illustrations of Irish history and topography, mainly of the seventeenth century* (London, 1904), 363–407, at p. 351.
33. Gerard Boate, *Ireland's naturall history* (London, 1652).
34. John Dunton (ed. A. Carpenter), *Teague land; or A merry ramble to the wild Irish (1698)* (Dublin, 2003), pp 127–9.
35. Rolf Loeber and Magda Stouthammer-Loeber (eds), 'Dublin and its vicinity in 1797', *Irish Geography* **35** (2) (2006), p. 135.
36. *CARD*, vol. 1, p. 19.
37. Butler, 'Itinerary', p. 32.
38. *CARD*, vol. 4 (Dublin, 1894), pp 553–5.
39. Maurice Craig, *Dublin 1660–1860* (Dublin, 1980), p. 289.
40. NAI, Pembroke estate map, ref. 2011/2/1/2.
41. L.M. Cullen, *An economic history of Ireland since 1660* (Dublin, 1972), p. 28.

3. Embanking of the Liffey and the construction of the Great South Bull Wall

It is reported in the *Calendar of ancient records of Dublin* 'That the river and port of Dublin will in a few years be choked up and the trade of this city entirely ruined unless some speedy method be found for erecting a ballast office for cleansing the river and channel of the port of Dublin and that almost one half of the depth of water that was formerly, is now lost by the irregular taking up of ballast ... it is therefore ordered by the authority aforesaid that the petitioners request be and is hereby granted'.

The town of Dublin at the time was managed by an Assembly or Corporation, which, depending on the political, military and social needs of the day, was made up of selected citizens. On 16 January 1708 it was ordered by that Assembly that Thomas Pearson be constituted and appointed master and treasurer of the committee of the directors of the Ballast Office.

The time was now opportune for decisions to be taken. The country was calm, peace reigned and the new leaders were in an unassailable position of authority. If they wanted to grow trade and the city, the only way to achieve this was through improving port access.

By the start of the eighteenth century the port of Dublin had two important issues to confront if it was to develop and expand as a modern trading hub: the first was the regular clogging-up of the port at Essex Bridge (Wellington Quay) as it became jammed with ships trying to enter and leave this small, shallow space; the second was the bar at the mouth of the Liffey, an impediment to shipping. Ships seeking to access the port to unload and load cargo also had two problems to overcome. The first was to access the river mouth safely, after possibly anchoring in the open, unprotected body of water that was the bay—using anchors that did not have the holding capacity that they do now—before taking the tide over the bar. Having negotiated the mouth of the river, the next task was to anchor safely in one of the often-crowded pools down at the confluence of the rivers Liffey, Dodder and Tolka. Then a decision had to be made as to whether to unload onto lighters or gabbards or to wait for a tide to work their way up (often against the prevailing westerly wind) to the congested space beside Essex Bridge at Capel Street, where the number of ships lying alongside dictated the turn-around times. As a result, fewer than one in four ships went on up to the Custom House. This situation would pertain for decades even though, as Louis Cullen has pointed out, the Custom House Quay was the very nerve centre of trade and therefore the task for shippers was to get up the river and as close to the quay as possible. This meant that sometimes there could be ships lying up to eight deep at the quays.

Geoffrey Corry (1969–70) has also noted the requirement for deeper water, as the tonnage of shipping increased in the late seventeenth and early eighteenth centuries, making the bar even more problematic. He quotes Boate from 1653: 'with an ordinary tide you cannot go to the key of Dublin with a ship that draws five feet of water'.

Embanking of the Liffey and the Construction of the Great South Bull Wall

This chapter will deal with two major works whose object was to improve Dublin as a port: the embanking of the Liffey on the south side, and the construction of the Great South Bull Wall. Specifically we will look at the narrow strip of ground bordered by the River Liffey between City Quay, only yards from the wall at Trinity College, down to the Grand Canal Docks entrance, and the line of the rail embankment from Westland Row station out towards the sea.

These issues, however, could not be dealt with in isolation. The question of the size of ships also impinged, in that they grew in bulk throughout Europe in this period. As the premier naval power, the Dutch had a huge influence on all matters marine. This was the period of enormous expansion in trade internationally, also led by the Dutch. Therefore size mattered. Another problem for the port upriver was ballast—the unregulated collection and disposal of material from the river used as ballast in ships when they were not fully laden with cargo. There was also the matter of rubbish disposal, sewerage and water for a growing populace and city. Finally, there was the problem of increasing congestion in Dublin's narrow medieval streets. This made it even more difficult for merchants to get goods on board vessels at the Custom House, and to remove goods from the area to their desired location away from the river. The quays were not solidly built or properly maintained, and carriages and horses caused not just congestion but also actual damage to the quays.

The issue of ballast was noted during the reign of Henry VIII, when it was collected from the Steyn River in 1534 on the fourth day after Easter. Regulation began with an order in 1557 instructing 'every vessel and gabbard [workboat] that henceforth shall come to the key and there discharge (cockle boats excepted) shall pay every time to the treasurer of the city eleven pence sterling towards the upkeep of said key'. Then an order was brought in to fine people for dumping rubbish directly into the Liffey: 'casting of filth into the Liffey a fine of two shillings'. By 1560 the city 'agreed that Giles Clyncher has authority over the river ensuring that no ballast be dumped into it, and he is to pay special attention to the south side of Poolbeg and monitor ballast at Ringsend'. In the same year appears the first mention of the city taking an official position on buoys in the harbour. The contract for putting out buoys and a perch (mark) on the bar of the Liffey is ordered in 1581, along with the cost of repairs to the walls and quays to be borne by the city. The city tried to impel the leaseholder of quays to repair them: for example, Thomas Fitzsimon shall 'make up his portion of the key in 1572' and 'that he shall be compelled to repair any defects and faults upon the slips of Merchants Key'. The net result of all this was that ships were avoiding Dublin because of the difficulty of accessing the port and city in terms of loading and unloading. The tides created delays which could be avoided by going elsewhere. The problem was still present in 1612, 'for as much as the examiners have also been humble petitioners unto the said assembly, praising as well a course to be taken for the cleansing of both quays now so choked up with filth [and] rubbish as no ships, boats or gabbards can come near to the slips'. Fresh orders were announced in 1618 to repair the slipway near the Inns for 'safety of boats and barques and the stones fallen into the river be removed and rings and other necessaries be put into the walls for tying up boats'. The taking of real control was still in the future, however, and there was much to do.

Embanking the River Liffey

The embanking of the Liffey began in earnest following the return from exile of James Butler, 1st duke of Ormonde, on the restoration of the monarchy. Influenced by what he had observed on the Continent, he encouraged the idea of wide thoroughfares along the river and an end to building down to the water's edge. He also encouraged the development of the fishing industry: 'You are to consider by whatever means the fishing trade may be most improved in the kingdom of Ireland'. Charles Grossett in 1778 cites the example of Holland, and in particular Amsterdam, which he said grew from a tiny fishing hamlet and 'now pretends to dispute consequence with the first trading city of the known world'. The embanking of the river was pursued piecemeal and was not completed until 1728. This section is specifically interested in the south bank from Lazy Hill (Townsend Street) to where the Liffey, joined by the Dodder, entered the bay.

The work about to commence had been carried out earlier elsewhere on an even larger scale. William TeBrake (1981) wrote that between 950 and 1350 in the estuary of the Rhine, at Rotterdam, land drainage and reclamation on a very substantial scale took place in an area 35km wide and 25km long inland which consisted of dunes, bog and trees but was in the main swampy. It was here that the Dutch perfected their skill in constructing dykes, digging canals and harnessing water while creating land that could sustain agriculture. The result of this work was that by the late fourteenth century some 50 villages with approximately 3,250 households existed in the reclaimed area. Amsterdam, slightly further to the west of the Rhine estuary, was no more than a fishing village as late as 1240. Giesebrecht, 3rd Count Amstel, built a large dam to keep out the sea, thereby allowing the port of Amsterdam to grow and develop. Four hundred years later, the Dutch were the premier trading nation in Europe.

The powers that be in Dublin would have been well aware of the Dutch expertise in land drainage and reclamation; indeed, it would have been impossible to ignore. When work first began on the Great South Wall, the machine used for driving piles was Dutch. British ships used Dutch pilot-books for navigation into the eighteenth century. Old houses show a Dutch influence in architecture. Even the timber lifting bridge erected over the two Grand Canal Basins was obviously a direct descendant of lifting bridges over the canals in Holland from 200 years before. It can safely be claimed, therefore, that Dutch influence was widespread.

In his *Lives of the engineers: an account of their principal works* (1670) John Smeaton writes: 'Our first lessons in mechanical and civil engineering were principally obtained from Dutchmen, who supplied us with our first windmills, watermills and pumping engines. Holland has sent us the necessary labourers to execute our first great works of drainage.'

Just as the story of Amsterdam consisted of land reclamation on a large scale, consuming vast numbers of trees for both piling barriers and for underpinning house construction, so did the story of the earlier building of Venice provide a similar guide for the Dutch. Some idea of the quantity of timber required can be gleaned from the fact that the piles underpinning the stone foundations of the Rialto Bridge over the Grand Canal used 12,000 trees driven into the sand and mud. Again, every building in Amsterdam was similarly built on timber piles. The version of the Rialto Bridge seen today is the fifth at least; all these trees were needed to carry the load of the enormous stone foundations so that the great weight of the single arch was bearable. This shoring up of usable ground began as early as the tenth century but continued on into the fourteenth and fifteenth centuries, according to Professor Michael Scott.

The merchants and city officials of Dublin could therefore have availed of knowledge going back hundreds of years on such technology. Their problem had been the long wait for the political stability that would allow full control so that decisions could be made and action taken.

In the seventeenth century the term 'quays' meant mooring posts, to which ships were tied up. Franc Myles has excavated some of the remains of these posts when preparing the site for the diving bell museum on Sir John Rogerson's Quay, and in excavations at Windmill Lane and Creighton

Fig. 3.1—Essex Bridge with Custom House on south bank of Liffey, with quays on both sides (photo: Brian Matthews).

Embanking of the Liffey and the Construction of the Great South Bull Wall

Street. The quays were largely of timber construction. The only area quayed in the early to mid-seventeenth century was at the Custom House; Le Gouz, a French visitor, admired the newly built quay in 1644. In the eighteenth century quays were constructed of stone and filled in behind with assorted materials; ships could then berth directly, as seen in Tudor's drawing of the Custom House dating from 1707 (Fig. 3.1).

The reason for embanking or walling the Liffey was to train the course of the river and make one navigable channel out of several. Trade could only grow if port facilities improved. The city was under pressure to meet the demand of a rising population, with the consequent demand for accommodation; furthermore, the drift of commerce and people was in a south-eastern direction. Corry called the area at the confluence of the Tolka, Dodder and Liffey 'a labyrinth of sands often altered in their course by the floods and storms'. The tides themselves also presented a variety of problems, in that high water at the bar of Dublin occurred 45 minutes before its arrival at the Custom House at spring tide, and half an hour earlier at neap tide. The Heinrich Moll map of 1714, though short on detail, shows the broad delta that was then the river mouth with its channels just as the work on the river walls was beginning. Confirmation of what actually existed in this area in the period comes also from Gilbert's documentary evidence, showing Arthur Annesley being given a lease for 90 years on the strand at College Green 'adjoining the seaside there' (Fig. 3.2).

Around this time the first enclosed docks along the waterfront in Liverpool opened in 1715.

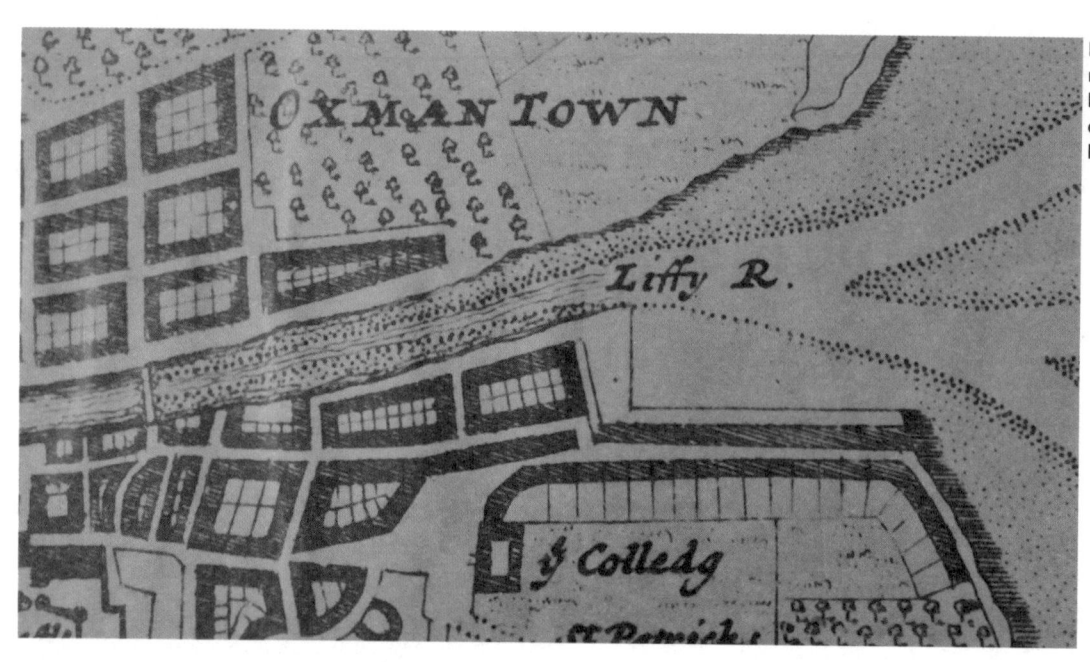

Fig. 3.2—Heinrich Moll's map of Dublin (1711) just before the walls were erected (courtesy of Marsh's Library, Dublin).

This presents an idea of where Dublin was in terms of port facility development. Liverpool forged even further ahead with its massive wealth generated in the slave trade, in which by the 1740s Liverpool merchants had overtaken both London and Bristol.

Real change began in 1708 when the Assembly obtained parliament's approval for the establishment of a Ballast Office at Dublin, under their direction. They were constituted conservators of the port of Dublin, and all ships 'resorting thither were to be furnished with ballast by the Ballast Office'. This heralded greater control of the collection and dumping of material in the river, which until that point had been unregulated. It would also raise revenue for the Committee of the Directors of the Ballast Office. Even then the work was not completely effective. Pool and Cash observed in 1780 that 'Dublin would have had a commodious and secure station for shipping if the entrance of the bay had not been so choked up, that vessels of burthen cannot come over the bar'.

Construction

Work began on the north bank in 1711, overseen by the Ballast Office. The resulting enclosure behind the wall became known as the North Lotts. The plan of the Lotts was drawn up in 1717 and was something of a 'wish list' in the early years, but it started to become a reality once the construction of the walls began, and by 1728 even more so. For this story the narrative follows the lead on the river walls rather than the occupation of the Lotts.

Sir John Rogerson began walling the south bank in the following years. This area became known as the South Lotts. In 1709 the Ballast Office reported that Watts and Kemmy on the south banks were committed to 'build up the wall nine feet high from the foundation'. In subsequent decades these walls or barriers would increase in height, as well as depth, before being faced with stone. The Ballast Committee also ordered dredging to clear 'shoals or banks'. At this very early stage the work was haphazard rather than structured, with men, materials and boats not always readily available.

Embanking of the Liffey and the construction of the Great South Bull Wall

The Committee of the Directors of the Ballast Office were of the opinion that a committee should be formally appointed 'to stake out the meares and banks of the strand' between Lazers Hill (Townsend Street) and Ringsend. The first step was to cut a new, more direct channel 100 yards wide from Lazy Hill to Ringsend. The Ballast Committee agreed in 1712 that 'it is absolutely necessary to enclose the channel in order to carry it directly to the Salmon pool' (below Ringsend). This was a statement of intent to create one navigable channel in the river all the way down. Further, they determined on a method, agreeing 'that the easiest and aptest way will be by laying kishes and filling them with stones, and backing them with sand and gravel which we have already found by experience for some years past to withstand all the force of the floods that come down the river. We have therefore contracted with several persons to furnish us with kishes.' Kishes were frames or baskets of wood which were filled with stones and dug into the riverbed at low tide in reasonable weather. (In their modern version kishes are wire cages filled with stones of varying sizes.) They were layered and interlaced on top of each other and behind each other, growing into a substantial—though at this stage still porous—barrier. One of the reasons why this barrier was able to withstand the incoming and outgoing tides and floods was the very fact that it was porous, acting as a release valve and not offering the substantive resistance of a solid wall, along with the fact that the walls were laid out in the direction of the flow of water. The engineers in the port remembered this when building the Great North Wall 100 years later. The ebbing tide, along with the flow of the Liffey, was not greatly resisted by the new barrier. This gave the structure a chance to grow and settle in, allowing silt and seaweed to help bind it together. Advice was tendered on the methods of filling the kishes to be used on the wall. The work proceeded in this manner, conditions permitting; it was subject to the weather, the tides and occasional flooding. Taking place outside the city walls, it was unseen by most of the citizens and progressed without any social impediment. The structure grew up to 12ft in height from base foundation to top. The supply of material for kishes, for building filling and for land reclamation was often problematic because of material being taken for supplying the South Bull during its construction.

In 1712 Sir John Rogerson applied to the Corporation to alter his lease on 133 acres on the strand to fee farm, in return for which he undertook to enlarge the new channel from Lazy Hill to Ringsend on the south side. In the following year Rogerson was 'thereby encouraged to wall in and enclose the same which means taking the gravel from the channel and along the same to back the walls as made, and filling and making keys etc thereon will help greatly to cleanse and bottom the channel and render it so deep that ships may get up to the Custom House'. In 1716 the Committee reported that the timber had arrived and 'kishes were due'. At the same time piling below Ringsend had begun and was continuing. In the meantime the workboats were supplemented by a purpose-built float: 'The gabbards belonging to the office being too few in number to carry on the several works now going on and to supply the necessary occasions of the office have built a large float carrying forty tons to bring stones to the said works'. By then the gabbards or workboats were working in the river along Sir John Rogerson's Quay as well as down in the estuary on the South Bull, assisting in putting in the rows of piles. The accounts for 1716 record the money spent on the new city wall between Mr Mercer's and Ringsend as £253 2s. 5d. Later in that same year the Committee advised: 'We are building a second float of 30 tons, the former not being sufficient for the office business, and are going on in laying kishes on the north side of the channel and backing them in order to prevent the floods overflowing that way'. Progress was steady but there were regular setbacks; when wall damage was reported at City Quay and Rogerson's Quay owing to flooding in

1716, the Committee ordered that 'the said walls be repaired by the city and raised to proper height'.

Meanwhile, having been granted in 1713 his 133 acres in fee farm on the strand, Sir John Rogerson had begun to extend his own quay down to the mouth of the Dodder. The ground enclosed was drained over time, and some of it was let as farmland. This was not a new science to progressive landowners. 'Mr Owney and Mr Draper of this place [Carlingford] have reclaimed vast numbers of acres from the sea where they have grown corn, planted potatoes which thrive well and turn a good account', wrote Isaac Butler during a visit. The quays in front were built on, with houses and stores and yards.

On the North Lotts behind the wall, the methods used to drain the water off were gravity and windmills: the water was simply allowed to drain away and windmills were used to further pump water out of the area. This has been confirmed by the archaeological investigation conducted by Melanie McQuade at Spencer's Dock. McQuade also recovered artefacts from the eighteenth and nineteenth centuries consistent with the documentary record. It is not unreasonable to assume that similar methods were used on the south side at Rogerson's Quay. Both the Brooking map of 1728 and the Rocque map of 1756 show windmills on both sides of the river, and the base of a windmill has recently been identified by Franc Myles at Windmill Lane, where excavations are ongoing. This particular mill is thought to be a corn mill. What is interesting is that the base is built on a timber raft, confirming Cormac Lowth's experience when working in construction there in the 1970s and '80s.[1] During excavations in Creighton Street in 2016 Myles uncovered the remains of an arubah mill erected on 150 ship's timbers. This is not surprising, as corn was grown on a large scale throughout the east coast and hinterland. Isaac Butler in his travels around the counties of Dublin, Meath and Louth attested to the proliferation of fields of corn, as did Arthur Young in his travels around Ireland some years later, besides supplying an excellent description of the operation of the tide-driven watermill for corn-milling located at the outflow of a small river at Portmarnock in 1744.

In Holland the 'very flatness of the land and the richness of its soil that is so easily overflowed every winter; so as the whole country at that season seems to be under water which, in spring, is driven out again by mills'. This observation, made by an English visitor in 1691, shows once again the Dutch leading in the use of windmills and in their proliferation in usage, adding that 'shortage of same would slow up process of drying out ground'. Muendel (1995), reviewing *Power from wind: a history of windmill technology* by Richard L. Hills, notes the author's contention that the scientific revolution experienced by Dutch millwrights of the sixteenth century was a result of their having perfected the design of the twisted windmill sail on a strictly empirical basis. Hills saw the beginning of a form of industrial revolution arising out of this design in that century, particularly on the Zaan promontory north of Amsterdam, where numerous windmills were constructed to support Holland's overseas empire. They were used to saw wood, to manufacture oil, rope and paper, and to hull grain and barley. The ability to saw timber mechanically gave the Dutch an advantage over other European empire-builders in allowing them to construct ships faster. The windmills, however, were also used extensively to pump water for land reclamation.

As late as 1698, Francis Place's paintings of various aspects of the city of Dublin show not one single windmill. By the mid-nineteenth century there were 9,000 operating in Holland alone; according to Hills, Britain and France had just as many, and Germany and Finland twice that number. Muendal also refers to the sixteenth- and seventeenth-century establishment of drainage mills in the Fens in eastern England. The lack of windmills therefore lengthened the time needed for drying out the ground and slowed up the opportunities both for agricultural use of the ground and for building on it. This applied more to the south side than the north side of Dublin, but the strip of land reclaimed was much narrower and the sheer tempo of human activity down in this port area may have rendered the matter moot. O'Sullivan and Downey (2012) note a substantial increase in the number of windmills erected after 1770, with the intensification of cereal production between 1770 and 1815, and they became prominent hilltop features, especially on the east coast of Ireland. The two windmills in Skerries are perfect examples.

There were three types of mills: post, block and tower. Tower mills reached up to four and five stories in height and are very much in evidence in Dutch seventeenth-century landscape painting. Most of the windmills used along the Liffey near the sea were post mills, though there is one tower mill still in Dublin, part of the Guinness complex near Thomas Street. The evidence indicates a preponderance of mills on the north side of the city in comparison to south of the river. Franc Myles's recent discovery of an arubah mill at Creighton Street is a first, and there is a dearth of knowledge about arubah mills in general. So far this is the only one to have been discovered. The mill itself is seen as a tube about 1m in diameter, with an outflow spout near the bottom. It is thought that the tube of stone filled with the incoming tide and operated a water-driven paddle. The ship timbers have been sent to Denmark for carbon dating, as they were Baltic pine. The results may add to our knowledge of such structures. The remains at Windmill Lane show that a mill was built here between 1790 and 1810. By this stage much progress in reclamation had been made. Large blocks of calp limestone were used and the structure sat directly on stilts. The ground consisted of redeposited material from the city latrines. This was the work of scavengers in the period and they are mentioned again and again in the *Calendar of ancient records*. Similar material has been unearthed in several archaeological excavations and it is safe to conclude that this strip was extensively used for dumping this material, to assist in the reclamation process. What can be safely concluded is that

Fig. 3.3—An 1817 illustration by Brocas, showing windmill in the distance on the south bank of the river (in Windmill Lane) (photo: Brian Matthews).

windmill technology was well known and widespread in use, but not so much in Ireland as in the rest of Europe (Fig. 3.3).

What took place along the river-banks can be seen today in the manner in which the ground level rises as you approach each of the rivers Liffey, Dodder and Tolka. In the case of the Tolka, the ground is higher at Annesley Bridge and then drops sharply on the city side on the North Strand. Further down the East Wall Road, again looking down the secondary streets illustrates clearly the low level of this enormous area. In Ringsend, too, it is very apparent on either side of the bridge but especially on the city side, where the eighteenth-century maps designated the ground as 'low ground'. Rocque showed the ground behind the wall at Sir John Rogerson's Quay as 'low ground' and this is exactly what it remains today. Further out on the sea road to Merrion the ground drops away from the sea road, which has been raised substantially over time to stem the sea; this is most easily observed at the Martello tower, which seems somewhat submerged.

When excavating a site from George's Quay down to Sir John Rogerson's Quay in 2010, McQuade found no material earlier than the eighteenth century in pits and slit-trenches dug to a depth of 2m. In 1815, however, two 'very ancient and rudely formed craft [were] unearthed from the river bed, when excavations were being made for laying the foundations of one of the bridges found four feet below the foundation of the old Liffey wall'.

The City Quay was complete by 1718. In the same year work had progressed sufficiently for Sir John Rogerson to build the Fountain Tavern behind his own wall. This indicates that the ground reclaimed by Rogerson was sufficiently stable to allow building (and he probably used timber as a raft for his foundations, almost certainly following the Dutch fashion) after he had topped and faced the river wall with granite stones. Another public house, the Long Stone, was erected in Townsend Street in 1754 and only closed its doors in December 2018. The locale was quite a busy one after the walls were erected and the ground around began to be stabilised.

In 1814, almost 100 years later, Ann Plumtre wrote that 'the walls of the quays are built of the same granite from Bulloch that has been mentioned in speaking of the pier' (South Wall).[2] By 1720 the Committee were able to report that Rogerson's work on the wall continued east downriver, that he would need more backfilling and that the channel was much improved. In this period the gabbards supplied Rogerson with filling when they had time to do so, as they operated between the two works on the river. For some time the Ballast Office used a yard down at Ringsend for storing timber. They had another on the north quays opposite Ringsend. The work was occasionally seen as contentious, with the results provoking different opinions.

And sometimes new opinions came from within the city establishment. A striking example of such was the report offered by Commander William Perry in 1721:

'The first considerable inconveniency to the port is, that the entrance or coming in over the bar, there is ordinarily not above seven feet depth at the time of low water … but about fifteen or sixteen foot at spring tides, and at neap not so much; so that no ship of any burthen, especially if there is any roll of the sea beating over the bar, can venture to run in without a good calculation of the time of high water but when they come upon the coast, let the violence of the weather and necessity be ever so great, must wait until the tides are risen; and if they happen to miss in their calculation of the depth, the ships and men's lives are in danger, and have been known to suffer thereby. Secondly, as for such cruising ships which sometimes put into the port, or other ships of any burthen, they have no place of safety where there is depth of water to anchor in after they are over the bar but in Poolbeg, which is an open roadstead or from half flood to the half ebb with but very little space for any considerable number of ships to ride in, clear of each other in time of bad weather: and when it blows hard from the sea [east] the waves beat in upon them over the sand called the South Bull, and if their anchor starts [drags] they may not have above half a cable's length drift before they come upon the shore or sand called the North Bull.'

Perry observed at first hand the practice of ships sending down their yard and topmasts when getting in over the bar. This was to reduce windage in the hope of lessening the chance of dragging anchors. 'None but small vessels of about eight or nine foot draught of water can at ordinary tides go up to the city, taking the top of high water for it … and the tide every ebb consistently falls away from them when they lie at the quays of the city, leaving them for the most part on the ground at low water.' Perry confirms the potential danger to the structure of ships' hulls if they dry out on the sands in Dublin Bay: 'They strike and thump with their keels, until the tide is more ebbed away from them, sometimes beating their bottoms out'. He adds further: 'So that by reason of their inconveniences, it is remarkable that for the particular trade, of the city, as to the carriage of coals etc they are obliged to build small ships and vessels of strength and lighters, on purpose for lying on the ground with their burdens'. These observations from a naval officer are graphic in their detail as to the dangers involved in accessing Dublin at the start of the eighteenth century, just as the first version of the Liffey walls was being completed and as the piling was just beginning.

When the quays were walled in, more ships than ever could lie alongside, no longer having to try to anchor in the crowded pools below. Rocque confirmed this to be the case, as his 1756 map shows ships all along both sides of the river. The work of backfilling and strengthening the walls would continue for decades.

The creation of Mercer's Dock and later George's Quay from infill behind a sea wall changed the topography significantly. The outcome was summarised by Pool and Cash in 1780: 'once under the dominion of water, Georges Quay with a large tract of many acres extending to Ringsend hath been within this century recovered from that element'.

The embanking construction method was tried and tested over time; it did mean, however, that the foundations and the accompanying granite facing stones that were later added did not go deep. This would improve when the use of the diving bell became commonplace later in the century. The tides continued to overflow these walls for decades until finally they were reinforced on both sides and heightened. In parts a second wall was erected behind the first and rubble placed between, according to Dr Elizabeth Shotton (2015), but no archaeological evidence has been produced to confirm this. There may be some confusion with the double wall on the Great South Wall. These walls were then augmented with Dalkey granite and calp stone from Clontarf (there were several quarries in the area, including one in the present Clontarf Golf Club on the Malahide Road at Donnycarney and another at Corr Bridge in Howth); later still they were faced with larger granite slabs, and later again capped with a granite wall. This process of reinforcement of the quay walls continued into the nineteenth century, as we shall discover when we shift our attention to the north side. Ruptures of the new sea walls that were being constructed would occur almost to the end of the century: 'A large boat overturned off Sir John Rogerson's Quay opposite Ringsend'; the 'amount of water so violent into the breach and confusion of the people such that fourteen persons perished, several that were taken up died of the fright' (Fig. 3.4).

DUBLIN MOVING EAST, 1708–1844

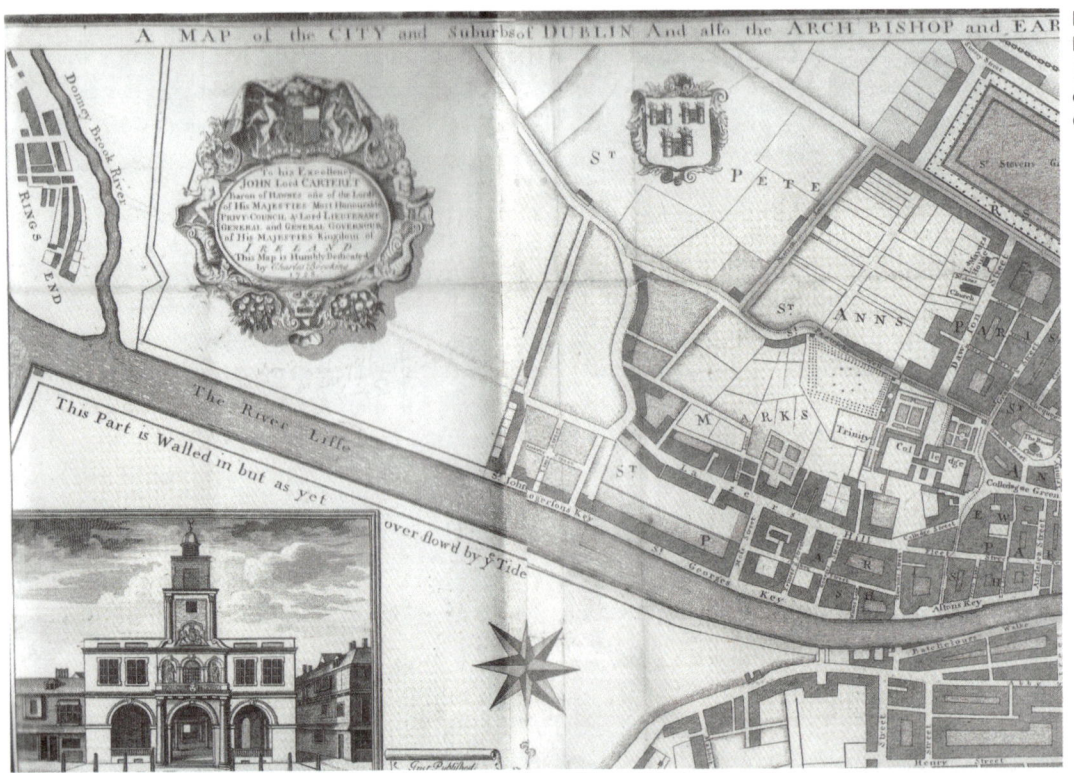

Fig. 3.4—Charles Brooking's survey map of 1728, showing walls complete (courtesy of the Glucksman Library, TCD).

Fig. 3.5—Ricciardelli's painting of Dublin (1750) shows walls complete, with water behind and haycocks sharing the space (courtesy of Louise Morgan and Brendan Maher, NGI).

30

Fig. 3.6—Charles Price's map of Dublin (1730) confirms one single channel (courtesy of the Royal Irish Academy).

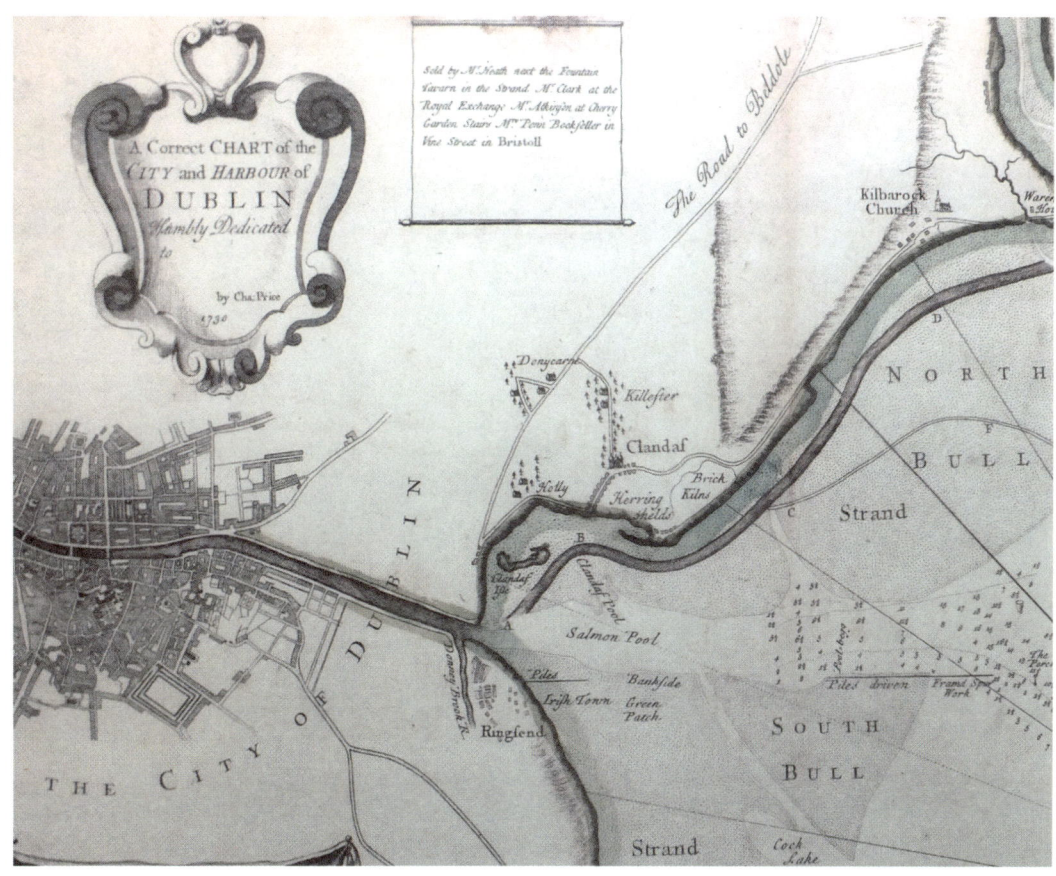

By 1728 the north and south walls containing the Liffey to Ringsend had been completed. It was noted by the Assembly that Thomas Brooking had finished his map of the city by January 1729. The work of improving these walls continued, however. It should be noted that often the right material was readily available for use behind the wall to assist in the reclamation process. A pamphleteer in 1787 wrote that there was an immense shoal of gravel and sand at low water extending from the Marine School down to the point of the south wall embankment. The same writer said that the Liffey had two channels east of the Marine School which embraced the large gravel shoal, and that the southernmost of these two was still 'discernible behind the Rogerson embankment and now serves to collect the waste waters which are let out through the sluice, and is yet of considerable depth', despite 'the distance of time since this ground has been reclaimed'. This comment confirms that some of the ground behind the south river wall was still somewhat waterlogged 50 years after the walling was completed, and that Ricciardelli's painting of 1750 was accurate in showing some water. It also explains why for decades afterwards this was still referred to in maps as 'low ground'. Close examination of Ricciardelli's painting, however, also shows several haycocks, which definitely imply that farming of some description was taking place. The pamphleteer summed up the results of the embanking in 1787: 'by means of Rogerson's and the north embankments, the merchant got his ship up almost to his dwelling, the citizen had his coals almost at his door, lighters, then called gabbards, went into disuse; a great deal of land was reclaimed at a great expense' (Fig. 3.5).

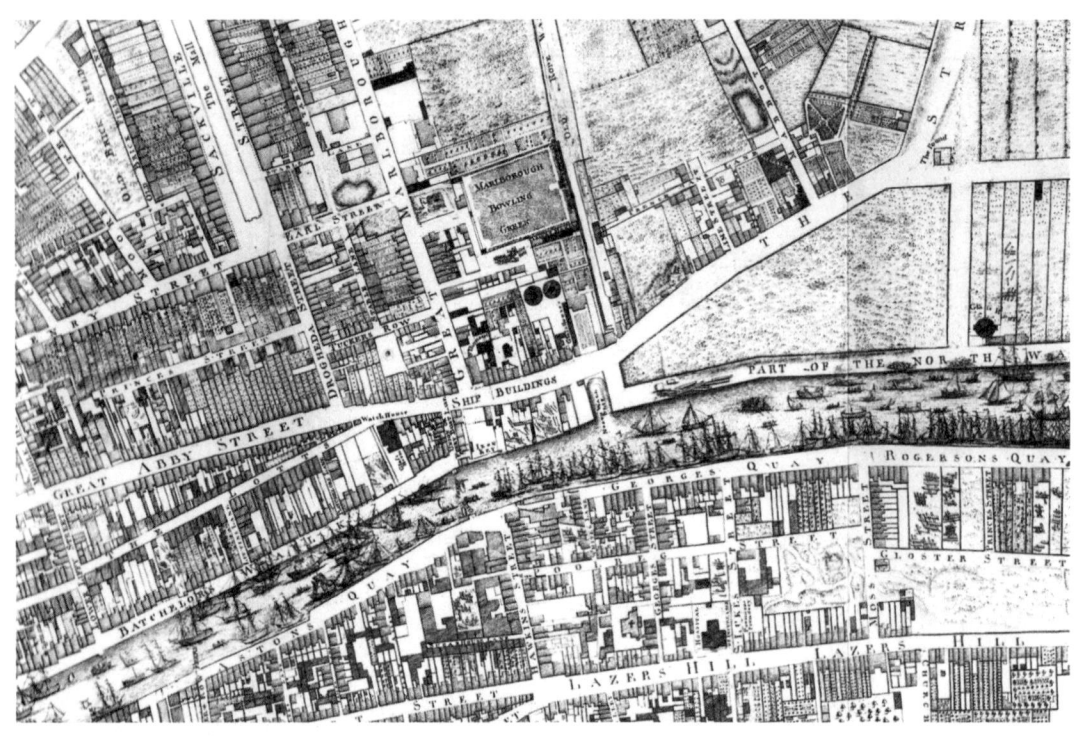

Fig. 3.7—John Rocque's survey of Dublin (1756) shows ships along the Liffey and growth on both sides of the river (courtesy of the Glucksman Library, TCD).

Working both in and under water became more practical from 1788, when the engineer John Smeaton devised an efficient air pump which allowed water to be displaced by air and permitted the occupied diving bell to work dry on the seabed. This was a huge improvement on earlier diving bells. William Steele invented a bell with an additional observation chamber and an airlock for passing written messages to those inside. In addition, this chamber allowed the observer to communicate with the surface via a speaking tube which overcame the problem of air pressure. The diving bell opened up enormous possibilities for working in both rivers and on pier head walls and jetties. In 1772 the Commissioners for the Navy received a letter from Digory Sonmin of Portsmouth Dockyard, outlining the cost of such a diving machine purchased for the *Resolution*, a naval sloop. The total expense being claimed for was £31 10s. This included the cost of double blocks (£3 3s.), leather bells (2s.) and leather bellows (£5).

The technology of the diving bell evolved over time to the one seen on Sir John Rogerson's Quay today, the workings of which were explained to this writer in 1985 by John O'Reilly of Howth, who had worked in this diving bell in the 1950s after having begun his apprenticeship in the Liffey dockyard in 1938 at fourteen years of age. He confirmed that the actual working methods had hardly altered in over 100 years.

Charles Brooking's map of Dublin in 1728 shows that the south bank of the Liffey had been walled or embanked by the late 1720s all the way down to where the Dodder met the Liffey, and that the wall had continued round the corner into the west bank of the Dodder by the late 1720s. The map certainly implied that there was water behind the wall. Either way it was prone to flooding. Streets had been drawn in behind Sir John Rogerson's Quay in the form of a square to include Hanover Street, and Lime Street is shown as partially developed, but the only buildings shown are major public ones (Fig. 3.6).

Fig. 3.8—Brocas view of Burgh Quay in 1817, showing coal being transported on the quays just above Sir John Rogerson's Quay, confirming that, 50 years after Rocque's map, shipping is clustered around the new Custom House (courtesy of the Glucksman Library, TCD).

In 1730 Charles Price's *A correct chart of the city and harbour of Dublin* confirmed the quay walls as straight all the way to the outflow of the Dodder, which he called the Donnybrook. The various channels were now gone. The map shows that the river had been embanked by 1730. Although it had been greatly narrowed, there were still some drying sands on either shore.

The 1750 painting by Ricciardelli shows the river embanked but also clearly illustrates that the land reclaimed at the back of the river wall was quite a bit lower in height than the wall itself, confirming the reference in several maps to 'low ground'. This is not surprising, as the volume of material required to fill the area to the top of the walls amounted to hundreds of millions of cubic metres. This 'low ground' can be clearly seen today in the area north of the line of Pearse Street towards the river around the Grand Canal Docks, a reminder of the original track up to Lazers Hill from the Ringsend spit in use before the wall at Sir John Rogerson's Quay (Fig. 3.7).

In 1756 John Rocque published his *Exact survey of the city and suburbs of Dublin*, in which is expressed the ground-plan of all public buildings, dwelling houses, warehouses, stables and courtyards. He included every single building in the city in his map—11,645 in total. It confirmed that more land had been filled in behind the wall at Rogerson's Quay in the 25 years since Brooking's map was published. Moving east along Rogerson's Quay, Rocque showed six houses with long back yards, while around the corner in Moss Street there were some eleven houses. After the Prince Street entrance there were eight more houses on Rogerson's Quay. The drift east was steady (Fig. 3.8).

Up west, next to Essex Bridge, there was a stretch that had not yet been embanked; there houses still came down to the water's edge. This is confirmed in a James Malton painting executed sometime later. Similarly, at Hawkins Street a few buildings remained at the water's edge, but the rest of the quays were clear. Having so much of the river embanked in the form of quays meant that Rocque was accurate in portraying ships both in the river and lying alongside. He also showed a large proportion of the ships downriver and towards Ringsend, confirming the eastward drift of the port activities.

Fig. 3.9—View towards Howth showing both river walls and shipping entering Dublin Port, executed in 1745 for Lord Howth (photo: Brian Matthews).

During this period coal was the largest single commodity brought into the port, and the new continuous wall at Rogerson's Quay, when completed, allowed for multiple ships to come alongside the quays. Shipping increased throughout the eighteenth century, as trade and the movement of people increased. Arthur Dobbs reported that 1,834 ships with a combined tonnage of 90,758 tons entered Dublin port in 1723 (Fig. 3.9). By 1784 the number of ships visiting the port stood at 2,803, a figure of almost eight ships per day coming into the harbour; in 1817 it had reached 3,483, while the tonnage had increased dramatically to 349,000 tons, in keeping with the increased size of ships.[3] The ships leaving the port did not always have just produce for export. The *Freeman's Journal* reported in January 1766 that 40 convicts were taken from Newgate prison and shipped on board the vessel *Oxford* under Captain McClean, bound for His Majesty's plantations in America.

The maps of Brooking and Rocque identify important moments in the development of Dublin. Brooking drew the city at the beginning of the eighteenth-century urban growth, and Rocque at the start of the work of the Wide Streets Commission and the radical changes that it brought to the topography of the city. Both maps were surveyed rather than compiled and both showed expansion outside the original city walls. Rocque wrote approvingly: 'the situation of Dublin is very agreeable and commodious; being a seaport, it hath a magnificent harbour through which a surprising number of vessels are continually passing up the river, which they cover from its mouth to the first bridge'. This ignored the fact that the bar still existed and the port remained subject to tidal access. The periodic massive flooding and tidal inundations also added to the concerns of the people and were usually made a lot worse when very high spring tides combined with easterly gales to push the water-levels even higher. Butler in his observations noted in 1727 that 'Equinoctial Lunation in conjunction with the south east storms raised the spring tide to a great height, the town of Ringsend

Fig. 3.10—The Marine School on Sir John Rogerson's Quay (courtesy of Louise Morgan and Brendan Maher, NGI).

was in some danger, the communication by land being cut off; a large part of Sir John Rogerson's East Quay being demolished, the waters rushed in with great violence'. In December of the same year a southerly gale drove a vessel onto the North Bull, with the loss of most of the passengers. In September 1728 a storm of great velocity blew from 5pm one evening until 3am next morning, driving several ships onto the North Bull, but none perished. On 29 and 30 September 1731 another powerful storm cast several ships adrift from their moorings onto the North Bull and three more onto the South Bull—another reminder of the difficulties of anchoring in Dublin Bay. The South Wall piling would not be completed for another three years. Rocque's map shows a high density of shipping in the river in 1756 (95 ships in all), confirming the advantage of the new quay walls, the strength of the port for trade and the fact that the river was navigable up to the first bridge (Essex Bridge).

Rocque also published *A plan of the city of Dublin and environs*, in which 'the mud-flats and rocky shoals of Dublin Bay and the channel of the river Liffey were shown in detail'. Ó Cionnaith (2012) was in error, however, when he endorsed Rocque's conclusion that 'the bay is both large and offers good shelter for ships from adverse weather and sea conditions'. Reliable primary sources offer the contrary opinion.

Nevertheless, the quays were being occupied, as seen from the addresses and occupations given in the city directory of 1752:

- John Butler, shipwright, at City Quay
- Luke Burke, sail-maker, at City Quay
- Clementine Clinton, rope-maker, at Rogerson's Quay
- Thomas Downes, shipwright, at Georges Quay
- William Murphy, shipwright, at Georges Quay
- Robert Owen, sail-maker, at Poolbeg Street
- Howard Moore, shipwright, at City Quay
- Christopher Dunn, master (captain) of the *Success*, London trader, at Lazers Hill
- James Lamb, master of the *Providence*, London trader, at Lazers Hill

Thomas Blair created a map in 1756 from the completed survey of George Gibson, titled *From an actual survey taken by George Gibson, Surveyor and Hydrographer, under the inspection of his father Robert Gibson, teacher of mathematics, a native and citizen*. Blair, too, showed the Liffey wall as completed down

DUBLIN MOVING EAST, 1708–1844

Fig. 3.11—Malton's view of a ship under construction beside the Marine School, Sir John Rogerson's Quay, Dublin, 1795.

to the Dodder at Ringsend. Malton's series of Dublin views at the end of the century includes one that shows clear industrial development, with the Marine School beside the Cardiff shipyard with a ship under construction (Fig. 3.11).

Towards the end of the eighteenth century Sir John Rogerson's Quay had become more developed. The Hibernian Marine School was for many years the most easterly building on the south bank of the Liffey, as seen from maps and charts. John Mercer, William Lydon and David Burleigh leased the site for the school from Luke Gardiner and Richard Benson on 1 May 1770. The site was a substantial one, measuring 300ft along the front, 547ft on the west side, 633ft on the east side and 300ft where it faced the lower road leading to Dublin from Ringsend. The Marine School was near the river 'on low ground and in winter at least in a damp and foggy atmosphere'. The charter for the school, issued on 1 August 1755, provided for the nomination and appointment of 'fit and able persons to be officers and schoolmaster of the said schools and nurseries doing the will of the said Corporation, to instruct and teach the children to read especially the Holy Scriptures, and to instruct them in the principles of the Protestant religion, established in our said kingdom'. It housed an average of 150 boys up to the year 1788. The Marine School, which featured in so many maps and artistic images, had been initiated in 1766 to train boys for the navy (Fig. 3.10). In 1768, ground was taken at the 'lower end of Sir John Rogerson's Quay for the purpose of erecting a house'. It is

36

Fig. 3.12—Ship for sale and ship bound for Bristol (photo: Brian Matthews).

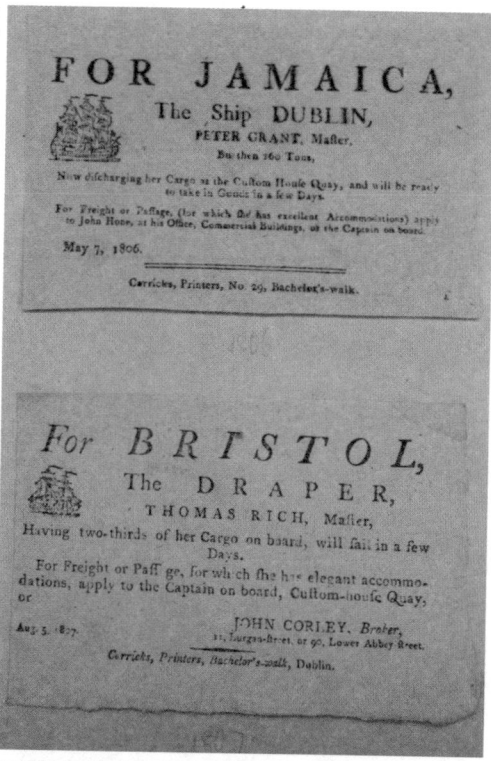

Fig. 3.13—Ships bound for Barbados.

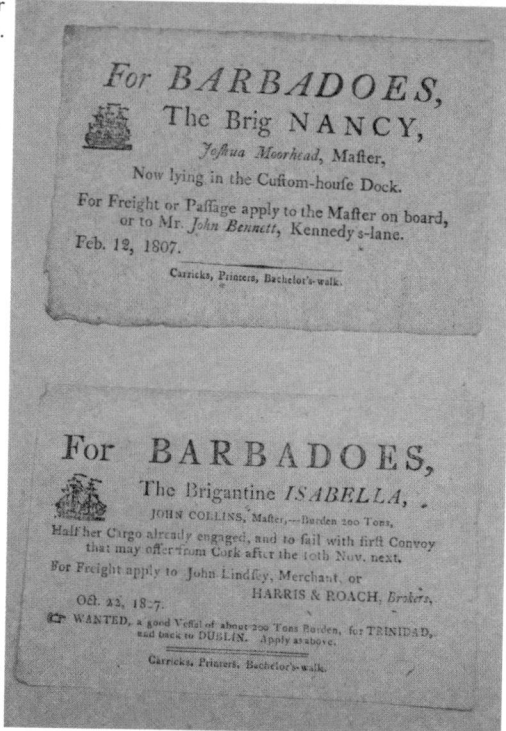

interesting to note that the ground that had been filled in behind the quay wall was now capable of supporting a substantial building, thus giving an outside time-line for construction on reclaimed land of about 40 years, but it is reasonable to assume that timber rafts were used for foundations, as in other major constructions in the city. The school opened in 1773.

In the Malton image note the ship under construction adjoining the school. Note also the narrow, sloping strand still in existence, abutting the river wall and the slanted wall. This was a substantial amount of building on reclaimed land made of sand, stone and gravel on top of river spoil and human waste from the city. While the pace of building may not have matched the pace of land reclamation, much building took place on the less-waterlogged land above Lazers Hill and around Merrion Square in the mid- and late eighteenth century. The Cardiff shipyard launched the largest ship built in Ireland in the eighteenth century at 500 tons. This shipyard was just down the river from Blair's yard, which launched a packet boat in 1765. Another shipyard also active in the area was King's. Although Dublin was growing in terms of both urban expansion and port development, most ships both visiting and being built in the city were still small, the exception being the HMS *Grampus* (1,063 tons), launched on 8 October 1782.

Though still containing much water, the area was productive for Rogerson. While bathers and anglers used this water space, it was leased to a Mr Pellissier as a private oyster-bed. This area was home to mariners, shipbuilders, brokers, rope- and sail-makers, chandlers and outfitters. It was also the haunt of revenue men, smugglers, military personnel, Royal Navy personnel, prostitutes, press-gangs, visitors and general travellers. The amount of land reclaimed totalled 125 acres (Figs 3.12–14).

The press-gang, which was empowered to operate in time of war and press men to serve in the navy, caused much difficulty for the authorities in terms of diminishing the manpower available to them for their works. This problem seems to have

Fig. 3.14—View of Sir John Rogerson's Quay in 1839, by John Berger (photo: Brian Matthews, courtesy of James Gorry, Gorry Gallery).

been present for much of the later eighteenth century. In 1793 the city offered 2,000 guineas as a fund to be dispersed to men signing on in the navy, every landsman to be given one guinea and to each able seaman two guineas. Landlords such as Lord Fitzwilliam, through his agent, were always apprehensive about losing men.

P.J. Duffy (2007) claimed that 'the most extensive modifications of the built environment in Ireland historically probably took place in the last half of the eighteenth century'. Taking into account the space reclaimed from the sea that would certainly be the case. Things did not always go smoothly, however, and projects of the size and scale that were attempted in the Liffey and Dodder were fraught with ongoing problems. In 1765 a letter written to the *Freeman's Journal* drew attention to the dangerous condition of the quay walls. As late as January 1792 the *Dublin Chronicle* reported that the duke of Leinster, leaving the city on a sea party, proceeded downriver and 'after shooting the breach in the South wall of the Liffey sailed over the Low Ground and the South Lotts and landed safely at Merrion Square'. The breach had been caused by a storm—a reminder that the coast of Dublin was, and still is, prone to powerful easterly gales. It also serves to make it clear that the land behind the quay wall was neither totally dry even at this late stage nor impervious to sudden flooding. It is to be noted that these floods were catastrophic in their volume and did fill up 'the low ground'.

On Sunday 3 July 1796 a boat race was staged between two yawls (two-masted boats)—one owned by Mr Peterson, having eight oars, and the other owned by John Draper, having six oars—from the Marine Hotel on Rogerson's Quay to the lighthouse and back. Charles Cosslett, coming to Dublin in 1794, arrived into the bay and describes how a boat came alongside and took the passengers ashore to land opposite the Marine Hotel at Sir John Rogerson's Quay. The hotel was sometimes called Burnett's Marine Hotel at the time.

An observation needs to be made with regard to the trade of the port at this time. While it is not possible to cover the century in its entirety, a glimpse of what was going in and out of the port after the walling of the river and a prolonged period of construction of the South Wall will illuminate matters and give the reader a greater understanding of city life in later eighteenth-century Dublin.

Karen Cheer (2008) provides quite an insight into the trading patterns of Dublin for part of 1785. Her research confirms the customs data of the time and is further backed up by newspaper reports. She notes that in reality the latter decades of the century were a 'vibrant economic era, one of progress, expansion and profit'. By 1785, ships carrying freight and passengers were sailing to the Caribbean, Canada and Charlestown and Philadelphia in America, while coastal traffic to Wales, Scotland and England increased significantly. Regular freight services to Liverpool also increased, as did the trade in coastal provisioning shipping at this time. This information was compiled by Richard Eaton, 'Collector of the Port of Dublin', and later 'Equalizer of Duties and Inspector of Hereditary Revenue of Ireland'.

In 1786 the Ballast Board was made responsible for the quay walls from the sea to Barrack Bridge at Watling Street and received the new title of 'the Corporation for the Preservation and Improvement of the Port of Dublin'. At this time the walls were not totally complete and some were in poor repair. John Semple won a competition in 1792 for design of a standard quay wall. Work began at Aston Quay under Francis Tunstall in 1794. There followed work on the north side, east of the newly built Carlisle Bridge; records show that the wall was 7ft 6in. thick at the base and 4ft 6in. at the top, and that it was 20–21ft high and built of stone. According to Dr Elizabeth Shotton, work was completed by 1820, but maintenance and repair continued for some years, according to the journals and ledgers of the directors of the Corporation for Preserving and Improving the Port of Dublin. The books show that George Halpin, the man in charge of all works within the remit of the Corporation, operated a constant building and repair programme on both sides of the river well beyond 1820.

It is not possible to write about work taking place both in the Liffey itself and below in the form of the South Bull Wall without considering the role played by George Semple, a man held in high regard in Dublin by those in power. Semple was highly esteemed for his technical experience and knowledge. In 1762 he compiled a series of maps of Dublin Bay for the Corporation, using a combination of other maps and charts. His *Treatise on building in water in two parts* (1776) contained much information and advice—both common-sense and technical—on a whole range of aspects of construction in or on water. It included detail on the design and rebuilding of Essex Bridge and on working in and under water subsequent to the excavation of the previous foundations. Semple contributed to and influenced all subsequent work in the area, especially the Grand Canal Docks and the Ringsend Bridge—which, unlike its predecessors, lasted. The South Bull Wall would only be completed in 1796. Semple's book was the fruit of his own experience, allied to the knowledge making its way into Ireland from the leaders in the field of construction in and around water as well as reclamation. In his section on the methods used by the 'antients and on particular qualities of lime, mortar and grout', he noted that in his excavations of the foundations of the Essex Bridge 'the bed of sharp gravel … was actually petrified into a close solid state'. This information, together with the experience that he and others gained from the building of the walls, would be put to use in the construction of the Great South Wall and the Grand Canal Docks. Semple included very clear drawings and diagrams, easily understood even by lay people, which were invaluable to those working in similar fields at the time as well as those who would follow. The book covered the building of harbour piers, walls and lighthouses, taking into account the tides, wind, waves, water surges and even the different shapes of piers at harbour mouths. He also included in this meticulous and detailed work a 'concise summary of the principles on which propositions are founded'.

The 1773 map of Dublin, which is Rocque's map with additions by Bernard Scalé (Rocque's son-in-law), has some notable features pertinent to the walled river. The full title of the map is *An accurate survey of the city and suburbs of Dublin with additions and improvements by Mr Bernard Scalé 1773 dedicated to the honourable the Dublin Society for the encouragement of arts and manufactorys and to the community of merchants of the city of Dublin*. It was the merchants who pushed for the improvement of port facilities and, as can be seen, they were the ones who commissioned the map, reinforcing the notion that the tides and improvements to the port were still uppermost in the minds of the merchant class. Again we are reminded that trade drove the intended improvements, but it was the Ballast Board that carried out the work. This was one of several maps in the eighteenth century dedicated to the merchants of Dublin. Note, too, that at this stage the most easterly building in the city was still the Marine School at Sir John Rogerson's Quay, where it was surrounded by deal and timber yards, while Lazers Hill is shown on the 'Low Road' to Ringsend and goes past the 'Low Ground' at the rear of Sir John Rogerson's Quay, now well removed from the river. This signalled the beginning of a new inland road down to the Dodder and on to Ringsend, and was a change from the old horse road on the strand at the water's edge. This would later become Great Brunswick Street and then Pearse Street.

Revd James Hall wrote in 1813 that 'there are several boats at different places perpetually crossing and recrossing with passengers at a halfpenny each'. This information confirms that by now along this stretch of the river there was sufficient depth to operate ferries all year round. Ferries had been operating on the Liffey for hundreds of years in the absence of bridges, and the city was very careful about who operated them, as a form of security within the environs of the city itself, controlling the movement of people across the river.

The work of repair and refurbishment of the river walls continued into the 1800s. The directors of the Corporation recorded that 'the quay walls now being finished under the direction of the inspector of works George Halpin … the board met on Friday 17 March 1820 for consideration of his services'. He was given a substantial increase in salary.

In his journal of 1825–7 Andrew Bigelow records: 'The labour and enterprise of the people have here succeeded happily in both widening and deepening its channel and in constructing some noble quays along its margin, what this stream has wanted in natural advantages has been supplied, as far as might be by the hand of man. Not only has great labour been expended in improving its channel and thereby facilitating navigation and not only has great taste been displayed in the quays along its sides'.

The river was now constrained to one navigable channel, and the quays now facilitated the free movement of goods and people. A channel originally 100 yards wide was now much narrower, as the walls were continually bolstered. The port had moved downriver to the east, and this move was confirmed with the building of both the new Custom House and Carlisle Bridge.

The dynamic of the city had been altered along with the port. The substantial military establishment was moved out of the city and up to the Phoenix Park in 1764, freeing more space for civilian development, though even this move did not produce total harmony, as a letter to the newspapers complaining of the noise of artillery practice showed.

It is understandable that on a building project of this magnitude there would be leaks, breaches and collapses of the walls, but all would be restored. Some quays would be totally replaced, including the new Custom House Quay later in the nineteenth century.

On a visit to Dublin in 1810 John Gamble noted that 'the quays when properly embanked will form a superior prospect to any of the kind in the universe'. Twelve years later, in 1822, Thomas Reid mentions 'those long elegant quays formed of fine hammered granite erected along the Liffey'. Work was continuing on the walls in 1824, as evidenced from a letter of 28 February 1824 from George Halpin, Inspector of Works for the Ballast Board, concerning a requirement for the Revenue Commissioners to pay for work to their wall adjoining the north wall at Commons Street. Men were also working on the north quay walls on 15 April 1824, having been paid £57 10s. 2d. A further payment of £46 7s. 9d. reveals that the walls were still being refurbished on 2 July 1824.

In 1833 the *Dublin Penny Journal* published an article about the quays of Dublin: 'the feeble citizen of four score, as he saunters along the quay of the north and south wall, recalls to his memory that in his boyhood those beautiful walks, which he now enjoys, were swampy impassable strands—that from Ballybough to Ballsbridge and from St Marks Church [Pearse Street] to Ringsend were under the dominion of the waves of the Atlantic'.

As Louis Cullen (1983) has observed, the building of the Custom House and the erection of the Carlisle Bridge, which the merchants had correctly foreseen as probable, gave an impetus to the continuing growth of the port eastwards down the river.

What had been a river estuary with many channels now contained only one, and it was deeper at all stages of the tide for ships. Shipping to Dublin—and consequently trade—had increased. As the century progressed, the population also increased as people flooded to the city, driving up demand for food, clothing, accommodation and work, all in an expanding economy. The single channel had been embanked on both sides and the work of backfilling and reinforcing the barrier continued. Meanwhile, the space had been occupied by streets and lanes containing dwellings, inns, brothels, sail-making lofts, rope-making operations, schools, a hospital, timber yards, boat-building and shipbuilding, general provisioning and chandlery shops. Terence Murray, one of several sailcloth-makers in the port, operated on St George's Quay but lived at Carey Lane, Drumcondra. Murray had adapted to the new reality. He lived in one new urban space and worked in another—one reclaimed from green pasture and the other from the tides. And of course throughout this period there was an inexorable rise in the demand for coal, which brought in most of the ships. Later in the century salt-making, metalworks and farming were undertaken in the area. All these activities signified people occupying the space where the tide had heretofore ruled. As the port developed and grew, so too did the occupation of the space between the river walls and Merrion Square and Mount Street down to Beggar's Bush Barracks, opened in 1824. The building of the barracks closed off another segment of the southern zone created by the embanking of the river and greatly added to the expansion of the area in human terms with the establishment of the military barracks.

Constructing the Great South Bull Wall

The second work of significance to be undertaken during the eighteenth century in the lower Liffey estuary to improve port infrastructure and consequently trade and growth was the erection of the Great South Bull Wall. This construction had an enormous impact on the port and the city. The combination of these two projects would be crucial in defining the manner in which Dublin expanded. As noted, at the end of the seventeenth century the maps of Phillips, Collins and Cullen show little evidence of activity or development down at the Ringsend end of the Liffey and in the Dodder basin. Not much seemed to have happened since the Restoration.

Fig. 3.15—St Matthew's Church, Irishtown, built in 1704, painted by Arthur Joy (1821) (NLI Prints and Drawings).

The 1706 Cullen survey of the Ringsend area for the Pembroke estate showed slight development. Two years later the Ballast Board took responsibility for all matters along the course of the Liffey to the sea. Having walled in the Liffey to make one navigable channel in an effort to facilitate access to the port at the Custom House, the second task was to constrain the Liffey as far as the bar by erecting a protecting wall for ships in the pools. The South Bull refers simply to the vast area of sandbanks below water when the tide was in and exposed for miles when it receded. The plan assumed that this work would also impede what was generally perceived as the spread of sand from the South Bull itself on to the bar, thanks to tidal action. It was also a fact that the wall would serve as some extra protection against invaders and predatory pirates—always a consideration, given the city fathers' obsession with security. The Assembly was told on 11 June 1745 that French privateers had taken several vessels in the Tusker Rock area (Wexford), among them three bound for Cork, reminding the Assembly that the harbour was undefended and open: while the Dutch threat might have abated, the French one was very much alive. The Ballast Board would erect a timber wall, generally referred to as the Pilings or Piles, and later a stone version, out to where the Poolbeg Lighthouse now stands, with a harbour, hotel and military depot on the wall halfway down, at the location of the Pigeon House today.

In February 1692/3 John Cullen drew a map for the Pembroke estate. It showed 28 dwellings at Irishtown and six at Ringsend, and a wooden bridge (at the present location of Londonbridge Road) as the only connection to the spit. There are ships in both the Liffey and the Dodder and smaller boats upstream in the Dodder, but little activity down on the spit.

In his 1693 pilot-book (published separately from his 1686 map of Dublin Bay) Captain Grenville Collins compared Dublin unfavourably with Chester. His depths showed 9ft at low water at Chester Pool ('you may anchor at Dort Pool eighteen feet; you will find nine feet of water at Low Water Spring Tides') but only 3ft in Dublin's Iron Pool. In 1704 John Payne was granted a lease of the oyster-beds down at Poolbeg (the pool, not to be confused with Poolbeg Lighthouse) for 21 years at £5 per half-year. This information is useful, firstly because it shows that the oyster-bed must have been very productive to generate such a healthy rent, and secondly because it confirms that the

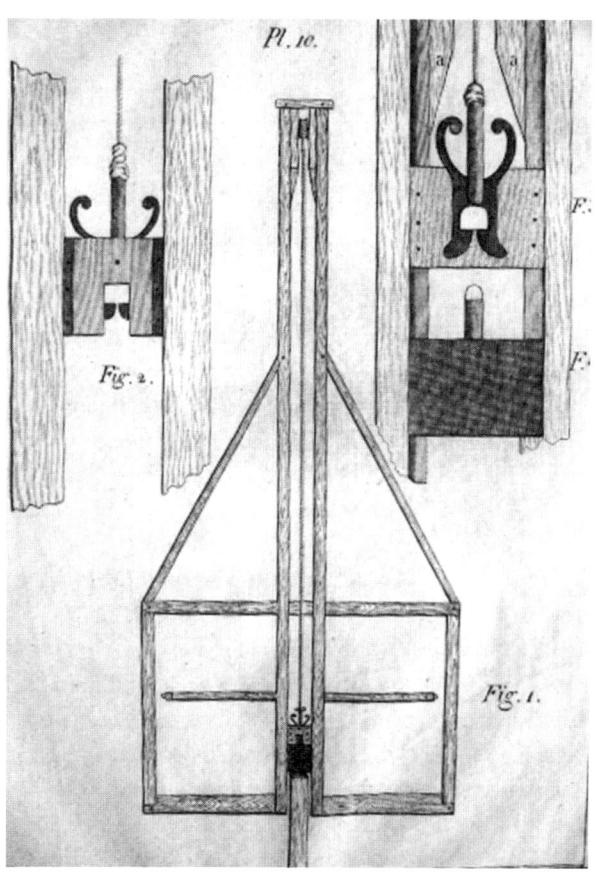

Fig. 3.16—George Semple's sketch of a machine for piling (TCD Early Printed Books).

area of the oyster bed was tidal and that the water was shallow enough to allow the gathering of the oysters on foot.

John Cullen completed another map of the area in April 1706 in which he confirmed the erection of the Church of St Matthew in Irishtown (Fig. 3.15). St Matthew's became an important landmark for ships attempting to pilot their way across the bar and records show that it was completed in 1704. It is clearly shown, with all the buildings in Irishtown to the west and north of it, and the area between it and the River Dodder was called the Irishtown bank. St Matthew's appears in maps, charts and paintings and is a useful source of evidence of location. In 1706 it was ordered that the church be given £50 by the city when the roof was put on. In 1710 money was allocated to help complete the building with a steeple. In the same year, three streets were laid out at Ringsend on the spit parallel to the Dodder—Thorncastle, Barrow and Maryann's streets, which fronted onto the waterfront of the river, then called Fitzwilliam Key (Pembroke estate map, NAI 1706). What Cullen had called in 1693 the 'City Strand' had now become 'Lord Fitzwilliam's Strand'.

To understand what took place, a chronological outline of the process is helpful. We will treat the wall in three separate sections: (i) the timber piles, (ii) the change to the stone basket barrier, which became a wall, and (iii) the separate wall which ran from the Pigeon House towards Sandymount but quickly vanished from the records, never to be heard of again.

In 1715 the directors of the Ballast Committee advised the Corporation that 'it is the opinion of merchants and other skilful men that the south side of the channel be piled, which will raise the south bank so high it will be a great shelter for shipping which lie in the harbour'. This reveals yet again that the city merchants were one of the main driving forces for change and improvement. It cannot be a coincidence that the entire creation of the city of Amsterdam up to that date and beyond was based on piling. The oldest extant painting of the city, completed in 1538 by Cornelius Anthonisz and now in the Amsterdam Historisch Museum, illustrates how the Dutch had built it—shoring up sandbanks and pieces of dry and semi-dry ground, and reclaiming more by keeping out the sea. More importantly from the point of view of this writer, the painting shows the piling set in two rows along the front of the town. This is exactly what happened on the South Bull. Before piling began in Dublin the Dutch had already experienced their 'Golden Age' as leaders in shipping, trade and discovery, as well as in canal construction and windmill technology, and their achievements were widely known. At this stage most houses in Amsterdam were built on timber rafts or piles, so it is no surprise that a Dutch engine for pile-driving is mentioned early in the Dublin development. Piling of individual vertical timbers using local machinery commenced in 1716. A Dutch engine for pile-driving arrived in 1717, but in the following year the project reverted to using the more reliable and robust Irish machine. This was not a unique instance of the seeking out of better technology to achieve a goal. In 1735 the Royal Dublin Society, on being informed of a new agricultural development, agreed to fund master carpenter James Moore on a trip to Scotland, where a new type of corn-threshing machine had been invented. His instructions were to make a scale model and then return to make a full-size model, which he did; it was bought and used by one of the directors (Fig. 3.16).

Work progressed to both east and west from the height of the South Bull during 1718–21.[4] The early construction consisted of piles set in three rows connected with woven wattle to form a casing 10ft deep, which was then filled to a height of 5ft with shingle and stones. A new method was adopted in 1721, whereby large frames of timber were assembled in a yard at Ringsend and floated down to the site on rafts. In 1726 and 1727 much larger frames began to be used for making bigger boxes to be filled with stones and gravel, permitting the creation of more rigid structures. This system continued in use until the completion of the timber wall in 1731. Meanwhile, the Committee reported on 20 June 1726 that 'thirteen frames were sent down last season and all bar one have weathered the winter'; one went adrift but was repaired. While the wall provided much-needed shelter in the harbour area in the pools to the north of the wall, it also had the positive effect of increasing the amount of dry ground to its south. The work was demanding of both men and materials; in 1726 it was reported that 'six gabbards and one float' 'had been graved to be ready for next season, twenty two tons of oak, and they had in storage 222 pieces of oak'. Timber for shipbuilding and structural work was sourced from Poland at this time. Polish timber was viewed as being of a superior quality, and was often more readily available than material transported overland.

The problem remained that the structure was not robust enough, and there were places where there was 2m of water in pools even at low water. The report in the following year itemised the purchase of 61 pieces of oak from Mr Gibton and 42 pieces from Montgomery and White, and the agreement to buy in another 640 pieces of oak from Poland. In the same report two additional gabbards are requested to expedite the task. This was necessary because of the high rate of attrition suffered by the boats and equipment, and because of the need for constant repair and maintenance of the piles. It must be remembered, too, that throughout this enormous project the weather played a vital role in that men could only work in certain conditions, and the work rate was also subject to the tides. In fact, the work was totally seasonal, as winter brought not only worse weather but also shorter hours of daylight for working.

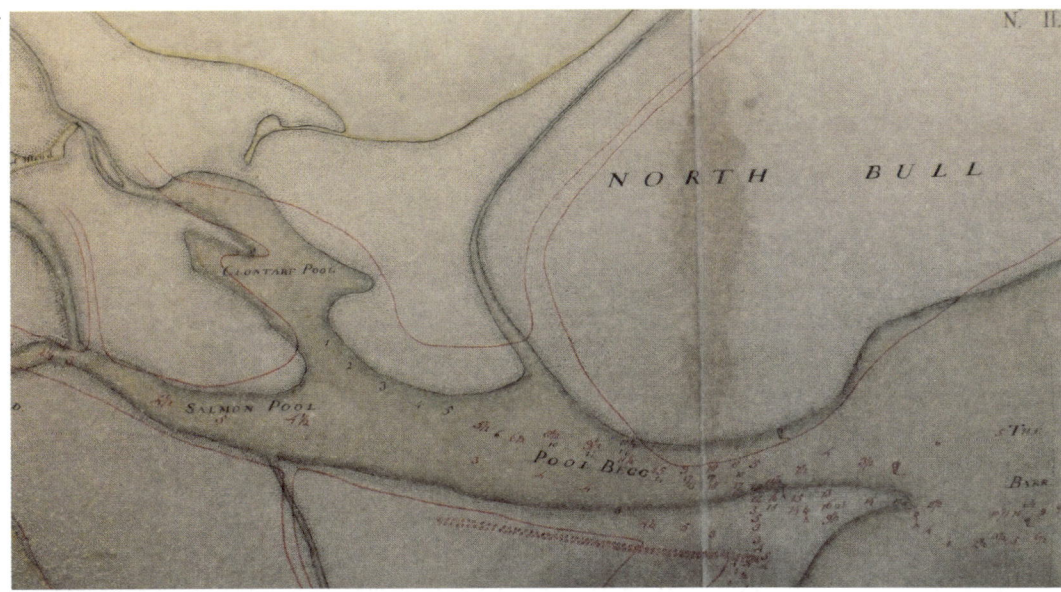

Fig. 3.17—Stokes's map of 1725, showing piling on the South Bull (Dublin Port Company).

Timber and ropes were valuable commodities in the period and were quickly collected—and not just by beachcombers. In November 1728 Captain Vernon of Clontarf Castle assumed the right to all property of shipwreck at Clontarf shore, including any timber from damaged frames from the piles. Timber was always seen as a valuable commodity, and Queen Elizabeth I had prohibited tree-felling for use in charcoal-burning (except in iron-making areas) because she was aware that there was not an inexhaustible supply of timber, as oak trees took so long to grow.[5] The city, jealously guarding what it perceived to be its own property rights, vigorously denied Vernon's claims to shipwreck material, and issued a denial of his claims to fishing rights at Poolbeg the following year. Vernon was not so easily beaten; he took his case to the House of Lords but lost his appeal for his rights over Crab Lake and strand (immediately opposite the wooden bridge to Dollymount Strand), although he did succeed in his appeal for the right to farm oysters. One side-effect of this whole episode was that Vernon constructed a series of stone pillars in the open strand, daily washed by the tides, to mark his property line. Two of these stone pillars can still be seen today, one just off the Clontarf Road at Castle Avenue and the other opposite Vernon Avenue. A third, which lies fallen nearby, can be seen at low tide.

It is evident that large quantities of expensive timber were required for the project, but warnings had already been sounded regarding possible problems, including structural damage. The Stokes map shows the position in relation to progress in 1725 (Fig. 3.17). Captain John Perry had written to the Ballast Office in 1721, warning that the piles will 'yet require repeated labour and expense to answer the service required and will be impossible in my opinion further to carry out and maintain the same to the distance which is necessary into deeper water unless some better method be taken for it'. This is exactly what happened. The problem was how to drive the piles through the pool water and into the sand.

To address this, the engineers now began to assemble even stronger piles in the form of series of timber stakes, up to twenty at a time, braced together both diagonally and horizontally; these sturdier structures were sunk and dug into the sand, and then filled with stones and gravel. Gravel for filling the frames was also taken from the Dodder, where there were enormous gravel banks, as shown on John Cullen's 1731 map. It was recorded that in the summer of 1786 men used pickaxes to remove gravel from the bank of the Dodder at the strand at old Donnybrook (Ballsbridge).

Inevitably, when piling on the South Bull was complete it was decided to build in stone, a double wall. It was always evident that nothing less than a stone barrier would suffice, both because of attrition from storm damage and because of the rotting of the timber piles. John Semple wrote twenty years later that 'these piles rotted and decayed in a very short time'. He quotes Sir Hugh Platt on the methods of preserving timber: 'the Venetians make use of one which seems very rational which was to burn and scorch their timber in a flaming fire ... others inform us, the Dutch preserve their gates, portcullises, drawbridges and sluices by covering them with a mix of pitch and tar ... I conclude the Venetian method is preferable.'

New method of construction

This wall was begun in 1748 and would take more than eleven years to complete. At this stage open water still existed for a distance along the Liffey from Ringsend Point eastward out to where the piles ended. This, however, only dealt with part of the overall problem.

In 1721 Perry had warned the Corporation that Liverpool had raised sufficient money by public subscription to build 'a dock or basin' and that Dublin faced similar difficulties to Liverpool. He asked the Assembly: 'Are there not other influences in the world that bear the same evidence of the increase or disadvantage to trade from the same causes ... and does not that town feel the benefit of it and the trade of Chester decline?'[6] Perry's concerns notwithstanding, by 1759 the only part unfinished was the very short section between Ringsend Point and Ringsend Bridge on the Dodder. In that year a petition was presented to parliament seeking more funds. The work would continue for another 35 years and be completed between 1792 and 1795.

The double wall consisted of a second barrier of frames filled with stone and gravel on the north side of the already completed structure. Operating this way allowed more protection from the elements for the workmen. Even so, Captain Bligh made additions and alterations to the wall in the early nineteenth century.

In 1731 the piling was complete but required a massive maintenance programme, which proved costly. Money—cash flow—was always a problem for the Committee, as well as the difficulties caused by ongoing flooding from heavy rains upriver in the Liffey and easterly gales allied to high tides.[7] They had only recently completed the north and south walls on the Liffey and these structures required continuous refurbishment. But other problems arose in the harbour which drew the Committee's attention away from the work, such as the incident in 1726 when a man-of-war ran aground and had to be refloated with the help of all the floats and gabbards. Damage to the piles could also come from other sources, such as 'a ship running against them' in 1755. On 21 January 1757 a ship was reported wrecked on the south side of the piles and gabbard no. 8 was 'drove on shore at Sutton and beat to pieces'.

Pressing, too, could lead to problems. Ships could press men from almost all walks of life into the navy to serve as seamen, and this played havoc with ordinary commerce, as men literally disappeared from view. At one point the presence of the warship *Lively* sent men to ground and halted the arrival of coal-boats—and of course the gabbardmen vanished, too. At the request of the Assembly, the captain negated the warrant of his press-gang and was in return presented with the freedom of the city in a silver casket.

Fig. 3.18—Blair's map of 1756, showing a new and separate new wall complete to Sandymount (Glucksman Library, TCD).

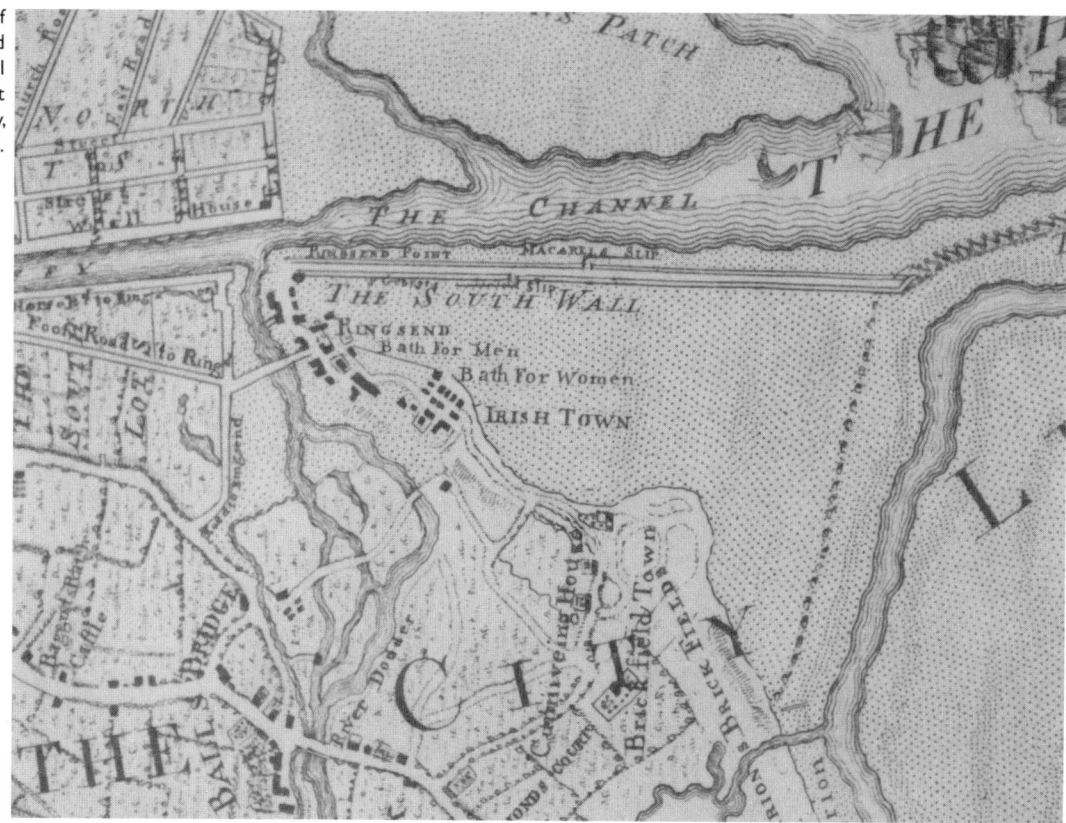

Another wall

For some reason which has never been explained, at this stage the Ballast Committee decided to build another wall from the site of where the Pigeon House is today in a southerly direction towards Sandymount. The sources provide no explanation as to why they did this; it is simply recorded that this other wall was built. On completion it was immediately ignored in the documents. Nevertheless, its existence can lead to confusion as to which work is being referred to in the sources. It can be identified from a number of old maps, including Blair's map, but this writer has been unable to discover anything further on this aspect of the construction in any official documentation (Fig. 3.18).

The stone wall

It now became imperative to construct a stone wall, which was begun from the location of the Pigeon House towards Ringsend in 1748 and finished by 1759. The Committee recommended in 1758 that as soon as this wall was completed an immediate start be made on completing the double wall down at the east end of the piles. This made sense: the barrier created by the piling was always susceptible to greater damage and the early indications were that the new double wall was more robust. By 1759 'the walls are now complete high enough to prevent water going over them on spring tides as far as the salt house'. Shortly afterwards, the walls were finished to Ringsend (where the salt house was located).

In 1760 work began on the construction of a lighthouse at the east end of the piles to replace the lightship; it was completed by 1767 (Fig. 3.19). The building of a stone wall commenced from

DUBLIN MOVING EAST, 1708–1844

the new lighthouse back towards the Pigeon House to meet up with the other stone wall. Advertisements in various publications in London, Dublin and Amsterdam announced that there would be a new light at the end of the pilings from 29 September 1767. Finishing this work and reinforcing the double stone wall—facing the wall with granite slabs and topping the surface with similar stones—would absorb another 30 years. When finished, this double stone wall built out to the site of the Pigeon House was able to take carriages.

Blair's map of 1756 reveals the state of construction of the entire structure and clearly defines the difference between the timber piles and the new double stone walls. This new work comprised two separate parallel walls to the north of the piles, the space between filled in with sand, stones and gravel. At the western end it shows that the wall was built out from Ringsend downriver for approximately half the distance to the Poolbeg Lighthouse (i.e. where it would be when completed). The rest of the construction was called the piles and stretched to the end. Blair showed the Liffey

Fig. 3.19—The lighthouse at Poolbeg (which opened in 1768) by William Sadler (courtesy of James Gorry).

wall as complete down along the river and angled south to the Dodder Basin.

The 1738 Dublin Directory barely mentions the existence of Ringsend/Irishtown, noting only that eight persons of any consequence lived there. There had not been a great increase in population since the Restoration, when a population of 59 of English descent and 21 of Irish descent was reported. This figure cannot be accurate, however, because there were boat crews, carpenters, labourers, revenue personnel and shore crews, as well as a multitude of clerks administering and working on the construction of the frames, the movement of same or the repair and installation, as well as constantly repairing the piles. It may be that most were non-resident or not permanently resident and thus not counted.

In 1740 a painting of Howth Castle and grounds was presented to Lord Howth. The painting—known more for its inclusion of the figure of Jonathan Swift supposedly attempting to court Lucy St Lawrence in the lower corner—is of interest to this work because it shows the piling extending a great distance out into the bay, with ships sheltering behind this new breakwater. It is the only known painting including the piles at this time.

In July 1744 the Committee reported to the directors that 'since our last report to your honours we have gone on with the repairs of our works on the south wall'. Two days later they stated that 'we have built a new floating light and fixed her to the end of the piles'.

On 22 April 1748 the Committee suggested to the directors that a double wall of stone should be built from the western end of the piles to Ringsend point.[8] This in fact became two separate walls, faced at the sides, with the gap between filled in and covered with large granite slabs. Some months later, in July, they reported 'reasonable progress'. The accounts sent to the directors in 1759 showed that the cost of building was £1,109 17s. 6d., and the wall was completed that same year. The following year, 1760, the Committee arranged for a blockhouse to be constructed at the junction of the timber and stone constructions; this became known as the Pigeon House.

Nevertheless, the notorious easterly gales inflicted damage on this man-made barrier in every season. Reports claimed that there was not one single season when no damage was done to the structure, noting in 1762 that 'several ships have fallen foul of them'. It has to be borne in mind that a ship entering the bay in boisterous seas would find it extremely difficult to identify the structure, even if the captain knew of its existence and current state of progress. This recurring damage also caused loss of filling inside the structure and it seems that quite often men wound up in the water, so the decision was taken to fix ladders to the structure in December 1764 'for the safety of the men and mariners'. The concern for equipment remained a priority in this period too, as the Committee 'has ordered a new pinnace and a small boat to be built' and considered the necessity of building a sloop and a large boat for carrying on the wall on a larger scale.

While the work on the piling barrier and then the double walls continued apace, the Committee had the job of juggling its resources and prioritising the location of men and workboats, and this included the many attempts to clean and dredge the Liffey along its course. This meant that for differing reasons over time men were assigned to work upstream at the Custom House quay on Wellington Quay. Another problem for the city and its people arose in 1772, when westerly winds made it too difficult for several colliers (coal-boats) to get up the river—days passed before they succeeded. It was then suggested that when this happened again (notice not *if* but *when*) the gabbards should be used to collect gravel and sand by dredging for use in the laying of pipes for water and other works. The attempt to clear the river at the Custom House continued into 1774 and the men working in the river collected 308 tons of stones from the shoals, consequently deepening the channel.

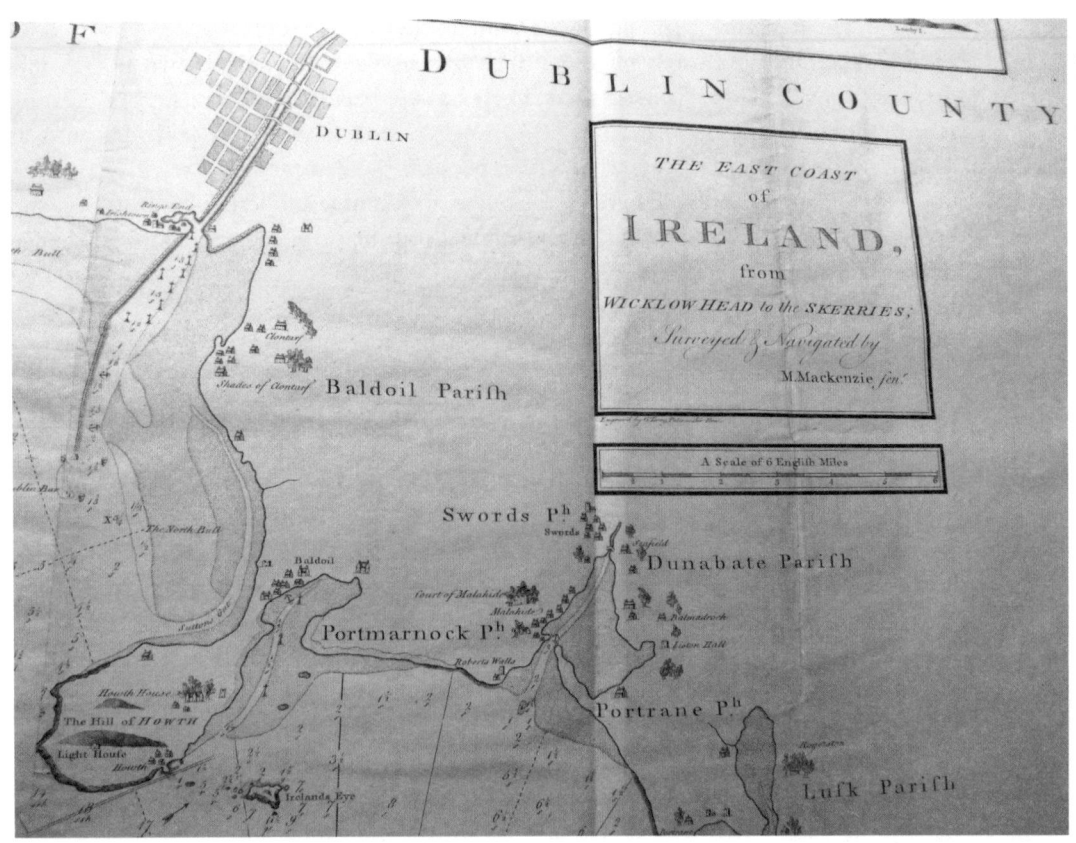

Fig. 3.20—Nautical chart of the east coast by Murdoch McKenzie (1776) (courtesy of Frank Pelly).

Nothing ever seemed to run smoothly in this monumental project, and attention was regularly diverted from the task in hand. On 5 March 1773, for example, a mob boarded the ship *Britannia* and destroyed and carried away an amount of worsted yarn.[9] It was not always bad news, however: when the ship *Trevor* was lost, Captain James Standon saved the cargo, valued at £7,000, and was rewarded with the freedom of the city. On another occasion in 1773 several tanners complained of drastic water shortages and the city was instructed to help out. These examples illustrate the many ways in which the city and its Ballast Committee got sidetracked into different areas of responsibility.

As the South Wall was being constructed, the engineer John Smith was asked to design and erect a lighthouse at its outer extremity. Begun in 1761, it was completed and operating by 1767. The idea of a lighthouse had been around for some considerable time. In 1700 the Assembly endorsed a report 'upon the business of erecting a lighthouse etc at Dublin'. The Committee reported on 24 June 1767 that the light 'will soon be finished and the floating light will be discontinued, and that they have placed the advertisements in three gazettes'. Months later, in early October,[10] they reported: 'We beg to inform your honours we have had a light on the new lighthouse every night since 29 September last and have pleasure to find it answers very well'. While all this work was being carried on under the instruction of the Committee, damage continued to be inflicted on its construction, as again in 1771 ships had been driven onto the piles.

In their efforts to make the port safer and more accessible, the Committee decided to mark the Kish Bank out on the eastern edge of the bay, eight miles offshore. They sent a deputation to Liverpool to find out more about how the city there was dealing with such matters. The envoys came back with a sample buoy and accompanying chain, which were copied and used for a period to mark the bank for shipping.

In 1770 Murdoch McKenzie, an innovative and pioneering naval surveyor, produced a map of Dublin Bay (Fig. 3.20). He was one of the very first Royal Navy surveyors to take over responsibility for producing charts; up to that time the use of Dutch and French charts had been universal. He arrived with a justified reputation for excellence, having surveyed the Orkney Islands in the 1740s. Without question the Orkneys would be one of the most difficult places to survey, simply because of the exposed Atlantic weather conditions and, more importantly, the strength of the tides, ten knots not being unusual. His charts were the first accurate British charts, and his was the first attempt to chart the coast of Ireland since Grenville Collins in 1693. McKenzie also invented the symbols and abbreviations still in use today. His treatise on maritime surveying was published in 1774. His chart included many depths and some excellent detail on the eastern coastline of Ireland, from Wicklow Head to the Skerries islands. This was part of his commission to survey the entire coast of Ireland for the Admiralty. The methodology he employed—the use of interconnecting triangles—would be used by those who followed him, including the Ordnance Survey of Ireland 70 years later.

Defence of the island, and particularly Dublin, was always uppermost in the minds of the authorities at the time and there were many reminders of why they needed to be prepared. Charles

Fig. 3.21—Troops stationed in the fort (NLI; photo: Brian Matthews).

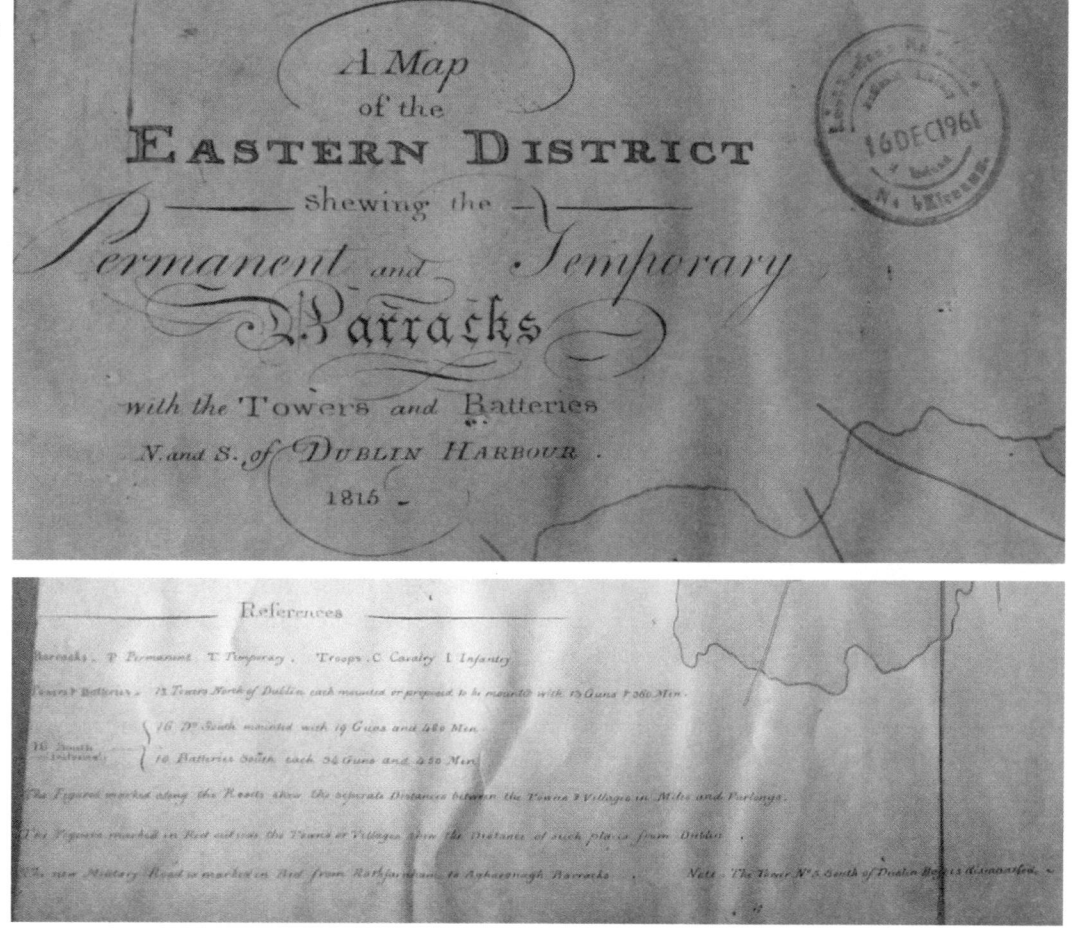

Vallancey, a military engineer, was posted to Carrickfergus after the French invasion of February 1760, when the French under Commodore Thurot landed near Kilroot and attacked Carrickfergus. After a parley, the governor managed to persuade Thurot to re-embark and sail away, and his ships were captured shortly afterwards off the Isle of Man. Vallancey later reported on various projects as a consultant on harbours, canals and bridges and became the man in charge at the erection of the pier at Kingstown.[11] In his report on the Boyne Navigation he notes the great spirit of Drogheda, remarking that 'the town has four vessels which sail to London'. On 18 August 1777 he submitted a report on the bay and harbour of Dublin (Fig. 3.21), with emphasis on defence of the city, in which he advised building a battery at the Pigeon House on the South Wall and erecting a fort at Ringsend (note that at this stage the construction was not complete) to store arms and ordnance (it was finally decided to place the arsenal in the Phoenix Park):

> 'Agreeable to your request I have carefully examined the bay and harbour of Dublin, and having consulted many experienced pilots and fishermen on the spot, I beg leave to submit the following remarks.
> The security of shipping in this channel depends chiefly on the local situation of the harbour, being a tide harbour, having a dangerous bar at the entrance and many sand banks without, and if an enemy ship was traversing the bay in the night, the only time for so hazardous an attempt, it is almost impossible such a ship can escape being wrecked if the lights in the bay were to be extinguished, or can such an attempt be done suddenly as the enemy boats must come up with the flood and having the moorings of the vessel must then remain in the narrow channel, until such time the tide ebbs, in order to carry off the prize.
> A battery erected at the lighthouse and another at the Pigeon House will certainly annoy the boats of the enemy rowing up the harbour with the flood.'

Vallancey added that the weakness of shore batteries in this case would be that enemy boats might keep to the north side of the channel (the side nearest the shore at Clontarf) while exiting on the ebb tide. He pointed out that the channel is half a mile wide off the lighthouse and from thence to the shore at Clontarf is two miles, so that the other possible deterrent would be a sloop or man-of-war. He confirmed that the physical situation of the harbour was its greatest security and that a shore battery would be an added bonus. As proof of this he remarked: 'I find the privateer which lately sailed in the channel never ventured nearer the shore than three miles'. Noting that 'The lighthouse is far advanced in to the bay and much exposed to the force of the sea', Vallancey suggested that a battery at the Pigeon House would cost about £5,000. He maintained that a battery at Ringsend 'would in no way defend the harbour as vessels cannot come up so far when loaded on account of the shallowness of the water'. He gave depths at low water of between 2ft and 5ft at Ringsend and 3–4ft at the Pigeon House, and cites the nearest available ports as Carrickfergus and Waterford. Vallancey also dealt with the other aspect of security—that of safety in bad weather: 'In a hard gale at east which causes the greatest swell in this bay, there is no place of shelter'. Vallancey drew in the ranges of battery fire from both of the proposed batteries at the Pigeon House and the lighthouse, showing clearly how perilous it would be to attempt to invade.

Only seven years after McKenzie's chart, Vallancey confirms the state and progress of the double wall from the spit at Ringsend to the Poolbeg Lighthouse, which at the time was nearing completion.

Fig. 3.22—Wide Streets Commission map of area no. 227 (courtesy of Mary Clarke, Pearse Street Library).

At this stage he showed the wooden piles as comprising about only a third of the entire structure. His suggested battery did become a reality later on and was only once in danger of being used—at the time of Daniel O'Connell's monster Repeal meeting that was scheduled to be held at Conquer Hill in Clontarf in 1843, when the gun crews went on high alert.

In 1778 an abutment on the south side of the wall was proposed, in order to bolster the wall itself against the easterly gales by diffusing the sometimes ferocious waves. The point of this proposal was to attempt to break down the big seas as they attacked the structure, and so the plan was to extend out a slope of huge stones in a southerly aspect to take the power out of the waves. This system works and is in use today in harbours everywhere. The following year Lord Ranelagh supplied 2,000 mountain stones 5–7ft long at seven shillings each, later reduced to five shillings each.[12] This same abutment was extended the full length of the wall over the next twenty years. For further appreciation of the expense of the project, a list of some costs associated with the work may be helpful:

- Cash paid for mountain stones—383 in all, with a continuous length of 4,452ft, at 8½d. per foot—totalled £157 13s. 5d.
- Cash paid for walling and filling stones from Bullock—3,382 tons at 20d. per ton—totalled £281 16s. 8d.
- Cash paid for hammered blocks from Bullock—24 at 8s. per block—totalled £10 4s.
- Cash paid for carriage of stones from Bullock in the period from 1 July 1766 to 14 October 1767 totalled £123 11s.
- Cash paid for quarry stones from Clontarf—488 tons at 2s. per ton—totalled £48 16s. Carriage on this delivery came to £8 2s.
- Cash paid to a stonemason for 278 days at 2s. 3d. per day totalled £31 5s. 6d.
- George Darley, stonecutter, was paid for two days at 3s. per day.

In 1779 the Committee found a new supplier of stones, a Mr Combs, and ordered 2,000 from him at 7s. each—2s. 6d. less than previously for the wall.[13] Some years later, in 1785, the Committee confirmed that between 1752 and 1781 they had paid out a total of £57,169 4s. 6d. for the construction of the wall and piles. This total included a rough mason's wall from Ringsend to the Blockhouse (Pigeon House/Fort) which had been completed ('rough' can be interpreted as meaning unfaced with granite stones). The Wide Streets Commission produced a map of the planned development of the zone down to the fort (Figs 3.22 and 3.23).

While all this progress was being made, the workmen on the boats struck in 1785 over pay

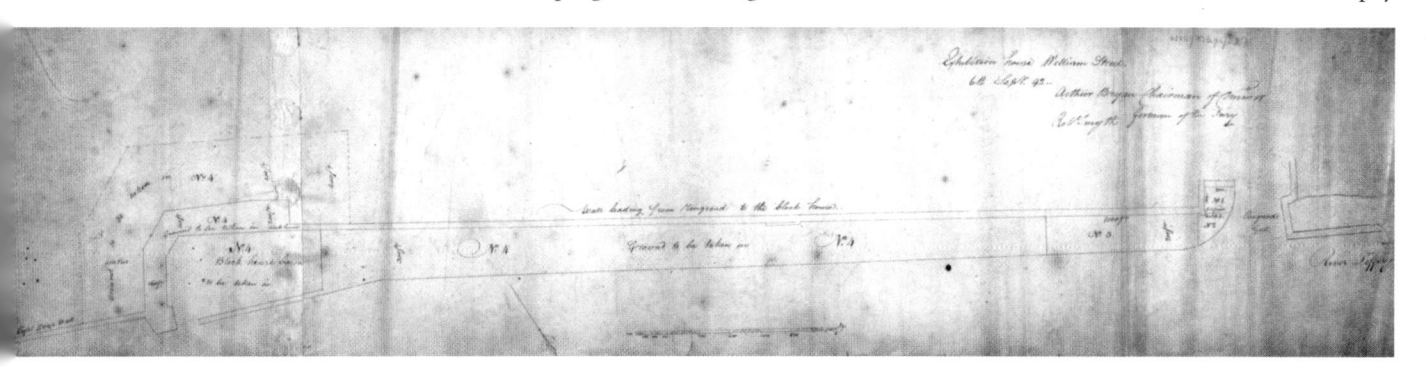

Fig. 3.23—Pigeon House Harbour, with the *Dorset* of Lord Lieutenant Marquis Cornwallis at her berth (courtesy of Louise Morgan and Brendan Maher, NGI).

rates; they were, however, quickly coerced or persuaded to return to work at the same rates, strikes not being acceptable as a form of employment bargaining then. The following year Hugh Murphy, a master shipwright, was leased land by the Committee for the purpose of building and repairing workboats. All this time damage continued to be done to both the Liffey wall and the South Bull Wall. Repairs to the wall from Sir John Rogerson's Quay to Ringsend Bridge are mentioned in 1787. The sum of £200 was allocated by the Committee, with the warning that, if repairs were not carried out speedily, 'considerable damage may ensue by the overflowing of the low grounds enclosed by the wall'. This comment is important because it shows that the land behind the wall was not completely secure from inundation, and that the time-line for building around the Grand Canal Docks and along Great Brunswick Street, as well as the erection of the Dublin to Kingstown Railway, was extremely close to these events.

One of the other omissions from the official records throughout the construction—and, indeed, in other major works—is the complete absence of any mention of horse transport of any description. It is a fact that most stones were floated across to the site by barge, workboat or raft, using the tides. Nevertheless, it is apparent that many horses, carts and carters—whose numbers had to be in the hundreds—were involved in the walling of the Liffey, the erection of the Great South Wall, the Grand Canal Docks and the embanking of the Dodder, as well as the movement of stone supplies along the Tolka and the construction of the railway embankment for the Dublin to Kingstown Railway. This would have been especially the case on occasions when barges, floats and gabbards were unable to collect and deliver the larger stones (such as the large stones used for facing the wall) owing to light or weather conditions.

In September 1767 the Assembly voted to present John Smith with a piece of plate valued at twenty guineas in grateful thanks for his excellent work on the planning and construction of the new lighthouse. The work of bolstering the defences around the wall and the lighthouse continued, however. This explains the stonework around the base of the lighthouse seen in the paintings of William Sadler, among several others who painted the scene many times in the last decades of the eighteenth century.

As the development of Dublin port attests, land reclamation on a grand scale was not beyond the imagination of man in the mid-eighteenth century. George Semple had proposed in 1762 that two large sea walls be built, one coming out from Booterstown into the bay for a distance of one mile and a second one, also a mile in length, coming out from Sutton Strand. With the South Wall as a border to the north, the total enclosed area would comprise 1,266 acres. This was thinking on a very ambitious scale, and the fact that Semple was not ridiculed speaks volumes for the ambitions of the men who operated in Dublin at the time. The northern section would have been even larger, comprising 2,444 acres. Together these would have added an absolutely massive area of land to the city. Semple created a series of maps overlaid on top of one another to compare improvements and changes in the harbour. These maps were never published, as far as is known; if they were, no trace of them has been found. There is the suspicion that Semple was not entirely altruistic in his motives and that this is why his proposal was rebuffed.

Throughout this period the overriding concern was the safety of the harbour and port of Dublin and its lack of protection, a concern that was reinforced by the continuing hazards to shipping. The *Freeman's Journal* of 15 November 1763 printed a letter outlining the loss of seventeen ships in the bay in 1761. Some few years earlier the traditional enmity between England and France had appeared as a threat to the city; the resulting nervousness was understandable in view of the fact that in 1760 the French briefly occupied Carrickfergus on the north shore of Belfast Lough. In 1777 John Paul Jones, the American hero and privateer, sailed into Belfast and captured the HMS *Drake*, while Gustavus Conyingham, an Irish-born officer in the American navy in command of the *Revenge*, caused mayhem in both the North Sea and the Irish Sea, where he took many prizes. The *Dublin Journal* reported on 29 May 1796 that on 12 May the 'armed frigate *Doris* under Captain Jones captured a French cutter of fourteen guns after a chase of 38 hours'.

The threat to the security of the state and the city was never far from the minds of the authorities, where it had been well entrenched since as far back as the reign of Queen Elizabeth I. The ever-present threat also indirectly encouraged ships to slip into secondary ports such as Malahide and others owned by the local landlord. In the mid-1700s over 200 called at Malahide, simply arriving on the high tide, drying out, unloading and then leaving at the top of the flood tide to catch the ebb. Isaac Butler, journeying around the east of Ireland in 1744, described Malahide: 'The gut that goes up to Malahide is very deep and large and will permit ships of a large burthen at high water as far up as the town of Malahide'. Some ships also lay against a quay wall then in existence at Robswall. This is seen in both Taylor's and Duncan's maps of Dublin in the nineteenth century.

By 1767 the Great South Bull Wall with the new lighthouse existed as a continuous structure, though it still required modifications and repairs. In 1787 a pamphleteer commented that all the work had provided was a breakwater. Nor was it perfect, as two newspaper reports in 1765 show the loss of a vessel and crew, and later in the year vessels were damaged within the harbour when the weather was bad. It must be remembered that although the new wall existed there was behind it a large body of water over which wind could build up to great strength and cause problems for vessels moving as well as those at anchor. More importantly, ships did not use chain but rope for anchoring.

This removes the curve in the anchor warp which exists in chain because of the weight coming up from the seabed to the ship, on top of which anchors were still using wooden stocks.

Rope was man-made and suffered weaknesses from that circumstance as well as from the quality of hemp. Hemp from Riga was favoured, as was Rhine hemp. Anchor cable was vital for ships; Captain John Weller reported in 1741 that when his cable broke in Dublin Bay he put out another anchor (called a bower), marked its location with a buoy and recovered the original, of which the cable had parted three fathoms (18ft) from the anchor. Ships' rigging also suffered damage in winds. Anchor hawsers and other ropes used in ships were seized using tar and whipping at the ends. Again, tar from abroad was preferred, and Stockholm Tar was much in demand in dockyards.

The Ballast Office report of September 1765 noted that the work of replacing the piles had commenced with a stone wall just as the lighthouse neared completion: 'we have begun another [wall] at the south side which we apprehended will be of great use in case of accidents happening to ships either in the harbour or on the South Bull; the necessity of carrying out these works obliged us to borrow £600 at four per cent and we beg leave to report it as our opinion to your honours that it will be necessary to borrow much more as will amount with said to £2000, for which we beg your honours will empower us to pass debentures'. Materials included large stone from Bullock Harbour and from Clontarf. An abstract of the accounts of the treasurer for the Ballast Office presented on 29 September 1767 stated: 'We lay herewith before your honours pursuant to your order last assembly an account of the sums of the money expended on the south wall and lighthouse from 1 July 1766 to this day 29 September 1767'. It mentioned the respective wages paid to the several proprietors, clerks, masons, carpenters and labourers. Again it is to be noted that there is no mention of horses and carts, for whatever reason. The Ballast Committee had reason to be pleased with what they observed, according to a commentator in 1787: 'the embellishment of the city of Dublin and the improvement of its harbour are now pursuing with a degree of ardour highly honourable to the nation, and laudable in those characters who principally patronise the works of public utility amongst us'.

The historian James Whitelaw in 1818 described the work (stretching from the Pigeon House east to the Poolbeg Light) as 'composed of two parallel walls constructed with large blocks of hewn granite without cement, consisting of alternate headers and stretchers so dovetailed into each other that no single block can be dislodged by any force except by breaking it. The intermediate space is filled with gravel and shingle to a certain height, over which a course of masonry is laid in excellent cement, and the whole is furnished with a course of granite blocks of large dimensions laid in tarrass, those at the edges of the wall being all headers and generally from six to seven feet. The parapet wall was later raised in height.' He observed that 'the wall [is] at present a spacious elevated road secured by parapet walls, which however from the badness of the materials are in a state of decay'. The Pigeon House Harbour—a drying-out harbour, i.e. tidal—was completed in 1784. The hotel had been finished in 1793 and a few years later became the officers' quarters for the fort. The fortress occupied an oblong space on the east and south of the basin and had a battery of 24-pounders defending the approach via the wall, with guns on carriages to cover all directions. Much of the outline structure of the harbour and fort is intact today. The Pigeon House Fort and harbour were open for trade by the last decade of the eighteenth century, as seen from maps and confirmed by witness statements.

By 1811 the Committee suggested that piped water be extended down to the Pigeon House Fort—which, according to a military map of 1816, housed over 400 men[14]—and also to all the space and population between it and the canal bridge at Baggot Street. Commercial shipping was excluded and had to relocate to Howth, and later to Kingstown. Archaeology has examined various sections of the complex, including the complete structure of the Pigeon House itself.[15] An excavation by archaeologists David McIleary and Fintan Walsh in the same area in 2013 found the truncated remains of a metalled surface and walling, which they identified as having been a formal part of the causeway to the fort.

The Wide Streets Commission did not have any direct impact on the area of Ringsend/Irishtown but it did have a major impact on areas adjacent to it and to its immediate west. The residential and commercial aspects of the city moved in a south-easterly direction. The mercantile emphasis also moved eastward and down the River Liffey. In 1780 Pool and Cash recorded their positive reaction to the nearly completed South Wall: 'The defects of the harbour are greatly remedied, by a prodigious work of stone and piles of wood, extending about three miles into the bay. This great and laudable work was executed in consequence of a statute made in the 6th of Queen Anne, called the Ballast Act.'

After the wall was finally finished, several visitors to Dublin reported on its existence and its effect on the harbour. One visitor recorded in 1797 that 'the packet lands her passengers in a fine and newly erected dock [the Pigeon House harbour] where now also a very spacious hotel is nearly complete' (Warburton and Whitelaw 1818, p. 57). This basin, 900ft long and 450ft wide, constructed to protect the ships in a south-easterly swell, 'has been built which at low tide is nearly dry'.

Nathaniel Jeffries in 1810 observed that 'the breadth of the pier is 250 feet, on which are erected a magazine, arsenal, and custom house'. He added that 'This new road facilitated a better experience for the traveller to Ireland coming in to Dublin Harbour'.[16] Note how the simple two-layered wall had now grown in width from a carriage road at this section. This was a sizeable piece of land reclamation in and around the Pigeon House area, creating a substantial space.

Revd James Hall also commented positively on the passengers' experience in 1813,[17] but a petition to the prince of Wales in 1811 noted that 'Dublin is situated on a small river, the navigation of which is impeded by a sandbank at its mouth that vessels of about 200 tons only can approach the quays'. It should be remembered that although more and more ships were calling to the port, most were small colliers delivering coal.

Thomas Reid, arriving in the port in 1822, had to wait for the tide to cross the bar, and several boats came alongside to take passengers ashore.[18] It was not long after this that the port engineers finished the North Bull Wall and shortly after that the bar was no more. We will look at this in more detail when we move to examine events on the north side of the Liffey. It was eventually done away with owing to both scouring and dredging. The protection that the wall offered is seen in a journal entry of Andrew Bigelow (1825–7): 'a work of this scale is sufficient to illustrate the public spirit and persevering enterprise of the citizens of this great metropolis. The shipping at the mouth of the river makes a fine display; literally a forest of masts.'

On the instruction of the Commissioners of Irish Fisheries, Alexander Nimmo surveyed Dublin Bay in 1823. Nimmo, a writer of note on aspects of survey and hydrography, was well qualified for the task. The standard was being improved all the time, thanks to the extraordinary chart of the bay which William Bligh prepared in 1801. Nimmo published his work *On the application of the science of geology to the practice of practical navigation* in 1825. Some changes were noticeable from earlier maps, such as the depth at the bar, which had begun to improve thanks to the construction of the North Bull Wall and to further dredging. Furthermore, the two hamlets of Ringsend and Irishtown had increased their footprint. Sandymount had become built up and now boasted a Martello tower (Fig. 3.24), and a wall had been finished along the strand at Ringsend beach to keep out the sea. Nimmo's

Fig. 3.24—Sketch of riders on Sandymount Strand, showing the fort and the Martello tower (photo: Brian Matthews, with the kind permission of the NLI).

Fig. 3.25—Brassington and Gale survey for the Pembroke estate (1830), showing later development (photo: Brian Matthews, with the kind permission of the NAI).

survey showed two baths complexes—Cranfield's and Murphy's—and some dwellings that had begun to appear south of the Grand Canal Basin and on the reclaimed slob and marsh of the Dodder upriver of the Ringsend Bridge. Still at this stage the made ground behind the Marine School on the quays remained labelled 'low ground'. Merrion Strand became Sandymount and was turned into a playground for walkers, bathers and riders.

The Pembroke estate in 1830 contracted Sherrard, Brassington and Gale to survey Ringsend and Irishtown once more. Much ground had been reclaimed and made productive, and good estate management required up-to-date estate maps (Fig. 3.25).[19] The first item to note is that both Cranfield's and Murphy's baths were still shown. In 1824 Daniel O'Connell was a regular patron of Murphy's Baths, as a letter to his wife clearly shows. For the first time it becomes clear that Cranfield's possessed a substantial footprint when compared to the space occupied by St Matthew's Church and the school next door. The new and solid stone single-span bridge at Ringsend was in place, at last connecting the area directly to the city. The ground west of Irishtown in the direction of the Dodder was shown as having two tenants: Clements had meadow measuring six acres four perches and two roods, and Verschoyle had seven acres three perches in pasture. Further along the bank in a northerly direction, Clarke had two acres and eighteen roods in arable land and meadow. All of this had been taken back from the Dodder Basin slob and marshland foreshore on the east bank. Not all land was used for agriculture, however; Verschoyle leased a further two acres on which was built Clarke's metalworks, which manufactured the metal water pipes used all across Dublin, and next door was the glassworks. Both of these factories consumed large quantities of coal and can be seen in some of the paintings as well as on maps. Overall the area of ground then covered by Ringsend and Irishtown extended to almost 50 acres. This represented a large increase over the original spit of nearly nine acres. As the two hamlets grew into villages they backed on to the water's edge, and some of the buildings backed on to the strand. In short, much land had been reclaimed and it was all in the possession of the Pembroke estate.

EMBANKING OF THE LIFFEY AND THE CONSTRUCTION OF THE GREAT SOUTH BULL WALL

When they began the monumental task of constructing the Great South Bull Wall, the city fathers had assumed that it would solve the silting problem and do away with the bar through the double action of the ebbing tide and the Liffey pouring down along the wall, acting as a giant scour. Unfortunately this was not to be the case. It would be quite some years into the future before the depth at the bar would increase substantially. A 1787 pamphlet noted that the South Wall was merely a shelter for shipping and a convenience for passing down the harbour by land; it had given no depth to the channel. Further, the author predicted that the new harbour in contemplation at the Pigeon House, when built, would not achieve the task asked of it in that it was always going to incur silting problems. The port had some idea that this would be the case when they issued contracts for the walls of a new tidal harbour, a harbour within a harbour, in 1792. Work was completed by 1793, but the lifespan of the new facility would be very short because it dried out at low tide. Military and political demands also played a part in the decision to relocate. The entire structure can still be seen today through the gun ports of the walls of the fort, as can the Pigeon House Hotel, which was finished in 1797. The fort on the bend in the wall was erected in 1798 because of security concerns, both internal and external, and there are still quite a number of built remains of the structure. The arrangement was formalised in 1802 with a lease, and by 1804 all commercial shipping had been excluded from the harbour. Nevertheless, ships did continue to call to the quay adjacent to the new harbour, as witnessed by one visitor in 1814. Ann Plumtre described 'a little cluster of houses between the old pier and the new one'. She was one of those passengers who had had the experience of having to anchor off the bar and wait for the incoming tide when arriving in Dublin.

In 1825 Benjamin Oakley, a visitor to Ireland, wrote: 'I took a car down to the Pigeon House about three miles standing in the bay. It has a small fort with a Custom House and used to be the landing place for the packets but now in disuse in consequence of the newly erected pier at the entrance of Howth Harbour.'

The wall had, however, made the port somewhat safer for shipping, as attested by the revenue figures. In 1784 customs duties to the value of £485,039 were collected from shipping; by 1800 the figure was £826,848, rising to £1,309,908 in 1816.

In 1800 the problem of lack of depth at the bar at the end of the Great South Wall remained. By this time several proposals had been advanced concerning the possibility of the construction of a Great North Wall to finish the job originally undertaken some 50 or so years before. The engineer Thomas Hyde Page added his assent to the idea, whose main proponent was Captain William Bligh: 'A second wall would probably be of very great advantage to the river', Page reported.[20] He confirmed the current position at the time, as the chief cause of the loss of shipping in the bay was 'the want of a port to run for at any time of the tide with deep water'. Page also launched the idea of the canal between Grand Canal Docks and Kingstown Harbour, an idea of which others had been in favour for 40 years or so. In addition, like others before him, he promoted the possibility of the erection of a large breakwater at Dalkey to create a refuge area in certain wind directions. While the canal idea might sound fanciful today, it should be remembered that the large port of Liverpool is entered through a canal and that London has her tidal barriers. What is odd is that no one mentioned the fact that the Liffey is made up of both fresh water and salt water, and they both occupy different levels as they exit into the estuary.

In a concise statement of the proceedings of the Ballast Board and the consequent state of the harbour published in 1833, it was observed: 'it is time we are desired to be content with a tidal harbour because London, Liverpool and Bristol possess no other, but would the merchants of those places content with their present difficult and dangerous channels of approach were they blessed with the means that Dublin possesses for their evidence'. Again the idea of a canal connecting Dublin and Kingstown was put forward, along with the floating jetty and a suggestion that the profits of the Corporation for the Preservation and Improvement of the Port of Dublin could be used as collateral for borrowings for the project. This suggestion was not as fanciful as it may first appear.

The Georgians were prepared to think and plan in broad strokes, thanks to the political and military control they exercised over the country. The embanking of the Liffey all the way downriver on both sides was a very large undertaking by any standards. It was minor, however, compared to the size of the work required for the Great South Bull Wall. The city fathers saw it as a task which they had no choice but to undertake, to beat off competition in trade with other ports such as Cork and Waterford but more particularly Drogheda, and later Belfast, which developed in an almost identical manner to Dublin. They saw that the way to do this was to improve port facilities. To achieve this they had to tame the Liffey by reducing it to one navigable channel and then to create some sort of protection for shipping. The construction of the Great South Wall was designed to offer this. The other and greater hope for the mole was that it would have a scouring effect on the channels and that the river outflow together with the ebbing tide would actually wash away the bar. The fact that this did not happen meant that for another 30 years the bar of Dublin would literally haunt the thinking of the municipal authority. While the bar was finally removed by 1825 thanks to the scouring effect and steam dredging, shipping also changed with the arrival of steamboats. The first steamboat navigated the Liffey in 1815, bringing more certainty to the schedules of shipping traffic.[21] The mole did make a difference, however, as shipping losses decreased but did not disappear. The other great change that these two works brought was the momentum for further intervention in the area, connecting the Grand Canal to the Liffey and the changes imposed on the Dodder Basin.

These projects took almost 100 years to complete—meaning that several generations of Dubliners grew up, lived and died while the works continued—and work would continue for decades to improve and upgrade them. These works were monumental but they were not carried out in isolation: the construction of the Grand Canal Docks and the embanking of the Dodder to allow the start of land reclamation in the Dodder Basin began just as the South Bull Wall was being finished, while over on the north side of the river massive changes were imposed on the landscape in the eighteenth century, especially in the last twenty years, which we will examine in due course.

Notes

[1] Cormac Lowth, lecture on 'Ringsend trawlers', delivered at the Poolbeg Yacht Club, October 2014.
[2] Ann Plumtre, *Narrative of a residence in Ireland during the summer of 1814 and that of 1815* (London, 1816), p. 59.
[3] Constantia Maxwell, *Dublin under the Georges* (London, 1994), p. 284.
[4] J.W. De Courcy, *The Liffey in Dublin* (Dublin, 1996), p. 374.
[5] Geoffrey Moorhouse, *Great Harry's navy: how Henry VIII gave England sea power* (London, 2005), p. 37.
[6] J.T. Gilbert (ed.), *Calendar of ancient records of Dublin* [*CARD*], vol. 7 (Dublin, 1898), p. 604.
[7] *Ibid.*, p. 257.
[8] *Ibid.*, p. 262.
[9] *CARD*, vol. 12, p. 272.
[10] *CARD*, vol. 11, p. 404.
[11] *Journal of the Royal Society of Antiquaries of Ireland* **123** (1993), p. 22.
[12] D.F. Moore, 'The port of Dublin', *Dublin Historical Record* **16** (4) (1961), p. 140.
[13] *CARD*, vol. 12, p. 49.
[14] Military map (1816), NLI.
[15] Antoine Giacometti, 'Pigeon House Fort, Ringsend, Dublin', *Excavations.ie*, site no. 2009:357.
[16] Nathaniel Jeffreys, 'Dublin harbour in 1810', from 'An Englishman's descriptive account of Dublin', in Thomas and Valerie Packenham (eds), *Dublin: a travellers' companion* (London, 1988), p. 256.
[17] Revd J. Hall, *Tour through Ireland, particularly the interior and least known parts, containing an accurate view of the parties, politics and improvements, in two volumes*, vol. 1 (London, 1813), p. 40.
[18] Thomas Reid, *Travels in Ireland in the year 1822, exhibiting brief sketches of the moral, physical and political state of the country with reflections on the best means of improving its condition* (London, 1823), p. 148.
[19] Jacinta Prunty, 'Estate records', in W. Nolan and A. Simms (eds), *Irish towns: a guide to sources* (Dublin, 1998), p. 121.
[20] Sir Thomas Hyde Page, *Reports relative to Dublin Harbour and adjacent coasts in consequence of orders from the Marquis Cornwallis, Lord Lieutenant of Ireland, in the year 1800* (1801), NLI P 1077(19), p. 9.
[21] Maxwell, *Dublin under the Georges*, p. 294.

4. Building the Grand Canal Docks and taming the Dodder

This chapter traces the construction of the Grand Canal Docks, the alteration of the course of the River Dodder and the reclamation of the Dodder Basin. It also looks at the effects of these actions on the city and the people. The main outcome was the binding of the Ringsend spit to the rest of the reclaimed area. These were the third and fourth major works undertaken in relation to the enhancement of the port facilities on the south side of Dublin Bay and the River Liffey, and both would cement the growing urbanisation of this area of Dublin in that period. Note also that during this short period of activity down in the port area a similar amount of construction was taking place north of the river: the Four Courts, Aldeborough House, the new Custom House, Carlisle Bridge, Annesley Bridge over the Tolka (moving the city boundary out another quarter of a mile), and the Royal Canal and its four bridges down at the Liffey end of the canal. To recap just one statistic, six bridges were built on the north side in a small area, all within a ten-year period. In short, the city was one vast building site. Developments across the river will be dealt with separately. The activity north of the Liffey took place in a larger space and mainly in a different century (post-1800), using different skills and technology and in a new political atmosphere.

In examining the Grand Canal Basin, all aspects of the task—including design, construction and the materials used, as well as the architects and engineers involved—will be considered. A vast quantity of material was removed to make these two large, deep pools. This major task was a commercial project but it had municipal encouragement and involvement. It was made somewhat easier by the fact that the previous two major construction works had generated a level of technical expertise and had provided much valuable experience, as well as increasing engineering knowledge and general confidence particularly among the ruling classes. The confidence that came with change was assisted by the work of the Wide Streets Commission (see below), which had by this juncture four decades of activity behind it. The establishment of the Wide Streets Commission for improving the streetscape of the city (for both practical and aesthetic purposes) was one of the more important changes that had occurred since the beginning of the river walls and the South Bull Wall. While the Commission did not have a direct bearing on the works here, it did influence the attitudes and thinking of landlords, builders, architects and the élite in society at the time.

The construction of the Grand Canal Docks did not happen overnight. It became part of a process and has to be viewed as part of the development of the Grand Canal. It must be borne in mind, too, that the Royal Canal, which was being completed across the river, was also envisaged as entering the Liffey.

The building of the Grand Canal Docks was completed in four years—a much shorter time than the embanking of Sir John Rogerson's Quay and the construction of the Great South Bull Wall. Many thousands of men were involved in all of these works. It might be argued that the work consisted simply of digging a huge hole and filling it with water, but the designers had to consider the impact of such a large project on the eastern edge of the city at the time. The Wide Streets Commission was by now in a strong and confident position, having seen many civic changes through, and they would have had some input into these projects. The builders also had to consider the practical aspects of linking the canal with the port, bearing in mind that the action of the main port of Dublin now took place down here between Ringsend, the Pigeon House and Sir John Rogerson's Quay. The aesthetic, too, had to be borne in mind.

The city needed more water—hence the Corporation's involvement—and the canal offered a solution. Sourcing water was also of vital interest to the Corporation for Preserving and Improving the Port of Dublin. A growing city population needed water, as did animals, especially horses. Industry and commerce too needed increasing supplies of water, as did the port itself, both for shipping and for the collection and delivery of goods. This was, after all, the Dublin of legislative independence, with its strong civic pride and sense of well-being. The Wide Streets Commission had no direct impact on the Grand Canal Docks but it certainly influenced the manner of development in the locale and the actions of the Fitzwilliam estate, which was the major landowner in the area at the time, as will be seen.

The Wide Streets Commission came into being to improve access and movement in and around Dublin. Many of the streets, lanes and alleys were unfit for purpose by the mid-1700s with the increase in people, carriages and goods (most especially coal) being moved around the city. Streets literally needed to be widened. This civic idea and theme had been floated by the viceroy, the duke of Ormonde, between 1660 and 1685. While the Assembly would eventually act in 1756, they had been looking at improvements earlier. One of their first projects was to be Parliament Street and its access to the Castle. The Assembly ordered maps of this section of the city in 1751 and again in 1753.[1] Both maps give details of the streets around Parliament Street, including details of the Custom House office, yard and stores footprint. The National Gallery of Ireland also has a map from this time with similar detail, dated 1752.[2] These documents show that improvement was in the air and it would begin at the heart of the establishment, Dublin Castle.

Canals also offered an opportunity to move goods in greater quantities than roads. A horse could pull two tons on a cart but it could pull 50 tons on a barge. The task of digging this great hole in the ground posed different challenges in that it was anticipated that it would be completed in a short space of time. To finish the task so quickly, a sizeable number of men had to be employed in the digging out and another sizeable number in removing the vast quantities of material. There were also a large number of horses and carts involved in delivering the large stones of limestone and granite in the quantities that were required. These people and their animals are left out of the official records; no reliable figures appear until well into the second quarter of the following century. The geology and archaeology tell us that the excavation of this vast hole would have involved enormous quantities of sand, sediment and river and tide detritus, as well as the residue from the dumping of material from latrines around the city when there was nothing but tide-washed strand down here, save for gravel banks. Being now sadly incomplete, the minute-books of the Court of Directors of the Grand Canal Company do not present a full record of the process.

Technology in the form of pumps had, however, been available for some time to assist in the construction and maintenance of the canal dock. As early as 1734 a Dr Stephens experimented on the value of a screw-pump, and the Royal Dublin Society minute-books record that he emptied a canal 60ft long and 20ft wide, filled with water to a depth of 5ft, in the space of five hours using a Dutch screw-pump.[3] Knowledge of the construction and maintenance of canals and docks had been available for over 100 years. One writer visiting Holland in 1691 noted that 'one horse shall draw in a boat more than fifty can do by a cart; whereas carriage makes a great part of the price in all heavy commodities'. He added that in constructing and sealing canals 'they had found the common seaweed to be the best material for these dykes which fastens with a thin mixture of earth, yields a little to the force of the tide, and returns when the waves give back'.[4]

Towards the end of the eighteenth century inland navigation was 'in a flux', 'for the canal companies had very little money, and Dublin port came right into the centre of the controversy because it was the terminal point of the two canals, and also because it too had very little capital'. 'This new body [The Board of Inland Navigation Act] was set up in 1800 and given an initial grant of £500,000, part of which was to be spent improving Dublin for the benefit of the canals.'[5] Ruth Delaney says that the Irish parliament, in its dying moments before its union with Westminster, appointed five Directors General of Inland Navigation with a fund of £500,000, and for the next 30 years this body controlled waterway development in Ireland.[6] Quite simply, the canal cost enormous sums of money, which the stakeholders were never to recover. This also applied to the Grand Canal Docks, not only because of the enormous cost of the project but also because, as ships grew in bulk at the end of the eighteenth century, the dry docks would soon be too small to cope, and the entrance to the basin via the locks similarly too small. In addition, steam and the revolution it would unleash would appear within a decade of the tiny pioneering projects then in experimentation. This also meant that steam-driven paddle-wheel ships would be too wide to negotiate the entry locks.

Grand Canal Docks

Long before the advent of the Grand Canal Docks, canals had been proposed for the centre of Dublin. In 1673 and 1674 Bernard de Gomme and Andrew Yarranton made proposals for the improvement of the port and the protection of the city from the sea. Yarranton prepared a map of Dublin that showed a series of canals crossing the city to the east of Dublin Castle. Both proposals favoured land reclamation in the area of these docks. Even at that early stage Dutch influence was pervasive, and the expertise of the Dutch was well known. Yarranton's plan was close enough to the reality of what transpired; when the Grand Canal eventually opened, it resembled his original ideas. Commander Perry, too, suggested a canal system connecting Sutton with the city in the 1720s. Later, in 1785, the engineer John Brownrigg, a protégé of Scalé, produced a plan to link the Grand Canal to the Liffey while he was employed as an engineer on the Grand Canal. This was an important influence as well.[7] Ruth Delaney pointed out that, once the Grand Canal was nearing completion at Ringsend, the Grand Canal Company petitioned parliament in 1791 for a 'grant to construct docks capable of accommodating 150 seagoing vessels'[8] (Fig. 4.1).

Construction of the docks commenced in 1792. Architects, engineers and surveyors played a key role, but so too did the holders of new skills such as soil-testers, of whom there were three in the city at the time: John Davis, Michael Landy and a woman, Matilda Pearce of Hawkins Street. Soil-testers were associated with the work of the surveyors who carried out test borings for foundations.[9] The testing of soil for foundations was important because so much land in the area was, and continued to be, reclaimed.[10] Another new technology employed was steam power. William Jessop, the engineer for the project, came to Ireland as assistant to John Smeaton, who was one of the leading canal engineers in England, to engage in various works. Jessop's correspondence with Boulton and Watt, the early builders of steam engines, shows that two large steam engines were

Fig. 4.1—Boats on canal, looking towards Ringsend (photo: Brian Matthews).

ordered to drain the three excavations through pumping. The 3hp Sun and Planet engine, with a 10½in.-diameter cylinder and a 3ft stroke, was one of the earliest used for pumping in foundation works.[11]

Only five years later steam was being used in the processing of corn, as reported by Joseph Archer in 1801. He records steam machines operating at Mr Stephens's corn mill in Cole Alley, a machine for grinding corn at Mr Keating's in Great Britain Street, another at Mr Jackson's in Phoenix Street and another used for a variety of purposes at a brewery in Francis Street.[12]

Valuable experience had been gained in working in and under water during the embanking of Sir John Rogerson's Quay and the building of the Great South Wall to the Poolbeg Light. Smeaton had been the engineer on the Clyde and Forth Canal and also designer and engineer for the building of the iconic Eddystone Lighthouse, whose design influenced that of Poolbeg Lighthouse.[13] Both men exerted great influence in the building and engineering community through their own involvement with building in Dublin in the following years.

The method of building itself was straightforward. The material was removed, the water on site kept pumped out, the floors and foundations placed, and the walls built and mortared. As the graving docks themselves were in progress, sea water was kept out by the use of timber piling. This operated much like the coffer-dam system of blocking off water or ingress.[14] With the foundation that he used on the graving dock water seepage was very small, to Jessop's satisfaction.[15] The stone used was Leinster granite and Dublin calp limestone. The granite, sourced at Dalkey, was a hard-wearing stone, impervious to normal weathering and with the advantage of having low levels of porosity and water absorption.[16] Limestone was the main stone used in the building of the graving docks.[17] Lime mortar, which could be set in water without loss of property, was used to bind the walls together and seal gaps. This helped to speed up the work rate. It had previously proved a boost to construction on the South Wall and was used to advantage later on during the further improvements to the quays, including Rogerson's Quay. Jessop recommended that gravel and mud be used to floor the basins, and muddy water, after settling, allowed fine mud to fill the pores in floor and walls, forming a seal.[18] Lime mortar had been used in the construction of Essex Bridge in 1753, so its stability was known.[19] Much of the Grand Canal Docks is very visible today, still extant but used in a different manner, including the dry docks along with some of the warehouses in the location (Fig. 4.2).

The upper basin was 2,000ft long. Mr Edward Chapman was executive engineer. Cowan and Gamble were the contractors for the graving docks, and Bergin and Hayes contractors for the basin walls.[20] Having two separate contractors for the works must also have speeded up the completion of the entire project, as they were almost in competition with one another.

As already mentioned, Smeaton devised a new method for breathing while working in water. This was a very timely development for the Grand Canal Docks, and for the ongoing work of both reclaiming land behind the Rogerson walls and the constant upgrading of the South Wall. Jessop remained contracted as a consultant engineer to the Grand Canal Company until 1802.[21] Mark Baldwin, reviewing *William Jessop, engineer* by Charles Hadfield and A.W. Skempton, said that Jessop

Fig. 4.2—Sketch by Arthur Joy of the entrance to the Grand Canal Docks from north side, 1821.

was 'quite probably the leading civil engineer in the period 1785–1805'.[22] His experience in Dublin would be invaluable later when he was involved in the construction of the West India Docks in London. It was Jessop who proposed a basin and graving docks where the canal met the Liffey, 'whence boats may occasionally discharge over the wall into the sea-vessels lying on the outside of it'.[23]

As the directors of the Grand Canal Company were responsible for the whole canal, their attention was obviously bestowed upon all of the works along its length, including bridges and aqueducts. There is very little mention of the ongoing work at Ringsend in the surviving minute-books of the directors, but it would appear that the work was well managed and proceeded without any difficulty. In 1792 Jessop was back in Ireland to give detailed instructions on the building of the wall foundations and was 'progressively happy with the work being undertaken'.[24] In his second report of September 1794, he expressed himself as pleased with progress at Ringsend and made helpful suggestions regarding the execution of works.[25] The issues dealt with by the board at their meetings consisted primarily of problems to be overcome up and down the length of the canal. It was natural that the directors should visit readily because the site was close by, and any problem that arose was dealt with immediately. The directors of the Corporation for Preserving and Improving the Port of Dublin had also regularly inspected the South Wall works thanks to their proximity. In addition, being a public–private partnership of sorts, there were two sets of people looking over the shoulders of the project managers and foremen. On 27 April 1796 they ordered that a drain be brought up the Dodder from the lowest water to the sewers of the graving docks. They further ordered that a plan and estimates of the piles to protect the pier ends be 'laid before the board', and 'that chains be fixed to the heads and tails of the sea locks to prevent accidents'; their instructions were given to Captain Evans, who was the project manager for the entire canal.[26]

During the construction, vast amounts of material were removed to allow a depth of 16ft of water in the basin. This material had to go somewhere and it is likely that it was used to build up the large and high banks surrounding the basin. A quantity surveyor has computed the amount of material removed at 515,587m^3. If this material was spread around the basin to a thickness of 4m, it would cover an area of 32 acres.[27] This conclusion is justifiable for several reasons. There is no mention of the material in any of the documentary sources, yet there is some detail on the delivery and shipping to the site of stone. Secondly, the land immediately around the basin is higher than much of the surrounding area. A walk within the docks shows, for example, that the 1930s apartment blocks on the Dodder bank at Thorncastle Street are below the level of the basin, and these flats are on top of the original Ringsend spit. A third possible reason is that four years is a very short time for such a project. After all, a year longer was spent on building the Marine School, a single structure, nearby on Rogerson's Quay. Lastly, no figures for wages or labour and no details of the numbers of men employed in various areas of activity are mentioned in the minute-books of the Court of Directors of the Grand Canal Company. This is a very different approach to the way the minute-books of the Corporation were recorded. Although it is possible that relevant details are contained in the missing minute-books, it is unlikely that they contain information on wages.

A German visitor to London wrote to a friend in Germany that on 22 April 1835 'we drove past the West India Docks, an immense basin artificially dug out with machinery, long, broad and deep enough to contain a great number of the largest merchantmen'.[28] This observation gives a near-eyewitness view of the scale of construction involved in the digging out of the Grand Canal Docks, particularly when it is accepted that there was no machinery available to assist with the massive drudgery of removing half a million cubic metres of material to create both of these inland harbours.

DUBLIN MOVING EAST, 1708–1844

This visitor was not the only person to comment approvingly on what was achieved. Some 40 years earlier, John Ferrar said of the Grand Canal Docks and basins that 'these works are the noblest in all Europe, cost above £100,000, of which Parliament paid one third'. He reported that they 'covered thirty five acres of ground of which twenty six were under water and the basins sixteen feet deep. The large one is four thousand feet long and three hundred and thirty feet wide. It is capable of holding four hundred square rigged ships, which is equal to the whole of the extent of the admired docks at Liverpool.' This is half the figure of 800 ships cited by another observer but both are inaccurate; perhaps 50–100 ships might be a more accurate number. The issue was not how many ships could fit in the space allocated but how to get them into place, since their extended bowsprits demanded swinging room. The turning circle of the ships was the overriding determinant on the use of the space.

Fig. 4.3—Painting of the opening of the Grand Canal Docks in 1796 (William Ashford) (courtesy of Louise Morgan and Brendan Maher, NGI).

The three graving docks were named after successive lord lieutenants, the eastern dock after Earl Camden, the central after the marquis of Buckingham and the west after the earl of Westmorland. This was decided at a meeting of the directors on 21 April 1796 and conveyed in an address to Earl Camden a few days in advance of the opening, when they justified their decision in the following terms: 'the design of the work originated during the vice royalty of the Marquis of Buckingham encouraged by the government of the Earl of Westmorland and completed during the administration of your Excellency Earl Camden'.[29] The facility which was to be on offer had been long overdue, as the port had previously had nothing of the sort. This is confirmed by Fred Rogers, in charge of the Plymouth dockyard, when in 1772 he reported to the Admiralty that the ship *Dublin* had been dry-docked for bottom-cleaning on 3 December. This was in the days before the protection of copper sheathing. Bigger ships had to go further for such service, while smaller vessels could lie over at low water on strands such as that behind the north quay wall on the Liffey at today's Point Depot.[30]

On 21 April 1796, before the official opening of the docks, the directors of the Grand Canal Company placed advertisements in the *Evening Post*, the *Freeman's Journal*, *Falkiner's*, the *Dublin Journal* and other papers published on the Friday or Saturday, requesting all those who came in carriages to the Company's breakfast on the Saturday morning to order their coachmen to cross the Ringsend Bridge 'after dropping their passengers and wait until called for'.[31] It was a measure of their expectation that there would be a large crowd for the official opening, and they were not disappointed. The Ringsend Bridge mentioned is the one located at Londonbridge Road, as the Stone Bridge at Thorncastle Street had at this time been swept away.

The opening of the Grand Canal Docks was one of the great occasions in the late eighteenth century for the population of Dublin (Figs 4.3 and 4.4). It was likely the largest single crowd of people ever gathered together for such an event in Ireland. The *Freeman's Journal* reported: 'On Saturday 23rd instant (St George's Day) was exhibited one of the grandest and most interesting spectacles ever witnessed by this kingdom. At eleven o'clock in the morning His Excellency the

Fig. 4.4—Sketch of the opening of Ringsend Docks, 1796 (artist unknown) (courtesy of Louise Morgan and Brendan Maher, NGI).

Lord Lieutenant, attended by his suite and accompanied by Sir Alexander Schomberg, made his way in to the Basin. The Vice-regal yacht made her way to the oration in the Great Eastern ship dock from whence she passed into the floating docks, into the middle of which she was in a few minutes warped by means of the mooring buoys and there cast anchor'. The report continued: 'About twenty vessels of considerable size and burthen, some of them 400 tons and upwards, entered after the Yacht and each of them saluted as they came in. They were followed by a considerable number of small craft and a variety of barges and pleasure boats handsomely decorated which gave great variety to the scene.' The paper recorded that 1,000 of the great and good sat down to a substantial breakfast in tents erected for the occasion; the rest waited while a good repast was consumed. Afterwards Lord Camden took a turn around the docks to the cheers of the huge crowds, the firing of cannon and the acclamation and salutes of the other vessels present. The reporter added: 'We suppose that the spectators did not amount to less than 150,000 and never were gratified with a sight that more delighted and elevated the mind'.[32] Bearing in mind the unemployment levels of the populace, it is no surprise that so many turned up.

Addressing the lord lieutenant on the day, the chairman of the directors of the Grand Canal Company observed that 'The great importance of this work will not be fully experienced until our canal shall be united with the river Shannon'. The work was conceived to allow real trade and commerce between the city and the west by water, and it was expected to have a profound impact on many aspects of Irish life, including internal migration and urban drift, an increase in the movement of coal inland, and the development of small clusters of commercial activity at the various depots along the canal. It would, along with the Royal Canal, redefine the city itself. Physically the entire complex became part and parcel of the port, and specifically of the Ringsend/Irishtown area. It also paved the way for the embanking and straightening of the Dodder. The development that was envisaged began with the building of warehouses and stores around the perimeter of the docks immediately on completion, some of which exist today in the form of offices and apartments.

The construction of the docks helped to focus the minds of the city fathers on the embanking of the Dodder by encouraging the beginning of land reclamation in the basin upriver from the Ringsend Bridge, which finally brought the area in from being an island spit that was cut off from the city periodically. On 26 April 1796 'it was resolved that the thanks of the directors … be sent by the secretary to the Commissioners of the Revenue for their very polite compliance with the request of the directors to permit the Revenue Cruisers to enter the floating docks on Saturday last'. The directors were so pleased with the comments made by the lord lieutenant that they recorded them verbatim in their minute-book: 'It gives me the highest satisfaction to be present at the opening of the magnificent works which have been brought to perfection by the spirit and assiduity of the Grand Canal Company and to be a witness of the advantages they hold out to the commerce and trade of this Kingdom'. They recorded their thanks to Captain Burgh, who had arranged the tents for the occasion, and were delighted, too, that the Danish consul attended.[33]

The Chevalier de Latocnaye, a French traveller who witnessed the opening, was impressed by what he saw: 'This inland navigation is now so far completed as to form a perfect water carriage from St George's Channel or the Irish Sea at the eastern side of Dublin into the river Shannon … and thus completely intersects the whole kingdom through its centre'.[34]

As de Latocnaye's remarks attest, the opening of the Grand Canal Docks was regarded as a major improvement to the city, and potentially the country. A visitor to Dublin in 1797, just one year after the opening of the Docks, wrote that 'the city of Dublin has been highly improved within the last two years by the completion of a very great undertaking, namely docks of great magnitude, now finished by the company of undertakers of the Grand Canal. The two or rather one great floating dock (there being no lock dividing them, the only division being a drawbridge of a peculiarly light yet durable construction) was capable of containing 800 sail of merchant ships and give sufficient space for each to carry on their trade with ample room.'[35]

This figure of 800 vessels is entirely fictitious. There is no way this number could ever have been accommodated. Ships require turning room, and if ships were lining either side of these docks there would not be enough space, especially if any breeze was blowing during such a delicate manoeuvre. Rocque had drawn on his map a total of 95 ships in the Liffey, and they were placed all up and down the river, from Essex Bridge all the way to the end of the South Bull. Nevertheless, the compliments kept coming. In 1835 a German visitor, Friedrich Raumer, observed: 'There are besides to this dock, three graving docks for building or repairing shipping; the dimension of the largest is 180 feet long by sixty feet wide; and they appear to me to be built upon the same improved construction as that of the great dock at Portsmouth, which I remember to have seen in the year 1795, a little after it was finished'.[36] The eventual cost of the project was five times greater than the parliamentary loan which had been underwritten. It should be noted that the largest of the docks, at 180ft in length, was to have a short shelf-life, as ships grew substantially in both length and beam at the end of the eighteenth century.[37]

The three graving or dry docks built as part of the entire project were built for ships in the eighteenth century but within a short span of years they would no longer suffice. Access for steamships became a problem in terms of width. As was noted in relation to a discussion for extending the canal at Limerick, 'A steam boat of approved construction with outside wheels, cannot be less than twelve feet wide in the beam and six feet more for two wheels, besides two feet more for clearage room (to prevent accidents to the wheels), making in all twenty feet'.[38]

There were other issues regarding the use of the Grand Canal Docks, such as depths in the River Liffey, depths in the lock chamber and, finally, the question of depths in the dock. What this means is that entering the lock from the river was straightforward, but when the lock filled with water and the vessel rose up the sill at the entrance to the Dock there was a difference because the sill was 6ft above the bed of the river whereas the bottom of the lock chamber matched that of the river. Sir John McNeill confirmed this when comparing the entrance to the entrance to George's Dock. This partially explains the not-so-extensive use of the Docks and Graving Docks. It is illustrated that ships can proceed ahead into the Custom House Docks by merely opening the gates.[39]

The problem of a bar at the entrance to the Grand Canal Docks remained and was dealt with every so often.[40] Veredker wrote that 'It is necessary periodically to remove the mud which accumulates at the entrance'. Nothing, however, could alter the fact that steam vessels simply could not enter the locks, which were too narrow.[41] These problems combined to make it difficult for ships to make use of the facility.

Niall McCullough wrote that the creation of the Grand Canal Docks, with its space for so many seagoing vessels, gave reason for a grid of streets around it, which filled up the remainder of Rogerson's slob at the back of the river wall that kept the Liffey out.[42] The completion of the work acted almost as an eastern book-end to the development of the south quays. Very quickly warehouses, stores and mills began to be built around the new waterways. The building of a lifting bridge over the narrow water between the two basins in turn helped to solidify the finishing of the substantial road that had been developing in the previous decades and would shortly become Great Brunswick

Fig. 4.5—Drawing of Semple's design for a drawbridge over the two basins (courtesy of Trinity College Dublin).

Fig. 4.6—Scenes on the ice by Hendrick Avercamp, 1620, with lifting bridge in the background, showing Dutch influence (courtesy of Louise Morgan and Brendan Maher, NGI).

Street (now Pearse Street). This bridge is assuredly based on the design of similar lifting bridges in Holland, which the Dutch had perfected over hundreds of years (Figs 4.5–4.7). The completion of the Liffey wall meant a natural growth of reclamation and building close to the river. The canal circling the south side of the city also created a natural boundary for ground within that circle to be developed. The Assembly never lost sight of the aesthetic possibilities of the canal and were determined to make the most of it, allocating £65 for tree-planting along the banks for the better enjoyment of the people in 1766; Patrick Edgar was given the budget and was tasked with the planting of trees costing 3s. 3d. each.[43]

There was one major landowner in a prime position to take advantage; this was Lord Fitzwilliam. As the Pembroke estate owned the land outside the Grand Canal Docks and back up the canal towards Leeson Street, it was also in a position to influence what happened to the layout of land around the waterway up towards Leeson Street. It was acquiring new ground for building by the acre, and each acre would hold multiple dwellings, a different story from the farming which would result in other sections of its holdings. It was entirely natural that the space on the right-hand

Fig. 4.7—Sketch of docks, looking north, with lifting bridge, by Arthur Joy (photo: Brian Matthews, with the kind permission of the NLI).

(south) side of Grand Canal Street going towards Ringsend would be ripe for both reclamation and development as the city developed southward and eastward to enclose this area. The entire decision-making process was carried out from afar, as the owners of the Pembroke estate lived in England. The tidying-up of Grand Canal Street, as it is known today, became an imperative when the new stone Ringsend Bridge was begun seven years later. Ann Plumtre wrote in 1814–15 of the Grand Canal in this area: 'Trees are planted on each side of the canal … passage boats built for conveying passengers and goods are constantly passing and repassing … there is an excellent hotel now established at Portobello'.[44]

The spit was bound to the city at long last, because now there was a road and a substantial stone bridge, built over the Dodder at Ringsend in the first few years of the nineteenth century. Semple designed it in elliptical style, i.e. the stone surround was a complete oval structure, meaning that the greater the pressure of weight on the foundations the stronger it remained. Thanks to this new bridge, those landing at the Pigeon House Harbour could avail of the direct road all the way to the heart of Dublin; the port activities and the development around the new Grand Canal Docks had demanded the completion of this road. As a result, the old horse road up to Dublin along the shore soon became a distant memory. The momentum was apparent and can be seen in the number of boats plying the canal. In 1801 Lieutenant Joseph Archer carried out a statistical survey of the county for the Royal Dublin Society and concluded that there were 400 boats in total.[45] It should be noted that a floating chapel became a fixture within a few years, signifying growth in the area (Fig. 4.8).

An advertising campaign began in May 1796, only a month after the official opening, to encourage building and occupation of the area, 'that to encourage the building of houses, warehouses, and stores adjoining the banks of the Grand Canal Docks the Company will give the builder of twenty units the use of the companies quarries at Gollardstown for the purpose gratis … providing they start by 1st July next'.[46]

Fig. 4.8—Floating chapel in the Grand Canal Docks at the end of the eighteenth century (courtesy of Louise Morgan and Brendan Maher, NGI).

The next major work to change Ringsend and Irishtown was the development of the marshland south of the causeway and the construction of a second bridge over the Dodder. This would begin with the embanking of the Dodder into one single controlled channel.

Walling the River Dodder and reclaiming the Dodder Basin

The walling of the Liffey, the reclamation of the land behind Sir John Rogerson's Quay and the development of a plan for the Grand Canal Docks naturally encouraged those who considered that the River Dodder, which entered the harbour of Dublin at Ringsend point, where it meets the Liffey, should also be tamed. It is important to bear in mind that these works did not follow on from each other but overlapped. Indeed, this was true of each of the major improvements made to the port. While the Liffey wall was being embanked, the land reclamation behind Rogerson's Quay continued, with streets being laid out that added to the network of streets spreading out from Merrion Square and surrounds, all following an inevitable movement to join up. The wall itself was upgraded and improved several times, not least in the 1790s. The Great South Wall was completed in 1796, permitting the establishment of the Pigeon House Harbour, hotel and, finally, military fort, as the wall at that point was expanded from twenty yards wide to 85 yards wide on more reclaimed land.

The third work in the upgrading of the port facilities was the building of the Grand Canal Docks. This study has engaged with the construction of the Grand Canal Docks before the embanking of the Dodder and the sealing off of the lower Dodder Basin. The work on the Docks was complete by 1796, while that on the Dodder was not completed until 1798. The building of the new stone Ringsend Bridge in 1803 finally joined the Ringsend spit to Dublin. Even then the work of draining and improving the reclaimed ground was to continue for some years.

The embanking of the Dodder was pursued for several reasons. First, the Dodder had a history

Fig. 4.9—Watermill on the Dodder near Irishtown, 1812, King sketchbook, (National Library of Ireland).

of flooding and of causing serious damage to property. Second, the Corporation saw the potential of the land that could be reclaimed on its doorstep, and the additional revenue and economic activity that it would produce. They had already seen what was possible further up towards the city, with so much ground taken back from the tides. Third, there was a build-up of material, a bar, at the confluence of the Dodder with the Liffey which the Corporation for Preserving and Improving the Port of Dublin saw as needing to be removed. The embanking of the Dodder was seen by the port authority as a natural extension of tidying up the area for port activities. Fourth, the Dodder had always been seen as a valuable source of water, supplying an increasing demand as the city grew. The Corporation recognised the right of Dubliners to a supply of water from the river through their ancient watercourse in 1715.[47] Lastly, it was a natural decision to extend the development of the port area to the lower Dodder area, as it lay between the landfall of packets and passengers at the Pigeon House and access to the city. Corporations like to be seen to be improving and developing their space. The Rogerson's Quay wall abutted the Dodder Basin on one side, while on the other a wall had been built from the Ringsend point up the river bank. In a manner of speaking, therefore, the task had already been begun. Most importantly, however, as the city and its population grew, more and more water was required for both domestic and industrial purposes, especially as there were now factories down on the Ringsend spit which consumed large quantities of water. These included metalworks, foundries, saltworks and glassworks. It must also be borne in mind that water was being removed from the river all along its course as it flowed towards the sea at Ringsend. The *Calendar of ancient records of Dublin* mentions the existence of corn mills along the river's course as early as 1551 (Fig. 4.9).[48] In simple terms, the volume of water in the Dodder today bears no resemblance to that of the late seventeenth and eighteenth centuries.

Much discussion had already taken place about the future of the course of the Dodder, with diversions directly to Sandymount and canals to Dunleary among the ideas suggested. In 1778 the

Dublin moving east, 1708–1844

Fig. 4.10—Thomas Matthews's survey map of the Dodder Basin, 1778.

Ballast Committee appointed Thomas Matthews to survey the whole basin. He produced a clear and detailed map that informed and guided development (Fig. 4.10). Within twenty years the project had been completed. The river was straightened and embanked, and the task of draining and improving the tidal slobs on either side then began. The land reclaimed joined up with other reclaimed ground around the Ringsend spit and fused over time into one continuous land mass up as far as Beggar's Bush. Having tamed and controlled the Liffey, the Corporation saw it as natural to do the same to the Dodder.

Fig. 4.11—St Mary's Church, Donnybrook, from the north. Note the steep river gradient (Gorry Gallery).

The work of the Wide Streets Commission in the second half of the eighteenth century was also an encouraging factor. It became a major influence on taste and design in both civic and private development. This can be seen in the way Lord Fitzwilliam laid out the canal area as it worked its way up from the docks around the eastern fringes of Dublin. This was to be a substantial contribution by the Pembroke estate to the creation of pleasing aesthetics, while at the same time the estate took full advantage of land reclamation. This in turn led to a better quality of development with a financially beneficial rental return. The simple creation of the extension of the canal down to the sea at Ringsend moved the boundary of the city outwards and this had an effect on this area in the Ringsend zone and surrounds. This, then, was the context in which the fourth great work took place.

The Dodder, while short, was vital to the capital, supplying water and power from Templeogue and Rathfarnham down to the sea. Its pattern of economically costly flooding over centuries, however, was of particular concern. This was due in the main to the steep river gradient, which on occasion allowed huge surges to build in the flow downstream (Fig. 4.11).

In 1728 the wooden bridge at Irishtown was carried away, along with a great deal of linen cloth bleaching on the banks.[49] A decade later, on 11 September 1739, the bridge at Donnybrook was 'thrown down'. Again, 'several ricks of hay and corn with many chairs, stools, and tables were seen floating in the Donnybrook River [the Dodder], it is imagined that many cabins were also carried away'.[50] The brickfields between Ringsend and Merrion were damaged to the tune of £1,000.[51] Later the same year, on 15 December, the floods combined with tides to cause the Ringhouse, on the east back of the Ringsend spit, to collapse.[52] Isaac Butler reported the damage done by continuous rain: 'Rathfarnham Bridge was washed away and that of Irishtown damaged, several others carried away … a great deal of linen cloth from the bleaching yards on the river'.[53]

The river was a useful location for the bleaching of linen, as was the Tolka. Because it could be classed as a sort of cottage industry, numbers active in the operation are not readily available, but Charles Cosslett in his travels in Ireland visited a Mr Bennett near Coleraine in 1793 and noted that 100 men were employed there.[54]

The propensity of the Dodder to flood could not be ignored. It was made clear to Lord Fitzwilliam by Edward Cullen, who produced a map in 1731 of the area from Ballsbridge to Ringsend Bridge. At the bottom of the map Cullen noted that if a breach of the river occurred at the brickfields south of Irishtown and other grounds lower than the river the damage would be great. This did happen on at least one occasion. The river devastated the brickworks on 30 July 1743.[55] The damage was not limited to the Pembroke estate; it injured various customers of the brick factory at a time of massive building in Dublin when a constant supply of bricks was needed. Today the following incident would be referred to as a flash-flood. It is the only eyewitness account of such an event so far located. One mid-afternoon in September 1732, Isaac Butler and his companion Mr Ransford were 'to the south of Ballsbridge about a quarter of a mile, the weather then calm and serene, no water in river course, we heard all of a sudden a murmuring noise when looking we perceived the main Dodder coming down, bracing all before it with great violence; in three quarters of an hour the whole strand was covered with water and the three arches of the aforementioned bridge, which before were dry, were filled with water, in particular the middle arch, through which the water poured in great quantity and with violence; it is very remarkable of this river that if any rain falls on the mountains, though it be fair in the valleys, the waters hasten down with great impetuosity, and in less than six hours (if the rain ceases) are all conveyed into the ocean at Ringsend and the river course becomes shallow and dry as before.'[56] This flooding added to the shoal at the entrance. The Ballast Committee was concerned at the obstruction caused by this flooding, which was exacerbated by the drop in ground level as it flowed towards the sea, 'forming shoals at Ringsend'.[57] The Committee was only too aware of the urgency of the problem as well as the scale of it; in the 1730s from Ringsend to Green patch it ran 'a great obstruction to ships', so the committee recommended 'a great number of hands be employed to remove it with all expedition'.[58]

In 1782 the *Hibernian Chronicle* (Cork) reported that 'the flood in the river Dodder on Thursday last was so exceeding high as to break down the south wall of Ringsend Bridge with a considerable part of the three arches; it also shook different parts that remain standing'.[59]

It was reported that the Dodder had overflowed its banks again in 1786, and people were reminded of just how precarious conditions were for the people of Ringsend/Irishtown: not only was the bridge gone but also there was major damage to various factories, and several mill weirs were swept away. As a further consequence of the flooding, Ringsend was left without a permanent bridge for a period of seven years: 'It is thought a temporary causeway or wooden bridge will be constructed for the convenience of the public where the bridge stood until the course of the Dodder is diverted near Sandymount', the *Freeman's Journal* reported in 1786.[60]

This press report is interesting for two reasons. First, it reveals that it was decided to erect a type of wooden platform/gangplank and, second, it shows that it was public knowledge that there was a plan to divert the river away from its course at the time.[61] It should be noted that this flash-flooding was largely reduced in the early nineteenth century when reservoirs were constructed upstream, taking the speed and volume out of the Dodder. This was all in the future. Meanwhile, it was as Weston Joyce described: 'Before the Dodder was confined between artificial banks it flowed at its own sweet will in numerous streams over a considerable tract of marsh and slob land at Ringsend

Fig. 4.12—Drawing depicting Ringsend Bridge after it was washed away (John James Barralet, c. 1747–1815).

and in time of flood caused much perturbation among the inhabitants'.[62] With all this flooding, a build-up of enthusiasm for changing the direction of the Dodder was understandable.

Ringsend suffered again when there was extreme flooding in the Dodder Basin in 1787. The impact was vividly described by John Ferrer, who wrote in his *View of ancient and modern Dublin* that Ringsend 'resembled a town which had experienced the calamities of war that had been sacked by the enemy or that had felt the hand of all-devouring time. The unfortunate inhabitants were in a manner excluded from intercourse with Dublin. They were attacked by the overbearing floods which issued from the mountains in irresistible torrents and completely demolished the bridge.'[63] The flooding was so bad that another writer described the scene as being like a large sea (Fig. 4.12).

The problems posed by the Dodder were exacerbated by the fact that the river altered course in the eighteenth century. It occasionally altered course naturally, but it was being interfered with long before that. The presence of corn mills on the Dodder was reported to the Assembly in 1551.[64] Again, on 18 April 1689 it was reported that 'the Dodder upstream at Templeogue was diverted from its course by James Talbot to the detriment of the city people'.[65] This would prove to be the case many times over the next 120 years. As early as 1706 Cullen's map of the area mentions the 'correct flow' and the 'former flow'. The Dodder as seen in the 1778 map by Thomas Matthews shows the estuary as having several channels. This was equally true 100 years earlier. Gerald Boate wrote in 1652 that the bridge was barely built when 'the brook in one of its risings quite altered its channel for a good way so as it did not pass under the bridge as before'. This stone bridge was built further upriver between 1629 and 1637, but the river that altered its course in one direction could just as easily change it back again. Guided by this consideration, in his 1731 map for the Pembroke estate Cullen included the suggestive comment: 'between the red lines leading from Ballsbridge to Ringsend Bridge is the design for the new river'. Evidently Lord Fitzwilliam planned to divert the Dodder for the benefit of the estate.[66] The same map shows the extensive gravel deposits formed in banks thrown up by the natural flood surges in the Dodder every so often.

Though it was prone to flood, the variety of the course of the Dodder was not commonly acknowledged or understood. In 1787 a writer observed: 'Many will be surprised to hear that this river, from Ballsbridge downwards, had within this present century a different course than appears now'.[67] Furthermore, he noted that its course had been altered at the instigation of the landlord, who caused an opening to be made in the bank 'where the channel now is, in order to supply Ringsend' with water.[68] It can be seen, therefore, that the untamed nature of the Dodder was an ongoing problem and that it had serious consequences for the landscape and for passengers entering Ringsend by ship, as well as for those living and working in the area. It is also apparent that the river changed course of its own accord, as evidenced by the build-up of the gravel banks, and that this incentivised and encouraged landlord plans and wider civic plans to alter the flow of the river.

In 1780 Samuel Sproule, an architect of Holles Street, which was built on the edge of the tide on reclaimed land, submitted 'A plan of the present and intended course of the river Dodder' to Lord Fitzwilliam. It included a scheme to use the new channel out through the slobs at Sandymount to address the issue of clearing and cleaning the river of raw sewage. It was a bold and grand plan and, although not acted on, it demonstrates that the idea of regulating the course of the Dodder was now actually being considered by engineers, surveyors and architects.[69]

In 1786 a bill presented to the Irish parliament by John Beresford, the Chief Commissioner of the Revenue, for promoting the trade of Dublin by rendering its port and harbour more commodious received royal assent. It included a provision to alter the course of the Dodder,[70] proposing to cut out a new channel from the Dodder south-east through the strand (at Sandymount) to the sea to avoid the sand bar at the confluence with the Liffey. This plan to avoid the sandbank was never acted on thanks to improved dredging methods which enabled the sandbank to be removed.[71]

Harry Gilligan in *A history of the port of Dublin* has maintained that the course of the Dodder was never altered although there was a plan to do so. He is incorrect. In fact, there were at least four proposals over a period, one of which has been referred to by Gillian O'Brien and Finola O'Kane: 'The diversion of the Dodder at the turn of the nineteenth century allowed for the prevention of floods and the installation of new industries'.[72]

As the number of schemes to regulate its flow suggests, controlling the Dodder was quite a challenge. In 1787 the writer of a pamphlet on the subject who had closely studied the river observed that it was supplemented by a number of perpetual springs: 'its waters are constant'. It was obvious from his words that he had walked the river on many occasions before putting pen to paper. He also said that 'The manufacturers from Irishtown have never been prevented from following their businesses in the driest of summers'.[73] Although the author of this text has never been identified, it is likely to have been George Semple and that he wrote anonymously because his 1762 proposal for extra sea walls for the bay and a plan to make thousands of acres available for reclamation behind these proposed walls had been rebuffed. It is also possible that he did not enjoy a good relationship with some members of the Ballast Committee. He was certainly experienced and had the technical knowledge gained over a long career working in and around the Liffey and the port, beginning with his excavations on the foundations of the Essex Bridge in 1753. The pamphlet is detailed and is written in Semple's style. It displays the forthright competence of someone who knows what he is talking about. This is especially evident in his commentary on the manner in which flooding in the Dodder undermined the foundations of the bridges—and Semple knew about bridges and their

Fig. 4.13—Current Ringsend Bridge (photo: Brian Matthews).

foundations. The number of people who were capable of thus presenting such an argument was never more than three or four, and the alternatives—engineers from England such as Jessop and Smeaton—were occupied elsewhere at the time.

Only one bridge over the Dodder onto the spit is shown in the early maps of the area. It is still referred to as the wooden bridge at today's location on Londonbridge Road, with the road continuing on to Beggar's Bush.[74] It is important to note that the bridge at Irishtown and the bridge at Ringsend are one and the same thing. One bridge served the two communities until the eighteenth century, when a proper stone bridge was built near the outflow of the Dodder at Ringsend. Prior to this the original and main access to the spit was via the Beggar's Bush road and across whatever bridge was operational at the Irishtown end of the spit. The barracks at Beggar's Bush was built in 1824. The causeway across the slob lands of the lower basin evolved over several decades. This was the route used by people for social reasons as well as for work, trade and transit. Horse-racing on the flat strand attracted large numbers down from the city. On 29 October 1765 there was a letter of complaint in the *Freeman's Journal* about the rowdy behaviour of the lower classes during the races.[75] The establishment of the causeway was triggered by the embanking of Sir John Rogerson's Quay in 1728, after which foot traffic began to create a road through the slob lands of the lower Dodder. It was gradually added to, and when the two connecting Grand Canal Basins were built so too was a proper lifting bridge for carriages, which finally established the road to the Dodder. There was also a huge gain in building the causeway up to the new Ringsend Bridge using the material from the two basins. This is especially evident today in the long gradient up and over the Ringsend Bridge. Eventually a stone bridge was erected on this section of the river (Fig. 4.13). The bridge was rebuilt in timber for the last time after 1802 when it was again washed away, on the same occasion as the Ormonde Bridge over the Liffey was washed away.

Access to the long strand which stretched all the way to Merrion Gates offered many leisure possibilities. Charles Cosslett, while staying in Dublin in 1794, wrote that 'About two o'clock I took

DUBLIN MOVING EAST, 1708–1844

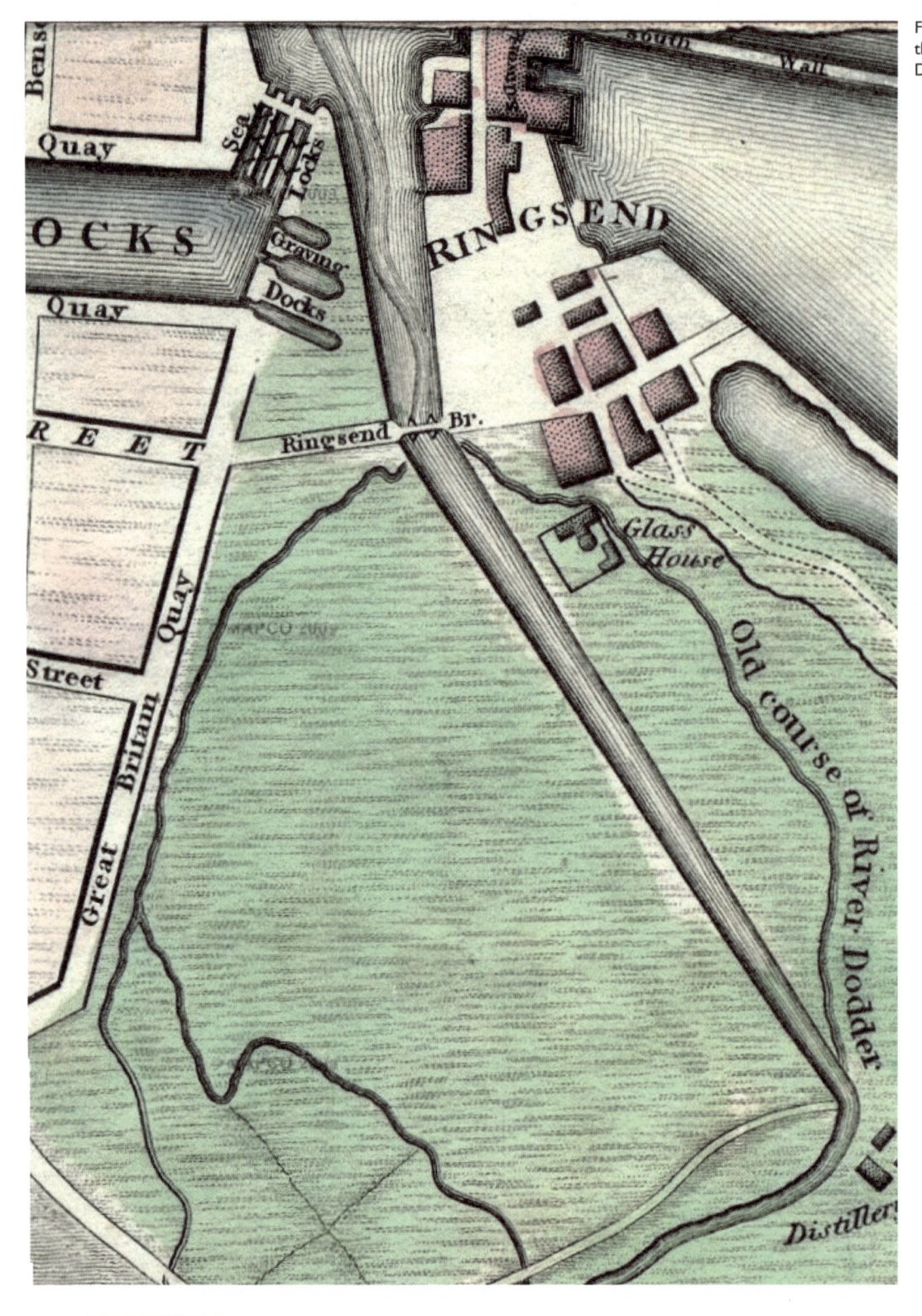

Fig. 4.14—Wilson's map of the city, showing the Dodder embanked, 1798.

a ride on the strand on my mare who I found in high order and spirits'.[76] On another day he 'rode to the rock [Blackrock] intending to bathe there … but set off immediately for Cranfield's near Irishtown where I bathed'.[77] He and a companion on one occasion agreed to 'take a ride, we both departed for our respective stables and after getting our horses ready, mounted and rode to the fields on the canal near Ringsend'.[78] On another occasion he records overtaking a friend also out riding on the Circular Road.[79] Cosslett is one of very few to write about such activities, providing a reminder of the number of horses in the city and the stables that catered for them and their riders.

There is little mention in the documentary sources of the work of embanking the Dodder. It may well be that, with plenty of ongoing first-hand experience in embanking and walling, the project just proceeded according to schedule without too many mishaps. It may be the case, too, that because it was a much smaller project than either Rogerson's wall or the South Bull Wall there was not the same interest in its progress. There are other examples of a lack of mention of certain events, such as no record of the opening of the Poolbeg Light in 1767. The same situation arose with respect to the Grand Canal Docks and it is fortunate that there is sufficient visual source material. The visual material is even more critical in this section. Two maps exist, one by Matthews in 1778, before any work had been done on embanking, and the other a city map by William Wilson (Fig. 4.14), showing the Dodder embanked in 1798. This gives a time-frame within which the work was completed. An additional nugget of information, which suggests that the redirecting of the Dodder had been completed two years earlier, is provided by an extract from the papers of the Corporation for Preserving and Improving the Port of Dublin, recording in 1796 that 'the branch of the Dodder which ran out between Tritonville and Irishtown was directed by the Corporation into the new channel'.[80] Moreover, the pamphleteer of 1787 confirms the situation: 'but the embankment, and the erection of the bridge, having obliged the shipbuilders to remove down to the point, they found themselves in want of room, and soon began to encroach on the water'. It might be suggested that he refers here to the embankment below the Ringsend Bridge. That, however, would not make sense. In this passage he is referring to the boatbuilders having to move downriver because there was no longer any waterfront available and no room to launch ships down under the bridge.[81] John Cowan's chart of Dublin Bay in 1801 also confirms the embanking of the Dodder. It is clear, then, that it was during this fifteen-year span that the work was completed. The second documentary source is Councillor William Vavasour's 'works that transformed the area'. Vavasour had taken a lease in 1792 of 60 acres between Beggar's Bush and Ringsend. The *Dublin Chronicle* reported that 'he intends immediately to reclaim by a complete double embankment of the Dodder which thus confined to a determined channel will thus form a handsome canal through it'.[82] It took six years to complete the task. This would concur with the 1798 date for Wilson's map. Either way, the work can be positively stated to have been complete by 1798.

Regarding the methods of construction, it seems logical that the work was carried out using the same methods as before. Crates or kishes of wood were made which were then filled with the plentiful supply of gravel available in the river, as seen in the maps. The walls did not need to be as high as the Liffey walls. Nor were they as substantial, as building on them was not immediately envisaged. They were in fact never reinforced in the same manner as the walls on the Liffey. Today the landscape shows clearly that the method used was the same as for the Liffey walls, as seen in the rise upwards of ground levels as the Dodder walls are approached. It can be seen today that they were faced with limestone.

The two major landlords in the area were Rogerson and Fitzwilliam. Landowners were

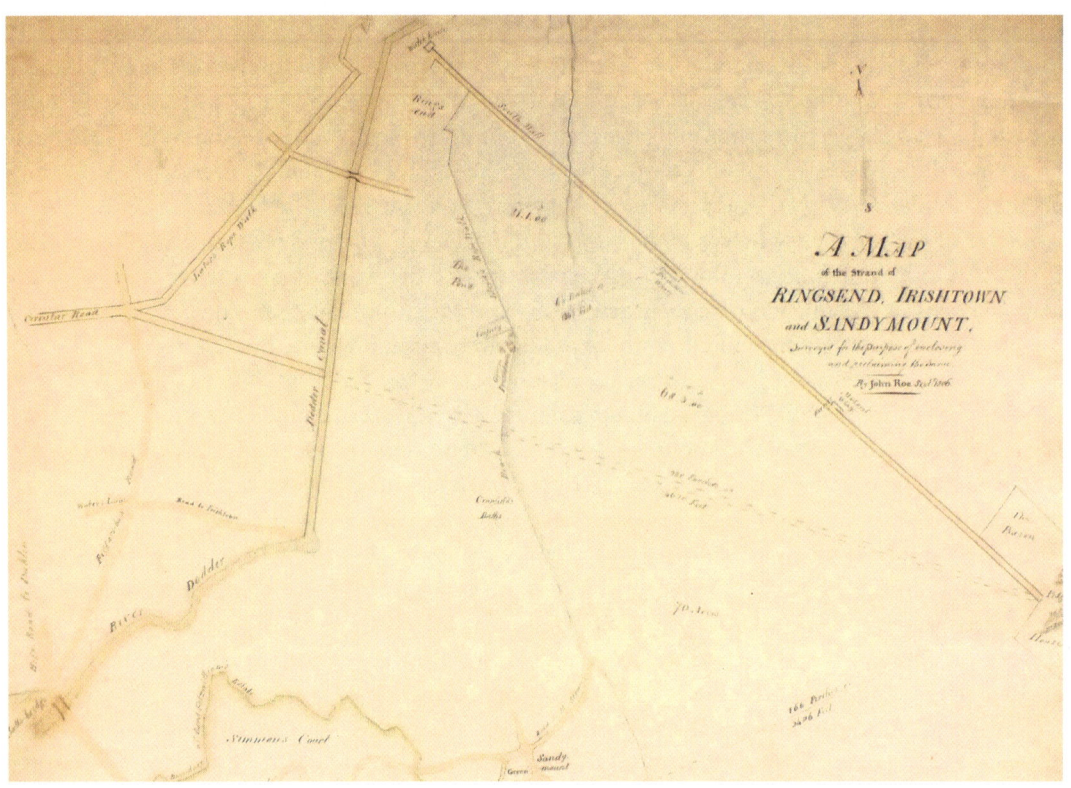

Fig 4.15—Pembroke estate map of Ringsend/Irishtown and Sandymount.

influential in the creation and remodelling of Irish towns, as seen in the walling of the Liffey by Rogerson and his reclamation of the ground behind. The Pembroke estate, too, was active. Its impact can be seen in the difference made to the Ringsend spit by the creation of three streets of dwellings, plots and yards in the space of thirteen years between 1693 and 1706.[83] There is no doubt that their motivation was the potential of land reclamation to yield additional money through rents. They were proactive in attempting to increase their landholdings. I disagree with Prunty, who claims that landlords 'were unable to transform the landscape unilaterally' but were prompted by motives of 'paternalistic responsibility' or 'prestige'.[84] Changing the landscape unilaterally is exactly what they did in the case of Dublin Bay. The Pembroke estate went from owning some nine acres on the original Ringsend spit in 1693 to in excess of 150 acres by 1800, when Ringsend was united with their other holdings on the fringe of the Dodder Basin. These acres changed from meadow and farmland to residential use and factories, which were followed in turn by larger multi-storey dwellings which brought incrementally larger rents to the Pembroke estate. These changes in land use also changed the employment pattern in the locality. Good land management required updated maps for the letting of land, and the Pembroke estate was well managed (Fig. 4.15). Survey maps also proved invaluable for planning new streets when the work of the Wide Streets Commission began in earnest.

The Pembroke estate was thus a major beneficiary as the city extended in an easterly direction, taking in Merrion Square and St Stephen's Green and ancillary streets. These were described in 1797 as 'delightfully situated; most of the houses having a view of Dublin Bay … the houses are all of a very large size, much uniformity has been preserved in building them'. The impact was even more marked at the Ringsend spit, where land reclamation took place on a large scale.[85] By the second

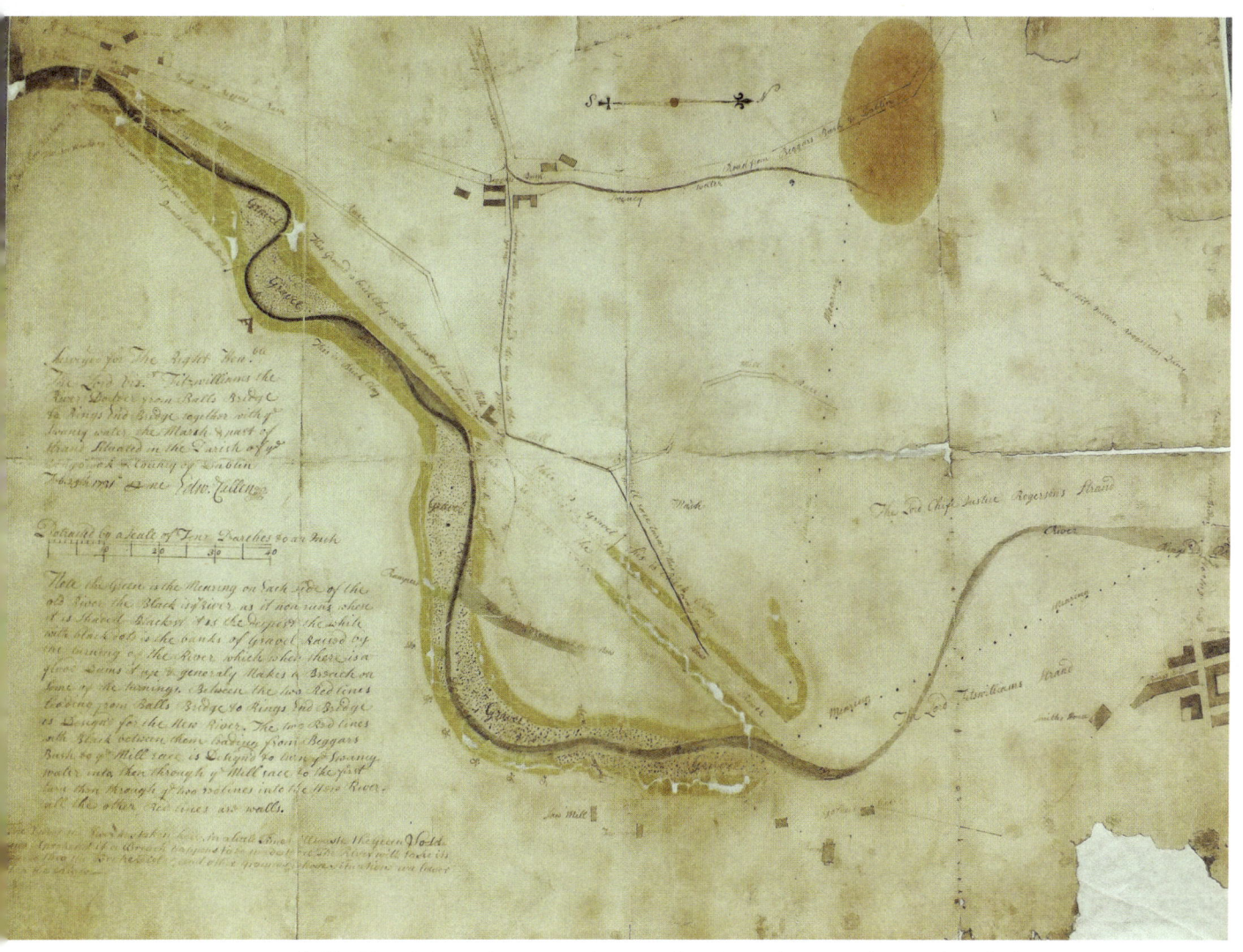

Fig. 4.16—Cullen's map of the Dodder, showing gravel deposits (NAI).

half of the eighteenth century the triangle of space between the South Wall, the strand on the coastal side of Ringsend and the sea had filled in to a large extent, thanks to the tidal build-up of sand creating another 25 acres.

Cullen shows in his 1731 map the location of the gravel beds in the river, and explains how they were formed through periodic flooding in the river: 'the white with the black dots is the banks of gravel raised by the turning of the river which is when there is a flood dams it up and generally makes a breach on some of the turnings' (Fig. 4.16). He further adds that 'between the red lines leading from Ballsbridge to Ringsend Bridge is the design for the new river'. This detail shows that there was a plan for the landlord to change the course of the Dodder. Cullen also denotes where Rogerson's land is located as well as Lord Fitzwilliam's.

In his survey map of Ringsend and Irishtown made in 1762, Jonathan Barker shows two slips at water's edge on the Irish Sea Ringsend strand, both at Thomas Street.[86] This illustrates that, along with activity taking place below the Ringsend Bridge on the Dodder, some fishing activities had moved to the south side of the spit. By now some streets had been built. The map also shows

85

DUBLIN MOVING EAST, 1708–1844

Fig. 4.17—Sketch of industrial development on reclaimed land at Ringsend, 1820.

shipbuilding taking place on the shore at Thorncastle Street. In his drawing of the makeshift bridge over the Dodder, Barralet depicts ships under both repair and construction on the shore here. The movement downriver on the Dodder of shipbuilding activities was confirmed by the 1787 pamphleteer. It included the area today occupied by the park south-east of Thomas Street and is depicted as 'My Lord's pond'. Barker shows the area west of Irishtown hamlet as salt-marsh, this on the west side of the Dodder, and names the shore west of Irishtown as 'Strand to the west of Irishtown village'. These details were to be confirmed twenty years later by Thomas Matthews's survey for the Ballast Office.

In 1778 the Ballast Office ordered Thomas Matthews to complete a survey of the Dodder from Ringsend to Ballsbridge for the purpose of embanking the river. The survey showed that upriver from the mouth of the Dodder and above Ringsend Bridge there was a huge spread of slob marsh which was all tidal. The enclosed area came to 43 acres, one rood and eight perches. Matthews included the high-water mark on the map. Within a few short years all of this would be taken in and walled by the Pembroke estate, and the river itself rerouted to run straight to the Ringsend Bridge. The estate owned the land to the south and west edges of this area too. The map titles this as 'Great area under the river Dodder'. The map also shows the South Lotts behind the Liffey Wall at Sir John Rogerson's Quay as being 'low ground', and the river wall continued around into the Dodder Basin, acting as a barrier to the high-water mark where Shelbourne Park sits today.

The Dodder, according to O'Brien and O'Kane, was diverted at the turn of the nineteenth century, and this, with the construction of the south wall, 'allowed for the prevention of floods and the installation of new industries'. One map in 1803 shows a large factory on the west bank of the spit on reclaimed land.[87] The Corporation established builder's stores and workshops, while new industries became the driver of development in the area (Fig. 4.17). O'Brien and O'Kane are in error, however, in claiming that the Dodder was diverted at the turn of the nineteenth century and that the finishing of the South Wall allowed for the prevention of floods. The wall never had anything to do with the flooding either of the Liffey or the Dodder. Furthermore, the Dodder has continued to flood on an irregular basis since the building of the South Wall.

The Pembroke estates embraced Merrion, Blackrock, Simmonscourt, Ballsbridge, Sandymount, Merrion Square and Fitzwilliam Square, as well as Irishtown, Ringsend and Beggar's Bush. This 'outward movement was made possible by the willingness of landowners to engage in speculative development of land for housing'.[88] Prunty further maintains that extensive suburbs developed in Ballsbridge, south of the Grand Canal.[89] The Fitzwilliams, being mainly urban landowners, operated in the usual manner of managing their landholdings, but in the areas of the two squares mentioned above they speculated in building houses. Here they followed a plan for a pleasing aesthetic to give an appropriate rent or return from such speculation. Merrion Square was laid out in 1762, using Merrion Street as the west side, and Fitzwilliam Square was laid out during the 1790s, being completed in the 1820s. In short, Prunty says that the Fitzwilliam sector was well developed.[90]

A good example of the Pembroke estate taking advantage was when in 1792 it negotiated to sell to the Corporation a strip of foreshore on the north side of the new South Bull Wall which it would never have been able to build on for £640, which was a considerable figure in the circumstances.[91] The estate would also take advantage of the embankment of both sides of the last stretch of the Dodder before it entered the sea, improving the ground on either side as it was reclaimed from sand-marsh and turned into rentable land. The estate was also able to turn the construction of the Grand Canal Docks and the canal itself to advantage, as it owned land on both sides of the canal up to Leeson Street Bridge as it tracked west. It should be noted, however, that the Fitzwilliams did not refrain from delegating the task of reclamation to others, as the *Dublin Chronicle* records. It reported on 31 May 1792 that 'the marsh between Beggar's Bush and Ringsend through which runs the Dodder on its way to the Ringsend Bridge is we hear taken by Mr (Councillor) Vavasour from Lord Fitzwilliam for 150 years at £190 *per annum*, this land which is inundated every tide'.[92]

Also in 1778, the Committee reported that, as well as getting Thomas Matthews to survey the Dodder Basin at the lower end, 'pursuant to your honours order of the 8th of February last we have had under consideration the expediency of altering the course of the Dodder by turning it to the southward of Ringsend Church' (St Matthew's, erected in 1704). They consulted the pilot committee, who unanimously agreed its potential benefit to the navigation of the port. Subsequently they commissioned Thomas Matthews to carry out his survey.[93]

Even though the Fitzwilliam landlords resided in London, they kept in touch with their agents and reviewed all suggestions made to them. Bryan Fagan was the agent between 1751 and 1761. When he died, his wife Elizabeth took over and ran the estates for the following sixteen years. Her daughter Barbara succeeded her; she married Richard Verschoyle and together they ran the estates until 1821.[94]

O'Brien and O'Kane noted that in the 1822 map of the area commissioned by the Pembroke estate there was a division between the type and size of plots in Ringsend/Irishtown. Both villages are consolidated in the map and there was a clear distinction between the residential and the industrial plots. While Irishtown had fewer industrial facilities, more were located in Ringsend at Thorncastle Street, with the plots perpendicular to the road, while the plots closer to the Liffey were wider and mainly industrial, with some residential. These industries can be seen in several paintings which include views of the area. The plots closer to the Dodder were residential, smaller and more compact.[95] At the same time the map shows that the seafront itself between the two villages was almost empty, but the plots on Bath Street and Pembroke Street contained the most number of dwellings with generally wider plots.

Rope-making gave employment in various parts of the city, but especially down here on the spit. Space allowed the operation to be carried on quite easily. It existed in a less formal way than in some of the great naval dockyards in England. When Charles Cosslett visited Portsmouth in 1794 he watched the rope-makers in action. He described the rope house there as consisting of three rooms 360 yards in length. The ground floor was where the longest cables were made and the shorter cables in the other two floors above, and on the ground floor 100 men were employed. To keep things in context, Portsmouth was a very large naval yard dealing with the whole of the Royal Navy and war with France was ongoing at the time. Nevertheless, it does give us an indication of the work available for men.[96]

To better appreciate what actually happened in the area, a reference to a well-known work on land reclamation will serve. Thomas Hitt's handbook *A treatise of husbandry on the improvement of dry and barren lands* was published in Dublin in 1760. The publication of such a book shows that the subject of land improvement and reclamation was of interest generally.[97] The *Dublin Guide* of 1787 shows just how aware Dubliners were of the potential: 'The immense quantity of ground lying from near Booterstown to Ringsend at present overflowed with water we are well assured could be rescued from the sea and converted into good land ... such work would long ago have been done in England or Holland'.[98] Kinahan wrote of land reclaimed in both the Liffey and the Boyne estuaries, and note should also be taken of Captain Bligh's involvement at Drogheda as well as Dublin. Comparisons between the two estuaries were made, particularly of the works on the deepening of the channel and the walling and enclosing of ground: 'as water from the enclosed slob was found unnecessary the walls were raised and the land cultivated'.[99] Kinahan recommended getting rid of the iron in the muds and marl dug out by the liberal use of liming.[100]

A good indication of how Ringsend/Irishtown developed in the eighteenth century can be seen by comparing Upper Buckingham Street, which has been described by Ruth McManus and Sinéad O'Shea. They quote Whitehead, who took the view that 'each society leaves its mark on the landscape, creating forms that reflect the aspirations and problems of its day. Urban landscapes are a physical record of past societies and of our own waiting to be read.'[101] This equally applies to Ringsend and Irishtown under the Fitzwilliam landlords throughout the period concerned. The presence of brickfields located between Ringsend and Merrion should be noted. This brick-making factory was fundamental to the growth of the city, since as it expanded so, too, did the brickworks.

'Dublin experienced prosperity and growth during the eighteenth century.' Political stability and a growing economy enticed ever-increasing numbers to settle in the city. Thus there was a determined effort to fashion a city worthy of its status as a capital and which could present itself as the second city of a growing empire.[102] It is reasonable to claim that much of the evolution of Dublin may be attributed to private landlords such as Gardiner and Fitzwilliam who developed building leases on their lands in order to reap long-term financial rewards.[103] This is clearly seen in the maps in Irishtown and Ringsend. Here land was reclaimed from the sea as well as from the Liffey and Dodder rivers. Jacinta Prunty points out that those maps were commissioned for the purpose of issuing new leases on both existing and newly developed property.[104] She makes the point that 'the

Fig. 4.18—OS map of the area, 1847.

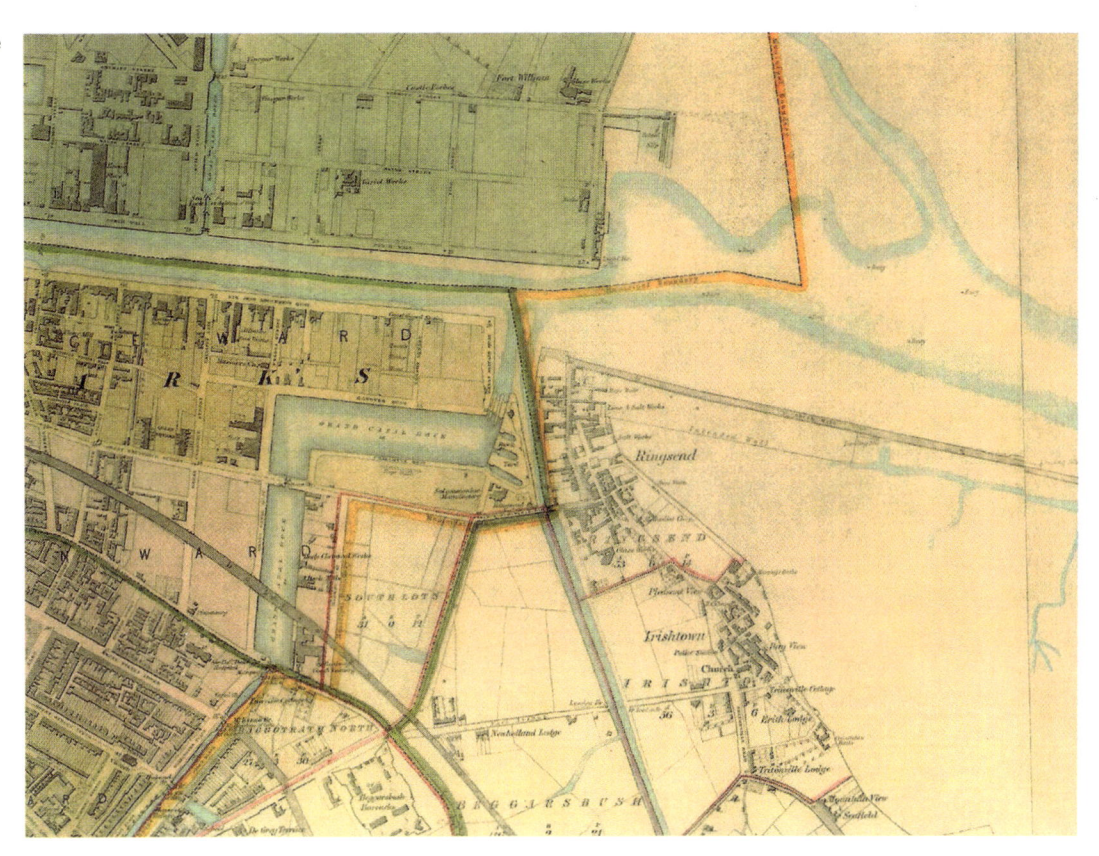

estate map where each plot was clearly outlined and numbered, with the details attaching to each, listed on an accompanying survey sheet, was an essential tool for good long-term estate management, and where urban property was concerned is invaluable to an understanding of town development'. The result is that the modern historian can readily differentiate between the types of houses constructed in Ringsend/Irishtown and those in Merrion or Fitzwilliam Squares and note the size differences as being one storey as against four storeys.[105]

Development occurred in various ways. A writer in 1787 observed: 'for a considerable while after Rogerson's embankment was completed, the houses along the point of Ringsend, the rear of which is next to the Dodder, had simple backyards; but as the embankment, and the erection of the bridge, having obliged the boat builders to remove down to the point, they found themselves in want of room, and soon began to encroach on the water. These encroachments were in some measure countenanced by a jetty or mole having been erected for the convenience of the revenue boats; at length, still nearer the bridge, an extensive permanent encroachment was suffered to be made, by the building of the Revenue dock.'[106]

Frank Gibney has listed fourteen great achievements of the period 1760–1800. He has put 'major improvements to the Port of Dublin' at the top of the list, followed by 'land reclamations of considerable area' and 'urban development of some two square miles of territory'[107] (Fig. 4.18).

The existence and geological content of the Ringsend spit was confirmed by archaeologists in 1983. The Dublin Regional Authority report showed how the area around Thorncastle Street was reclaimed from the tidal mudflats and sandbanks. While several dwellings are listed in the

Sandymount/Ringsend area in the Down Survey, the area was not extensively settled and reclaimed until the eighteenth century. No structural features were associated with the seventeenth-century soil. Razor shell and limpet throughout the upper levels of the sand subsoil indicate that the area was open sandbanks until the widespread deposition of the more recent garden soil. That life was tenuous is seen by the population of Ringsend in 1669, with 59 English and 21 Irish living there.[108] As port activities moved east, opportunities arose for all sorts of employment, though most of it was temporary; it included boatbuilding, sail-making, rope-making, chandlery, innkeeping and hackney-driving, on top of anything else that could be exploited from the port activity, while all the time watching out for the press-gangs. At this stage up to nine ships arrived in the port every day on average.

Fishing remained a constant source of food and employment down the centuries. The fishing both in the bay and on the east coast underwent a massive change as several Devon fishing-trawlers arrived in Ringsend in 1818–19. This transformed fishing and the change was seen in increased catches; the boats were able to operate with smaller crews, leaving more money for the men, and were able to stay out almost all year round. Their design was vastly superior and they had a mechanical winch system which allowed fewer crew to operate the trawling gear (three men and a boy). The design of these boats was based on the hull design of the Bristol Channel pilot cutters, vessels which traditionally went out to sea to meet ships coming in to the western approaches of the English Channel. Within a year, nineteen boats from the south of England and some of their crews were ensconced at Ringsend. Some of these boats lasted another 60 years while giving rise to a programme of Irish-built versions of these fishing-boats. This explains the non-Irish surnames abounding in the area for decades to come—indeed, up to today.

John Pigeon probably ran the first outdoor catering company in the country off the South Wall, supplying both ships' passengers and boating day-trippers in the bay with prepared foods, as well as ferrying them up and down the river from Ringsend. As the century progressed and sea bathing became a very popular activity, the locals were able to exploit this too, particularly after the opening of both Murphy's and Cranfield's baths for men and women on the seafront at Ringsend/Irishtown. A reminder, however, of just how difficult life could be is seen in the reports of Barbara Verschoyle, agent to the Pembroke estate between 1776 and 1821. In 1801 she described the women still gathering cockles off the strand while their menfolk were away at sea.[109]

What can be said with certainty is that by the end of the eighteenth century the Dodder was embanked on both sides down to the sea. The new elliptical stone Ringsend Bridge was erected in 1803, and the ground on both sides of the embankments had begun to be drained and reclaimed. The spit was now tied to the city permanently, and within a few years the second stone bridge at Londonbridge Road was constructed in 1836, and it too would last. The way was now open to finish reclaiming the area eastward from the city all the way to Beggar's Bush, and every advantage was taken by the Pembroke estate, which built on a massive scale in the entire area over the following decades.

As with all construction work, however, maintenance is required, and this applied to the walls in the area of the Dodder Basin too. George Halpin, Inspector of Works for the Board of the Corporation for Preserving and Improving the Port of Dublin, reported to the Board that the walls were in a 'ruinous state' from Ringsend to the Board's coalyard in 1822.[110]

The Dodder remained unfinished business in the sense that much of its water flow was being dissipated on its route to the Liffey. Like both canals, it also continued to absorb sewage while being a supplier of drinking water. In 1844 engineer Robert Mallet carried out a major survey of the Dodder with a view to possible reservoir construction. This was to create a more even flow for the mills along the river. His report to the Drainage Commissioners makes for interesting reading. Mallet pointed out that immediately down from Clonskeagh 'is Rochfort's Iron Mill, and below it Portis's Iron Mill, then at Donnybrook exists McGuirk's Saw Mill, the tail race of which, without re-entering the river, passes on into Duffy & Sons calico print works. An insignificant streamlet, the Swan water, rendered foul by sewerage, here joins the Dodder upon the left bank.'

Mallet lists the mills on the river that depended on water for their operational survival:
- four paper and mill board mills,
- ten flour and oil mills,
- three woollen and cloth mills,
- one cutlery mill,
- five iron manufactory mills,
- one cotton mill,
- two calico printing mills,
- one sawing timber mill.

The mill-owners constantly complained of a shortage of water to properly carry on their business. Mallet researched the rainfall of the area and recommended the building of one reservoir at first and three more if demand continued to rise. The reservoir site was to be up at Glenismole.[111]

The Grand Canal needed to be given a final £150,000 towards liquidation of its debts between 1813 and 1818.[112] The Grand Canal Company had a debt overhang of £600,000 and an income of just £15,000. This was an impossible situation to rectify by the usual commercial methods.[113]

Gibney has said of Dublin in 1760 that the main developed area of the city along its eastern limits did not extend beyond a line east of St Stephen's Green, Merrion Street and Lincoln Place over to Townsend Street.[114] He said that over the next 40 years the physical area of the city would almost double and that this growth would be almost entirely along the perimeter. The city now had a new perimeter, which in a short time was filled in with streets and houses as it grew out eastward. The entire landscape had been transformed by 1800 in this part of Dublin; while work and improvement would continue, the way had been paved by the work done before the close of the eighteenth century. And while all this activity had been taking place on the south side of the Liffey, there was much happening on the north side.

The *Dublin Penny Journal* had this to say in 1833: 'Ringsend might then be deemed an island, for, before the Dodder river was enclosed by banks, the sea rolled over where rich pastures now relieve the eye in the vicinity of Irishtown … In this place then there is, at present being, an individual who has resided there nearly a century.'

Even after all that had taken place, the authorities continued to fret over the port, with good reason. Having expended so much energy and money, two items remained unresolved which hindered Dublin's progression as a deepwater port: one was the continued existence of the bar and the other was a bank at the exit of the Dodder into the Liffey. There was also potential danger to shipping without a harbour of refuge in the event of storms in Dublin Bay. Charles Dupin, a French engineer visiting Dublin, reported that 'unfortunately the entrance to these docks [Grand Canal Docks] is precisely at the conflux of the Liffey and another small river; and the effect of this conflux is to form constantly a bar which hinders ships of any size from entering the docks'.[115] This writer can confirm that the bar remains, as he ran aground on it coming out of the Grand Canal Docks in

2010 on board a boat drawing 6ft.

There would be report after report suggesting alternatives to the status quo. The whole business of a ship canal connected to Dún Laoghaire and Sutton/Howth continued to be mooted into the nineteenth century. Thomas Rogers in 1800 suggested the same in his pamphlet *Remarks on shelter or safe anchorage between Ireland's Eye and Howth with a plan for a harbour and a canal from thence to Dublin for large ships*. Henry Flynn, too, wrote on the subject; in his 1834 pamphlet *A glance at a question of a ship canal* he included a map of his proposed route of the canal. He also included a map of Alexander Nimmo's proposed canal route, which shows the canal ending at Ringsend. He shows Cubitt's proposed line running north of Nimmo's, away from the shore, and ending at the Pigeon House, and he shows Kilaly's proposed canal across the land to the Grand Canal Docks and along the shore. The interesting thing is that just as this pamphlet was being circulated the new Kingstown Railway was already nearing completion, itself running along the shore on ground taken back from the sea, in the exact area of the proposed canals.[116]

Conclusion

The result of this work was to increase the total area under the control of the Corporation. As the land now enclosed and primed for reclamation was actually reclaimed, it was used first for agriculture and later for development in the form of dwellings, factories and streets. The area benefited from the expansion of trade and the increase in population, which necessitated more accommodation and vital services. It would also benefit from the outward growth along the seashore on the Irishtown and Merrion strands and the additional houses then constructed inland of this line, filling in towards Sandymount. In essence the completed works encouraged the development of the suburbs of Sandymount, Merrion and parts of Ballsbridge. The port grew and this boosted the traffic in and out, creating a variety of occupations to accompany such expansion in supplying all sorts of materials and services. These included ropes and cordage, sail-making, victualling, including butchery and meat supplies, and the provisioning of ships, alongside all aspects of the growing use of coal as the new steam technology expanded in use. It changed the social opportunities for the general populace in that the lower classes in the city could now walk down to the strand at Ringsend and Irishtown and engage in the popular pastimes of bathing and gathering shellfish.

As the Grand Canal and the Docks became established and traffic grew, schedules too expanded but were constrained by limitations. By 1824 the Grand Canal Docks boasted of having Mr Hugh Pollen as dock master at Ringsend,[117] although the reservation remained that 'they are far from sufficient for the increased size and number of ships trading to the port'. The 1846 report added that 'the entrance into the Grand Canal Docks is all blocked up by sandbanks and that there is but one public crane'.[118]

Notes

[1] A map dated 9 November 1751 and titled 'A survey of the present street immediately leading to His Majesty's Royal Palace or Castle of Dublin' and a map dated 15 January 1753 and titled 'A design for opening proper streets or avenues to His Majesty's Royal Palaces in Dublin' (both on show at an auction preview in the Gresham Hotel by Fonsie Mealy, fine art auctioneer, on 12 December 2016).

[2] Map, 'Survey of the present streets leading from the river Liffey to Dublin Castle', 1752 (NGI 20831).

[3] Royal Dublin Society minute-books, vols 1–3 (1731–46), at 4 July 1734.

[4] 'A late voyage to Holland; with brief relation of the actions at the Hague; also remarks on the manners and customs, nature, and comical humours of the people; their religion, government, habitations, way of living and manner of treating strangers, especially the English, written by an English gentleman attending the court of the King of Great

Britain 1691', in Thomas Park, *The Harleian miscellany: a collection of scarce, curious and entertaining pamphlets and tracts* (London, 1808), vol. 2, p. 59.

5. Geoffrey Corry, 'The Dublin bar—the obstacle to the improvement of the Port of Dublin', *Dublin Historical Record* **23** (4) (1969–70), 137–52, p. 147.
6. Ruth Delaney, *A celebration of 250 years of Ireland's inland waterways* (Belfast, 1986), p. 15.
7. *Dictionary of Irish Architects 1720–1940*, Irish Architectural Archive online database (www.dia.ie).
8. Jaimie McNamara, 'A case for the conservation of the graving dock', unpublished MA thesis, Trinity College Dublin (2012), p. 12.
9. Frank Gibney, 'A civic achievement: Dublin 1760–1800', *Dublin Historical Record* **15** (1) (1956), 1–10, p. 5.
10. McNamara, 'A case for conservation', p. 5.
11. *Ibid.*, p. 19.
12. Lieutenant Joseph Archer, *Statistical survey of the county of Dublin with observations for the RDS* (Dublin, 1801), p. 204.
13. Harry Philips, 'Early history of the Grand Canal', *Dublin Historical Record* **1** (4) (1939), 108–19.
14. *Ibid.*, p. 119.
15. Grand Canal Company minute-books, vol. 13, 16 September 1796 (NAI).
16. McNamara, 'A case for conservation', p. 21.
17. *Ibid.*, p. 21.
18. *Ibid.*, p. 17.
19. *Ibid.*, p. 23.
20. John Ferrar, *A view of ancient and modern Dublin* (Dublin, 1807), p. 39.
21. Delany, *Ireland's inland waterways*, p. 78.
22. Mark Baldwin, 'Review of *William Jessop, engineer* by Charles Hadfield and A.W. Skempton (London, 1979)', *Technology and Culture* **21** (2) (1980), 246–50.
23. McNamara, 'A case for conservation', p. 89.
24. *Ibid.*, p. 19.
25. *Ibid.*
26. Minute-book of the Court of Directors of the Grand Canal Company, 27 April 1796 (NAI).
27. Information courtesy of Stephen Harris, FSCSI, FRICS, Director, D.L. Martin & Partners, Mount Street Crescent, Dublin 2.
28. Friedrich Raumer, *England in 1835 volume 1, being a series of letters written to friends in Germany during a residence in London and excursions into the provinces by Friedrich Raumer, translated from the German by Sarah Austen and H.E. Lloyd in three volumes* (London, 1836).
29. Minute-book of the Court of Directors of the Grand Canal Company.
30. Fred Rogers, letters to Admiralty requesting cables, stores and anchors, Box 879, National Archives at Kew, London.
31. Minute-book of the Court of Directors of the Grand Canal Company.
32. Ferrar, *A view of ancient and modern Dublin*, p. 39.
33. Minute-book of the Court of Directors of the Grand Canal Company, 26 April 1796.
34. Chevalier de Latocnaye, *A Frenchman's walk through Ireland 1796–7, translated from the French of de Latocnaye by John Stevenson, 1917; with an introduction by John A. Gamble* (Belfast, 1984), pp 280–7.
35. Rolf Loeber & Magda Stouthamer-Loeber, 'Dublin and its vicinity in 1797', *Irish Geography* **35** (2) (2006), p. 145.
36. Raumer, *England in 1835*, p. 247.
37. McNamara, 'A case for conservation', p. 13.
38. James Dawson, *Canal extensions in Ireland recommended to the imperial legislature* (Dublin, 1819), p. 21.
39. Henry Veredker, *Letter to the Tidal Commission from the secretary of the Corporation for Preserving and Improving the Port of Dublin in answer to complaints by Captain Washington* (Dublin, 1846), p. 13.
40. *Ibid.*, p. 6.
41. *Ibid.*
42. N. McCullough, *Dublin: an urban history* (Dublin, 1989), p. 70.
43. *CARD*, vol. 11, p. 322.
44. Ann Plumtre, *Narrative of a residence in Ireland during the summer of 1814 and that of 1815* (London, 1817), p. 96.
45. Archer, *Statistical survey of the county of Dublin*, p. 118.
46. *Dublin Journal*, 17 May 1796.
47. *CARD*, vol. 7, p. vii.
48. *CARD*, vol. 10, pp 446–7.
49. F.E. Dixon, 'Weather in old Dublin', *Dublin Historical Record* **13** (3–4) (1953), 94–107, p. 96.

50 *Ibid.*, p. 96.
51 NAI, Pembroke Estate papers, 97/46/1.
52 *Ibid.*
53 Isaac Butler, 'Weather Diary 1716–1734', p. 29.
54 Diaries of Charles Cosslett (1793–4), in the archive of St Malachy's College, Belfast.
55 NAI, Pembroke Estate papers, 97/46/1 2/5.
56 Butler, 'Weather Diary', p. 377.
57 *CARD*, vol. 13, p. 90.
58 *CARD*, vol. 8, p. 244.
59 *Hibernian Chronicle* (Cork), 22 August 1782.
60 *Freeman's Journal*, 22 April 1786.
61 Anon., *Remarks and observations on the intention of turning the course of the river Dodder in order to show the inexpedience of that measure* (Dublin, 1787), p. 8.
62 Weston St John Joyce, *The neighbourhood of Dublin, its topography, antiquities and historical associations* (Dublin, 1912), p. 3.
63 Ferrar, *A view of ancient and modern Dublin*, p. 39.
64 *CARD*, vol. 1, pp 446–7.
65 *CARD*, vol. 5, p. 489.
66 NAI, Pembroke Estate papers, 97/46/1 2/5.
67 Anon., *Remarks*, p. 16.
68 *Ibid.*, p. 17.
69 NAI Pembroke Estate papers, 2011/2/1.
70 26 George III c.19.
71 H. Gilligan, *A history of the port of Dublin* (Dublin, 1988), p. 54.
72 G. O'Brien and F. O'Kane (eds), *Portraits of the city: Dublin and the wider world* (Dublin, 2012), p. 165.
73 Anon., *Remarks*, p. 9.
74 NAI, Pembroke Estate papers map, 23 April 1706.
75 *Freeman's Journal*, 29 October 1765.
76 Cosslett diary (1794), p. 11.
77 *Ibid.*, p. 13.
78 Cosslett, Diary B (1793–4), p. 12.
79 *Ibid.*, p. 11.
80 Charles Halliday, *The Scandinavian kingdom of Dublin* (Dublin, 1881), p. 242.
81 Anon., *Remarks*, p. 22.
82 See *Embanking the Dodder* (www.dublincity.ie/sites/default/files/content/WaterWasteenvironment/waterprojects/Documents/6 A11.1 to A12.2 pdf).
83 Jacinta Prunty, 'Estate records', in W. Nolan and A. Simms (eds), *Irish towns: a guide to sources* (Dublin, 1998), p. 121.
84 *Ibid.*
85 Loeber and Stouthamer-Loeber, 'Dublin and its vicinity in 1797', p. 146.
86 NAI, Pembroke Estate papers map, 16 G 18 (6).
87 Michael Swift, *Historical maps of Ireland* (London, 1999), pp 86–7.
88 Jacinta Prunty, 'Improving the urban environment: public health and housing in nineteenth-century Dublin', in J. Brady and A. Simms (eds), *Dublin through space and time* (Dublin, 2001), p. 166.
89 *Ibid.*, p. 167.
90 *Ibid.*, p. 170.
91 Gilligan, *History of the port of Dublin*, p. 60.
92 *Dublin Chronicle*, 31 May 1792, cited in Halliday, *The Scandinavian kingdom of Dublin*, p. 242.
93 *CARD*, vol. 13, p. 10.
94 Prunty, 'Improving the urban environment', p. 166.
95 *Ibid.*
96 Cosslett, Diary D (1793–4).
97 Thomas Hitt, *A treatise of husbandry on the improvement of dry and barren lands* (Dublin, 1760).
98 *The Dublin Guide* (Dublin, 1787).
99 G.H. Kinahan (assisted by Alexander McHenry), *A handy book on the reclamation of waste lands, Ireland* (Dublin, 1882), p. 27.

[100] *Ibid.*, p. 27.
[101] Ruth McManus and Sinéad O'Shea, 'Upper Buckingham Street: a microcosm of Dublin, 1788–2012', *Studia Hibernica* **38** (2012), p. 141.
[102] *Ibid.*, p. 141.
[103] *Ibid.*, p. 142.
[104] Prunty, 'Estate records', p. 123.
[105] *Ibid.*, p. 124.
[106] Anon., *Remarks*, p. 22.
[107] Gibney, 'A civic achievement', p. 10.
[108] Phil Comerford, 'Thorncastle Street through the ages', *Dublin Historical Record* **67** (1) (2014), p. 32.
[109] *Ibid.*, p. 33.
[110] Journal of the proceedings of the Corporation for Preserving and Improving the Port of Dublin, vol. 11 (3 December 1819–2 May 1823), p. 323.
[111] Robert Mallett, *Report to the Commissioners on the proposed formation of reservoirs on the river Dodder, county of Dublin, for the prevention of sudden floods and accumulation of water for the constant supply of mills on that river and on the city water-course* (Dublin, 1844), pp 14–18.
[112] Ruth Heard, 'Public works in Ireland, 1800–1831', unpublished MLitt. thesis, Trinity College Dublin (1977), p. 46.
[113] *Ibid.*, p. 55.
[114] Gibney, 'A civic achievement', p. 10.
[115] Baron Charles Dupin, *Narratives of two excursions to the ports of England, Scotland and Ireland in 1816, 1817, and 1818 together with a description of the breakwater at Plymouth* (London, 1827), p. 52.
[116] Pamphlets in the Charles Halliday collection, National Library of Ireland.
[117] *The Gentleman's and Citizen's Almanack (as compiled by the late John Watson Stewart) for the year of our Lord 1824* (Dublin, 1824), p. 159.
[118] Minute-books of the Commissioners of the Ballast Board (9 vols), vol. 3, Part 1, Tidal harbours, p. 41a. Dublin Port Company Archive, Damastown.

5. The Dublin to Kingstown Railway, including the building of Dunleary Harbour

The next major work to be completed along the south bank of the Liffey was the Dublin to Kingstown Railway, but before looking at the railway we must examine the context of its arrival. It arrived almost on the tail of the new packet harbour built on the south shore of Dublin Bay. What would be called Kingstown had been known as Dunleary; its name was changed to honour King George IV, who departed from there in 1821. It was known as a fishing centre, and Thomas Eyre, who succeeded Neville as surveyor general in 1752, re-established the link with civil works by supervising harbour works at Dunleary and subsequently at Balbriggan and Skerries.[1]

Mail-boats usually departed from the Pigeon House to either Holyhead or Parkgate near Chester. Sometimes incoming passengers had to disembark at Dunleary by getting aboard wherries (small boats) and being rowed or sailed ashore. Occasionally they did the same at Skerries, and more often at Howth.[2]

Prior to this the packet station had been at the equally new harbour at Howth, which turned out to be unsuitable. With the advent of packet-boats to Kingstown, the traffic generated in both directions quickly adapted to using the railway into Dublin. It makes sense, therefore, to look briefly at this context before proceeding.

The threat from France existed up to Napoleon's final defeat at the Battle of Waterloo in 1815. Britain's war with the USA also ended in 1815, but the French were always seen as the major threat, probably because of France's close proximity and the fear of the export of French revolutionary ideas and bloody revolt. On account of this threat the military took control of the Pigeon House harbour, and commercial traffic was eventually barred from accessing it. This meant that a new mail-packet station had to be provided and Howth was eventually chosen. The harbour at Howth proved unsuitable, however, and Dunleary was then further developed. Ten years later the mail contract with Howth ran out and was awarded to Kingstown, as it was now known. I intend to look at the Howth aspect separately while dealing with the north side and to examine the role of Kingstown Harbour as part of the railway chapter, primarily because one led to the other.

It makes sense to take into consideration the changes in building methods and new technology now becoming available as part of the Industrial Revolution. There was a significant growth in the consumption of coal, much of which would pass through Dublin port, although coal also came through several other harbours, such as Howth, Skerries, Balbriggan and Kingstown, and was even landed on beaches such as at Bray, Co. Wicklow. The increased use of iron in building and construction and the arrival of steam power followed.

In this digital age, some understanding of the development of steam as a source of power is needed to appreciate the full impact of its arrival. Just as today the digital phenomenon is all-encompassing, so too was this new source of power in the early nineteenth century, reaching out to shipping, railways, farm machinery, printing machinery, machinery in factories, draining, dredging and lifting machinery. And, just like today, its technological advance was unstoppable. It led to heating in factories and also for domestic uses, as well as pipes on the walls of houses and factories, and of course metal pipes for carrying water under the city street. All this activity would feed the requirement for even more iron, which necessitated even more coal for the foundries.

One of the changes brought about by the Act of Union of 1801 was the manner in which political business would henceforth be done. Professor Patrick Duffy, in a lecture to the Royal Irish Academy in August 2016, said that prior to the Act of Union political decision-making was driven by the landowning and ruling classes, while subsequent to the Act all decisions emanated from London. With the exodus of a good portion of the ruling class to London, the city of Dublin sank into some decline, and slums eventually took over parts of previously genteel zones. Slums were part and parcel of European urban life and not particular to Dublin. The Act is usually the reason given for this, but I maintain that the real impetus for the spread of slums was the fact that so many of the gentry no longer required townhouses in the city because they could now so easily access Dublin. One of the side-effects of this was the beginning of migration out of the city by the better-off, creating new suburbs such as Rathmines, Rathgar, Pembroke, Clonskeagh, Kilmainham and Clontarf, while the poor of the city moved inward in ever-greater numbers. But they also began to move out and occupy ground along the southern shore of Dublin Bay, starting close in at Sandymount. Another valid reason for the flight of the better-off, and one not much alluded to, was the overpowering stench in the city because there was no proper method of clearing away all sorts of effluent; almost all visitors to the city remarked on it.

Dublin had a justifiably bad reputation in this respect but too often what was achieved has been ignored. There were achievements in engineering, technology, building, architecture and artistic endeavour, such as the arrival of the Zoo and photography before mid-century. The construction of the Dublin to Kingstown Railway was one such major achievement.[3] Socially, too, great changes occurred, as recorded by John Trotter, a Protestant cleric: 'It has however lost much of its splendour, as well as most of the notables and gentry since the union'.[4]

The railway consisted of a raised embankment to carry the rails out of the city as far as Serpentine Avenue and thereafter at ground and sea level. It also involved the building of a large island of material 20ft high at Westland Row to contain a terminal station. This building up of a raised embankment had already been completed in similar fashion in the Leeson Street to Rathmines Road section during the construction of the Grand Canal, and was therefore nothing new or daunting for the builders of the railway embankment some 30 years later. The railway involved the use of coal, iron and steam—the three main ingredients of the Industrial Revolution. Its construction also consumed vast quantities of stone, both granite and limestone, from Dublin quarries and occasionally from further afield. All this stone had to be transported to the various sites along the line as the building progressed, and the large quantities used are easily appreciated today from the window of the DART.

The development of steam as a power source

Steam as a means of harnessing power had been discovered, developed and expanded in recent years, particularly for pumping water out of mines. The future of steam lay in its ability to generate power to drive and propel machinery in factories, on land in the form of railway transport, and at sea both for propulsion and for dredging. Steam, however, was not totally new to Dublin. Before the turn of the century a steam pump had been employed in pumping water out of the Grand Canal Docks, and steamship propulsion was known from the second decade of the new century. As a means of propulsion it was opening up all sorts of possibilities, alongside the Industrial Revolution.

Baron Charles Dupin, a French engineer, wrote of his fact-finding trip to England in 1819: 'The works of hydraulic construction in England are distinguished by the constant use of the steam engine, for draining … and all the manual operations which require the continued exertion of great and long efforts … A lighter provided with a steam engine which works the dredging apparatus … worked by the agency of steam not only have the basins been dug and cleansed out …'.[5] It is another suburb of London that Messrs Huddart and Brown have established the one his rope manufactury, and the other his manufactury of iron cables. Huddarts ropes are twisted and laid by the agency of steam.'[6] He added that 'Mr Rennie is now constructing in Woolwich a yard, a smithery with a forge adapted to it. The lifting of tilt hammers and all the machinery belonging to this forge will be put to motion by the steam engine.'[7] He later mentioned seeing large industrial planes powered by steam.[8] Dupin concluded his tour with this remark: 'In England the steam engine, the hydraulic press and several connotations of these two present the principal agents of English industry, possessing the strength of 200–300 horses'.[9] Steam power enabled constant experiment and advance in technology. Sir John Rennie built the first steam vessel for the Royal Navy in 1839 which included a screw-propeller for drive.[10] In the same year in Scotland experiments were being carried out on an iron ship and the possible effects of the metal on compasses.

Industry, too, was beginning to exploit this new source of power in Ireland. According to Dickson, in 1802 there were eight flour mills in south County Dublin and seven in the city, of which three were equipped with steam engines,[11] and he says that the first steam engine was built earlier still, in 1791, by Henry Jackson in Dublin.[12] The *Calendar of ancient records* reports the presence of boring tools and a steam engine in 1807, recording that Andrew Coffey, city engineer, 'has agreed with Aydon and Ewell of the Shelf Ironworks to buy the necessary iron pipes' and that he applied to Bolton Watts and Company 'respecting the steam engine' but that no decision had been made yet.[13]

Agriculture, too, saw changes thanks to steam and its possibilities. Andrew Meikle invented the first steam-powered threshing machine about 1786 and the technology continued to be improved over the following years. By 1834 John Avery and Hivem Pitts had invented a method of separating the grain from the chaff while threshing. One of the results of such machinery was riots in England in 1830, caused by the fear of unemployment after years of high taxes and low wages.

The first steamship arrived in Dublin in 1815, *en route* to London, immediately illustrating new and exciting possibilities. All these possibilities came together in a few short years and would utterly change the way people lived and worked and how goods were transported, besides making a difference to the political situation, to the military situation and the policing of the country, and to the structure of Dublin and the manner of the expansion of suburbs. It created new forms of employment directly and opened up opportunities for other areas of work and commerce indirectly, and it changed the daily lives of many of Dublin's citizens.

In the sixteenth century, as mining expanded, the increasing quantities of minerals extracted from the earth had to be transported over ever-greater distances. The answer was to lay rails to link mines with ports and factories, and of course to carry coal to foundries for the smelting of iron. An early example was the 3km-long track with wooden rails near Nottingham in 1604.[14] Iron rails had begun to replace wooden ones by 1732, with cast-iron rails appearing in 1787.[15] As matters progressed, the parliament in London became involved and the Act of 1800 for the Surrey Iron

Railway was passed in 1801. As the technology developed, the problem of the earlier iron rails being too brittle was overcome by John Birkinshaw, who was using rolled iron rails up to 20ft long by 1820.[16]

In 1712 Thomas Newcomen and Thomas Savary invented a steam engine for pumping water from a mine. The engineer John Smeaton improved this apparatus.[17] The same Smeaton was involved in technological development over a 40-year period, submitting papers on the use of water and windmills and circular motion, for which he was awarded a gold medal from the Royal Society.[18] He completed the masonry work on the Eddystone lighthouse, one of the most challenging engineering projects imaginable, and he took himself over to Holland to study Dutch methods and machinery. He also came up with improvements to the blast furnace, designed a pump for ships[19] and added improvements to the air pump for use in diving bells.[20]

The French engineer/designer Nicolas Cugnot progressed matters by building a self-propelled gun-carriage for the French army in 1769. Around this time the Industrial Revolution was getting under way and the possibilities began to be realised owing to the availability of capital and men of vision. In the 1780s James Watt took things a step further with his steam engine which could pull wagons up an incline in a mine. Finally, the first steam train pulled eight three-ton coal wagons with 50 passengers aboard for 23 minutes in 1812. The developing technology continued to gather pace with a non-stop list of firsts in rail travel.[21] By 1825 George Stephenson and Ralph Dodds had succeeded in developing the locomotive for the Stockton and Darlington Railway, as well as building the railway itself. This was an impressive development, given that only two years previously the Stephensons, father and son, had set up a factory in Newcastle for building steam locomotives. The engine pulled a passenger coach and up to 100 other people clinging to empty coal-wagons at fifteen miles per hour for twenty miles. Within five years several railways were in operation.[22] Stephenson followed up with the Canterbury and Whitstable line, which was the first to operate regular passenger services and to sell season tickets.[23] Here in Ireland two freight tramways were built—one at Arigna Mines, built in 1818, and the other from Killiney to Kingstown Harbour, laid out in 1819—and were in use before the Limerick and Waterford railway was sanctioned in 1826.[24]

The effects of the railway were unprecedented in social and economic terms. Its affordability allowed more and more people to avail of it. It would lead to intercity transport, reducing the scale of the horse and carriage transport system that had operated for the previous 80–90 years, such as that supplied by Bianconi. Franco Tanel observes that this was a profound social development in a time when most people never travelled far from their homes during their entire lives.[25]

The advent of the railway would also have a profound effect on the military situation in Ireland in that men and equipment could be more easily moved around on the railway as well as on the continually improving roads, thereby exercising greater control over the territory. It had a profound effect on politics, too, for the same reason, and allowed greater crowds to be amassed at times in various locations. It brought about the single time zone in the entire kingdom, allowing timetables to be printed. London would have its own rail by 1835, a year later than Dublin. The reason for the delay was the broad range of opposition to it from the coaching trade and dockworkers, who feared for their jobs.[26] The development of so-called railway mania in the 1840s was boosted by the seal of approval conferred by Queen Victoria when she travelled by train from Slough to Paddington in 1842. This also had the effect of triggering legislatively improved facilities for fare-paying passengers.[27] Twenty-seven years after Stephenson, locomotives were attaining speeds of 70mph while horses and carriages continued at a sedate pace. This is a clear indication of the cross-fertilisation of ideas and confidence, as the Industrial Revolution fed railway technological improvement and it in turn showed the way in shipping/steam engineering. The invention of the railways changed the course of history.[28]

Fig. 5.1—Badge on steamship company on Eden Quay (photo: Brian Matthews).

Railways were not developing in isolation. It is timely to expand here on the shipping aspect, because the railway was to be located within the port zone and steamships would ply their trade only 400m away from the train running out to Kingstown to deliver and collect passengers from the steam packets going to the new harbour there. Steam itself as a new power source was creating questions in the minds of men regarding the application of this potential in new ways, at sea as well as on land. In 1815 the first steamship began to operate between Liverpool and Glasgow. The steamship *Argyle* called at Dublin port in May 1815 on its way to London, where it was renamed *Thames*.[29] Smyth says that the following year the *Hibernian* sailed for Holyhead from Howth on 13 September, after the formation of the Steam Packet Company.[30] Baron Charles Dupin, on a tour of the ports of England, Scotland and Ireland, reported that steamboats went up and down the Clyde from Glasgow to various towns every day, depositing and collecting passengers, some of them travelling as much as 120 miles.[31] In Dublin in 1823 men with an eye on the future inaugurated the City of Dublin Steam Packet Company, which was incorporated by an act of parliament ten years later.[32] The British and Irish Steam Packet Company followed in 1825. At this time steam was new and exciting and offered endless possibilities. From the establishment of the Dublin Steam Packet Company less than twenty years elapsed before the single screw-propeller became a reality in shipping technology (Fig. 5.1).

Thomas Newcomen (see above) appeared in steamship history when in 1783 one of his engines powered a vessel in France built by Claude de Joffroy, showing that the technology was not restricted to Great Britain. According to Greer and Nicholson, the first steam engine in Ireland was installed in a Lisburn spinning mill in 1790.[33] Several other countries also built steam-powered vessels in this and later years. As 1801 dawned, Alex Hart built a boat powered by steam which towed other boats along the Firth and Clyde Canal, and two years later the *Charlotte Dundas* towed two 70-ton barges for 30km along the same canal. Steam technology and its applications were being constantly tested and examined. This applied equally on land and at sea, although it is fair to say that steamship propulsion was slightly ahead in development terms at this juncture. In 1814 Sir Marc Isambard Brunel, father of Isambard Kingdom Brunel, a French royalist who had settled in England, invented machines for sawing timber and others for making blocks for ships' rigging; he persuaded the Admiralty to experiment with steam tugs for the purpose of towing warships and by 1822 they possessed two.[34] The bar at Dublin was dredged with the aid of a steam dredger between 1819 and 1825, and a steam dredger was operating at Drogheda in 1830. The records show that the master of the vessel 'was employed under the continuing threat that he would be sacked on the first report of bad conduct by a commissioner'.[35]

Dunleary Harbour as we know it today was begun in 1816. On its completion in 1842 it was the largest harbour in the world.[36] It was primarily built as a refuge for shipping, the bay having a notoriously dangerous reputation and Howth already positioned as the main packet harbour (Fig. 5.2).

Fig. 5.2—Early rough sketch of Dunleary harbour by Thomas Cooley, 1825 (photo: Brian Matthews, with the kind permission of the NLI).

Two maps of Dublin provide much helpful information, one by Major Alex Taylor in 1801–5 and the second by John Taylor in 1828. The first thing to note is that in the earlier map Dunleary has only got one stub of a pier, confirming all documentation, and there is a continuous sprinkling of houses along the Merrion Road outwards, while a hamlet exists from Blackrock in to Williamstown and up the hill behind Williamstown. By 1828 both piers are portrayed and some additional development has occurred in the above-mentioned areas, as well as further development at Dunleary.

The start-up costs included provision for 200 trucks and wagons, twenty quarry cranes, and a stationary steam engine and another mill. A thousand men worked at the quarries and the harbour site, and up to 300 wagons arrived there each day, mainly from Dalkey but also from the smaller quarry at Glasthule.[37]

The directors of Inland Navigation in control of these matters at first recommended a wall from Dalkey Island to the shore for protection and for use by small vessels only, the harbour being too small for larger, square-rigged vessels. Thomas Hyde Page suggested a pier off Sandycove in deep water, plus a shorter pier between Codling Rock and the shore. The directors rubbished the suggestion, along with the various canals along the shoreline into the city, as being too long and expensive. They also turned down the idea of a pier between Howth and Ireland's Eye and concentrated instead on ways to scour out the Liffey and the bar.

It was the double tragedy of 1807 that focused minds. The *Prince of Wales* and the *Rochdale* both foundered close to shore while carrying military personnel for foreign service and lost over 500 lives between them.[38] A campaign led by Richard Toutcher convinced many of the worthiness of the asylum harbour idea, including the Dublin Chamber of Commerce, sailors, merchants and shipowners in Dublin, Liverpool and Bristol, and of course all those involved in the coal trade. In 1814 Robert Verschoyle, a Dublin merchant, wrote to Robert Peel asking for the new harbour at Dunleary. In 1815 an Act was passed to plan for the same and in 1816 it received permission to go ahead.

Again, as in the case of Howth and its construction, Rennie was chosen as engineer-in-chief and John Aird as site engineer; Richard Toutcher was assistant engineer because he had a lease on the quarry. The first stone was laid in the summer of 1817. George IV left Ireland in 1821 from Dunleary and was seen off by enormous crowds, who came out from Dublin for the occasion. The king had arrived in the steamship *Lightning*. His yacht, the *William and Mary*, requested permission to overwinter in order to encourage the use of the harbour—not just as an asylum harbour—and to showcase the advent of steam.[39]

While a royal visit was seen as a tremendous boost to the country at large, the port authorities never lost sight of the bottom line or of their property, as seen in the letter sent to the yacht *William and Mary* on 23 July 1821:

'Having been informed that you are in possession of an anchor from which his Majesty's ship *Erne* parted about two years ago in Dublin Bay I have to request as senior officer of the port that same may be delivered into my charge for the good of his Majesty's service, L B Phillimore Senior officer at the Port of Dublin'.[40]

Rennie suggested early on that a west pier be erected to halt the drift of sand from Blackrock Strand to Merrion Strand.[41] In 1802 he had said 'that under all circumstances … Dunleary or rather a little to the east of it was the most perfect place for the asylum harbour'.[42] The cost of building the new pier over ten years was £595,193, of which £84,198 19s. was for the funicular railroad from Dalkey.[43]

The other major source of power at the time was the horse, and horsepower was used extensively in all major projects for the movement of large quantities of material, e.g. timber or stone. The 1840 census of Ireland provides one of the few sources of information on the number of horses available for work. In the agricultural statistics it lists the number of horses in the whole country as 576,115, and the total number of mules and asses at 92,365. Images of horses in the late eighteenth and early nineteenth centuries largely consist of paintings of racehorses, but these figures show that there were plenty of workhorses in the country.

The construction of Dunleary Harbour— renamed Kingstown after King George departed from it in 1821[44]—was closely intertwined with the future railway project. The harbour was begun by Rennie in 1816, almost at the same time as Howth was being completed. The voyage time to Howth was more than an hour shorter than to Kingstown, but its harbour was silting up and was very awkward to negotiate at its entrance, a situation that still pertains today.[45] By 1826 Kingstown had superseded Howth as the mail-packet port of choice through the sheer volume of usage.

Henry Inglis arrived in Kingstown in 1830 'on a fine spring morning … I saw waters as elegant in urging the claims of their hotels … and a new race, the drivers of the jaunting cars … No sign of wretched suburbs which stretch in many other directions.'[46] This reveals that the town was already an attractive location away from the ugly sights and smells of Dublin—particularly Ringsend, which had always attracted negative comment from visitors and passengers.

William Bald, surveyor, civil engineer and cartographer, as late as 1837 was still arguing for a sea canal to Dublin, quoting the success of Amsterdam, Glasgow and Rotterdam. Noting the property losses of £400,000 (and 135 lives lost) each year in the Irish Sea and St George's Channel, he asserted that this sum could provide ten asylum harbours larger than the Royal Harbour at Kingstown.[47]

When the Dublin–Kingstown line opened in 1834 only three other railways were operating, all of them in England, which explains the objections to it and the general apprehension regarding this new mode of transport. It fired much public discourse and, as can be imagined, would have been the subject of conversation in most homes in Dublin and beyond.[48]

The Drummond Commission was established in 1836 to study and report back to parliament on the most suitable methods of introducing rail transport to Ireland. The very setting up of the commission indicates that rail development in Ireland was likely to be different from that in England. Drummond recommended that two lines be established, one Dublin–Belfast and the other Dublin–Cork, by separate companies. Though proposed in 1837, they did not materialise till 1852.[49]

The arrival of the railway would have had a much more immediate impact on the citizens than steamships. The ships were slightly away from most citizens, down on the river, and were nowhere near as noisy. If you had no business down in the port there was no need to go there, but it was impossible to avoid or ignore the physical presence of the railway, running along 20ft above street level with screeching brakes, hissing steam, the screaming of metal on metal and the puffing of the locomotive.

While the Kingstown Railway was not a work directly of the Corporation for Preserving and Improving the Port of Dublin, it was indirectly connected with them in that it was enabled by their actions. Its development and success were directly connected with the new harbour, and it in turn fed the success of the harbour and its shipping traffic. Moreover, it was developed on land which had been reclaimed from the sea and had been drying out for 100 years. It was thanks, therefore, to the actions of the Ballast Office Committee (and later the Corporation for Preserving and Improving the Port of Dublin) that the railway found itself in a position to instigate construction. While it was a private enterprise, it came at the end of a series of major civic works around the city, so that there was an abundance of confidence and expertise available. It ran parallel to Sir John Rogerson's Wall along the Liffey; this entire area had been flooded to a depth of several feet in 1792. The railway was constructed along Great Brunswick Street, which by the time of building had the Grand Canal Docks at one end while at the other (western) end was now sited a major music hall or theatre, opened in 1829 just opposite Pearse Street Garda Headquarters and twenty yards from the north wall of Trinity College on the edge of the strand. In the middle of this street was built the Westland Row terminus, next door to the substantial St Andrew's Catholic Church and complex, also finished in 1834. The station at Westland Row, originally planned for Mount Street, involved the building of a very large flat-topped mound or island there, 100 yards wide and approximately 300 yards long, on which to locate the terminus with all its ancillary buildings and services. This construction involved the gathering and reinforcing of an enormous amount of material to make it stable enough to take the weight of the trains, and employed large numbers of men, horses and carts.

The station and the church would help to bring a new suburb into being in the immediate area, linking the growing Grand Canal Docks zone nearby with the higher ground of Merrion Square and Lincoln Place, Holles Street and Mount Street. Development had continued in spite of the serious flooding 35 years earlier. The theatre would become the site of another 100 years later, the Old Queen's, which in turn would be home to the Abbey Theatre until it was rebuilt after the fire of 1951. The use of the area around Westland Row changed, as great numbers of people came in to the terminus to travel. As Ray Egan (2014) pointed out, the area between the belt of streets at the river and port and the more upper-class residential zone of Merrion Square and environs became industrial. This all confirmed the gradual swing to the east and south of the river, as well as significantly locking in place the new Great Brunswick Street (Pearse Street) approach to the new developments down towards Ringsend.

Fig. 5.3—Westland Row Station in 1834, with Cumberland Street and Great Brunswick Street adjacent (courtesy of the NLI).

We must remind ourselves that 100 years previously this had been a track across the 'low ground' which prior to the Liffey wall at Sir John Rogerson's Quay had been flooded twice daily by the tides; it now became a main artery of the city, encouraging housing in due course in all the new little streets running off it, thanks to the bridges built over the roads to carry the tracks. The railway influenced the creation of new villages along its line, new summer homes for the wealthy and permanent new large houses for that same class where they decided to live along its route. It was an important boost to urban and suburban development while at the same time providing an extremely popular social outlet for all who could afford a trip out of Dublin. Niall McCullough (1989) noted the way the construction of the Grand Canal Docks had helped to create a grid of streets in the locality after its completion. The advent of the railway similarly affected the strip along the embankment containing it and, as can be seen from maps, this new area of development was next door to the Grand Canal Docks and its grid of new streets, so defining new boundaries within the area, which all added to further development (Fig. 5.3).

The success of the new Liverpool and Manchester Railway, Murray contended, had an effect on the business class in Dublin, who woke up to an opportunity to connect the new Kingstown harbour with the city by rail rather than the much-touted canal. The idea of a ship canal had been put forward on several occasions in the past. While today the idea of connecting the port of Dublin to Kingstown by canal might seem far-fetched, at the time it was logical, with the entry to Liverpool successfully operating as a good example of what was possible.

On 9 February 1825 Dublin merchants, traders and freeholders submitted a petition to parliament for a tram road near Mount Street, according to the journal of the House of Commons.[50]

A meeting was held at which it was decided to apply to parliament for a charter for a company. At that meeting £78,000 was immediately subscribed. James Pim, a Quaker businessman, had already paid for a survey in 1831 carried out by Alexander Nimmo, the Scottish civil engineer who worked on many projects in Ireland. A second petition followed, and on 6 September 1831 the bill was passed and received royal assent.[51] Over the next couple of years one of the most consistent opponents was the Grand Canal Company, who rightly saw it as a serious competitor and hindered its fund-raising efforts until the idea of the canal was finally done away with.[52]

The *Belfast Magazine and Literary Journal* had this to say in 1825, flying the flag for the development of railways:

'We conclude therefore by calling the attention of all who are interested in promoting the means of internal communication in this country to the formation of the railways; not merely those which would connect Belfast, Dublin and Enniskillen ... Let landlords and tenants consider with what safety and despatch, and at how small expense, the grain, butter, pork, live cattle and other production of the interior could be conveyed to Belfast or other seaports (such as Dublin or Drogheda), while building materials, manure and other articles for the improvement of the country could be had with equal ease in return.'[53]

Construction

With the harbour operating as both a harbour of refuge and a packet harbour, the connection with Dublin and the establishment of roads to the city, the growth of Kingstown as a town in its own right was now well under way. Work began on the railway in 1831, the first sod being turned on 11 April, spearheaded by the innovative engineer William Dargan.[54] Dargan was one of the great engineer builders of the nineteenth century and had been project manager for Thomas Telford on various jobs, but most notably on the final miles into Holyhead on the connecting road from London. When Dargan came back to Ireland in 1823 he won the contract to build the road from Howth to Dublin.[55] Later he would invest in the Royal Marine Hotel in Kingstown and also in the Grand Hotel in Malahide, showing his total confidence in the beneficial effects of the railways on both towns.[56] Dargan was a problem-solver and proved it over and over.

Construction began at several places; the many thousands of tons of granite used came from the Dalkey quarries, while limestone was sourced in Donnybrook. Moving large quantities of material, especially stone, was not a new task for the engineers on the project; the walling of the Liffey, the South Wall and the Grand Canal Docks had all absorbed huge quantities of stone, and both the Liffey and the Great South Wall continued to do so. Dargan was one of the new breed of engineers taking control of major civil engineering projects and contracts whose fortune flourished in this period. He agreed to build the railway and included in his contract price all the stone wall embankments in the city, retaining walls along the seashore, all ditches, bridges and cuttings, and the laying down of the tracks.[57] The railway was funded with subscriptions for capital shares to a total of £200,000, issued in £100 shares—a substantial figure in 1831—and the project received royal assent on 6 September 1831.[58] By its opening in 1834, however, the line had devoured £370,000.

The promoters of the railway had carried out some market research on the traffic along the road from Merrion Strand out to Blackrock, and their findings were presented to a meeting of the proprietors of the railway on 25 November 1831. Between February and October 1831 the following movements were recorded along the road at Blackrock:

- 29,256 private carriages
- 5,999 hackney coaches
- 113,495 private jaunting cars
- 149,754 public cars
- 20,070 gigs
- 40,485 saddle horses

The meeting also expressed the hope that 'Kingstown will become a spot to which all classes will be attracted by the opportunity for the enjoyment of healthy exercise and a pure atmosphere and beautiful romantic surroundings'.[59]

The Board of Commissioners had been set up in 1831, the year construction began, with the purpose of lending money for the building of bridges, roads, harbours and land drainage—in fact, any project that would provide employment in the execution and benefit the public on completion. The secretary of the railway company applied for a loan, and after much negotiation the company was allowed to borrow the sum of £75,000. The Commissioners exacted a price for the loan, however: they insisted that the company accept their nominee, Charles Vignoles, as chief engineer. Vignoles was an engineer with a solid reputation which would prove to be justified on the project. He was a great asset and practically redesigned the line in his attempt to save money. This was of great help, given the strict and tough terms for repayment of the loan and interest.[60]

The railway at this time was new technology and an as yet unproven transport system. The cost per mile was expected to be £62,000, quite an increase over the cost of the Liverpool to Manchester line, which was £50,000. Not all monies invested were private. The Board of Works eventually loaned the project £115,000 and this loan was paid off.[61] A contemporary report on the new line said: "The work of building the Dublin and Kingstown line, which had its cost enhanced very much by the high price demanded for private interests, the requirements necessary to secure perfect safety, and to assure the unaccustomed mind, the number of roads and thoroughfares to be bridged, and the extent of the interference with private demesnes, such as Lord Cloncurry and Sir Harcourt Lees, was carried out in the face of much prejudice, misrepresentation and calumny'. This is in reference to the insistence on a tunnel by these two gentlemen. Also strenuously objecting was Thomas Gresham, founder of the Gresham Hotel in Sackville Street. He had bought Nos 21 and 22 Sackville Street in 1817 and began operating a hotel from there. He owned another hotel and house property in Kingstown; it had been proposed that the company build and operate a hotel nearby, and he did not want any competition.[62] The press, too, were against the proposal.[63] Mr P. Hicks, visiting Dublin in 1818, 'called at Mr Harcourt Lees to see his place which is on the bay. It is built on a rock overhanging the sea. After we went to see the new pier at Dunleary this it is said will be a very good harbour.'[64] It is therefore possible to allow that Harcourt Lees might have had a valid reason for imposing supposed extra work and expense on the rail construction.

There was a bonus for the contractor, who in his excavations came upon a separate source of granite, which was very handy for stonework in the piers and bridges.[65] The first plan had been to begin the railway terminus at Thomas Clarendon's riding school at 200 Great Brunswick Street. This proved to be too close to Trinity College, so the site then chosen was the present one.[66]

The new Catholic St Andrew's Church at Westland Row, next door to the terminus for the new railway, was opened in 1834, having cost £13,000. This was an interesting choice of location for a Catholic church, and such a large one at that, as the area was still relatively sparsely populated.

Fig. 5.4—DART crossing road bridge towards Westland Row Station (photo: Brian Matthews).

It seems as if it was a case of the Catholic Church making a political statement, filling the space of Dublin with churches in competition with the building of Protestant churches, sometimes before there were enough parishioners to fill them.

The construction of the embankment consisted of two enormous retaining walls, pinned and infilled with material to a height of 20ft above ground level, on which the trains would travel. The retaining walls were 6ft thick at the base, tapering to 2ft 9in. at the top. The fill consisted of earth, stones, gravel, sand and waste. Of course, the sheer mass of material when compacted led to several episodes where the retaining walls burst, and from then on tie-irons and cross-stays were inserted (Fig. 5.5). This problem was also alleviated as the ground underneath dried out and stabilised. The project would include several bridges close to the city and port, crossing the Grand Canal, the Dodder River and various streets and roads (Fig. 5.4). Much of the material used in the filling of the embankment came from lakes out at Simmonscourt Fields which have since disappeared. The embankment would completely alter the landscape of the area. The terminus was also built 20ft above ground. Iron, being the new material of choice, became a major component in the building of the terminus. It was Stephenson who suggested that a succession of arches could be beneficial for use as stores or dwelling houses. The original plan called for six sets of rails, the two outer lines to be used for wagons to transfer goods and for the operation of cranes. From Barrow Street the line has two tracks.[67]

Between 1834 and 1841 a total of 660 miles of railway were constructed in England and Ireland. This involved the movement of a total of 70 million cubic metres of material, much of it moved from cuttings to embankments. John Skempton said that construction on this scale had no precedent.[68] The technical information was flowing back and forth across the Irish Sea, as the railway under construction in Dublin had the added novelty of being built on land reclaimed from the sea. Skempton wrote that locomotives and stationary engines were used on some earthworks operations, and there would also have been several small steam engines to pump out the excavations.[69] He further notes that some 4,030 men and 460 horses, along with two locomotives, were employed on the Midland Counties Line in 1838. On the same line the following year 5,140 men, 510 horses and

Fig. 5.5—Embankment retaining walls with tie-bars (photo: Brian Matthews).

one locomotive were involved. According to Skempton's research, embankments were usually formed from the material taken from nearby cuttings, the excavated material being carried in horse-drawn wagons that ran on rails from up to two miles away from the front end of the works.[70]

These embankments were built up in two ways. One method was to build in layers up to 4ft deep, compacting each in turn; the other was to build all in one go and allow the weight of the material to do the compacting. Whichever method was employed, the earth wagons went to the end of the works and tipped their load out. These wagons were like early dump trucks except on rails.[71] Each wagon could carry 1.25 cubic yards, and a typical workforce or gang consisted of 40–80 men and from six to twelve horses. Two shifts were operated in summer, using the longer daylight hours; while occasionally in winter there might be two shifts, one shift was the norm. This, Skempton said, was the way Stephenson operated on the Stockton to Darlington line in 1822.[72] Stephenson was the first to use the method of building embankments in one layer to the full required height. He used this technique on the Liverpool to Manchester line in 1827, along with the tipping wagons, 100 of which he had ordered to be built for the purpose.[73] Skempton offers some detailed information on the quantities of material shifted: on a section of the London to Birmingham line only 1.4 miles long, the embankment—30ft wide on top and 45ft high—consumed just one million cubic yards. This figure allows a comparison to be made with the Dublin to Kingstown line in terms of the length of its embankment out to Lansdowne Road, which covers a similar distance although lower in height. So half the figure may suffice for Dublin. On the other hand, a whole island measuring almost 300m by 200m had to be erected, and therefore the figure of one million cubic yards may not be far off the mark.

The *Dublin Penny Journal* of 30 August 1834 records: 'To preserve the ordinary traffic of the public thoroughfares, the railway starts at an elevation of about twenty feet from the surface, and spans in succession over each street by flat elliptical arches. For the more important streets, smaller arches for the footways have been made on each side of the principal openings. The intervals between the streets consist of high retaining walls of limestone, obtained from the Donnybrook Quarries. The space between the walls has been filled with sand, gravel, dry rubbish and similar materials: the cartage gave employment during the whole of autumn, winter and spring, to hundreds of the proprietors of carts and cars.'[74]

The width between the walls from Westland Row to Barrow Street is nearly 60ft, calculated to receive four lines of rails: two for the railway itself and the outer ones on either side to be used for coal, granite, timber and general merchandise wagons which would operate separately from the passenger traffic.

As already mentioned, the retaining walls burst on a number of occasions, owing either to lack of compaction or to water seepage. Slippage was a problem for most railways during construction. Skempton records at least seven major slippage incidents both during and—more importantly— after construction. They tended to occur on higher embankments and deep cuttings.[75] On the Swindon embankment, after the second episode of slippage or mini-landslide, Brunel, who would later work on the railway tunnels at Bray Head, had a row of timber baulks driven down 8ft into the ground below the level of the toe of the slope. This did not work, so he then had a series of pits, 6ft square, dug at intervals of 24ft to a depth of 2ft below the surface and filled with rubble. Slippage was a major problem for the various railway projects, generally arising from clay filling and poor compaction, but each problem was solved sooner or later. Of course, water and clay always made a potentially dangerous cocktail.[76]

Skempton wrote that the rail lines are carried 'across the quays and a part of the Grand Canal Docks by a granite bridge of three oblique arches ... one arch is intended for a future street ... to pass parallel to the docks, one for the business of the quays ... the third is to pass the boats of the trade and is provided with a towing path'. Some engineering difficulties were overcome at Barrow Street Bridge. Here the width between the parapets contracts to 30ft feet, as from that point only two lines are in operation. As the lines leave the city, the height of the embankment decreases until it ends at Haig's distillery (Lansdowne Road). As Dixon wrote at the time of construction, 'The railroad here approaches the surface of the country', adding that a little further out are located buildings being erected for the repair and construction of the locomotive engines, coaches and wagons, 'and other necessary shops and conveniences for the company'.[77] The locomotives came at first from George Forrester and Co. of Liverpool and from Messrs Sharp, Roberts and Co. of Manchester. The carriages for the passengers were in three classes. 'Most of these have been made in Dublin by Mr Dawson of Capel St., and by Messrs Courtney and Stephens of Blackhall Place.'[78]

New industry would emerge in supplying both personnel for maintenance and equipment such as coaches, rails, sleepers and locomotives. New types of employment arose across a series of tasks and skills. The company workshops would come to rest in Grand Canal Street, occupying the old Kinahan's distillery there. By 1840 the works for repair and servicing of locomotives and carriages had moved from Serpentine Avenue to Grand Canal Street.[79]

Thus, not long after the Grand Canal had opened out onto the Liffey and the sea, the area was also hosting a completely new form of transport. The canal companies had had no choice but to oppose the growth of the railway, as its speeds were always faster than could ever be achieved on canals.

DUBLIN MOVING EAST, 1708–1844

The locomotives and rolling stock from England were not always a success. In 1834 the Horsley Iron Company in Yorkshire supplied a disaster of an engine that had to be junked.[80] By 1841, only one year after the company moved its engineering works to Grand Canal Docks, the very first Irish-built locomotive was manufactured there, making this the first railway in the world to build its own engines.[81]

On 4 October 1834 a train drawn by the locomotive *Vauxhall* and comprising just a few carriages carrying dignitaries made a number of short runs along the line. Five days later, eight carriages drawn by the locomotive *Hibernia* made the trip from Westland Row to Salthill in just fifteen and a half minutes.

A traffic survey on the Kingstown Road on 12 and 13 February, just before the train came into service, showed that 36,287 carriages, 7,272 hackney coaches, 133,537 private cars, 24,175 gigs, 46,164 saddle horses and 69,133 carts used the route in both directions.[82] Murray wrote that the committee stationed clerks at Blackrock to ascertain the traffic that might be expected (see above). The resulting figures are interesting not just in terms of information for the committee at the time but also for the reader today. It gives some idea of the number and range of horses in use at a time when horses and various vehicles are never mentioned in many of the reports on aspects of public activity.[83] It must be remembered, too, that every single mention of horses involved an accompanying human being, so the figures also give an indication of human traffic (Fig. 5.6).

The other interesting thing about these figures is that they show how much road traffic the harbour was creating between Kingstown and Dublin. They also confirm the growing number of dwellings out along this coast road. These houses, being the properties of the wealthier citizens, employed large numbers of domestic servants and outdoor staff in gardens and stables, and therefore

Fig. 5.6—*Competing coachmen* by Robert Richard Scanlan (fl. 1826–76) (courtesy of the Gorry Gallery).

110

a substantial number of servants and estate workers must have been housed elsewhere in the area.

At first granite blocks were used as sleepers but soon proved too brittle, causing damage to rolling stock and rails. Timber quickly replaced the granite, which was then used to shore up the sea wall further out. Gaslight was planned along the line but initially proved too expensive; financial circumstances finally allowed it to be installed in April 1835.[84] The coaches were of four class types: first class was closed, there was an open and a closed second class, and third class was open. 'Open' meant partially exposed to the elements.[85] These coaches were replaced with improved facilities within ten years.[86] Vignoles is reported as saying in 1833 that 'one of the peculiar advantages of the Rail Road is that females may travel in the carriages as securely and as privately as in their own cars'. This promotion of female safety as a benefit of rail travel was a successful marketing ploy.[87] Another positive impact of the railway during the construction phase was the money spent locally by the many men working on the project, as well as those bringing in material and moving stone along the line. The presence of all these men helped to reduce potential crime.[88]

A train departing Westland Row and other views were reproduced in the *Dublin Penny Journal* of 21 June 1834. Its front page carried an engraved picture of the embankment under construction for the Kingstown Rail, showing a bridge over a street near the docks close to the drawbridge at Ringsend.[89] The Wide Streets Commission paid close attention to the construction, insisting on a minimum span of 30ft for the bridges and the inclusion of side arches for pedestrians—this at a time of small foot traffic in the area.[90] Some bridges are of the skew pattern, meaning that they are at an angle to the rail rather than at 90 degrees.[91] The *Dublin Penny Journal* article said that speeds of travel of 3–4mph by canal were the norm, while railways delivered 10–15mph; in addition, unlike the canals, rail travel was not subject to frost or drought, and railways were much cheaper to build than canals. The article noted that a locomotive of 8hp could pull between 30 and 50 tons at 12mph.[92] Allowances must be made for the over-enthusiasm but such was the style of journalism at the time. 'Let the country be intersected with railways passing through the most important districts and terminating in the principal seaports and from leading lines, let branches be extended to neighbouring towns of mines and other places of importance; and a new impulse will be communicated to the energies of the nation. At proper stations stores and warehouses may be erected and markets may be established for the purchase of the articles produced in the neighbourhood and the sale of others in return. Now the promoting of internal communication would materially facilitate the establishment of manufacturers of almost every kind.' Indeed, it reads like a company prospectus, yet the writer accurately portrayed the future development opportunities. The article concluded: 'The commercial history of Great Britain amply demonstrates that its present pre-eminence is mainly attributable to the facilities which the steam engine has afforded to our manufactures, that by reducing the cost of production, the population at large have become consumers'.[93]

The *Daily Journal* during 1834 published two woodcuts supposed to have been made for the opening of the line. One is of the rail embankment crossing over a road, with ships' masts in the background. More interesting, however, is the first known painting of the train moving, about 1840, which also shows some large houses (Fig. 5.7).

From its first day of service to 1 March 1836 the line carried 1,237,800 passengers. By January 1835 the company had drawn up timetables, such was the popularity of the service.

The railway had a large impact socially on the population of Dublin, as seen, for example, in the case of the Kingstown Races. On Monday 6 April 1835 the trains left Westland Row 'packed to

Fig. 5.7—Train *en route* to the city in an early painting by J. Saul, 1840 (courtesy of the Gorry Gallery).

suffocation and, in spite of the efforts of the police, with the roofs covered by those who, determined to go, would not be dislodged from their dangerous position'. Some 18,585 passengers paid a total of £532 16s. 8d. The railway had a huge effect on the Kingstown Regatta, too. It must be remembered that in those days people actually watched yachts racing from the shore. Up to 1912 the public in their hundreds paid sixpence each to access the pier at Skerries to see the boats racing on a Sunday in July.

One of the main impacts of the railway was on the spread of suburbs, as people were enabled to live at a distance from their place of work. Shortly after it opened, great building activity began in Blackrock, Kingstown, Dalkey and Killiney, as well as Williamstown (Fig. 5.8). At this time the occupation of Sandymount began in earnest, as the railway acted both as a transport system and a barrier to the sea. Development along the road to Dublin from Kingstown can be seen by comparing William Duncan's 1821 map of Dublin with the Ordnance Survey map of 30 years later. The railway also had the effect of making changes to the working man's conditions of employment. Because the workers in these new developments were from Dublin and couldn't afford train fares, the company arranged for special fares and these workmen's tickets became a substantial part of the company receipts. Traders and hawkers were given preferential treatment to travel to and from the city to get goods for sale.[94] The arrival of the railway had been opposed by the jarvies, who feared for their livelihood, but in fact it proved a boon to their business, adding additional trade to and from stations.

The development of rail travel meant that postal services improved nationally, beginning with shortening the time it took for news to reach Dublin from London. It also facilitated emigration

The Dublin to Kingstown Railway, including the building of Dunleary Harbour

and migration. The improvement in communications with London began a change in both the military and political management of Ireland.

As the railway industry grew and expanded, so too did the requirement for expertise in surveying and the building of railways across all sorts of topography, from rivers and canals to roads and bogs, and the building up of embankments in various circumstances. In Ireland this was the start of civil engineering as a separate science. The new technology employed and experience gained in the construction and operation of the Dublin to Kingstown line were to prove invaluable, particularly as the Dublin to Drogheda Railway, opened ten years later, also involved the erection of embankments and bridges across rivers, canals and roads.

The railway was a success: it paid its debts and it paid out a first dividend of 5%. Later dividends were higher, making for an average of 9%—a healthy return on railway stock at the time.[95] The Kingstown line demonstrated the range of possibilities for railways and increased public confidence in rail transport. The railway created a new momentum for the pace of development in and around the city and along the shore towards Kingstown. Both Kingstown Harbour and the mail-packet helped grow the success of the railway line, which in turn boosted the usage of the harbour and the growth of the town itself. It helped to create the beginnings of a new commuter class living away from their employment, while allowing new opportunities to arise for social outlets. New dwellings outside the old perimeter of Dublin in turn encouraged further development and expansion in the supply, servicing and maintenance of the large houses. Much of the physical evidence of Victorian building is still to be seen all along the roads into the city from the southern seaside suburbs of Dalkey, Dún Laoghaire and Blackrock today.

The railway was not developed in isolation. Francis Cullen writes that 'In the year 1834 the port authorities had for twenty years been busily engaged in adapting their facilities to suit the needs of the newer and larger steamships' and that a succession of London engineers were kept busy

Fig. 5.8—Williamstown and Booterstown, showing reclamation of shore (courtesy of the NLI).

adapting the berthing space for the increasing number of vessels. As steam packets made up the bulk of the traffic into and out of the port in the 1830s, changes needed to be made.[96] So the original space down along Sir John Rogerson's Quay was being changed and adapted well into the nineteenth century, only 400m away from the new railway line.

One very visible effect of the new railway was the ability to move large numbers of people to and from Kingstown. The Kingstown Races were the first to be held in Ireland where the punters arrived by train, only a matter of months after the opening (see above). In May 1835, 'once again the Rock Road was jammed with early traffic as crowds headed out from town. In addition the railway company, which ran trains every fifteen minutes, with eleven coaches to the engine, brought 8,000 passengers to the station one mile below the course.'[97] It was a matter of some relief that the meeting passed off 'peacefully and with perfect good humour'. This comment is interesting because with such numbers attending the organisers could have reasonably expected some trouble. One of the stewards was Edward Hayes, a Kingstown hotelier, illustrating the fast-growing seaside and travel aspect of the new harbour and town.[98] In 1837 crowds came at the rate of 1,500 per hour, from 11am till 3pm. The following year, 1838, it was recorded that 'Good order was kept by a party of the new Dublin Metropolitan Police'.[99]

The military and security opportunities could not be ignored either. The ability to move large numbers of troops from one place to another by rail even faster than had been possible by canal, which itself had been an improvement over road transport, would have greater impact over the following ten to fifteen years, with the building of the other termini at Broadstone and Kingsbridge binding the country closer.

The Kingstown Railway left a physical imprint on the space which had earlier been reclaimed from the tidal inundations in the form of the embankment and the rail/road bridges as part of the embankment. It involved the building of nine bridges over roads, one over the Grand Canal Dock and another over the Dodder. Some bridges were skew bridges (meaning at an angle rather than at right angles to roads), such as at Grand Canal Dock and Grand Canal Quay.[100] Not long after the railway was completed, a new stone bridge was built across the Dodder at Londonbridge Road, south of the one at Ringsend. This bridge facilitated the building of a more permanent road to Beggar's Bush and the final fastening of the Ringsend spit to Dublin, allowing for the easy movement of troops between the fort on the South Wall and the new barracks built in 1824. Furthermore, it allowed for further reclamation and occupation in Sandymount and up towards Ballsbridge.

The iron foundries expanded to cater for the needs of the water mains installation, the laying of gas mains pipes below ground level and the infrastructure that followed on from the railway—coachworks and the repair, maintenance and manufacturing of locomotives. New jobs were created for ticket-sellers and clerks, personnel managers, boilermakers, drivers and labourers on the actual line and in the construction of stations along the line. A little further upriver on the Dodder another bridge was built at today's Aviva Stadium, assisting the city to spread its tentacles outwards. New engineering was being brought into being, too; for example, Peter Barlow in 1817 wrote of experiments carried out by the Royal Navy, testing iron bolts, bars, wires and cables, while Telford was creating new types of lathes to be used in the building of suspension bridges, including the Halfpenny Bridge over the Liffey, the first iron bridge in Dublin (1816). All this experimentation would lead to changes in how new technology was later applied on a large scale at Westland Row terminus. Barlow himself was also experimenting on railway bars in 1817.[101]

Just prior to the Act of Union, as the Grand Canal Docks were begun, the largest building

Fig. 5.9—Map showing some of the many proposed canals from Kingstown to the port at Dublin (photo: Brian Matthews).

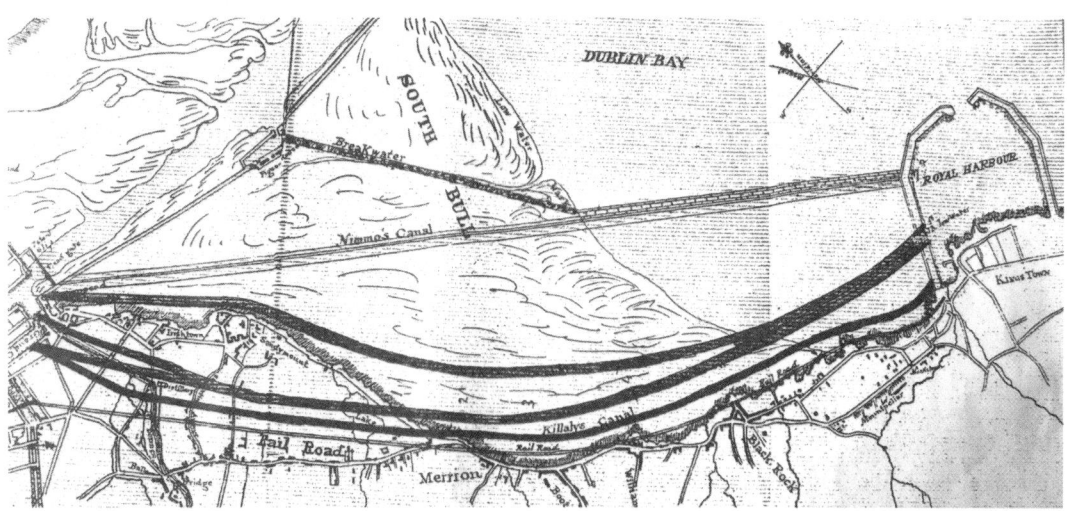

constructed in the area in recent years was opened, on Townsend Street/Lazy Hill on the edge of what had earlier been the strand. Known as the Westmorland Lock Hospital, it was similar in scale to the Marine School, built just a few years earlier, and was dedicated to the treatment of venereal disease. The hospital had 300 places, all for women, and was segregated between Catholics and Protestants. Most of the patients were prostitutes and its location was no accident, being at the port and not too far from Beggar's Bush Barracks and the troops based in the city around the Castle (and of course well away from the more genteel areas being developed further inland, such as Merrion Square). Years before, James Caulfield on his travels had described Malta as 'one vast brothel', reminding us of the perennial association of men, women, ports and army barracks.[102]

The subject of the railway has to be seen also in the context of its impact on the harbour at Kingstown. The harbour was developed in tandem with the railway and each fed and fostered the other. The harbour now became the packet port and, together with the railway, created a strong incentive for development all along the strip of coastline into Dublin. Sir John Rennie wrote in his autobiography: 'The harbours which I made are described in my book on British and Foreign Harbours, they were a portion of Kingstown in Dublin bay'.[103] That the harbour was a focus of much attention can be seen from the several suggested canal connections between it and Dublin (Fig. 5.9). It quickly became a destination for those Dubliners who could afford to take the train out to Kingstown for a day of leisure away from the city. John Barrow wrote of 'the rapidly improving town of Kingstown, the length of the road is five and a half miles, which is usually run in under fifteen minutes. The fare is sixpence to one shilling first class and the number of passengers from Dec 1834 to this time is exceeded half a million.'[104]

Ann Plumtre, staying in Dublin in 1814/15, reported that 'to the south are the villages of Blackrock, Dunleary, Dalkey and Monkstown'. These villages were affected by the trade coming in to Bullock Harbour and by the improvements firstly to Dunleary Harbour and then the complete construction of the new one. They were also affected by the continuous growth in traffic in and out of the city on the two main roads as the harbour and the railway were built.[105]

Another issue was that by 1824 the Grand Canal was supplying water to a wide variety of consumers. The governors of Sir Patrick Dun's Hospital were granted a supply of water direct from the canal that year, helping to firmly establish urban occupation on the edge of the old tidal grounds just before the advent of the railway.[106] In the same year the Corporation reported that six miles of metal pipes for water had been laid within the previous twelve months.[107] An appreciation of the cost and value of piped water can be gleaned from the entry in the corporation records issuing directions to Mr Richard Quintan 'to use every exertion to ascertain what water closets are supplied by piped water and not in charge of the water collector having reason to believe there are numbers so circumstanced'.[108]

John Barrow wrote in 1835 that he 'took up quarters at the Royal Hotel' (Kingstown), describing it as 'a very splendid establishment filled at this time with summer residents from Dublin'.[109] Thomas Cromwell, arriving by ship, described the south shore as 'a rich cultivated bank covered with villages and cottages extending to Dalkey … Dunleary and Blackrock surrounded by villas, woods and pastures'.[110] He also noted that Sandymount had by now become a 'principal place for bathers for the city'.[111] D.L. Cooney recorded that, as people moved out of the city in all directions, Sandymount in particular benefited from the quiet exodus. The area once known as 'brickfield town', which housed the brick-makers and their families as they supplied the building bricks for Dublin's expansion, became swamped by more genteel-minded immigrants to the area, who quickly got the name changed to the more respectable Sandymount.[112]

Just before the arrival of the railway, the archbishop of Dublin, Richard Whately, moved his residence from the city to Kilmacud. His daughter Jane recorded that the distance from Dublin enabled him to be at the palace for transacting business between breakfast and dinner and that he always returned home with a holiday feeling.[113] Even earlier, by 1823 the idea of the attractiveness of Dunleary as a place to live away from the city appeared to have taken hold, as land facing the promenade was laid out in plots, giving impetus to the idea of suburbia allied to the harbour and railway later.[114] O'Grada wrote that both Clontarf and Blackrock competed for visitors throughout the 1780s and their roads were improved on that account. Blackrock had already come within the orbit of everyday city travel in the 1770s thanks to Lord Kildare's decision to reside there, showing how easy it was to access the city providing you had horses. The Ringsend to Blackrock shore road was opened in 1788 and by 1791 the new coach system carried ten passengers at a time.[115]

Jonathan Binns, who arrived at Kingstown and stayed at the Gresham Hotel in Sackville Street, observed that Dublin was a 'city of lamentable contrasts', referring to the extremes of social status.[116] He noted that the rents in Sackville Street of shops with houses attached 'varies from £200 per year; some being from £300 to £1,000'.[117] As regards commerce, Binns remarked that 'the decrease in trade may be principally attributed to the general change which took place upon the establishment of a steam communication between the Irish capital and this country … prior to this imports came in great quantity, now however the generality of the country shopkeepers go to England at a trifling of the expense, and purchase for themselves.'[118] The result of all this activity was that by 1845 the population of Kingstown was given as 7,229, making it a sizeable town. Nearby Blackrock contained 2,372 inhabitants.[119] A visitor to Kingstown in 1837, just three years after the advent of the railway, wrote that 'the road to Dunleary to Blackrock is a pleasant road laid out with well built mansions, gardens tastefully laid out. This confirms the Fitzwilliam Estate strategy of parcelling out sites and plots for development thereby encouraging suburban growth'.[120] An Edward McFarland painting of 1853 shows the beginnings of development around Monkstown.

William Marrot, another visitor to Ireland in 1841, wrote that he 'arrived at the Kingstown pier on board the government steamship *Sprightly,* where we had to remain till six o'clock in the morning when the first train starts for Dublin'. Describing 'Kingstown, where all the mail packets from Liverpool and Holyhead sail from', he remarked that 'the harbour is large and spacious and the pier, which adds greatly to the attraction of the town, is 2,000 feet long and the quay fifty feet wide; there is also a church and RC chapel, some great inns and many fine houses and beautiful villas'. Marrot further noted that the 'railroad to Dublin which had lately been opened is the cause of this being now quite fashionable watering place, and of a Sunday in particular Dublin people make a great promenade of the quay and pier'. Two days later he returned to Kingstown on the train and enjoyed a band playing music on the pier for an hour, during which time he saw the arrival and departure of two packets. In Dublin he visited the Zoo and on same day saw the Oyster Parade, noting that most oysters came from Howth; he also went to the Theatre Royal in Hawkins Street, crossing the Carlisle Bridge on foot and recording its size as 210ft long and 40ft wide.[121]

Henry Inglis recorded in 1830 that 'the facilities of steam navigation are now so great that the country dealers throughout Ireland, who formerly made their purchases in Dublin, now pass over to England and there lay in their stocks'.[122] This is a clear indication of one change in commercial practice encouraged by the new harbour and its proximity to the city.

On the water new opportunities were exploited. Friedrich Raumer, a German visitor to London and Dublin in 1835, reported that 'while running up the Thames from the tunnel to London bridge, our boatman told us that, on Easter Sunday, a steamer had taken 2375 people from London to Greenwich, where the sum of fifty L was taken from 12,000 persons all to see the new railway'.[123] Raumer also visited Lambeth and saw the steam printing presses by which '*The Penny Magazine* among many others is printed. Twenty presses moved by steam, worked with such unwearied rapidity that a thousand sheets were printed in an hour.'[124] The consumption of coal to feed the furnaces naturally went up correspondingly. Raumer quoted coal imports in 1800 of 364,000 tons and by 1830, before the full explosion of steamships and railways, of 940,000 tons.[125]

In 1833, the year before the first railway in Ireland, William Laird built the first iron paddle-steamer, the *Lady Lansdowne*, for the City of Dublin Packet Company, and this ship would operate as a pleasure-craft on the River Shannon at Lough Derg for the next 34 years.[126]

South of the Liffey, 1834–44

The appliance of steam as a power source became more widespread, changing methods in farming and more especially in industry. During this ten-year period after the advent of the Kingstown Railway, occupation and construction continued in the area, including further mills and warehousing at Grand Canal Dock and immediately behind the first streets parallel to the Liffey, as well as housing of various grades in the zone between the river and Denzille Street (Fenian Street), as this street connected directly with Sir Patrick Dun's Hospital, Boland's Mills (Treasury Building) and Beggar's Bush Barracks. Technological improvements in dredging, shipping and railways continued and were seen in the greater speeds of ships and trains, as well as in the power of dredgers and cranes. In short, there was a technological avalanche which continued to gather momentum during the nineteenth century. As iron began to be used to build ships and, later, masts and rigging, there was an even greater demand for the metal and a consequent increase in the consumption of coal—all affording opportunities in employment, albeit mainly unskilled labour. By the time that the Dublin to Drogheda Railway was completed ten years later, there had been considerable development in railway technology as regards surveying and engineering. Bridges would now contain an element of iron in their construction, as would the building of both termini. Another tangible result of the railway's integration into the city and suburban infrastructure can be seen in the building of suburban railway

DUBLIN MOVING EAST, 1708–1844

Fig. 5.10—The Lock Hospital, Townsend Street, for the treatment of venereal diseases (courtesy of Louise Morgan and Brendan Maher, NGI).

Fig. 5.11—Hibernian Bank 1824 badge in Dame Street (photo: Brian Matthews).

stations at both Blackrock and Seapoint in 1841.[127] In the middle of all this new technology thrived one old enemy—the Lock Hospital in Townsend Street for the treatment of venereal disease, standing not far from the commercial (banking and insurance) aspect of the city (Figs 5.10 and 5.11).

Probably the best way to appreciate just how immense were the changes that had been imposed since 1708 on former tidal lands is to look at what now occupied the old track (now Great Brunswick Street). Where the tide used to come in twice a day, a main artery of the city now ran all the way east from College Green, across the bridge at Grand Canal Docks, over the stone Ringsend Bridge towards Irishtown and on out to Merrion. The city was now joined to the spit, and reclamation and building continued alongside industry and housing throughout its length.

Industries undreamt of at the outset were now part of the area between the docks and the rail embankment, such as canals, docks, engineering works for railways and shipyards. Coal was the single most important cargo coming into Dublin and was now more vital than ever, both for steamships and for locomotives. The boundary of the city had been moved eastward by 1.5km, from College Green to the coast of the old Ringsend spit. John Trotter, looking down from Rathfarnham, wrote

118

Fig. 5.12—Beggar's Bush Barracks, 1835 (photo: Brian Matthews).

that it was a 'thickly inhabited coast near Dublin'.[128]

Along this thoroughfare there existed not only the ancillary businesses connected to the port (coal supply, shipping and chandlery) but also the new services associated with the railway and its allied activities, along with the full range of occupations in the various dwellings and retail and service outlets, including theatres and music halls.

If we look at Great Brunswick Street as an example of development in the area, the Pettigrew and Oulton Almanack and Directory of 1844 is very informative. This street now housed twenty persons in the legal profession, either barristers or solicitors. There were six persons carrying on the coal trade, factoring or wholesaling. At least four were occupied in dealing with all aspects of the horse trade (stabling, saddlery, harness-making and coach-building). We can trace the developing technology in the fact that at No. 42 was Joseph O'Reilly, plumber, force pump, bath and water-closet manufacturer.[129] Richard Leavy at No. 70 was director of music at the Theatre Royal, Hawkins Street. Pearse Square began to be developed in 1839 with the first few houses adjacent to Great Brunswick Street. It is no surprise that so many establishments connnected with horses are mentioned in the almanac; this was, after all, the primary manner of getting around beyond a walking distance for most, and it reflects the great numbers of horses required for various purposes around the city.

The completion of the Beggar's Bush Barracks (Fig. 5.12) also added to the human occupation of the area just above the Londonbridge Road Bridge, which shortly became a proper stone bridge to match the stone structure lower down the Tolka, stitching the Ringsend spit to the land.

All was not calm and peaceful, however; trade unionism was desperately trying to gain a foothold among the employed, and jobs and openings were very jealously guarded. Sawyer Thomas Hanlon was beaten to death in broad daylight by a crowd attending a funeral in Thomas Street in 1829. He and his work partner had been under threat because they would not join the sawyers' union. (Sawyers were men who sawed logs and large baulks of timber into planks, usually in a saw-pit, with one working the large saw from below and the other from above at ground level.) The two men were working for a building contractor (William Fagan of Bridgefoot Street) for a much lower rate of pay than the union demanded. The sawyers' union was especially militant, and the problem had arisen over the previous ten years. In 1820 another contractor, Edward Carolan, was approached by a deputation of workers and shot one of them dead. Seven years later an attempt was made to kill him in an acid attack. Industrial relations were often tense, as in the case of Morton of Ringsend, a notorious employer of child labour. During one dispute one of his apprentices was shot dead outside his works in 1825.[130] Four men were hanged at Green Street jail as a consequence, two that same year and two in 1840.[131]

By the 1830s the area of the Ringsend spit had been transformed from an isolated narrow finger of ground into an area of made ground absorbed by the city, comprising some 50–60 acres. Nevertheless, just as their antecedents had struggled to survive hundreds of years previously, so too did the modern inhabitants. A writer who witnessed events on Merrion Strand between Irishtown and the Martello tower watched as members of the 59th Regiment carried out target practice on the shore at low water. Behind the targets, placed some 150 yards away, numerous boys aged from eleven to fourteen collected the spent bullets—for sale, he was assured by other observers. One of the boys, about eleven years old, was wounded; the attending military surgeon dug the bullet out and the writer then accompanied the boy to his home in Ringsend. Just like gathering cockles, gathering bullets was a local occupation for earning money.[132]

In 1808 the Bank of Ireland, which had opened in 1783 at St Mary's Abbey, moved across the Liffey to open at No. 2 College Green, just at the end of Great Brunswick Street, and by 1845 across the street at No. 34 Dame Street, such was the increase in business being done by banks. That it could contemplate occupying such a large edifice showed the growth and strength of the city's economy and its need for banking facilities. Branch banks were equally required nationwide, as seen in the expansion of branches: 22 opened in twenty counties in the same period.[133]

There had always been a boat- and shipbuilding aspect to this area of the port; pictorial evidence appears before 1800 in the Barralet sketch, showing ships under construction through the remains of the first stone bridge at Ringsend, and in Malton's westward view, showing a large vessel under construction on Sir John Rogerson's Quay. As the city and port expanded, so too did boat and ship construction. Yards were run under the names King, Teall, Morton, Clements, Marshall, Good and Hills, among others. By 1820 in this corner of Dublin there were almost 100 sawyers employed in sawing baulks of timber into planks. Some yards operated on the bank of the Dodder, while others used the Grand Canal Docks.

In 1779 the privateer *Fame* was launched for owners Samuel Dick and Edward Forbes, according to the *Freeman's Journal*, which reported that the event was attended by great crowds. *Fame* subsequently operated mainly in the Mediterranean. After 1800 lifeboats were built in the area by Clements, and were stationed at Clontarf, Sandycove, Sutton, Howth and Pigeon House Harbour. Others were later stationed at Dunleary and still later moved to the new Kingstown Harbour. Clements not only built vessels but also owned several over time, such as the *Annesley* and the *Kate* in 1825. He sued for the loss of an express cutter on the packet run in 1818, when Revd Charles Beresford came aboard with a letter from the GPO containing instructions for Clements to convey him to Holyhead. Beresford insisted on continuing on to Caernarvon, where the vessel was wrecked on a sand bar at the entrance.

While boats were being salvaged, repaired and built, the workmen were attempting to unionise in direct confrontation with the law. At the same time, after the arrival of the Devon trawlers, the Dublin Fishery Company was set up, thanks to increased fishing catches and varieties. By 1829 the

Corporation was trying to levy tolls on people using the fish market and the fishermen were battling against these charges. Interestingly, those opposed included fishermen from Howth, Skerries, Balbriggan, Malahide and Rush as well as Ringsend. One of Clements's trawlers, the *Volunteer*, saved a ship eighteen miles out to sea off Howth, towing her into Dublin under sail. Captain and crew were awarded £50 for their service, a substantial sum at the time; all lives were saved, and the full cargo of coal too.

Robert Morton ran his boatyard from near the drawbridge on Great Brunswick Street between the two basins. In August 1825 the launch of a new schooner, a packet of 130 tons under Captain Cawley, was announced. Sadly, another death occurred during the building as a result of union unrest. The papers reported that an apprentice by the name of Marchant was bludgeoned to death beside the gas factory. Workmen from the gas factory attempted to intervene to no avail; despite being brought to Sir Patrick Dun's Hospital the unfortunate Marchant died. Morton, the press added, was to build the first ever steam packet for the Dublin–Wexford trade, with her engines built in Ireland for the Rogers Bros. At one time Morton had three contracts to build a Bordeaux packet, a steam packet and a canal boat, while having two boats in the dry dock at Grand Canal Docks.[134]

After Morton came Henry Teall, who called his yard the Brunswick Boatyard.[135] Its exact location was recently confirmed as being Barrow Street and Ringsend Road, and it opened onto the Inner Basin of the canal.[136] Teall announced in 1841 that a new trade vessel built with iron ribs was launched for the City of Dublin Steamship Co., and also a new smack of 50 tons.[137] He eventually moved down to the point on the shore at Ringsend with a slip in 1843. Like all boat-builders, he had difficulties with the 'combinations' or unions, and was the victim of direct sabotage when his vessel *Bessey* had a hole bored in her side below the water-line on the North Wall and consequently sank.[138] Just like Morton earlier, Teall carried loaded pistols about as a precaution, though even a precaution could turn out wrong. Teall was involved in an altercation at a brothel in French Street (now Upper Mercer Street), where he pointed one of the said pistols at two women, Margaret Douglas and Mary McGrane. On 7 April 1844, the day of his appearance in court over the episode, his wife gave birth to his daughter Jane.

A full appreciation of the turn of events is provided by the fact that the Dublin Coal Gas Works were located at Grand Canal Docks on the street. In short, not only had this strip been transformed from tidal waters to reclaimed land and then to canals but also it had gone through the new technology of iron and steam to railways and finally to gaslighting. This had been the track over the 'low ground' and now it was a proper street with dwellings, factories, yards, theatres, buildings and businesses on both sides of its full length. The new railway terminus at Westland Row had 'an abundance of cars … in constant attendance'.[139]

The Ringsend spit, now fastened to the rest of the city, was no longer a barren strip of sand and shale with a smattering of dwellings in three rudimentary streets with one church, St Matthew's. It now housed the Ringsend Iron Company, engineering and millwrights, smiths, boilermakers and iron shipbuilders; James Pommoret ran a saltworks, John Hill ran a saltworks and limeworks, Mr Page also ran a saltworks and Mr Grierson ran the chemical works at Bridge Street. Mr Wilson operated one ropeworks and Mr Hanton a second. There was a medical dispensary and a Catholic school, and in Pembroke Street a Catholic chapel.[140] In short, it now had all the accoutrements of a suburban town on the edge of the city.

Nearer the river in 1844, only 100m from Great Brunswick Street, a shipwright was domiciled at No. 2 Creighton Street, Peter O'Brien and Edward Smyth at No. 1, Captain Stone, shipmaster, at

No. 7 and Mr Mackinson, also a shipmaster, at No. 10. This information confirms occupations particular to the port and its activities in housing along the river, all on the ground reclaimed from the sea.[141] Yet another symptom of major change in the way people lived and worked can be seen in the life of Peter Martin, who lived at Queen's Square (now Pearse Square), Great Brunswick Street, just beside Grand Canal Docks, while his workshops were at St Michael's Hill when he was overseeing the construction of Conciliation Hall, a very large building beside the Corn Exchange on Burgh Quay which would later house the *Irish Press* newspaper.[142]

In essence, what had been a sandbank of nearly nine acres 100 years earlier was now vastly expanded in terms of acreage, all reclaimed ground; this was then connected when the new stone elliptical bridge was begun in 1803, followed by the stone bridge at Lansdowne Road in 1837 and soon after by the second bridge to the spit at Londonbridge Road. At the same time, the area became home to the new Beggar's Bush Barracks in 1827, a substantial military establishment which was just up the road from the fort at the Pigeon House. As always, commerce was ahead, and the first known public house was established adjacent to it in 1803.

An area once occupied by the tides became occupied by people for work, rest and residence. It even included a Wesleyan Methodist chapel at Thomas Street, Ringsend. An area some 1.5km long by some 400m wide had become land—a very substantial increase in Dublin's footprint in the period. Moreover, the development of the area and the reclamation around the meeting of the Dodder and the Liffey had encouraged people to move out further from the city as defined by the 1728 walls, most certainly along the coast to Kingstown but also inland of both the rail line and the Blackrock Road, to create a second road behind connecting Stillorgan.

While huge change had occurred in the area, there nevertheless remained a reminder of its past: 'Grand Canal St, Denzille St, Lombard St and Townsend St still suffered from flooding and damp at high tides in wet weather'.[143]

Notes

1. Ruth Heard, 'Public works in Ireland 1800–1831', unpublished MLitt. thesis, Trinity College Dublin (1977), p. 4.
2. C.C. Ellison, *The hopeful traveller: the life and times of Daniel Augustus Beaufort LLD, 1790–1821* (Kilkenny, 1987), p. 112.
3. Garret Lyons, *Steaming to Kingstown and sucking up to Dalkey: the story of the Dublin and Kingstown railway* (Dublin, 2015), p. 23.
4. John Trotter, *Walks through Ireland in the years 1812, 1814 and 1817* (London, 1819), p. 15.
5. Baron Charles Dupin, *Narratives of two excursions to the ports of England, Scotland and Ireland in 1816, 1817, and 1818 together with a description of the breakwater at Plymouth* (London, 1827), p. 3.
6. *Ibid.*, p. 8
7. *Ibid.*, p. 12.
8. *Ibid.*, p. 13.
9. *Ibid.*, p. 105.
10. Sir John Rennie, *An autobiography* (London, 1867), p. 288.
11. David Dickson, *New foundations: Ireland 1660–1800* (Dublin, 2000), p. 284.
12. *Ibid.*, p. 233.
13. *CARD*, vol. 16, p. 23.
14. Philip Marsh, *The exploration of rail travel* (London, 2015), p. 8.
15. *Ibid.*
16. *Ibid.*, p. 10.
17. John Smeaton, *Reports of the late John Smeaton, FRS, made on various occasions, in the course of his employment as a civil engineer* (4 vols) (London 1812–14), vol. 1, p. xxi.
18. *Ibid.*, p. xvii.
19. *Ibid.*, p. 365.

[20] *Ibid.*, p. xxiv.
[21] *Ibid.*, p. 11.
[22] *Ibid.*, p. 12.
[23] *Ibid.*, p. 16.
[24] Kevin Murray, 'Dublin's first railway. Part I—from the inception to the opening', *Dublin Historical Record* **1** (1) (1938), 19–26, p. 19.
[25] Franco Tanel, *Trains: an illustrated history from steam locomotives to high-speed rail* (London, 2013).
[26] *Ibid.*, p. 18.
[27] *Ibid.*
[28] *Ibid.*, pp 18–19.
[29] Hazel Smyth, *The B & I* (Dublin, 1984), p. 5.
[30] *Ibid.*, pp 6–7.
[31] Dupin, *Narratives of two excursions*, p. 45.
[32] Roseanne Dunne, 'Number 25 Fitzwilliam Place', *Dublin Historical Record* **49** (1) (1996), p. 60.
[33] Desmond Greer and James Nicholson, *The Factory Acts in Ireland, 1802–1914* (Dublin, 2003), p. 2.
[34] P. Kemp (ed.), *The Oxford companion to ships and the sea* (Oxford, 1976).
[35] Ned McHugh, *Drogheda before the Famine: urban poverty in the shadow of privilege 1826–1845* (Dublin, 1998).
[36] David Edwards, 'The construction of Dún Laoghaire harbour', *Dublin Historical Record* **57** (2) (2004), 204–10, p. 204.
[37] Arnold Horner, 'Dún Laoghaire's great harbour', *History Ireland* **21** (5) (2013), 24–7, p. 26.
[38] Edwards, 'The construction of Dún Laoghaire Harbour', p. 205.
[39] *Ibid.*, pp 206–7.
[40] 'Journal of the proceedings of the Corporation for Preserving and Improving the Port of Dublin', vol. 11, p. 245 (National Archives of Ireland).
[41] Edwards, 'The construction of Dún Laoghaire harbour', p. 206.
[42] Horner, 'Dún Laoghaire's great harbour', p. 24.
[43] *Ibid.*, p. 25.
[44] Lyons, *Steaming to Kingstown*, p. 21.
[45] Murray, 'Dublin's first railway. Part I', p. 20.
[46] Henry Inglis, *Ireland in 1834: a journey throughout Ireland during the summer and autumn by Henry D. Inglis* (2 vols) (London, 1834), p. 4.
[47] Margaret Storrie, 'William J. Bald FRSE, *c.* 1789–1857: surveyor, cartographer and civil engineer', *Transactions of the British Institute of Geographers* **47** (1969), 205–31, p. 219.
[48] Pamphlet, *Concise statement of the Ballast Corporation and the subsequent state of the harbour, an inquiry into the promised and probable consequences to the trade and commerce of the proposed railway between Dublin and Kingstown, and an investigation into the project of constructing a ship canal connecting the asylum harbour at Kingstown with a floating dock in the river Anna Liffey* (Dublin, March 1833).
[49] Charles A. Fisher, 'Evolution of an Irish railway system', *Economic Geography* **17** (3) (1941), 262–74.
[50] Lyons, *Steaming to Kingstown*, p. 23.
[51] *Ibid.*, p. 26.
[52] *Ibid.*, p. 28.
[53] Z.A., 'On railways', *The Belfast Magazine and Literary Journal* **1** (2) (March 1825), 163–74, p. 174.
[54] Murray, 'Dublin's first railway. Part I', p. 24.
[55] Horner, 'Dún Laoghaire's great harbour', p. 26; Fergus Mulligan, 'William Dargan: an honourable life', *Irish Quarterly Review* **104** (413) (2015), p. 40.
[56] Mulligan, 'William Dargan', p. 47.
[57] Murray, 'Dublin's first railway. Part I', p. 24.
[58] *Ibid.*, p. 20.
[59] *Ibid.*, p. 19.
[60] *Ibid.*, p. 23.
[61] John T. Dunne, 'The first Irish railway, by shriek and smoke to Kingstown', *Dublin Historical Record* **43** (1) (1990), 44–6.
[62] Lyons, *Steaming to Kingstown*, p. 36.
[63] Murray, 'Dublin's first railway. Part I', p. 20.
[64] P. Th. Hicks, 'Journal of a tour of P Th Hicks from Gloucester through Wales and Ireland 1818' (TCD, MS 968).
[65] Kevin Murray, 'Dublin's first railway. Part II—the line in operation', *Dublin Historical Record* **1** (2) (1938), 33–40, p. 34.
[66] Lyons, *Steaming to Kingstown*, p. 28.

67 Murray, 'Dublin's first railway. Part II', p. 33.
68 A.W. Skempton, 'Embankments and cuttings on the early railways', *Construction History* **11** (1996), 33–49, p. 33.
69 *Ibid.*, p. 33.
70 *Ibid.*, p. 34.
71 *Ibid.*, p. 35.
72 *Ibid.*, p. 36.
73 *Ibid.*, p. 36.
74 P. Dixon Hardy, 'The Dublin and Kingstown Railway', *Dublin Penny Journal* **3** (113) (30 August 1834), 65–8, p. 65.
75 Skempton, 'Embankments and cuttings on the early railways', p. 41.
76 *Ibid.*
77 *Dublin Penny Journal* (30 August 1834), p. 66.
78 *Ibid.*, p. 67.
79 Murray, 'Dublin's first railway. Part II', p. 35.
80 Lyons, *Steaming to Kingstown*, p. 80.
81 *Ibid.*, p. 82.
82 Dunne, 'The first Irish railway', p. 46.
83 Murray, 'Dublin's first railway. Part I', p. 22.
84 Murray, 'Dublin's first railway. Part II', p. 35.
85 *Ibid.*, p. 35.
86 *Ibid.*, p. 36.
87 Murray, 'Dublin's first railway. Part I', p. 25.
88 *Ibid.*, p. 25.
89 *Dublin Penny Journal* (21 June 1834), p. 401.
90 Lyons, *Steaming to Kingstown*, p. 38.
91 Murray, 'Dublin's first railway. Part II', p. 34.
92 *Dublin Penny Journal* (21 June 1834), p. 402.
93 *Ibid.*, p. 403.
94 Murray, 'Dublin's first railway. Part II', pp 38–9.
95 *Ibid.*, p. 40.
96 Francis J. Cullen, 'Local government and the management of urban space: a comparative study between Belfast and Dublin 1830–1922', unpublished Ph.D thesis, NUI Maynooth (2005), p. 50.
97 Fergus D'Arcy, 'The Kingstown Races', *Dublin Historical Record* **45** (1), 55–64, p. 56.
98 *Ibid.*, p. 56.
99 *Ibid.*, pp 58–60.
100 Rob Goodbody, 'Bridges', in A. Carpenter, R. Loeber, H. Campbell, L. Hurley, J. Montague and E. Rowley (eds), *Art and architecture of Ireland, vol. 4. Architecture 1600–2000* (Dublin, 2015), 145–8, p. 147.
101 Peter Barlow, *Treatise on the strength of timber, cast and malleable iron and other materials for application in architecture, the construction of suspension bridges, railways* (London, 1851).
102 Lewis Hardy, *Memoirs of the life of James Caulfield, Earl of Charlemont* (Dublin, 1810).
103 Rennie, *An autobiography*, p. 415.
104 John Barrow, *A tour around Ireland through the sea counties in the autumn of 1835* (London, 1836), p. 375.
105 Ann Plumtre, *Narrative of a residence in Ireland during the summer of 1814 and that of 1815* (London, 1817), p. 8.
106 *CARD*, vol. 18, p. x.
107 *Ibid.*, p. 104.
108 *Ibid.*, p. 81.
109 Barrow, *A tour round Ireland*, p. 372.
110 Thomas Cromwell, *The Irish tourist or excursions through Ireland, province of Leinster*, vol. 3 (Dublin, 1820), p. 21.
111 *Ibid.*, p. 26.
112 D.L. Cooney, 'Dinner in Sandymount', *Dublin Historical Record* **64** (2) (2011), 192–3, p. 192.
113 Diarmuid O'Grada, *Georgian Dublin: the forces that shaped the city* (Cork, 2015), p. 117.
114 *Ibid.*, p. 117.
115 *Ibid.*, p. 101.
116 Jonathan Binns, *The miseries and beauties of Ireland* (2 vols) (London, 1837), p. 2.
117 *Ibid.*, p. 5.
118 *Ibid.*, p. 7.
119 *Dublin Almanac* (1845).
120 Diary of a tour in Ireland *c.* 1837, NLI MS 194, p. 30.
121 William Marrot, 'A tour through the south of Ireland in the autumn of the year 1841', NLI MS 46839.

122 Inglis, *Ireland in 1834*, p. 5.
123 Friedrich Raumer, *England in 1835 volume 1, being a series of letters written to friends in Germany during a residence in London and excursions into the provinces by Friedrich Raumer, translated from the German by Sarah Austen and H.E. Lloyd in three volumes* (London, 1836), p. 181.
124 *Ibid.*, p. 191.
125 *Ibid.*, p. 54.
126 Information courtesy of the Maritime Museum of Liverpool.
127 John P. Clancy and John Montague, 'Railways', in R. Loeber, H. Campbell, L. Hurley, J. Montague and E. Rowley (eds), *Art and architecture of Ireland, vol. 4. Architecture 1600–2000* (Dublin, 2015), p. 161.
128 Trotter, *Walks through Ireland*, p. 8.
129 Pettigrew and Oulton, *The Dublin Almanac and Directory, 1844* (Dublin, 1844), pp 616–18.
130 F.A. D'Arcy, 'The murder of Thomas Hanlon: a nineteenth-century Dublin labour conspiracy', paper read to the Old Dublin Society, 4 November 1970.
131 *Ibid*.
132 Anon., 'Rambles of a discontented gentleman: the bullet gatherers', *Irish Monthly Magazine, politics and literature* **2** (19) (May–December 1833), 417–20.
133 Information courtesy of John McGrath, Bank of Ireland Archive, Dublin.
134 Cormac Lowth, *Boatbuilding in Dublin* (forthcoming), pp 50–3.
135 *Ibid.*, p. 55.
136 *Ibid.*, p. 56.
137 *Ibid.*, p. 58.
138 *Ibid.*, p. 62.
139 Barrow, *A tour around Ireland*, p. 375.
140 *Dublin Almanac 1845*, p. 821.
141 Pettigrew and Oulton, *The Dublin Almanac and Directory, 1844*.
142 Vincent Ruddy, *Monster agitators: O'Connell's Repealers, 1843 Ireland* (Dublin, 2018), p. 86.
143 Park Neville, *Report to the lord mayor of the city of Dublin on the sewerage of the city and the general state of public works* (Dublin, 1853), p. 4.

6. North Dublin before the Ballast Act

We will examine what took place on the north side by first noting what Dublin was like before 1708 and the activities of the Ballast Board. This will include looking at the area occupied by man in the approach to the seventeenth century. Consideration will be given to the changing political climate and to the effects of the Industrial Revolution on the city and its people, and their work and leisure activities. Note will be taken of the different speed and content of development in comparison to the south side and the reasons for same. Attention will also be paid to the plans which were laid with the 1717 map of the North and South Lotts, which envisaged massive occupation extending all the way out to Clontarf. We will then trace how the North Wall on the Liffey and the East Wall were completed up to 1728, the impact on topography and the opportunity for further interference. The story will look at the occupation of the space inside the walls after 1728, creeping out eastward and northward as it filled in the area around O'Connell Street and environs by the end of the third quarter of the eighteenth century. There followed a series of major structures completed within the walls in the last quarter: the Four Courts complex, Carlisle Bridge, the Custom House, the Royal Canal, Aldeborough House and Annesley Bridge. These individual structures and complexes had both a separate and a collective effect on people and the city. The year 1800 and the new century brought new technologies, new skills and expertise, new forms of transport, and the movement away from the Liffey of packet-boat activities to Howth and then Dún Laoghaire. A boom took place in the building of schools, medical facilities and churches, as the State became more involved in the everyday lives of the citizens. The Great North Bull Wall was built in less than four years, creating an enclosed harbour and removing the bar at last, and Howth Harbour was completed, before losing out to Kingstown as mail port. The final major construction to be imposed on this landscape was the Dublin to Drogheda Railway. The effects of these actions will be examined in relation to the city and the citizens.

Vandra Costello wrote that 'Dublin city developed piecemeal over the centuries without the benefit of any great master plan, and the only means of planning control of the urban environment was by the insertion of various duties and conditions into leases given to lessees and developers', those early developers being the religious houses around which settlements developed.[1] This is not totally accurate, because the very fact that the Corporation, through the work of the Ballast Committee, planned and executed the walling of the Liffey and the Tolka proves that there was in fact a plan of some magnitude. It may not qualify as a master plan in that in 1707 they did not outline, for example, the Royal Canal. They did, however, plan the North Lotts in 1717, and those plans included the reclaiming of land from the sea, out north of the Tolka to Clontarf. Further, it was always a given that the building of dwellings large and small would occur firstly on the higher ground above the tide line within the new enclosure of the walls. This is clearly evidenced by the building along the approximate 5m line above sea level. Indeed, Costello's claim may be partially true, but the reality was that boundaries such as those on the north side after the walls were built had to allow for expansion.

As can be seen from John Speed's 1610 map of Dublin, the city enclosed by the walls on the north bank of the Liffey was small and medieval. There was some fragmented development outside the walls along the edge stretching from the Capel (Essex) Street Bridge in a north-westerly direction towards what would become Dorset Street—until the late 1700s a major route north out of the city. This map gives the first idea of what Dublin actually looked like.

Speed's map shows most settlement on the south side of the Liffey. After 1170 the Old Norse and Irish moved across to Oxmantown and settled in that area around where Collins Barracks stands today, downriver from the Law Society's premises in Blackhall Place and Queen Street.[2]

Before the Reformation, the major landowner and developer on the north side of Dublin was St Mary's Abbey, a Cistercian house. Founded *c.* 948 as a Benedictine monastery, it passed to the Cistercians in 1139. The Cistercians were a strong presence in Ireland as creators of large granges, where all manner of agricultural and industrial activity was organised and carried out. Strongbow donated Clonliffe to St Mary's; Adam de Phepo, too, gave it some of his property. This meant that the land under the management of the Cistercians ran all the way out from west of Four Courts Bridge to Baldoyle and its port.[3] (By a quirk of history, the abbot was also officially the admiral of the port of Baldoyle, and the maritime connection is kept alive today in the anchor on the flag of Sutton Golf Club.)

The Reformation changed all that, as this great property, extending all the way out to the coast, was parcelled out to Henry VIII's friends and loyalists. In 1619 Baron Moore received a portion of the lands of St Mary's Abbey and he made the abbot's house his home until later in the seventeenth century, when Drogheda Street (Sackville Street) was laid out, followed by Earl Street, Henry Street and Moore Street.[4]

Sir Humphrey Jervis began to build and develop the area around Capel Street in the seventeenth century. From this point the north side of the city began to change, though still mainly behind the walls, such as they were. When Jervis began, there was little on this side of the river in the stretch outside the walls, and the ground rose gently in gradient until approximately North King Street as it rose to Broadstone Hill and, east of that, Henrietta Street and Dorset Street, all to be developed in the future. Further east, the seashore was at Busáras and Amiens Street and so was overrun by tides twice a day. Further east again, Summerhill was the high ground above Gardiner Street and out to Clonliffe Road, which slopes upwards as it reaches the Drumcondra end. So this area was identical to the south side—marsh, sand, slobs, tidal and mostly unproductive.

Sir Humphrey Jervis completely altered his ground by creating an elevated 457m-long wall, using much of the stone left from St Mary's Abbey, which narrowed the channel.[5] Dickson said that Jervis helped to initiate the reclamation of the tidal flats, a vast area to the east of his land, later called the North Strand.[6] John De Courcy wrote that Jervis used stone from the abbey to build the Essex Bridge (Capel Street) in 1678, named for his patron, Arthur Capel, earl of Essex.[7] Meanwhile, on the other side, William Hawkins, another Cromwellian soldier, drove the reclamation of the riverside between Dame Street and the river. He paid for 450m of double riverside walling east of the custom house (that is, the original of the three custom houses), thereby protecting College Green from most—but not all—tidal inundations. This included Lazers Hill (Townsend Street, then on the strand track down to Ringsend).[8]

All this would begin a period of transformation. In building the North Wall and the East Wall the Ballast Board created a new boundary perimeter for Dublin. The ground inside this wall would be drained and reclaimed over the next 150 years and become host to agriculture, housing and industry.

While Speed's map, being only a map of the city, offered little detail of the north side of the Liffey, William Petty's 1665 map was a county map, and he added details such as various villages, hamlets and townlands. He also confirmed the existence of a bridge over the Tolka at the edge of the bay and well inshore of Clontarf Island at Ballybough. This vicinity was known as 'Mud Island', home to waterfront inhabitants who survived on the margins of the city. As Dickson said, there was no mention of parishes north of the river; they did not exist.[9] Captain John Vernon had title confirmed to his estate in Clontarf in 1663.[10] The *Calendar of ancient records of Dublin* records a statement that 'This city being since His Majesty's happy restoration increased to that magnitude that it is larger without the walls than within'.[11] This statement seems accurate, though Thomas Phillips's 1685 map does not show development reaching out this far.

Sinéad O'Shea and Ray Egan have each examined closely a specific street within the city. Egan looked at Denzille Street (Fenian Street) between Merrion Square and Pearse Street, while O'Shea completed her thesis on Upper Buckingham Street, which runs from Summerhill down to Seán McDermott Street.[12] In addition, Brendan Twomey examined Smithfield and the parish of St Paul's of North King Street and Queen Street.[13] All three works offer a very good appreciation of what took place in each specific area and the effects more generally. O'Shea and Egan both looked at development on reclaimed land, while Twomey examined one of the original parts of the city during the eighteenth century. A clear picture emerged of the development of each locale, each work illustrating how the areas were occupied and built on, by whom and for whom, and the impact of all this on society.

Notes

[1] Vandra Costello, 'Public spaces for recreation in Dublin 1660–1760', *Garden History* **35** (2) (2007), 160–79, p. 160.
[2] David Dickson, *Dublin: the making of a capital city* (London, 2014), p. 16.
[3] J. Collins, *Life in old Dublin* (Dublin, 1913), p. 8.
[4] Seamus Sently, 'Ghosts of Moore Street', *Dublin Historical Record* **25** (2) (1972), 54–63, p. 54.
[5] Dickson, *Dublin*, p. 88.
[6] *Ibid.*, p. 89.
[7] John De Courcy, 'A bridge in its time: the River Liffey crossing at Church Street in Dublin', *Proceedings of the Royal Irish Academy* **90**C (1990), 243–57, p. 255.
[8] Dickson, *Dublin*, p. 87.
[9] *Ibid.*, p. 76.
[10] *Ibid.*, p. 81.
[11] *CARD*, vol. 5, p. 20.
[12] Sinéad O'Shea, 'Upper Buckingham Street', unpublished BA thesis, St Patrick's College, Drumcondra (2013).
[13] Brendan Twomey, *Smithfield and the parish of St Paul, Dublin, 1698–1750* (Dublin, 2005).

7. Walling of the north bank of the Liffey to 1728 and beyond

In 1707 the Assembly was warned that the river would be completely choked in a few years unless action was taken.[1] A report submitted to them in March 1708 encouraged them to act.[2] In 1710 the committee appointed to view the north side of the Liffey met with the people who leased the ground there to try and get them to pile the river-bank, but they refused to contribute.[3] In 1717 the committee let out the North Lotts, which stretch north to Clontarf, well north of the proposed east wall along the Tolka.[4] The story of the North Lotts may be seen as the removal of one island (at Clontarf) and the imposition of another (the base for Amiens Street railway station) in the period of interest.

The Assembly ordered that kishes (crates or boxes made of wood, usually oak or larch, filled with gravel and stones) be set towards Mourny's Dock.[5] They were laid out in an interlaced fashion and the structure was backfilled with larger stones and gravel to add strength to the barrier. It was then faced over time with stone, and later with granite. Meanwhile, the land side of the structure was reinforced with more and more filling and support and grew to a height of up to 15ft. It was able to resist flooding surges because it was porous and allowed some leakage and because the boxes were laid one way and then another. Moreover, the barrier was laid out in the general direction of the outflowing Liffey and the ebbing tide, so pressure was not such a serious issue. In any case, the committee reported that the structure suffered fewer breaches in the building. In July 1716 it is reported that while the ground below Ringsend had been staked out, the kishes on the north side of the channel were laid up to the land as far as possible 'as it is thought necessary and will be so strong when backed and finished as may prevent the floods from breaking through to the northwards for the future, and keep the current in its right channel'.[6] Later that year they reported the building of a second float of 30 tons for moving kishes, which they were continuing to lay on the north side and backing them.[7] Shortly afterwards they confirmed that they 'Have carried the kishes as far westward as we designed and likewise as high at that end being three rows and have filled them with stones and are backing them and do design them to continue east at the same height'.[8] This is a rare detail in the records of construction.

At the same time the Assembly auctioned lots for lease across the north side out to Clontarf. These would become vital as the city expanded over the years (Fig. 7.1).

The origin of all development on the north side after the construction of the north and east walls can be traced to the following report from the Ballast Office in 1717: 'We ... have surveyed the Strand and are of the opinion that the strand on the north side of Ballybough River [the Tolka] from the highest ground on the north end of Clontarf island to the next angle on the west side of Clontarf House [Hollybrook Road] on the road containing seventy seven acres to be divided with the Strand on the south side of the Ballybough River containing in all 441 acres. That the Ballybough

Dublin moving east, 1708–1844

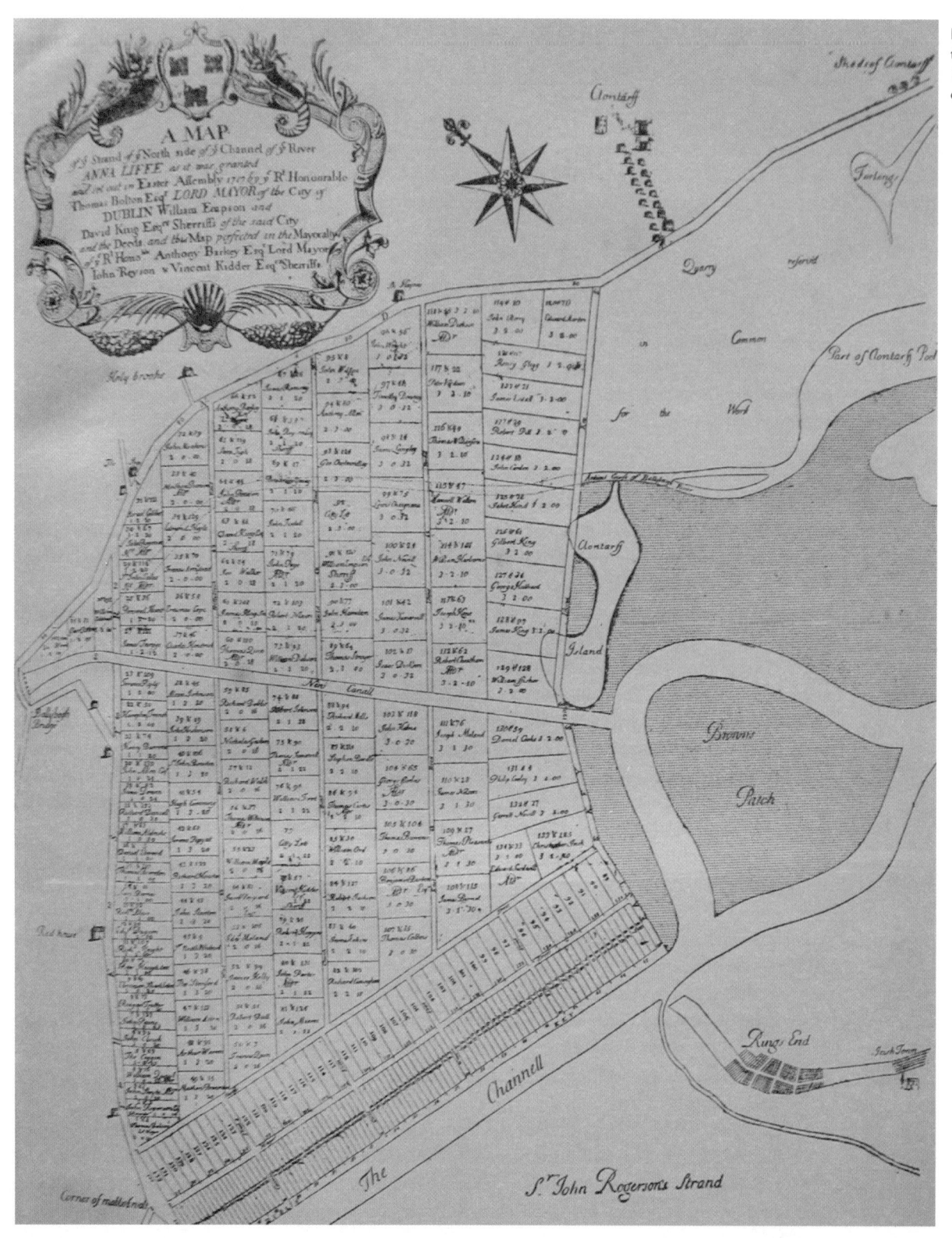

Fig. 7.1—Map of the North Lotts, 1717 (courtesy of the NAI).

River be carried on the south side of Clontarf Island in a straight line from the first angle on the east of Ballybough Bridge in a new channel and the canal to be eighty feet wide.'[9] The Ballast Committee added their recommendation that the front Lotts be divided into 88 and the rear ones into 44, making a total of 132 Lotts. The council kept two Lotts (nos 77 and 92) for public use. They further recommended that the Strand be used for the raising of stones and carrying out the works. This plan for the North Lotts, for the area between Mabbots Mills and the sheds of Clontarf, was presented to the Assembly on 5 April 1717. It is interesting to note that there was a plan to divert the course of the Tolka a full 70 years before a similar plan was unveiled to alter the course of the Dodder.[10]

The directors reported a sluggish reaction to the scheme in that the owners of Lotts were slow to part with their money. Meanwhile, progress continued on the erection of the wall: 'We have laid and filled with stones on the strand this summer 400 kishes and have bought 500 more, some of which are already used'.[11] Later on it is reported that 'We have bought 1200 kishes to be delivered this summer and men are employed in filling and laying down kishes on the north bank of the channel'.[12]

On 18 July 1718 it is reported: 'We have laid down the kishes on the north side of the channel as high and as far eastward as opposite to Ringsend Point [Point Depot] and are filling them and backing with stones as fast as we can and likewise laying down kishes from the east end of the aforesaid kishes in a line towards the island [Clontarf Island]; we have a good quantity of kishes by us and do expect more every day according to agreements formerly made for them, which will be a means of securing these kishes already laid down on the north of the channel'.[13] Clontarf Island was located where the entrance of the Port Tunnel is today. This gives a clear picture that the north wall had been laid out with kishes as far as envisaged in the plan and that the beginning of the wall had been started, turning left at today's Point Depot and running along in a straight line to where the Port Tunnel exits today. This was good progress, as the work depended on low tides and good weather, and shorter hours of daylight reduced the amount that could be done in winter.

It is interesting to speculate on the reasons behind Commander Perry's proposal to create a canal to Dublin Port via Sutton when the walls at this stage were proceeding apace; moreover, the piles too had been begun and the Assembly received a report in January 1721 that 'The frames and piles are a good shelter to ships as lie in Poolbeg and to fishing boats that fish in the harbour'.[14] In any case, the Assembly addressed Lord Carteret, the lord lieutenant and governor-general of Ireland, to the effect that 'We are fully confirmed in our opinion that Captain Perry's scheme for making his proposed entrance would prove prejudiced and even destructive to our trade and navigation'.[15]

By 17 January 1724 it was reported that 'We are carrying on the wall of the north strand between the west end of the quay of the said strand already built and the east end of Mr Mourney's dock and have made good progress there, the building of which when we are finished with good stones at ten pence halfpenny per ton by one Browne on the strand which is a penny per ton cheaper than the stones cost the Ballast office'.[16] In this instance the directors are confirming that these stones are for facing purposes on the north wall. It is added that 'We pay eleven pence per hogshead for roach and ten pence per hogshead for slack lime to Mr Montgomery and Mr Conyingham for the work of the said wall'. Mr Robinson, stonemason, is paid 9d. per perch for work. 'Computing that one foot high and twenty one feet long and eighteen inches thick to each perch and we are obliged to pay labourers for digging and clearing the foundation of the said wall … The sand for making the mortar and the gravel we have brought by the Ballast Office gabbards at two pence per ton for dredging and bringing the same to the strand wall, and 1 penny per tun to labourers for throwing the sand and gravel out of the said gabbards.'[17]

It should be noted that as this work was proceeding down on the strand in the estuary of the three rivers, away from the houses and buildings just outside the city walls, it was out of sight of most of the populace of Dublin. Probably the only people to see this construction making its way across the landscape would have been seafarers and travellers.

In 1724 it was decided to appoint Mr Luntly to manage the work of the wall and to keep an account of the tons of stones, sand, gravel and hogsheads of lime to be used.[18] The Committee further ordered that a back wall be built on the north side to preserve the wall built by the city, and that the space between the two was to be equal to the quay at the end of the said ground and was to be filled up and paid for by the city.[19] Further, ballast in gabbards was to be used to fill up behind the wall on the north side, and they reported that Mr Thornton's dock on the west side of the north wall was nearly finished.[20] A timely reminder of the dangers of Dublin Bay came in the form of the stranding of the ship *Friendship* on the North Bull in January 1728. In this particular incident not enough attention had been paid to the buoys and other navigation marks in the channels.[21]

Another problem with which the Assembly had to deal was shipwreck and who had legitimate claims to same. This was a major issue around all coasts at the time because wreckage and cargo washed up could be very valuable, especially timber and cordage. In November 1728 Major Vernon of Clontarf Castle assumed the rights to all property of such wreckage at Clontarf.[22] He cannot have been too sure of his ground, however, because when both he and Lord Howth came into possession of some of the piles that had come adrift from the construction of the Great South Wall they eventually returned them.[23]

It was noted in January 1729 that Thomas Brooking '[h]as completely finished his map of the city'.[24] This map, together with the lack of any other information in the *Calendar of ancient records of Dublin* on the wall on either side of the channel, allows the assumption that the walls were complete. This is supported by Charles Price's map, which also shows the straight channel.

It must be apparent to the reader at this stage that huge quantities of large stones were required for the continuing work on the walls on both sides of the river. Much use was being made of the south coast of the bay at Blackrock, but it was very exposed. The intention was to supply stones from here but only when some protection could be offered to boats and rafts floating them across to the sites. In the meantime, 'It was agreed with Mr Murray of Clontarf for stones until a pier can be built at Blackrock at ten and half pence per ton'.[25]

The tide always remained a problem and continually overflowed the walls, especially on the north side. Temporary flooding of much or little of the new enclosure continued for years. A 1743 Committee report of ground 'Which is now pasture and meadow made useless to the farmer' obviously refers to flooding.[26] It would become a rarity as the walls were banked up and reinforced and the ground inside dried. In Holland it was the practice to work with the natural elements. The English gentleman in Thomas Park's pamphlet noted the flatness of the land and 'the richness of the soil that is easily overflowed every winter; so as the whole country at that season seems to be under water, which in spring is driven out by mills [windmills]'.[27]

Damage to the walls was not unknown; at Ormonde Quay, owing to a hackney mishap, a horse fell into the River Liffey and drowned in 1738.[28] In the same year a vandal cut loose the perch at the North Bull mark for shipping in the lower estuary channel.[29] On 6 December the following year, upriver at Bachelor's Quay, a ship broke loose from a mooring post and smashed down on

Fig. 7.2—Essex Bridge at the beginning of the improvement of the city under the Wide Streets Commission; note the ships at the Custom House on the other side of the bridge, and unfinished walls on the river on the west side, with unpaved streets (photo: Brian Matthews, with the kind permission of the NLI).

another; both then came down on top of six more, tearing them away from their moorings and causing much damage. This episode was unique in that there was no storm at the time, nor was there much in the way of wind.[30]

During 1744 the wall is described as being in a 'Ruinous state and the Ballast Office owes a large quantity of ballast to the said wall which will be delivered as soon as possible to prevent any further damage'.[31] Later in the year it was delivered.[32] The owners of the North Lotts leases asked for some assistance in the cost of repairing the north wall, 'It being in a bad condition'.[33] By 1791 a total of £45,000 had been granted by parliament for making docks on both sides of the river.[34]

The work of building and backfilling the walls continued, and the Committee submitted the names of applicants for financial help in repairing their sections of the north wall. The Committee was willing to pay one penny per ton of sludge or sand that 'Shall be dredged up and laid on the quays enclosing the north strand not to exceed £100 in any one year that the part of the said wall or bank that encloses the said channel being the south wall on the north side be repaired at the cost to owners on the north strand occasionally offset by payments from the Ballast Office at no more than £40 in any year'.[35] This refers to the work of banking up behind the walls, to both the north and the east, and is today seen in the street levels as the streets approach both the Tolka and the Liffey (Fig. 7.2).

While the new barrier for creating a single channel for the Liffey was completed by 1728, the work of reclaiming the ground behind it would continue for many years, as would the upgrading of the wall itself. The barrier was in fact the first version of the wall. Work continued, and 100 years later the port ledgers and light account books show that George Halpin, master builder of the North Bull Wall and of lighthouses around the country, was in charge of repairing and reinforcing both Liffey walls. Windmills were established on the north side to assist in draining the ground just inside this new barrier. Rocque included one in his map of the city. Building on this new ground was not long in taking place, but the first phase of reclamation was a measure of farming which helped to stabilise the ground.

Notes

[1] *CARD*, vol. 6, p. 371.
[2] *Ibid.*
[3] *Ibid.*, p. 420.
[4] An auction preview of a copy of the 1717 map was displayed by Fonsie Mealy, auctioneer, in the Tara Towers Hotel on 14 December 2016. This writer later found out that the original map is in the National Archives, Dublin.
[5] *CARD*, vol. 7, p. 5.
[6] *Ibid.*, p. 14.
[7] *Ibid.*, p. 21.
[8] *Ibid.*, p. 28.
[9] *Ibid.*, p. 30.
[10] *Ibid.*, pp 32–3.
[11] *Ibid.*, p. 51.
[12] *Ibid.*, p. 62.
[13] *Ibid.*, p. 70.
[14] *Ibid.*, p. 183.
[15] *Ibid.*, p. 333.
[16] *Ibid.*, p. 250.
[17] *Ibid.*, pp 250–1.
[18] *Ibid.*, p. 252.
[19] *Ibid.*, p. 394.

[20] *Ibid.*, p. 403.
[21] *Ibid.*, p. 409.
[22] *Ibid.*, p. 436.
[23] *Ibid.*, p. 445.
[24] *Ibid.*, pp 443–4.
[25] *Ibid.*, p. 490.
[26] *CARD*, vol. 9, p. 121.
[27] 'A late voyage to Holland; with brief relation of the actions at the Hague; also remarks on the manners and customs, nature and comical humours of the people; their religion, government, habitations, way of living and manner of treating strangers, especially the English, written by an English gentleman attending the court of the King of Great Britain 1691', in Thomas Park, *The Harleian miscellany: a collection of scarce, curious and entertaining pamphlets and tracts* (London, 1808), vol. 2, p. 598.
[28] *CARD*, vol. 8, p. 396.
[29] *Ibid.*, p. 280.
[30] *Ibid.*, p. 359.
[31] *CARD*, vol. 9, p. 148.
[32] *Ibid.*, p. 150.
[33] *Ibid.*, p. 144.
[34] *CARD*, vol. 8, p. 233.
[35] *CARD*, vol. 9, p. 191.

8. Inside the new enclosure after 1728

Even before the new walls were complete, activity had begun in the old town. Capel Street was built by 1710, facilitating further development. Luke Gardiner bought tracts of the lands of St Mary's Abbey in 1714–21, allowing the extension of Capel Street to Dorset Street and Dominick Street in the mid-eighteenth century, but Henrietta Street proved the trigger for further development.[1] It was at that time on higher ground, which was always viewed as a healthier place to live, and offered very attractive views. John Rocque's map of 1756 shows the connection between Great Britain Street (Parnell Street)/Summerhill, Dominick Street, Dorset Street and Rotunda Gardens.

David Dickson said that Luke Gardiner gained ownership of nearly all of the old St Mary's Abbey estate between 1722 and 1729.[2] As the first half of the century unfolded, Luke Gardiner more than any of his contemporaries influenced the development of Dublin. He bought St Mary's Abbey in 1729/30 from the earl of Drogheda and the earl of Duncannon.[3] By 1734 he was the most extensive property-holder on the North Lotts; the street system extension was planned by the landholders, especially Gardiner. He was also a public figure, which allowed him an even greater influence. Nuala Burke maintains that this gave him an advantage in attracting clients to his new suburbs.[4] In fig. 22 of her thesis, Burke shows the Gardiner land bank extending from the Tolka to the Liffey and from the North Wall to the edge of Glasnevin, out past Dorset Street to a vast swathe of the new Dublin yet to come. The only drawback was that while the North Lotts, as per the map of 1717, was neat and tidy, that is all that it was.

The North Lotts represented one of the major steps in the development on the north side. In approximate terms it was bounded on its southern flank by the Liffey wall, completed in 1728 down to the Point (today's Point Depot) and then running in a west/north direction towards St Lawrence Road, Clontarf, from the East Link Bridge, and over towards North Strand by Fairview Strand. It included the triangle between the Tolka and Fairview Strand but did not include part of the site of the Custom House.[5] De Courcy said that in 1710 the Ballast Office Committee began building a wall down along the Liffey towards the site of East Link Bridge, and by 1718 work was in progress along the line of the East Wall Road.

The Corporation plan had been to get the leaseholders to develop the space by reclaiming the land and constructing the north and east walls themselves. This was, however, space (it wasn't even ground yet) on which there was no immediate sign of a return on investment, and many of the Lott-holders allowed their Lotts to be repossessed for failure to abide by their leases. Gardiner picked up these leases when they came up for resale; a man with deep pockets, he played the long game. Some Lotts were not very accessible and consequently drainage and reclamation was a much slower process than had been the case on the south side. When the wall was first built it was not a wall as we know it today, solid and somewhat watertight. Rather it was a construction of interwoven baskets of stones and gravel on top of, beside and behind one another, interlocked for strength. By the nature of its construction it was porous, and would remain so for some years until backed in front and packed and padded behind. On the water side of this structure large stones formed an extra, more solid layer. Over time the wall or barrier was reinforced with banked-up material, growing both higher and deeper. This can be seen all up and down the walls of both the Tolka and the Liffey, with a substantial dip in ground levels behind these walls today. During the next 100 years and more the ground was drained and reclaimed. As it dried out, it was divided up and turned to agriculture, then houses and factories. From the mid-nineteenth century a particularly large tract of the space would be given over to extensive railway marshalling yards.

Historians are fortunate that there is much documentation available in the form of papers from the Gardiner estate. Just as the Fitzwilliam estate was the major landowner on the south side of the river in the eastern quadrant, Gardiner was the pre-eminent landowner on the north side in the north-eastern quadrant, while also owning land south of the channel. A look at a sample of leases confirms the range of interests of the estate.

- Lease granted to Mary Kenny by Luke Gardiner on ground between Lazy Hill and the Strand on 16 January 1712.
- Lease and release forever to Luke Gardiner by twelve of the members of the committee constituted and appointed at a general assembly of the proprietors of the Lotts on the North Strand on 9 May 1729 (just one year after the completion of the initial barrier), pursuant to an act of parliament—an act for the more speedy and effectual enclosing of the Strand on the north side of the Liffey.

As the walls now defined the new city boundary, especially along the north bank in the area of Capel Street, it followed that structures were erected on the ground as it became stable, and so development crept out along Capel Street and created streets, lanes and alleys off it up into Bolton Street and onto the fields of Dorset Street. At the same time in the early 1700s the same thing happened to Parnell Street and its surrounds. In 1764 Mr Foy of Moore Street, a maker of sedan chairs, got married. The Dublin Infirmary for curing diseases of the skin opened at 29 Moore Street; it was maintained privately by William Wallace, a surgeon of Jervis Street Infirmary, who lived at 4 Great Denmark Street.[6]

Following hot on the heels of the occupation of this space came the demand for water supply, and the provision of street and pavement surface also became an urgent necessity. The Paving Board was set up in 1774 to supply this need and to control the manner in which the citizenry used the streets in terms of taking over footpaths and streets with building extensions and protrusion at both street level and above as well as markets, which the Corporation saw as needing to be regularised. This was yet another body at work in the city, along with the Pipe Water Commission and the Wide Streets Commission, on top of all the activity over the following fifteen years or so on major structures. Much excavation was required, involving many men with shovels collecting stone and sand, as well as carters to deliver the material to sites. The Paving Board had 30 horses at their disposal for carrying out works. Thomas Brownrigg was partnered with Thomas Sherrard, surveyor and secretary to the Wide Streets Commission, and based in Capel Street. By 1799 Brownrigg was surveyor to the Paving Board. Sherrard meanwhile designed the new bridge to be built across the Tolka to move the boundary and road half a kilometre east and to create a new sea-walled road to

Fig. 8.1—Clontarf Sheds and an unfinished road (artist unknown) (courtesy of the NLI).

the north. He managed to balance his work for the Board with his survey work for the Grand Canal and the Royal Canal, as well as a private practice. He only resigned in 1806 to focus on the growing canal system.[7] Richard Edgeworth, an inventor who had analysed the methods of road construction and examined how the wheel hubs, wood types and suspension springs of carriages coped with various surfaces, presented his findings to the Royal Dublin Society, receiving help in his research from the Paving Board [8] (Fig. 8.1).

In 1773 the Bank of Ireland opened for business on the north side at Mary's Abbey, on the corner of Boot Lane between Capel Street and the Four Courts. By now this area had become an important commercial hub. Merchants were located down here, as was the private bank of Newcomen until the 1780s. As one of the older parts of the city, however, with stores and warehouses adjacent, many premises were a fire hazard. There was also the problem of sewage disposal, and the bank paid £50 towards the supply of a sewer to connect and empty in the river, to add to all the other raw sewage going in at the time. When the bank opened it had nineteen staff; within twenty years it had 180. Pool and Cash wrote in 1780 that 'the eastern side of the city … is about entirely laid out in contiguous streets … for the residence of the gentry'.[9]

- Leases for one year or three lives to John Gosson, a coachmaker at Bolton Street, on 28 March 1798 by Luke Gardiner, and extended on 20 February 1804 by Charles Gardiner; the lease was extended yet again by Count Alfred D'Orsay and others in trust in the will of the earl of Blessington on 4 November 1833.[10]

Fig. 8.2—Drumcondra Bridge over the Tolka and turnpike (photo: Brian Matthews, with the kind permission of the NLI).

- Lease and release of two fields near Dorset Street to Richard Ennis, and subsequently to Charles Mallows, on 1 June 1757 by Charles Gardiner.[11] Lease for seven years of one field in Drumcondra Lane (Bolton Street) to William Marshall on 19 June 1756 by Charles Gardiner; also the renewal of a lease on the west side of Drumcondra Lane to Edward Croker on 7 April 1762 by Charles Gardiner.

These last two entries are interesting in that they confirm the topography in each location at the time, as well as the spread of landownership of the Gardiner estate. Land and leases continued to change hands outside the direct connection of the Gardiner estate, however, as can be seen below.

- Lease for nine years for a piece of ground in a new street to be laid out and called Moore Street on 13 August 1707, to Thomas Overend by Charles Campbell.

Ann Plumtre described Dublin in 1814–15 as 'beyond Sackville St is Rutland Sq and ascending further Mountjoy Sq. With a great number of new streets, like there is in the south nearby completed, others straggling and unfinished.'[12] As regards the northerly exit from the city (Fig. 8.2), she says that 'the road runs for a long way at the edge of the North Bull … of the two roads heading towards Howth the sea road is more interesting. The inland road through Raheny is not so.' She cautions that 'It is not advisable, however, to take this road at the flow of the tide since it is at the very edge

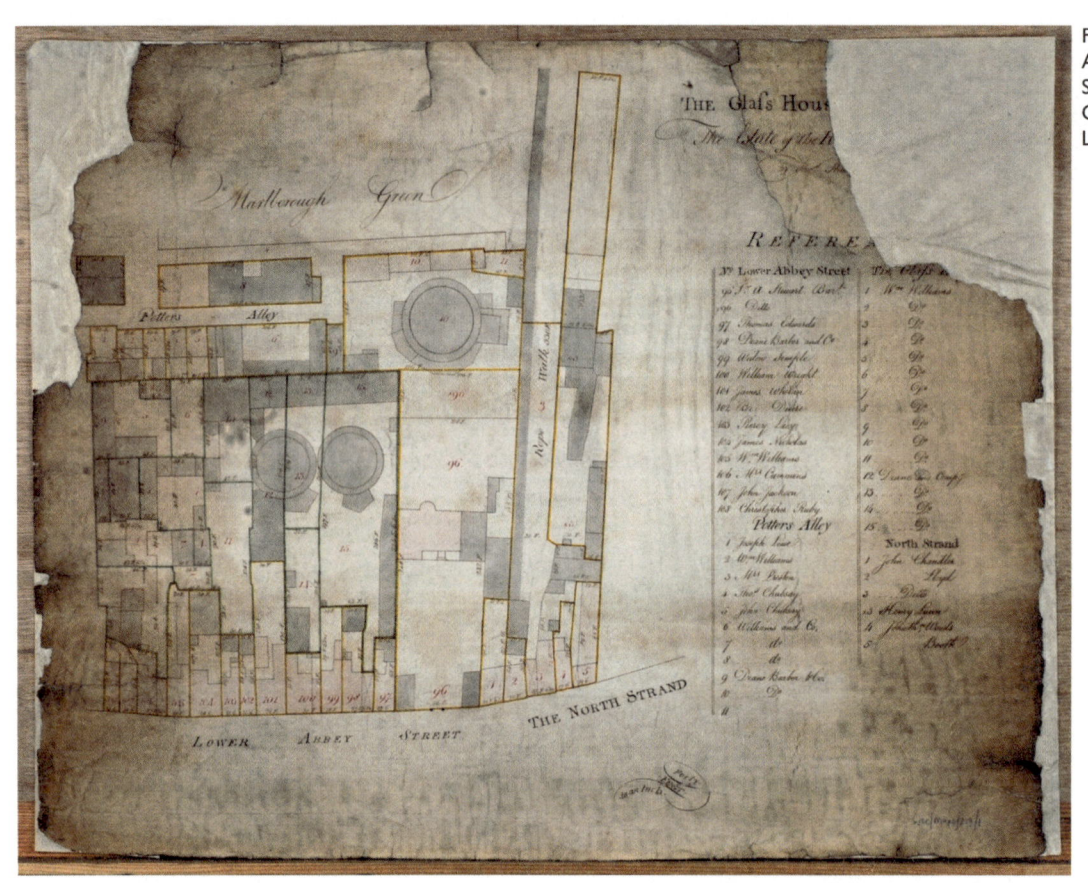

Fig. 8.3—Occupation in Abbey Street and North Strand (courtesy of Mary Clarke, Pearse Street Library).

of the water … with barely space for two carriages to pass …', whereas at low water 'there is ample space of sand for a legion of carriages'.[13] Ways to improve road construction were constantly sought. In the preface to his *Remarks on the present system of road making*, McAdam suggested that a foundation of crushed rocks of a uniform size coated with a binding agent to keep out water greatly improved construction.[14]

All the while much of the north side remained under cultivation, with numerous dairies and fields for tillage and livestock, supplying vegetables, poultry, eggs, pork and beef to the Dublin market. Up in the area of Dorset Street and Bolton Street existed one of the main entry roads into the city. This was the edge of the city, the outer perimeter on this side, and all carriers on the northern road were exempt from tolls on any cattle or goods whatsoever passing in or out of the Toll Houses in Dorset Street.

When Mirza Abu Taleb Khan visited Ireland, he described the streets as 'usually divided into three sections, both sides flagged for foot persons, middle paved with stones [cobblestones] for horses and carriages'. He wrote that 'Many of the best streets are entirely occupied by shops large glazed windows'[15] (Fig. 8.3).

- Lease for seven years to James McLoughlin, grocer, at Montgomery Street on 28 January 1836.[16]

Fig. 8.4—Cavendish Row, Rutland Square (elevation) (courtesy of Mary Clarke, Pearse Street Library).

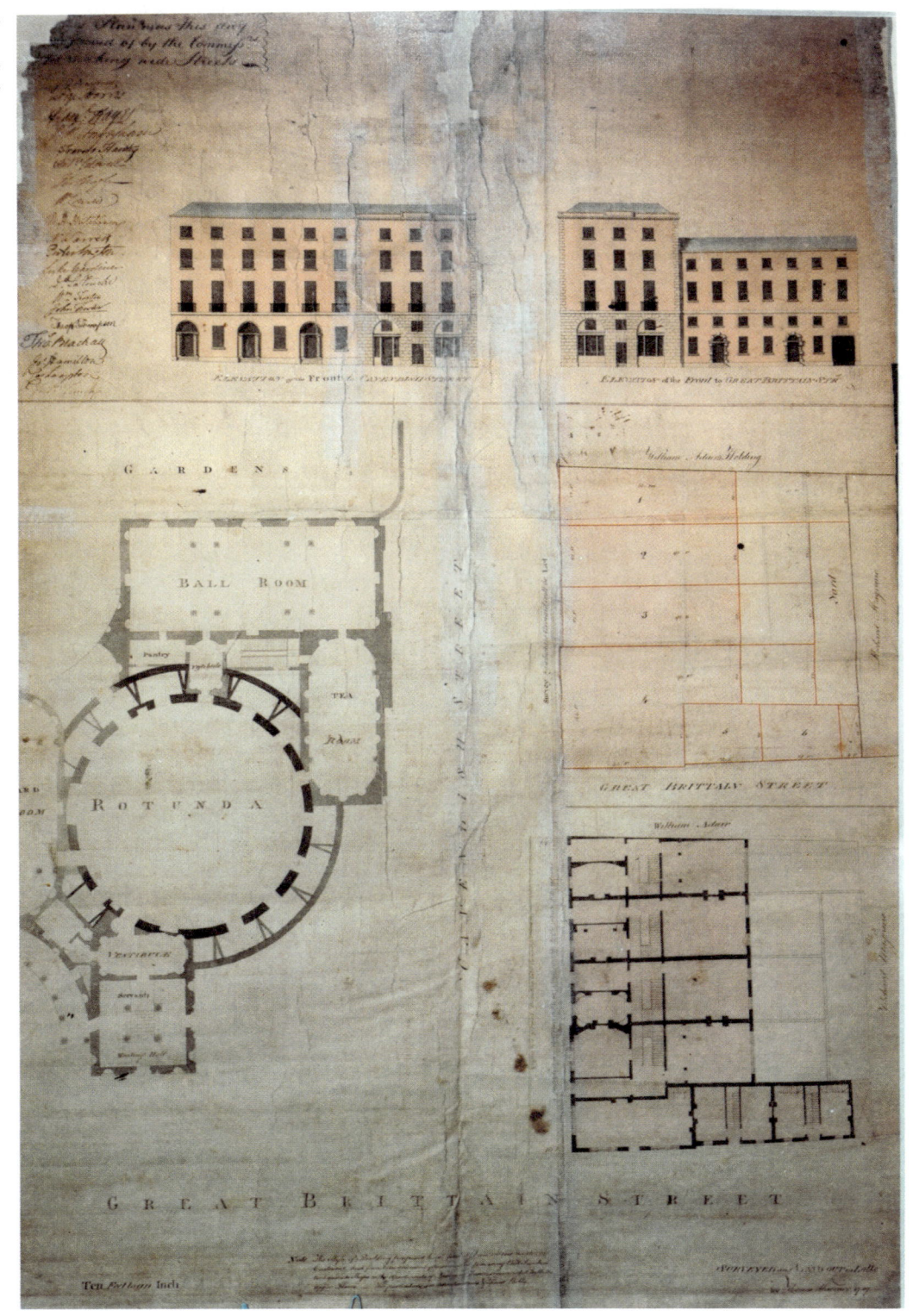

- Lease for seven years of 32 Montgomery Street, on 28 January 1836, to Patrick Wade of Montgomery Street, publican, by Robert Connor, one of the masters of the High Court of Chancery[17] (much as shown for Cavendish Row on Fig. 8.4).

The 1717 Bolton map of the North Lotts showed a minute eastward development; there is one building called the Red House and the Ship over at Fairview, one building called Hollybrook at today's Hollybrook Road, and just two buildings on the space adjoining Ballybough Bridge.[18] Among other names, including Luke Gardiner, the map lists Sir John Rogerson as the owner of two plots, as well as showing that the foreshore overrun by tide on the other side of the channel was titled Sir John Rogerson's Strand. The other valuable nugget of information to be taken from the map is the manner in which the Assembly thought and planned. In this case the amount of space stretching eastward beyond the Tolka is vast, but the Assembly were already planning to reroute the course of the river to suit the Corporation.

Meanwhile, north of the river, when the wall was complete it created an automatic boundary along the Liffey which invited the continuation of a similar retaining wall along the Tolka, as it, too, entered the myriad of channels created by the confluence of the three rivers in this area of Dublin. It could be said that while on the south side the Ringsend spit became absorbed by creeping land reclamation, something similar occurred on the north shore in relation to Clontarf Island.

Fig. 8.5—Summerhill turnpike (photo: Brian Matthews, with the kind permission of the NLI).

P.J. Stephenson advocated the use of Dublin directories and almanacs to closely examine street completion and building during the second half of the eighteenth century. Writing about Seán McDermott/Gloucester Street, he noted that it is not shown on the Rocque map of 1756 but appears in C.T. McCready's *Dublin street names* of 1776 as Gloucester Street.[19] In 1770 there was no evidence of any houses in Cumberland Street. Revd Thomas Paul of St Thomas's Parish in Marlborough Street gives his residence as Gloucester Street, having previously lived in Marlborough Street; allowing for the delay in printing, Stephenson estimates that the home was built in 1771/2, meaning that the 1770 almanac is accurate. In 1758 the first stone of St Thomas's Church was laid;[20] it opened in 1762. About 1729 a committee at St Michan's began to gather funds to build a good-sized church in Mary Street/Upper Liffey Street. This church has since disappeared.[21]

In 1802 the Royal Dublin Society asked Hely Dutton to report on all aspects of the city. There may have been some dissatisfaction with Lt Joseph Archer's report of the previous year. Dutton opened his report by comparing Speed's 1610 map of Dublin with Wilson's city map of 1798 and

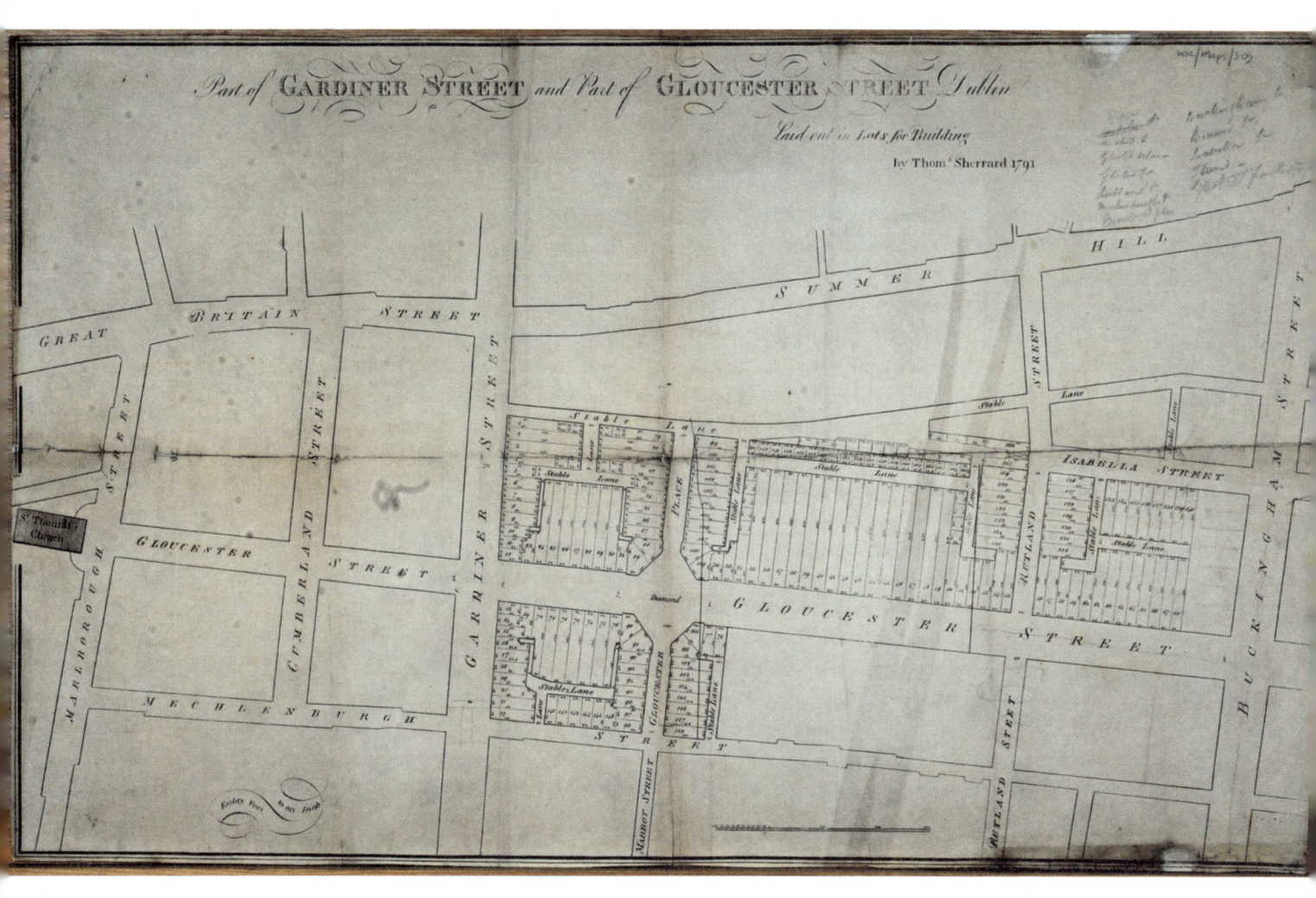

Fig. 8.6—Environs of Gloucester Street and Gardiner Street (courtesy of Mary Clarke, Pearse Street Library).

noted 'the great growth and increase in the city without the walls'. He wrote that 'Mary's Abbey was then the extent of that part of the town and northeast from thence now stands'. He supplied a list of streets now added to the city: 'Capel, Abbey, Mary, Stafford, Henry, Great Britain, Summerhill (Fig. 8.5), Marlborough, Henrietta, Bolton, Dominick, Paradise Row, Eccles, Rutland Sq, Great Denmark, North Great Georges, Mountjoy Sq, Gardiner Street, Beresford Place, as well as Cumberland, Gloucester, Meckleburg, Earl, Sackville, these with a great number of other streets and lanes out in that quarter'.[22]

Stephenson maintained that the completion of the Carlisle Bridge led to more house construction in Upper Gloucester Street shortly after, between Marlborough Street and Cumberland Street. Upper Gloucester Street ends at the Gardiner intersection. Lower Gloucester Street begins there and ends at the strand at Portland Row.[23] He is confirmed in his argument by the Wide Streets Commission maps of the area.

The east end of Seán McDermott Street is called Killarney Street. Both sides of Gloucester Street were built on in the Georgian era and the Diamond was laid out Fig. 8.6).[24] The surveyor Samuel Byron's 1789 plan of Dublin shows Buckingham Street joining the Strand to Summerhill.

Upper Gloucester Street had 45 houses in it; in Lower Gloucester Street there was a spurt of building and then a pause, which carried houses down to Gloucester Place. By the 1830s only 40 houses were occupied and the rest were vacant lots, which remained the position for the following 25 years. Killarney Street was all vacant but Buckingham Street had only one vacant site.

Stephenson showed that from early on Gloucester Street hosted an aristocratic element, such as the Hon. Richard Annesley, the marquis of Sligo, Viscount Headfort of Kells, George Molyneaux of Granard, Viscount Maxwell of Cavan, John Stewart MP and Hans Hamilton MP. After the Union in 1800 some of the above remained in the area and some new blood moved in, such as Viscount Strangford and Viscount Avonmore, who was an MP in the new Commons at London. A gradual change came about, however, in that merchants moved in, such as wine merchant James Tandy at No. 6 Lower. Several lawyers and barristers arrived too, as did medical practitioners such as Dr William Brooke. Thirty years later the landed and private gentry, as Stephenson called them, were still prolific in the street, with the Hon. Lady Claremorris and the Hon. Mrs Preston at No. 18 and No. 14 respectively, while Mrs Brabazon of Drogheda and Joseph Booth of Darver Castle were in Nos 35 and 33 Lower. George Darling, engineer to the Dunleary Harbour Commission, had his office at 19 Upper Gloucester Street. One of the teachers in the Finaiglian Seminary in Aldeborough House lived at No. 3, and another teacher of French and Italian, Mr de Pothonier, was at No. 33 Upper. At the eastern end of the street was a Classical and Mathematical Academy, a boys' preparatory school and a day school in the same block. Later, in 1846, the Presbyterian community opened a meeting-house at No. 62, near the junction with Buckingham Street. The street did not begin to decline until mid-century, when several houses were let as tenements and boarding houses, which eventually led to prostitution and the establishment of a substantial red-light district here. While at this stage there was no army contingent hereabouts, the port was only a few minutes' walk away.[25]

In 1779 Philip Lockome visited Ireland. In the introduction to his book he tells of two ways of getting to Dublin: one through Park Gate, some twelve miles from Chester, and the other via Holyhead—a shorter sea voyage but an extra 80–90 miles overland to Holyhead. He confirmed that the Queen Street Bridge was rebuilt in 1764 and that the Essex Bridge (Capel Street) was built eleven years earlier. He describes Lord Charlemont's house at Parnell Square (now the Hugh Lane Gallery): 'though it cannot be described a large house, nothing can be more elegant, nor any situation more delightful, it stands upon a little eminence, exactly fronting Mosse's Hospital [the Rotunda] is situated in Great Britain St near the north extremity of Dublin'. The hospital was, he records, the first charity of its kind in 'his majesty's dominions' and 'above 10,000 poor objects have been delivered here since within twenty years', it having been founded in 1745.[26]

A very specific building wave took place in this area in the last quarter of the eighteenth century, according to Jenny S. Price. She describes Dublin in the eighteenth century as having islands of activity in the general geography of the city; for example, the textile trades were concentrated in the Liberties area of today's Dublin 8, with the majority of those in work living and working in the same premises. She maintains that 100 years later the situation was different, with commuting becoming a fact of life and contributing to the creation of new urban areas, now called suburbs. She says that Dublin was in the process of changing from a pre-industrial to a modern city. This was especially true in the new space on the north side, because planning became a feature of what took place. Price maintains that the modern city is characterised by three things: commercial, industrial and residential zones. She argues that the commercial zone was the centre of the city, with its shops and retail businesses.[27] Because of its size and population, Dublin comprised a market itself—or critical mass, as marketers today would call it.[28] In a population density chart (fig. 1) she shows the north-east quadrant as having a density of 21–35 persons, but beyond that, out in the new zone towards Clontarf and Howth, less than 21 persons, which would indicate rural values. In fig. 2 she shows professional services as located north of the river in the Sackville Street area, and this would become more pronounced when the new Four Courts building was completed, as those concerned with the law courts shifted their emphasis to the north side. Commerce in general she shows south of the river, while what she calls 'Food and Drinks industries' are located in the western segment, influenced by the Guinness Brewery.

Henry Delmaine employed more than 40 families in his delft manufactory on the North Strand and the produce was sold in the Indian warehouse on Lower Abbey Street (the old strand road along the river) (*Dublin Journal*, 31 May 1755). Glass was made on the North Wall slip and also at the junction of Abbey Street and the North Lotts. This operation employed 150 people by 1794.[29] One glasshouse set up in 1754 was capable of producing eighteen gross of bottles per day (*Dublin Journal*, 18 June 1754).

The food produce coming in to feed this growing city each week amounted to:
- 2,268 barrels of wheat,
- 1,597 barrels of oats,
- 1,179 barrels of beer,
- 451 barrels of barley.[30]

There is no mention of corn, however, which was being grown on a huge scale, as witnessed by Isaac Butler and Arthur Young and by the members of the Royal Dublin Society, who sent a man to Scotland to view, examine and build a model of a working corn-threshing machine in the early part of the century. It is therefore reasonable to assume that corn, too, was coming into the city in large quantities.

Price wrote that the linen industry was concentrated around the newly built (1728) Linen Hall in the north-west of the city.[31] In essence she said that in the eighteenth century workplace and home were by and large the same premises for both the richest and the poorest. It would take the arrival of the railway to build greater momentum for a shift of the population out towards new suburbs.[32]

In his account of his tour of Ireland in 1752 Richard Pococke wrote of Carlingford and environs: 'This is properly the port of Newry from which the vessels go up four miles higher to Newry walls and unload into gabbots [gabbards or lighters]; they say 400 vessels commonly come into this harbour every year; this and the oyster fishery for Dublin is the chief support for the town and a great number of boats are constantly carrying limestone from the quarries on each side of the mouth of the harbour to Newry, to be burnt for the buildings'.[33]

Michael Williams, writing in 1970, infers that the picture of the evolution of the rural landscape is not fully presented if land reclamation and waste enclosure are not taken into account. This is of interest because the area we are examining became agricultural first before it was converted to industrial, residential and institutional uses. He goes on: 'For those who are interested in the evolution of the landscape of the country, this place of colonisation which brought about new patterns of fields, farms, roads is of vital importance because of the new intensity and the extent of the change. It is also a period in which a new landscape was deliberately created, contrasting markedly with the slow, piecemeal, even haphazard alternative of previous centuries'[34].

Ann Plumtre in 1814 wrote that 'both to the north and south such vast additions have of later

Fig. 8.7—House at Blessington Street Basin supplied for the water superintendent (photo: Brian Matthews).

years been made to the city, that they may almost be labelled new towns'.[35]

Williams added: 'This applies in the sense that green countryside ran right to the sea boundary and the walls create new areas which use the space for agricultural purposes'.[36] But a by-product of change of use is that commerce enters the picture in the form of property-dealing, as seen in the extensive growth in that field of activity (Fig. 8.8).

It is clear that as people arrived in Dublin for all the usual reasons—famine, bad harvest, hope of opportunity or a lack thereof, or having been demobbed by the navy or army—throughout the

Fig. 8.8—Buildings to be let, showing active commerce in property in April 1826 (WSC 323) (courtesy of Mary Clarke, Pearse Street Library).

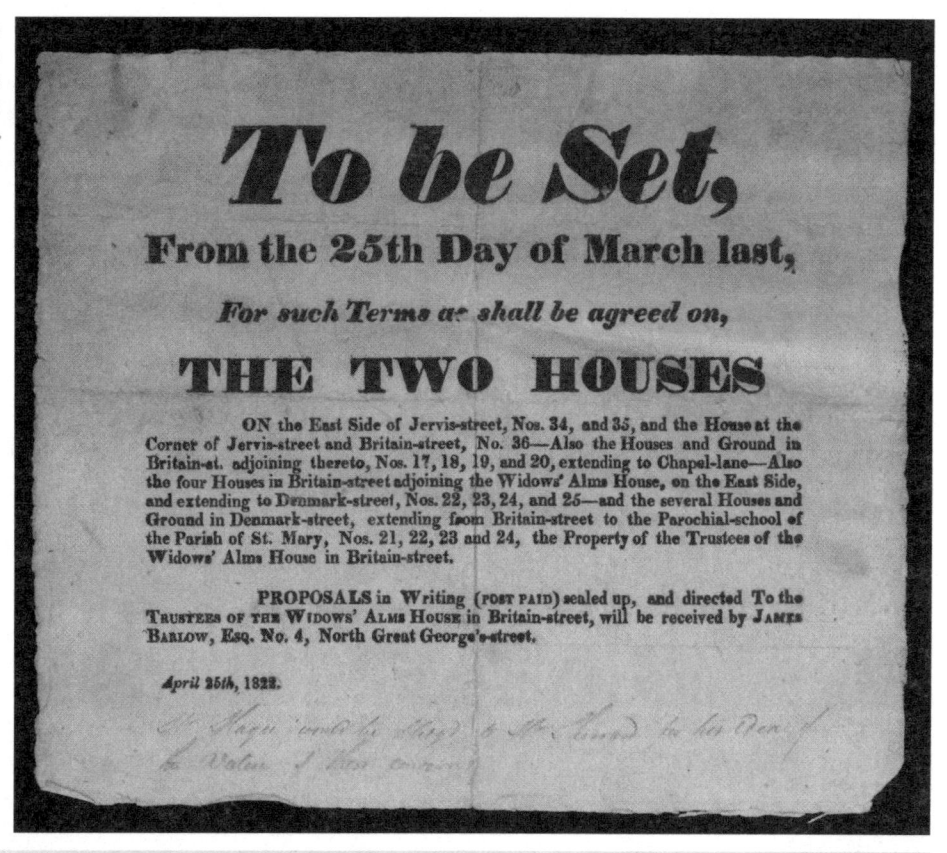

To be Set,

From the 25th Day of March last,

For such Terms as shall be agreed on,

THE TWO HOUSES

ON the East Side of Jervis-street, Nos. 34, and 35, and the House at the Corner of Jervis-street and Britain-street, No. 36—Also the Houses and Ground in Britain-st. adjoining thereto, Nos. 17, 18, 19, and 20, extending to Chapel-lane—Also the four Houses in Britain-street adjoining the Widows' Alms House, on the East Side, and extending to Denmark-street, Nos. 22, 23, 24, and 25—and the several Houses and Ground in Denmark-street, extending from Britain-street to the Parochial-school of the Parish of St. Mary, Nos. 21, 22, 23 and 24, the Property of the Trustees of the Widows' Alms House in Britain-street.

PROPOSALS in Writing (POST PAID) sealed up, and directed To the TRUSTEES OF THE WIDOWS' ALMS HOUSE in Britain-street, will be received by JAMES BARLOW, ESQ. No. 4, North Great George's-street.

April 25th, 1828.

Fig. 8.9—Charlemont House, Marino, the country seat of Lord Charlemont (courtesy of the NLI).

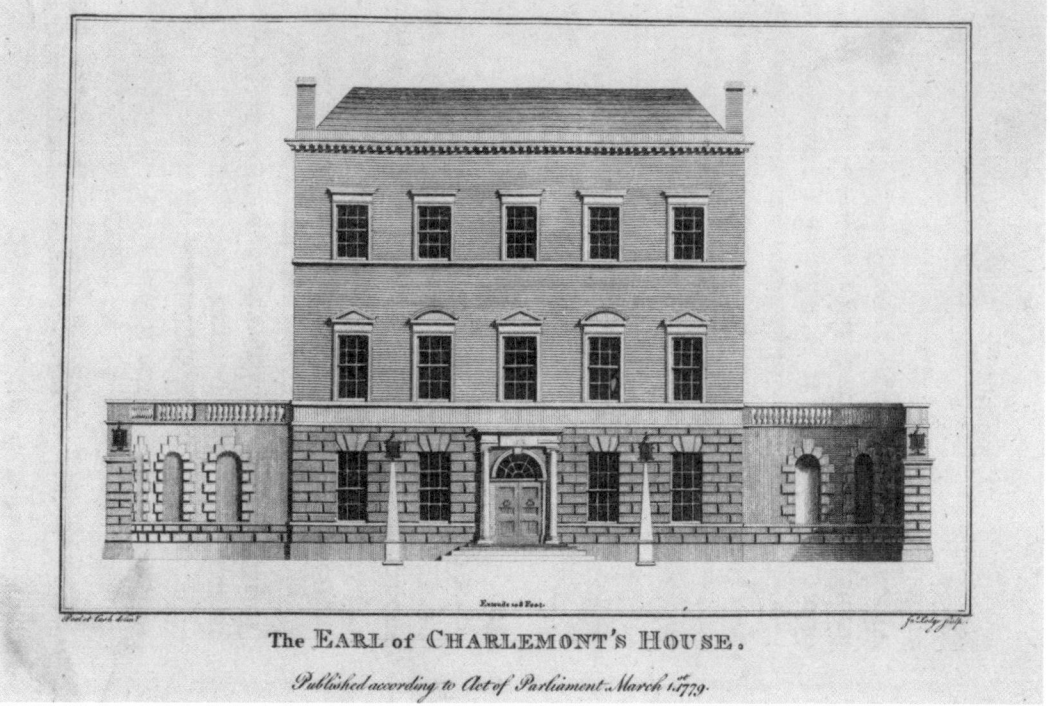

The EARL of CHARLEMONT'S HOUSE.
Published according to Act of Parliament March 1st 1779.

Dublin moving east, 1708–1844

Fig. 8.10—Clontarf Crescent on Howth Road, at the junction of the Malahide Road and the sea road at Clontarf and the inland Howth Road to Killester, Raheny and Sutton (photo: Brian Matthews, with the kind permission of the NLI).

Fig. 8.11—Clontarf Castle, rebuilt in 1835 (courtesy of the NLI).

eighteenth century, more accommodation, food, clothing, transport and work were needed. A certain number of the newcomers succeeded in getting work as labourers on the many building projects taking place in the city. A good number, too, found employment in the houses being built for the wealthier segments of society (Figs 8.9 and 8.10). By the last quarter of the century a whole series of major constructions had been completed along the inner perimeter of the walls of 1728, and these we will now examine. These, too, created more opportunity for people, and some required new skills and a wider range of job descriptions.

While Dublin grew outwards and expanded, the very people who could afford to erect townhouses in the city near which they had their country seats found that, thanks to expansion, better roads and bridges, and carriages with springs, the gap had greatly closed, turning the suburbs into a reality. Hence Vernon saw fit to rebuild Clontarf Castle (Fig. 8.11) and take advantage of the new roads out to Clontarf.

Notes

[1] John H. Martin, 'Aspects of the social geography of Dublin city in the mid-nineteenth century', unpublished MA thesis, University College Dublin (1973), p. 14.
[2] David Dickson, *Dublin: the making of a capital city* (London, 2014), p. 141.
[3] N. Burke, 'Dublin 1600–1800: a study in morphogenesis', unpublished Ph.D thesis, Trinity College Dublin (1972), p. 220.
[4] *Ibid.*, p. 293.
[5] J.W. De Courcey, *The Liffey in Dublin* (Dublin, 1996), p. 268.
[6] Seamus Scully, 'Ghosts of Moore Street', *Dublin Historical Record* **25** (2) (1972), 54–63, p. 56.
[7] Finnian Ó Cionnaith, *Exercise of authority: surveyor Thomas Owen and the paving, cleansing and lighting of Georgian Dublin* (Dublin, 2016), p. 109.
[8] *Ibid.*, p. 116.
[9] R. Pool and J. Cash, *Views of Dublin* (Dublin, 1780), p. 27.
[10] NLI, Gardiner Papers, 36,516/18.
[11] *Ibid.*, 36,524/3.
[12] Ann Plumtre, *Narrative of a residence in Ireland during the summer of 1814 and that of 1815* (London, 1817), p. 54.
[13] *Ibid.*, p. 76.
[14] John Loudon McAdam, *Remarks on the present system of road making* (London, 1823), p. 116.
[15] *The travels of Mirza Abu Taleb Khan in Asia and Europe during the years 1799, 1800, 1801, 1802 and 1803 written by himself in the Persian language and translated by Charles Stewart* (2 vols) (London, 1810), p. 116.
[16] NLI, Gardiner Papers, 36,535/14.
[17] *Ibid.*, 36,553/1.
[18] Rt Hon. Robert Bolton, map titled *Strand on north side of channel of river Anna Liffie as it was oriented and set out in Easter Assembly 1717 by Rt Hon Robert Bolton Lord Mayor of the city of Dublin, William Empson and David King esqs Sherrifs of the said city and the deeds and this map perfected in the mayoralty of the Rt Hon Anthony Berkey Esq Lord Mayor, John Rayson and Vincent Kidder Esqs Sherrifs.* (Original map on pre-auction show in the Gresham Hotel, 12 December 2016, by Fonsie Mealy, Fine Art Auctioneer, as Lot No. 460.)
[19] P.J. Stephenson, 'Seán McDermott Street', *Dublin Historical Record* **10** (3) (1948), 83–8, p. 85.
[20] *Ibid.*, p. 86.
[21] *Ibid.*
[22] Hely Dutton, *Observations on Mr Archer's statistical survey of the county of Dublin* (Dublin, 1802), pp 109–10.
[23] Stephenson, 'Seán McDermott Street', p. 87.
[24] *Ibid.*, p. 88.
[25] *Ibid.*
[26] Philip Lockome, *A tour through Ireland wherein the present state of that kingdom is considered* (Dublin, 1780), p. 36.
[27] Jenny S. Price, 'Dublin 1750–1850: spatial distribution and organisation of economic activity', unpublished MSc. thesis, Trinity College Dublin (1997), p. 11.

28 *Ibid.*, p. 3.
29 *Ibid.*, p. 56.
30 House of Commons Journal, vol. XI (1759–60), p. 815.
31 Price, 'Dublin 1750–1850', p. 41.
32 *Ibid.*, p. 102.
33 G.T. Stokes (ed.), *Richard Pococke's Tour in Ireland in 1752* (Dublin, 1891), p. 7.
34 Michael Williams, 'The enclosure and reclamation of waste land in England and Wales in the 18th and 19th centuries', *Transactions of the Institute of British Geographers* **51** (1970), 55–69, p. 56.
35 Plumtre, *Narrative of a residence in Ireland*, p. 50.
36 Williams, 'The enclosure and reclamation of waste land', p. 56.

9. Clustering structures along the north side of the Liffey

The purpose of this chapter is to illustrate how Dublin in the late eighteenth century became hemmed in by a new boundary consisting of a chain of building complexes constructed down along and inside the recent perimeter of the new Liffey walls on the north side of the river. These structures became individual focal points for development. In the early eighteenth century, after the consolidation of the new walls, development began to creep up along Capel Street and Bolton Street, opening and solidifying the northern route out of the city. It also crept east along Parnell Street and Henry Street towards Sackville Street or the Mall, as it would be known at first. By the middle of the century occupation was spreading outwards more slowly. We are concerned here with how and why these complexes were erected, and their effect on the immediate area and on the greater surrounding area. We will also note how each structure created its own economic and social cluster of activity in the immediate vicinity, as well as attracting other activities from outside that zone.

One example is the Four Courts, created as a complex in the last fifteen years of the eighteenth century at a time of awakening civic pride and city improvement via the work of the Wide Streets Commission, which became a growth area for work connected with practice of the law. People involved in this profession settled in the surrounding area, and the locating of the prisons close by also drew occupation in. As the activity around the Four Courts grew, it had a direct and immediate influence on the creation of the King's Inns up the hill behind the courts complex, which in turn reinforced the legal associations of the area which persist today. Each structure created an individual island of development while adding to the sum of the parts of each of the others.

The construction of these major buildings along the new edge of the city created a second perimeter inside the wall, which had been completed by 1728 as far out as the bridge at Ballybough. The building of the wall on the north side allowed the drying out of the grounds within; this was followed by an outward spread of occupation up Capel Street into Mary Street, Liffey Street, Parnell Street, over to Moore Street and into Sackville Street. There was certainly room for the buildings to be erected and to create their own micro-economy and social structure, but the sum of the buildings created greater momentum for urbanisation than each individual structure.

Looking downriver, there came into being, all in the last fifteen to twenty years before 1800, the Four Courts, Carlisle Bridge and the opening up of Sackville Street, the Custom House, Annesley Bridge and Aldeborough House. Inside this new perimeter, running all the way to Ballybough Bridge, was the Royal Canal, which acted as another magnet for occupation and also created a new internal boundary within the 1728 enclosure. It has to be noted that it wasn't just a case of digging the canal across mostly tidal space; it also involved the construction of four stone bridges across the canal, each then contributing to new road connections in the area. These would have the same effect as an anchor tenant in a shopping mall today. The construction of the North Circular Road inside the new perimeter of the canal created another inner boundary within the new enclosure. Dillon

Cosgrove dated the North Circular Road from 1768.[1] At that stage it ended at the top of Portland Row, where Aldeborough House was built on the edge of the strand. The erection of Tyrone House in Marlborough Street must be included in our examination, as it had already added to the cluster effect in the northern Georgian quarter of the 1750s at Marlborough Street. Tyrone House was built just above the water-line of the bay and river, along the edge of the Parnell Street development as it filled in to the north and east. The location here of a large private house with an influential owner was virtually guaranteed to attract further private dwellings in this quarter. It was not long before St Thomas's Church of Ireland church was built only 150m away. Another large structure that had an impact on all the citizenry of the north bank was the Rotunda Lying-in Hospital, also finished by the mid-1700s. All these structures created a strong momentum for occupation along the north bank of the river.

It might be fair to ask what, if anything, was going to happen once the Liffey became one single channel. The answer was always going to be that the ground would be saved and built on, because this was the original plan in 1717 with the letting of the North Lotts. It should be noted that the actual walling on the north side began in 1711, and so, armed with these beginnings, the Assembly were most certainly planning on an enormous expansion of the city. During the second quarter of the eighteenth century the spread outwards continued to Sackville Street and beyond. During the third and fourth quarters, occupation of the area originally enclosed continued apace northward and eastward, as we will demonstrate. It will also become apparent that these structures had a knock-on effect, as we saw in the case of the Grand Canal Docks or the Kingstown Railway south of the river. The work of the Wide Streets Commission, starting in mid-century, would also add greatly to the momentum in terms of civic pride and development.

The Four Courts

While the Four Courts building might appear to be on the edge of our brief, it is very much connected to what was happening in Dublin at the time, being one of the major projects under way in the last segment of the eighteenth century, a direct result of the work of the Ballast Board in their walling of the river into a single channel. The city then was literally a giant building site, with so many projects under construction. The Four Courts were sited on land from Chancery Lane to Church Street on old Cistercian property, once part of St Mary's Abbey. These major projects certainly moved the emphasis onto this mainly made ground on the north side of Dublin and had a major impact on life and work around the city.

In 1695 William Robinson, surveyor general, was directed to rebuild the courts, which were on the south side up near Christchurch Cathedral, and completed the task at a cost of £3,421 7s. 8d. The courts were rebuilt again in 1755 but became dilapidated, and Luke Gardiner was asked to arrange the design and construction of new courts, this time across the river, where there was room to build.[2] The foundations were laid in May 1786 by the duke of Rutland and the chief justices. James Gandon was already in the city, having arrived in Dublin in 1781 to oversee the work on the Custom House.[3]

The new site on the north bank also provided an opportunity to create some sort of repository for State and civic documents. Thomas Cooley, because of his work on the Royal Exchange, was asked to design such a structure. This design eventually became absorbed into the Four Courts design by Gandon after Cooley's death in 1784.[4] McParland maintained that as early as the 1750s there were some small private dwellings as well as some derelict buildings occupying the site.[5] When

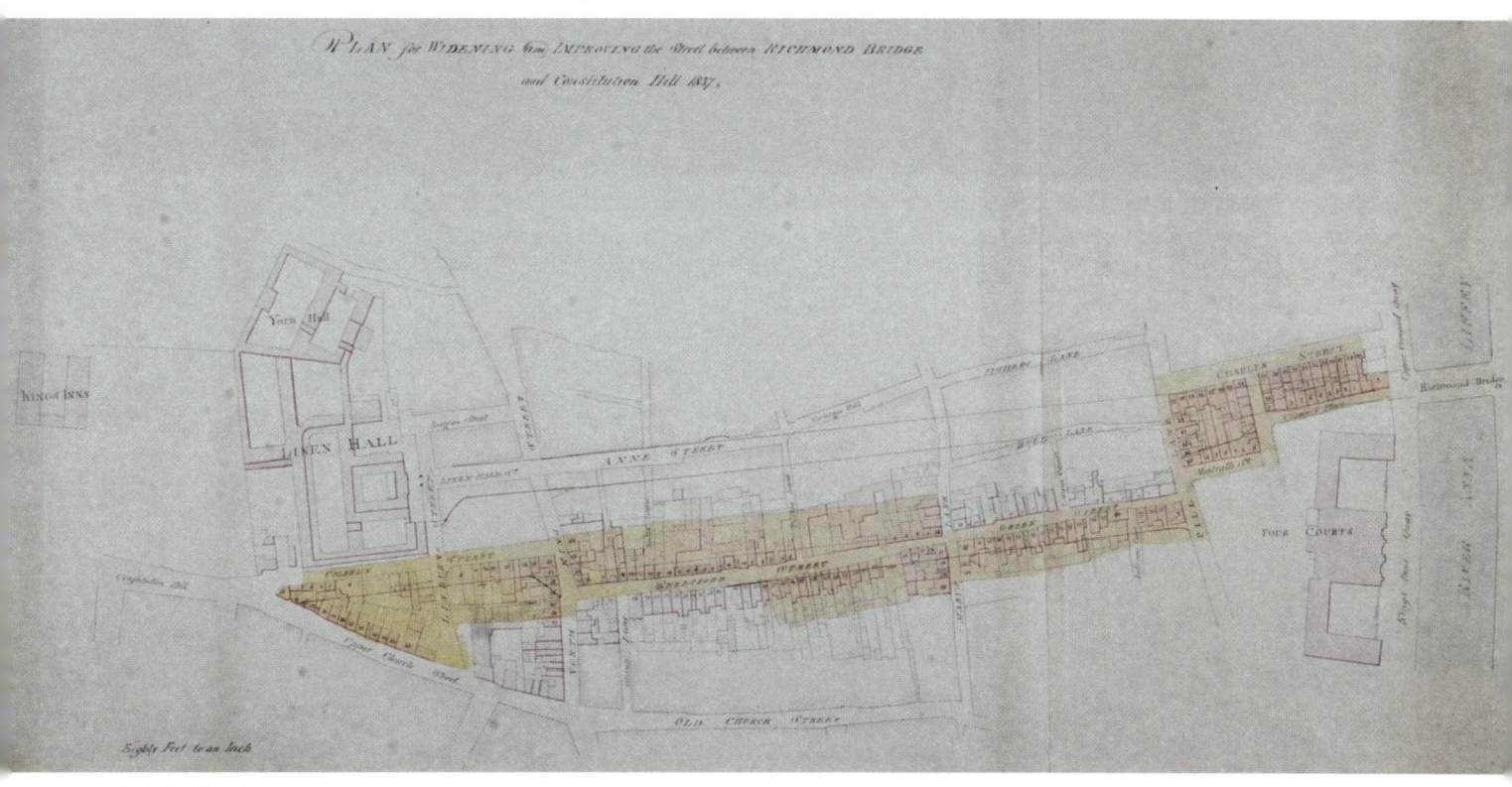

Fig. 9.1—Plan of streets spreading north from the Four Courts (Wide Streets Commission map, courtesy of Louise Morgan and Brendan Maher, NGI).

Gandon took control he had to clear the area before beginning on the foundations.

As work progressed, costs were met by grants of £3,000 each year, later increased to £6,000. The duke of Rutland, a great promoter of the project, died in 1787. Following many petty problems and interferences, the grants were upped to a single allocation of £30,000, of which £10,000 was to be expended annually to keep momentum going. Later, in 1793, another grant of £6,000 was made.[6] By 1794 the great dome was visible across the city skyline and immediately became the new identifying landmark of the city. The courts were sufficiently ready for use to allow the first term to begin on 8 November 1796; the wings and façade were finished in 1802.[7] The entire footprint of the structure stretched for 450ft along the river front and was 170ft deep.[8] The Four Courts took fourteen years to complete, at a cost of £200,000[9] (Fig. 9.1).

The Four Courts brought a new focus to this area to bolster what already existed, slightly east of the complex, around the main access to the city via Capel Street. It was already a vibrant quarter, with two theatres in Capel Street at the time. Merchants, shipping agents, brokers, coach-builders and ostlers were all located nearby. The momentum for more housing and educational facilities was seen in the growth of small schools, and it should be noted that it was here in North Richmond Street that the Christian Brothers set up school in the 1830s. Life was vibrant in the environs, as seen in the advertisements for Lee Love's nine-night run at the Theatre in Capel Street, beginning on 6 February 1796, and for Mr Bannister's series of performances at the Theatre Royal, also in Capel Street. On 31 May the same year Miss Hegarty and her sisters announced that they had room for a few more pupils at their French and English boarding-school in Prussia Street.[10]

Maire Kennedy wrote that just as the hub of streets and alleyways near the old Custom House on the north side filled up, as seen in the many coffee-houses which appeared in the area, the same thing happened in the hub around the Four Courts, serving lawyers and judges, as well as laymen when the new Custom House began to operate from its new location.[11] This was also the route taken by the better-off citizens of Dublin on their way to the Phoenix Park and its new Zoological Gardens, as an alternative to the North Circular Road. Thanks to general activity, the markets in the area experienced a resurgence and were formalised by the early nineteenth century. So the conclusion can be safely drawn that the Four Courts complex had an impact on the area, helping to build it up and increase its size.

One way of looking at the impact of the Four Courts is to view the number of those involved in the practice of law who now lived in the area. The almanacs over a couple of decades quite clearly show that the list grew to 30 attorneys who gave their address as Capel Street, close to the complex. Several others resided on Ormond Quay and Bolton Street, again close by. The courts also hosted many servants and employees, such as F. O'Dwyer, sixth clerk, who lived on Inn's Quay.[12] Bankers, too, moved into the area, such as John Finlay at Ormond Quay; of course, the Bank of Ireland had set up at Mary's Abbey in 1783, before the courts were completed.[13] S. Chapman, cashier to the bank of Sir William Alexander & Co., also lived at Capel Street. By 1820 the area hosted a wide variety of occupations, such as B. Eaton, carpenter, at Blackhall Place, George Holmes, shoemaker, at Capel Street, John Franklin, cutler, at Lower Ormond Quay, T. Bell, starch manufacturer, at 8 St Mary's Abbey, and R. Wright, felt-maker, at Ormond Quay.[14] Capel Street also contained Mr Acheson, apothecary, at No. 142, R. Allen, clock- and watchmaker, at No. 40, Archer and Burnside, booksellers and stationers, at No. 18, and Henry Bingham and son, ironmongers, at No. 144 (Henry Bingham Jr also ran a hosiery at No. 145), while umbrella-maker George Boles worked and lived at No. 30.[15] There was another umbrella-maker at 4 North King Street. John Browne, Lottery Office-keeper and stockbroker, was at 5 Capel Street, and John Burke, goldsmith and jeweller, was at No. 141.[16] Further up Capel Street into Bolton Street lived John Chartre, wax bleacher and manufacturer of wax and spermaceti candles; he used whale oil, which had to be imported, to supplement the tallow for his candles.[17]

The Four Courts consumed vast quantities of paper, which had to be made and supplied, along with ink and quills. The courts gave employment to clerks and secretaries in great numbers, and tipstaffs for each judge. One effect of the new courts was that members of the legal profession would spread out in their abodes across the newer streets of North Strand, Summerhill and the grid of streets between. The 1820 almanac lists 25 solicitors as living in Capel Street.[18] Paula Lynch wrote that Samuel Ferguson, antiquary, poet, Gaelic student and lawyer, lived at 20 North Great George's Street in 1834. In fact, 21 of the 50 houses in the street were occupied by members of the legal profession.[19] Of note is the fact that Sir Isaac Butt, lawyer, lecturer and writer on economic matters, especially those of Ireland, lived for some time at No. 41 in the same street. Lynch says that groups of lawyers also had apartments in No. 42, one such group being the Goddard Brothers.[20] The other main result of the building of the Four Courts was that it led directly to the construction of the King's Inns just up the hill over the following decade, thereby solidifying the legal character of the area (Fig. 9.2).

In the early 1790s a grand jury found that prostitutes in Newgate Prison at North King Street had easy access to male prisoners, while at the debtors' prison, the Four Courts Marshalsea, the governor was found to have boosted his income by renting space to pimps who kept their prostitutes in the jail. While brothels operated all over the city, at least one existed in Capel Street at the same time.[21] James

Fig. 9.2—The Four Courts, the legal quarter and its environs (Wide Streets Commission map, courtesy of Mary Clarke, Pearse Street Library).

Murphy maintained that debtors' prisons, county jails for persons awaiting trial and houses of correction or industry attempted to instil habits of industry in the poor[22] (Figs 9.3 and 9.4).

Marshalsea prisons were used to incarcerate debtors, and the one that operated near the Four Courts during the 1790s was a place of such corruption that it was unhealthy for the transaction of court or legal business. Disease—particularly jail fever, a strain of typhus spread by people coming

DUBLIN MOVING EAST, 1708–1844

Fig. 9.3—Four Courts painted by William Sadler the Younger (1782–1839), showing large crowds around the building (courtesy of Louise Morgan and Brendan Maher, NGI).

and going in the prison—was rife, and court officers were afraid when attempting to serve documents. Newgate prison, on the south bank, was also within the sphere of the courts, indicating the level of human activity down here not long after the Four Courts opened.[23] Even the new penitentiary that opened on three and a half acres at Grangegorman in 1820 was within walking distance of the Four Courts.[24] Given the substantial scale of corruption and prostitution in the area, it is no surprise that pickpockets were a problem in Capel Street—a sure sign of the presence of money.[25] The *Dublin Penny Journal* in 1832 described the environs of the Four Courts: 'during Term time it is crowded with lawyers and pickpockets, strangers and stragglers, the fleeced and the fleecing, the hopeful and the hoping, the anxious and the careless', and warned that, at such a period of bustle, a visitor 'should look to his pockets'[26] (Fig. 9.5).

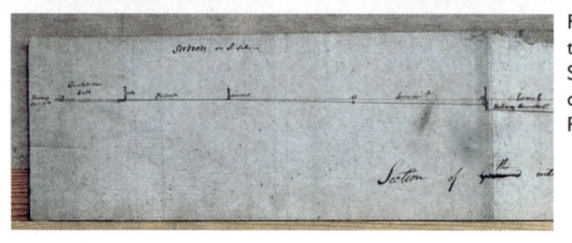

Fig. 9.4—Constitution Hill to King's Inns (Wide Streets Commission map, courtesy of Mary Clarke, Pearse Street Library).

Fig. 9.5—Ground laid out from Constitution Hill down to the river under the supervision of the Corporation for Preserving and Improving the Port of Dublin (Wide Streets Commission map).

156

Fig. 9.6a—Sketch of the Linen Hall in the nineteenth century (courtesy of Louise Morgan and Brendan Maher, NGI).

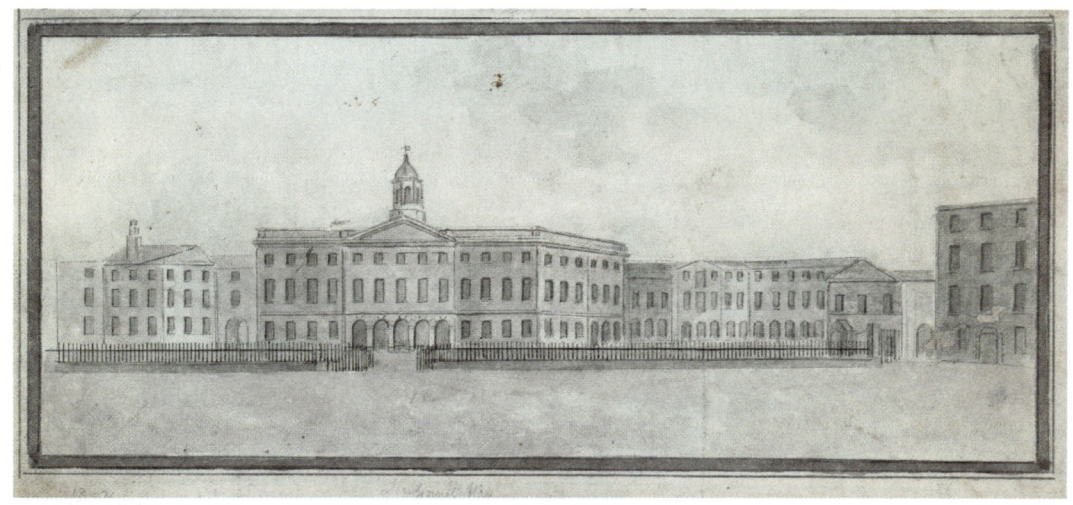

Fig. 9.6b—Linen Hall Arch as it now is in Bolton Street (photo: Brian Matthews).

Meanwhile, the Corporation for Preserving and Improving the Port of Dublin continued its activities in close proximity to the Four Courts through its responsibility for the river and walls, as this involved constant upgrading of the walls and balustrades.

The above clearly shows that all sorts of businesses, trades and professions moved into the area, encouraged by the advent of the large complex of the Four Courts and the substantial bureaucracy in its orbit (Fig. 9.6a&b). It is also a good time to remind ourselves that this was the era of living over the shop or business. The figure of 1,000 lawyers in 1760 had by 1800 become 1,500, according to O'Grada, who also noted that Sackville Street housed 'a notable sprinkling of lawyers no doubt attracted by the proximity of the Four Courts'.[27] This meant that while the political element of the city was now at College Green (until it moved to London after 1800), the legal was now firmly established on the opposite bank.

Carlisle Bridge and Sackville Street

Capel Street Bridge, completed in 1676, was named after Arthur Capel, earl of Essex, lord lieutenant from 1672 to 1677. It resisted the Liffey flash-floods for the next 80 years but suffered attrition. It was rebuilt in 1755, at a cost of £20,000, as a humpbacked five-arched bridge, as seen in Malton's drawings, confirming the plans of George Semple. Parliament Street would be the first work undertaken in the city by the Wide Streets Commission, which was funded by the imposition of a 1s. duty on every ton of imported coal. In 1674 a syndicate that included Sir Humphry Jervis paid £3,000 for twenty acres of the land of the former St Mary's Abbey for the purpose of building a grid of streets in the area of today's Jervis Street. This was the true beginning of Dublin's modern north side. It was Jervis who built the bridge and the quay alongside, at the suggestion of the viceroy, James Butler, duke of Ormonde, after whom the quay was named. Jervis then built Capel Street, which became a major artery for northbound traffic. At this time the top of Capel Street was rural countryside. Patrick O'Kelly said that 'nearly all bridges down to modern times were erected and sponsored by some promoter of the common good, who took upon himself the promotion and fulfilment of such works of public utility'.[28]

George Semple, designer and builder of the Capel Street Bridge, was a pioneer in building, especially in water. His *Treatise on building in water* (1776) was a blueprint for mastering many quandaries in relation to construction in water, providing detailed instructions and technical back-up. When rebuilding the Essex Bridge at Capel Street he literally wrote the book on bridge construction. He undertook test borings down into the riverbed, hitting rock at a depth of 23ft 3in. Above that rock he showed three layers or strata of different material, all corresponding with the findings produced centuries later by the Irish Geological Survey. Below the bed of the river, which was at a depth of 11ft 9in., there was 3ft 5in. of 'pretty close gravel'. Under that was 3ft 6in. of 'softer and finer gravel', and below that again 4ft 7in. of 'rather closer gravel'.[29] An interesting piece of information discovered when digging out the foundations of the previous Essex Bridge was that 'the middle of it was an actual petrification of about a foot thick, but not so hard in the bottom as in the top'.[30] This was important because of the construction of the Liffey walls and the Great South Wall and so a certain amount of petrification or solidifying of the gravels and foundations could be expected to occur. This knowledge and expertise was most useful when construction took place (Figs 9.7 and 9.8).

Later in the eighteenth century, as the city grew both in population and in terms of horse traffic and carriages, those in authority did not enjoy the extra time and effort required to get to and from parliament or the castle or Trinity College, Capel Street Bridge being then a bottleneck for all

Fig. 9.7—Eighteenth-century ink drawing of Carlisle Bridge immediately after construction. In the background are the five arches of Essex Bridge at Capel Street (courtesy of Louise Morgan and Brendan Maher, NGI).

Fig. 9.8—View from College Green and the Parliament building via Westmorland Street towards Carlisle Bridge, with Sackville Street in the distance (photo: Brian Matthews, with the kind permission of the NLI).

movement of people and wheeled traffic. Demand began to build for another bridge in a more easterly location. By that stage all the space between where it would be sited and Capel Street Bridge had been filled in. Houses, shops, factories, stores, yards, stables, abattoirs, markets and even the odd school and hotel had moved in to occupy the space which had been under the tides and along the water's edge. Indeed, development had moved even further east along the North Strand, out along Summerhill and in between along Gloucester Street. Great Denmark Street, Great George's Street and Henrietta Street, as well as Sackville Street, were built on and occupied.

One of the early promoters of a new and more easterly bridge was Luke Gardiner.[31] There is no doubt that he was enormously influential, which is just as well, because the project required such endorsement. He stood to benefit to an unheard-of extent if the bridge came about, as it would help to further develop the area of which he was a major landowner, raising the value of lands and property. In essence, if the city grew, so would his income (Fig. 9.9).

In 1761 a sixteen-page pamphlet was published under the title *Reasons for a new bridge in reply to an attack*, and *Falkiner's Journal* promoted the idea that since both Trinity College and the parliament were outside the city a new bridge should be built to facilitate access to and from both. The Wide Streets Commission was granted approval to build in 1782 and in 1791 the first stone was laid by John Beresford. Construction of the bridge involved the use of concrete and coffer dams; the balustrade was of metal and can be seen today in Drumcondra outside Clonturk House, with the foundry stamp of Clarke of Ringsend visible.[32] The bridge opened in 1794 and was named after Frederick Howard, earl of Carlisle, lord lieutenant from 1780 to 1782. Cromwell puts its cost at £3,000.[33] It was an enormous success, as seen in the sheer volume of traffic it carried. The main

Fig. 9.9—Early nineteenth-century view of Carlisle Bridge from the south-west by William Sadler (photo: Brian Matthews, with the kind permission of James Gorry, Gorry Gallery).

Fig. 9.10—Balustrade from Carlisle Bridge relocated to Drumcondra (Clonturk House) (photo: Brian Matthews).

carriageway was only 40ft wide, however, and the structure would only be fit for purpose for a limited period (Fig. 9.10).

The bridge changed utterly the work and social patterns of activity, making all parts of the city much more accessible in both directions. It created a new and direct access to Trinity College—a very important city and national institution at the time, where most of the élite had some connection, located just opposite parliament—on the south side and the port area downriver, and to the new residential squares and ancillary streets around today's Dublin 2. One of its unseen benefits was the ease with which the military were able to get around the city during the run-up to and the actual 1798 rebellion. That so many of the citizens of Dublin used the bridge with immediate effect is seen in the fact that the authorities used it as a place of public execution after the rebellion as a warning to all. Dr John Esmonde of Sallins, father of Jesuit priest Bartholomew Esmonde,[34] was one of those hanged there.

The increased volume of commercial and general traffic soon made it obvious that the bridge would have to be enlarged, as it was too narrow and humpbacked like the Capel Street/Essex Bridge.[35] *Falkiner's Journal* then argued against doing so, asking 'Why all this outcry about a bridge?' and 'Will the building of this bridge be really a prejudice to the public or will it not?'. The author expands the argument and finally homes in on the crux of the matter: 'If, on the other hand, the public emolument is to be the consequence, it is the established maxim in all societies that public good is to supersede private benefit'. He says that Dublin, having grown in attractiveness and opulence, 'has from some particular circumstances extended itself to the eastward in an extraordinary manner'[36] and gives a very clear picture of the circumstances of the city at the time: 'Thus has this city extended itself eastward on the south side of the river, while the rising ground and healthful soil on the north naturally led gentlemen of property to vie with their neighbours on the south and hence such convenient and elegant buildings have been raised …'.[37]

The single most important aspect of the building of the bridge was that it moved the city east. Of all the major structures put up on the north bank of the Liffey, the Carlisle Bridge had the greatest personal impact on the citizens. It had a great influence, too, on how the city developed north-eastwards in the last years of the eighteenth century and into the first quarter of the nineteenth. Its construction meant that ships could no longer come up to the Custom House and so a new version would have to be built, shifting the emphasis of the port eastward and downriver. The bridge's most immediate effect was the opening up of Sackville Street, with the subsequent opening of the General Post Office and its concomitant social and commercial activity. It also transformed the hospitality sector over the next twenty years. By 1815, as Maire Kennedy records, the coffee-houses in the area, such as the Dublin Coffee House on Lower Sackville Street and the one run by Mrs Martha Dodd from 1793 in Earl Street, had moved on from merely serving coffee to offering drawing rooms for dinners and breakfasts.[38] Sackville Street quickly became home to several hotels, bringing visitors to the area. John Gamble reported in 1818 that 'Sackville St is a broad and commodious one and the coaches drive up and drive away without confusion'.[39]

It made sense to expand and enlarge Sackville Street from a mall to a wide thoroughfare for pedestrian and rider alike. The Mall, as it was known, had emerged in the 1740s and had became firmly established in 1772, when a new law banned cab stands from it and forbade its use as a market-place.[40] It also made sense to use up the space all the way down to the newly walled river. The area just to the east around Beresford Place was already connected to the river, so opening up Marlborough Street was also an obvious move. This type of development allowed landlords such as Luke Gardiner to build at will and speculate. In some of the old prints of the area the bridge was

Dublin moving east, 1708–1844

within sight of the parliament building. The old maps also show that Marlborough Street was not connected to the river directly, but it, too, was altered and added to the northside quays. The sheer width of Sackville Street made it the perfect location for the erection of the GPO and an ideal site for Nelson's Pillar.

At the top end of Sackville Street, at the junction of Parnell Street and Parnell Square, occupation spread all round the environs of Mountjoy Square and filled in the grid of streets up to Hardwicke Street up the hill. The arrival of the bridge also allowed easier access to the Rotunda Hospital (Fig. 9.11).

Benjamin Oakley, an English visitor to Dublin in 1819, wrote that from the Carlisle Bridge 'you see the noble Custom House enveloped in a forest of masts'. In Sackville Street, he said, the Post Office 'is another ornament to this fine city … Nelson's Pillar adjacent to it'.[41] Oakley was back in Dublin in 1825 and called to the Post Office to engage with 'Mr Ferguson the superintendent of all the mail coaches'.[42] Ann Plumtre wrote that the foundation stone for the new GPO was laid while she was in Dublin on 12 August 1814.[43]

Fig. 9.11—Early nineteenth-century view northwards along Sackville Street and beyond, including the GPO and the recently erected Nelson's Column. The illustration shows the scale of development towards Rutland Square (courtesy of Louise Morgan and Brendan Maher, NGI).

Fig. 9.12—The Halfpenny Bridge (Samuel Frederick Brocas, 1816), showing how both quays have expanded (courtesy of Louise Morgan and Brendan Maher, NGI).

Nuala Burke says that the building of the Carlisle Bridge and the opening of Sackville Street necessitated the raising of the levels of the quays on the north bank of the river, because the level of the new street was 5ft higher than the flags of Bachelor's Walk.[44]

Another result of the construction of the bridge was the general upgrading which began to take place upriver on other bridges and their approaches. In the period around 1815, as John De Courcy reports, there was a general will to enrich the setting of the Four Courts buildings around the courts themselves, which were completed in 1805. The Richmond Bridge was coming to completion at this time—another public structure of some civic significance. The wall along Inn's Quay and the Whitworth and Richmond bridges were fitted with new balustrades which now used a coping of granite on top of cast-iron balusters, which came from the Mallet foundry.[45] It is apparent, therefore, that the Corporation was determined to stitch the two sides of the new city closely together (Fig. 9.12).

The *Dublin Penny Journal* in 1835 called Sackville Street the 'greatest leading street in the city', and described 'the long continued line of quays extending right through the centre of the city from

> **The Halfpenny Bridge**—a toll-bridge over the river—was the brainchild of John Beresford and William Walsh. The Carlisle Bridge had not been open for long before the idea of making another access across the Liffey between it and the Capel Street Bridge began to be discussed as a necessary utility. This time the promoters had to deal with the ferry operators, who had a long history of service in the metropolis but who were eventually paid off. The bridge, cast in Coalbrookdale in Shropshire, opened in 1816 at a cost of £3,000 (Fig. 9.12). The first iron bridge in the country, it came with iron lamp-brackets.[46] It was named the Wellington Bridge after the duke of Wellington, in honour of his victory at Waterloo, but became known as the Halfpenny Bridge because that was the price of the toll. Its erection relieved some of the traffic pressure on the Carlisle Bridge by allowing large numbers of pedestrians access to both sides of the quays. The technology in the iron industry was racing ahead at this stage. In North Wales, Telford began building his first iron suspension bridge over the Menai Straits just three years later, setting in motion the use of suspension bridges everywhere across Europe.[47] Shortly after this, in the mid-1820s, Dublin's first locally manufactured iron bridge, cast at the Phoenix Ironworks, was erected at Kingsbridge.[48] At this time the Corporation recommended that one William Walsh be given an extension to his lease, presently for 70 years, of a further 29 years, as 'he is an improving tenant, having expended a large sum of money in erecting the Metal Bridge, which is not only permanent but ornamental and will under the covenant of the lease revert to the city at the expiration of his term'.[49]

Ringsend Point to the Military-road, a distance of nearly three miles. In the direction of the Bay, the Custom House, arising at a little distance in all the beauty of classical architecture, and surrounded by ships and other vessels of considerable size which approach quite close to the bridge.'[50] On 5 November 1824 the Corporation ordered that 'the harbour master be directed to prevent cattle on the north side between Carlisle Bridge and the Canal Docks', whether for aesthetic reasons or because there was so much traffic in the area of the bridge.[51]

Thanks to the advent of the Carlisle Bridge, Sackville Street attracted 'coxcomical captains, pert coxcombs, ancient beaus, battered belles, and banker's clerks', the whole tribe of pen and ink and the very dregs and sweepings of the shops at Merry Eve, according to the Dublin satirist of November 1809.[52] Another visitor described those occupying Sackville Street on his visit in 1810 as 'Peers, pastry cooks, perfumers, bishops, butchers, and brokers in old furniture, together with hotels of the most superb description and a tolerable sprinkling of gin and whiskey shops'.[53] Sackville Street and its environs were allowed to improve as residential areas thanks to the banning of brick-making; glass-making, too, was restricted, as limekilns had been earlier, all being obliged to move further out of the city.[54] Note that a limekiln was located at Summerhill.[55]

Maintenance work on the bridge continued into the nineteenth century before the volumes of traffic demanded its rebuilding on a grander scale. The Ballast Board expended £1,260 13s. 6d. in 1819, according to the port ledger for that year.[56] Maintenance work also continued on other bridges, as shown by a payment to John Clarke of £111 8s. on 30 December for repairs to a balustrade carried out on 27 October.[57] One of the main results of the construction of the bridge was that it shrank the size of the city and allowed the Bank of Ireland to move across to its new location at College Green. At the same time it reflected the reduction in importance of this zone for the very reason that the emphasis was moving east.[58]

The GPO and Nelson's Pillar

The news of Nelson's victory at Trafalgar arrived in Dublin on 8 November 1805, eighteen days after the battle. The freedom of the city was given to Richard Spear of HMS *Conqueror* 'for his distinguished gallantry' at Trafalgar. Spear's family operated a ship's chandlery at Capel Street. It was decided to honour Nelson for his victory and his deliverance of the country from French tyranny by erecting a suitable monument. By 1807, £3,827 had been collected for a statue. The city voted £200 towards it, with the proviso that any money raised through visitors would be given to Dublin charities. The first stone was laid on 15 February 1808 and it was opened on 21 October 1809 by the duke of Richmond, the lord lieutenant.[59] The Pillar was a source of pride for many in the city and a massive, imposing structure, showing strength and endurance; it was in fact a political statement. The location aided the siting of the GPO close by not long after, strengthening the position of Sackville Street on the cityscape as a major focal point for the metropolis. The fact that the monument was open to the public to access the viewing platform at the top meant a steady stream of customers to see the panorama of Dublin and beyond. The visitors that it attracted to Dublin and to the street were also greatly welcomed by those with something to sell in their stores.

Bigelow during his 1817 visit notes the GPO, 'which is erecting on a magnificent scale and which when completed will form not only a great embellishment to Dublin. The mail coaches are provided with guards who, with the driver, are well armed and they travel at the rate of eight miles per hour, including the necessary delays.'[60] Writing about the new Post Office in 1820, Cromwell said that 'Dublin Mails all leave the GPO every evening at eight pm, and carry two guards each and occasionally a trooper or two besides, as an escort, side panels are sheet iron or copper'.[61] These remarks clearly illustrate the level of crime.

On the other side of Sackville Street began the building of the Catholic Pro Cathedral in Marlborough Street, just 200 yards from the Protestant St Thomas's. It was not just a church; it was a building complex involving several buildings along Marlborough Street, similar to what was built in Westland Row and in Gardiner Street. This building, too, was a political statement—of rising Catholicism in the very heart of the city. Cromwell said that the cost of the Pro Cathedral was estimated at £50,000 and that there were nine other Roman Catholics chapels across the city.[62]

Postal services were formalised with the use of coaches, which meant that the postal service took an interest in roads. An 1805 act permitted the Post Office to set standards for road design, including quality, size and gradients, as well as surveying rebuilding for carriages of all descriptions. The postmaster general was required to be proactive in surveying roads to lay out suggested improvements. The Board of Works later confirmed the impact of roads on agriculture, noting that 'whenever a road is constructed flourishing farms at once spring up'. Bianconi set up his national coach service in 1815 and by 1840 was covering 3,000 miles of roads. Corresponding improvements in and around the city allowed people and produce to enter and leave Dublin more easily.[63]

In a very short time three major constructions had been placed along Sackville Street, ensuring that it became the premier thoroughfare in the city, mostly on tidal and unstable ground.

The Custom House

The Custom House 'which stands on Eden Quay ... is 375 feet in length, and 205 feet in depth, and exhibits four decorated fronts, answering almost directly to the four cardinal points of the compass. On the east of the Custom House is a wet dock, capable of containing forty sail of vessels; and along the quay that bounds it on the east and north is a range of capacious and commodious houses. It is a curious circumstance that about two hundred years since the entire space that the eye can command from right to left, in this position including the ground on which stands the Custom House, the houses on Bachelors-walk, the two Ormonde-quays, and Inns-quay, was entirely covered with ouse, and overflowed by the tides, to within about eighty yards of Trinity College on the south.'[64]

The Corporation had been dealing with the question of the location of the Custom House since 1744, when representations were put forward by the earl of Harcourt to the House of Commons. A committee was formed to begin examining the matter. One witness, Mr Grayson, said that 'he would be glad of a Custom House nearer the sea' and that 'the further a ship comes up the river, the better for the merchant but not for the mariner'.[65] Another witness said that only four ships could 'lay their sides to the quay' and that 'they cannot discharge, if they lay eight or nine deep'.[66] The Custom House in its original site was no longer fit for purpose by the third quarter of the eighteenth century. It was generally agreed that a move to a new site was sensible, 'It being allowed on all hands that it is necessary that a new Custom House shall be built somewhere'. The Assembly had two options: use the old site or move to a new one.[67]

In 1773 the Custom House on the south bank of the Liffey was found to be unsound, and a report prepared for the lord lieutenant concluded that, given the choice between repairing and refurbishing the present building and building a new one for the city and port of Dublin, it would be better to build afresh. The question would be where. The location at Wellington Quay was no longer tenable. The report noted that the increase in building over the past 30 years 'has so enlarged the town on the east, Essex Bridge nearly divides the town in equal parts and the upper half that is west of Essex Bridge has the advantage of four bridges'.[68] The council, after much deliberation and the interviewing of witnesses, concluded that 'The present is inconvenient to trade and prejudicial to his majesty's revenue'.[69]

In 1773 John Beresford, Chief Commissioner of Excise in Dublin, began the long battle to relocate the Custom House to a new site downriver on the north side. Beresford ran the Revenue service for a period of 30 years, which put him in a unique position to encourage such a move.[70] In 1781 he wrote to James Gandon, who had been introduced to him by Viscount Carlow, giving him an order for designs for a Custom House and pleading with him to come to Dublin.[71] Gandon did not enjoy the most comfortable or harmonious beginning to the project. Not everything had been agreed and there was violent opposition to it. He was also apprehensive about the willingness (or lack thereof) of Irish workers to stay on the job. So volatile and confused was the situation that he went armed to work each day.[72] Nevertheless, he stayed on and also completed designs for Carlisle Bridge, for which Beresford laid the foundation stone in 1791, the King's Inns, for which the foundation stone was laid in 1795 by the earl of Clare, and of course the Four Courts. He returned to Dublin after the 1798 rebellion to erect the portico of the Irish House of Commons building in Westmorland Street.[73]

The first stone of the Custom House was laid by John Beresford on 8 August 1781. Viola Barrow says that every available stonemason was engaged in the work.[74] A visitor to Dublin in 1788 wrote: 'I paid a visit to the Custom House, with the assistance of Mr Gandon was led through every part of this very ponderous edifice, it will be the first of its kind in Europe'.[75]

Benjamin Oakley described the Custom House in 1819 as 'a noble building'; 'in the interior is a noble room seventy feet long, sixty five feet wide and thirty feet high'. Moreover, 'Just by is a fine dock and wooden wharves with very extensive warehouses, so constructed as to resist the ravaging effects of fire, the roof and centre part of the building being found entirely of iron'[76] (Fig. 9.13).

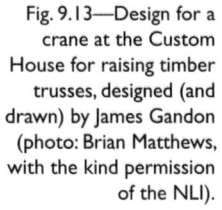

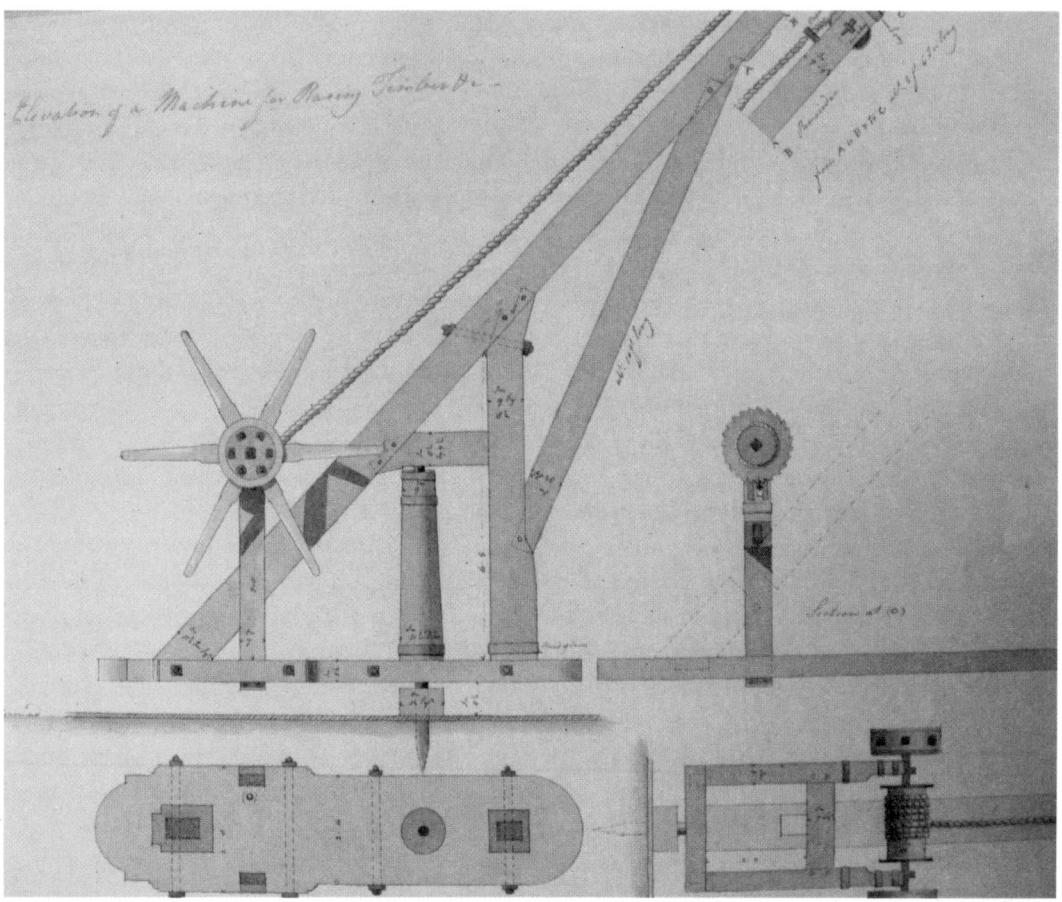

Fig. 9.13—Design for a crane at the Custom House for raising timber trusses, designed (and drawn) by James Gandon (photo: Brian Matthews, with the kind permission of the NLI).

David Dickson says that the new Custom House set the tone for a whole district, giving it a defining feature in architectural and physical terms but also as a working establishment. In addition, it would begin the process of giving encouragement to the occupation and building down along the Liffey and inland, as seen in the building up to Mayor Street and Sheriff Street.[77] Indeed, enough progress on walling, reclaiming and occupying the space had occurred by 1791 for the *Freeman's Journal* to report that 'The rage of building towards the sea has arrived to such a degree of order that even the marshy and swampy grounds near the North Wall are reclaiming'.[78]

There are no figures available to indicate how many people worked in the Custom House or, indeed, supplied it with goods and services. It is possible, however, to offer a reasonable speculation. By 1800 it was operating in the heart of a new zone at the eastern extremity of the city. It was backed by the development around Beresford Place and the lower end of Gardiner Street, which was filling up with substantial houses. Shipping had increased, making the business of the Custom House more extensive. Shipping, like the legal profession, consumed vast quantities of paper, ink and quills, as well as ledgers and account books, and clerks to record all these transactions. Such a large building meant many fires, requiring a continuous supply of coal. All the activities of the port were now more adjacent to the Custom House, leading to an increase in the number of taverns, both legal and illicit, as well as rooming-houses for both seamen and passengers. And of course wherever there were men and mariners there would be women to look after their wants, and when difficulties arose there was the Westmorland Lock Hospital to resort to. Literally hundreds of people were conducting business here every day. No sooner was it finished than talk of further development in terms of docks beside it turned into action, and St George's Dock became a fixture on the landscape.

Some indication of the numbers of persons both using and employed in the Custom House can be gleaned from the instructions issued to the housekeeper in 1845. The housekeeper was in charge of the house porters and charwomen and reported directly to the collector and controller. He was in charge of the 'building and of the general stock of coals, bogwood, soap, candles, and all other activities necessary for the public service', and had to exercise supervision of the men and women 'employed in and about the house'. His duties included opening and closing the building and ensuring that the charwomen 'lay fires in the several offices' and 'sweep, wash and keep clean the offices and furniture therein'—'And also the water closets'. The house porters are to attend to supplying coal and bogwood from the vaults, 'sweeping and cleaning the several halls', and 'pumping the necessary supply of water into the said water closets and other cisterns about the building'. Mention of water closets is interesting here because they were obviously installed years after the construction, and this is one of the rare mentions of the operation of the same.

The housekeeper was also responsible for the maintenance and service of fire equipment. 'The fire engines with all their tackle and apparatus ... at all times ready for use in case of fire; the permanent crew for working them to consist of the four house porters and four boatmen of the upper stations', and 'the fire equipment to be tested monthly'. Another part of the job was to live in the apartment allotted, and 'daily check on the several watchmen and others appointed to guard the building are at their posts and alert at their stations'. By far the most interesting aspect of the employment, however, was that 'You are strictly forbidden to belong to any Orange Lodge or any political society'. This reflects the thinking of the period and is a reminder of the civil disorder caused by the Order over the previous 30 years.[79]

Visitors commented on the building. John Gamble noted in 1810 that 'the river is open to view in the whole of its course through the city and the quays, and when properly embanked will form a superior prospect ... the Liffey is navigable to the Custom House'.[80] Ann Plumtre said that the Custom House stood on the quay 'almost at the eastern extremity of the town ...', and described the locale as 'a dirty, disagreeable, badly inhabited part of the town, abounding with those minor public houses which are the resort of sailors'. The observation is interesting in that it shows that port activities in this area of reclaimed land were extensive enough to support a sufficient population to use these pubs, well away from those on offer on the other side of the river.[81] Baron Charles Dupin, visiting Dublin on a tour of ports of England, Scotland and Ireland, commented on the new docks and stores being built alongside the new Custom House: 'workmen are employed in digging new docks near that magnificent edifice the Custom House ... the first stone of these was laid in the summer of 1817'. In 1834 Henry Inglis, too, noted that the Custom House was 'magnificent'.[82] John Barrow the following year described the aspect thus: 'the Custom House has no equal, the spacious quay in front of it and the docks with the shipping give life to the scene'[83] (Figs 9.14 and 9.15).

In 1822 the Board of Works moved to office space at 5 Talbot Street, where it remained until 1831, when the new Commissioners for Public Works took over and were assigned offices in the Custom House.[84] Another side effect of locating the new Custom House downriver was that it enabled the Bank of Ireland, previously up at Capel Street Bridge, to relocate downriver to not far from the new Carlisle Bridge,[85] reflecting the inexorable eastward shift of the city and the reduction in importance of the original site in commercial terms.

CLUSTERING STRUCTURES ALONG THE NORTH SIDE OF THE LIFFEY

Fig. 9.14—A James Hore painting looking north towards the Custom House, including a view of Beresford Place to the left (photo: Brian Matthews, with the kind permission of James Gorry, Gorry Gallery).

Fig. 9.15—Lifting bridge and shipping (including a steamship) on the dock at the Custom House (courtesy of the NLI).

The drift of the city in an easterly direction was now well under way. This encouraged more development in the direction of the outer North Lotts, which would continue for the next 50 years. Almost immediately after its completion, the quay at the new Custom House became operational and was soon a hub of commercial activity. In 1824 the Liverpool Steam Packet Company announced that the *City of Dublin* would sail from the North Wall at 8pm on 6 January 1824; those wishing to make the trip were directed to apply to the office at 17 Eden Quay. Across the river, the first steam packet directly to Bristol would sail from Sir John Rogerson's Quay at 9pm on Saturday 7 August 1824, and passage could be arranged at the office in 33 Lower Sackville Street, opposite the Post Office. It is worth noting here that the new Post Office had become sufficiently embedded in the public mind to be referenced as a location aid.[86] Note, too, how trade and shipping have become part of the life of the north bank of the river east of the Carlisle Bridge.

Annesley Bridge

Tutty cites the Act of Parliament of 1792 as the real beginning of development in the North Strand area, quoting it as follows:

> 'It would be of advantage to the Public if that part of that space of ground overflowed by the sea at High Water, eastward of Ballybough Bridge, between the Wall enclosing the ground formerly taken in from the sea called the North Lotts, and the Weir Wall on the North Strand, were enclosed and taken from the sea. It is intended that the said new communication shall be made in a direct line from the Strand Road leading from His Majesty's Custom House, to the said ground overflowed by the sea and across the same to the road adjoining the said Weir Wall on the North Strand nearly at the end of a place called Fairview on the said Strand. In order to make the said new and more commodious communication between the city of Dublin and the country on the other side of the bridge called Ballybough Bridge it will be necessary to build, erect, and make a new bridge and causeway, eastward of Ballybough Bridge aforesaid.'[87]

The House of Commons Journal records that the new bridge, called Annesley Bridge, is to be built by the trustees of the road from Dublin to Malahide, who were given the power to borrow £2,000 for the purpose.[88] Lord Talbot of Malahide was a trustee. Permission was granted for further borrowings of the same amount.[89] The new bridge came into being in 1793 (Fig. 9.16).

The area had been known as 'the Strand' until the arrival of the bridge, and according to Diarmuid Hiney was a favourite haunt of the gentry and wealthy to parade their 'victories, valuables and vanities'. Fairview was until the end of the eighteenth century known as Ballybough; this only changed with the erection of the bridge. Some building had taken place on the northern shore of the Tolka but very little. Erlington House was around since before 1748. In the early years of the eighteenth century communities of Jews, Huguenots and Baptists moved out here away from the city. The Huguenots settled along Richmond Road and the Baptists on Philipsburg Avenue, where they used a small chapel.[90] The Jews came out about 1718 and settled in Philipsburg Avenue. In that same year they leased a plot of some 2,500m^2 for use as a cemetery; they eventually purchased it in September 1748[91] and it remained in use until 1900. By 1760 the number of Jews living in Dublin warranted a synagogue on the north side and one was opened in Marlborough Green, off Lower Abbey Street.[92] At the junction of Philipsburg Avenue and Richmond Road on the strand beside

Fig. 9.16—Edwin Hayes (1835) painting of Annesley Bridge. This is the original arched bridge, with a fishing vessel in the foreground (photo: Brian Matthews, with the kind permission of James Gorry, Gorry Gallery).

the Jewish Cemetery stood from 1830 an RIC barracks until it moved out to Hollybrook Road at Clontarf.[93] The view over the strand from here at the time would have included an excellent picture of Clontarf Island, then but 750m to the east along the East Wall road.

There were also several factories in the locale. Four glass-making operations were here: one near the bridge at Ballybough, another further down the Tolka just before Annesley Bridge, and Chebsey's glasshouse and Mulvanney's glass factory. This explains the development of housing in the area, in that the workers lived locally.[94] Hiney says that there was also a factory making farming implements from the 1830s, and another which printed linen.[95]

The Annesley Bridge became the new northern border to the city, following the original plan laid down by the mapping, planning and sale of the North Lotts. Indeed, the Lotts had originally envisaged occupation all the way out to near Castle Avenue, a further 2km. In time their foresight would be vindicated. The Corporation knew what they were attempting. Villages, towns and cities had grown from time immemorial along rivers, at crossroads and bridges; rivers in particular had allowed for weirs and for mills, fostering further growth.

In 1797 Thomas Sherrard was ordered to draw a map, which he titled 'Survey of the ground from the sea by the new bridge' (Fig. 9.17a). It shows the new triangle of ground now enclosed by the road north from the bridge, and the road then turning south-west, now called Fairview Strand, and the last section as the same road curls in a more southerly direction across Ballybough Bridge, finally following the bank of the Tolka eastward back to Annesley Bridge. The map shows a sea wall along Fairview Park, glasshouses halfway between the two bridges on the south side of the Tolka, and a strip of dwellings along the strand at the bottom of Philipsburg Avenue on the north side of the road going toward Ballybough Bridge.[96]

The Corporation for Preserving and Improving the Port of Dublin was also responsible for the repair and maintenance of the wall along the Tolka from Ballybough Bridge, and then for the walls

Dublin moving east, 1708–1844

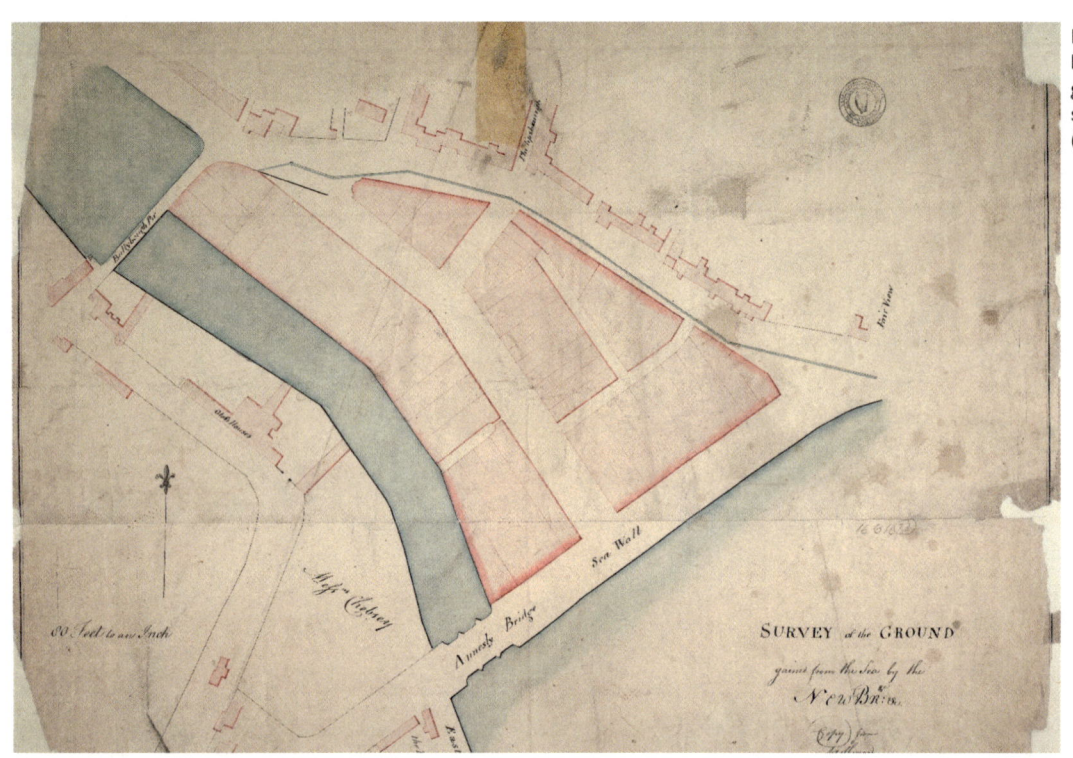

Fig 9.17a—A 1797 survey by Thomas Sherrard of ground gained from the sea by the new bridge (NLI 16 G 16 (37)).

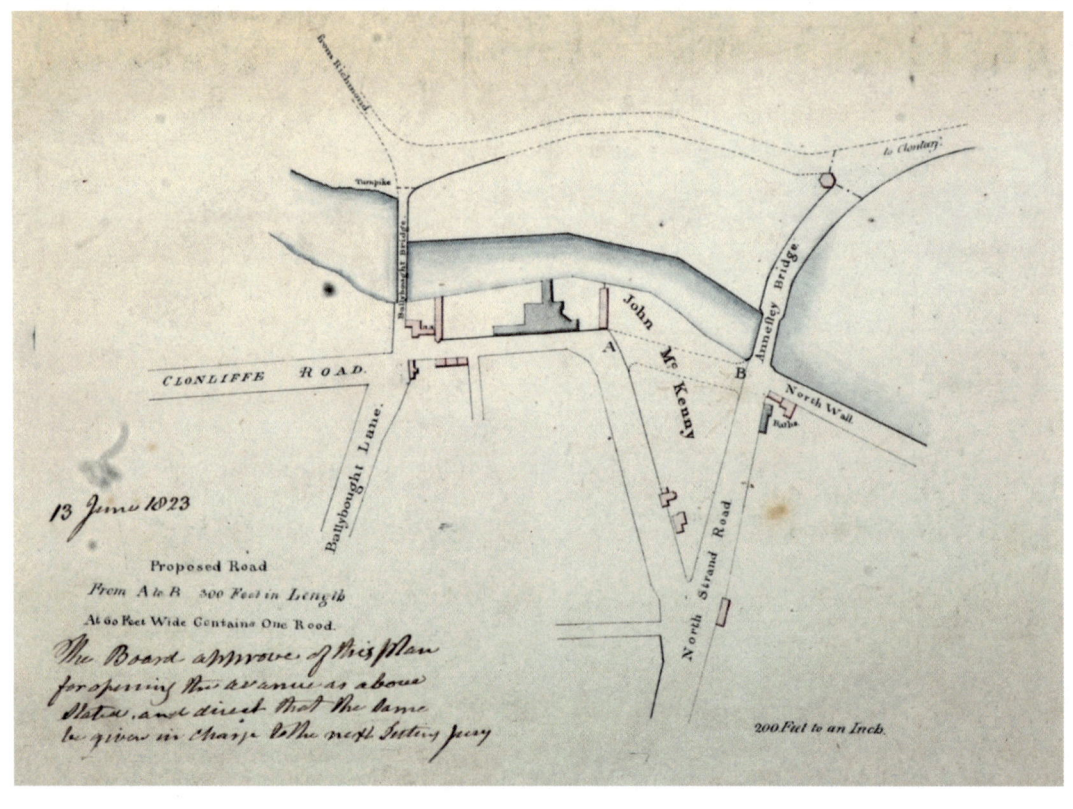

Fig. 9.17b—A 1797 map of the area around Annesley Bridge (NLI 16G 16 (37) 1797).

threading eastward towards Annesley Bridge and beyond in the direction at the time of Clontarf Island and the Liffey. Stones for the North East wall were recorded on 3 March 1826 as being purchased at a cost of £17 5s. 10d.[97] On 11 June 1824, men were employed to work at the wall along from the bridge at a cost of £23 19s. 7d. The same meeting recorded that George Smith was paid £378 19s. 2d. for stones, and noted deliveries of lime valued at £14 0s. 3d. The following week the payment for men working at the wall was £23 16s. 8d. Earlier, on 21 May, men employed on the North East wall were paid £13 13s. 8d.[98]

Some other costs will shed light on the volume of repair and upgrading work that was being carried out on the walls in the area. On 9 January 1824 George Smith was paid a total of £314 4s. 7d. for supplying stones to the North East wall.[99] On 26 March 1824 Thomas Healy was paid £26 14s. 6d. for supply of stones, while Smith, Gaffney and Clements were paid £5 18s. 8d., £11 12s. 2d. and £1 14s. 6d. respectively for freight of stones. On 24 October 1824 payments are recorded to workmen for cartage of land at Annesley Bridge to the value of £6 16s. 8d.[100] Earlier in the same month the gabbardmen delivered ballast to the bridge for £25.[101]

The Ballast Board on 16 August 1824 received a letter from Thomas Sherrard at Blessington Street, requesting from the Wide Streets Commission that the Board 'supply 1500 tons of material for filling the new line of cross road between Ballybough Lane and Annesley Bridge, to be landed at the quay wall at the south end of said bridge and to know if the Ballast Master would please furnish same and at what time and rate per ton'. The answer was '7 pence per ton deliverable drawn on the wall, or if down to the new line of the road [0.5km west] 11 pence per ton'[102] (Fig. 9.17b).

At the end of all this work the bridge was complete and the new border on the north-eastern edge of the city had been moved some 0.5km due east down from Ballybough Bridge. This new edifice would lead to further development and change out here, but it would take a little time. As Lt Joseph Archer reported to the RDS in 1801, Ballybough was then a village 1¼ miles north-east of the Castle, situated by the seaside. Clontarf, he said, was a large and pleasant village 2¼ miles from the Castle on the seaside, 'much used in the bathing season. A large number of handsome and well built houses are about.' He adds that Mr Weeks has altered the course of a stream and converted it into a large pool reservoir for the use of bathers,[103] and that Drumcondra village, also two miles north of the Castle, was well inhabited, with a number of gentlemen's seats. Each of these locations would become enmeshed into the city fabric over the next 30–40 years, losing their complete separateness.

There was a difference of opinion as to who owned what on the North Strand because the trustees were encroaching on the strand near Annesley Bridge in 1794. On 14 October John Beresford claimed a lease; the arbiters in the dispute found that 70 acres of strand were in fact due to the city and that 112 acres were in dispute, going to arbitration. The Corporation were of the opinion that putting the strand into a state of reclamation 'would greatly benefit the emigration of the river' (the Tolka).[104] In reference to the 1717 North Lotts map or the Bolton map, the tenants were bound 'to close a canal from Ballybough Bridge through the strand to comprise eighty feet at one end and 120 feet at the other end' but it 'has not been built'.[105] In fact it was completed, as is seen today.

Contained in a map of Dublin in 1820 is the information that between Annesley Bridge and Ballybough Bridge is water, and 'Mud Island' is named east of the Royal Canal at Ballybough. Amiens Street to Annesley Bridge is still called the Strand, and ribbon development can be seen between the two bridges.[106]

What were the effects of the arrival of the bridge? First, it extended the eastern boundary of the city for 0.5km down from Ballybough Bridge. Second, it improved access to the city from Clontarf, Howth, Raheny, Coolock, Malahide and the whole hinterland there, and laid the foundations for a new road system out of the city along the shore to Clontarf. Third, it created pressure to extend the road network, which also extended the building up of areas such as Fairview, Clontarf, Killester, Raheny, Donnycarney, Sutton and Howth. It automatically brought closer to the city those élite landowners who had homes not that far out in these areas of development, such as Clontarf or Drumcondra. This, of course, is exactly what the Corporation had envisaged when drawing up the plan of the North Lotts. In addition, the new bridge, being further east than Ballybough Bridge, acted as a buffer of protection from the sea, permitting development to take place around the old Mud Island.

The advent of the Drogheda Railway in 1844 moved the eastern boundary of the city once again. A new stone and iron bridge was constructed across the southern exit of the Tolka (the northern exit being through the outer arch of the railway bridge at Clontarf, 1km distant). 'The Tolka flowed before me now through the middle arch, the central part of the railway embankment where it crosses the sea.'[107] The bridge brought an end to the existence of Mud Island, an area around Ballybough Bridge which had played host to smugglers, criminals and people who lived on the margins of city society down here in a maze of channels and creeks. This space was now moved inland to become just ordinary suburbia over the coming decades. This allowed housing to be built down the Clonliffe Road and similarly down the Richmond Road on the east bank of the Tolka. Aside from this, it contributed a substantial extra acreage to the city originally foreseen in the North Lotts plan of 1717. It also ensured the new road access to the city from Clontarf, Raheny and Malahide, altering the old way of Summerhill. This bridge, along with Carlisle Bridge and the four bridges over the lower Royal Canal, transformed the potential of the entire area.

Aldeborough House

The house was built for Edward Stratford, 2nd earl of Aldeborough, on today's Portland Row, just adjacent to the Five Lamps at North Strand (Fig. 9.18). While it faced directly onto the street outside, it had substantial gardens (for a city house) at the back, facing west. Stratford had inherited part of the Paul estate, added to his holdings by accumulating long leases from the other heirs. The first written reference to the house was in his own diary of 8 May 1792, where he mentions viewing part of the estate of the late Colonel Paul at the North Strand, to build on.[108] According to O'Boyle, it seemed likely that, with the ever-expanding estate of the Gardiners next door, the area would become fashionably built up, and Stratford intended to take advantage by building not just the house but also developing streets surrounding his house; one such still bears his name. Work began on 1 July 1793.[109]

The construction of the house, of seven bays and three storeys over a high-ceilinged basement, employed a team of 46 builders, including three stonecutters, twelve carpenters, thirteen bricklayers, ten brick labourers and seven of Stratford's own labourers. Carpenters were paid 19s. 6d., bricklayers received 16s. 3d., and two of the three stonecutters received £1 5s. each. The *Dublin Evening Post* reported on 3 June 1794 that the total cost would amount to £50,000.[110] Throughout the construction the earl was short of money, and more than once his clerk of works wrote to him of materials vanishing from the unprotected site and workmen not attending owing to lack of funds.[111] It is interesting to note that the latest invention for heating was employed, the Rumford Stove supplied by Ferris and Orr ironmongers of Pill Lane.[112]

Fig. 9.18—Front view of Aldeborough House, Portland Row, off the North Strand (photo: Brian Matthews).

One of the strange aspects of the entire project is the fact that as construction proceeded so too did the building of the Royal Canal, and in fact the canal would be finished before the completion of Aldeborough House. This would involve the loss of the view from the house; the canal was only 200m away, and the long ramp leading up to it, to allow carriages to drive up to the bridge that would be built over it, began to rise 50m from the front door of the house. So far research has not uncovered whether Stratford ever objected to the canal; possibly he was too busy in London.

In 1813 Professor von Feinaigle, a teacher of international fame, arrived in Dublin and immediately gave a series of lectures and demonstrations on his methods of teaching, especially on increasing memory capacity.[113] His public lectures soon gathered support for a school that he would run. His supporters took two houses at Clonliffe, near the Circular Road, Mountjoy Square.[114] The promoters included Bindon Blood of No. 8 Charlemont Street (interestingly, Bindon Blood was the name of the great port engineer who literally transformed engineering by his early use of giant blocks of pre-cast concrete for the new Liffey walls), Thomas Williams, Bank of Ireland, Richard Williams of Drumcondra Castle and Dr Harty of 32 Gloucester Street. The two houses proved inadequate for the numbers applying. Aldeborough House, which had been lying idle since the Union, was bought for £4,800 for use as a combined day and boarding-school for boys.[115] It was fitted out for the purpose, even with a chapel, and the name was changed to the Luxembourg.[116] The fact that it catered for both day pupils and boarders shows that a comfortable segment of society lived close to the school. The fact that the fees were high meant that it attracted wealthy patrons into the area. By 12 March 1814 the Clonliffe establishment had been taken over by the late proprietress of the Clontarf seminary, Miss Austin, for the boarding only of females.

Von Feinaigle died in 1820; at that time there were about 130 pupils enrolled in his school.[117] His son-in-law took over the operation but was totally inept, leading to closure some few years later. The house remained vacant from then on. In its successful days, however, the school had acted as a beacon for improvement in the area. Another school run on similar lines was opened in 24 Jervis Street by a Dr T. Finn, hosting 100 pupils, 80 of whom were Catholics.[118]

Not long after the house was completed, Hely Dutton was in the area on behalf of the Royal Dublin Society, examining roads and paths. He reported that footpaths were 'too badly neglected, which don't really exist as such but off the road become swamps of mud which could have been filled to make paths by using the scrapings of the roads'. He adds that 'opposite to Lord Claremont's demesne on the North Strand another pregnant proof may be seen of this neglect; in fact it may be seen on every road in the county of Dublin. I must express my surprise, that the stinking swamp between Gloucester Street and Aldeborough House has been so long permitted to annoy the neighbourhood of Summerhill and the adjoining streets; in warm weather it is sufficient to breed a pestilence.'[119] His task, as set and paid for by the Royal Dublin Society, was to verify and question the work carried out the previous year by Lt. Joseph Archer. He confirmed that there existed a network of streets around Aldeborough House and Portland Row, but not all were finished or occupied. Nevertheless, as this was ground taken back from the tide, any occupation kept up the momentum for the creation of new zones in the expanding city.

The importance of Aldeborough House was that it was built as a private dwelling, whose wealthy and influential owner was quite aware that his home would attract others into the area, which is exactly what took place over the following twenty years. Its erection solidified the role that Amiens Street and North Strand would play in helping to develop the area, as it lay inside the Royal Canal and the recently completed North Circular Road, which ended just up the slope outside the house on Portland Row. Where the élite go, the lower orders will follow, as night follows day. This allowed for development around the house at the eastern boundary of the street network which was working its way out east and north of Sackville Street.

The change taking place on the north side of Dublin was gaining momentum. In 1820 Cromwell wrote that Temple Street, Gardiner Street and Mountjoy Square had been recently completed and noted that 'the upper windows command an extensive aspect of Dublin Bay'.[120] In 1834 Henry Inglis reported that 'The Zoological Gardens have lately been constructed' at the other end of the North Circular Road, at the entrance to the Phoenix Park.[121]

By 1844, as the Drogheda Railway was completed and the new station in the Strand—now called Amiens Street—was opened, the area around had filled in with grids of streets and lanes hosting a variety of dwellings and businesses. The proximity to the new northside port structures and quays was reflected in the occupations of some local residents. The 1844 *Pettigrew & Oulton Dublin Almanac* lists four shipmasters in Coburg Place alone. In Potters Alley off Marlborough Street in 1840 glass material was being cut using steam in Irwin's glass manufacturers, while around the corner in North Earl Street the firm of Sherwood were supplying water closets and forcing pumps, according to the 1840 *Dublin Almanac*. A large part of this locale around the North Strand remained in agricultural use, however, growing vegetables and supplying poultry and pork for the city, as well as eggs, milk and beef.

In 1822, according to one visitor, Thomas Reid, the city was home to 178,824 persons. Reid also described the quay walls as 'long elegant quays formed of hammered granite erected along the Liffey', although his arrival in Dublin had been delayed, as the bar was still an impediment to shipping.[122] Andrew Bigelow, wandering around the area, expressed his surprise at finding so many shops open on the Sabbath; he noted, too, that 'Dublin exhibits a deplorable spectacle at night in the numbers of females abroad who are abandoned to infamy'.[123]

As this zone was being built on and occupied, the popular pastime of bathing in the sea now moved down eastward to the corner of the north and east walls, and also to the shore at Annesley Bridge. The poor, excluded from using the facilities at Rutland Square and Mountjoy Square, took full advantage of the seaside here.

The Royal Canal

The Royal Canal created a new form of transport on the north-eastern fringe of the city. It brought focus and opportunity for expansion to this area lately reclaimed from the tides, helping to create a new grid of streets between it and the North Circular Road/Portland Row. Goods and people now moved in and out of Dublin in a new manner. New buildings connected with the operation of the canal appeared, together with new forms of employment along the route. The canal was able to boost the establishment of a whole new manner of commerce, in the movement in both directions of people and goods. It was built during a period of population growth in the city, when water became more important than ever for people, animals (particularly horses) and industries such as glass-making, smelting, tanneries, brewing and distilling, which consumed large quantities of fresh water. The canal in part satisfied this need.

The canal needed men to design, plan, build and maintain it, to build and operate the boats that used it and to run the horses along the tow-path; stabling, feed and shelter for both men and horses were also required, as well as houses for lock-keepers. This would lead to the building of mills, warehouses and harbours close to the city.

The first and most immediate effect on the space out here on the North Strand wetlands was that the canal presented a new barrier which had to be crossed, necessitating a series of new bridges. Down here at the Liffey end of the canal four stone bridges were built. They would be completed at the same time as the new Carlisle Bridge across the Liffey and the new Annesley Bridge across the Tolka, making a total of six bridges completed in a very short space of time in an area of newly reclaimed land on the north side of the Liffey (see below). An iron lifting bridge on the holding dock next to the Liffey would be added later, as would another on the inner end of the holding dock and another stone bridge at the Jones Road entrance to Croke Park. This was a very substantial building programme on top of the other major works being completed in the city at the time, and even today would cause major upheaval. The construction of the bridges over the canal meant that the roads over them became formalised, improving access to the city. The canal allowed the movement of large quantities of turf to be brought into the city, which consumed enormous quantities of coal, offering some relief to the poor more often.

When the construction of the Royal Canal began, the site was well away from everything. It was in the middle of the new area blocked off by the north and east walls, still not completely drained or reclaimed but operating primarily as occasional farmland. To the north lay the Tolka, 0.5km away. To the east was the not-so-new North Liffey Wall, and out to the north-east was the East Wall as it ran over towards the almost-finished Great South Wall. By the end of construction this end of the canal was still crossing an area where little had changed, nor would it for another twenty years. During this period the space was semi-agricultural, helping to supply the dairy and food needs of the populace. Witness statements confirm that there were fields and meadow east of the road to

177

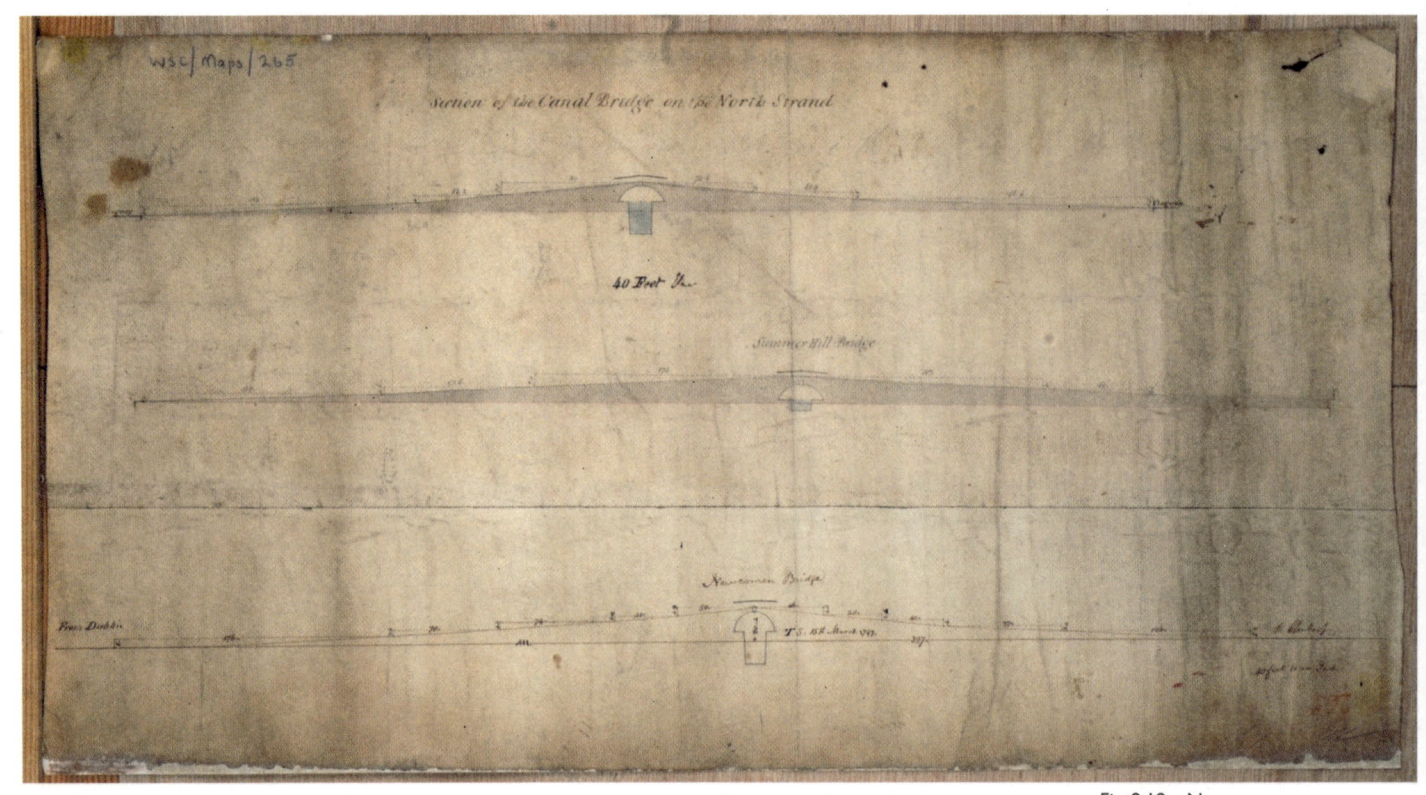

Fig. 9.19—Newcomen Bridge, showing how ramp was built by raising the levels on either side. (Wide Streets Commission, courtesy of Mary Clarke, Pearse Street Library).

Clontarf. The same aspect would have seen dozens of masts of ships, because there was nothing to obscure the view. If one turned south-west, the newer city was 0.5km distant, and due west was just a greenfield prospect. Roads across this landscape were few, poorly constructed and maintained, but improving. The canal itself would snake across the ground originally walled off from the bay and so was flat for some distance going west. In fact, it did not begin to climb very much until almost at Glasnevin at Cross Guns Bridge. It required embanking along the walls to retain the water.

The only building of any consequence anywhere in the vicinity would have been Aldeborough House, still at the time under construction. It stood at the lower end of a slope coming down from Summerhill on Portland Row, and at the bottom of the slope coming down from Newcomen Bridge, the first bridge over the canal as it worked its way west from the Liffey. The views from the house would have been truly panoramic, including ships in the harbour with Clontarf, Sutton and Howth in the distance, but this all changed dramatically with the construction of the canal—more specifically Newcomen Bridge and the ramp up to it (Figs 9.19 and 9.20).

Newcomen Bridge would have the most impact on the ground because it required a long rise up to the arch itself and the same on the northern side, to facilitate traffic to and from Malahide, Sutton, Clontarf, Raheny, Donnycarney and Howth. The other bridges did not need such a substantial ramp. The road to Howth was to have a direct impact on the idea of building the new harbour out at Howth a decade later. Newcomen Bridge came into existence at very much the same time as Annesley Bridge over the Tolka, 0.5km to the north.

The material removed from the digging of the canal was simply used to shore it up, and for the ramp at Newcomen Bridge. Close to the river the material was used to pack the back of the Liffey

Fig. 9.20—Photograph of Newcomen Bridge from south, showing at bottom right the walking slot for horse and driver (photo: Brian Matthews).

wall and for the eastern embankment between Mayor Street and Newcomen Bridge, and to create two embankments on either side coming away from the Liffey. While the section inland to Newcomen Bridge did not require much in the way of an embankment, the next strip up to the stadium at Croke Park needed substantial shoring up to safely contain the water. All this is visible today from the DART. At this time, as the city was snaking its way out in a north-easterly direction, the ground was being used for various forms of agriculture, mostly smallholdings. Dairies are frequently mentioned, supplying the city with milk. Visitors to Dublin often mentioned Lord Charlemont and, of course, his Casino at Marino.

In 1814 and 1815 Ann Plumtre, a summer visitor to Dublin, explored much of the city and its outer areas. On her way to Howth she described Clontarf as a village, with 'a number of delightful villas scattered about'. She further wrote about the view of the bay from a house in North Strand, 'one of the intended new streets in Dublin, of which only five or six houses are yet built'. The accompanying drawing by her friend Mrs C, who lived in one of these houses, shows fields, cabins and cottages, and has been used extensively in publications without ever being explained or contextualised. It does, however, confirm that agriculture was extensive in the area after the initial North Wall and East Wall were erected, and in the intervening period while the area totally dried out.[124]

Canals were expanding at a phenomenal rate across England and enthusiasm was growing equally here in Ireland. Patrick O'Kelly wrote that one of the main reasons for the building of the Royal Canal was to bring coal to rural Ireland: 'Coal is of good quality; and easy to be worked and, as much of it can be drained without steam engines, it can be got at a small expense'.[125] Canals, like the developing road system and the rail system, would prove a boon for the ruling of Ireland, and in

Fig. 9.21—Lifting iron bridge and mechanism at Royal Canal Dock (photo: Brian Matthews).

1798 the military took full advantage. Lord Cornwallis moved troops from Dublin to Tullamore to combat the French, who had landed at Killala, and found the arrangement so satisfactory that an agreement was drawn up to pay £900 per month to keep boats in readiness for government use in the future.[126] Whatever the reasons, the construction of the canal went ahead but always carried a whiff of failure during the operation, between runaway costs and technical faults. Proof that it never quite achieved what had been its primary objective was the delay in accessing the final connection to the Liffey (Fig. 9.21).

The success of canals in England was based on the mass movement of goods, which increased as the Industrial Revolution took hold. A horse and cart could not shift anything akin to the tonnage that a canal barge could carry. Patrick O'Kelly quoted a report of the House of Commons Committee (1745) to the effect that 'the average load of a cart drawn by one horse in Ireland is 450 lbs'.[127]

There were 181 subscribers to the Royal Canal, investing from £100 to £3,000 each, and they mainly consisted of gentry and aristocracy, such as the duke of Leinster, Lord Longford, Sir John Blacquiere and Sir William Newcomen. It was estimated that the overall cost of building the canal would be £197,098. The company petitioned parliament for funds and were granted £66,000.

Work on the Royal Canal began on 8 October 1789. While it is well known that the entire project was continually problematic, even the initial figures for construction costs were quite unbelievable, coming to £1,868 per mile as compared to the Grand Canal's £10,968 per mile.[128] The original surveyor was John Brownrigg, whose name crops up in several areas of engineering work in Dublin in the period. In December 1789 Richard Evans, who had been engineer on the

Grand Canal, joined the project as engineer at an annual salary of £200. Sir Thomas Hyde Page and William Jessop were both consulted and had opinions regarding routes and the problems entwined in same. Both names were well known in the small pool of engineers in Dublin at the time.[129]

Work commenced at Cross Guns Bridge (also known as Westmorland Bridge) in May 1790 and proceeded in both an easterly and a westerly direction. In the early years small local contractors carried out the work.[130] About 2,000 men (as against the 3,944 men reportedly working on the Grand Canal) were employed, working in gangs or teams of 140, and were paid tenpence per day. The work was straightforward: lines were pegged out and sections were allocated to different contractors, who then got on with the digging.

In 1763 Charles Vallancey had written a useful treatise on inland navigation, on the art of making rivers navigable, on making canals in all sorts of soils, and on the construction of locks and sluices. He included advice on boring regularly to test soils beneath the position of the floor of the canal to check for bog or rocks, and also advised using cross-cuts to check for soils.

A series of letters between John Smeaton, engineer, and Redmond Morres, one of the subscribers to the Grand Canal, left no room for error in the planning and execution of work on canals: 'Let all the substitute parts have a particular officer assigned to them, in order to relieve the attention of the engineer from everything except the mechanical constructions and deposition of the works and workmen and to see that his orders are duly put into execution'. There was also to be 'a purveyor to look out for and provide materials and agree for the carriage thereof to the places ordered by the engineer'. Each project also required 'a land engineer to measure the lands staked out or proposed for purchase'.[131] Sadly, there was a failure to apply this advice during work on the Royal Canal.

The first section to be built was that between Ashtown and the Liffey. As a major construction it was a shambles; work was shoddy and inconsistent, especially in the lock chambers, because the overseeing engineer, Richard Evans, was nearly always away on the Boyne Navigation and there was no one to take his place. One of the problems of construction at the time was the proper use of mortar. For this and other reasons several locks had to be replaced and a couple of bridges had to be rebuilt, most notably Newcomen Bridge, where two men were killed when the arch collapsed because of insufficient bonding in the stonework.

The major issue for engineers was to make the waterways watertight. This involved the making of puddle clay, finely 'chopped loam' usually mixed with coarse sand or gravel to deter rats. This was then mixed with water to create a pliable plastic material, and up to nine or ten layers were laid on. One hundred years earlier an English visitor to Holland, observing canal technology, noted that 'They have found the common seaweed to be the best material for these digues [dykes] which fastens with a thin mixture of earth, yields a little to the force of the sea, and returns when the waves give back'.[132]

The formula for hydraulic mortar had been known since Roman times, when it was used in the construction of the artificial port of Rome at Ostia. More recently, between 1670 and 1680, exactly the same formula was used in the Canal du Midi in south-west France. Masons added volcanic ash to the usual mix of lime and sand to create cement that would harden under water, but being a versatile and durable material it was also used on land. Thus the technique was known to some degree in Dublin in the late seventeenth and early eighteenth centuries. In Ireland and England— and in Europe, too—engineers would have tried and tested various combinations of ingredients to achieve the same results without having to import Pozzolan from Italy, as the builders of the Canal du Midi did.[133]

By 12 November 1790 enough progress had been made for the lord lieutenant, the earl of Westmorland, to lay the first stone in the first lock; the ceremony was attended by a large crowd. The first lock was not completed until 3 June 1791, however, and the cost was £1,846 9s. 4d. This did not bode well for the budget.

By 1792 work had commenced on the floating docks down at the Liffey's North Wall, and £23,000 was allocated to this aspect of the canal, £7,000 of which was an advance. In the same year Sir Thomas Hyde Page arrived in Ireland at the company's request to find total chaos, particularly on the Dublin section. Levels were often wrong, the positions of some lock chambers were incorrect and some of the timber lock gates were rotting. It would appear that anything that could go wrong did go wrong. Now the original estimate of John Binns, the promoter, proved to have been a spurious exercise at best, and the route to be followed was taken from a 1755 survey map. His method of costing work had been to approach some of the contractors on the Grand Canal and ask them what they charged.

By the early 1800s there was detailed technical advice available in such matters as instructions for the proper laying of foundations for canals, including foundations which were to be 12in. below the bottom of the canal.[134] Advice was also included on the gradient of approach roads to bridges as a descent of one in four from the puddle on the crown of the arch.[135] Each bridge over the canal had to provide for a ramp ascending to the top of the bridge from both sides. The gradient needed to be accurate, for neither foot passengers nor carriages would be able to get up the rise if it was too steep. This access had to be available to carriages in all weathers. A massive amount of material was required to build up this slope. Note, too, that the bridges had to allow space for carriages to pass comfortably on each bridge and approach ramp.

On 22 May 1801 Brownrigg reported that the canal was in full working order from North Strand up to Broadstone.[136] He identified the sea lock at the Liffey, implying that it was finished but that the proposed docks had not been completed at this stage.

During the construction of the Grand Canal on the south side of the Liffey the builders added another basin at Portobello, not just as a harbour for river traffic but also as a source of water supply; the same occurred on the north side, at Broadstone, just up from King Street (Fig 9.22). The ground in and around Blessington Street was purchased from the owners for use as a reservoir. In 1807 the contract was signed and excavation was ready to begin. Mr Swan, Lord Palmerston's agent, agreed a deal with the Royal Canal Company to supply them with earth from the excavation at Blessington Street basin (at a cost of fivepence per cubic yard) to be removed to their harbour at Broadstone, to assist in raising the retaining embankment around the harbour above Upper Dominick Street.[137] A stroll around confirms the short distance between the two works. It must be noted in case of confusion that the canal leading to the harbour was a branch line or spur, and the canal proper continued to operate in the interim. The Blessington basin or reservoir opened in 1809.

While money was changing hands for soil, it was also changing hands in the other direction for water. In June 1806 the city paid the Royal Canal Company £11,156 5s. for water. This was a very substantial sum, amply illustrating the scale of demand for water in Dublin and its consequent value.[138]

The water quality in the Royal Canal became progressively worse as the decades slid by and nothing was done about it, although accusations flew back and forth between the various responsible bodies. The problem, which was plain to every citizen, was simply ignored. Medical science, however, was revealing the danger of dirty water. In 1819 the Assembly resolved 'to prevent the disgraceful

Fig. 9.22—The Broadstone harbour by Samuel Frederick Brocas (c. 1792–1847), across the road from the King's Inns, now filled in (with the kind permission of the NLI).

Fig. 9.23—The excavation for the canal cut at Castleknock (Irish School, early nineteenth century) (photo: Brian Matthews, with the kind permission of James Gorry, Gorry Gallery).

practice of persons bathing in the canal',[139] a practice later termed 'indecent'.[140] Nevertheless, in 1828 humans and dogs bathing in the two canals were still causing concern.[141] During this period both cholera and typhoid epidemics cut down large swathes of the population, and fear roamed the streets. In 1835 the lord mayor complained about the quality of the water in the Royal Canal, claiming that it was 'impure' thanks to the spillage of manure and also to the use of gastar (a type of protective anti-fouling compound) on the hulls of the canal boats.[142]

While there is a shortage of contemporary documents on the actual workings of the canal itself, we can make up for the dearth with odd documents such as the 'Estimates for completing Royal Canal Custom House Lock …' in the archives in Belfast, for example. Also available are a selection of images in the Prints and Drawings collection at the National Library of Ireland which illustrate how work proceeded along the canal (Fig. 9.23).

Trade began on the canal in 1796, the same year in which the Grand Canal Docks opened on the other side of the river. On 2 December 1796 the first passengers were carried between Dublin and Kilcock, fares being lower than either coach or car travel. Trade boats carrying merchandise began to operate, and the cost of transport was 1½–2d. per ton per mile. After a slow start, business improved and a wide variety of goods were transported, including fuel, building material, agricultural produce for the Dublin market and general merchandise. The canal still faced competition from the improving road network, and it was not helped by the fact that it had to close periodically (in some cases for several months) owing to the continuously rising demand for water.[143] This fact would be used to promote the railways when their time arrived.

Patrick O'Kelly wrote that the carriage of peat for fuel gave rise to much activity on the canals and encouraged the draining of large tracts of land in the midlands.[144] Turf was sold directly from canal boats, which did not have to contend with the vagaries of getting into Dublin port.[145] The canal made turf freely available to the Dublin market in large quantities at competitive prices,[146] which had the effect of keeping down coal prices. The Broadstone Harbour, when complete, became a major depot for the sale and distribution of turf. Prior to that, the Irish Turf Company had another yard at the Whitworth Road.[147] By 1839 the tonnage of turf delivered had reached 82,988. This supply of fuel was very important to the citizens of Dublin as a reserve against the inevitable coal shortages. As the roads of Ireland (especially those in and out of the capital) improved, road hauliers tried to compete with the canals by selling turf in the market at 6d. less per ton.[148]

Another of the commercial and social benefits of the Royal Canal was the increase in the potato trade, which was solid thanks to the low rates charged on it from 1800 at the instigation of the directors. Fees were ½d. per ton per mile on the Royal Canal, while the Grand Canal charged 1½d. per ton per mile.[149] The canal also transported live pigs, corn meal, casks of butter, stone, bricks, coal, manure and general merchandise. Of the 131,972 tons carried in 1833, live pigs accounted for 36,002 tons, turf for 22,992 and potatoes for 31,746.[150]

That passengers and goods of a wide variety were utilising the canal can be seen in the notice placed in the *Freeman's Journal* in October 1839 by Matthew Walsh, advertising Sligo oysters for sale in the Dublin market via the five canal boats owned by John McCann at Broadstone. McCann operated at Liffey Lock, down at the North Wall, under the trading name of John McCann & Sons.[151] The canal also carried coal slack to the turf-manufacturing plant set up by McWilliams at Cappagh Bog to make an early version of peat briquettes, which were then transported to Dublin.[152]

Warehousing and facilities for the distribution of goods followed the building of the canal, on a larger scale in Dublin than elsewhere. Between 1821 and 1830 leases for a number of mills were granted between Drumcondra Road and Blanchardstown. Clarke mentions a mill and corn mill at the North Wall first lock, both supplied with water from the canal. This is also the location of the windmill owned by Thomas Duffy which famously burnt down and features in various etchings of the period. Clarke confirms that in 1822 a lease was issued for the mill site at Drumcondra and Glasnevin Road to make glass, and Mallet got a site at the same location to build an iron foundry which went on to supply substantial amounts of iron product to the city, including the railings outside Trinity College.[153] Water was in such demand for industry, for the city and for the canal itself, however, that it automatically restricted further growth.[154]

Collins quotes the *Picture of Dublin* of 1812 describing the Royal Canal: 'The Royal Canal, like the Grand Canal, extends from the city to the river Shannon, and like that, has been injured from the same cause (a too expensive establishment and jobbing) … The canal is now vested in the Director-General of Inland Navigation, under whose management much has already been affected and much more is expected … The accommodation to passengers who travel in the packet boats is certainly very respectable. The boats travel about three and a half miles an hour … There are two cabins in every boat, and two separate fares … A boat leaves the Royal Canal House at the Broadstone for Mullingar every morning at six o clock in the summer and seven in the winter and another boat leaves Mullingar for Dublin.' This gives an indication of passenger traffic on the canal up and down to the midlands. Fares for the full trip were 8s. 4d. in first class and 4s. 10d. in second class.[155] *Saunders's Newsletter* reported on 2 February 1818 that on 31 January the first boat, the *Lanesborough Trecker*, arrived from the Shannon to the Broadstone Harbour amid cheers from spectators, with a fiddler playing merrily on the deck.[156] By the late 1820s iron boats built in Ringsend were in use, each having a capacity of 50 tons.[157] The *Almanack* of 1824 shows that the canal was open from the River Liffey to Tarmonbarry. It gave details of boat movements on the canal: they arrived from Mullingar on Monday, Wednesday and Friday at 7am and also left Dublin for Mullingar at 7am. 'Establishments have been formed for the conveyance of passengers onward from Tarmonbarry.'[158]

Fifteen years after the canal opened, Watty Cox presented the canals as a political story: 'The Royal Canal arose with the revolution of 1782; that year, they were to promise the circulation of our domestic industry, and facilitate a commercial intercourse with our manufacturing towns, which were to appear in every direction. In this view they were to act as rival to England; and to erase the danger, which England apprehended, the Union was resorted to; the expedient answered, our manufacturers have disappeared, the canal is useless, only as a military road, and the proprietors are begging.'[159]

Canal-building was more widespread in England owing to the higher level of industrial development and activity, but substantial work did occur in Ireland eventually. Just as in road-making, the influence of the landlords was again evident. Lord Talbot of Malahide attempted to construct his own canal between the sea and the hinterland north of Swords, using the river and Broadmeadow Estuary at Malahide/Swords. He also changed the route of the Malahide to Dublin road, which used to run right in front of the castle, to bypass his demesne. In Maynooth the landlord was able to insist on altering the route of the Royal Canal to include a harbour at Maynooth (Fig. 9.24).

One of the main effects of the Royal Canal was the laying out of boundaries in the defining of the new size of the space enclosed on the north side of the Liffey. The bridges erected over it also assisted in further development, defining how thoroughfares would develop and contributing to building along and around them. The first one built, Newcomen Bridge, cemented the new route across the north strand to Annesley Bridge over the Tolka, constructed almost immediately after it.

Fig. 9.24—Maynooth Harbour in front of the college, with castle on right (photo: Brian Matthews, with the kind permission of James Gorry, Gorry Gallery).

The road out to Raheny, Malahide, Howth and Clontarf was now established, even though care was needed not to become bogged down by the tide at Clontarf (Railway Bridge). The next bridge inland from the bay, at Summerhill (Fig. 9.25), led to the bridge over the Tolka at Ballybough. Ballybough, of course, was the former location of Mud Island, which was now absorbed into the greater space bordered by the Liffey and Tolka walls. East of the Summerhill Bridge was another stone bridge across the canal at the Jones Road entry to Croke Park. The bridge over the canal at Lower Dorset Street and Drumcondra Road was named Binn's Bridge after John Binns, a director of the Royal Canal Company in 1791.[160] The Jones Road Bridge was a later addition; the road was preceded by a path through the fields to Clonliffe House, which was the other building owned by the Feinaglian School of Aldeborough House.[161] This allowed connection with the access that the Drumcondra Bridge offered via the road to Swords and the north. The Whitworth Hospital was constructed in 1818, showing the extent of development.

The area just east of the Custom House, which had all been reclaimed from the tides, was now a construction site not only for an exit of the Royal Canal out into the Liffey and the sea but also for proposed new docks on a similar but smaller scale to the Grand Canal Docks, and this development was being driven by the Revenue Commissioners. Their plan, with the approval of John Beresford, was to create stores, sheds and controlled warehouses with vaults around these new docks. To this end Whitmore Davis, surveyor to the Revenue Commissioners, submitted a plan in July 1810. He suggested that the proposed stores and floating dock should 'consist of a range of vaults underground … to be adequate to store 1360 pipes of wine or spirits … 1364 hogsheads of sugar and 609 hogsheads of tobacco'. He added that 'the quay between the stores and the docks was laid down at 500 feet, that between the Liffey and dock 80 feet, the dock to be 696 feet long by 349 feet wide, which would support 26 vessels in single line', and further submitted 'that the accommodation

Fig. 9.25—The Summerhill canal bridge and towpath (photo: Brian Matthews).

between the present and proposed quay should be as convenient as possible'. He concludes with 'I would beg leave to recommend the placing of a range of sheds along three sides of the dock'.[162] John Rennie (later Sir John Rennie) was asked to look over the plan by Revenue. Rennie had some suggestions, such as 'framing the roof of buildings to be made of cast iron, many buildings in Manchester and Glasgow have been constructed in this manner',[163] but in the main supported Davis's proposals. These plans were largely executed and most of these structures, including the vaults, still exist today, the entire area now converted to leisure activities around the Custom House Docks Scheme.

There is a difference of opinion as to when exactly the connection was made between the canal and the Liffey. Maps of the city show it as connected by 1800, and *Wilson's Dublin Directory* clearly claims that in 1800 'The canal is now complete from the river Liffey to Newcastle'.[164] In 1823 a letter to the board of the Corporation from the directors of the Royal Canal Company reported that an accumulation of gravel in the Liffey at the entrance to the Company's docks at the North Wall obstructed the passage of vessels and requested that it be removed. The board acknowledged receipt and ordered George Halpin to comply.[165]

Halpin reported on 28 January 1822 that the Royal Canal between the bridge opposite Mayor Street and Newcomen Bridge was 'in many places considerably washed away' and that during the high tide on Friday 28 January 'water moved within a few inches of the top of the banks'.[166]

Over the subsequent years, on the other side of the walls separating the canal basin from the Liffey, the need for upgrading work to be carried out on either side of the river became evident to all. The Ballast Board reported in 1846 that 'evidence shows that the quays foundation is so generally imperfect that they will not in their present state admit of the river being further deepened'.[167] The

Corporation added 550yds of timber frontage to the north quay. It also reported other work, consisting of 'rebuilding of a great part of the quay walls'.

The story of the Royal Canal did not end overnight or all that quickly. By 1819–20 it was well established, and it was proposed to extend it into the Erne waterway and Lough Neagh systems. At this time the industrial revolution in Great Britain was literally exploding rather than just expanding and the development of steam was seen everywhere, although the proposer of a plan to extend the Royal Canal into Ballinasloe saw the arrival of steam power as an ally to the canals rather than as lethal competition. The arrival of the train, however, dealt a killer blow to a transport system which had never made any financial sense in the first place and whose erratic water supply in the early years did nothing to help. Trains could always transport more people and so it would prove with the Midland Railway operating in the same theatre as the Royal Canal.

Having purchased the canal in 1845 for £318,860, in January 1846 the Midland Great Western Railway began to build a railway station behind the harbour at Broadstone—signalling, for those paying attention, the inevitable demise of canals as a form of transport in Ireland.[168]

The Royal and Grand canals had the effect of promoting the new arrangement of hotel accommodation rather than the old *ad hoc* inn-type accommodation. The first hotel along the route of the Grand Canal was opened in 1794 at Sallins and was quickly replaced by a second at Robertstown, which led to a small urban cluster. In 1802 another hotel was begun at Tullamore. Closer to the city, the Portobello Hotel was built in 1807. The Royal Canal saw the establishment of the Moyvalley Hotel and the opening of a hotel in Phibsborough, beside the Broadstone Harbour.[169] In Dublin the Royal Canal also became useful as a boundary when the new Mountjoy Prison was opened in 1850, not long after the Drogheda Railway, adding another major civic work to the occupation of new suburbs.

The Royal Canal and its bridges changed the topography of north Dublin. It encouraged development around new streets, bridges and roads. New industries, fostering new skills, grew out of it, along with new forms of employment. Mills and hotels were erected along its length. Its construction improved the water supply for the city from the canal itself and also enabled the basin reservoir at Blessington Street to be built in the new sector of the city. It was one of several important components which collectively helped to fill the new city that had expanded since the walls of 1728 and assisted in the overall plan for the North Lotts.

Notes

[1] Dillon Cosgrove, 'Clonliffe', *Journal of the Royal Society of Antiquaries of Ireland* (5th ser.) **14** (1904), p. 363.
[2] James Culliton, 'The Four Courts, Dublin', *Dublin Historical Record* **21** (4), p. 116.
[3] *Ibid.*
[4] Edward McParland, 'The early history of James Gandon's Four Courts', *The Burlington Magazine* **122** (932) (1980), 727–33, p. 727.
[5] *Ibid.*
[6] Culliton, 'The Four Courts', pp 122–3.
[7] *Ibid.*, p. 124.
[8] *Ibid.*, p. 124.
[9] J. Collins, *Life in old Dublin* (Dublin, 1913), p. 6.
[10] *The Dublin Journal*, 29 May 1796.
[11] Maire Kennedy, 'Dublin's coffee houses in the eighteenth century', *Dublin Historical Record* **63** (1) (2010), 29–39, p. 35.
[12] *The Gentleman's and Citizen's Almanack*, compiled by John Watson Stewart (Dublin, 1800), pp 166–9.
[13] *Ibid.*, p. 7.

[14] *The Gentleman's and Citizen's Almanack*, compiled by John Watson Stewart (Dublin, 1820), pp 196–8.
[15] *Ibid.*, pp 45–50.
[16] *Ibid.*, pp 50–1.
[17] *Ibid.*, p. 56.
[18] *Ibid.*, p. 168.
[19] Paula Lynch, 'A Dublin street—North Great George's Street', *Dublin Historical Record* **31** (1) (1977), 14–21, p. 16.
[20] *Ibid.*, p. 18.
[21] Diarmuid O'Grada, *Georgian Dublin: the forces that shaped the city* (Cork, 2015), p. 205.
[22] James H. Murphy, *Ireland: a social, cultural and literary history, 1791–1891* (Dublin, 2003), p. 38.
[23] O'Grada, *Georgian Dublin*, p. 171.
[24] *Ibid.*, p. 173.
[25] *Ibid.*, p. 129.
[26] *Dublin Penny Journal*, 27 October 1832, pp 141–3, at p. 143.
[27] O'Grada, *Georgian Dublin*, p. 82.
[28] Patrick O'Kelly, 'Road transport before the coming of the railways', unpublished Ph.D thesis, London School of Economics (1921), p. 59.
[29] George Semple, *A treatise on building in water, in two parts* (Dublin, 1776), p. 20.
[30] *Ibid.*, p. 40.
[31] David Dickson, *Dublin: the making of a capital city* (London, 2014), p. 163.
[32] Rob Goodbody, 'Bridges', in A. Carpenter, R. Loeber, H. Campbell, L. Hurley, J. Montague and E. Rowley (eds), *Art and architecture of Ireland, vol. 4. Architecture 1600–2000* (Dublin, 2015), p. 147.
[33] G.N. Wright, *A historical guide to the city of Dublin* (Dublin, 1821), p. 274.
[34] Louis McRedmond, *To the greater glory: a history of the Irish Jesuits* (Dublin, 1991), p. 139.
[35] Michael J. Tutty, 'Bridges over the Liffey', *Dublin Historical Record* **35** (1) (1981), 23–33, pp 29–30.
[36] J.F. Daly, 'O'Connell Bridge and its environs', *Dublin Historical Record* **14** (3) (1957), 85–93, p. 85.
[37] *Ibid.*, p. 86.
[38] Kennedy, 'Dublin's coffee houses of the eighteenth century', p. 30.
[39] John Gamble, *Sketches of history, politics and manners, taken in Dublin, and the north of Ireland* (London, 1818), p. 61.
[40] O'Grada, *Georgian Dublin*, p. 80.
[41] Manuscript diaries of Benjamin Oakley during three tours in Ireland 1819, 1825 and 1827, NLI MS 11,938; 1819 diary, pp 83–4.
[42] Oakley, 1825 diary, p. 152.
[43] Ann Plumtre, *Narrative of a residence in Ireland during the summer of 1814 and that of 1815* (London, 1817), p. 43.
[44] Nuala Burke, 'Dublin 1600–1800: a study in morphogenesis', unpublished Ph.D thesis, Trinity College Dublin (1972), p. 434.
[45] John De Courcy, 'A bridge in its time: the River Liffey crossing at Church Street in Dublin', *Proceedings of the Royal Irish Academy* **90**C (1990), 243–57, p. 255.
[46] Tutty, 'Bridges over the Liffey', p. 30.
[47] 'Suspension bridges', *Irish Penny Journal* **1** (34) (20 February 1841), 267–8, p. 268.
[48] Goodbody, 'Bridges', p. 147.
[49] *CARD*, vol. 18, p. 52.
[50] *Dublin Penny Journal*, Vol. 3, Supplement: Views in Dublin (1835), pp. ix–xvi.
[51] Journal of the proceedings of the Corporation for Preserving and Improving the Port of Dublin, vol. 12 (9 May 1823–25 August 1826), p. 238.
[52] O'Grada, *Georgian Dublin*, p. 55.
[53] *Ibid.*, p. 82.
[54] *Ibid.*, p. 110.
[55] Registry of Deeds, King's Inns, Dublin, book 89.
[56] Port Ledger, p. 130 (Dublin Port Archive Vault at Glenbeigh Records Storage, Damastown, Dublin 15).
[57] *Ibid.*, p. 157.
[58] Sarah Ward-Perkins, 'Bank of Ireland—old Parliament House', *Dublin Historical Record* **37** (2) (1984), 42–53, p. 42.
[59] Andrew O'Brien, 'The history of Nelson's Pillar', *Dublin Historical Record* **60** (1), 15–23.
[60] Andrew Bigelow, *Leaves from a journal: Bigelow's sketches of rambles in some parts of north Britain and Ireland chiefly in*

the year 1817 (Boston, 1821), p. 123.
61 T. Cromwell, *The Irish tourist or excursions through Ireland, province of Leinster*, vol. 3 (Dublin, 1820), p. 151.
62 *Ibid.*, p. 147.
63 Ann Mullin and Kevin Whelan, 'Roads', in A. Carpenter, R. Loeber, H. Campbell, L. Hurley, J. Montague and E. Rowley (eds), *Art and architecture of Ireland, vol. 4. Architecture 1600–2000* (Dublin, 2015), p. 143.
64 *Dublin Penny Journal*, Vol. 3, Supplement: Views in Dublin (1835), pp. ix-xvi
65 'Considerations on the removal of the Custom House humbly submitted to the public'(pamphlet, Dublin, 1781), p. 6. NLI P1380 (3).
66 *Ibid.*, p. 11.
67 *Ibid.*, pp 3–4.
68 Timothy Dawson, 'Crane Lane to Ballybough', *Dublin Historical Record* **27** (4) (1973), 131–45, p. 132.
69 'Considerations on the removal of the Custom House', p. 11.
70 Dickson, *Dublin: the making of a capital city*, p. 219.
71 G.F. Cumming, 'James Gandon: his work in Ireland', *The Irish Monthly*, pp 319–20.
72 *Ibid.*
73 *Ibid.*, p. 322.
74 Viola Barrow, 'Dublin Custom House—the river heads', *Dublin Historical Record* **29** (1) (1975), 24–7, p. 24.
75 'Notes of a tour in north Wales and Ireland 1788', TCD MS 891, p. 36.
76 Oakley, 1819 diary, pp 61–2.
77 Dickson, *Dublin: the making of a capital city*, p. 221.
78 O'Grada, *Georgian Dublin*, p. 116; *Freeman's Journal*, 26 June 1791.
79 Mr Hartnell, *Instructions for the housekeeper of the Custom House at Dublin* (Dublin, 1845), NLI 3A 5935.
80 Gamble, *Sketches of history, politics and manners*, p. 20.
81 Plumtre, *Narrative of a residence in Ireland*, p. 17.
82 Henry Inglis, *Ireland in 1834: a journey throughout Ireland during the summer and autumn by Henry D. Inglis* (London, 1834), p. 14.
83 John Barrow, *A tour around Ireland through the sea counties in the autumn of 1835* (London, 1836), p. 374.
84 Ruth Heard, 'Public works in Ireland, 1800–1831', unpublished MLitt. thesis, Trinity College Dublin (1977), p. 80.
85 Ward-Perkins, 'Bank of Ireland', p. 43.
86 *Freeman's Journal*, 6 August 1824.
83 Michael J. Tutty, Review of *History of the parish of Drumcondra, North Strand, St Barabbas*, by Arthur Garret. *Dublin Historical Record* **24** (2) (1971), p. 43.
88 House of Commons Journals, vol. 19, 32 G 3, c 37.
89 *Ibid.*, 33 G 3, c 26.
90 Diarmuid G. Hiney, '5618 and all that: the Jewish cemetery, Fairview Strand', *Dublin Historical Record* **50** (2) (1997), 119–29, p. 123.
91 *Ibid.*, p. 124.
92 *Ibid.*, p. 126.
93 *Ibid.*, p. 119.
94 *Ibid.*, p. 121.
95 *Ibid.*, p. 122.
96 NLI, MS 16 G 16 (37).
97 Journal of the proceedings of the Corporation for Preserving and Improving the Port of Dublin, vol. 12, p. 413.
98 *Ibid.*, p. 161.
99 *Ibid.*, p. 102.
100 *Ibid.*, p. 236.
101 *Ibid.*, p. 219 (1 October 1824).
102 *Ibid.*, pp 99–100.
103 Lt. Joseph Archer, *Statistical survey of the county of Dublin with observations for the RDS* (Dublin, 1801), p. 87.
104 *CARD*, vol. 14, pp 379–80.
105 *Ibid.*, p. 381.
106 G.N. Wright, *An historical guide to ancient and modern Dublin* (London, 1821).
107 Dillon Cosgrove, *North Dublin: city and environs* (Dublin, 1909), p. 31.
108 Aidan O'Boyle, 'Aldeborough House', *Irish Architectural and Decorative Studies: the journal of the Irish Georgian*

Society **4** (2001), 102–41, p. 109.

[109] *Ibid.*, p. 111.
[110] *Ibid.*, p. 112.
[111] *Ibid.*, p. 112.
[112] *Ibid.*, p. 120.
[113] Michael Quane, 'The Feinaiglian Institution, Dublin', *Dublin Historical Record* **19** (2) (1964), 30–44, p. 32.
[114] *Ibid.*, p. 34.
[115] *Ibid.*, p. 36.
[116] *Ibid.*, p. 37.
[117] *Ibid.*, p. 40.
[118] *Ibid.*, p. 40.
[119] Hely Dutton, *Observations on Mr Archer's statistical survey of the county of Dublin* (Dublin, 1802), p. 148.
[120] Cromwell, *The Irish tourist*, vol. 3, p. 145.
[121] Inglis, *Ireland in 1834*, p. 9.
[122] Thomas Reid, *Travels in Ireland in the year 1822, exhibiting brief sketches of the moral, physical and political state of the country with reflections on the best means of improving its condition* (London, 1823).
[123] Bigelow, *Leaves from a journal*.
[124] Plumtre, *Narrative of a residence in Ireland*, p. 12.
[125] O'Kelly, 'Road transport before the coming of the railways', p. 264.
[126] *Ibid.*, p, 298.
[127] *Ibid.*, p. 115.
[128] Headland Archaeology, unpublished report for Waterways Ireland, p. 6.
[129] *Ibid.*, p. 9.
[130] *Ibid.*, p. 7.
[131] John Smeaton to Redmond Morres, *Letters between Redmond Morres esq one of the subscribers to the Grand Canal and John Smeaton esq engineer in 1771–2* (Dublin, 1773), p. 33. Pamphlet collection NLI LO 14121.
[132] Thomas Park, *The Harleian miscellany: a collection of scarce, curious and entertaining pamphlets and tracts* (London, 1808), vol. 1, p. 597.
[133] Chandra Mukerji, 'Tacit knowledge and classical technique in seventeenth-century France: hydraulic cement as a living practice among masons and military engineers', *Technology and Culture* **47** (2006), 257–77.
[134] Peter Clarke, *The Royal Canal: the complete story* (Dublin, 1992), p. 306.
[135] *Ibid.*, p. 307.
[136] Headland Archaeology report, p. 11.
[137] *CARD*, vol. 16, p. 25.
[138] *Ibid.*, p. 72.
[139] *CARD*, vol. 17, p. 226.
[140] *Ibid.*, p. 248.
[141] *CARD*, vol. 16, p. 80.
[142] *CARD*, vol. 19, p. 209.
[143] Peter Clarke, 'The Royal Canal 1789–1791', *Dublin Historical Record* **46** (1) (1993), 46–52, p. 51.
[144] O'Kelly, 'Road transport', p. 292.
[145] Minute-book of the Royal Canal Company, August 1824, p. 96.
[146] *Ibid.*, p. 95.
[147] Clarke, *The Royal Canal*, p. 95.
[148] *Ibid.*, p. 96.
[149] Clarke, 'The Royal Canal 1789–1791'.
[150] Clarke, *The Royal Canal*, Appendix C, p. 156.
[151] Brian J. Goggin, *The Royal under the railway: Ireland's Royal Canal 1830–1899* (Derby, 2014), p. 22.
[152] *Ibid.*, p. 24.
[153] Clarke, *The Royal Canal*, pp 94–5.
[154] Minute-book of the Royal Canal Company, August 1824, p. 93.
[155] Collins, *Life in old Dublin*, pp 91–2.
[156] *Saunders's Newsletter*, 2 February 1818.
[157] Goggin, *The Royal under the railway*, p. 28.
[158] *The Gentleman's and Citizen's Almanack (as compiled by the late John Watson Stewart) for the year of our Lord 1824*

(Dublin, 1824), p. 159.
[159] Dickson, *Dublin: the making of a capitol city*, p. 273.
[160] Cosgrove, *North Dublin: city and environs*, p. 43.
[161] *Ibid.*, p. 62.
[162] Whitmore Davis, surveyor to Revenue Commissioners: Submission and plans for development on North Wall, 1 July 1810, PRONI, D562 7763.
[163] John Rennie: Dublin, the North Wall Docks, comments on plans for same by Whitmore Davis, PRONI, D562 7763.
[164] *Wilson's Dublin directory, 1800* (Dublin, 1800), p. 153.
[165] Journal of the proceedings of the Corporation for Preserving and Improving the Port of Dublin, vol. 12 (9 May 1823–25 August 1826), pp 70–1. NAI.
[166] *Ibid.*, vol. 11, p. 323.
[167] Commissioners for the Ballast Board (9 vols): contents of vol. 3, Part 1, Tidal harbours, p. vii.
[168] Clarke, 'The Royal Canal 1789–1993', p. 51.
[169] Livia Hurley and John McKeown, 'Canals and inland navigation', in A. Carpenter, R. Loeber, H. Campbell, L. Hurley, J. Montague and E. Rowley (eds), *Art and architecture of Ireland, vol. 4. Architecture 1600–2000* (Dublin, 2015), p. 150.

10. Churches, schools and hospitals on the north side of Dublin

After the new north bank of the Liffey was completed in 1728 and the wall continued round to Ballybough Bridge, an enormous amount of space became available to drain, occupy and build on. The original idea of the North Lotts became a real possibility for developing the city outwards. People could now realistically imagine what was envisaged. It is clear that the higher ground was built on first, as the growth began to creep out from the edges of the old medieval town around Capel Street and its environs. This was inevitable, because the bridge and therefore Capel Street provided the major access in and out of the city and to both Trinity College and parliament.

Churches, schools and hospitals are the best prisms through which to examine the outward spread of the city, as they provide better evidence for settlement than any other activities. This chapter will examine their effect on the citizens and on the landscape. As observed earlier, the nineteenth century saw the emergence of new kinds of government and administration and a new kind of state, one that intervened more directly in the lives of its citizens.[1] In examining the totality of these aspects of development in the new city, it becomes obvious that the pace of occupation, building, conversion of structures and movement of people was frenetic in its reaction to changing circumstances. It was in essence an explosion of activity, all occurring alongside the great urban structures of social and civic importance such as roads, railways and harbours, as the State became more directly involved with the city population.

The larger edifices of the Four Courts, Carlisle Bridge and the Custom House, as already noted, each acted as a focus of activity, bringing changes in living and working that had an impact on the city in social terms. Churches, schools and hospitals had a similar effect as they began to proliferate. They each represent local activity and were vital to the growth in the new space. They cannot be seen in isolation, as each had an impact on the others. It is the intention to concentrate on these developments primarily on the north side, showing how they affected the space and the people who came to occupy it.

Change had begun with the passing of the various Relief Acts which permitted Catholics to vote in parliamentary elections, to buy and sell land, and to have Mass-houses. Catholics were not allowed to refer to their places of worship as churches; they were to be called chapels, and no church bells were allowed.[2]

Social pressure also arose in the form of the men returning from the army which had been fighting all across Europe against Napoleon. Huge numbers had been enlisted; James Murphy maintains that the Irish accounted for as much as one sixth of the total British land forces. Sadly, there is no detailed information on unemployed sailors released from the navy.[3]

It will be seen that the development worked along the higher ground at first (as seen in the 5m line referred to in the section on geology), and then took hold along roads, rivers and canals and adjacent to bridges, as it spread out from the original medieval town in an easterly and northerly slant. By the end of the first decade of the 1800s the roads out of the city had become firmly established: the Queen Street to Stoneybatter route; the Church Street route up past King's Inns, past the harbour at Broadstone and on to Phibsborough and beyond; the Capel Street route to Bolton Street, Dorset Street and the Lower Drumcondra Road, on towards the north; from Marino the Malahide Road out to Donnycarney, on to Coolock and then to Malahide; and the new Clontarf to Howth roads, both the shore and the inland versions, both facilitated by the recent Annesley Bridge. Coach and hackney travel was by now available on all these routes, making life easier for the wealthier citizens who had homes outside the city as well as within. And it wasn't only disembarking passengers from England who occupied all the hotels now located on made ground; internal travellers, too, used these establishments, as well as the ordinary citizens.

Hospitals were mostly built on a voluntary basis up to the turn of the nineteenth century, and the whole process of the dispensing of medical help was based on volunteers. The nineteenth century would bring more formal civic structure to the question of medicine, with dispensaries and clinics added to the growing provision of medical assistance available from municipal resources. The development of medical science added to the momentum of change, with greater medical knowledge and new discoveries. Most hospitals were built close to where people lived. The decision-makers had the sense to locate these institutions in areas where they could do most good—the Lock Hospital in Townsend Street just off the quays, for the treatment of venereal diseases, being a case in point. The section on hospitals and medicine will take into account the typhoid and cholera epidemics of the early nineteenth century, and under the same heading we will include orphanages and facilities for the blind and the deaf.

Many new churches were added to the number on the north side of Dublin in the later eighteenth century, but much building took place after 1800. It will be seen that these new churches both contributed to the building up of parishes and created new parishes, as well as attracting clusters of population wherever they were established, and they often added impetus through Sunday Schools and other schools. Churches also appeared as parts of hospitals and schools, such as the Rotunda Hospital, Aldeborough House and the Loreto College in North Great George's Street—private houses which in each case became a school. Churches also implied parishes, in that the people who used the churches lived locally. This also applied to schools and hospitals. They are therefore a sound barometer of the spread of occupation in the space of the north city.

As schools, too, are to be used as measures of the outward growth of the city, we have to look at why and how education was also essential in creating clusters of communities.

It is the contention of the writer that, while the city grew out in an eastward and north-eastward direction in the eighteenth century, much of this growth consisted of dwellings. Schools, like cottage industries such as weaving, were then located mainly in homes. Hospitals as we would recognise them today—such as the Rotunda and Jervis Street—were few in number, but dispensaries and clinics were quite prolific, and the new century brought more formalised medical arrangements. Churches, particularly Catholic churches, had seen very little growth in the years before 1800, but the Act of Union created an expectation for Catholic Emancipation. A certain amount of civic development took place, albeit on a small scale. In terms of schools, churches and hospitals there was some building, but as regards hospitals it was a case of mostly volunteer supply and often with a built-in political motivation, such as the rescue of Protestant orphans and poor with some volunteer assistance. This, in fact, applied in the case of both schools and hospitals.

One of the few areas of growth in Protestant churches was the creation of the new parish of St Thomas in 1749, when St Mary's grew too large. By 1800 there were five parishes on the north bank of the Liffey, where one had sufficed 100 years before.

The Protestant churches remained largely static in number in and around the city, with a few exceptions, the demand for such churches having already been met. In the nineteenth century, however, as more affluent citizens were able to move out of the city to more pleasant surroundings, new places of worship were required. The facility of a synagogue on the north bank of the Liffey was required, and in 1834 the old building in the Liffey Street zone which had been occupied by the Bank of Ireland before its move to College Green became a synagogue for the following 60 years.[4]

This subject is too big to apply to the entire city, so we will attempt to confine our examination to the north side, looking at the area roughly walled in by 1728 and including the North Lotts, as well as the suburban growth of the first decades of the nineteenth century. All three aspects—churches, schools and hospitals—were subject to the political and religious conditions pertaining up to Emancipation and for some fifteen years afterwards.

With the Act of Union the State would become more involved. Education, the vote and Catholic Emancipation became important issues and would have to be faced by those in authority. They could not continue to ignore the growing number of Irish—mostly Catholic—in the English navy and army, although mutiny did not necessarily have to be driven by religion, as seen in the naval mutiny at Spithead at the end of the eighteenth century. And with the early murmurings of education for the masses in England, for how long could the tide of demand be held back here in Ireland? When Napoleon was finally defeated and the French threat greatly reduced, along with the ending of the war with America, politics on both islands would inevitably revert back to non-security matters.

The outcome of all this was that all three of these activities became much more formalised and prolific. It is of interest that, as the city absorbed more and more people, the chasm between the poor and the better-off remained, but slums and poverty are not the subject of this examination. The intention is to trace activity, opinion and attitudes during the approach to Emancipation and for some years after, to note how all three aspects were inextricably linked, and to examine their impact on the spread of the city and its citizens.

Churches and religion

Catholic Emancipation was an issue for the majority population in the opening years of the new century, along with education and tithes. The subject of education began to be tackled in various ways and Emancipation was finalised by 1829, but tithes took longer and caused much aggravation because of the sheer unfairness of the system of administration and the corruption involved. Only five years after Emancipation, clergyman William Ryder arrived with a military detachment at Mrs Ryan's home in Rathcormac, Co. Cork, to collect the sum of £2. In an ensuing skirmish, her son and eleven other people were killed and over 40 injured.[5]

There was no shortage of opinion on the state of Ireland and her people. Noel Baptist Wriothesley summed up the situation as he saw it: 'although forming part of the wealthiest empire in the world, the mass of its inhabitants scarcely has the necessities of life'.[6] 'Surrounding barbarism tempts its aristocracy to emigrate, civil discord drives out its thriving peasantries and starvation greets its paupers: yet their numbers and their miseries continue to multiply.'[7]

Alice Murray wrote that 'England hated Roman Catholicism because it seemed to be fraught with danger to the state ... It was an alien rule in the midst of an alien population, for it consisted of representatives of the ruling caste.' She did allow, though, that every other expanding European state behaved similarly.[8] In the early nineteenth century, however, this area was a battleground of an ongoing war to win people to one or other religion, because this was seen as the key to political control and the future good governance of the country. Daire Keogh wrote that 'it is difficult to exaggerate the extent of sectarian tension in nineteenth-century Ireland'. The Bible-promoting foot-soldiers, primarily Protestant and Methodist, spread across the land, and the Catholic Church fought against their hegemony. As Keogh maintained, the conversion of Ireland to biblical Protestantism was seen as vital to the process of making Ireland British. In this Keogh echoed writer Desmond Bowen, who also described it as a war that had expanded with a sermon by Archbishop William Magee in October 1822 in which he claimed that the Church of Ireland was the only legitimate ecclesiastical body and that it should bring the entire population, including Catholics and Dissenters, into its fold.[9]

Alice Murray saw Ireland's problems as arising not from religion but from its being disadvantaged by the manner in which English commerce saw off competition and the possible growth of Irish industry by using their influence and power via politics, which often translated into religion. She made clear that, since the time of Charles I, Ireland was not allowed to become wealthy to compete with England. Her main point was that Ireland was in a less favourable position than that of an English colony.[10]

Methodism had been very active since the visits of John Wesley from the middle of the eighteenth century. D.N. Hempton said that the Wesleyans and the Quakers had had a softer journey than other proselytisers, such as ultra-Catholics, evangelical Anglicans and Calvinistic Presbyterians, because the Wesleyans hosted preachers who delivered in Irish and the Quakers managed to convey a more neutral stance.[11] Methodism offered a rich ground to be tilled by their missionaries, as seen in the fact that Wesley made 21 visits to Ireland. By 1789 he had over 14,000 followers.[12] Methodism had a simple tenet: if Ireland was to obtain peace, it must be converted. They saw the way forward as lying in the joint efforts of Wesleyans and the Anglicans who were willing to preach the Gospel,[13] but the Catholics were resisting via their clergy: 'But more than all the rest is the control they are under to their crafty, intolerant clergy'.[14] When in 1812 the question of Catholic Emancipation was before the House of Commons, the Methodists succeeded in getting a spokesman elected. His task was to derail all attempts at Emancipation.[15] Joseph Butterworth was their voice until he died in 1826.[16] He took a very active part in parliament in vehemently opposing any concession on Emancipation, but Irish Catholic nationalism was as 'rigid and unyielding as the system it opposed'.[17] The fear remained for Methodists that Emancipation was only the beginning for Catholic nationalism, and that it would end with taking back the land seized 200 years previously.[18]

It would be unfair to give the view only of Protestant antipathy to Emancipation. In 1812 Revd John Evans began to gather a list of names of Protestants, including some dozens of clergymen from Belfast, Ballymena, Newry, Markethill, Ballyclare, Loughbrickland, Lurgan, Warrenpoint and several other locations, which was to be handed in to parliament in support of the call for Catholic Emancipation.[19]

It was not always just religion that was the perceived problem. Race or nationality arose, too, in the area of opinion and discussion. How were the Irish perceived, and how did that blend into the whole religious aspect? James Hardy quoted the earl of Charlemont: 'a great change has happened

Fig. 10.1—Remains of the Greek Orthodox church in Gloucester Street (now Seán McDermott Street) with (below) its Greek inscription, 'Glory to the One Wise God our Saviour' (translation by Dr Philip Kay) (photo: Brian Matthews).

since my boyish days when, as I well recollect, an Irishman was the standing jest of the theatre, when England ever appeared the imperious and not always the enlightened mistress; whilst Ireland remained her humble untaught domestic, to be dragged after her in war, or in peace, just as she thought proper … England clad in the commerce of the world, Ireland restricted to be soliciting manufacturing and called on by her superior to weep when she wept, to smile when she smiled or go mad when she did.'[20] This is the opinion of one of the most influential landowners in Dublin at the time, who, coincidentally, was also in favour of Catholic Emancipation. Observers noted, however, that religion and politics were for the most part inextricably linked. John Barrow said of Ireland: 'I have avoided, as much as it is possible in Ireland, the all-engrossing topics of religion and politics, the difficulty of doing which is increased since they have both become so intimately intertwined'.[21]

The State was quite capable of dealing with difficult or awkward situations, one of the more obvious examples being the manner in which Maynooth was allowed to be set up to train Irish priests. It was founded in 1793 on the back of the French Revolution, with the State deciding that it was more palatable to deal with home-grown, more malleable priests than with the possibility of importing extreme rebellion, poisonous ideology and the potential loss of control of an important colony through the influence of priests educated in Europe, especially France. Very soon Maynooth housed 205 students.[22]

As the achievements constructed on the ground are examined, they become even more impressive in light of the overall context of the time. It was not just about Protestant versus Catholic. Also in the city then were churches catering to Methodists, the Welsh community, the Greek

Orthodox community (Fig. 10.1) and Episcopalians, all in this area of reclaimed land on the north side of the city. As we shall discover, it was amongst children, especially orphans, that much of a proxy war for hearts, minds and loyalty was waged.

Ann Plumtre, visiting Dublin in the summers of 1814 and 1815, noted that there were sixteen meeting houses for Dissenters, ten Catholic chapels, six friaries and six nunneries but no synagogue.[23]

Vast sums of money were collected and spent on new churches. They required labour on a large scale, as well as a wide range of technical skills in the construction, finish and fitting out, employing carpenters, masons, plaster craftsmen and ironworkers. Stone, timber, ironmongery and glass had to be transported to site, offering opportunities in supply. This would have involved a great number of horses, and consequently a great number of carters. The Malton view of Sackville Street of 1803 shows clearly the sheer density of horse-drawn traffic in the metropolis at the time; note that a total of nine different types of vehicles are included.[24] Each church was a mini-industry involving a wide range of services, run by volunteers and mainly parishioners, a focus for communal development which otherwise might not occur. It was often the case that the church building was one of several in a complex. It is a given that these parishioners lived near their churches, especially in the case of the less-well-off Catholics, those without horses or carriages. People also supported religious activities in other ways, however, such as public fund-raising sermons, and those blessed with personality, charisma and a good voice could command great crowds. Walter Kirwan gave a sermon that raised £921 for the Female Orphan House in 1793, as observed by one witness, who noted the 'great crowds' and the 'numberless carriages'.[25]

The Methodists were fully engaged in the city throughout the first four decades of the nineteenth century. Their founder, John Wesley, had arrived in Dublin in 1747, at which time the

Fig. 10.2—Methodist church, Great Charles Street (now Pavee Point) (photo: Brian Matthews).

Fig. 10.3—Methodist Church, Langrishe Place, off Gardiner Street (photo: Brian Matthews).

Methodists engaged a building in Marlborough Street, close to Abbey Street. They later adapted it for their use and continued to use it for another 50 years.[26] They located another chapel close to the new Royal Barracks at Blackhall Place, as they had members of the congregation among the military.[27] By 1805 they had acquired a site at Great Charles Street (behind Summerhill) and built a church. When they moved from this location twenty years later, the Jesuits attempted to buy the building but could not complete the purchase because it would have been used as a Catholic church, and the landlord would not permit the sale for this reason. This building is today used by Pavee Point, the Traveller Community organisation (Fig. 10.2).

The Wide Streets Commission had an issue with the aesthetics, but the Methodists firmly refused to fit in with the Commission's plans.[28] In 1821 they built a new chapel just metres from the original Marlborough Street location, on Lower Abbey Street, in the heart of the growing north side of the city.[29] They later purchased a chapel in Hardwick Street which had started life as a convent chapel for nuns, who then sold it to the Jesuits, who in turn sold it in 1843. It housed a primary school and a teacher-training facility.

The separate group of Methodists who had occupied the chapel at Great Charles Street ran into financial difficulties and had to move to Langrishe Place (Fig. 10.3). Great Charles Street is just off the north side of Mountjoy Square, near the junction of Summerhill and Gardiner Street and North Circular Road.[30] Thus they did not move very far, perhaps 300m, which allows the assumption that there were potential adherents in the locale.[31] Meanwhile, in 1838 the Welsh Calvinistic Methodist Church, called the Bethel, was built in Talbot Street.[32]

The Jesuit presence in the city comprised two distinct periods, one pre-1800 and one post-1800. The earlier period saw them spread over the city until the eighteenth century. Specifically on

Fig. 10.4—Trinitarian Church, North William Street (photo: Brian Matthews).

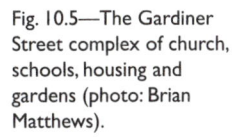

Fig. 10.5—The Gardiner Street complex of church, schools, housing and gardens (photo: Brian Matthews).

the north side they were based at Mary's Lane, Chancery Lane and George's Hill, all at the same location just inland of the later Four Courts. Louis McRedmond notes that in the seventeenth and eighteenth centuries the term 'chapel' mostly meant a Mass-house rather than a church. These were often unobtrusive or disguised in city side streets, as was especially true of the Jesuit chapel at No. 3 George's Hill, which they had moved into sometime before 1718.[33] There was always a danger for Catholics in the city, particularly for priests; John Garzia, a Jew and a priest-hunter, had a Fr Murphy arrested in 1718 and gave evidence to the judge that Fr Murphy 'kept a school in Dublin and taught grammar and philosophy'.[34] Murphy was convicted.[35]

The small Jesuit community provided schooling in the city and by 1770 Fr Betagh Macaile had founded a boarding-school beside the original chapel, extending the project to evening, day and Sunday school classes for the poor of the area, numbering 300 boys. This was done with the help of the Roman Curia, in the knowledge that if Catholic boys and girls were not given the education in Catholic schools they would resort to Protestant ones. The boarders were charged twenty guineas per annum. Fr Mulcaile also encouraged the establishment of the Presentation Convent at George's Hill in 1794; he is buried in its crypt.[36]

In 1816 Fr Kenny, a Jesuit then based in the George's Hill locale since the Jesuits' return to Dublin, bought the chapel in Hardwicke Street, formerly the property of the Poor Clare nuns and later of a secular priest at No. 38 Gardiner Street. During this time the area was beginning to be occupied by Catholics and the chapel was too small for the growing congregation. The Pro Cathedral was then built but did not satisfy the growing demand.[37] Dr Murray, then Catholic archbishop of Dublin, who lived close by on Mountjoy Square, suggested that the Jesuits build a larger church. Murray undertook a massive church-building programme, seeing 97 churches completed or under construction before his death in 1852. He also sought to expand the number of convents, using the nuns' role in the community to expand Catholic influence.

He began with Mary Aikenhead of Cork, professing her as the first sister of the Irish Sisters of Charity.[38] He procured them the house which became the Trinitarian Orphanage in North William Street in 1817; it was taken over by the Carmelites in 1827 (Fig. 10.4). In 1818 Mary Aikenhead opened a new convent in Stanhope Street.[39] This left the Sisters of Charity free to take over the running of one of the free schools which Murray had begun to build in Gardiner Street, thanks to a legacy of £4,000—a very large sum of money at the time—left to him by Dr Everard, archbishop of Cashel; this school was the first to offer free schooling to large numbers of girls in Dublin.[40] In 1831, owing to ill health, Mother Mary Aikenhead moved to a convent in Sandymount for the sea air.[41] This confirms two things: that another convent had been founded in a new suburb and that the suburb of Sandymount had by then become somewhat established.

In the south of Dublin at Ranelagh, well outside the city, the convent of St Joseph existed since at least 1819, as an 1823 letter to Dr Murray from the prioress, Mary Catherine Meade, mentions a member of the community who had been there for four years.[42] This convent ran two fee-paying schools which allowed poor girls to avail of free education, suggesting a healthy population in the area.[43] Murray, who was then living at 41 Cumberland Street on the north side,[44] also encouraged Catherine McAuley to establish the Sisters of Mercy, who would go on to open schools, orphanages and hospitals. He would likewise promote the Vincentian Fathers and the Society of St Vincent de Paul.[45]

Dr Murray bought the site beside the church in the area known as Mountjoy Fields, owned by the earl of Blessington. As he had more ground than was necessary, the balance of the land was leased to the Jesuits for the church of St Francis Xavier. While the church was under construction, the Jesuits lived across the road at No. 36 Gardiner Street. The old church was turned into a school, which became the start of Belvedere College.[46]

St Francis Xavier's was a large construction and a showpiece for Catholicism, especially as it was the first to be built in the city after Catholic Emancipation (Fig. 10.5). No expense was spared and opulence was much in evidence as a powerful political statement. Its fitting out was elaborate and very costly, as seen in the extravagance of the altar, which cost £13,000 and was made in Rome under the eye of Fr Esmonde (son of the Dr Esmonde executed in 1798). During its construction, he wrote to Dublin from Rome in 1838 to 'try and raise several hundred pounds or double that amount in order to complete the great work' in the quest for perfection.[47] Even the holy water fonts used stone brought from Kilkenny and Carlow.[48] The church, when finished, contained a gate that separated the nave from the transept. Reflecting custom and practice at the time, the pews inside the gates were occupied by those who could afford to pay a subscription for the privilege; those too poor to do so stood in the nave. This illustrates the stratification of Irish society at the time even within the Catholic Church.[49] The area became fashionable with wealthier Catholics and was home to a growing Catholic middle class.

The Jesuit accounts book provides valuable information on the trades in the city at the time of building: payments to Mr Buckley for plastering and stucco work to 22 December 1831 came to £1,311; Mr Dunne was paid £496 4s. 7d. for supplying slating for part of the roof in the period April–June 1831; Mr Chigwell was paid £278 11s. for flagging 134 yards of the transept and 470 yards in the nave of the church. Wages for carpenters who were employed on a daily basis to 22 December 1832 amounted to £400 17s. 2d.[50] The dwelling house fit-out costs mounted up after the church opened: sash windows to December 1834 cost £738 13s. 6d.[51] Timber for the church ceiling joists and roof cost £4,012 15s. 4d. to the end of 1832, supplied to Linehan and Ham. Martin and Son supplied fifteen and a half tons of red deal at £4 5s. per ton and five tons of yellow pine at £3 10s. per ton. Mr Murray of Hammond Lane supplied 91ft of iron railing for the front of the church at a cost of £106 12s. 2d.[52] Sawyers to saw the large baulks and oak logs were paid £143 0s. 1d. At the same time Mr Tobin, plumber, was paid £355 0s. 10d.[53] (By this time the term 'plumber' had become universal within the building trade.) Mr Olligan was paid £793 14s. 9d. for the supply of granite for the stonemasons between 1830 and June 1833. A vivid picture can be drawn of activity, of the movement of goods and supplies around the city, and of the variety of work available for men on a substantial project.

The final cost of the church was £18,000, according to Alfred Jones. This figure does not include the cost of the altar, or that of its shipping from Rome to Dublin. This clearly implies the existence of a substantial middle class with the money to fund such projects. There are lists of contributors and a separate one for subscribers for the years 1829, 1830, 1841 and 1850. The numbers listed are 138 for 1829, 96 in 1830, 109 in 1841 and 128 in 1850. Interestingly, most names are not repeated; some are from outside the parish, such as Mrs Henry Grattan, Sir John Ennis and Lady Ennis, and some are from outside the city, such as Aylmer, Esmonde, Dillon and Bellew. This pattern was replicated in other church-building operations, such as Westland Row and the Pro Cathedral in Marlborough Street, and to a lesser extent in the outer fringe locations where there was a smaller population of substance.[54] Of course, not all churches cost amounts anywhere like these figures for Gardiner Street. The accounts book gives a figure of £2,020 10s. 11d. collected in the church between 3 May 1832 and 16 August 1835.[55]

The residence for the Jesuit community was completed on the north side of the church in 1834. Thus the church became not just a singular church but a complex of buildings, constructed, occupied and serviced, drawing in more people to the locale. This, too, was replicated in St Andrew's (Westland Row) and the Pro Cathedral (Marlborough Street), where each structure formed another mini-cluster of economic and social activity while contributing to the overall expansion of the city. Two aspects alone are worth noting in such places at the time: the consumption of candles and the consumption of soap in the laundry for washing clerical garb, both contributing to forms of employment,[56] although laundry work usually involved women on very low wages.

One aspect of the Jesuit community, small though it was, was that it offered employment to a number of non-religious staff to run the community. An idea of how deep the religious ethos ran in Catholic society in this period of the reawakening of the Catholic Church is given by the working conditions for lay staff, whose religious duties were specified by Fr Browne:

'Obligatory on all members of staff who live in the house
- Daily Weekdays, Mass each morning 6.45am.
- Sundays, Mass 7am
- Weekly religious instruction for all members of the staff every Wednesday at 12.15pm.
- Monthly, Communion on the first Sunday of every month to be received at the end of the 6.30am Mass at St Aloysius's altar. All are to be in the church no later than 6.45am. In attendance at daily Mass all are to assemble in the transept in front of St Aloysius's altar.
- Repeated violations of any of the above regulations particularly with regard to attendance at daily Mass will incur dismissal.'[57]

Only a few years later the Jesuits opened Belvedere House and school, beside the new church in Gardiner Street. The school included a separate oratory. A chapel was opened at Oriel Street, down towards the river, in 1850.[58]

Loreto College, which opened for enrolment in North Great George's Street in 1836, housed a chapel which contained some particularly fine plasterwork. The house had been built in 1755, as the city crept out northwards along the higher ground above the tidal flats of the Liffey down in Marlborough Street.[59] Belvedere College was founded in the growing area, taking over the mansion built in 1786 by the earl of Belvedere. It was bought in 1843 for £1,800 and converted. The house sits at the top of what was planned to be a tree-lined avenue with a long prospect down towards the river. The Jesuits became much involved in the area, both in schooling and in church-building. Again the school had a chapel. And again fees were paid for schooling, confirming the growth of a more comfortable middle-class Catholic cohort in the area, as this was a day school and remained so until today.[60]

Catholic opinion was encouraged by *The Irish Magazine*, which railed against loyalist politicians, yeomanry officers, city magistrates and the Orange gentry who had been closely identified with the State in 1798—and Beresford in particular, who had used the stables of his house in Marlborough Street for the scourging of suspects. It was vicious writing, adding to the already bitter sense of disappointment which Catholics felt over the results of the Act of Union.[61]

In 1830, the year following Catholic Emancipation, the editor of *L'Avenir*, a Paris newspaper, wrote: 'Catholicism in Ireland has at least stayed clear of the siren of the seduction of political power. It nominates its bishops; it founds its convents, and manages to do all with a degree of autonomy free of the baleful supervision and interference of a hostile non-Catholic government.'[62]

In connection with the fact that the French Catholic clergy were fund-raising for the relief of Irish Catholics in response to information in *L'Avenir*,[63] Dr Kelly, the bishop of Tuam, wrote to Archbishop Murray, describing conditions and telling him that 'the distress is worse than ever'.[64] Murray himself wrote to the editors of the paper in gratitude for their efforts in August 1831.[65] He acknowledged the generosity of the French and added that 'the French Catholics not only met temporal needs but prevented the poor accepting aid proffered by proselethyzers; not only life but faith was saved'. This comment certainly illuminates the attitudes prevailing at the time and the battle not just for hearts and minds but also for bodies.

Friedrich Raumer, a German visiting Dublin in 1835, recorded that 'the grants for Protestant schools irritated the excluded Catholics who are now sensible to the want and value of better education'.[66] He later added that 'it is equally certain that two thirds of the schools existed in practice for the benefit of Protestants alone: ... in short, Protestants hold that it was their right and their duty to educate Catholic children as Protestants'.[67]

Shunsuke Katsula has addressed the religious tensions of early nineteenth-century Dublin in the approach to Catholic Emancipation. 'Ireland in 1820 was about to enter into a decade of sectarian hostility affecting all levels of Irish society. Dublin was no exception.' He added that 'the inbuilt divide between Catholic and Protestant evangelism was creating alarm in both religions. Politics saw the arrival at a by-election for Parliament of pro- and anti-emancipation candidates.' The 'anti' man was an Orangeman. He was backed by the Orange Order, causing the reaction of commercial boycotting. At the time, the Corporation was anti-Emancipation and itself excluded Catholic participation (even though by now Catholics were legally entitled to participate).[68] When the police force was formed it consisted of 7,000 men, 5,000 of whom were Orangemen.[69] The perception was that the army, too, was controlled by Orangemen, which led the duke of Cumberland to dissolve the Orange Order in February 1836; the Grand Orange Lodge of Ireland closed itself down the following year.[70] When Daniel O'Connell was elected lord mayor of the reformed Corporation of Dublin in 1842, the newspaper *The Pilot* posed the question: 'Was it possible that the Corporation, the old stronghold of Orange Ascendancy, was in the hands of the people?'[71]

Religion percolated into every single aspect of city life: the Rotunda lying-in hospital, established in 1745 and opened in 1757, included a Protestant chapel. Perhaps this explains the zeal with which the Catholic Church continued with its church- and school-building programme.

The result was that, as the new century unfolded, literally dozens of organisations were formed to hold the line, while there was a small dissenting Protestant view that was more liberal and outgoing, seeing the current state of the country as totally unjust and potentially unstable. There were few influential Catholics as part of the establishment, and one could say that they kept their heads down, much as the Protestants of the new state a century later would do.

The various Lords Gormanston were the exception. The Prestons remained Catholic during the eighteenth century and actively resisted laws to regulate Catholic status. They organised and raised funds for legal fees to defend Catholics, led by Jenico Preston, the 10th Viscount Gormanston.[72] He also campaigned and made speeches on behalf of the Catholic Association[73] and to mobilise voters between 1825 and 1828.[74] Interestingly, the Prestons appeared to be able to overcome impediments to social progress for Catholics, as seen in the election in 1733 of Lord Gormanston to the Royal Dublin Society, much against the norm.[75] Nevertheless, the Prestons and people like them constituted a very small group in terms of society.

Reaction and resistance were visibly apparent at official and government level. The *Calendar of ancient records of Dublin* records that on 30 January 1829 it was 'resolved that a committee be appointed to enquire into the alarming consequences that are threatened to the Protestant interest in the country by the shelter afforded them to those dangerous and unconstitutional societies of Jesuits who have taken every advantage thereof and extended their establishments and intolerant doctrines with impunity so as to become highly alarming to the loyal and well disposed inhabitants of Ireland and that the Committee do prepare petitions for both Houses of Parliament'.[76]

Catholics began to play a greater role in the life of the city after Emancipation in 1829 and later, gathering momentum with the reform of the archaic and sectarian Dublin Corporation in 1840, and there was a spate of Catholic church-building after 1829. Martin maintained that the morale of Dublin had been sapped by the Act of Union in 1800. The phrase 'grass growing in the Dublin streets' gained traction among many but was not quite accurate. This is to ignore the Catholic church-building which occurred before 1829 and also the church-building in which the Established Church of Ireland had engaged.[77] The Church of Ireland church of St Stephen, known as the Pepper Canister church, was built in 1824 on land donated by the Pembroke estate, which also contributed to the building cost. The Lower Mount Street area had begun to be developed in 1789 and the building of the church shows the stage of settlement and occupation at which it had arrived. The houses in these streets, at one remove from the less-salubrious activities of the port area not far away, were taken by Established Church adherents.[78] Martin wrote that 'It took several decades before the elegant and lively capital of the Anglo-Irish Ascendancy gave way to the dull and economically retarded city of the rising professional and business class'. He quotes Thomas Cantisell, a reformer who suggested improvements for the sanitary condition of the city, to the effect that 'Dublin was

Fig. 10.6—Trinity Church, Gardiner Street, one of the largest churches in the city (later used as a dole office until recently), built on reclaimed ground by the river (photo: Brian Matthews).

the worst sewered, lighted, cleansed and watered city in the empire'.[79]

In Abbey Street there were four churches, two beside each other opposite the VHI, another beside the VHI and another 100m west on the same side in red brick. Certainly by 1820 there was a Wesleyan chapel at Rutland Street.[80] The Irish Auxiliary to the London Society for Promoting Christianity among the Jews kept an office at 16 Upper Sackville Street.[81]

The church at Gardiner Street, just up from Beresford Place adjacent to the Custom House, has gone through several phases of identity. The old Rope Walk, as Gardiner Street was originally known in 1786, became one of the finest streets in the city as planned by the Wide Streets Commission. The Protestant Episcopal Church, designed by Frederick Darley in 1838, opened in 1839 (Fig. 10.6). The building was mainly funded by a wealthy donor called Vance, who put up £15,000 towards the cost on the basis that the first pastor, John Gregg, a renowned orator in both Irish and English, could raise the balance. He succeeded, thanks to a series of public speaking engagements.[82] The church had the capacity to hold between 1,750–2,000 people. The reason for its large size was that substantial numbers of the aristocracy and their servants still lived in the area north of the Liffey when it opened its doors on 12 November 1839.[83]

Bible societies sprang up, such as the Hibernian Bible Society, established in 1806 'to encourage a wider circulation of Holy Scriptures'.[84] The Irish Evangelical Society was set up in 1842 'for promoting the spread of the gospel in Ireland, by assisting Pastors and supporting itinerant preachers'.[85] The Continental Society 'for assisting local native ministers in preaching the gospel and distributing bibles' was based at 7 Lower Abbey Street.[86] The Hibernian Wesleyan Methodist Missionary Society was located at 28 Lower Gloucester Street, promoting Methodism.[87] The Irish Unitarian Christian Society, established in 1830 and fostering Unitarian worship, was based at 57 Great Strand Street (Parnell Street today).[88] Out at Malahide, which was turning into an outer suburb (and this would be solidified with the arrival two years later of the Drogheda railway), a new Catholic chapel opened in the main street in 1843, with Fr James Carey as parish priest.

Fig. 10.7—St Andrew's, Westland Row: complex of church, schools and meeting-rooms, covering a whole block (photo: Brian Matthews).

The Dominican congregation which had been a presence on the south side of the Liffey at Bridge Street and Cooke Street, west of Merchants Quay, moved across to the other side, opening a small chapel in Little Denmark Street in 1780.[89] They then located four houses together in Lower Dominick Street, including a yard previously used by coach-makers. The cornerstone was blessed by Dr Cullen on 8 September 1852 and St Saviour's was due to cost £15,000. The fund-raising consisted of a 'weekly house to house collection through the city'. In this particular case the church was fortunate in that the Murphy family of Mount Merrion bequeathed a total of £15,000 from three separate members of the family. This was an enormous sum of money, especially for one single family to donate.[90] In 1858 John Hogan wrote in the *Irish Quarterly Review*: 'The friar preachers are building a beautiful church in Lower Dominick Street, not for a fashionable congregation, or the wealth and rank of Dublin, but for the poor, devout, toil-hardened population of Britain Street and Liffey Street and the nameless lanes and alleys that intersect these thoroughfares'.[91] The original church on Little Denmark Street had its origins in 1835 and was completely cut off from view, hidden by houses and trees; it was accessed via one of the houses. The new, large church was situated not very far from the Pro Cathedral in Marlborough Street, illustrating how the whole north city space was becoming dotted with churches.

Churches were mini-clusters of employment. In Protestant churches those receiving payment included the sexton and his assistant, the bell-ringer, the organist, the vestry clerk, the parish clerk, the surgeon, the beadle, the bellows-blower and the fire-engine keeper. Catholic chapels, too, gave employment, to sacristans, clerks and organists, and both denominations also used laundries for vestments and consumed candles and paper, ink and quills, as well as bread for wafers and wine for chalices. Books, too, had to be supplied, as well as altar books and ledgers to register births, marriages and deaths.[92]

A closer look at the building of both St Andrew's in Westland Row and the Pro Cathedral in Marlborough Street will illustrate the situation as it pertained in Dublin in this period of highly charged activity and political stress.

Dr Murray laid the foundation stone for the first version of the proposed St Andrew's Church on 22 April 1814, close by the site of the present church in Townsend Street. It was then decided to relocate the church to a new site—the present one at Westland Row.[93] The architect was James Bolger and the estimated cost of the project was £16,000. The stone for the new church was set on 30 April 1832 and the church was dedicated on 2 January 1834. The altar and tabernacle came from Rome. By 1841 expenditure on both the church and the presbytery buildings had come to £26,188. By 1846 a tower was added, costing another £1,000.[94] As the church was being finished, two separate presbyteries were added. Then two large vestries were begun. These contained extensive rooms for the use of confraternity meetings, and over them were schoolrooms for female students from the parish. Meanwhile, the boys' school at Hanover Street was abandoned and the 500 pupils were left with no schooling in 1844. The parish faithful were again canvassed for subscriptions; £2,608 was collected and a boys' school adjoining the church was built.[95] In a letter to the parish in 1859, Revd W. Meyler confirmed that the schools could now accommodate up to 1,000 pupils. They had been completed at a cost of £2,605 4s. 2d. This figure included furniture, lower apartments for caretakers, rooms for the headmaster and recreation grounds. The purpose of the school was also to provide education for those using 'Kildare Place and similar schools', in which the Catholic clergy supposed that there was too much Protestant influence. He thanked his Catholic parishioners and also Mr Marsh of York Street, who had donated £2,000 to his school fund. Most importantly, he offered effusive thanks for the support—including financial—of the Protestant inhabitants of the locale,[96] and it should be noted that this was not the only parish in which such generosity was shown by Protestants towards Catholics. It is therefore apparent that St Andrew's was not just a church; it was a centre for the Catholic population of a growing parish, including opportunities for schooling and social activities, while the church became the nub of parish life through religious ceremonies and rites, as well as also taking on the State role of registering births, marriages and deaths. The structures built employed much labour and material in the locality and continued to consume goods and services (Fig. 10.7).

The erection of the Pro Cathedral, too, was a major project in all respects. It had an impact on the political and social context of the north side of Dublin while it came to occupy a key location (Fig. 10.8). The site for the church was bought for £5,755 in 1803 by Valentine O'Connor, almost 30 years before Emancipation. The site contained a house owned by Lord Annesley, which lay directly behind the Sackville Street-facing house of Lord Drogheda and faced directly onto the house of Lord Tyrone in Marlborough Street. The house was bought at public auction. The site was partly paid for by a collection to the amount of £2,832 7s. 3d. The house was then let to the Barrack Board for housing troops at a rent of £300 a year. By 1808, the £2,267 12s. 9d. collected was used to pay the balance of a loan on the purchase price.[97] In 1810 the debt on money borrowed was down to £250. The Barrack Board vacated the building in 1814, allowing the site to be cleared under the supervision of John Sweetman of Raheny and Paris.

A fund-raising committee made up of 21 men was formed. They used to meet in Liffey Street church and then began to meet in D'Arcy's tavern on Earl Street. Payments to the fund-raising committee included a legacy of £3,111 7s. from a Mr Cardiff. A city-wide house-to-house collection

Churches, schools and hospitals on the north side of Dublin

Fig. 10.8—The Pro Cathedral, Marlborough Street, complex of houses, church, stores for Revenue and accommodation for priests and staff (photo: Brian Matthews).

Fig. 10.9—St Thomas's, Marlborough Street (courtesy of Louise Morgan and Brendan Maher, NGI).

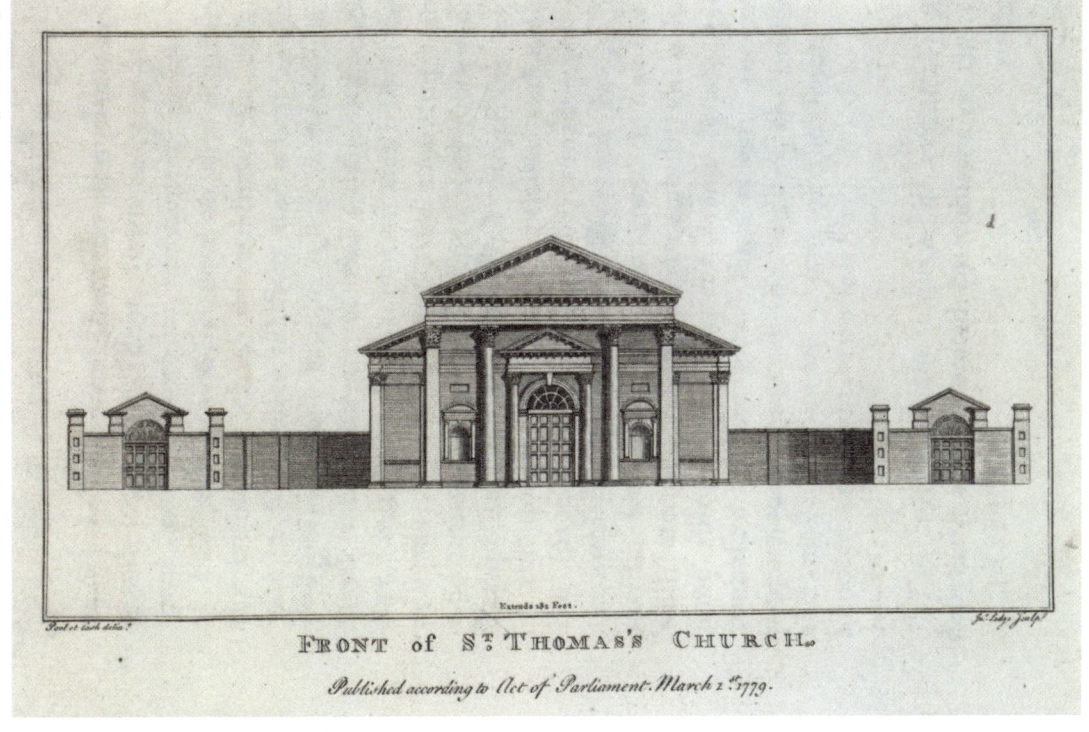

209

Fig. 10.10—St George's, Hardwicke Place (photo: Brian Matthews).

was proposed, which by 1823 had raised enough so that £31,000 could be expended on the building, and it was estimated that £12,000 more was needed to finish it. This would include a gallery for the organ and choir.[98]

As this work proceeded, it should be noted that the most recent and closest in geographical terms to the new construction was the Church of Ireland church of St Thomas in Marlborough Street, only metres away (Fig 10.9). It was an audacious move to site the new church in the very heart of the city, across the street from the heart of Dublin—the GPO.

While the fund-raising was continuing, a competition was held for a design for the proposed church, with a sum of £50 to be awarded to the winning architect.[99] The foundation stone was laid on 28 March 1824. However, the vaults below the structure had been completed in 1816. In 1817 the church leased the vaults to the Revenue Commissioners for £300 per annum, an arrangement that lasted until 1824.[100] This was not unusual; St George's at Hardwicke Place (Fig 10.10) had a similar arrangement with the Revenue Commissioners. In 1823 the plastering was done on the interior. The high altar relief was carved by Smyth of Dublin for £150 and the organ was made by Lawless, also of Dublin, for £100. By 1824 Dr Murray was in a position to tell the parish meeting that the total number of priests based in the church was nine, not including deacons.

At this juncture Sir G. Neville, owner of the house next door to the church, offered to sell it for £1,500. After some negotiating, the church became the owner of this substantial house for the accommodation of priests and a variety of indoor staff.[101]

The church was dedicated in 1825. The south portico was complete by 1837 and the others by 1841. By 1841 all debts attached had been cleared and the bell hoisted. The total cost of the complex was £45,000.[102]

When the time came to open the church, 3,000 tickets at £1 each and 2,000 tickets at 10s. each were put on sale. Such was the demand that £2,346 was raised. Among those Protestants who attended the opening were the Guinnesses and the earl of Howth. It was decided to mark the occasion by having a dinner in the house next door, but again demand was so strong that the event had to be relocated to Morrisson's Hotel in Dawson Street. The cost of the dinner was 30s.[103]

The Pro Cathedral again was a complex of buildings and not just a single church. It made a strong political statement, just 150 yards from the Church of Ireland church in Marlborough Street and just 150 yards from both the GPO and Nelson's Pillar on Sackville Street, the premier street on the island at the time. Jackob Venedy visited the Pro Cathedral for Mass in 1843, noting the admission price of 'sixpence for the upper class section, the plebs paid only two pence'. He found the separation of the rich from the poor offensive.[104] At this time Marlborough Street hosted a mix of residents and commercial enterprises. John Tomney at No. 42 built coaches; a few doors away Robert Kelly ran a saddle- and harness-making operation at No. 54, while at No. 4 lived the architect for the Drogheda Railway, who kept his office close by at No. 44 Gloucester Street.[105]

While the Act of Emancipation came into force in 1829, two things remained unchanged. One was tithes, which would remain a bone of contention for years to come, and the other was the attitudes and influence that continued to hold back Catholic expression. Friedrich Raumer said that in 1831 'there arose a universal resistance to tithes in Ireland. With the aid of an extremely expensive and empowering military force, and the most rigorous measures employed during two months, scarcely a tenth of the tithes had according to Mr Stanley been collected.'[106] Raumer further said that the situation was even worse owing to the fact that 'Catholics have to pay tithes to Protestant clergymen who have no flocks'.[107]

The Additional Curates Fund Society for Ireland was established in 1839 for the maintenance of additional (Protestant) clergymen in those parts of the country most in need of such assistance.[108] The Swiftian Readers Society was founded for Ireland in 1822, and by 1844 it had 'sixty-six males going about reading the Scriptures among the poor, using pious men of humble rank'.[109] The Sunday School Society of Ireland, based at 16 Sackville Street, was established in 1809 for promoting Sunday Schools.[110] In 1843 the incorporated Society for promoting English Protestant Schools in Ireland was founded.[111]

During Daniel O'Connell's push for Repeal of the Union there was equally a counter-push, and in 1843 this was seen in the holding of many anti-Repeal meetings, such as at the Rotunda in June of that year. Good attendance was reported and a large section of those present were from the humbler walks of life, but the body of the house was composed mainly of Orange freemen.[112] By this time a new social class had appeared, that of the poor Protestant with poor prospects for work and accommodation, and consequently shrinking the income of the Established Church, leading to the formation of new organisations to assist them in various ways.

The Charitable Association, established in 1806, was run out of No. 7 Great Denmark Street and had an office in 49 Upper Sackville Street; it called on people in the area, giving assistance. Some of those who ran the Association lived locally at Mountjoy Square, Dominick Street, Amiens Street and Dorset Street. So we can see that the HQ of the Association was on newly built ground and that those who ran it also lived on newly built ground.[113] The Protestant Orphan Society, instituted in 1829 for destitute orphaned children, did not admit any child who had had a Catholic parent.[114] The North Strand Episcopal Chapel and Sunday and Daily Schools were established in 1786 'for instruction of the poor, of every religious denomination, in such branches of learning as are best suited to their station and condition but especially for supporting them with a scriptural education'. The chaplain operated out of No. 10 Newcomen Terrace, adjacent to the Newcomen Bridge on the canal at North Strand. By 1844 the school catered for 130 children. The address confirms that there were dwellings on either side of Newcomen Bridge across the Royal Canal by this date.[115] It is to be noted that, while some of these organisations post-dated 1800 and the new political circumstances, it is apparent that the battle continued even after the fact of Emancipation.

All this information tells us three things about society in north Dublin by the year 1844. First, much of the territory within the 1728 new perimeter and beyond was now occupied and built on. Second, a section of Dublin society which could be referred to as an underclass was suffering from political and economic change triggered by the Act of Union, made worse by the downturn of the economy after the defeat of France in 1815. Third, there is evidence of a growing Protestant poorer class. Nevertheless, despite the devastating poverty in the city, there were obviously a substantial number of Catholics who could afford to donate money to this huge church-building programme.

The location of proposed new churches was not always straightforward, however, as seen in a letter from Barbara Verschoyle, agent to Lord Pembroke, in which she writes that the residents of the Baggot Street area would murmur against the erection of a Catholic church on the site at the corner of Baggot Street and Fitzwilliam Street, as 'beggars and poor people who surround Catholic chapels would be in the area'; she thinks, however, that the new house of refuge in Baggot Street 'might be allowable'.[116]

St Mary's chapel of ease at Mountjoy Street, beside Dominick Street and Parnell Square, was built in 1830. It was called the Black Church because of the calp stone used. It was very close to the Dominick Street church and complex, being only 200 yards away (Fig. 10.11).

Fig. 10.11—St Mary's, the 'Black Church', Mountjoy Street (photo: Brian Matthews).

The church of St John the Baptist (Church of Ireland) was finished in 1866 to replace an earlier church in Castle Avenue on the edge of the old graveyard there. The parish is bordered by Coolock and North Strand, and the earlier church had been in use since 1609. The Catholic church of St John the Baptist on the Clontarf Road was built in 1836.[117]

By holding services in private houses, the charismatic Revd J. Grainger of the parish of St Thomas, off Marlborough Street, grew his congregation from 800 to 2,000 in three years, mainly at 7 Seaview Terrace, off North Strand.

St Paul's on Arran Quay was built in 1835 to replace the old church at the rear of what is now Nos 11 and 12 Arran Quay. Statues and the bell were added in 1843.[118] A mere ten minutes' walk away on the south bank was the Catholic church of SS Michael and John, which opened in 1815, some £5,000 having been collected for it.[119] The original organ cost £700,[120] and a vestry was added in 1836. To build a Catholic church literally beneath Christchurch Cathedral was a bold political statement at that time.

The Presbyterian congregation used to gather in a church at the corner of D'Olier Street and Hawkins Street, then moved to Seán McDermott Street (Gloucester Street) before moving out of the city to the new suburb of Clontarf at the bottom of the Howth Road twenty years later.[121]

Construction of St Peter's (Church of Ireland) in Baldoyle began in 1831 and it opened on 6 December 1833.[122] St Peter's up on the North Circular Road opened in 1834.

The church of St Nicholas of Myra out in Kinsealy on the Malahide Road opened in 1832, not in suburbia but in the midst of an agricultural area.

On 7 September 1836 the first stone was laid for the North Strand Episcopal Church. The

Fig. 10.12—Church of St Laurence O'Toole, built on the tidal sands (photo: Brian Matthews).

Presbyterian Community moved further out toward newer suburbs and built a church on Adelaide Road in 1841, while a new Methodist Church was completed on St Stephen's Green West in 1842. The Bethseda Chapel was located on Dorset Street.[123] There was a Jewish synagogue at St Mary's Abbey, a Baptist meeting-house at Lower Abbey Street and a Moravian meeting-house at Bishop Street.[124]

By 1843 the parish of Kingstown and Cabinteely was well established; Revd A.J. Fagan acted as convenor of the O'Connell meeting at Kingstown, although Revd Bartholomew Sheridan, who lived there and had overseen the building of the church in 1835, did not attend. Suffice it to note that Kingstown was by now a well-established suburb of Dublin with a growing Catholic population.

By the 1840s the port church of St Laurence O'Toole was under construction (Fig. 10.12). Charles Kenneddy, a prominent and charitable Catholic, presented Dr Murray with a site of 20,000ft² to build a church where, it was remarked, Neptune had ruled. Kenneddy also donated £1,000 towards the cost of building.[125] After fund-raising, albeit at a more modest level than on other, higher-profile projects, the first stone was laid on 13 June 1844. The tower was added ten years later, and by 1855 the entire cost totalled £9,854. It was far below the huge sums spent on Marlborough Street, Westland Row and Gardiner Street, yet it too was a substantial complex and a large church, and this figure included the provision of two schoolrooms for boys and girls.

CHURCHES, SCHOOLS AND HOSPITALS ON THE NORTH SIDE OF DUBLIN

Fig. 10.13—Complex at All Hallows, Drumcondra (photo: Brian Matthews).

Fig. 10.14—Clonliffe College, Clonliffe Road (photo: Brian Matthews).

In 1841 the college of All Hallows for the training of Catholic priests was founded at Drumcondra (Fig. 10.13). Daniel O'Connell subscribed £100 and also donated his time and legal expertise to the setting up of the college. Close by, on Clonliffe Road, was established Clonliffe College, also for the training of priests (Fig. 10.14). In this area, then, were located two massive institutions of the Catholic Church. Their construction was on a very large scale, employing many in both labour and supply and consuming a wide range of material, all contributing to Dublin businesses. Many, too, would be employed in the running and the ongoing supply of both establishments. Both institutions housed hundreds of seminarians and both included a large church as part of their substantial complexes. Neither college offered free training and at the time neither was cheap, and this again signifies a large, well-off coterie of Catholic parents who could afford the fees. These colleges, together with the very substantial training college at Maynooth, confirmed the serious purpose of the Catholic hierarchy and its growing financial strength, which in turn reflected a growing well-off section of Irish society.

It is apparent, therefore, that by mid-century the race to build new churches across the space of interest was almost run. A place of burial for Catholics became a reality in 1831, when the Catholic Association purchased land at Glasnevin for a cemetery. This was another major institution on this side of the city, providing a focal point for citizens and having an impact on the use of the various roads in and out of the city, as well as increasing the use of internal thoroughfares.[126] There would be a more sedate expansion subsequently as the suburbs themselves grew.

More and more people now lived out here in the area which had once been under the tides, and along slopes up towards the fields on higher ground. There were shops, small workshops, houses, public houses and factories, and service outlets to look after all of the above, including horses to be used, maintained and replaced along with their corresponding drays, carts and carriages.

By 1851 Dr Murray had laid the foundation stone for the new Catholic church in the growing suburb of Sandymount on the south side of the city. Again this encouraged a cluster of occupation and small shops to supply people with their daily needs. On the other side of the city, at Clontarf, two Masses were said on Sundays, signifying a substantial population in the parish. The same applied to Fairview, while Coolock and Ballymun had just one Sunday Mass. By helping to build communities, the churches added momentum to urbanisation, as did schools and hospitals. The quality of housing improved over the coming decades, along with indoor plumbing, for example. These improvements required new skills in fitting out structures.

In this period of the expansion of church-building, enormous sums of money were expended on these projects, mostly paid for by Catholic donations. At the same time, large sums of money were being donated to Daniel O'Connell's Repeal movement, much of it originating in Dublin. Substantial Catholic donations also contributed to the building and furnishing of a new structure next door to the Corn Exchange on Burgh Quay. To be known as Conciliation Hall, it was to hold 4,000 persons. This is a reminder that, despite all the poverty in the city, there was a solid segment of working people who could afford to make these donations, at a time when a teacher earned £20 per annum and a farm labourer £10, while a junior clerk in the Custom House was paid £50.[127]

With the passage of time, there was a growing differential in the numbers of adherents of particular churches. The number of Established Church followers had dropped in comparison to Catholics from almost equal numbers in the city in 1834 to 61,833 against 174,957 in 1750.[128] This shift had a political impact when the Municipal Corporation Reform Act (1840) gave the franchise to all £10 freeholders (of whom Catholics had a majority of two to one). Removing the franchise from 4,000 Protestant freemen, it dealt another blow to working-class Protestants. Daniel O'Connell was elected to the office of lord mayor in 1842.

As church-building reached its peak in the 1840s, the world outside was going through another technological transformation. Michael Farraday discovered the principle of the dynamo, successfully generating an electric current in 1831, signalling another light and power source to be developed which would have an enormous impact on society. In 1837 Pitman invented his shorthand system, which would change news-reporting and commerce generally. The invention of the Colt six-shooter in 1844 would transform warfare and policing worldwide, including here in Ireland. The arrival of the railways allowed the State greater control on a national basis, being able to move the military around with greater speed. In 1846 a New York printer invented the rotary press, capable of producing 10,000 sheets every hour.

While these developments would not be seen immediately by many in Ireland, they were part of a continuing industrial revolution and desperate thirst for knowledge and improvement at the time, and education became part of this great drive. To fully appreciate the speed of industrial invention and improvement, note the example of the first screw-propeller: invented in 1827, it was successfully applied to the building of the *Great Britain*, an iron steamship using screw propulsion to cross the Atlantic in 1843.

Thomas Tredgold wrote on roads and railroads and carriages, on warming and ventilating public buildings and hothouses, and also contributed notes to tracts on hydraulics by John Smeaton, but iron was his primary interest. 'I have attempted to supply a practical treatise on the strength of cast iron ... best appreciated by those who consider the serious consequences of a failure in the application of this material. It is used for the principal supports of churches, theatres, dwelling houses, manufacturers and warehouses, for bridges, roofs and floors and for the moving parts of the most powerful engines.'[129] Improvements in the manufacture of iron enabled the manufacturers to reduce its price, 'so far indeed that it can now be employed, instead of foreign timber, for many important purposes in buildings and machines, at a very small additional expense, with a considerable addition of soundness and durability'.[130]

The growing use of iron as a building material meant that iron foundries began to increase in number and also in size. While on a smaller scale in Ireland than in industrial England, they afforded new opportunities for employment in a new industry. John Martin wrote that Dublin was influenced by the virtual absence of an industrial revolution. Perhaps his opinion is accurate but only in that the engines driving it were absent; its results, effects and impact were everywhere in evidence.

Schools and education

In the first four decades of the nineteenth century, schools would proliferate to fill the same space that was occupied by churches and religious establishments. Between the Act of Union and the National School system of primary education, established in 1831 as a result of correspondence between Chief Secretary Edward Stanley and the duke of Leinster, lay a period of intense activity in terms of attempts to provide some form of education.

Tyrone House, one of the early large homes located north of the Liffey in Marlborough Street but no longer a private dwelling, had become the administrative centre of education by 1836. The State contribution to education began with grants of £50,000, rising to £120,000 by 1848, towards buildings, books, teacher-training and inspectors. This was a major step in the involvement of the State in education, and subsequently in the education of all of the people, including Catholics.[131]

The intention here is to look at education and schooling, noting how it altered between the latter part of the eighteenth century and the first four decades of the nineteenth century. This section will consider how, from having been primarily the constituency of the wealthier citizens, it developed and spread out to include all classes of society. We will also note the growing desire of the poorer citizens for any form of education. This requires tracing the impact on society and on the topography of this tidal space within the 1728 new walls, and noting how the occupation of the space by schools crept outside those same walls and up along the main city thoroughfares and on into the nearest villages, helping to turn them into new suburbs.

The presence of a school meant the presence of people in the immediate locale, just as was noted in relation to churches. In plain terms, most people did not travel far for church, school or work, and certainly not for medical assistance. As we look at the aspect of schooling and education in the nineteenth century and how and why it grew, note must be taken of the position in the previous era.

In the eighteenth century there were many schools, such as the Royal Charter Schools, set up in the city, all on a voluntary or purely financial basis; the State had no involvement. The city élite were home-tutored. Most schools were individually owned and run by the teacher/proprietor. Much education was not just charitable but free. There was little or nothing on offer for Catholics, although they might be given schooling in the smaller individual schools, which were mostly fee-paying and mostly run by Protestants. But hand in hand with the desire and expectation of Catholic Emancipation went the desire for education. The Catholic hierarchy, too, fed this growing yearning. After the years of war with France and America, non-national security issues bubbled to the surface. The eighteenth-century position is summed up by Thomas Moore from a Catholic perspective.

Thomas Moore, poet and ballad-writer, was born in 1779 in Aungier Street and describes the reality faced by Catholic parents who had no way of registering the births of their children and had to find alternative methods of marking the events.[132] He says that 'at a very early age I was sent to a school kept by a man of the name of Malone in the same street where we lived'. This 'wild odd fellow, of whose cocked hat I have still a very clear remembrance, used to pass the greater part of his nights in drinking at public houses and was hardly ever able to make his appearance in the school before noon'.[133] Later Moore added: 'As soon as I was old enough to encounter the crowd of a large school, it was determined that I shall go to the best then in Dublin, the grammar school of the well known Samuel Whyte, whom a reputation of more than thirty years standing had placed at the time at the head of his profession'.[134] The usual route at the time for a Catholic to receive an education was to be taught by Protestant teachers and be educated in the Protestant religion.

The Charter School in Clontarf, founded in the eighteenth century, housed 120 live-in boarders being educated in the Protestant religion in 1814, according to Ann Plumtre.[135] Like the other Royal Charter Schools, it was set up both to protect the Protestant population and to create a new Protestant wave of loyal apprentices for trade and commerce. The schools grew out of the Incorporated Society for Promoting English Protestant Schools. The operation of each was entirely Protestant, and the orphans, often Catholic, who were educated and trained in the Protestant way of life were often sent to locations well away from their old abodes. Many children also came from destitute Catholic backgrounds, and it was an offence to interfere with the taking of such children from their parents. By 1758 there were 46 such schools across Ireland.

Clontarf is of particular interest because it was operating by the mid-eighteenth century on the strand, well outside the boundary of the city north-east of the Tolka and long before the erection of Annesley Bridge and the new sea road to Clontarf. It started life out in the country, but by the time it closed in 1831 the area had become a suburb within walking distance of the city[136] (Fig. 10.15).

It was set up in 1748 on land leased by John Vernon. The earl of Harrington laid the foundation stone and contributed £50 towards its establishment. Rocque shows the school *in situ* in his map of 1756. The plan was to house 194 boys, train them as apprentices to trades and educate them as

Fig. 10.15—Charter School, Clontarf (Welcome Collection).

Royal Charter School, Clontarf

Protestants. This was made clear in a sermon given at Christ Church Cathedral on 24 April 1796 by the bishop of Elphin to an audience that included the earl of Camden.[137] Most boys were indeed apprenticed to Dublin city tradesmen in such a manner.

By 1782 there were 194 boys there, all occupied in weaving and carpet-making; twelve extra looms had been installed in 1781. When John Howard visited in 1787, the numbers were down to 53.[138] The children were often apprenticed out as servants: for example, in 1805 John Kelly, aged thirteen, left to serve Mr Samuel at Hollybrook Park in Clontarf for five years, and in 1808 Philip Thomas, aged twelve, went as a servant to Philip Despard of the Crescent, Marino. Neither boy had to travel far from the school for their employment. It needs to be said that the school was a school in name only, as the boys worked long days and received little education.[139] Today it would be termed an industrial school, where the children worked for outside contractors and the income they earned was paid to the staff.

Richard Pococke, an annual subscriber to the Incorporated Society in Dublin for promoting English Protestant working schools in Ireland, became bishop of Meath in 1765 and bought No. 11 (now 13) Henrietta Street from Lord Loftus for £3,000. At the time this was the most exclusive address in Dublin, known as Primates' Hill because of the number of senior clerics with houses there. His will stipulated: 'then I do leave all my estate real and personal for founding a school for papist boys from twelve to sixteen years old who shall become Protestants and be bred to linen weaving, and instructed in the principles of the Protestant religion'.[140]

All changed with the Act of Union. Parliament now ruled both islands and this, combined with the widening effects of the Industrial Revolution, much-improved communications and new forms of employment and commerce, completely altered the social and political context of the first quarter of the new century. A demand for education now entered the public discourse. Schooling became more formalised, leading to a full national education programme over a 25-year period.

In 1811 the government, seeking to be seen as even-handed, set up the Kildare Place Society. This was intended to run non-denominational schools, with well-trained teachers, which pupils of different religions could attend without danger to their own religious beliefs. Though honourable in its aims, the plan unravelled because almost all teachers were Protestant and the Bible was a text used for all pupils.

The Dorset Institute, founded in 1815 at 49 Sackville Street, 'afforded work for women and schooling for children' locally, and by 1844 it provided for 112 women, 100 young girls, 67 infants and fifteen deaf and dumb persons.[141] Over at Russell Place, off the North Circular Road, the Old Man's Asylum for respectable and reduced Protestants was established in 1810; it provided accommodation for 24 men and its secretary was at 31 Lower Gardiner Street.[142] A school for the deaf and blind opened in Glasnevin on 18 June 1816.[143] Yet another organisation based in Upper Sackville Street was the Richmond National Institution for the industrious blind at No. 37.[144] St Joseph's Asylum for aged and virtuous single females stood at No. 7 Portland Row. In 1809 an asylum for aged and infirm female servants of good character was set up at 21 Lower Dorset Street.[145] Each of these organisations provided some level of learning.

Thomas Reid wrote in 1822 that 'employment and education are indispensible to the well being, if not the very existence, of a free state, so obvious are the advantages'.[146] Concerning tithes, he said that 'There should be no check put upon industry by heavy local taxes and exorbitant demands of Tithe'.[147] He showed that there were various views in society as regards educating Catholics: 'On the progress of education in Ireland, a difference of opinion has long existed and still continues'.[148] He added, however, that 'There can be only but one opinion, schools are wretchedly conducted; those such as Charter and Royal Schools absorb money which could be spent elsewhere'.[149] Reid was wary of the promotion of religion: 'Proselytising has ever been the bane of peace and social happiness in Ireland'.[150] He asked, 'What danger has the constitution to fear from emancipating the Catholics?' He maintained that there was none. 'Can anyone in his sober senses imagine that giving them an interest in the country could make them wish for a revolution?'[151] Observing society in Dublin and the activities of the Orangemen, he remarked, 'None but Orangemen are "the right sort", not those "harmless Protestants"'.[152]

Education would be a major focus of attention for the following 40 years. Access to education was the key to personal growth and development, and people were hungry for it; control of it bestowed political power. Education became a battleground in the struggle to control society in the run-up to, and in the aftermath of, Emancipation. The same would apply to medical and hospital care.

In 1827 the Catholic Association proposed the building of a model school to train Catholic teachers,[153] and Daniel O'Connell recommended that £1,500 be appropriated for the same. Mr Hicky of 40 Jervis Street wrote to O'Connell urging that a site for the school be found on the north side, claiming that there was 'an extremely numerous and poor school population' in that area and 'an almost total lack of free school education'. A fund-raising committee for the Christian Brothers

Fig. 10.16—The Christian Brothers' O'Connell School, North Richmond Street (photo: Brian Matthews).

obtained premises in Jervis Street in St Mary's parish and opened a school in 1827.[154] Dr Murray had an established relationship with the Brothers, as he had already encouraged them to open a school in Hanover Street at a site that he provided to school the poor in the docklands. He was active in harnessing the assistance of some of the better-off parishioners of St Andrew's to help the school, where 'several hundred are daily instructed'.[155] Some 550 boys were enrolled at Hanover Street.

On 8 June 1828 Daniel O'Connell laid the foundation stone for a new school of the Christian Brothers at North Richmond Street, which opened for enrolment in 1832. It was to be a case of a 'Catholic education, on Catholic principles, with Catholic masters and the use of Catholic books'[156] (Fig. 10.16).

In 1831, after a long list of enquiries into education, Edward Stanley moved a scheme to vote a sum of £30,000 to the lord lieutenant for education purposes, providing for a National School system.[157] Finances were to be administered by a Board of Commissioners of National Education, appointed by the lord lieutenant and including two Catholic bishops. The Commissioners would be assisted by inspectors of schools. Provision was made for the separate religious instruction of each denomination.[158] From the Catholic perspective it was an improvement on the 1811 situation. There was the inevitable opposition but it petered out, and the new scheme was seen as more efficient and useful than the schools run by the Kildare Place Society and by the old 1733 Incorporated Society for Providing English Protestant Schools in Ireland.[159]

The Murray papers include an account of the St Mary's Orphanage at North William Street, formerly the Trinitarian Orphanage, founded in 1794.[160] It is easy to understand the battle for the hearts and minds of the young when reading the letter requiring the children of Catholic soldiers in the army to attend Protestant Schools and Protestant worship. The fathers of such children were made to comply by their commanding officers.[161] At the other end of the social scale, Dr Murray received an invitation to attend the regatta aboard the yacht of the lord lieutenant and his wife, the duchess of Northumberland.[162] The bishop's inclusion on the guest list of the Protestant social and political élite may be an indication of how much attitudes had changed—or that the millions of Catholics could no longer be ignored.

Besides settling at George's Hill behind the Four Courts and then moving to the Hardwicke

Fig. 10.17—School complex with chapel, Mountjoy Street (photo: Brian Matthews).

Place/Dorset Street locale, the Jesuits found the time and money to buy and build Clongowes Wood College, just south of Dublin in north Kildare, as a fee-paying boarding-school for boys in 1814. Belvedere College opened on 16 September 1841. Originally a private house, when built in 1775 it stood in a rural setting with no building nearby. The earl of Belvedere spent £24,000 on the house but the Jesuits paid a lot less for it.

Irish Methodists for years had their own teacher-training institution at No. 38½ Hardwicke Street. It was originally occupied in 1752 by one Major Favreiere, who gave the site to the Poor Clares of North King Street. The Jesuits took possession in 1816 after the nuns moved out to Harold's Cross.

According to D.A. Levistone Cooney, the Methodist School at Clonliffe, out on the northern fringe of Dublin, had 210 pupils; it was managed by Revd E. Benson, with Principal James Henry and teachers Florence Smith, Margaret Mitchell and Elizabeth Reid.[163]

The *Almanac* of 1844 shows that the Misses Harding were operating a boarding- and day-school at 11 Lower Abbey Street.[164] Mrs Walshe ran a day- and boarding-school at No. 11 Lower Dominick Street, Mrs Burke ran a seminary at No. 72 Upper Dominick Street and Mrs Keating also ran a day- and boarding-school at 113 Upper Dorset Street.[165]

Religious orders such as the Jesuits and the Dominicans moved into the area after Emancipation. The Loreto College opened in 1836 in North Great George's Street, down the street from where the Jesuits were becoming established. This was one of the earliest establishments of the order led by Mother Frances Teresa Ball. This facility, too, was a fee-paying school, and the increasing number of such schools confirms the growth of a middle class with the cash reserves to pay for such schooling.

Nearby, the needs of those in Mountjoy Street (Fig. 10.17) and in the vicinity of the King's Inns and Bolton Street were met. Consideration has to be taken of the flood of people coming into the city before the Famine, swelling the number of inhabitants, which explains the sheer number of institutions offering some form of learning. There were over 250,000 people in Dublin and a good portion of them were in work, which accounts for how so many of these institutions were able to charge money for their services.

The spread continued over at Lower Gloucester Street, where Mrs Lyons operated an Italian, French and English boarding- and day-school out of No. 37, while at No. 39 Mistress Hannah Mahon ran the Sunday and Daily female school.[166] At 19 Mountjoy Street Lower Miss Jane McCullagh ran a male and female infant school.[167] On Mecklenburgh Street (the section from Gardiner Street to Lower Buckingham Street) at No. 87 was John Hickey's seminary for general education, while down the street at No. 17 Edward Dove also ran a seminary for general education.[168] In King's Inns Street Miss Maxwell had a ladies' seminary, a male free school, a female free school and an infant free school at No. 3.[169] We can see, then, that the sheer numbers of teaching institutions which had been established in the new part of the growing city were filling up the space alongside churches. This meant that the numbers of people now occupying the area were increasing.

There was a school for girls in Coleraine Street, next door to the Inns, managed by Mistress Hamilton Drought in 1824; the pupils, who paid one penny per week for lessons, included 39 Catholics, nine Protestant Episcopalians and two Presbyterians but no Quakers.[170] A secondary boarding-school for Quakers opened in 1840 at 29 Camden Street, charging £45 per annum.[171] All these institutions signify clearly that the frenetic opening of schools, whatever their size or religious ethos, was fast occupying the new ground on the north side of Dublin and also in other expanding new suburbs.

There were sufficient numbers living out in the area of Artane/Donnycarney by 1825 for the Christian Brothers to set up a school in the old Artane Castle. This confirms that the Malahide Road had by then created a stronger connection to the city.[172] At that time the area was becoming more settled as a suburb and the more affluent were commuting to work in the city.

John Taylor's map of 1828 shows the Royal Charter School still at Clontarf, and the school at Donnycarney. Other items of interest are the mill at the bridge in Portmarnock, the quay for the use of ships still extant at Robswall, Malahide, and a windmill on the north bank of the Liffey (at the Convention Centre). Two quarries are marked—at Corr Bridge, Howth, and the Black Quarry at Clontarf—and another watermill at St Ann's Estate, Clontarf.[173]

The map made in 1801–5 by Major Alex Taylor of His Majesty's Royal Engineers confirms development out as far as Drumcondra Bridge, and all the way out to Ballybough Bridge on both sides, and on the west side mainly on North Strand Road. The village of Clontarf is shown along the shore and up Vernon Avenue; Raheny is a distinct entity and so is Coolock. What stands out in this map is that Great Brunswick Street has not yet appeared as a street.[174]

It can be concluded that education, having been the preserve of the few in the eighteenth century, became the preserve of many by the third and fourth decades of the nineteenth century. The Catholic Church waged an ongoing war for the education of the Catholic majority of the population. Having established a massive church-building programme in the city and surrounds, it followed it up with the establishment of schools. By the end of the 1840s this new space had been well and truly occupied by society in the form of churches and schools.

Hospitals, medical treatment centres and public health

In this section we will examine the effects of the changes in dealing with health issues across the new space primarily on the north side of Dublin. We will note how, just as the city had been supplied with churches and schools, so too would further occupation of the space occur thanks to the location of hospitals, infirmaries, dispensaries, homes, orphanages, penitentiaries and smaller institutions offering care and relief. We will also note the expansion well outside the traditional boundaries of occupation of 1728, which helped the growth of suburbs.

By 1800 the population of Dublin was still growing, but owing to the scale of the Catholic underclass the populace was always open to all sorts of epidemics, such as typhus, cholera, influenza, dysentery, scurvy and the effects of famine. This impoverished underclass was the weak spot in society because of poor diet and overcrowding in cold, damp, windowless accommodation with unhygienic conditions, such as no proper sewage disposal or clean water supply. Because this cohort of society consisted of many beggars, disease was easily spread as they mingled with other citizens, and the same group were least immune to any and every outbreak of disease.

The other side of the picture is that many people were working and supporting families, thanks to an expanding metropolis, a massive church-building programme which lasted over four decades, a large increase in the number of schools offering all forms of education, and the major works which were undertaken in the first quarter of the new century. More ships were using the port of Dublin than ever before. There were also the benefits of the industrial activity in society generally, even though the massive industrial complexes of England were absent here. The economy was widening and expanding.

In public health, too, changes were afoot. The State would be confronted with a litany of public calamities in health threats, from famine to 'flu. Doing nothing was not an option; the State had to deal with these challenges, which could not be contained within any particular class or any particular area. The typhus and cholera epidemics were especially democratic in attacking all classes of society. The State, however, had faced similar catastrophes in the past and had taken decisive action. When plague threatened in the 1600s, the Assembly bought a house in George's Street for use as an isolation hospital, strictly controlling access to it.[175] The city also operated a quarantine station on Clontarf Island, and ships' passengers and crews were only allowed ashore after a period of isolation. Smallpox, too, had been a great killer in the period 1661–1746, during which it is stated that 20% of all deaths were caused by it. Inoculation was tried successfully on the prisoners in Cork Gaol, but those inoculated in Donegal in 1781 were not so fortunate—51 of the 52 died.[176]

In the eighteenth century medicine consisted very much of a volunteer form of relief for those who became sick. Many institutions were set up by well-intentioned individuals and they offered some relief. The period up to the typhus outbreak in 1817 was one of more sedate activity; the pace of change quickened with its arrival, as it brought widespread fear and rumour in its wake.

A potato famine during the summer of 1801, a 'flu epidemic in 1803 and another partial failure of the harvest in 1811 drove hordes of people from the land to the towns, mainly to Dublin. Just after this the French wars proved a boon to agriculture in terms of the supply of horses, men and grain. Within two years of Waterloo, however, in the same year as the typhus epidemic, another bad harvest arrived alongside falling agricultural prices, putting additional strain on the island. Almost immediately there was another famine in 1822. Ruddy wrote that the population of the city was meanwhile doubling every 39 years.[177] Unemployment was such a vital aspect in the spread of fever that the government, on examination of the typhus outbreak of 1817, 'devoted almost an entire report to devising schemes to provide work'.[178] In addition, attitudes did not help matters; as Luke Gardiner had said, 'Those who rendered our people idle are the first to ridicule them for their idleness'.[179] Thomas Campbell Foster took the opposing view: 'the people here have only themselves to blame'.[180] Weather, too, was always a factor in making matters even worse. O'Neill quotes Peel, writing in 1816: 'If there is a severe winter, the want of fuel will be a greater source of misery than the want of food'. The State apparatus could not ignore these major social disruptions, over which they had not much control, and so became more involved in public health thanks to such epidemics.[181]

The Asylum for the Recovery of Health and for the Care of the Diseases of the Skin was located at St George's Place, North Circular Road, near Dorset Street.[182] The Dublin Infirmary for Diseases of the Skin at Moore Street was established in 1818.[183] Not far away, St Mary's Hospital, also known as the Dublin Eye Infirmary, was set up in June 1819, and within four years had attended to 44,000 patients. Again, the nearby Cow Pock Institution at 62 Sackville Street had inoculated 83,123 patients and dispensed 64,577 packets for infection between its opening in 1804 and the end of November 1823.[184] Inoculation would be one of the great breakthroughs in medical development. It came as a result of inoculation trials, using those who were not in a position to object to being guinea pigs.

The other major change in medical thinking that came about in the last few years of the eighteenth century was the idea of placing institutions out on the fringes of the city for the beneficial effects of space and fresh air. Similarly, sea bathing was thought to be of benefit to physical well-being, and people practised it enthusiastically all along the coast of the bay. Drinking seawater, too, was considered to be good for one's constitution, and Howth seawater in particular was most popular.[185]

The sheer number of institutions illustrates the scale of what was taking place on the ground. All these establishments needed to be built from scratch or converted from one already built. They had to be fitted out. Then they had to be supplied with the relevant supplies, both medical and domestic, and on a substantial scale. Most important of all, they had to be manned to dispense and administer the service, and the people who did the dispensing mainly lived in the locale near their work. Cleaning, laundry, food supply and general catering, heating, water and waste disposal, and the supply of paper, candles and quills for keeping records all required manpower in these institutions which were mainly new to both society and the city. There was work available for all levels of skill.

The relocation of the lying-in hospital from the south side to the higher ground above the Mall in the 1750s and downriver from Essex Bridge was a bold move. It was established on Great Britain Street, up from Capel Street, as this part of the city began to fill in rapidly. Note the streetscape of Parnell Street or Great Britain Street to the side of the Rotunda Hospital in Fig. 10.18.

As the eighteenth century turned into the nineteenth, water was provided to the citizens via old wooden pipes, newer metal pipes now locally produced, public fountains and directly from the two canals. Canal water presented problems and remained a difficulty until cleanliness took hold as a medical concept. In any case, the supply from the Royal Canal was irregular. But the laying of metal pipes continued all across the city in an attempt to supply water for both industry and private accommodation.

Sir Patrick Dun's Hospital, adjacent to the Grand Canal, opened on 8 October 1808 for medical instruction. It was located at what used to be just above the high-water mark on the side of the river.

The Westmorland Lock Hospital in Townsend Street, originally set up on 20 November 1792, took over the site of a Hospital for the Incurables that had originally opened in Townsend Street in 1744, sixteen years after the Liffey walls were completed. It dealt with sexually transmitted diseases and was well placed down at the port and not too far from the army barracks at Beggar's Bush, close

Fig. 10.18—The Rotunda Hospital, erected on the north side in the 1750s, showing the development of Great Britain Street (courtesy of Louise Morgan and Brendan Maher, NGI).

to the Grand Canal. Located on the edge of the river beside the port and docks, it had to deal with tidal offerings, damp swamp vapours and the effluent of 300 patients, as well as 'filth and abomination of the most licentious in surrounding lanes'.[186] There was public outrage when the extent of sexual relations between male and female patients was discovered; some years earlier the problem had been that soldiers who were supposed to be acting as guards at the hospital were found to be taking advantage of the women patients.[187] It reopened in March 1820 for the relief of female outpatients exclusively.

Mosse's Hospital opened in 1745 in George's Lane, south of the river, before relocating to the top of Sackville Street in 1757. From then until November 1822, some 105,051 women gave birth there (to 55,704 boys and 50,979 girls).

Also on the north side was the Whitworth Hospital, set up in 1818 opposite the fourth lock on the Royal Canal, which included two wards for private patients. Its managing committee was composed of people who lived at Gloucester Street, Dorset Street, Eccles Street, Capel Street, Mountjoy Square and Rutland Square.[188]

Each of the above, along with the placing of churches and schools, helped to fill in the area north of the Liffey.

In 1834 Henry David Inglis wrote of a visit to Ireland just two years after the end of the cholera epidemic. He described 'Ragged wretches that are sitting on the steps'.[189] Lifestyle, too, had changed: 'the facilities of steam navigation are now so great that the country dealers throughout Ireland who formerly made their purchases in Dublin now pass to England and lay in their stocks'. He noted that, whereas in 'London every fifth or sixth shop is a bacon and cheese shop, in Dublin luxuries of a different kind offer their temptations. What would be the use of opening a bacon shop where the lower orders, who are elsewhere the chief purchasers of bacon, cannot afford to eat bacon, and live upon potatoes?'[190] 'After the cattle have been fed, the half-eaten turnips became the prerequisite of the crowd of ragged boys and girls without. Many and fierce were the scrambles for these precious relics'.[191]

Inglis also visited the Dublin Mendicity Society and reported a total of 2,145 persons availing of the charity, of whom 200— almost 10%—were Protestant.[192] This again confirms the expanding Protestant element in the urban poor. He noted that the financial support for the charity consisted of subscriptions from mainly the middle classes, but not much support from either the wealthy or Catholics. In fact, he wrote, Catholics only donated one shilling for every 50 shillings donated by Protestants.[193] This is a very interesting figure in the light of the vast sums of money raised in this period by the Catholic Church for building both churches and schools, and for Daniel O'Connell for his major movements up to 1843. Inglis does remark 'on the multitude of jaunting cars', and his comments remind us of the great population of the city, the volume of traffic and the sheer numbers of horses. He cites one instance where he counted 27 hackney coaches and sixteen cars in the funeral cortège of a person of 'the humbler walk of life'.[194] He had earlier noted that all coach-makers were in full employment. The comment on the volume of traffic and the number of horses was borne out nine years later by the scale of both in the massive attendances at O'Connell's monster meetings in Dublin and around the country.

The medical profession was very slow to allow Catholics to enter it, as noted by Laurence McGeery.[195] The voluntary hospitals were the preserve of Protestant surgeons and physicians. In the early 1840s only thirteen of the 107 public hospital positions were held by Catholics, and only 5% of the medical officers were Catholics. This reflected a rearguard action by the Protestant powers to hold the line.[196] The most significant public health reform in the nineteenth century was the extension of the modified English Poor Law to Ireland in 1838; however, as Leany said, 'in reality little changed; politics and religion continued to be prioritized over individual ability in medical appointments'.[197]

The typhus outbreak of 1817 lasted until 1819. It affected all classes and showed that no section of society was immune from its effects. As always in Irish society, the poorer sections—dwelling on the margins, poorly clothed and poorly housed, on a sub-standard diet, with human waste and dirt outside their doors—were the weakest and fell first. The more genteel elements of society also suffered greatly, however, but for a different reason—that of having no natural defence against contagion.

The spread of the epidemic, crossing all class divides, created great fear everywhere. People vainly attempted to evade it by moving out or away from their homes. Some of the better-off even moved to England. One section of society that was particularly badly affected were those who worked to alleviate the suffering of the sick: doctors, surgeons, apothecaries, the nursing staff of the time, those who worked in hospitals and dispensaries, and clergymen of all religions.

The disease did not confine itself to the city. Revd Ham, the parish priest of Coolock and Clontarf since 1808, lived at the Sheds at Clontarf and died of typhus on 4 August 1818. His own funeral, while a display of great affection for him in terms of the crowds attending, showed no regard for the public advice on reducing contagion by avoiding crowds such as wakes and funerals. His funeral procession went from Clontarf through Summerhill, Great Britain Street, Capel Street, Stoneybatter and on to Mulhuddart. In November of that year Revd D. Ferrell of Denmark Street Chapel died.[198] John Barrelet, a dentist of Lower Sackville Street, succumbed to typhus on 13 October 1818.[199] On 22 May in the same year Miss Cecelia Lacy of King Street Convent died of typhus. Three weeks earlier Revd John Smyth of Baldoyle and Howth parish died. He had been educated at the Catholic Jesuit college of Stoneyhurst in England and switched to Maynooth for ordination.[200]

Then he moved to Baldoyle. His first task in the area was to build two schools in Howth for 150 males and 150 females. He followed this up by building the Catholic church in Howth.

Records show 796 hospital admissions in September 1817 and 1,712 by March 1818; in October of that year 3,000 were admitted and 2,394 the following January, but by June 1819 numbers had dropped to 996.[201]

On 30 May 1818 local Boards of Health came into being under an Act of Parliament for the setting up of fever hospitals. Within two years there were four in Cork and six in Tipperary. They had the authority to manage and implement decisions concerning outbreaks.[202] By 1820 a General Board of Health for the whole country had been established as a permanent body to act as a medical watchdog, to collect statistical information on local conditions, and to advise and recommend remedial action. Though mainly advisory, it did offer medical relief in emergencies. These boards were reacting not only to typhus and cholera but also to outbreaks of relapsing fever, dysentery, scurvy and smallpox. All of these had the worst effect on the weaker strands of society, the poor, the hungry and the poorly housed—in other words, the people with the least reserves to counter such epidemics and whose culture and customs of gathering for wakes and funerals only made things worse. In short, the casual labouring classes had little to offer in the way of resilience. The effects of outbreaks were multiplied by the placing of manure dumps immediately outside the doors of dwellings which were often badly ventilated already. The window tax—imposed in 1799 and extended in 1816—exacerbated the problem, causing windows to be blocked up. In some cases the rear courtyards of multiple-storey buildings became open-air receptacles for human waste from basement to ground-floor level. At this time the city still had communal depots for holding the waste collected by the city scavengers, close to society with the accompanying smells and flies.

In his thesis on Victorian travel writing in Ireland T.J. McAuliffe focuses on aspects of attitudes and perceptions. He maintains that in this period travel writing can be viewed as 'a homogeneous genre which is entirely complicit with British colonial policy'.[203] As a clear exponent of this he proposes Caesar Otway, who traversed Ireland and beyond and wrote about his travels. Otway, born in 1780 in Tipperary, attended Trinity College and became a Church of Ireland clergyman at the Magdalene Asylum in Leeson Street, Dublin, in the 1820s and 1830s. He displayed anti-Catholic themes in his writing and in his preaching. As a cleric, he carried respect and status among the Protestant population. He wrote in the *Dublin University Magazine* at the time of the resignation of Robert Peel on 5 May 1835, 'The Protestants of Ireland have been sold by the Whigs for O'Connell's support'.[204] The essential problem for society at large—the Protestant society and its representatives—was the pull of national Ireland, in whatever form it was felt, against the ingrained antipathy towards Catholics as people. This conundrum was being acted out everywhere, and McAuliffe says of Otway that 'His pride in his nationality and his animosity towards his fellow nationals' exemplified the problem faced by Protestants in the city. He maintains that in all of his writings Otway displays a predicament of vacillating between descriptions of Irish antiquity and self-conscious commentary on the native population, echoing what Sir Samuel Ferguson had written, 'A dialogue between the head and heart of an Irish Protestant'. Both writers appeared torn between their own arguments.[205] But these attitudes became upended with the outbreak of the cholera and typhoid epidemics, both of which raced through all strata of the city's inhabitants, showing no favouritism towards any particular class or location or religion. This only compounded the panic created by cholera, according to Asa Briggs.[206]

In 1804 the Cork Street Fever Hospital opened with 80 beds, and the facility to increase to

Fig. 10.19—The Richmond Hospital (photo: Brian Matthews).

120 in emergencies. By 1809 the hospital had the ability to increase to 140 beds, and with the typhus outbreak had 240 beds for the sick.[207]

By 1815 the position in Dublin regarding aid for the poor sick amounted to dispensaries, infirmaries, houses of industry, fever hospitals and lunatic asylums, with a small number of institutions catering for specific diseases.[208] Much had changed since the House of Industry was set up in 1773; this was extended in 1813 and opened as a fever hospital, and in 1815 the Richmond Lunatic Asylum opened (Fig. 10.19).

The State became more involved in public health in the late eighteenth century, and this involvement was put on a more solid footing thanks to legislation. It began by allying voluntary subscriptions with government grants, with the result that by 1846 Dublin had at its disposal one infirmary, six fever hospitals and fourteen dispensaries, with over 632 dispensaries nationwide.[209] O'Neill maintained that the crisis rather than government policy drove the construction of fever hospitals. Either way, the hospitals, dispensaries and infirmaries became part of the cityscape and part of the thinking of the citizenry of Dublin. The House of Industry Hardwicke Hospital, too, was available to the public in times of emergency, and the crisis pushed forward the opening of another hospital of the House of Industry, the Whitworth, in 1817.

The Richmond, the Whitworth and the Hardwicke were known as the Hospitals of the House of Industry, a title dating from 1772, and were governed under a special act of parliament. When the public failed to maintain them, the Irish parliament made grants in aid, and the charitable institutions received £22,000 per year. When the Poor Law Acts came into force in 1838, these hospitals were

Fig. 10.20—The Richmond Hospital, badge over the front door (photo: Brian Matthews).

separated from the workhouse. A board of governors was appointed by the lord lieutenant, and it was provided that the imperial government should make a contribution to them and to certain other hospitals. In 1840 the grant was £18,000, specifically for maintenance and not for expansion or extension. The old Richmond, which had been a nunnery, was taken over in 1807 but remained as it was, without funds to improve it, for another 80 years.

In an attempt to tackle the typhus epidemic, Dr Steevens's Hospital and the Richmond Penitentiary were converted into temporary fever hospitals, as was Sir Patrick Dun's Hospital, which was actually a teaching institution.[210] A committee composed of doctors and governors of various fever hospitals was set up to co-ordinate the fever relief scheme and to improve the medical inspection system.[211] The figures of 700,000–1,500,000 persons infected, resulting in 44,000–65,000 deaths, are agreed to be on the low side. Whatever the accuracy of the figures, the actions taken to tackle the outbreak displayed the massive effect it had on the city and its people. The city was divided into four zones and a cleansing operation was put into action. This involved whitewashing cabins and cleaning streets, and the sick were encouraged to go to the various fever hospitals.

Dublin, with its population of 250,000, finally got a second lying-in hospital—the Coombe—in 1829.[212] This is a reminder that the Rotunda lying-in hospital, which had been founded in 1745 (85 years earlier), was situated for some years by South Great George's Street and moved to Parnell Square in 1757.[213] O'Grada offers valuable information on men and work in the city and surrounds in his statistical information culled from the original books of the Rotunda. This information confirms that 32% of all fathers whose wives were giving birth in the Rotunda were labourers, while 22% were servants, giving an accurate idea of the level of unskilled labour pursuing work in Dublin.[214]

In 1822 another famine occurred in the west and south of Ireland, further straining resources. Again people came to Dublin, putting more pressure on the system of relief. Further, in 1826 the collapse of the textile industry in Dublin and the consequent loss of earnings caused hunger and cold and the inability to pay rent or clothe families, leading to a fever outbreak among the weakened and susceptible people. By October of that year 6,000 patients had been seen, the epidemic lasting until the following summer. This caused the building of extensions to the fever hospitals already in existence[215] and in addition a nunnery and an encampment were taken over, bringing in a further 400 beds. The figure of some £15,792 is generally accepted as having been spent on relief.[216]

One of the ways in which the State sought to alleviate the problem was by setting up the Board of Works to create mass employment on structural projects.

There was a Female Penitent Asylum at 77 Marlborough Street housing 45 females. In 1830 a Penitent Asylum opened in Brown Street.[217] In the same year Mother Mary Aikenhead moved to a convent at Sandymount for the sea air because of her failing health. She did, however, manage, with the assistance of Doctor O'Farrell, to plan a Catholic hospital for the city, and St Vincent's opened on St Stephen's Green in 1834—the first hospital in the world to be owned and staffed by women.[218]

Cholera came to Ireland in 1832. It, too, had a devastating effect on all aspects of life in the city, from commerce to social activity. It would later create in society a reliance on the State to provide assistance in terms of general healthcare. People moved from place to place to try to avoid it. Many left Drogheda and moved to Dublin to get some relief. The affluent were advised that the best chance of safety was to provide for the poor, and some of the recommendations in a proclamation were to avoid visiting family and not to go to a place of worship or any crowded place.[219]

The disease, which had been widespread across Europe, brought mortality rates of around 40%, as death usually occurred within 24 hours. The spread was made easier thanks to contaminated water and the fact that all those contaminated became carriers. It was first reported on 25 March 1832. By the following July the death-toll totals had reached 1,574, and by Christmas they numbered 4,478.[220]

O'Neill wrote that, just as new roads and steamships opened a weak economy to foreign producers, the same roads and steamships also enabled the contagion. Commerce was greatly affected and many businesses closed down; in Balbriggan two cotton mills closed because they could not access material from Liverpool. Rumour and lack of knowledge of the causes of cholera made people afraid to eat fish and cockles, and fishermen in Howth and other fishing ports suffered as a result. In the city paper and woollen mills closed down.[221] Quarantine restrictions put 2,000 heads of families out of work in the parish of St Mark and put 8,000 on relief.[222]

Extra doctors were employed mostly in Dublin, both because it had the largest population and because of the extra influx of people from other parts, especially in both Grangegorman and Townsend Street. Mother Mary Aikenhead's Sisters of Charity nursed the sick in the temporary accommodation at Grangegorman, while Mother Catherine McAuley's Sisters of Mercy, founded just before the outbreak, nursed at Townsend Street.[223] The death rate was estimated to be anywhere between 40% and 76% of those infected. Infection was spread by flies and unclean hands.[224] Another facilitator of contagion was the sheer numbers in the city and people congregating everywhere, such as in hostelries and hotels. There were fourteen hotels alone on the north side of the city operating in this new space and more than 26 insurance offices, signifying not just employment but people and mingling.[225] John Barrow had recorded that the Bitton Hotel in Sackville Street 'is one of the most magnificent in Europe'.[226] Jakob Venedy wrote of the masses of beggars who were everywhere in the city; in particular they followed the money, thus spreading contagion.[227]

The Richmond Penitentiary opened in 1811 at Grangegorman Lane, close to the rear of the Four Courts.[228] The Dublin Female Penitentiary on the North Circular Road, set up for the religious and moral improvement of women and enclosing a chapel of the Established Church in which 'there is ample and commodious accommodation for the public',[229] by 1821 had accommodation for 34 residents, as did the Bow Street Female Penitents Asylum, while the General Asylum on Townsend Street housed 37 females.[230] The Lock Penitentiary at Dorset Street, also known as the Bethseda, operated as a workhouse from 1794.[231] Workhouses became part of the landscape of the country and city with the enactment of the Poor Law Union of 1839. The North Dublin Workhouse opened in North Brunswick Street in May 1840, with a capacity for 4,100 inmates.[232]

Close to the Richmond, the House of Refuge was established in 1811 at Stanhope Street for 'industrious and distressed young women of good character', 50 at that time under the Sisters of Charity.[233] Other institutions in the area included St Mary's Asylum for 'fallen women', founded in 1833 on the Drumcondra Road under the patronage of Dr Murray. Slightly nearer to town was St Joseph's Asylum for 'aged and virtuous single females' at 7 Portland Row, founded in 1836, again with Dr Murray as patron. Close by, St Mary Magdelene's Asylum on Lower Gloucester Street had begun life at Lower Mecklenburgh Street in 1822.[234] An Asylum for 'aged and infirm female servants of good character', founded in 1809, was run at 21 Lower Dorset Street. The Old Man's Asylum 'for respectable and reduced Protestants', set up in 1810 and housing 24 men of good character, was at Russell Place off the North Circular Road.[235]

The St Thomas Dispensary opened in 1825 for the sole purpose of administering to the poor of the parish of St Mary, prescribing for upwards of 6,000 people. The consulting doctor was Dr Mollan, who resided at Gloucester Street. Another dispensary, St George's, opened in 1827 at Dispensary Lane, off Dorset Street, and some of its patients even received visits to their homes. The poor were offered vaccinations every Tuesday. Revd F. Brilge, who lived at 56 Dorset Street, was attached to the dispensary. There was also a dispensary at 176 Great Britain Street, off the lane at Henry Street, established in 1836 and a parochial dispensary was sited at 26 Upper Abbey Street.[236]

As already noted, State intervention became the norm during the first four decades of the nineteenth century, with the result that by 1845 Medical Officers and dispensaries existed across the city and beyond to the newer suburbs. A.G. Guinness MD was Medical Officer for Clontarf and Raheny, William Fossett was in Drumcondra, Mr Geoghegan looked after Baldoyle and Howth, Mr B.G. Darley was responsible for Coolock, and there was another dispensary at Sandymount.[237] In Swords two dispensaries were established, one urban and the other rural.[238]

The State was also responsible for other structures which were imposed on the land in the nineteenth century—the various Martello and signal towers built as a system of coastal defence during the war with France. Fifty were built up to 1815, 27 of which were around Dublin, from Balbriggan down to Bray. On the north shore they were built at Sutton, Howth, Ireland's Eye, Malahide, Portrane, Loughshinny, Skerries and Balbriggan. One interesting aspect of the internal defences in the Martello towers is the inclusion of internal narrow spiral staircases. After hundreds of years of military development, the idea of the spiral stair which could be defended by one man still held sway.[239] The towers were manned until the threat of the French subsided but each became part of the landscape in their respective areas. William Duncan's 1821 map of Dublin shows the towers at Sutton, Dalkey Island and Sandymount. The tower at Sandymount was constructed on reclaimed land along the new wall to Merrion Road. The map also features the Half Moon Battery and the Pigeon House Fort on the South Wall, also built on ground retaken from the sea.[240]

The dynamic of the occupation of the streets of Dublin was always shifting. Dr William Drennan, who lived in Gloucester Street in 1791, viewed his street as one of the best in the city at that time, on the northern edge of Dublin Bay on North Strand. Over the following four years, however, he changed his opinion, viewing Gloucester Street and other 'genteel' streets as being taken over by the lower orders.[241] This street had, according to the *Dublin Chronicle*, been sketched out by Mr Byrom to be 80ft wide, extending to the Circular Road, with intervening streets between it and Summerhill. Among these are those named Nugent Street and Grenville Street, boosting the clustering around Aldeborough House.[242]

The more comfortably off continued to occupy the area, however, including Lady Hassard at 39 Summerhill, Revenue inspector John Fea at No. 10 and Miss Ecshaw at No. 35. Countess Belvedere was at 6 Great Denmark Street and Alderman Archer at 9 Gardiner Place, while John Ball lived at 18 Upper Gardiner Street. Nor had Mountjoy Square and Henrietta Street—the bastions of the upper orders—been abandoned. W.J. Guinness lived at 12 Mountjoy Square and the earl of Blessington in Henrietta Street, while Major-General Chabot had a house at 13 Lower Dominick Street, a few doors from Lord Howth. Just outside Mountjoy Square the Hon. Hans Blackwood kept house at 23 Great Charles Street, just off the bottom of the North Circular Road. In fact, P.Th.

Hicks on his tour of Ireland in 1818 noted that Rutland and Mountjoy Squares 'are in my opinion the two primary squares in Dublin'.[243] This observation was made at the height of the typhus epidemic and while most of Merrion and Fitzwilliam squares were nearing completion. The 1824 *Almanac* shows that, while some of the MPs had sold up and decamped for London along with some of the élite, many remained. In addition, the finer streets also began to be occupied by the professions and successful traders. Gloucester Street had by now been partially occupied. Miss Archbold lived at No. 39, Mrs Arturre at No. 9 and Miss Anderson at No. 30. Lower down towards the river, Alderman Bloxham had a Dublin abode at 26 Gardiner Place as well as a home at Booterstown, a burgeoning new suburb, while Sir William Betham kept house at both Montpelier House in Monkstown and Westland Row. In this they were following a trend led by Lord Fitzwilliam, who 'left his land in small parcels for building country houses'.[244] This shows that the drive to decamp to England after 1800 has been somewhat overstated in terms of numbers.

The owners of larger houses originally well outside the city now found these seats more adjacent to it, as suburbia crept northward. Austin Cooper, who owned Abbeyville in Malahide (later the home of Taoiseach C.J. Haughey), had a house at 4 Merrion Square; Lord Charlemont, as well as having Marino, also had a Dublin house at 22 Rutland (Parnell) Square; Benjamin Booker had his seat at St Dulough's on the Malahide Road and in the city at 102 Mecklenburgh Street; James Barlow's town house was at 4 North Great George's Street while his country house was at Sybil Hill, Raheny; and Lord Howth of Howth Castle also had a city dwelling, at 34 Lower Dominick Street, as did Sir Bagnell Burdett as well as Merchamp in Clontarf. It is therefore clear that the confines of the city were spreading, and quite substantially, across reclaimed land. In other words, the North Lotts had been taken over. At this stage Telford was improving the road into Dublin, as was confirmed by Hicks in 1818: 'I got clear of Howth about half past seven when I took the road for Dublin which the whole way in is very good'.[245] It is perfectly obvious, then, that with the city and these new suburbs melting together many of the élite did not actually need to own a city centre property, as the city had extended out to make their original country seat so much closer to town.

Information useful to this work also comes from parish detail. David Dickson provides pie chart information on both St George's parish, showing a population of approximately 5,000 souls, and St Thomas's parish on Marlborough Street and its environs, with 10,000 souls. In St Mary's parish, meantime, the number is 20,000. All of these parishioners now occupy mostly reclaimed land. St George's is especially interesting in that it was green fields not long before. The other point of interest in Dickson's pie charts is the make-up of the various classes living in each parish, shedding more light on life in eighteenth-century Dublin. St Thomas's parish is made up of 50% lower class and servants and 50% middle to upper class; in St Mary's parish the vast majority comprised lower class and servants; and St George's, the newest parish with its new church, has a majority of upper- and middle-class parishioners.[246] Between them, the parishes of St Thomas and St George boasted a total of 15,000 persons where no one had previously been living.

The conclusion, then, which can be drawn from the information in the three sections of this chapter is that during the first four decades of the nineteenth century huge changes took place on the space within the old walls of the Liffey and the Tolka, constructed in 1728, along with the North Lotts. Great change had occurred outside those walls too, from the initial ribbon of development connecting the two along the roads, rivers and canals and using bridges as natural locations of settlement. People now lived and worked where before there was merely tidal foreshore and green fields. The ever-increasing population of the city acted as the driver for the building of more houses, which in turn triggered the further development of places of supply for the occupants. All this led in turn to the further development of churches, schools and hospitals—each new edifice on the landscape helping to build a new city on the north side of Dublin.

Notes

[1] Virginia Crossman, 'The growth of the state in nineteenth-century Ireland'. In J. Kelly (ed.), *The Cambridge History of Ireland. Vol. 3: Ireland c. 1730–c. 1880* (Cambridge, 2018), p. 552.
[2] Vincent Ruddy, *Monster agitators: O'Connell's Repealers, 1843 Ireland* (Dublin, 2018), p. 31.
[3] James H. Murphy, *Ireland: a social, cultural and literary history, 1791–1891* (Dublin, 2003), p. 37.
[4] Sarah Ward-Perkins, 'Bank of Ireland—old Parliament House', *Dublin Historical Record* **37** (2) (1984), 42–53, p. 43.
[5] Ruddy, *Monster agitators*, p. 45.
[6] Baptist Wriothesley Noel, *Notes of a short tour through the midland counties of Ireland in the summer of 1836, with observations on the condition of the peasantry* (London, 1837), p. 1.
[7] *Ibid.*, p. 2.
[8] Alice Murray, *A history of the commercial relations between England and Ireland from the period of the Restoration* (London, 1903), pp 11–12.
[9] Daire Keogh, 'Review of *The bible war in Ireland: the Second Reformation and the polarisation of Protestant–Catholic relations in Ireland 1800–1840* by Irene Whelan', *Irish Historical Studies* **35** (138) (2006), 251–2, p. 251.
[10] Murray, *A history of the commercial relations between England and Ireland*, pp 4–8.
[11] D.N. Hempton, 'The Methodist crusade in Ireland 1795–1845', *Irish Historical Studies* **22** (85) (1980), 3–48, p. 33.
[12] *Ibid.*, p. 35.
[13] *Ibid.*, p. 36.
[14] *Ibid.*, p. 37.
[15] *Ibid.*, p. 38.
[16] *Ibid.*, p. 40.
[17] *Ibid.*, p. 43.
[18] *Ibid.*, p. 43.
[19] Revd John Evans, 'Petition of the Protestants of Ireland in favour of Catholic Emancipation', *Belfast Monthly Magazine* **8** (45) (April 1812), 323–6.
[20] Francis Hardy, *Memoirs of the political and private life of James Caulfield, Earl of Charlemont* (London, 1810), p. xiii.
[21] John Barrow, *A tour around Ireland through the sea counties in the autumn of 1835* (London, 1836), p. 11.
[22] T.J. Morrissey, *The life and times of Daniel Murray, esteemed archbishop of Dublin 1823–1852* (Dublin, 2018), p. 48.
[23] Ann Plumtre, *Narrative of a residence in Ireland during the summer of 1814 and that of 1815* (London, 1817), p. 9.
[24] National Gallery of Ireland, 'Drawings of Dublin' exhibition.
[25] Diaries of Charles Cosslett (1793–4), Diary B, p. 12 (St Malachy's College, Belfast).
[26] Revd D.A. Levistone Cooney, 'The Methodist chapels in Dublin', *Dublin Historical Record* **57** (2) (2004), 152–63, p. 152.
[27] *Ibid.*, p. 153.
[28] *Ibid.*, p. 153.
[29] *Ibid.*, p. 155.
[30] *Ibid.*, p. 159.
[31] Paula Lynch, 'A Dublin street—North Great George's Street', *Dublin Historical Record* **31** (1) (1977), 14–21, p. 19.
[32] Levistone Cooney, 'Methodist chapels', p. 162.
[33] Louis McRedmond, *To the greater glory: a history of the Irish Jesuits* (Dublin, 1991), p. 101.
[34] *Ibid.*, p. 106.
[35] Irish Jesuits Archive, Vol. 1. History of Irish Province, 1560–1814 (Dublin, 1962), p. 80.
[36] McRedmond, *To the greater glory*, pp 109–10; E.E. O'Donnell, *The Jesuits in Dublin* (Dublin, 1999), p. 29.
[37] Maureen Ryan, 'The Church of St Francis Xavier, Upper Gardiner Street, Dublin', unpublished MA thesis, University College Dublin (1994), p. 6.
[38] *Ibid.*, p. 7.
[39] Morrissey, *The life and times of Daniel Murray*, p. 60.
[40] Ryan, 'The Church of St Francis Xavier', p. 8.
[41] Morrissey, *The life and times of Daniel Murray*, p. 62.
[42] *Ibid.*, p. 97.

[43] *Ibid.*, p. 109.
[44] *Ibid.*, p. 71.
[45] *Ibid.*, p. 103.
[46] Ryan, 'The Church of St Francis Xavier', p. 10.
[47] *Ibid.*, p. 37.
[48] *Ibid.*, p. 12.
[49] *Ibid.*, pp 15–16.
[50] Jesuit Archives, Lower Leeson Street, Dublin: Accounts book, p. 21.
[51] *Ibid.*, p. 24.
[52] *Ibid.*, p. 58.
[53] *Ibid.*, p. 107.
[54] Jesuit Archives: Cm/Gard/41/1, Cm/Gard/2/5/1 and Addenda no. 88, list of benefactors for the years 1829, 1830, 1841, 1850, p. 15.
[55] Jesuit Archives: Accounts book, p. 106.
[56] Ryan, 'The Church of St Francis Xavier', p. 27.
[57] Jesuit Archives: CM/Gard/2/5/1, p. 14.
[58] Levistone Cooney, 'Methodist chapels', p. 157.
[59] Lynch, 'North Great Georges Street', p. 19.
[60] *Ibid.*, p. 17.
[61] David Dickson, *Dublin: the making of a capital city* (London, 2014), pp 271–2.
[62] Seamus Deane, 'Montalembert letter on Catholicism in Ireland', *Field Day Review* **7** (2011), 250–71.
[63] Mary Purcell, 'Dublin Diocesan Archives: Murray papers', *Archivium Hibernicum* **37–8** (1982–3), p. 30.
[64] *Ibid.*, p. 29.
[65] *Ibid.*, p. 33.
[66] Friedrich Raumer, *England in 1835 volume 1, being a series of letters written to friends in Germany during a residence in London and excursions into the provinces by Friedrich Raumer, translated from the German by Sarah Austen and H.E. Lloyd in three volumes* (London, 1836), p. 44.
[67] *Ibid.*, p. 45.
[68] Shunsuke Katsula, 'Conciliation, anti-Orange politics and the sectarian scare: Dublin politics of the early 1820s', *Dublin Historical Record* **64** (2) (2011), 142–59, p. 142.
[69] Vincent Ruddy, *Monster agitators*, p. 47.
[70] *Ibid.*, p. 48.
[71] *Ibid.*, p. 65.
[72] Gormanston Papers, NLI MS 44,448/1.
[73] Gormanston Papers, NLI MS 44,450/2.
[74] Gormanston Papers, NLI MS 44,450/3.
[75] RDS Minute-books, vols 1–3 (1731–46), 22 February 1733.
[76] *CARD*, vol. 18, p. 550.
[77] John H. Martin, 'Aspects of the social geography of Dublin city in the mid-nineteenth century', unpublished MA thesis, University College Dublin (1973), p. 29.
[78] Neal Doherty, *The complete list of the streets of Dublin* (Dublin, 2006), p. 297.
[79] Martin, 'Aspects of the social geography of Dublin', p. 83.
[80] T. Cromwell, *The Irish tourist or excursions through Ireland, province of Leinster*, vol. 3 (Dublin, 1820), p. 145.
[81] Pettigrew & Oulton's *Dublin Almanack and General Register of Ireland* (1845), p. 318.
[82] Ciaran Clancy, 'Gardiner St. employment exchange: the historical background and development', *Dublin Historical Record* **43** (1) (1990), 47–51, p. 47.
[83] *Ibid.*, p. 48.
[84] Pettigrew & Oulton's *Dublin Almanack and General Register of Ireland* (Dublin, 1844), p. 309.
[85] *Ibid.*, p. 309.
[86] *Ibid.*, p. 311.
[87] *Ibid.*, p. 311.
[88] *Ibid.*, p. 313.
[89] *St Saviour's Church, Dublin, 1861–1961* (centenary book, kindly lent to the author by Fr Crotty, acting prior), p. 74.
[90] *Ibid.*, pp 5–9.

[91] *Ibid.*, p. 12.
[92] D. O'Grada, *Georgian Dublin: the forces that shaped the city* (Cork, 2015), p. 49.
[93] Dublin Diocesan Archive: Church building, Diocese of Dublin, Account book, 1800–1916, p. 2.
[94] *Ibid.*, p. 1.
[95] Dublin Diocesan Archive: History of Dublin parishes, south city, and RC chapels, 1749, p. 153.
[96] Revd W. Meyler, *Letter to the people of the parish of St Andrew* (Dublin, 1859), p. 6.
[97] N. Donnelly, *Short histories of Dublin parishes*, p. 87. Catholic Truth Society of Ireland.
[98] *Ibid.*, pp 96–7.
[99] *Ibid.*, p. 89.
[100] *Ibid.*, p. 92.
[101] Dublin Diocesan Archive: History of Dublin parishes, north city, and index 1,11,111, p. 99.
[102] Dublin Diocesan Archive: Church building, Diocese of Dublin, 1800–1916, p. 1.
[103] N. Donnelly, *Short histories of Dublin parishes*, p. 98.
[104] Ruddy, *Monster agitators*, p. 40.
[105] Pettigrew & Oulton's *Dublin Almanack* of 1844.
[106] Raumer, *England in 1835 …*, p. 31.
[107] *Ibid.*, p. 35.
[108] *St Saviour's Church*, p. 305.
[109] *Ibid.*, p. 310.
[110] *Ibid.*, p. 318.
[111] *Ibid.*, p. 312.
[112] Ruddy, *Monster agitators*, p. 144.
[113] *Ibid.*, p. 325.
[114] *Ibid.*, p. 322.
[115] *Ibid.*, p. 319.
[116] Mary Purcell and David Sheehy, 'Dublin Diocesan Archive: Murray Papers. Letter no. 10', *Archivium Hibernicum* **4** (6) (1986), pp 3–63.
[117] T. Dawson, 'The road to Howth', *Dublin Historical Record* **29** (4), 122–32, p. 125.
[118] Dublin Diocesan Archive: Church building, Diocese of Dublin, 1800–1916.
[119] Brendan Grimes, 'Patrons and architects and the creation of Catholic Church architecture in nineteenth-century Dublin', *Dublin Historical Record* **61** (1) (2015), p. 9.
[120] Dublin Diocesan Archive: Church building, Diocese of Dublin, 1800–1916.
[121] Dawson, 'The road to Howth', p. 124.
[122] Thomas J. Johnston, Ven. John L. Robinson and the Very Revd Robert Wyse Jackson, *A history of the Church of Ireland* (Dublin, 1953), p. 9.
[123] Pettigrew & Oulton's *Dublin Almanack and General Register of Ireland* (1845), p. 352.
[124] *Ibid.*, p. 637.
[125] N. Donnelly, *Short histories of Dublin parishes*, p. 97.
[126] Ó Gráda, *Georgian Dublin*, p. 164.
[127] Ruddy, *Monster agitators*, pp 250, 265.
[128] *Ibid.*, p. 66.
[129] Thomas Tredgold, *Principles of warming and ventilating public buildings, hothouses & c.* (London, 1838), xviii.
[130] *Ibid.*, xix.
[131] Ruddy, *Monster agitators*, pp 45–6.
[132] Thomas Moore, *Memoirs, journal and correspondence of Thomas Moore*, vol. 1 (London, 1853), p. 3.
[133] *Ibid.*, p. 4.
[134] *Ibid.*, p. 6.
[135] Plumtre, *Narrative of a residence in Ireland*, p. 43.
[136] Helena Kelleher Kahn, '"Objects of raging detestation": the Charter schools', *History Ireland* **19** (2) (2011), 24–7, p. 25.
[137] Bernadine Ruddy, 'Clontarf Charter School', *Dublin Historical Record* **57** (1) (2004), p. 72.
[138] *Ibid.*, pp 70–1.
[139] *Ibid.*, p. 72.
[140] Michael Quane, 'The journal of Richard Pococke', *Journal of the Royal Society of Antiquaries of Ireland* **80** (1) (1950), p. 43.

[141] Pettigrew & Oulton's *Dublin Almanack* (1844), p. 326.
[142] *Ibid.*, p. 326.
[143] *Ibid.*, Annals section.
[144] *Ibid.*, p. 326.
[145] *Ibid.*, 308.
[146] Thomas Reid, *Travels in Ireland in the year 1822, exhibiting brief sketches of the moral, physical and political state of the country with reflections on the best means of improving its condition* (London, 1823), p. 360.
[147] *Ibid.*, p. 361.
[148] *Ibid.*, p. 362.
[149] *Ibid.*, p. 363.
[150] *Ibid.*, p. 365.
[151] *Ibid.*, p. 367.
[152] *Ibid.*, p. 368.
[153] Morrissey, *The life and times of Daniel Murray*, p. 139.
[154] *Ibid.*, p. 56.
[155] *Ibid.*, p. 54.
[156] Brother Michael Paul Riorden, successor to Brother Edmund Ignatius Rice.
[157] Morrissey, *The life and times of Daniel Murray*, p. 140
[158] Johnston *et al.*, *A history of the Church of Ireland*, p. 257.
[159] *Ibid.*, p. 258.
[160] Mary Purcell, 'Dublin Diocesan Archives: Murray papers', *Archivium Hibernicum* **37–8** (1982–3), no. 18.
[161] *Ibid.*, no. 16.
[162] *Ibid.*, no. 37.
[163] D.A. Levistone Cooney, 'Methodist schools in Dublin', *Dublin Historical Record* **56** (1) (2003), 41–52.
[164] Pettigrew & Oulton's *Dublin Almanack* (1844), p. 593.
[165] *Ibid.*, pp 644–7.
[166] *Ibid.*, p. 667.
[167] *Ibid.*, p. 709.
[168] *Ibid.*, p. 700.
[169] *Ibid.*, p. 686.
[170] Michael Quane, 'Quaker schools in Dublin', *Journal of the Royal Society of Antiquaries of Ireland* **94** (1) (1964), p. 59.
[171] *Ibid.*, p. 62.
[172] Dillon Cosgrove, *North Dublin: city and environs* (Dublin, 1909), p. 108.
[173] Map by John Taylor (1828), Glucksman Map Library, TCD.
[174] Map by Major Alex Taylor, Royal Engineers (1801–5), Glucksman Map Library, TCD. (Copy; original held in the British Library.)
[175] John F. Fleetwood, *The history of medicine in Ireland* (Dublin, 1983), pp 56–7.
[176] Elizabeth Malcolm and Greta Jones (eds), *Medicine, disease and the State in Ireland 1650–1940* (Cork, 1999), p. 30; *Hibernian Journal*, 16 March 1781.
[177] Vincent Ruddy, *Monster agitators*, pp 16–17.
[178] Timothy P. O'Neill, 'Fever and public health in pre-Famine Ireland', *Journal of the Royal Society of Antiquaries of Ireland* **103** (1973), p. 2.
[179] Ruth Heard, 'Public works in Ireland, 1800–1831', unpublished MLitt. thesis, Trinity College Dublin (1977), p. 215.
[180] Thomas Campbell Foster, Commissioned letters on the condition of the people of Ireland published in *The Times* between August 1845 and January 1846. NLI.
[181] O'Neill, 'Fever and public health', p. 8.
[182] *The Gentleman's and Citizen's Almanack (as compiled by the late John Watson Stewart) for the year of our Lord 1824* (Dublin, 1824), pp 212–14.
[183] *Ibid.*, pp 212–14.
[184] *Ibid.*, p. 211.
[185] Ó Gráda, *Georgian Dublin*, p. 92.
[186] *Ibid.*, p. 168.
[187] *Ibid.*, p. 169.
[188] *The Gentleman's and Citizen's Almanack* (1824).

[189] Henry Inglis, *Ireland in 1834: a journey throughout Ireland during the summer and autumn by Henry D. Inglis* (London, 1834), p. 10.
[190] *Ibid.*, p. 11.
[191] *Ibid.*, p. 12.
[192] *Ibid.*, p. 17.
[193] *Ibid.*, p. 17.
[194] *Ibid.*, p. 6.
[195] Laurence McGeery, *Medicine and chemistry in Ireland* (Dublin, 2004), preface.
[196] Enda Leany, 'Vested interests: science and medicine in nineteenth-century Ireland', *Field Day Review* **2** (2006), p. 290.
[197] *Ibid.*
[198] Hugh Fenning, 'The cholera epidemic in Ireland, 1832–3: priests, ministers, doctors', *Archivium Hibernicum* **57** (2003), 77–125, p. 148.
[199] *Ibid.*, p. 139.
[200] *Ibid.*, p. 135.
[201] O'Neill, 'Fever and public health', p. 10.
[202] *Ibid.*, p. 12.
[203] Timothy J. McAuliffe, 'A study of travel writing in early Victorian Ireland', unpublished MA thesis, NUI Galway (1997), p. 5.
[204] *Ibid.*, p. 13.
[205] *Ibid.*, p. 19.
[206] Asa Briggs, 'Cholera and society in the nineteenth century', *Past and Present* **19** (1961), 76–96, p. 79.
[207] O'Neill, 'Fever and public health', p. 7.
[208] *Ibid.*, p. 5.
[209] *Ibid.*, pp 5–6.
[210] *Ibid.*, p. 10.
[211] *Ibid.*, p. 11.
[212] Cormac O'Grada, 'Dublin demography in the early nineteenth century: evidence from the Rotunda', *Population Studies* **45** (1) (1991), 43–54, p. 46.
[213] *Ibid.*, p. 44.
[214] *Ibid.*, p. 45.
[215] O'Neill, 'Fever and public health', p. 16.
[216] *Ibid.*, p. 16.
[217] Pettigrew & Oulton's *Dublin Almanack* (1845), p. 539.
[218] Thomas J. Morrissey, *The life and times of Daniel Murray, esteemed archbishop of Dublin 1823–1852* (Dublin, 2018), p. 62.
[219] O'Neill, 'Fever and public health', p. 20.
[220] *Ibid.*, p. 20.
[221] *Ibid.*, pp 20–1.
[222] *Ibid.*, p. 21.
[223] *Ibid.*, p. 22.
[224] *Ibid.*, p. 16.
[225] *The Gentleman's and Citizen's Almanack* (1824).
[226] Barrow, *A tour around Ireland*, p. 375.
[227] H.R. Klieneburger, 'Ireland through German eyes 1844–1957: the travel-diaries of Jakob Venedy and Heinrich Böll', *Studies: An Irish Quarterly Review* **49** (196) (1960), 373–88, p. 376.
[228] *Dublin Almanack* (1845), p. 539.
[229] *Ibid.*, p. 539.
[230] O'Grada, 'Dublin demography in the early nineteenth century', p. 195.
[231] *Ibid.*
[232] Vincent Ruddy, *Monster agitators*, p. 82.
[233] *Dublin Almanack* (1845), p. 333.
[234] N. Donnelly, *Short histories of Dublin parishes*, p. 133.
[235] *Dublin Almanack* (1845), pp 334–8.
[236] *Ibid.*, p. 349.

[237] *Ibid.*, p. 511.
[238] *Ibid.*, p. 512.
[239] Muiris O'Sullivan and Liam Downey, 'Martello and signal towers', *Archaeology Ireland* **26** (2) (2012), 46–9, pp 46–7.
[240] Gilbert Library, Pearse Street, Dublin.
[241] O'Grada, 'Dublin demography in the early nineteenth century', p. 55.
[242] *Ibid.*, p. 37; *Dublin Chronicle*, 31 July 1788.
[243] P. Th. Hicks, 'Journal of a tour from Gloucester through Wales and Ireland 1818', TCD MS 968.
[244] Dr Pococke's tour, TCD MS 887, p. 106.
[245] Hicks, 'Journal of a tour'.
[246] Dickson, *Dublin: the making of a capital city*, p. 259.

11. Gas in Dublin in the nineteenth century

John Clayton, the dean of Kildare, was interested in research, but the demands of a growing family came first. He died in 1725, and in 1740 his father sent the results of his research to the Royal Society, and thus Clayton came to be credited with discovering the process of distillation of coal. This research was carried out totally independently from that of William Murdock (see below).[1]

Falkus wrote that 'Gas was one of those manufacturing enterprises developed first in Britain in the middle of the industrial revolution between the French and Napoleonic Wars'. The result was that by the close of the first half of the nineteenth century supply had been brought to all major towns, and even to smaller towns of 3,000 or more inhabitants. Gas was another major change to arrive with the new century, along with steam power and the use of iron on a massive scale in building. Moreover, gas would become a major consumer of iron and coal. Gas for lighting would be supplied to consumers through metal pipes laid underground, just like water.[2] Like electricity, the gas enterprise grew on the basis of demand for lighting and subsequently developed other uses, such as for heating, cooking and power generation. It came into the market to replace tallow, candles and whale oil.

Towards the close of the eighteenth century there was a definite search under way for some improvement in the provision of artificial light, as seen in the competitions set by the Royal Society from the 1770s and highlighted by the Rumford Medal in 1800 for 'the author of the most important or useful discovery which shall be made and published … on heat and light'.[3] As society expanded in all its forms, from factories to theatres and concert rooms, the cost of lighting increased exponentially, and it included not just the price of tallow and candles but also the employment of staff to manage these candles in crowded spaces. Street lighting, too, was a major cost factor. The large factories in the north of England would provide the path to an answer. These factories were multiplying and growing in size. One in particular, the cotton factory of Phillips and Lee in Manchester, was lit up for ten hours a day during winter, as were many others. The cost in candles and tallow was high; McConnell and Kennedy's factory spent £750 in 1806.[4] Moreover, tallow and candles were dangerous on account of the risk of fire.

By 1790 matters were being taken more seriously thanks to the efforts of William Murdock, an employee of Boulton and Watt, steam engine manufacturers, who was experimenting at his home in Redruth. By 1792 Murdock was testing how a 'viable plant could be constructed and operated to make, store, distribute and use coal gas as light'.[5] He read a paper to the Royal Society on 25 February 1808, claiming to be the first to apply the use of this gas to economic purposes.[6]

At the same time in France, Philippe Lebon, scientist and engineer, was independently testing his own theories.[7] Lord Dundonald produced coal gas as a waste product from his coal tar works at Culross, but it was Lebon who first demonstrated gas lighting before a public audience in 1801.[8] A subsequent demonstration was attended by William Henry, who gave a series of lectures in

Manchester, and it was thanks to this that Phillips and Lee installed gas to light their factory. (Lee, who was not averse to taking risks, had already used cast-iron frames, and two years later introduced steam heating to the plant at Salford.[9]) The factory of Phillips and Lee at Manchester was at the time reputed to be the largest in England.[10] The cost differential was substantial—£650 per annum for gas as against £3,000 for tallow and candles.

The successful lighting of the plant and its attendant publicity generated many enquiries, and then another major works, called Burleigh, was fitted out. In these early days, as in all new technological developments, there were setbacks, but by 1805 the subject of gaslight was attracting newspaper attention and several manufacturers began to make smaller machinery for shops and commercial operations on that scale.[11]

In April 1812 the London and Westminster Chartered Gas Light and Coke Company was set up as the first gaslight company. This helped to build momentum and the subject of street lighting by gas began to spark the public imagination. It would, however, require a broader commercial vehicle to deliver such service.

As interest in all things gas naturally increased, greatly augmented by the exotic aspect of light flames out of air, commerce came into the equation. Boulton and Watt were anxious to retain some semblance of control of the market for distribution of gas, and other interests wanted to carve out a share for their investors. There was no regulation, and it was obviously not feasible to have several different companies digging up the streets to put in their several pipelines. This led to the passing of a bill in 1812 and the granting of a Royal Charter of Corporation, and, as Hutchison said, the gas industry was born.[12] The Dublin Gas Light Company was incorporated by act of parliament (1st of George IV) for lighting the city and suburbs with gas.[13]

All the while, the technology was being improved; this included the problem of the removal of impurities from the gas, which was solved thanks to the involvement of water. There were issues of odour, but these had existed for tallow and candles too.

The worst fears of the public were realised when an explosion occurred in 1813 at the Peter Street works of the Gas, Light and Coke Company in Westminster, causing widespread alarm. The cause of the explosion was quickly investigated, however, and recommendations were made and effected, restoring confidence. The nub of the matter was the manner in which gas had been stored.

The first street lighting appeared in St Margaret's, Westminster, on 1 April 1814.[14] By 1816 companies in Preston and Liverpool had begun operations, and within ten years few towns of any importance did not have gas companies.[15] Falkus sums up the situation by saying that the expansion of the gas industry arose out of French inventiveness, German entrepreneurship, London society capital and London demand.[16] When Charles Dupin was in Glasgow, he reported that 'preparations are making on a large scale for lighting with gas all the streets of that great city'.[17]

Here in Dublin the Crow Street Theatre was lit by gas in 1818, and public lighting arrived in Dublin in 1824, the same year as the first gas cooker was made.[18] Iron was a substantial component in the setting up of gas infrastructure.

There were a reputed 6,000 whale oil or tallow lamps in Dublin in 1817.[19] McCabe claims that the earliest reference to gas in Dublin occurs in 1817. Private groups were sponsoring bills but were opposed by the Corporation on the grounds that gas pipes under the streets would somehow contaminate the water supply. There was only so much delay that would be tolerated, however, and in the short time-span of 1823–5 the Hibernian Gas Light Company built their works at Great Brunswick Street (Pearse Street), beside the lifting bridge over the canal. The Dublin Coal Gas Light

Company had works at North Strand, while the Patent Oil Gas Light Company had works at the Academy Cinema in Pearse Street. Exactly what the authorities were concerned to avoid in London occurred in Dublin, with the laying of gas mains side by side by several gas companies. Finally a treaty was arrived at to curtail the waste and duplication. On 5 October 1825 the first street gaslight installation was recorded. Gas was then installed along all the important routes and in business premises and civic buildings. One of the earliest buildings to be lit was the Mansion House in 1824.

Gas is mentioned in 1818 when a bill was requested to be laid 'before Parliament by the Commissioners for paving, lighting and cleansing the streets of Dublin, for lighting this city with gases'.[20] In 1824[21] a letter to the *Freeman's Journal* was 'recommending to the public the reviving contrast exhibited by the brilliant gas lighting of Rutland Square last night, compared with the black darkness of all the other streets of Dublin'.

Fig. 11.1—Gas company badge on gable in Hawkins Street (photo: Brian Matthews).

The *Gentleman's and Citizen's Almanack* of 1824 contains advertisements for three gas companies in Dublin:
- the Dublin Gas Light Company (Fig. 11.1), based at Foster Place;
- the Patent Oil Gas Company of Ireland, with offices and works at Great Brunswick Street, adjoining St Mark's Church;
- the Hibernian Gas Light Company at Great Brunswick Street, adjoining Grand Canal Dock (this was close to the Brunswick Boatyard on Grand Canal Dock).[22]

Despite the stops and starts suffered by the companies trying to roll out the service, consumption rose inexorably as the years passed. In 1836 the Alliance Gas Company was established by act of parliament, with works at Sir John Rogerson's Quay. Then in 1844 another group tried to impose some form of control on the market with their Dublin Consumers Gas Company. This would lead eventually to one united gas company.[23]

When Daniel O'Connell held a Repeal 'monster meeting' in Catherine Street, Limerick, some 412 persons sat down to dinner in a pavilion specially erected for the event. There were two galleries, both capable of holding 1,000 people. The *Limerick Chronicle* reported that the dinner was 'brilliantly illuminated by gases'.[24]

Nevertheless, for all the progress of gas as a power and heat source, one area where pace was lacking was the domestic market in Dublin. As late as 1872 a pamphlet recorded that 'in England and Scotland, where gas is looked upon as one of the necessities of life, it is supplied at a rate so low (in comparison with Dublin) that even mechanics and labourers are enabled to use it universally while giving the producer a large profit'. The writer notes that in Manchester there are 33,000 small consumers while Dublin has just 2,700.[25] The growth remained in the public area, and the architectural paraphernalia of supplying gaslight began to change the streetscape of the city. It is interesting to note that the gas industry began its rise to prominence in the capital down in the zone of the Grand Canal Docks, on the land taken back from the sea less than 100 years previously.

By 1844—almost mid-century—gas had become a familiar system in the city and a whole new range of employment became available, besides all the labouring work involved in digging trenches, laying pipes and backfilling. There were engineers, who decided where the pipes went, and a whole new bureaucracy, creating an even greater demand for paper and ink. The pipes required new types of fitters—a skilled occupation using new tools—while carters gained new customers as they delivered pipes to sites. New firms sprang up, supplying gas facilities to go with water supplies, and thus it was that heating, lighting and plumbing became associated as coming from one source of supply and fit.

Notes

[1] Colm McCabe, 'History of the town gas industry in Ireland 1823–1980', *Dublin Historical Record* **45** (1) (1992), 28–40, p. 28.
[2] M.E. Falkus, 'The early development of the British gas industry, 1790–1815', *Economic History Review* (new ser.) **35** (May 1982), p. 217.
[3] *Ibid.*, p. 218.
[4] *Ibid.*, p. 219.
[5] Kenneth Hutchison, 'The Royal Society and the foundation of the British gas industry', *Notes and Records of the Royal Society of London* **39** (2) (1985), pp 248–9.
[6] *Ibid.*, p. 249.
[7] *Ibid.*, p. 220.
[8] *Ibid.*, p. 221.
[9] *Ibid.*, p. 222.
[10] *Ibid.*, p. 250.
[11] *Ibid.*, p. 224.
[12] *Ibid.*, p. 253.
[13] *The Gentleman's and Citizen's Almanack (as compiled by the late John Watson Stewart) for the year of our Lord 1824* (Dublin, 1824), p. 167.
[14] *Ibid.*, p. 231.
[15] *Ibid.*, p. 232.
[16] *Ibid.*, p. 233.
[17] Baron Charles Dupin, *Narratives of two excursions to the ports of England* (1819), p. 43.
[18] McCabe, 'History of the town gas industry', p. 29.
[19] *Ibid.*, p. 33.
[20] *CARD*, vol. 17, p. 289.
[21] *Freeman's Journal*, 7 January 1824.
[22] *The Gentleman's and Citizen's Almanack* (1824), p. 229.
[23] McCabe, 'History of the town gas industry', pp 34–5.
[24] Vincent Ruddy, *Monster agitators: O'Connell's Repealers, 1843 Ireland* (Dublin, 2018), p. 93.
[25] John McEvoy, *The gas question in six parts, in October 1872* (pamphlet, NLI P 1134), p. 3.

12. Howth Harbour

At first glance Howth appeared to be a sensible choice of location for a packet harbour. Besides shortening the voyage to England, it did away with 'the awkward passage in and out of Dublin Bay'.[1] The packets would no longer have to take the bar into consideration.

We must remind ourselves that the reason for transferring the location away from the Pigeon House was that the military had taken control of the harbour there and did not encourage civilian traffic because of the implied threat from France (much as today's airspace in countries such as France and Spain is controlled by the military). Since the French Revolution England had possessed a hair-trigger sensitivity to French ambitions.

It also, however, presented the problem of connecting the city with the proposed packet harbour. As it was to be nine miles from Dublin, it would certainly have an impact on the territory between the two. We will examine just how much of an effect it did have, both topographically and socially.

The first requirement was the building of a proper road for the use of horses and carriages, to carry both the mails and the passengers in both directions. The roads would be built in conjunction with the construction of the harbour, but they would take a little time to finish. Roads had already existed between Baldoyle, Portmarnock and Malahide, as observed by Isaac Butler. That people could readily get around if they had either horses or carriages was attested to by Charles Cosslett in January 1793, when he came out from the city to attend a ball at Malahide Castle, where he danced with Miss Magill of Baldoyle.[2]

Howth as a location was proposed by Thomas Rogers in an 1805 pamphlet in which he described its advantages for 'the extension and improvement of commerce' and as a 'military station', 'an asylum for merchantmen' and a safe harbour for (military) transports and 'small frigates'. (Note that the French and Irish rebellions were of very recent memory.) He added that 'the piers that I have proposed between Howth and Ireland's Eye agree with the sentiments of Sir Thomas Page; but he observes they should be differently curved'.[3] William Dawson, too, backed the choice of Howth in his proposal to the Directors of Inland Navigation.[4]

In that same pamphlet, discussing the harbour of Dublin, Rogers argued that the continued existence of the bar was still restricting trade. He also observed that there was no shelter in the bay at low water and that easterly winds posed a great danger, and therefore he suggested Howth as an option for security of shipping.[5] 'The object I allude to is that of forming the Sound of Ireland's Eye into an extensive harbour with a canal from thence to the port of Dublin.'[6] The western boundary of the Sound is the extensive strand of Baldoyle, over which the tide spreads for some square miles and through which there is a small channel leading to the village of Baldoyle.[7]

Parliament sanctioned the building of a packet harbour in 1805.[8] It was assumed that it would 'merely be an extension to an existing pier erected by Lord Howth in 1718'.[9]

Howth Harbour remained outside the control of Board of Works, having in 1823 been placed under the control of the Holyhead Roads Commissioners, a body set up to amalgamate the control of Howth and Holyhead harbours, the Menai Bridge and the multiplicity of turnpike trusts which controlled the Howth–Holyhead–London roads.[10]

One need not be a nautical expert to appreciate the potential danger at Howth. Ann Plumtre, visiting Howth in 1814–15, observed that 'on the east side is a perpendicular mass of rocks called the Stags, considered as very dangerous to shipping: an additional recommendation of the spot chosen for the new harbour gives ships making for the harbour must pass close to this rock'.[11] She also noted that the easterly storms would be able to damage the east pier because of the force of the wind and seas coming round Howth Head. Her sound concerns apply to this day, as the pier is being reinforced again in 2018. The depth in this new harbour had better be right or carnage would ensue. She concluded that the harbour should have been located at Dunleary but that Lord Howth, like many others, had benefited directly from voting for the Act of Union.[12] On subsequent visits to Howth she met and spoke with workers who openly sneered at the entire project.[13] Howth was adjacent to Baldoyle, which Cromwell described in 1820 as 'a pleasant little bathing place with an open beach'.[14] He also confirmed that at that time there were two lighthouses at the Baily.[15]

From the very start there were doubts about the suitability of the harbour at Howth as the packet harbour for Dublin, and silting was a constant concern.[16] It was a political football, however, and Ruth Heard maintained that it had the open backing of the lord lieutenant. This led to the problem of how to deal with George IV when he came to Ireland in 1821, ostensibly to visit the country but actually to visit his mistress at Slane. Expedience ruled: he arrived in Howth on the royal yacht *Lightning* on 9 August and left from Dunleary (subsequently renamed Kingstown). That it was a big occasion for Howth can be seen in an advertisement placed in the *Freeman's Journal* three days prior to the royal arrival, listing the fishing wherries of one Joseph Rickard and offering trips to go out to meet the royal yacht at ten shillings a head.

As the eighteenth century drew to a close, the French threat aroused political nervousness among the establishment in London. They greatly feared that the whiff of revolution might cross the channel and take hold. The threat would not fade until after Waterloo. The decision to move the mail-packet operations from the Pigeon House was forced on the Corporation by the military take-over of the space there, and the increase in military personnel and ordnance, although some packet-ships still called to Ringsend. The harbour and fort were soon held by 400 men. There was nothing new or novel in the idea; it had been mooted by, among others, Charles Vallancey, military strategist and engineer, some 25 years earlier.

Once the decision was taken, there followed much discussion and promotion of either Howth or Dunleary, along with a regurgitation of the ideas of connecting canals to either location from the city. Several ideas were put forward for Howth, including one for the building of the harbour between Ireland's Eye and the mainland, cutting a canal through the isthmus at Sutton Cross and running a canal into Dublin along the north shore of the bay, behind Bull Island. One obvious problem in the Howth location was the rocks lying off Ireland's Eye and the present east pier. The gap between is small. In the period immediately before the arrival of steamships, controlling a sailing-vessel coming down the sound, when ships required hundreds of metres to turn and manoeuvre, was always going to be hazardous. In addition, if anything went amiss on a ship when turning into the harbour, there was the Baldoyle spit—a sandbank jutting well offshore and sited to leeward of the harbour. There was no shortage of advice; Dawson, an amateur engineer, also warned about the harbour.

In 1811 an anonymous pamphlet referred to the harbour works as a 'wanton waste of money'.[17]

245

Dublin moving east, 1708–1844

DUBLIN AND DROGHEDA RAILWAY, FROM BALDOYLE STRAND.

Fig. 12.1—Baldoyle Strand, looking towards Howth and Ireland's Eye (courtesy of the NLI).

The author claimed that newspapers did not print his letters to them, warning of 'insurmountable natural impediments, improper plans and places, in capacity or interested views of those who here hitherto attempted it'. He said: 'When I heard of the Howth plan, the whole struck me as big with absurdity, and I thought it a lavish and wanton expenditure of public money'. He continued: 'After looking at both Howth and the wrecks of the *Rochdale* and the *Prince of Wales* with alarm, I plainly saw that Dunleary not Howth was the spot on which a harbour ought to have been erected'.[18] As well as those already outlined, there was the additional problem of rock in the new harbour which would have to be dealt with. The anonymous writer questioned Lord Howth's role, asking whether the new road through his land was totally for the transportation of stone or for more open access to his larger estate and access to Dublin. Either way, by 1813 some packets were using the harbour with its incomplete pier. These would have been under sail, as steam had not yet arrived.[19] The self-styled 'ordinary citizen' claimed to have sought the opinion of mariners and captains and remarked on the precarious nature of the structure given the dangers of an easterly gale in the sound of Howth, referring to November 1808, when the pier under construction was damaged by waves, 'At the period when the sea made dreadful incursions on the Howth projections'.[20]

William Dawson insisted that by connecting Ireland's Eye with the land the 'enclosure would give complete shelter'. He noted that Howth was ten miles nearer Holyhead than Dalkey Sound, and that mail-boats 'will cross the channel in six hours, and will suffer no delay from tide, bar, rock or sandbank'. Dawson also maintained that no part of the coast could be 'so easily or for a trifling expense guarded against an enemy'.[21] He observed that the road from Howth to Dublin 'is the proper line except from Raheny to Kilbarrack at the ruined church on the strand'[22] (Fig. 12.1).

Construction

The decision to proceed was eventually taken in 1805 and £10,000 was granted towards the building. The construction took ten years to complete, from 1807 to 1817. John Rennie signed on in 1809 as consultant engineer after Captain George Taylor, who had been with the project from the start, resigned in 1807 over the build-up of silt inside the east pier at the elbow. Work stopped for a period because of this and began again in 1810.[23] After a survey, Rennie advised that the site was badly

246

chosen but that, as a considerable amount of work had already been carried out, it made sense to continue.[24] While the packet harbour was deemed a failure, and correctly so, it left many positive effects. One of these was that it established the road to Howth, leading to the growth of Clontarf, Sutton, Raheny and Howth itself. It also helped to establish Howth as a seaside resort and as a major fishing harbour, and allowed for the growth of the herring industry in the period when the herring fleets and migrant workers would go round the coast following the fish. Howth benefited, too, from the newer type of fishing-vessels after they began to come up from Devon and Cornwall, the better boats allowing year-round fishing and adding to the size of the fish market in Dublin.

The first lease for St Ann's Estate and the signal for the area to attract settlement by the élite of the city's citizens came on 16 May 1747, John Vernon of Clontarf Castle and estate granting 27 acres and seventeen perches to Paul Hale and William and John Hale, with 'liberty to use the wharf and quay facing the premises', at a yearly rent of £25 15s.[25] The arrival of wealthy residents north of the Tolka signalled road improvement and access, which was reinforced by the construction of Howth Harbour. In turn, these two aspects encouraged further village development along the shore and along the inland route in Clontarf and Raheny.

Ida Delamere gave a figure of 600 men employed in the harbour works, but this included granite-workers from Dalkey and Killiney who came over to work the granite facing slabs.[26] The other stone for the works came from the quarry at Kilrock, up at Balscadden, and some came from the quarry at Corr Bridge.

Ann Plumtre described the village of Clontarf as hosting 'a number of delightful villas scattered about'. It is clear, therefore, that persons other than fishermen and their families inhabited Clontarf.[27] In her narrative of her Irish visit she reported what she had seen in Bristol, describing the movement of 'stone from the quarry above down to the canal below, by means of an iron railway down an inclined plane, with machinery which in conveying the loaded cart makes that draw the empty up'. She had actually ridden up in the system at the site at the Kennet and Avon Canal.[28] This system was also used at Howth, from Balscadden to the pier workings, and later at Dunleary, from Dalkey down to the east pier there, and continued to be used for the supply of stone for the Great North Bull Wall between 1819 and 1824.

Though a large stone construction, the man-made project was just as susceptible to gales, and 80 yards of the east pier was washed away in 1809. To this day, the public are prohibited from walking down the east pier in a bad easterly gale, as the seas come over the top of it. After this, John Rennie advised the building of a second (west) pier. Howth at the time was a tiny hamlet, housing only some Howth estate workers and some fishermen. The building project attracted day visitors and sightseers and this planted the seeds of a busier future for Howth, especially when the mail-packet began to operate.[29]

In letters addressed to Henry Yew at 19 Mecklenburgh Street for the Commissioners for Howth Harbour, Rennie gave estimates for works of £44,500 in total, £30,000 of which was for 100,000 tons of rubble and stone. This letter was one of a series, from February 1811 to 3 July 1817. In another letter of 1812, Rennie quoted John Aird, resident works engineer, who 'has stated in various letters that sand has accumulated within the east pier of Howth and as far as he can discover … this sand comes from the spit at Baldoyle'.[30] Later in the same letter is a mention of stone coming to Howth from Runcorn, on the other side of the Irish Sea.[31] Two of the letters deal with the purchase of a diving bell. One other letter is a response to Rennie from Bolton, Watt & Co., Soho, London, regarding the purchase of a steam engine, which they supplied to John Aird, site engineer.

Ann Plumtre described a visit to Howth: 'I went one day over to Howth in hopes of seeing the Diving Machine at work. The machine is made of cast iron … a vast chest or coffer having no bottom. In the top are four bulls eyes to give brightness and the air pipe is so managed that nothing is to be apprehended from the want of a sufficiency of air or a proper ventilation of it; there are seats at each end … the object of which is laying the foundation stones for the bend of the new pier.' Tellingly, she added: 'since 1814 I knew that the idea of the harbour at Howth ever being brought to answer the destined purpose is so much abandoned, that making a harbour on the southern shore of the bay is determined on … at Dunleary'.[32] She said further that 'this is nearer to Dublin by two miles than Dalkey would be; there is already a little fishing harbour which is to be enlarged by an additional mole, and at all states of the tide there will be sufficient depth of water for the packets to come in. Passengers coming by the packets very often choose to be rowed ashore to Dunleary and there to land rather than wait for the vessel going into the harbour, while jaunting cars and jingles are in attendance to carry them to the city.' She noted that at the time mail-packets were using Dalkey as well as the Pigeon House. Her comments reinforce the idea of the near-inevitability of Dunleary coming into its own as a packet station, though it would take another twenty years for it to officially occur.[33] The main point is that it had already entered the public consciousness.

At the time of Ann Plumtre's visits to Howth, Benjamin Richey, deputy clerk of the Crown, was paid £21 15s. 11d. for prosecuting John Gaffney and others charged with plundering a vessel wrecked off Baldoyle.[34] This episode highlights the dangers of the spit at Baldoyle.

Road access to Howth had improved by now, with both the inland road and the sea road in use. In 1815 it is recorded that John Gavin was maintaining 520 perches of the Strand Road of Clontarf, beginning at the road leading from Raheny to Crab Lake. William Colville was maintaining 120 perches of the Dublin to Howth road inland, while Leland Crosthwaite was maintaining 340 perches of the road from Clontarf to Howth.[35]

On 1 August 1818 Howth became a packet station, in spite of the reservations expressed by ships' captains about the viability of the harbour.[36] This was not unusual; owners did not often take into consideration the warnings or advice received from their own officers. At the same time support was growing for the possible use of Dunleary as a harbour of refuge—not to be confused with a packet harbour.[37]

Work on the harbour did not finish until 1819, however, as the ledger of the Corporation for Preserving and Improving the Port of Dublin records payment of £339 10. 9d. to the Commissioners of Howth Harbour on 7 January 1819 'for finishing the lighthouse at the harbour' (Fig. 12.2).[38] At this time Irish Lights had not yet become responsible for lights for shipping around Ireland; this function was still in the control of the Corporation. We know that the harbour entertained packets by 1820 because Thomas Cromwell confirms this in his writings.[39]

Thomas Telford built the road between Dublin and Howth after the Howth Commissioners were abolished in 1823 and were replaced by the new Holyhead Roads authority.[40] By then there was considerable pressure to substitute Dunleary for Howth as packet harbour and as a harbour of refuge. It is to be remembered that those pushing for Dunleary saw it primarily as a harbour of refuge for the bay and secondly as a packet harbour. In the same year Captain Charles Malcolm, captain of the royal yacht, joined the Board of Harbour Commissioners for Dunleary, two years after the king had left from the harbour.[41] This could be taken—and was—as an ominous sign for the future of Howth.

Expenditure on Howth from the Consolidated Fund between 1800 and 1831 amounted to

Fig. 12.2—Badge on lighthouse, east pier, Howth (photo: Brian Matthews).

£372,995 with an additional £12,349, while the figure for Dunleary was £499,400 with an additional £404,489.[42] The Post Office decision in 1834 to relocate the packets stopped any further investment in the improvement of Howth Harbour.[43]

Benjamin Oakley visited Dublin in 1819 and arrived via Howth Harbour: 'after 22 hours tedious passage arrived at Howth, went to Moira Hotel, Sackville Street'. He said that he 'took a long walk, first crossing the Carlisle Bridge at the end of Sackville Street'.[44] The Custom House was a 'noble building; in the interior is a noble room seventy feet long, sixty-five feet wide and thirty feet high'.[45] At the end of his tour he left Dublin from Howth: 'I got into a stage to convey on to the packet [at Howth]'.[46]

Not all attempts at safe passage were successful, however. Captain Davies of the Holyhead packet *Countess of Liverpool* wrote: 'I had the good fortune on the night of the 19th instant to save from shipwreck the master and crew of the sloop *Nicholas of Whitehaven*, bound for Newry with a cargo of coals; she struck about eight o'clock on the South Rowans off Ireland's Eye and instantly went down. I took the crew off the topsail yard; several of the boat's crew also assisted.'[47] As regards that same night, the six-man crew of a fishing-boat from Baldoyle subsequently wrote to the Board 'stating their exertions trying to save the lives of the crew of the sloop *Janet of Stranraer*, lost on Wednesday 19 and recommended by the Pilot master'.[48]

The following week it was recommended that five guineas be sent to Lieutenant Browne, harbour master at Howth, for the crew of nine who left Howth on the morning of Wednesday 8 December 1819, taking off the crew of the brig *Bryan*, which was lost.[49] It was also ordered that the

Fig. 12.3—Balscadden Ladies' Swimming Place (courtesy of the NLI).

boat crew from Howth Harbour be awarded four guineas for saving the crew of the *Sally of Whitehaven*, lost on the bar at Baldoyle, which action was certified by the harbour master, (now) Captain Browne.[50]

Courage and bravery in very difficult circumstances could also prove awkward for persons attempting to save lives. On 1 October 1824, 'it appeared that the Pilot George Landers could not by any exertion within his power have saved the lives of the persons who were lost except by risking the safety of the vessel. He was admonished for his apparent show of inhumanity.'[51]

When Oakley returned to Dublin in 1825, he reported: 'weighed anchor at four am [Holyhead] and arrived at Gresham's Hotel, Sackville St., about noon'. This signifies a fast passage across the Irish Sea under steam to Howth and confirms how steam propulsion had developed.[52] His return passage was no less speedy: 'At 8.30 the mail had me landed at Howth, where I embarked in a steam packet; I was the only passenger on board … arrived Holyhead three o'clock'.[53] He considered that the new, fast packet-boats 'may have a beneficial effect in quelling insurrection and rebellion', as they could do away with the need for a large standing army in Ireland on a permanent basis. He had earlier watched the embarkation of three troops of the 15th Hussars from Dublin for Liverpool, even going on board to inspect arrangements for the horses, with which he was very impressed.[54]

Kevin Rickard wrote that in 1826 the route carried 6,465 passengers, 1,134 children, 1,705 deck passengers, 420 carriages, 34 two-wheelers and 153 horses.[55]

In 1832 the respected engineer Alexander Nimmo created a chart of the east coast of Ireland and then wrote a comprehensive book of sailing directions for mariners, including details on Dublin, Howth and Kingstown. On Howth he remarked that 'vessels not drawing more than ten feet may

Fig. 12.4—The Inn at Baldoyle (Grainger's today) (courtesy of Louise Morgan and Brendan Maher, NGI).

enter at low water springs and moor at the wharf'. He added: 'It was constructed for the accommodation of the Holyhead packets, and is chiefly used by them and the fishing wherries that supply the Dublin market'.[56] Nimmo also wrote that 'Near Howth pier the channel has only three feet at low water'. Here he refers to the ground just west of the west pier—a reminder that ships needed to get their angles of turn correct for the harbour or else risk running aground.[57]

The sea road to Howth had cemented itself into the topography so well that in 1838 the Catholic Church of St John the Baptist was built, at a cost of £1,000, just beside the sheds at Clontarf.[58] T. Dawson maintained that in the nineteenth century Sutton was famous for its oysters and mussels just off the beach (at Santa Sabena School) and delivered to the Dublin market on an ever-improving road.[59] And it was on this road that George IV travelled to Dublin when he arrived in Howth Harbour in 1821.[60] Reid in 1822 recorded that the Galway herring fishery was a twice-yearly event, as it was in Howth, and described 'vast shoals annually are astonishing … larger and esteemed a much better quality, than those taken on the coasts of Scotland'.[61] It can be seen, therefore, that the herring fishery was a building block in the development of Howth Harbour, especially as the shoreside paraphernalia of dealing with the catch was still on the west pier until the late 1970s, including the herring sheds.

By 1844 and the arrival of the railway to Drogheda, but prior to the rail spur to Howth, there was a hotel at Howth, as seen in this announcement in the *Freeman's Journal* on 1 January: 'Festivities at Howth for Earl of Howth coming of age; organiser of the celebrations is the proprietor of the elegantly fitted hotel in that town, Mr McDowell'.[62] In 1845 there was a post office in the village, run by Ellen Sweetman, who also ran a lodging house, and by now Mr P. McKenny was operating the Royal Hotel.[63]

Howth Harbour did change things on the north side of the city in several ways. It helped to

Fig. 12.5—McFarland's view of the harbour from the end of the east pier to the village and the Dublin road (courtesy of the NLI).

create new roads in the area. It established the harbour as a major fishing port for the following 200 years and, by extension, helped promote the town as a seaside attraction (Figs 12.3, 12.4 and 12.5). The arrival of the packet-ships saw the erection of the Royal Hotel, thanks to the business brought to Howth, and jarvies began to operate for passengers on the peninsula.[64] It also encouraged the building of many early nineteenth-century houses (still to be seen) on both roads to Howth and on the peninsula, thereby stitching it to the city and offering a similar but smaller-scale development of substantial dwellings for commuters. Most importantly, it helped to develop the growth of the villages on the roads out to Howth, such as Clontarf, Killester, Raheny, Kilbarrack, Baldoyle, Sutton and the town of Howth itself. The more comfortably-off members of Dublin society had earlier seen these northern outreaches as an attractive location to inhabit. In 1793 Charles Cosslett accompanied his friend Mr Pollocks to his house 'beyond Raheny where Captain Wilcock, being a very particular acquaintance of his, made free of his melons'.[65]

The military, too, were living out in these new northern suburbs: General Luscombe at Killester House in Killester and at 155 Leeson Street, Lt. Col. Charles Pepper at Hollybrook Park in Clontarf, Captain Low at Hollybrook Lodge and Captain Thomas Montgomery at Manor House, Raheny (now a girls' school).[66] This gives a good indication of the condition of the roads, as the military always had to be able to access the city easily. Hugh Hanna, Royal Navy Coast Guard station commander, lived at Fortview Avenue in Clontarf. Close by, at the Clontarf sheds, Catherine Farrell ran the post office and a lodging-house. William Preston, who was based at the Custom House, also lived at Clontarf. Another who depended on the roads to Howth was Edward Hogan, owner of the

Fig. 12.6—New rail spur extending to Howth, 1853 (courtesy of the NLI).

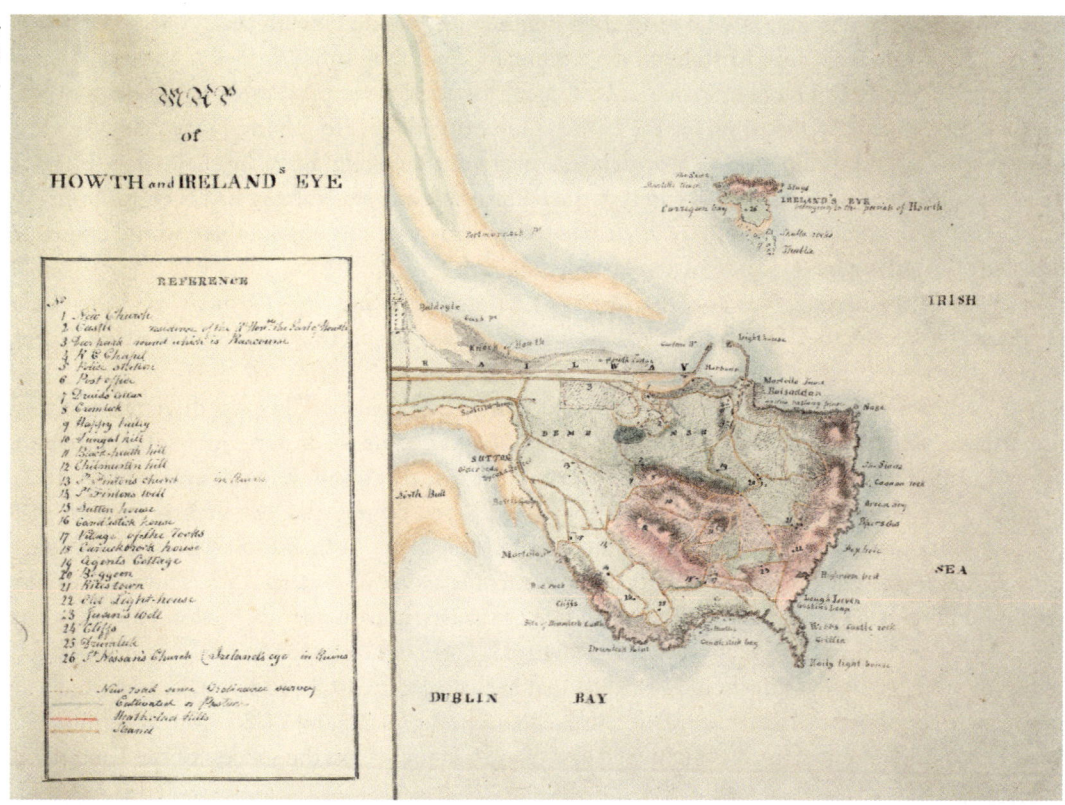

Fig. 12.7—Fishing-boats rounding the lighthouse. Note that the lighthouse has yet to be rebuilt, using stone from the lighthouse at the Bailey (John Faulkner c. 1825).

Howth and Sutton oyster-beds, who resided on Phillipsburg Avenue, close to James Cruise, Professor of Drawing, while next door Mrs Glynn ran a seminary for young ladies.[67]

In 1801 the Royal Dublin Society, a body bent on constant improvement in all walks of life, instructed Lt. Joseph Archer to survey the entire county of Dublin. He reported that Baldoyle was a 'pleasant fishing and bathing town', Howth was a small town enjoying 'a fine air', Killester a 'pleasant village' and Raheny a 'large village'.[68] In fact, the countryside around Raheny had been for some 50 years or more an attractive location for a select few to holiday near the sea, and these would influence others to follow and be the cause of an expanding village.[69]

By 1824 the harbour was operational (Figs 12.7 and 12.8) and the *Almanack* listed the *Royal Sovereign*, the *Ivanhoe*, the *Vixen* and the *Meteor* as packet-boats connecting with Holyhead. The agent at Howth was Lt. Browne, Royal Navy.[70]

Roads were vital for connection and communication and road-building was therefore of prime importance, particularly roads that lasted. It was reported that some roads were not well constructed. In his statistical survey for the RDS in 1802, Lt. Archer wrote that some were poor owing to 'rutting because gravel not sorted in the pit'. He further asked: 'does it ever strike the makers of roads that the round smooth stones laid on a hard surface can never unite … Which caused horses to become lame and carriage springs to break, so that roads become worn in two tracks'.[71] Howth Harbour energised the tidying up of roads on the north side of the city, in particular those along the coast but also the north road out of Dublin towards Drogheda. This could be seen in the improved public transport available by 1824. It should be noted that in that year it cost 3s. 11d. to take a jaunting car from the packet-boats at Howth, while it cost 1s. 4d. from Ringsend and 2s. 2d. from Dunleary. Ten years later this differential in cost might well have had an influence on the success of the Kingstown railway.[72]

George Montgomery, who arived in Howth on 29 June 1826, outlined the cost of using the mail-packet to Howth in a letter to the earl of Pembroke:

- Carriage £2 2s. 2d.
- Bill at Howth 5s. 6d.
- Howth to Mount Merrion £1 1s.

On his departure from Howth on 24 July 1826 he listed the prices as follows:

- Three full passengers £3 3s.
- 2 men £1 1s.
- One carriage £2 2s.
- Shipping 10s. 6d.
- Steward 10s. 6d., including a cabin man.[73]

This area received a further boost in terms of building and settlement with the arrival of the Dublin–Drogheda Railway in 1844, and another with the extension of the spur to Howth itself shortly afterwards (Fig. 12.6). This connected the village and, more importantly, the harbour at Howth directly to the city. With access by both road and rail, Howth became a much-visited day-trip location. Thomas Carlyle visited the Hutton family of Baldoyle: 'tall silent-looking Fr Hutton (for they live at Baldoyle this side of Howth) meets me at the station there (Baldoyle station): car is to follow us to Howth, where I am to bathe'. He does not seem to have enjoyed the experience: 'bad bathing ground, tide being out, wound heel in the stones (slippers were in the bathing machine but people didn't tell me), Cornish pilchard sloops fishing here, dirty village'. The good Huttons, changing the arrangements, 'have decided to send me by their carriage. Poor little streetkin of Baldoyle fronting

Fig. 12.8—New lighthouse (1817) on east pier (photo: Brian Matthews).

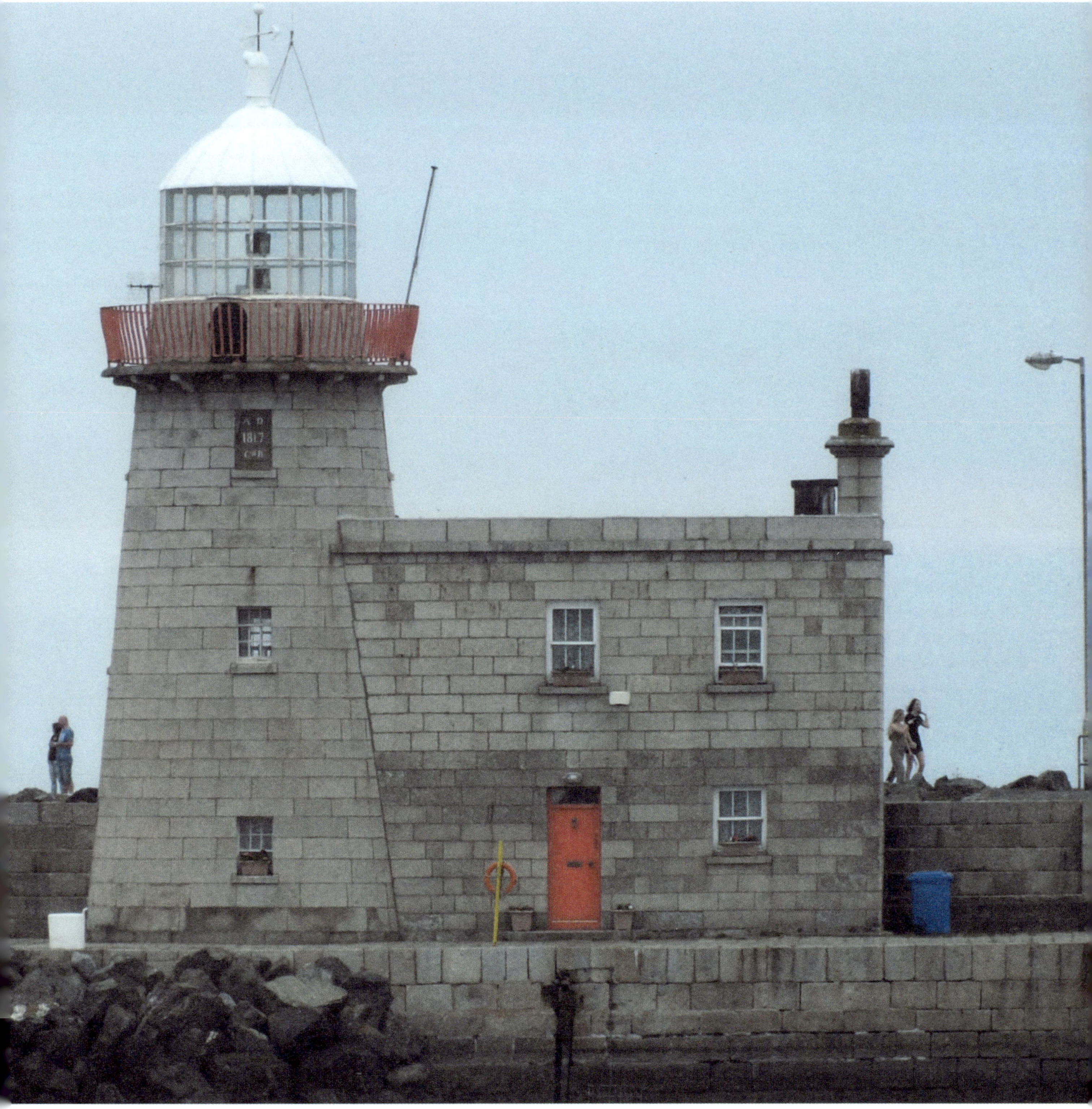
1817

a wide waste of sea sands (fisher people I suppose).'[74] Obviously the tide was out (Fig. 12.9).

The other road on the shore, below Lord Charlemont's demesne at Marino on the Malahide Road, helped to establish Malahide, which would enjoy even more growth as both a seaside resort and a suburb of Dublin when the railway arrived only ten years after the Post Office contract moved to Dunleary.

It was inevitable that the harbour at Howth would be unsuccessful; it could not fight the natural impediments, which remain the same today, and the harbour after a few decades again needs to be dredged.

'A mile north lies the picturesque rocky isle called Ireland's Eye and in the sheltered sound between is the costly, capricious, beautiful but almost useless artificial harbour of Howth.'[75]

Fig. 12.9—View of Howth Harbour and lighthouse for earl of Whitworth by Rowbotham and engraved by Daniel Havell (courtesy of Howth Yacht Club).

Notes
1. Ruth Heard, 'Public works in Ireland, 1800–1831', unpublished MLitt. thesis, Trinity College Dublin (1977).
2. Unpublished diaries of Charles Cosslett (1793–4), Diary B, p. 7 (St Malachy's College, Belfast).
3. Proposal contained in Thomas Rogers's pamphlet *Observations on the reports laid before the Rt Hon. and Hon. Directors General of Inland Navigation in Ireland, for the improvement of Dublin Harbour* (Dublin, 1805), p. 70. NLI P1134 (16).
4. William Dawson, *Plan for a complete harbour at Howth town for the use of His Majesty's packet boats; merchant ships, in case of storm; and fishing vessels to supply Dublin market* (Dublin, 1805), p. 2. NLI JP 1486.
5. Rogers, *Observations on the reports*, p. vi.
6. Ibid., p. 51.
7. Ibid., p. 55.
8. 45 George III c 113 (1805), p. 111.
9. Heard, 'Public works in Ireland, 1800–1831', p. 111.

[10] *Ibid.*, p. 117.
[11] Ann Plumtre, *Narrative of a residence in Ireland during the summer of 1814 and that of 1815* (London, 1817), p. 79.
[12] *Ibid.*, p. 78.
[13] *Ibid.*, p. 77.
[14] Thomas Cromwell, *The Irish tourist or excursions through Ireland, province of Leinster*, vol. 3 (Dublin, 1820), p. 91.
[15] *Ibid.*, p. 21.
[16] 'Letters of John Rennie & John Rennie Engineers on the building of Howth Harbour', *Dublin Historical Record* **61** (1) (2008), 2–4, p. 2. Fingal County Council, correspondence collection 1809–1822.
[17] Anon., *Considerations on the necessity and importance of an asylum port of Dublin and remarks on the harbour erecting at Howth and that which is the object of various petitions proposed for Dunleary, by an ordinary seaman* (Dublin, 1811), pp 4–5. NLI P653 (5).
[18] *Ibid.*, p. 5.
[19] Heard, 'Public works in Ireland, 1800–1831', p. 133.
[20] *Considerations on the necessity and importance of an asylum port of Dublin*, p. 5.
[21] *Ibid.*, p. 6.
[22] *Ibid.*, p. 7
[23] Kevin Rickard, 'Howth and its maritime past', *Dublin Historical Record* **70** (1) (2017), 19–35, p. 20.
[24] Heard, 'Public works in Ireland, 1800–1831', p. 111.
[25] Joan Ussher Sharkey, 'St Anne's—the Guinness estate', *Dublin Historical Record* **57** (2) (2004), 132–45.
[26] Bernadine Ruddy, 'The disturbance at Howth Harbour', *Dublin Historical Record* **65** (1–2) (2012), p. 50.
[27] Plumtre, *Narrative of a residence in Ireland*, p. 8.
[28] *Ibid.*, p. 4.
[29] Ruddy, 'The disturbance at Howth Harbour', p. 51.
[30] 'Letters of John Rennie & John Rennie Engineers on the building of Howth Harbour', p. 3.
[31] *Ibid.*, p. 4.
[32] Plumtre, *Narrative of a residence in Ireland*, p. 207.
[33] *Ibid.*
[34] County of Dublin, extract of presentments at Easter Term, 1815 (Royal Dublin Society library), p. 9.
[35] *Ibid.*, p. 64.
[36] Rickard, 'Howth and its maritime past', p. 21.
[37] *The Gentleman's and Citizen's Almanack (as compiled by the late John Watson Stewart) for the year of our Lord 1824* (Dublin, 1824), p. 112.
[38] Port ledger 1819, p. 175 (Dublin Port Archive Vault, at Glenbeigh Records Storage, Damastown, Dublin 15).
[39] Cromwell, *The Irish tourist*, p. 37.
[40] Heard, 'Public works in Ireland, 1800–1831', p. 120.
[41] *Ibid.*, p. 121.
[42] *Ibid.*, p. 126.
[43] *Ibid.*, p. 113.
[44] Journal of Benjamin Oakley (auditor of Drury Lane Theatre, London), including descriptions of three tours in Ireland (1819, 1825, 1827), pp 60–1. NLI MS 11,938.
[45] *Ibid.*, p. 61.
[46] *Ibid.*, p. 85.
[47] Journal of the proceedings of the Corporation for Preserving and Improving the Port of Dublin, vol. 11, p. 27. NAI.
[48] *Ibid.*, p. 28.
[49] *Ibid.*, p. 32.
[50] *Ibid.*, p. 228.
[51] *Ibid.*, vol. 12, p. 221.
[52] Journal of Benjamin Oakley, p. 183 (1825 tour).
[53] *Ibid.*, p. 209 (1825 tour).
[54] *Ibid.*, pp 206–7 (1825 tour).
[55] Rickard, 'Howth and its maritime past', p. 23.
[56] Alexander Nimmo, *New piloting directions for St Georges's Channel and the coasts of Ireland* (Dublin, 1832), p. 111.
[57] *Ibid.*, p. 112.
[58] T. Dawson, 'The road to Howth', *Dublin Historical Record* **29** (4) (1976), 122–32, p. 125.

59 *Ibid.*, p. 129.
60 *Ibid.*, p. 130.
61 Thomas Reid, *Travels in Ireland in the year 1822, exhibiting brief sketches of the moral, physical and political state of the country with reflections on the best means of improving its condition* (London, 1823), p. 296.
62 *Freeman's Journal*, 1 January 1844.
63 Pettigrew & Oulton's *Dublin Almanack and General Register of Ireland* (1845), p. 839.
64 Rickard, 'Howth and its maritime past', p. 21.
65 Diaries of Charles Cosslett (1793–4), in St Malachy's College, Belfast (no page numbers).
66 *Dublin Almanack* (1845), p. 839.
67 *Ibid.*, p. 839.
68 Hely Dutton, *Observations on Mr Archer's statistical survey of the county of Dublin* (Dublin, 1902), pp 87, 92, 95.
69 Diarmuid Ó Gráda, *Georgian Dublin: the forces that shaped the city* (Cork, 2015), p. 93.
70 *The Gentleman's and Citizen's Almanack* (1824), p. 70.
71 Dutton, *Observations on Mr Archer's statistical survey*, pp 134–6.
72 *The Gentleman's and Citizen's Almanack* (1824).
73 George Augustus Montgomery, list of expenses and costs in Ireland, NLI MS 1432.
74 Thomas Carlyle, *Reminiscences of my Irish journey in 1849* (New York, 1882), p. 11.
75 Caesar Otway, *A tour in Connaught* (London, 1839), p. 93.

13. The Great North Bull Wall

The harbour at Dublin immediately before the Great North Bull Wall

The further development of trade, commerce and growth in the city hinged on the facilities of the harbour and port, just as it had 100 years earlier, but larger ships were restricted in their use of Dublin port because of the continued existence of the bar at the mouth of the Liffey. The size of ships had grown, which meant a corresponding increase in the depths needed by these vessels as they accessed the port. In addition, ships needed deeper water at the quayside in the Liffey.

The Great South Wall offered a measure of protection, albeit precarious—any kind of a strong easterly wind crossing the bar and getting in behind the wall was fraught with danger, as the list of losses in the bay confirmed. Furthermore, ships approaching the bay had nowhere to run for safety before either trying to anchor or chancing the entrance; ships could not answer their helm like motor cars do today, with all their ropes and rigging aloft creating windage. The bay had one other serious drawback: the holding ground was sand. The use of two anchors was quite normal but no guarantee of safety.[1]

As we have seen, in the eighteenth century George Semple had proposed the enclosure of vast areas of Dublin Bay behind a wall (Fig. 13.1). As far back as 1721 Commander Perry had proposed a canal on the north side behind the North Bull Sands to provide access to the city. On the other side, too, there had been a number of promoters of the idea of accessing the Liffey via the Dodder, and of a canal coming south from the Dodder across the strand around Sandymount just beyond Irishtown. The reason was the existence of another bar—this one at the exit of the Dodder into the Liffey, still in existence today. This writer can attest to the fact, having run aground exiting the Grand Canal Docks in 2010.

As the eighteenth century ended and the nineteenth began, another spate of ideas, proposals and suggestions were floated to deal with the issue. Captain William Bligh came to Dublin and produced a report for the Directors of Inland Navigation in 1800, along with a map suggesting a north wall over at the Liffey outflow almost parallel to the Great South Wall. Sir Thomas Hyde Page agreed with Bligh's proposal to run a north wall downriver parallel to the south wall (Fig. 13.2). He also made some observations on the bay and on methods of anchoring, and commented on facilities for ships seeking asylum over at Dunleary and Bullock. His suggestions were followed in 1802 by John Rennie's proposal for a North Bull Wall.

Another proposal was that a harbour be constructed at Douglas in the Isle of Man, 'accessible at all times to the largest vessels'.[2]

The public were asked to interest themselves in the whole matter of a harbour of asylum and the port of Dublin: 'the public too ought to be roused to a sense of their own interests, and shall have the utility of inland navigations clearly and distinctly pointed out to them'.[3] Submissions and

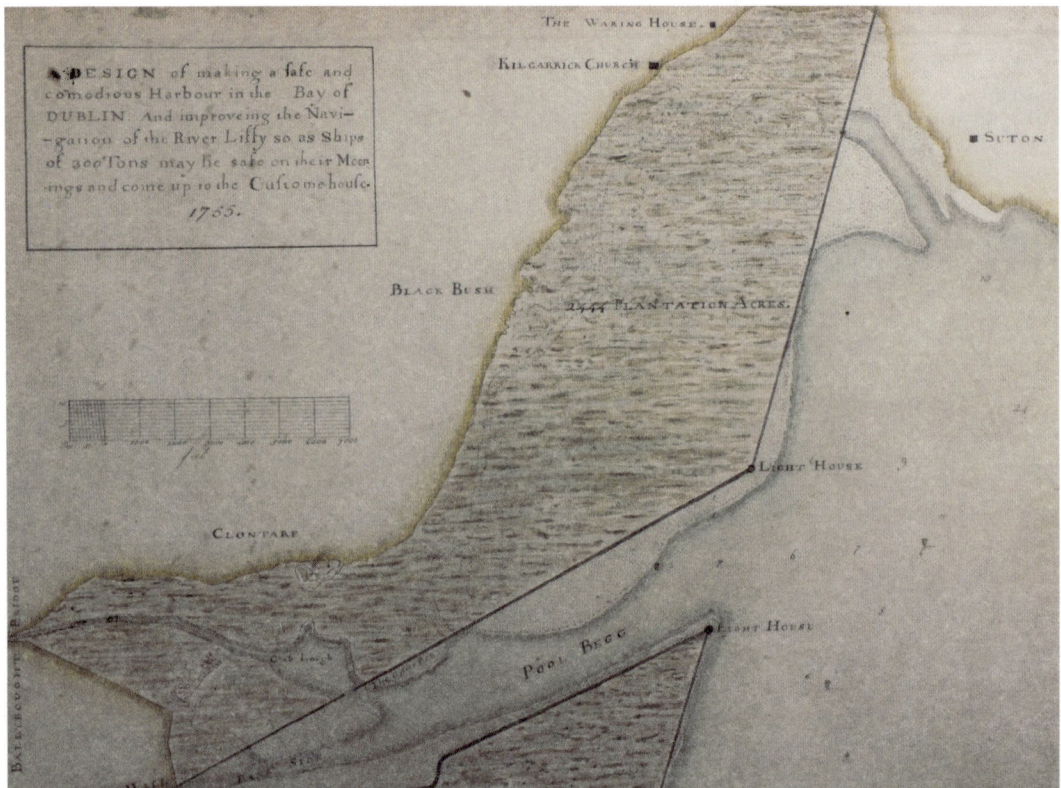

Fig. 13.1—George Semple's map of the proposed wall enclosing the harbour (Dublin Port Company Archive).

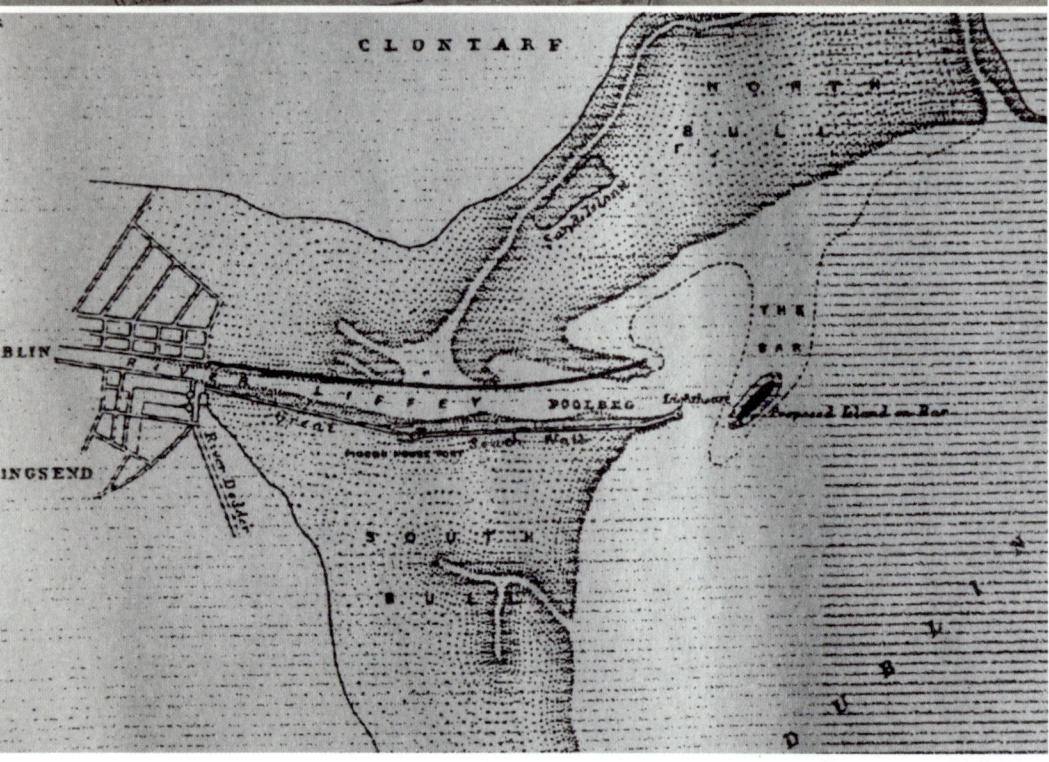

Fig. 13.2—Bligh's proposed North Wall, along with that proposed by Sir Thomas Hyde Page, 1800–1.

> **The Corporation for Preserving and Improving the Port of Dublin** replaced the Ballast Committee in 1786. The Corporation, whose membership included the lord mayor and three councillors, would now dictate policy and take decisions in relation to all aspects of Dublin port and the River Liffey up as far as Barrack Street Bridge (two bridges beyond the Four Courts). In 1792 another department, called the Anna Livia Department, was added to their remit, and in 1810 the lighthouses became the third statutory body of the Corporation.
>
> The Corporation continued with one set of directors but used to hold two separate board meetings each month. The affairs of the Anna Livia Department were included under port business, hence the references throughout the Journals. The lighthouses kept a separate set of journals. There was always an element of overlap and for this researchers must be grateful in that not all material has vanished.

suggestions were welcomed by the various interested bodies. This can be seen as equivalent as today's County Council public consultations.

'J.M.', another contributor to the harbour debate in February 1804, offered his opinion that, no matter which proposed walls were erected, the scour effect would never be sufficient to remove the constant deposits of material from both bulls at the entrance to the Liffey on the bar.[4] His suggestion was a series of dams and sluices across the Liffey at Ringsend.[5] He suggested to William Gregory, secretary to the Directors of Inland Navigation, that 'The Great South Wall does credit to the Ballast Office Corporation, as it affords very necessary shelter to the shipping in Poolbeg; but it has scarcely improved the depth of water'. He agreed with Bligh that a parallel wall to the Great South Wall was the answer.[6] J.M. also recommended that a dam and weir be built across the Tolka to add to its power of flow, which would then run out into the Liffey parallel to but north-east of the Royal Canal.[7]

Thomas Rogers, in his proposal for selecting Howth as the location for a new packet harbour in 1805, wrote that the idea of a canal into Dublin should be a matter of 'subsequent consideration'.[8]

Revd William Dawson wrote in 1805 that 'A wall from the north side of the bay to the river in whatever course it might take would be much more likely to accumulate the sand than the south wall', adding that 'Any wall from the north side of the bay east of Clontarf sheds, to the river channel, Spit Buoy, must still leave the North Bull open for ships'.[9]

With this level of public discourse on the subject, allied to the fact that the port authorities were most anxious to complete the task outstanding, it is safe to conclude that it was much discussed at meetings of the Board. Sadly, the minute-books of the directors are lost.

As late as 1833 another pamphlet investigated the project of building a ship canal 'connecting the asylum harbour at Kingstown with a floating dock in the Anna Liffey'. Mr Killally, an engineer of some expertise in canal-building, especially on the Grand Canal, is mentioned as having written on the subject too.[10] The subject of connecting Dunleary to the city via the Dodder or Grand Canal Docks made another appearance: 'It has been suggested by very able engineers that a deep cut might be made from the Grand Canal Docks … along the shore till it meets with a depth of water sufficient to admit the largest West Indiaman'.[11]

William Jessop, one of the most respected engineers in the British Isles at the time and engineer to the Grand Canal Docks, also had suggestions on the subject. He proposed something similar: 'I find the most practicable mode will be to install a canal through the enclosed lands from the south end of the Docks to meet the strand at Old Merrion and from thence to extend it along the strand to Dunleary … I will propose that by means of two locks, one for large, the other for lesser ships …

into a basin 150 yards by fifty yards'.[12]

As late as 1846 Sir John McNeill proposed that a canal be cut across the sands outside Irishtown from the docks for 'about 600 yards'. He also suggested waiting on the results of the experimental testing of the screw-propeller against the paddle-steamers before deciding on the size of basin required.[13]

The Great North Bull Wall

By 1819 the Corporation for Preserving and Improving the Port of Dublin had finally decided to begin construction of 'the Great North Wall' using their own funds.[14] They could not put off the decision any longer. Howth had not proved a successful alternative to the Pigeon House Harbour as a packet station. Dunleary was now coming to the fore as a possible refuge harbour, leaving the port of Dublin to be dealt with. Almost 100 years after beginning the Great South Wall, the Corporation realised that it would require more velocity in the water than was then available to remove the bar, or so it was assumed. The certain arrival of steamships promised further challenges.

The purpose of this chapter is to examine the reasons for the wall's construction, to explain the manner of its construction and why it took less than five years to build. It is also important to illustrate why it appears unfinished. Finally, a look at the wall's impact on the port itself, on Clontarf and on the city as a whole will be included.

The construction of a North Wall for the purpose of using the ebbing tide to assist in scouring out the bar at the entrance to the port at Poolbeg Lighthouse presented different engineering challenges. Where was the best location? How long should it be? What angle should it present to the shore? What size should it be—how high and how wide? Should it retain any part of the actual North Bull (that is, the giant sand bar, parts of which often remained dry at high water)?

In July 1812 John Rennie was called on to report on the state of the harbour. He suggested that a new wall be extended from the north shore near Clontarf towards the Poolbeg Lighthouse, leaving an entrance some 550 yards wide (Fig. 13.3). He also suggested the embanking of the South Bull. After a lapse of seven years, the Clontarf wall plan was adopted.[15] This was a very different proposal from the one put forward by Captain Bligh, who had suggested a second wall to run parallel to the South Bull Wall.

The construction of the North Bull Wall was one of the last of the great projects in which the port authorities had been involved over a 100-year period. In purely physical terms it finally enclosed a large body of water, offering a greater measure of protection to shipping, but the issue of the bar remained. Many mistakes had been made along the way, such as the building of the Pigeon House Harbour on the Great South Wall. The decision-makers and builders must have known that it would be tidal and therefore was always going to be restrictive to ships, yet they went ahead anyway. The development of Howth Harbour would also prove to be problematic because its entrance was tight, with rocky hazards on the right side on entering and drying sand bars immediately to the west of the harbour mouth. In addition, the harbour was never deep enough, never contained sufficient swinging room and had extensive sand bars close to the harbour road.

Dunleary was not built as a packet base but became one by default. It was developed as a harbour of refuge, somewhere to run to in the event of bad weather. It did not change the dangers in the bay but, combined with the arrival of steam and therefore greater control of shipping schedules and a substantial improvement in the prediction of arrival times, it reduced the major problem with which the city and port had had to contend for hundreds of years. From then on the bar receded in

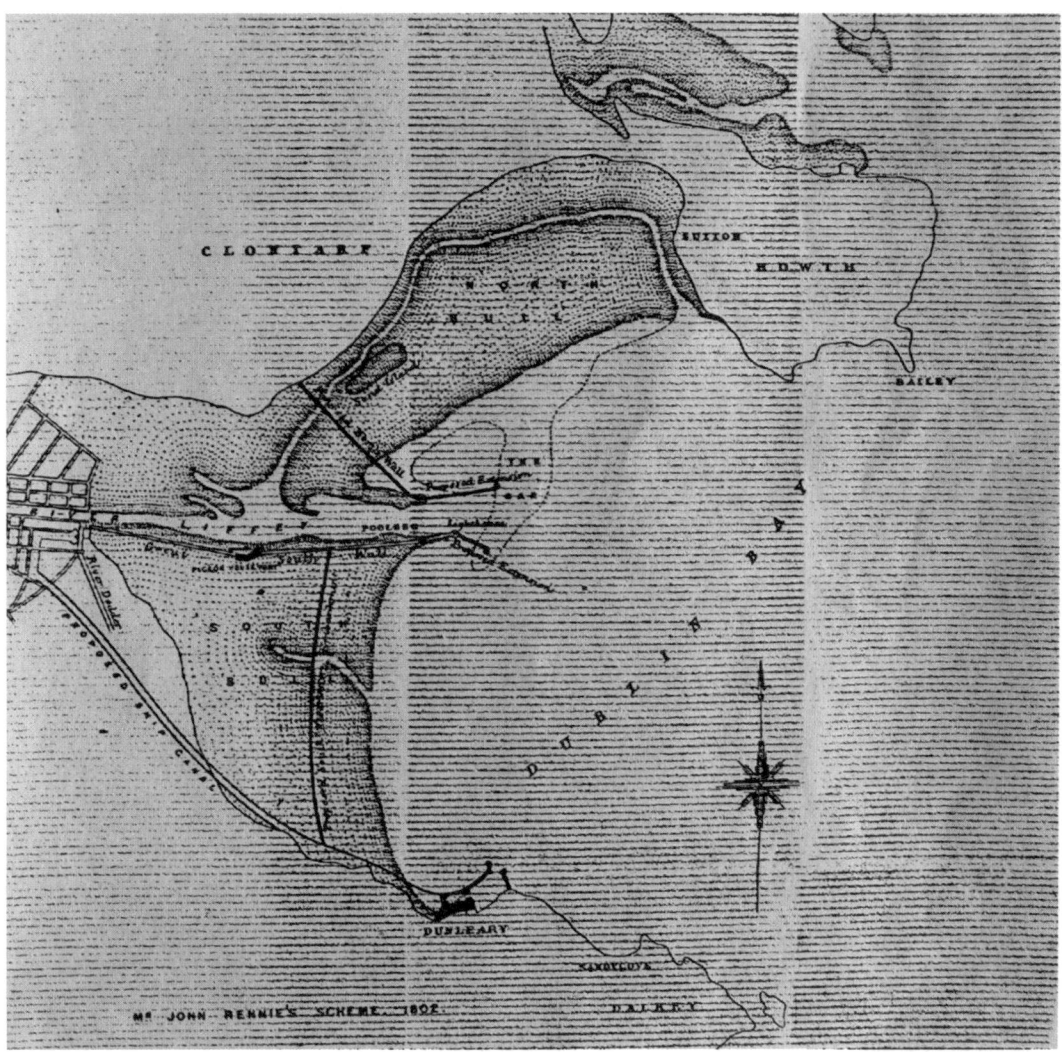

Fig. 13.3—John Rennie's proposed North Wall, 1802 (NLI).

importance as a major issue. After the enclosure of the second protecting wall, the hoped-for scouring effect finally worked, and steam dredging also had a powerful impact on the project.

Now the authorities could turn their attention to the matter of a harbour of refuge, where ships that failed to reach the Liffey could obtain shelter from easterly gales and storms. The immediate effect of the new North Bull Wall was to allow for an expansion of ideas in terms of planning extensions to the port facilities on the north side, even if these were not completed for another 35 years. It would allow for the acceleration of land reclamation on that side; in fact, it was on the north shore that most of the port activity of reclamation and subsequent building would take place. Another effect was the final disappearance of Clontarf Island, beginning in this period. It would finally vanish thanks to the constant removal of material from it in spite of regulation, and it would be absorbed in land reclamation along the East Wall Road (just at the road entrance to the Port Tunnel today).

Before dealing with the myth that Captain Bligh designed or built or had anything to do with the North Bull Wall, we need to look at another proposal for action in the area—in May 1800, a

> **Captain William Bligh**
>
> Captain William Bligh of the Royal Navy played no part in the construction of the Great North Wall, as it became termed by the Corporation. He died in London in 1817, two years before the work began. He came to Dublin in 1800, however, and produced two maps, one showing his proposed North Wall, to complement the South Wall, and a chart of Dublin Bay with its many soundings, laying the groundwork for what would take place some years later. There are many myths about Bligh. His skill as a navigator in the days when navigation was expanding as an exact and demanding science and his talent as a cartographer were recognised by Captain Cook, who specifically asked him to come to the Pacific as sailing master on the *Discovery*.[16] His chart of Dublin Bay remains to this day a work of great accomplishment—the first (and best) comprehensive chart with soundings.
>
> A question mark remains, however, over his chart of a wall drawn to accompany the South Wall. He drew it as parallel to the other, making for a very narrow channel at a time when steamships were non-existent; how sailing-ships were supposed to beat upriver against wind and tide in narrow confines has never been explained—and this from a ship's captain. Equally, the effect of scour on the topography would have been devastating to the floor of the river, and where might it have gone? Bligh had to have some idea of the existence of calp limestone, especially in light of his comments on ships taking the ground in Dublin.
>
> Bligh's chart of Dublin Bay was more finished, more complete and much more detailed than anything that had preceded it. The difference between it and Murdoch McKenzie's 1776 work and John Cowan's of 1800 is immediately apparent even to someone not used to looking at such information. Bligh took a vast number of soundings and all in only three months—a remarkable achievement.[17] He noted that Clontarf Island, for so long an aspect of the landscape of the bay, was now much reduced in size. He also included other banks and shoals, such as the Kish Bank, today marked by a lighthouse some eight miles out east of the harbour. Of course, by this time society had been nibbling away at it for material.[18] Bligh did not do all this work himself: he could not have, because it was too much for one man. He had a team of well-qualified cartographers to assist him. The astonishing fact is that he completed his task in the winter months, when days were shorter and the weather more inclement than in the summer. And the boats used to take the soundings used only sail and oar power.
>
> Bligh's opinion was that, with due care and caution, Dublin Bay was not so dangerous, but his view was coloured by his experience of operating a large sailing-ship with a Royal Navy crew of usually well-disciplined men who took immense pride in their skill. He recommended that a ship should pay out 150 fathoms of anchor cable while anchoring in the bay (one fathom = 6ft) to stop the anchor dragging. In his report he accused the owners of merchant ships of cutting back on such cable and supplying poor-quality anchors to their masters, claiming that this added to the losses in the bay.[19]
>
> The proof of the respect in which Bligh was held by the Admiralty is that he retired a Vice-Admiral of the Blue in 1814, a very solid career end for one who had come up through the ranks and had been involved in two mutinies.

proposal to 'demonstrate beyond the possibility of a doubt that the increase of water-carriage in the country is, of all other improvements, the most essentially requisite to its future prosperity'.[20] In the appendix to this report William Jessop leaves no doubt as to just how crucial the issue was to the well-being of trade and growth in the city: 'But alas! Without a better harbour than the present, what foreign trade can Dublin ever expect to possess'. Bligh did not arrive in Dublin until later that summer. At this stage the bar was two miles wide and a quarter mile deep, allowing a depth of only 5–6ft at low tide.

The Corporation for Preserving and Improving the Port of Dublin applied to the Directors General of Inland Navigation for funds to further improve the port. The Directors consulted a number of experts on the problems of the port and possible solutions. Lord Cornwallis requested from the Admiralty the services of a good surveyor and cartographer to make an up-to-date detailed chart of the bay and port. Bligh was chosen because his reputation as a hydrographer and cartographer was first-rate. He was instructed to report to the Directors rather than the Corporation. Others who had also examined and reported included Sir Thomas Hyde Page, Captain Daniel Corneille, John Rennie and Captain Joseph Huddart, who all supplied different answers.[21]

Bligh arrived in October 1800 and reported his findings to the Directors on 12 January 1801. The work would have entailed many days out in small boats with anchor and leadline, taking soundings. A heavy, cylindrical lead weight, hollow at the bottom and packed with grease or tallow, on a long line with knots and ribbons spaced out along the length, was dropped over the side of the boat and fed out; when the line went slack, the depth was read off the knots and ribbons. Whatever stuck to the grease or tallow was then visible. Of course, it goes without saying that Bligh was not alone; there were likely to have been half a dozen small craft working in pairs around the bay to get the task done. One of those assisting him was Michael Spatks.[22] The chart produced is scaled at four inches to the mile. It describes extremely accurately the entire bay, with all topography and tidal streams, and includes the chart datum of low-water springs (data during spring tides). Bligh had some recommendations for Dunleary, Dalkey, Bullock and Howth as possible harbours of refuge. He also took samples of the infamous bar and found it to be sand.

Bligh concluded that the worst time for shipping in attempting to enter the port was during east-north-easterly high winds. He was opposed to any canal along either the north or the south shore, mainly on the basis that a project of that magnitude would divert both attention and funds away from where they were needed, which was in the port itself. Most importantly, Bligh suggested a new north wall running down the north bank of the Liffey—an extension to the then-current north wall on the river. He envisaged this extended wall as continuing out into the harbour and finishing in an area opposite the Poolbeg Lighthouse. His chart shows little detail on land but includes the baths down at the end of the East Wall, behind which he shows just marsh and slobs. He was also concerned that the constant dredging of the river was creating an uneven seabed which was dangerous to ships when they took to the ground at low water, stressing their hull construction. His report complained of the smell coming from the open sewers emptying into the river and recommended that they be arched over.[23]

It must be added that Bligh was not asked to formally submit a detailed plan; the map of his proposed wall is evidence of this because it portrays none of the fine detail seen in his chart of the bay itself. In fairness to Bligh, his map was almost an afterthought and has to be seen as such. Just how he thought that ships in this pre-steam age were going to be able to sail upwind against the prevailing westerlies in a very narrow space which automatically precluded tacking is beyond this writer's understanding.

The Corporation deferred any decision on Bligh's report in order to consider another proposal by two Board members, George Maquay and Leland Crosthwaite, for a new wall to originate from the shore at Clontarf and run eastward to finish within a few hundred yards of the Poolbeg Lighthouse.[24] This idea was not new, having been suggested as far back as 1786 by William Chapman before being revisited and revised by these two and further tweaked by Corneille, another engineer. Francis Giles and George Halpin, Corporation employees, were also thinking along these lines.

Bligh's idea might not have worked, but this will never be known. What is certain, however, is that what was built in the end from Clontarf succeeded, and the bar disappeared. The long-considered scour effect was actually effective, though only because it was greatly helped by the use of a steam dredger. The reservations about Bligh's suggested wall included the fact that the enclosed body of water would have been too narrow, creating a whole new danger to shipping in any kind of stiff breeze, and at the wrong angle could create very turbulent seas at the entrance. There was also some concern that the sheer volume of water pouring out of a narrow, constrained, walled channel could either move or damage the structures.

The first steam dredger employed by Dublin Port was operating by 1819. This is remarkable, given that it was only four years since the first steam-driven vessel had arrived in Dublin. This changed everything in the port. It meant that work could proceed at a pace less subject to the vagaries of the weather. It also meant the imminent arrival of steam-powered vessels, more independent of tide and wind and more amenable to schedules. It is ironic that the age of steam coincided with the eventual construction of the North Wall and led to the deepening of the mouth of the Liffey. The effect on trade—which after all this time was the main reason for improving the port facilities—was enormously positive. One result of the increase in traffic was that the North Wall quays began to be developed and shortly afterwards the first hotel appeared on North Wall, though this facility had been available for quite some time on the south side at Sir John Rogerson's Quay.

Halpin and Giles

The Great North Wall was designed and built by Francis Giles and George Halpin, employees of the Corporation for Preserving and Improving the Port of Dublin. Giles was an engineer and had worked with Sir John Rennie in England on the new road from London to Holyhead; Halpin was not, but he was an exceptional builder and manager of both projects and men. He had been working for the port authorities since 1800, when at the age of 21 he took over the role of being in charge from Francis Tunstall, who had died. He later became Inspector of Works. The port secretary, Henry Veredker, later referred to Halpin as an engineer, however: 'The Corporation have directed their engineer, Mr George Halpin, to report and make a judgement on the report of Sir John McNeill on the area of George's Dock as it joined the Liffey'.[25] The Corporation employed 'an eminent engineer, Mr Giles, to make accurate plans and surveys, on a sufficient scale of the river and harbour, in order to show the actual state of the port, and to determine at any future time what changes have taken place'.[26]

If there is a towering figure in the history of the city in terms of building, engineering and architecture across all aspects of construction it is George Halpin. James Gandon is rightly lionised for his achievements but Halpin is his equal and, just like Gandon's, all of his work is there today for citizens to appreciate. The list includes lighthouses, the corn exchange on Burgh Quay, the Bank of Ireland in Wexford, the reinforcing of the Great South Wall and the restoration of the quay wall up to Queen Street Bridge on the Liffey.

Throughout the construction of the wall Halpin was also going around the country, for example monitoring the work at the building of Mullaghmore Harbour, and he showed clearly that he was very much in control of his responsibilities. In a letter dated 30 June 1824 he told the Board that he had uncovered the supply of false weights in ballast boats supplying sand, where the lighters filled the bilges with water.[27]

The Corporation did not have to approach government for money as they had enough to fund the project themselves. Their 1819 ledger confirms Ruth Heard's claim that they held £30,752 16s. 4d. in government bonds, on a five-year bond.[28] They also held a loan in favour of the Wide Streets Commission for £11,000 as of 5 January 1819.[29] The interest received on this loan was entered at

THE GREAT NORTH BULL WALL

Fig. 13.4—Francis Giles's 1819 map, showing wall which was acted on and completed (courtesy of Lar Joye).

£550—a not-insubstantial sum at the time, nor indeed a small rate of interest.[30] It has to be remembered that at this stage the port was generating income from port fees, pilot fees, shipping tonnage, ballast collection and delivery, and quay fees, all the above itemised in the ledgers. Water was also charged for but within quay fees. The port authorities made no exceptions in exacting payment, even exacting pilot fees from the Commissioner of His Majesty's Navy for services to the cruiser *Shamrock* and *Whitworth* of Messrs McMahon, and Eustace pilots, at 16s. 3d. and £1 12s. 7d. respectively.[31] The 1819 ledger mentions a sum of £11,251 16s. 9d. for tonnage fees that year alone.[32] Quay wall revenue amounted to £3,971. Note that a ship not only paid port dues but also paid for the use of the quay wall that it occupied for the duration of its stay. These dues can be substantial and explains why ships are often seen at anchor out in the bay today, avoiding dues.

Documentary evidence for this earlier period is sadly lacking. It would seem that reports of committee meetings and directors' meetings have disappeared, leaving only some maps and ledgers for 1808, 1824, 1827 and 1830. Just very recently this writer discovered that copies of some port books were made at that period. These were presented to the National Archive and are currently stored in the basement of the Four Courts. This collection of material has never been fully catalogued and therefore the precise amount of material involved is not yet known. Happily for the purpose of this work, two journals covering the years 3 December 1819–25 August 1826 still exist and are helpful. We also have the 1819 drawing by Francis Giles for the proposed North Bull Wall (Fig. 13.4).

Construction

What is known is that in 1818 Francis Giles surveyed the area 'with great care and detail'. In May the following year Giles and George Halpin together 'reported further on the direction of the North Bull Wall, which being favourably received the work was immediately set on foot, and vigorously carried on for the following five years'.[33]

The construction of the North Bull Wall would have a dramatic effect on the harbour and port of Dublin just at the precise moment of the arrival of steamships and the consequent expansion of the use of steam for power. It had long been supposed by some that the way to increase the depth at the bar was to improve the scour effect of the tide going out combined with the Liffey outflow. The improvement would have a knock-on effect on safety (although it would not solve the problem of the lack of a harbour of refuge in Dublin Bay). It would assist trade, as the figures would confirm. It also had the side-effect of improving security for the city, in that any enemy (usually perceived as the French once the American problem had been dealt with) would find it much more difficult to attack the port. The war with the USA lasted from 1812 to 1815, and Napoleon returned to power in the same year. General Vallancey's original idea was to set up a battery at the position of the bend in the South Wall so as to sweep the area with cannon fire in the event of foreign incursion. His range would have reached quite a distance over towards Clontarf, but the advent of the North Bull Wall made things even more difficult for any invader, who could now be trapped between both walls. Vallencey's map is in the NLI manuscripts collection.

As far back as 1762 George Semple had floated the idea of building walls out from the north shore and taking in vast acreages into public ownership through reclamation. Canals had been suggested skirting around to the city from Sutton, and several others, including Rennie and Sir Thomas Hyde Page, had suggested another wall on the north shore coming out to enclose a large tract of Dublin Bay.

George Halpin decided to bypass the usual management of the workmen on the project and came up with a novel arrangement that allowed the completion of the wall in five years as against the 100-year construction span of the Great South Wall. He saw that the men's work rate would be severely slowed down if they adhered to the normal daily routine of walking out to the site from the city to begin work and then in the evening reversing the exercise. He informed the Board 'that work on the platform and abutments of wrought stone round the Poolbeg lighthouse will have to be done while advantage can be taken of the ebb tides. The great distance from Dublin and Ringsend from whence men employed will have to come [each day], their strength will be much exhausted before they can reach the work—and other inconveniences may arise by they being too late.'[34] He therefore recommended that a vessel of about 200 tons be bought, fitted out and moored near the Poolbeg Lighthouse, for the purpose of providing the men with a place to sleep and eat while the work was going on. As similar difficulties would arise when the Great North Wall came to be built, this vessel could be retained for the like accommodation of the men who would be employed at that work. (Near the end of the project Halpin constructed a shed on the wall to house the men instead.) This was an unheard-of procedure at the time, and the result was similarly unheard-of. Halpin's suggestion was acted on because he was enormously respected within the Corporation for his building, engineering and man-management skills after twenty years' service. Evidence for this is seen in his application for a raise on 8 November 1822 and its being granted by return of post.

The 267-ton Russian ship *Alexander of Petersburg*, seven years old and timber-built, became available in Liverpool. Captain Joseph Grantham, pilot master of Dublin, was instructed to go and purchase the vessel if satisfied with her condition. The cost of the ship was £630.[35] This vessel was more of a hulk than a seaworthy ship but she made it across the Irish Sea in one piece. She was then fitted out with beds, blankets, sheets and rugs and was moored off the Poolbeg Lighthouse by June.[36] The accounts for the port show that this vessel was paid for by the Lights section at the time. Thus the men were on site at all times; records of their victuals and beers are recorded under the title 'Incidents' in the port ledgers of 1819–24. George Halpin also charged the Board for the supply of a horse, and his allowance in quarterly sums amounted to £8 10s. 7d., as per the dates supplied.[37] Another unexpected aspect for the period was the fact that men worked at night on the site: the entry for 21 January 1820 records that boatmen were paid £1 10s. for receiving lighters at night, while Mr Pephoe charged £8 5s. 6d. for supply of candles to the *Patrick*.[38] At the time carpenters were paid 4s. per day, ship's carpenters 4s. 2d. per day, stonecutters and masons 3s. 1d. per day, and labourers 1s. 7d. for a day's work.[39]

The expenses recorded give some idea of the scale of the project. On 17 December is recorded £6 for the annual allowance for hats and coats for the boatmen, while the payment for mason work came to £1 5s. 8d. and the gabbardmen were paid £12 18s. 8d. for moving ballast to the wall.[40] The first mention of the steam dredger *Patrick* is here included, as employees on board were paid £5. The 24 December meeting records that George Smith was paid £166 4s. 4d. for stones for the wall and £129 17s. 11d. for extra work at Bullock Harbour. Almost all the stone for the project came from either Bullock Harbour or Sandycove. The name George Smith cropped up in the payments regularly for the following four years and he was paid far more than any other supplier of stone for the project. Other entries of interest include £1 5s. 8d. for glazing for the *Patrick*, evidence that a steam dredger was operating to remove the bar as early as the end of 1819. The cost of men working at the site came to £37 1s. 2d. George Halpin, as Inspector of Works, was paid £45 17s. 2d., aside from his allowance for a horse. Of interest, too, is the figure of £40 12s. 2d. for men working on the wall over Christmas, as seen in the entry for 31 December 1819. It shows that work was proceeding apace from the point of view of the project, but also reveals that socially there were not the same holiday expectations for Christmas as in later times. It also shows that Halpin was determined to complete the project in a timely fashion. The dredger, too, operated all through Christmas and £226 16s. 9d. was expended on new buckets for it.[41]

Danger was ever present in and around the bay, and the owners of pilot boats Nos 3 and 6 applied for extra money for help extended to the *Robert Nelson* and Captain Dixon when his ship struck the Kish Bank, which request was granted.[42] The Board meeting of 17 December 1819 records that the lifeboat crew requested payment 'for their exertions in striving to save the crew of a sloop lost on the North Bull'. They were awarded a half-guinea for each crew member and one guinea for the skipper.[43]

The Corporation was meticulous in the detail of carrying out its duties, in the protection of its responsibility and in the extraction of payment. The Grand Canal Company was billed £413 12s. 6d. for the removal of 5,515 tons of mud landed at the entrance of the Grand Canal Docks. This confirms a theory that material removed from the basins was dumped around them.[44] The Corporation also insisted in being paid port dues if any passengers were carried on troop ships.[45]

Throughout the period of the building of the Great North Wall the steam dredger *Patrick* continued operations, as is evident from the expenditure items listed, including £74 0s. 7d. charged to the Coals Account of the Corporation for the *Patrick* on 13 February 1824. Repairs, too, were a constant entry for boats, floats and gabbards; the following week John Clements was paid £42 7s. 5d. for repairs to the stone boat at the wall.[46] Again it is to be noted that George Smith brought stones to the value of £110 11s. 2d. to the wall, as itemised to the Board on 6 February 1824.[47]

As the work on the wall proceeded, Halpin prepared to change the manner in which the men were accommodated. He wrote to the Board outlining the fact that the brig *Alexander* 'is getting into such decay I beg leave to submit for the consideration of the Board that she be advertised and sold by auction as she is now, before she gets worse, in the event of which I also submit that a shed be built for the boatmen'. Arthur Guinness for the Board ordered a shed to be built 'without delay'.[48]

One of the vital pieces of information in the journals is the following, giving a clear indication that the construction was approaching completion. The Board ordered in February 1824 that Halpin be instructed to give notice 'to the persons furnishing and quarrying stones to the Great North Wall that the Corporation will require only small quantity, and that they are not to carry stones in the expectation of being taken by the Corporation'.[49]

The last entry in the journal for men working at the Great North Bull Wall was recorded for the Board meeting of Friday 4 February 1825, when the cost involved was £1 13s. 4d. There would, of course, be further repairs, maintenance and other work requiring the return and attendance of men, but the last of the construction could be safely said to be complete. In today's terminology it would be called the 'snag list'.

While the wall was built of stone at the inner end, at Clontarf it was connected to the shore by a wooden bridge. This allowed the tide to flow around the north side of a growing Bull Island. The Bull Island was always there in the form of a sandbank, but it seems clear that it was augmented by the reconfigured tidal streams after the completion of the South Bull Wall down to the Poolbeg Lighthouse. The island was owned partly by the St Anne's estate (the north-east end) and partly by the Vernon estate (the inner end). In 1822 the secretary to the Board of Commissioners for Preserving and Improving the Port of Dublin submitted an account from Messrs Bergan and Co. for the building of a wooden bridge at the Great North Wall by contract amounting to £2,212. The Board ordered a draft to be drawn for £2,000 in favour of the Ballast Master, to be handed to Messrs Bergan and Co. on account.[50]

The completion of the North Bull Wall did not of itself fully scour out the bar at the entrance as had been hoped, but in combination with dredging success was finally achieved. The engineers understood tides and the potential problems better than is generally acknowledged today. This is evidenced by the wooden bridge at Clontarf but is also seen at the other end, at the railway bridge spanning the road. There are two arches; only one was necessary at the time of construction but the second one was added so that the tide could flow in and out of the pool behind the new railway embankment created at the time of building. These two arches and the rail embankment meant that, less than twenty years after the completion of the wall, another huge inner wall was constructed, increasing the pace of change and development on the space out here on an area literally miles from the original medieval city.

The designers and builders of the Great North Wall knew something that had eluded Bligh. They knew about forces and pressure and the power of water in gigantic quantities moving from one location to another. It was recognised that Bligh's proposed wall, intended to run parallel to the Great South Wall, could have had catastrophic results because of the funnel effect of the Liffey exiting along with the tide ebbing. This was confirmed on 29 November 2017 during a presentation on the Port of Dublin given to the Royal Dublin Society by the current harbour-master, Captain Michael McKenna,[51] who informed the audience that the Great South Wall did move in certain conditions and was constantly monitored using modern laser measuring equipment.

Giles and Halpin realised that such an enormous body of water would be trapped within the two proposed walls with only a narrow opening to let water escape, and with great foresight they decided to order the outer 800 yards of the wall to be built up to only half the height of the rest of the wall. This had the effect of acting as a release valve, allowing much water to escape over the lower construction.

The idea of a release valve for the water was obviously not understood by Dillon Cosgrove, who wrote in 1909 that 'The extreme portion of the breakwater is very rudely constructed'. He did, however, see clearly how the wall had offered expansion for suburbia on its completion and even 80-odd years later. 'The North Bull and its pier are sure to share in the growing popularity of Clontarf.'[52] This is amply seen in the purchase of the St Anne's estate in the early 1830s by the wealthy Guinness family. As Cosgrove records, the estate 'has been in the possession of the Guinness family for upwards of seventy years'.[53]

In 1832 Alexander Nimmo, a highly respected engineer, wrote a pilot book of sailing directions for the Irish coast, including Dublin Bay. He said that 'The anchorage in Poolbeg has of late been further protected by a rough mole carried across the strand on the north side, from the shore, near Clontarf, towards the lighthouse and the tide of the ebb has materially deepened the direct passage into the Liffey, over the bar'.[54] It is interesting that Nimmo makes no mention of the effect of dredging here; seven years earlier, when he was consulted on improvements to the port of Drogheda, he had proposed the use of a steam dredger. Wilkins claims that this was the first time that such a vessel was recommended in Ireland, but the steam dredger had by then been on station in Dublin for over six years.[55]

Francis Cullen wrote that 'this major engineering work provided the foundation upon which the nineteenth-century port would develop'. He added that 'after 1830 due to moderate funds at the disposal of the port authority engineering work was mostly confined to dredging of the Liffey Quays and the creation of wooden wharves to maintain depth'.[56] In 1834 William Cubitt, engineer at Belfast port, along with William Dargan proposed deepening the quays in Dublin along the North Wall, but while the work was begun it was not completed until 1876.[57]

In 1846 Henry Veredker, the secretary of the Board, wrote to the Tidal Harbour Commission in rebuttal of accusations by a Captain Washington of waste, ineptitude and lack of proper governance in the work of the Corporation. The long response dripped with irony. Veredker did note, however, that 'the Corporation observe, with pleasure, that the Commissioners concur in the unanimous opinion of engineers respecting the many improvements effected by the Corporation in the Harbour of Dublin; and particularly those from the Great North Wall, inasmuch as that work originated with, and was steadily carried on under the control of, the Corporation contrary to the opinion then entertained by engineers employed by the government'.[58]

Results

The North Bull Wall allowed for the continued development of the area and helped to create new port facilities. It further solidified the development of Clontarf as a new suburb away from the city, and it became an attractive Victorian area. It became more active in terms of officialdom, too, with the arrival of lifeboats stationed out here. While the second wall enclosed the harbour, danger remained in certain weather conditions. William Waring and the twelve-man crew of the Clontarf lifeboat were awarded half a guinea each for assistance given to the brigantine *Star of Liverpool*, driven onto the North Bull in a gale on 2 September 1824.[59]

The net result of the North Bull Wall was the enclosure of the harbour. This immediately improved the security situation, which coincided with a reduction of the French threat after Waterloo. The port could now expand its trade in and out, as it clearly did over the following few years.

Fig. 13.5—Clontarf: the Sheds (Irish School, early nineteenth century) (NLI).

Fig. 13.6—Clontarf Road Crescent. (Irish School, early nineteenth century) (NLI).

- In 1803 the tonnage entering the port was 373,790 tons.
- In 1845 the tonnage entering the port was 653,680 tons.
- In 1803 the largest vessel entering was 406 tons.
- In 1846 the largest vessel entering was 1,134 tons.[60]

The deepening of the entrance allowed this larger tonnage to come in, which had a beneficial effect on employment and commercial activity in Dublin, most obviously on the north quays. There also occurred a change in shipping figures in tonnage terms and numbers of ships docking on the north wall now as against the south quay wall. Veredker in 1846 gives the following information: 2,613 vessels docked on the north side, comprising a tonnage of 437,057 tons, while 2,156 docked on the south quay wall, comprising a gross tonnage of 216,663 tons. Docking facilities, too, had been much improved along the quays. There were now a total of fourteen cranes in operation and two shears

THE GREAT NORTH BULL WALL

Fig. 13.7 (top)—Clontarf Island and front at Clontarf, 1812 (photo: Brian Matthews, with the kind permission of the NLI).
Fig. 13.8 (above)—Clontarf, looking west at wooden bridge on Bull Island, by Edward McFarland (courtesy of the NLI).

273

for the use of heavy machinery and steam locomotives, all available free to users.[61]

We should note that the underlying trade into Dublin had not altered in 200 years. Coal was still the predominant commodity imported. Veredker confirms that of the 2,156 ships docking on the south quay wall more than four-fifths were laden with coal. The figures left just 10,000 tons for all other imports, which by this time were dealt with via the Revenue stores east of the Custom House at George's Dock.[62]

By its very nature the Great North Bull Wall moved the harbour out in an easterly and northerly direction and added impetus to the task of upgrading the north Liffey wall and the deepening of the adjacent quays, which allowed the potential of the north side of the port to be realised. The Corporation and the expanding railways were presented with the opportunity to create a vast rail hub on what had been tidal space.

More houses began to be built along the sea front at Clontarf, up along the inland Howth Road and along the Malahide Road. The arrival of the Drogheda Railway and the subsequent spur to Howth would further present Clontarf as an attractive suburban alternative to life in the city. This represented extraordinary growth and expansion, all helping to create a new type of land occupation by a city population (Figs 13.5–13.8).

The result, therefore, of the Great North Bull Wall on the city went beyond the harbour, port, shipping and trade; it closed the gap between the city and the new burgeoning suburbs on the north side of the Liffey. Thanks to improved roads to Howth, passing through the villages of Clontarf, Raheny and Sutton, travel time in and out of Dublin, whether on foot or on horseback, was reduced. The edge of the city had moved a long way from Capel Street Bridge. It is good to be reminded of the vision of the Assembly in their selling of the North Lotts over 100 years earlier, especially as the same Lotts came all the way out to Clontarf, well beyond the original new expanded border of 1728. The North Lotts had originally envisaged going out as far as Castle Avenue, and included 60 Lotts outside the proposed new canal of the Tolka. This was breathtaking ambition in 1717.

North Dublin was now ready for the next great intervention on the tidal space over at Clontarf at the outer fringe of the original North Lotts plan: the Dublin and Drogheda Railway.

Notes

[1] J.M., *Observations on the defects of the port of Dublin in which the former proposals for remedying them are considered, and new and comparatively cheap means of permanent improvement are suggested, addressed to the Rt Hon. and Hon. the Directors of Inland Navigation in Ireland* (Dublin, 1804), pp 23–4.

[2] Pamphlet, *The national importance of a great general harbour for the Irish Sea, accessible at all times to the largest vessels, proposed to be constructed at Douglas, Isle of Man* (1836). NLI P1222 (6).

[3] Pamphlet, *Facts and arguments respecting the great utility of an extensive plan of Inland Navigation in Ireland, with an appendix containing the report of William Jessop Esq., civil engineer, respecting the practicability and expense of making an artificial harbour for large vessels in the bay of Dublin, by a friend of National Industry* (Dublin, 1800), p. 4.

[4] J.M., *Observations*, p. 8.

[5] Ibid., p. 35.

[6] Ibid., p. 8.

[7] Ibid., p. 36.

[8] Thomas Rogers, *Observations on the reports laid before the Rt Hon. and Hon. Directors General of Inland Navigation in Ireland for the improvement of Dublin Harbour* (Dublin, 1805), p. 71. NLI P1134 (16).

[9] Pamphlet, *Considerations on the necessity and importance of an asylum port in the bay of Dublin and remarks on the harbour now erecting at Howth and that which is the object of various petitions proposed for Dunleary, by an ordinary seaman* (Dublin, 1811), p. 16. NLI P653 (5).

[10] Pamphlet, *Concise statement of the Ballast Corporation and the subsequent state of the harbour, an inquiry into the promised*

and probable consequences to the trade and commerce of the proposed railway between Dublin and Kingstown, and an investigation into the project of constructing a ship canal connecting the asylum harbour at Kingstown with a floating dock in the river Anna Liffey (Dublin, 1833), p. 2. NLI P1222 (5).

[11] *Facts and arguments*, p. 21.

[12] William Jessop, appendix to *Facts and arguments*, pp 69–70.

[13] Sir John McNeill, *Report on the present state and proposed improvement of the Grand Canal Company's extensive floating and graving docks at Ringsend* (Dublin, 1846), p. 5. NLI P1222 (6).

[14] Ruth Heard, 'Public works in Ireland, 1800–1831', unpublished MLitt. thesis, Trinity College Dublin (1977), p. 113.

[15] Commissioners of the Ballast Board (1846), nine volumes, contents of Vol. 3, Part 1, Tidal Reports, Part 1, p. 41. Library of the Oireachtas.

[16] Gerald Daly, 'Captain William Bligh in Dublin, 1800–1801', *Dublin Historical Record* **44** (1) (1991), 20–33, pp 20–1.

[17] Ibid., pp 23–4.

[18] Ibid., p. 25.

[19] Ibid., p. 26.

[20] *Facts and arguments*, p. 4.

[21] Daly, 'Bligh in Dublin', p. 23.

[22] Ibid., p. 24.

[23] Ibid., p. 30.

[24] Ibid., p. 32.

[25] Henry Veredker, *Letter to the Tidal Commission from the secretary of the Corporation for Preserving and Improving the Port of Dublin in answer to complaints by Captain Washington* (pamphlet, Dublin, 1846), p. 16.

[26] Ibid., p. 25.

[27] Journal of the proceedings of the Corporation for Preserving and Improving the Port of Dublin, vol. 12 (9 May 1823–25 August 1826), pp 180–1.

[28] Port Ledger (1819), p. 11. Dublin Port Company Archive Vault at Glenbeigh Records Storage, Damastown, Dublin 15.

[29] Ibid., p. 12.

[30] Ibid., p. 47.

[31] Ibid., p. 19.

[32] Ibid., p. 30.

[33] Commissioners for the Ballast Board 1846, 9 vols, contents of Vol. 3, Part 1, Tidal Harbours, Part 1, p. 41a.

[34] Lighthouse journal, 18 March 1819, p. 83. NAI, Four Courts.

[35] Lighthouse journal, 25 March 1819, p. 87.

[36] Lighthouse journal, 17 June 1819, p. 111.

[37] Port Ledger (1824), p. 76.

[38] Journal of the proceedings of the Corporation for Preserving and Improving the Port of Dublin, vol. 11 (3 December 1819–2 May 1823), pp 18–19, 21 January 1820.

[39] Accounts of Dublin Port, commencing 6 January 1813, no. 5, p. 11.

[40] Port Ledger (1824), p. 7.

[41] Journal of the proceedings of the Corporation for Preserving and Improving the Port of Dublin, vol. 11, p. 4.

[42] Journal of the proceedings of the Corporation for Preserving and Improving the Port of Dublin, vol. 11.

[43] Ibid., p. 9.

[44] Ibid., p. 16.

[45] Ibid., pp 18–19.

[46] Ibid., p. 123.

[47] Ibid., p. 116.

[48] Ibid., vol. 12, p. 201.

[49] Ibid., p. 115.

[50] Ibid., vol. 11, p. 103.

[51] 'Dublin Port past, present and future', presented by Captain Michael McKenna MsC, Dublin Port Harbour-master, in the Minerva Room, RDS, on 29 November 2017.

[52] Dillon Cosgrove, *North Dublin: city and environs* (Dublin, 1909), p. 124.

[53] Ibid., p. 125.

[54] Alexander Nimmo, *New piloting directions for St Georges's Channel and the coasts of Ireland* (Dublin, 1832), p. 109.
[55] Noel P. Wilkins, *Alexander Nimmo, master engineer, 1783–1832: public works and civil surveys* (Dublin, 2009), p. 260.
[56] Francis J. Cullen, 'Local government and the management of urban space: a comparative study between Belfast and Dublin 1830–1922', unpublished Ph.D thesis, NUI Maynooth (2005), p. 85.
[57] *Ibid.*, pp 74, 85.
[58] Veredker, *Letter to the Tidal Commission*, p. 3.
[59] Journal of the proceedings of the Corporation for Preserving and Improving the Port of Dublin, vol. 12, p. 228.
[60] Veredker, *Letter to the Tidal Commission*, p. 27.
[61] *Ibid.*, p. 7.
[62] *Ibid.*, p. 5.

14. The Drogheda Railway

Introduction

The last of the great works to be imposed on the space reclaimed from the sea throughout the eighteenth and early nineteenth centuries was the building of the Dublin to Drogheda Railway. It was another essential component in the growth of the north city and a direct consequence of the work of the Corporation since 1711, when the Liffey walls were begun on the north side. Yet again the boundary of the city was moved in an easterly and northerly direction. The massive rail embankment had a large impact on the immediate area it traversed and also helped to fill in development along the suburban section and beyond. From the terminus, a huge man-made island 35ft in height, it ran north for 2km before joining up with land at the same level east of the seaside Howth road at Clontarf. The inland Howth road then became protected and cut off from the sea, making ribbon housing development along it easier, as seen today. The embankment also finally cut the Crescent at Marino off from the sea. While the railway ran for 30-odd miles, it is the intention here to concentrate mainly on the section between Dublin and Malahide (Figs 14.1 and 14.2).

The line took a coastal route to Drogheda, requiring many substantial embankments along the way, especially at the city end between the terminus and Clontarf. It was built over or contained some 75 arches similar to those on the Kingstown line; it crossed the Royal Canal south of the Newcomen Bridge on a new bridge made of iron, and it crossed over the River Tolka on another iron bridge. It finally crossed the seashore at Clontarf via a stone bridge, set at an angle to the road underneath. The bridge contained two arches; the inland one facilitated people, horses and carriages, while the outer one allowed the Tolka to partially drain out in a northerly flow from behind the embankment. The Tolka also drained out along the East Wall road under the railway bridge before joining the bay. The line then at the original Clontarf station crossed the inland Howth road on another iron bridge.

The embankment at the city end consisted of two distinct sections; the first was within the old 1728 walls of Dublin on the north side up to the bank of the Tolka, while the second began after crossing the Tolka and proceeded across the tidal strands and channels inshore of Clontarf Island (located at the entrance to the Port Tunnel). Inside the old walls this embankment created another new inner perimeter. At this stage development was scant on the east side of the rail embankment on the northern side of Newcomen Bridge, with few individual structures, but over on the west side of the North Strand Road substantial development had taken place all the way to Annesley Bridge and across to Ballybough Road. At this stage the Fairview Strand and Richmond Road environs had also filled in. While the large parcel of ground behind the new embankment was not put to use at once, it would only be a matter of time.

What the erection of the embankment did immediately was to protect and foster growth in this area, leading to joining up both Richmond Road and Clonliffe Road with Dorset Street and

Fig. 14.1—Raised embankment using calp limestone (photo: Brian Matthews).

Fig. 14.2—Rail station above ground level in Sheriff Street (photo: Brian Matthews).

the Drumcondra Road as it exited the city, by secluding it from the sea. What had been Mud Island was now absorbed into the occupation of this area at the bottom of Clonliffe Road. This had always been part of the plan, as seen in the original 1717 map of the North Lotts.

The railway brought Clontarf, Killester, Donnycarney, the Malahide road and Raheny—and of course Marino and Fairview—much closer to Dublin. These suburbs now lay within walking distance of town, especially since both the Howth and Malahide roads had been much improved. Within a short time the presence of the Amiens Street terminus created a rail hub to the east; this would shortly develop into marshalling yards, which would in turn foster commerce, trade and increased port activity down in this quarter. Just as the North Circular Road had encouraged building on both sides, so would Victorian cottages and small dwellings begin to appear between the embankment and the North Strand Road. No notice is taken today of this major structure which was the new station, because it is seen by all every day from bus and car. We can only imagine its impact on the eye while it was being built, higher than most dwellings.

The construction of the embankment was far from being an insurmountable task. William Dargan, when in Belfast digging out the channel for shipping, had arranged for the spoil to be dumped nearby, and this became a seventeen-acre island (later a public park and zoo).[1] Construction was also facilitated by the fact that the Black Quarry in Clontarf, at Clontarf Golf Club, was close to the line proposed. The stone was used on the structure and on the Clontarf rail bridge. It was also used by Vernon in the rebuilding of Clontarf Castle in 1835 and on the 'Black Church', St Mary's in Dorset Street. The quarry is to the right-hand side of the rail tracks between Killester and Clontarf stations at the north end of Clontarf Golf Club. The Vernons had been using the quarry for some 200 years at least. After his dispute with the Corporation in the eighteenth century, Vernon erected a series of seven stone cairns on the tidal shore at Clontarf to mark the boundary of his property. The last two still standing are seen near the Yacht public house and near Vernon Avenue.

When the time came to begin the construction of the railway between Dublin and Drogheda in the late 1830s, the thinking about rail transport had changed radically. The Kingstown railway had proved a success in a very short time and so there was more enthusiasm. The railway was completed a full ten years after Kingstown. Much valuable experience in civil engineering had been gained in the interim. The problems which arose south of the river, such as bulging embankments or splitting granite sleepers, had all been solved by the engineers. The conditions, too, had altered because now locomotives were being sourced in Dublin and soon after in Drogheda, as were coaches, thanks to the engineering workshops down in Grand Canal Docks.

Why build a railway between Drogheda and Dublin? Well, Dublin was the capital and Drogheda was a thriving port which at one stage, 100 years or more earlier, could possibly have usurped Dublin's position as the main port on the east coast. Drogheda was also on the main road to Belfast, which had been going through a very similar transformation to Dublin as it expanded. Moreover, much of the trade from all over north Leinster passed out through Drogheda and so it was a natural choice. There was also the issue that the Dublin fish market had grown significantly since the arrival of the Brixham beam trawlers in 1819 to Ringsend, completely changing fishing practices to the benefit of the supply to market. Note, too, that a series of fishing harbours with fleets were located along the proposed line. Lastly, there was a sizeable selection of very wealthy landowners along the route of the proposed railway. Some of these landowners, such as Talbot in Malahide and Hampton in Balbriggan, had a direct influence on the harbour in their area. Now that eyes had been opened by the rampant success of the Kingstown line, those with imagination could see the very real possibilities.

It was also a case that there was capital available and men willing to invest in railways.

Joe Lee wrote that, in the aftermath of the early mania for railway construction, in 1836 the government appointed the Drummond Commission to recommend a system of railways for Ireland. As late as February 1836 the promoters of the Dublin–Drogheda railway still hoped for a State grant of two-thirds of the set-up costs needed, but with so many subscribers it became unnecessary to count on State aid. In April that year they had 5,000 surplus applications for shares.[2] By 1842, however, Charles Vignoles regarded Irish railway development prospects as 'Hopeless for a long time to come' because of the depressed state of the money market.[3] Many of the backers of the Dublin–Drogheda line were from the industrial north of England and were merchants, ship-owners and mill-owners. They subscribed 43% of the capital and Irish investors put in the other 57%.[4] While raising money was not especially easy, there was money in the country. Bank deposits went up from £6,000,000 in 1840 to £10,000,000 twelve years later. This increase in the mid-Famine years shows that not all were merely surviving. Twelve years later the figure had doubled again.[5]

'We conclude therefore by calling the attention of all who are interested in promoting the means of internal communication in this country to the formation of the railways; not merely those which would connect Belfast, Dublin and Enniskillen ... Let landlords and tenants consider with what safety and despatch, and at how small expense, the grain, butter, pork, live cattle and other production of the interior could be conveyed to Belfast, or other seaports such as Dublin or Drogheda, while building materials, manure and other articles for the improvement of the country could be had with equal ease in return.'[6]

P.J. Geraghty wrote that although the railway was commenced on 18 June 1838 it was built substantially during Famine times, which had an effect on its financing and progress. The Dublin–Drogheda line was the brainchild of Drogheda businessman Thomas Brodigan of Piltown, Drogheda, who had written to the *Freeman's Journal* on 17 April 1835 recommending a rail link between the two. Brodigan was no mere enthusiast; he went to England to see the various operations in action. The engineer William Bald was working in Drogheda at the time on the harbour walls and quay improvement. In August 1835 a meeting was held in Dublin to move the project along. An engineer was needed to examine the route and another English engineer, William Cubitt, was appointed. Cubitt arrived in Ireland and went over the ground with surveyors George Woodhouse and Patrick Byrne. He recommended a coastal route which would have a gradient of 1:400 and he estimated costs at £650,000. His report was handed to the promoters on 9 January 1836.[7] The inland route suggested and actively touted by others was dealt with after some squabbling and resorting to parliament. Daniel O'Connell was selected as chairman of the Commons Committee. The coastal route won out in the end. A prospectus for this route was issued and support gained from Manchester business interests.[8] Revisions to plans included the abandonment of the portion of the line between Sackville Street and Amiens Street in Dublin, the lowering of the embankment across Clontarf Strand from 20ft to 6ft in order to avoid local objections, and a diversion of the line closer to the town of Skerries in order to avoid putting in a tunnel at Milverton (a quarry outside Skerries).[9]

Cubitt, who was to be the main witness for the inland route, proved to be something of a liability, as he had to admit that he had allowed embankments which were too steep on the coast road at Antrim and the cuttings had slipped; he had also had a similar problem while working as director of the grand jury between 1809 and 1816 in Mayo, where a bridge had failed in front of witnesses to whom he was making a demonstration. The Committee came out in favour of the coastal route on 30 June[10] and it received royal assent on 13 August 1836. Shortly afterwards, on 10

October 1836, the first meeting of shareholders took place in Northumberland Buildings, Eden Quay, in Dublin.[11] Some landowners were unhappy with the values given for their land by the railway under the original act of parliament and sought more, while the Admiralty still had not given formal consent to the building of the embankment at Clontarf. On top of these niggles, the Malahide Turnpike Trust raised objections to the railway, as it saw loss of revenue for its own operation of the road.[12]

To make things worse, John McNeill, the chief engineer, had a running battle with the Company over the non-payment of his fees, which lasted from February 1837 to the end of 1839. The Company appeared to be strapped for cash, as not all who had pledged money had handed over funds.[13] Cubitt, too, had not been paid, although he was eventually. Because of the uncertainty of the times the Company had problems raising capital, but 1838 brought improved conditions and tenders were sought for a section of line between the Royal Canal and Portmarnock. On 18 June two contracts were awarded to William Weeks of Enniscorthy for £49,830 to build approximately six and a half miles of line.[14] By March 1839 Weeks had been removed for selling stone from the company quarry and pocketing the money.[15]

Construction

'The Commissioners state their conviction founded upon the information thus obtained that the important public objects anticipated from the establishment of railways in Ireland are not to be accomplished by separate isolated lines, but by a well combined and judicious system in which the joint traffic on many places and districts should pass to a great extent over one common line.' This was not just about railways and their impact on the commercial life of Ireland; it was also very much a political statement about governing and control: 'The present condition of the population of Ireland, with a view of the peculiar circumstances which affect it, are next reviewed, and some important facts are added showing the influence of railways in developing resources of a country, and improving the moral and physical state of its inhabitants'. It is necessary to note here that one of the Commissioners was Thomas Drummond, who at the time was very much in charge of running the country from Dublin Castle. It is interesting, too, that while dealing with such new technology, still unknown to a great degree, the Commissioners had the vision to see an Ireland criss-crossed by the myriad tracks of future railways as a physical development but also as a binding agent from the political standpoint.[16]

The bridge over the Royal Canal was designed by John McNeill and involved the use of iron latticework, which became extremely popular as a form of structural building in iron. The span across the canal was 44m, the largest of its type in the world at the time, not exceeded until the Boyne Viaduct in the 1850s.[17]

The chief engineer for the project, John McNeill, was born at Mount Pleasant in Louth in 1793. He was in the Louth Militia in 1811–15. He then aided Alexander Nimmo to carry out a coastal survey of Ireland. Nimmo helped McNeill to get a position with the renowned Thomas Telford, and he became an expert in road-building on the Holyhead Road for the Parliamentary Commissioners. In 1836 he came back to Ireland to work for the Irish Railway Commissioners in surveying and laying out a system in the north of the country. He arrived in Dublin as engineer to the Dublin to Drogheda railway in 1840 and remained there until it opened in 1844. McNeill used George Halpin to prepare whatever calculations or documents were required (the same Halpin who also worked for the Corporation in port activities and on banks and lighthouses; see Chapter 13).

By August Halpin's son, George Junior, was appointed engineer to the Company at £250 per annum—a very good salary, showing the esteem in which the name Halpin was held.[18]

McNeill was also engineer for the Hibernian Steam Coach Company, the first to introduce steam coaches onto Irish roads. In November 1842 McNeill, who had been a serving member of the Institute of Civil Engineers, was appointed the first professor of civil engineering at Trinity College. During his tenure he revised his work on calculating the volume of earthworks, *Tables for facilitating the calculation of earth work in the cuttings and embankments of railways, canals, and other public works* (1846).[19]

The Dublin–Drogheda rail line was recommenced after some delay at Kilbarrack near Sutton in November 1838 after the act of parliament was passed on 2 July 1837. The improved roads to the north from the city were beneficial for the construction of the railway, facilitating the movement of goods, men and supplies, as well as visitors inspecting the works and progress and all others who needed to access the site.

Giving evidence before the Devon Commission in December 1843, Sir John McNeill stated that there were '7,000 to 8,000 men employed by him on building the Dublin to Drogheda railway'. He said that 'the mode of conducting the work was systematic and careful; settlement was made every month with the contractors, and if it was necessary to have work done originally contemplated, plans and estimates were made and it was all contracted for'. The railway was costing £14,000 per mile. The source evidence was taken before Her Majesty's Commission of Enquiry into the state of the law and practice in respect of the occupation of land in Ireland.[20]

Having promised that he would ensure that a resident engineer, who would receive an annual salary of £130, would be on site at all times, McNeill appointed George Hemans in April 1840.[21] He would also employ a master mason, a master carpenter and an overseer for earthwork at a salary of one guinea per week (paid by the Company). He agreed to inspect the works personally and to attend more often if it was deemed necessary, for which he could charge five guineas a day plus his travelling expenses. In addition, he would use some of his own pupils from time to time to work on the engineering aspects and would not bill the Company for their time.

In October 1840, new contractors Messrs Jeffs recommenced work on the line at Hollybrook (Clontarf) and were employing 180 men by November.[22] The contract for the section from Raheny to Malahide was given to William McCormack in February 1841 for £43,000. McNeill's proposal for a metal bridge over the line at Killester was met by objections from the residents of Hollywood Park as well as the Turnpike Trustees. The cast-iron bridge was erected the following September.

As the railway industry grew and expanded, so too did the requirement for expertise in surveying and the building of railways across all sorts of topography, from rivers and canals to roads and bogs, and the building up of embankments in various circumstances. This is precisely what happened in Dublin. The Kingstown to Dublin line was first situated on top of a raised embankment and thereafter was laid on reclaimed land on a causeway out to Kingstown. Over on the north side some ten years later, when the line was designed to go from a new terminus at Amiens Street to Drogheda, the first couple of kilometres became a massive undertaking.

In 1840 Peter Bruff wrote a useful handbook on how to survey land for a railway, *A treatise on engineering fieldwork, comprising the practice of surveying, levelling, laying out works and other field operations connected with engineering*. This work was symptomatic of the time; in most parts of the British Empire the only expertise came from a 'How To' book.

Bruff gives a picture of an emerging new profession as a branch of engineering. He says that surveyors' earnings varied according to the topography and the quantity of detail required to be represented. His own enquiries show a range from 6d. to 1s. per acre, though in some places it may be done for 2d. while very complicated districts might cost 18d. He concludes, however, that 9d. per acre would be considered fair overall in Ireland.[23] The expense of copying plans on the three-chain scale, in the best manner (inclusive of stationery), varies from 1d. to 3d. per acre.

For all the exactitude of surveying, with its precise angles and mathematics, Bruff surprisingly reveals that 'A common practice with many chain surveyors to facilitate their work when employed on railways is to form triangles at the commencement and at intervals on the base line, and do little better than fudge in the intermediate parts or, at least, pay very little attention to the immediate lines of construction, knowing that the errors which accumulate as their work advances will be stopped at the close on each successive triangle, a practice which cannot be too much discountenanced'.[24]

John Quested was another surveyor who added to the textbooks for surveyors with his *A treatise on railway surveying and levelling* (London, 1846).[25] His section on levelling says that it 'may be considered as the act of finding by artificial means such a line from one point to another as, being drawn parallel to the horizon, will define either the rising or falling acclivity or declivity of these parts with regard to each other. Its application to the construction of railroads and canals is all-important, and it is highly essential to the surveyor, but is an operation requiring more care and strict nicety than mathematical skill.'[26] He adds that 'The reason being the spherical form of the earth precludes the possibility of any line being level, there being two levels, the true level and the apparent level'—in other words, what is and what appears to be. Elaborating his argument, he calculates the difference between the two by using the measurement of the circumference of the Earth in inches rather than miles, showing a rate of 63,360 inches per mile. He presents the difference as 7.9981 inches or nearly 8in. per mile.[27] This is the essential figure for surveyors to take into account when working on railways. Quested lists the instruments required for work on railway surveying in the area of levelling: spirit level (these were becoming more refined and accurate all the time), levelling staves, chain and pins, small hand-bill, and a small piece of iron plate 2in. or 3in. square. Of course, the theodolyte was a valuable instrument in general use and it, too, was becoming more accurate as time passed.

Working for the railways was novel to say the least, according to Frank McKenna, who reminded readers that while in 1824 there was no such thing as a railway worker, less than 25 years later (1847) the permanent staff of railway companies across Britain numbered 47,000. No numbers are available for Ireland, but two successful lines with many stations created an entire range of railway employees and suppliers. The new system demanded a new order not seen before. Once the Company became established, three features of employment became requirements: obedience, literacy and punctuality.[28] These new work practices and iron discipline became the new normal, accepted by the men. Railways were not like the docks, where petty thievery was an accepted feature of the work.[29] Men were now employed in a totally different manner: they got a job for life and were employed all year round, not just in the good times or in fine weather.[30] This was an enormous social change for a class of employee used to working per hour or per day. Again, the poor and uneducated could only get employment on the railways as stokers, labourers, line repairmen and that kind of thing. Nevertheless, it was a new type of work, and the Company paid much better wages to its labourers than almost every other industry.

As work proceeded along the route there were some accidents, and here the Company showed a new-found compassion towards workers killed or disabled. Donations were made to local

Fig. 14.3—Rail bridge over the Royal Canal using metal lattice (photo: Brian Matthews).

dispensaries; contributions were made directly to injured parties and to the widows of men killed. The men also contributed to funds for colleagues who had suffered loss, and in consequence a Friendly Society was established for their benefit. While the higher wages on the railway of 12s. per week (as against 6s. for agricultural workers) brought money into each locale, overcrowding and unhygienic conditions in cottages and makeshift cabins risked medical outbreaks.[31]

The Ordnance Survey map of 1837 shows the embankment in progress across the tidal space east of the East Wall at the estuary of the Tolka. It would alter the exiting of the Tolka, from ebbing out over towards Clontarf to down along the East Wall and partially out through the railway bridge at Clontarf.

By 1842 McNeill proposed moving his engineer Hemans to the very crucial Clontarf works, with its bridge, embankment and terminus all demanding extra attention. He replaced Hemans with Mr Power, all to keep tighter control over the works. No doubt he had been influenced by his close working relationship with George Halpin and how he operated on the North and South Walls by having the men on site and by permanent inspection.

McNeill reported to the shareholders in March 1842 that 'Mr McCormick is now working part of the night and in three weeks or a month Messrs Jeffs will also have men employed throughout the whole night; they now have got the deep cutting at Killester in a most excellent state, and so well arranged for the work, that they can employ from 160 to 200 men at the same time on one face and can remove twenty-five wagons by the locomotive power, which he now employs at one run, so I fully expect he will be enabled to make very great progress in this, the heaviest part of the work, in the ensuing six months. Mr McCormick has purchased the timber for the viaduct, to be erected over the Malahide channel, and is now actively employed in making preparations to complete the important work during the summer.'[32]

The first permanent rails were ordered from the Blaina Ironworks on 21 October 1842. McNeill ordered 75-pound rails, which were to prove up to the task. He also developed a new technique for

Fig. 14.4—Malahide Viaduct from Edward McFarland's sketch-book, 1853 (courtesy of the NLI).

laying the rails. The Irish iron foundries also got business. On 2 February 1844 McNeill wrote to the Ringsend Foundry: 'We commence to lay the line from Balbriggan northward and expect to proceed at the rate of two miles a week in that district alone besides three miles a week in other localities. I hope therefore you will not let us be disappointed'. In the same month he reported to the shareholders that 'the timber bridges and viaducts are completed, as are also the metal bridges with the exception of those over the Royal Canal … and the one over Sheriff St., which is to be of cast metal'.[33]

It was at this stage that McNeill began to use a new method of construction. It was quite simply layering or doubling to increase strength in the ironwork of bridge construction. Known as latticework, it can now be seen along the two rail lines north and south of the city. McNeill first used it in 1843 on a light road bridge at Raheny, just north of Clontarf, adjacent to Mount Temple School. The second time was on the bridge across the Royal Canal, only a couple of hundred yards north of the terminus at Amiens Street (Fig. 14.3). This was and is a substantial bridge, with a span of 146ft and weighing 350 tons exclusive of platform. The contract was awarded to Thomas Grendon's foundry and engineering works, established in 1835 on the South Quay, Drogheda, and employing 600–700 workers, making ships, locomotives, weighing machines and all classes of ironworks. They also made wheels and later supplied ready-made sections for bridges. At one stage they built and supplied nine steamships to the Grand Canal Company, one being of 800 tons.[34] The cost of the bridge's erection came to £7,121 11s. 5d. It is interesting that it cost slightly more than the entire Amiens Street terminus. New technology always attracts doubters and this bridge proved no exception. When the chocks were removed and the piles knocked down, however, the bridge remained intact as the first trains came and went. Eleven years later engineers spotted that the supports were suffering damaging stress and a German visitor in 1856 described it as being a serious problem. Intermediary piers were installed under the bridge to spread the load and this took care of the problem.[35]

Further out, the viaduct at Malahide estuary was also causing problems; having been begun in March 1842, it was completed one year later, McCormick being the contractor. The causeway bridge was a major structure, some 534ft long with eleven bays, each 48ft long, the whole being 28ft wide and 20ft high—'A noble piece of work, unrivalled in the annals of modern timber bridges' (Fig. 14.4). On 2 November 1843, however, a severe storm caused major damage to the piles on the northern side, undermining the entire structure, but it was repaired in full, if not to McNeill's complete satisfaction in terms of time spent on repairs.

The railway had a new ally in steam from the end of the first quarter of the nineteenth century. The City of Dublin Steam Packet Company was set up in 1823 and was incorporated by act of parliament in 1833, when the capital was set at £24,000. In 1833 it began life on Burgh Quay, in what is today the corner building opposite the new bridge.[36]

In 1843, as construction progressed on the line, across the Irish Sea John Braithwaite on the Eastern Counties line carried out successful trials of the American Steam Excavator. This machine, powered by a 10hp engine, was the fourth of its type to be made by Carmichael, Fairbanks & Otis and had been used on the Western Railroad (from Worcester, Mass., to Albany, New York). It dug and loaded 500 cubic yards per day, equivalent to the work of 30 men but at half the cost. The bucket on the excavator had a capacity of one and a quarter cubic yards. It is not known whether this technology was known or available to the promoters of the Dublin to Drogheda line, as no mention of it was made in any of the surviving correspondence.

The first locomotives for the line were bought from Sharp and Roberts at £1,500 and £1,510, and they arrived in 1843. The following year another ten engines arrived. In 1845 three engines were bought from the firm of Thomas Grendon & Sons, Drogheda. This was a milestone in engineering and heavy industrial development.

The pressure to finish on schedule was enormous, but McNeill was as good as his word and the line was ready on time. On 18 March 1844 a special train left the Royal Canal with 565 passengers and the band of the 34th Regiment, who entertained the passengers *en route*. At Malahide they got a six-gun salute and at Skerries a twelve-gun salute. At Drogheda the welcome and celebration included a ringing of the bells of St Peter's Church, and the Drogheda Temperance Band played some airs. On the return to Dublin there was a supper held at McNeill's house in Rutland Square. Writing to his friend General Pasley, McNeill said that he expected to have the entire second-line rails laid by the end of May. A further trip was arranged on 4 April 1844 and again on 8 April, when a celebration dinner was hosted at Simcock's Hotel in Drogheda. The engineer, shareholders and directors were now very confident in the line, and so on 12 April the directors invited a select number of dignitaries and leading citizens to sample the delights of this new mode of transport. Present were the lord lieutenant, Lord Talbot of Malahide, Baron Lefroy, G.A. Hamilton MP, James Hamilton, Thomas Brodigan MP, Revd Mr Taylor of Ardgillan demesne, Sir John Burgoyne and the architect William Caldbeck. Groups assembled at various points along the route to cheer and marvel at this unusual sight; flags were flown from vessels and the coastguard fired salutes.[37] Note that at this stage the starting point was not Amiens Street.

At the above-mentioned dinner in Simcock's Hotel to celebrate the coming of the railway, McNeill toasted Daniel O'Connell: 'I should be wanting in my duty if I did not express my sense of what we owe Mr O'Connell, and I am sure the Company would be wanting in gratitude if they did not feel and acknowledge the benefits conferred on them by Mr O'Connell'. Because O'Connell was still very active politically, having held a monster meeting in the Mall, Drogheda, as recently as

Fig. 14.5—Clontarf Viaduct by McFarland, 1853 (courtesy of the NLI).

1843, he did not get to sample the railway until 23 May, when a special run was arranged on a train sensitively named the *Saint Patrick*.[38] It stopped at Raheny and the company alighted to have supper at Edenmore House. On this occasion 1,200 tickets had been sold in advance, which gives some idea of both the popularity and the novelty of the train. Another result of the coming of the railway was that it allowed vast crowds to assemble in various locations, such as for political rallies of the kind hosted by O'Connell.

There was, however, some suspicion of sabotage on the line, just as there had been on the canal, for whatever reason. McNeill alluded to this in February 1844. In the same letter he also mentions the turntable—a large circular device making it possible to turn a locomotive around in the opposite direction. The one at Amiens Street is *in situ* today, right beside the DART line at Connolly Street, just off the platform.[39]

The railway officially opened on 25 May 1844, initially running from Drogheda to Royal Canal—a temporary station until the new terminus at Amiens Street was opened on 29 November 1844. The stations serviced by the trains included Clontarf (Figs 14.5 and 14.6), Raheny, Baldoyle, Portmarnock and Malahide. This was a further boost to the growth of northern suburbia, now aiding the travelling or commuting workers, just as had happened on the south coast of Dublin Bay with the line to Kingstown. At the opening of the railway 'the workmen engaged on the line and their friends' were entertained at a public dinner on a 'magnificent scale'.

The original estimate for the line had been £20,000 per mile, but in the end the work came

Fig. 14.6—Clontarf Viaduct (Brian Matthews).

in at £14,000 per mile, thanks to the gradient change from 1:400 to 1:180 and the alterations in the route facilitated by some landlords, such as Taylor at Ardgillan Castle.[40] The line was well tested by some storms soon after it began operating but the only result was some minor damage to the embankment at Rogerstown Estuary, which was immediately repaired. Water supply for the engines in Dublin came from the Royal Canal, pumped by a hydraulic ram supplied by Mallet & Co.[41] In Balbriggan a viaduct was built with eleven arches, 35ft above ground and spanning 30ft. By March 1845 the company had carried over one and a half million passengers.

Out at Malahide the Company saw an opportunity and opened the Grand Hotel in May 1844. In another effort to exploit commercial opportunities, they carried all livestock free of charge to the Royal Agricultural Society's show in Dublin in 1844. They also allowed the carriage of horses to and from the Lusk and Bellewstown Races. Into the future they would occasionally offer free trips to the public, practising some early marketing and promotion by giving the public a free taste for rail travel (Fig. 14.7).[42] That the benefits and changes brought about by the railway were appreciated can be seen in 'that the special thanks of the society [RDS] be presented to the directors of the Dublin and Drogheda Railway, for the very liberal and kind manner in which they conveyed to the late Cattle Show of the society, animals destined for exhibition there'.[43]

Malahide, according to Thomas Cromwell in 1820, was a bathing village and 'Dublin families holiday here during the bathing season'. It had grown as a small resort thanks to being a small port with an attractive strand not too far from the city. The railway enhanced its attractions, making it easier to connect daily with the city, and the terminus at the city end brought passengers right into the heart of the new north city, further cementing the growth of the whole area.[44] This is confirmed by the establishment of new trades and industries offering new goods and services, such as Sherwood water-closet manufacturers and forcing pumps, located at North Earl Street, demonstrating that houses were being constructed in sufficient numbers out on the north city edges, that there was a market for the products and that an adequate piped water supply existed locally.[45] Nearby, in Potters

Fig. 14.7—View down to Skerries in 1844 (courtesy of the NLI).

Alley off Marlborough Street, was the Irwin Glass manufactory, which advertised the cutting by steam of glass material (also of use to house-builders).

The branch line to Howth was not left long in abeyance. On 24 January 1845 McNeill was instructed to furnish an estimate for a branch line from Kilbarrack to the pier at Howth. It was given royal assent in 1845 and opened for passengers on 30 May 1847, further reinforcing the development of the villages and suburbs out on the northern fringe of Dublin as station halts were added to the line, beginning close to the city at Killester, Raheny, etc. McNeill ran a very tight ship but greed for more profit on the part of contractors was exposed a couple of years later when Jeffs, one of the original contractors, was found to be falsifying the numbers of men employed and to be running the system of payment by token instead of cash, whereby the men so paid could only use the tokens in the overpriced shops operated by the contractors themselves.[46]

The Company was planning further expansion. A meeting was held in the Company offices at 22 Marlborough Street on 6 April to start the project of the branch line to Kells. Two days later a prospectus was issued.[47] Just three years later the Navan line was used by McNeill to provide famine relief for the poor of Meath.[48]

Five years later, in 1852, a pamphleteer presented *Suggestions on the present condition of Ireland and government aid for carrying out an efficient railway system*, writing that the 'remarkable feature of railways is the extent to which they have created trade, and called into existence a hive of industry, and how they have planted thriving towns'.[49] In Dublin, however, the very lack of connection between the different rail lines shows that each company was merely interested in profit; public convenience was a poor second, according to Francis Cullen.[50]

Railways now formed part of everyday life. The sight and sound could not be avoided or ignored in the city, as trains arrived and departed on both sides of the Liffey. The railway benefited towns,

Fig. 14.8—Baldoyle Station, looking towards Dublin in 1844 (courtesy of the NLI).

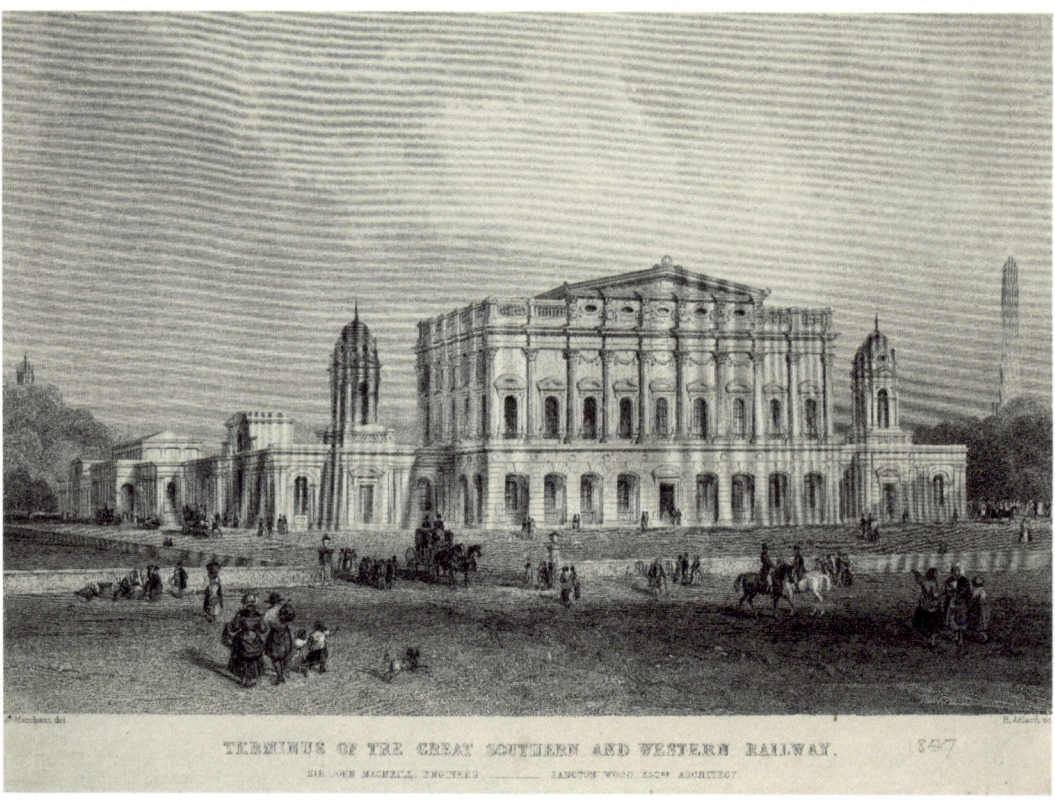

Fig. 14.9—Kingsbridge Station c. 1847 (courtesy of the NLI).

Fig. 14.10—Broadstone Station (courtesy of the NLI).

villages and blossoming new suburbs along its routes and encouraged further development, as can be seen in the immediate effect of the Howth branch line. It created a whole new range of workers and employees—manning the offices, stations and trains, supplying locomotives, rails and carriages, and servicing and maintaining all this new infrastructure (Fig. 14.8).

The city had a new boundary even further east, half a kilometre down from Annesley Bridge over the Tolka. Over at Clontarf the rail embankment was east of the inland Howth Road. The embankment offered protection for Fairview, Marino, the lower Howth Road and the lower Malahide Road, and up the rise in both cases. It pushed Clonliffe Road and Richmond Road even further inland away from the sea, aiding the reclaiming and developing process. This boosted building along both roads. Just 100 years earlier this area had been under the control of both the tides and unruly smugglers and bandits. Now it held Clonliffe College on Clonliffe Road and All Hallows just off the Richmond Road, two very substantial Catholic institutions training men in their hundreds to be priests both at home and as missionaries.

North County Dublin farmers found it easier to supply the Dublin market, and all the fishing harbours along the line from Drogheda to the city now sent in fish to an expanding fish market. The rail line automatically encouraged greater settlement out in Clontarf and Killester. It also helped to fulfil the original desire and vision of the Corporation, with their 1717 plan of the North Lotts. That the railways were a new force to be reckoned with can be deduced by the fact that Charles Bianconi, a shrewd operator, altered his routes in the following few years to use the cross-country roads to feed passengers to railways.[51]

The Drogheda railway cannot be viewed in isolation but rather as part of a momentum of change in transport, in engineering skills and in the design of new types of public buildings. Its immediate effect was the building of both Kingsbridge and Broadstone stations (Figs 14.9–14.11).

Fig. 14.11—Broadstone Station near original harbour and (inset) date badge over main door (photo: Brian Matthews).

These buildings involved the use of masses of cast iron.[52] Now the city had rail constructed at four corners and new termini to serve the public in terms of transport. On top of that, the Midland Rail Company bought the Royal Canal Company, heralding the demise by slow strangulation of the canal through lack of attention and simple maintenance.

The demand for coal continued throughout the middle of the nineteenth century thanks to population growth and industrial demand. Coal was landed all along the Dublin coast, at Balbriggan, Baldoyle, Kingstown, Malahide, Rush and Skerries. When coals were to be discharged at any of these creeks belonging to the port of Dublin, 1s. per ton was deposited with the collector of revenues. Boats named in the instruction book for captains in the manner of charging duty and tariffs on ships included the *Agnes* (110 tons) and the *Betsy* (112 tons), indicating the size of boats in the trade. There were exemptions: Joseph Mundell was excused duty on swearing that coal coming into Dublin was for use in his glass, sugar and salt manufactory.[53]

Conclusions: 1844

The net result of the works carried out in the area from 1711 on the north bank of the Liffey was an expanding Dublin. It grew out from the original medieval town, all the way from one block east of Capel Street Bridge to Annesley Bridge and beyond. The Assembly which arranged the original North Lotts sale would have been satisfied with the scale of the take-up. One indication of the occupation of the space under examination is the fact that a total of 75 arches were required in the construction of the embankment out as far as the Royal Canal forming a viaduct. Many of these, as on the south side and in London, provided storage and garage facilities, stabling for horses and workshops for small industries, many still in use similarly today.[54]

Clontarf, previously a small port, had become a growing suburb of Dublin, 2km outside the new 1728 walls. The sea road at Clontarf was now protected in the Fairview area behind the railway embankment, and landowners were bolstering the coast road piece by piece. The road to Malahide, too, was now protected from the sea, similarly allowing development to creep up along and almost parallel to the inland Howth Road. This brought this entire area within walking distance of the GPO, the accepted epicentre of the city when quoting distances. The town houses previously maintained by the élite became surplus to requirements. The new heart of Dublin on this side was now Sackville Street, with the new bridge across the river, the GPO, Nelson's Pillar and the Gresham Hotel, among so many other hotels in the area. Just twelve months before the opening of the Drogheda Railway the new Arnott's department store opened in Henry Street, its size proving that, despite all the poverty of Victorian Dublin, there was sufficient confidence for such an investment.

Science, too, was making great strides that had an effect across society, such as photography, which by 1844 was no longer an unknown quantity. Steam trains went on to become faster in the next ten years, and steamship technology brought iron ships and iron rigging along with the screw-propellor. Water and gas supplies continued to be rolled out to more consumers. The city became host to the great Victorian desire for knowledge and education, as seen in museums, the art gallery and the botanic gardens. Public transport by carriage, foot and train opened up the city to the urban dweller, with or without money, to avail of time by the sea at Howth, Malahide, Blackrock and Kingstown. Those on foot could avail of Irishtown Merrion Strand for seaside activity, or walk up along the quays to the Phoenix Park to enjoy the green space and view the Wellington Monument. The railways had brought about a new phenomenon of enormous crowds, seen in the numbers gathering for various events. Socially, too, great crowds became almost normal, as seen in the gatherings of Daniel O'Connell, especially the one that had to be cancelled at Clontarf, at which some 300,000 persons were expected.

While change in everyday life might not have been immediately felt by the average Dubliner, information was pouring out onto the city streets about medical breakthroughs such as anaesthesia in 1842, changes in food production and consumption leading to refrigeration, the advent of the tin can, the bicycle and the vulcanising of rubber, which heralded yet another form of transport and a social activity. The invention of the six-shooter would change warfare and create further demands for more mechanised weapons. Steel was invented in Essen by Krupp, with the obvious effect on building seen at its most extreme in the Chicago skyscrapers after the fire. How did the Dubliner know about such things? The newspapers of the time, of which there were plenty, kept him informed. The rotary press added further to printing technology, allowing 10,000 pages to be printed in an hour by 1846.

Dublin was obviously a completely different metropolis in 1844 from what it was in 1708, having grown to at least twice the size. More importantly, new suburbs had grown on both sides of the city, southward along the shore out to Kingstown, and northward to Howth and Malahide, with the villages in between becoming more settled. Growth also occurred in Rathmines, Ranelagh and Rathgar. Clontarf was greatly affected by the railway, as it opened up occupation of the area. By 1845 the Richmond Road locale boasted Richmond Road, Waterfall Avenue, Salisbury Place, Convent Avenue and Richmond Avenue in this space north of the Tolka, between the river and Fairview.[55] Nearby on Ballybough Road were several grocers, vintners and provision dealers. At Ballybough Bridge resided the grocer Butterworth, the builder Conroy and J. & M. Kenny, who operated the chemical works.[56] Michael Byrne now operated the tavern at Dollymount, just north

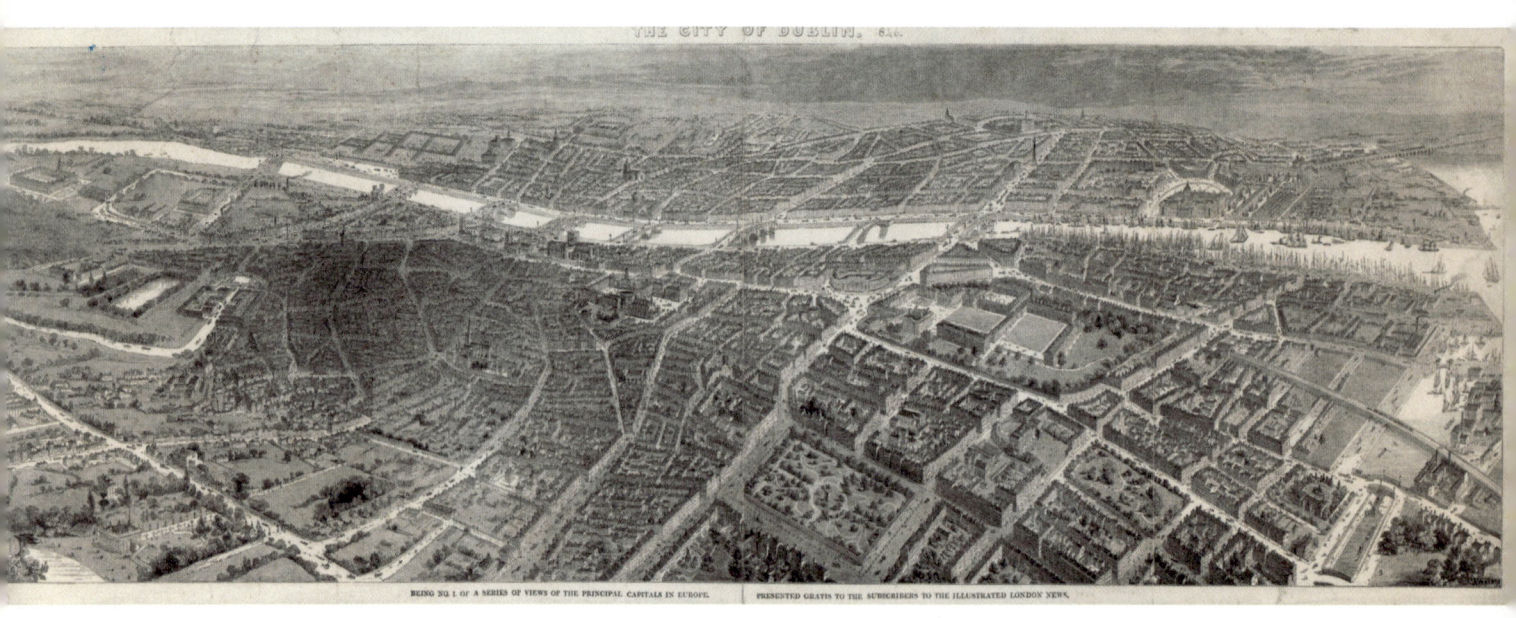

Fig. 14.12—View of city from south-east in 1846, showing scale of change (courtesy of the NGI).

of the recent wooden bridge to the Bull Wall. Very close was the new post office at the Sheds.

The horse remained the primary method of transporting people and goods around the city and suburbs. The 1844 almanac advertised stabling for 80 horses and 40 carriages at 157 Great Britain Street. People moved around either on horse or on foot outside the two rail routes north and south of the city. Momentum continued to build in all aspects of settlement around and outside the core of the city. Savings banks opened at Balbriggan, Castleknock, Blackrock and Clontarf.[57] There were branches in the city at Meath Street, Lurgan Street and Abbey Street. The very existence of such facilities shows that money was being saved and people were using the service to some degree. Likewise, the post office system by now had branches at Baldoyle, Clontarf, Drumcondra, Fairview, Raheny, Malahide, Skerries, Swords, Rush and Santry, a high proportion of them run by women.[58] Institutions such as museums, galleries and the zoo became part of city life.

This story began with Europe just awakening from the brutality of the seventeenth century, and it ends with the arrival of massively improved roads and streets with water and gas beneath them, and with the transition from sail to screw-propeller propulsion. The canals on both sides of the city had been superseded by the railway. Coal had become an even greater import to the city, employing thousands of people in its delivery to the customer. Iron was now an established building material, requiring new skills and employees to provide product. Water was coming into houses not just through taps but also for use in baths and in central heating.

The city now occupied a space measured in extra kilometres (Fig. 14.12). What had once been green fields and tidal flats was filled with houses, schools, churches, railway stations, hospitals, police barracks, seminaries, banks, hotels and post offices, quite apart from every conceivable retail emporium offering goods and services previously unheard-of. It had beyond doubled in size in the period and the original scheme which might have seemed a credible stretch had been mostly achieved in real terms.

It brings us full circle that, having finished the building of the line to Drogheda, the Howth spur and the lines running both south and west from the city, the railway then turned back to the Liffey and the port and began to create the hub and extensive yards adjoining.

Notes

1. Fergus Mulligan, 'William Dargan: an honourable life', *Studies: An Irish Quarterly Review* **104** (413) (2015), 40–50, p. 43.
2. Joe Lee, referring to the *Dublin University Magazine* **14** (1842), pp 36–7.
3. *Ibid.*, p. 39.
4. *Ibid.*, pp 43–4.
5. Lennox Barrow, 'The use of money in mid-nineteenth-century Ireland', *Studies: An Irish Quarterly Review* **59** (233) (1970), 81–8, p. 83.
6. *Ibid.*, p. 84.
7. P.J. Geraghty, 'The Dublin and Drogheda Railway: the first great Irish speculation', *Dublin Historical Record* **66** (1/2) (2013), 83–132, p. 83.
8. *Ibid.*, p. 86.
9. *Ibid.*, p. 87.
10. *Ibid.*, p. 88.
11. *Ibid.*, p. 89.
12. *Ibid.*, p. 90.
13. *Ibid.*, p. 90.
14. *Ibid.*, p. 91.
15. *Ibid.*, p. 93.
16. 'The second report of the Irish Railway Commissioners', *Journal of the Statistical Society of London* **1** (5) (September 1838), 257–77, p. 258.
17. Rob Goodbody, 'Bridges', in A. Carpenter, R. Loeber, H. Campbell, L. Hurley, J. Montague and E. Rowley (eds), *Art and architecture of Ireland, vol. 4. Architecture 1600–2000* (Dublin, 2015), p. 147.
18. Geraghty, 'The Dublin and Drogheda Railway', p. 94.
19. P.J. Geraghty, 'The battle of the Boyne: a Victorian engineering controversy', *Journal of the County Louth Archaeological and Historical Society* **25** (4) (2004), 400–25, pp 400–1.
20. The Devon Commission, Part 1 (Dublin, 1845), pp 85–6.
21. Bernadine Ruddy, 'Mount Temple School, Clontarf', *Dublin Historical Record* **61** (2) (2008), 183–93, p. 96.
22. *Ibid.*
23. Peter Bruff, *A treatise on engineering fieldwork, comprising the practice of surveying, levelling, laying out works and other field operations connected with engineering* (London, 1840), p. 69.
24. *Ibid.*, p. 77.
25. John Quested, *A treatise on railway surveying and levelling* (London, 1846), p. 58.
26. *Ibid.*
27. *Ibid.*, p. 59.
28. Frank McKenna, 'Victorian railway workers', *History Workshop* **1** (1976), pp 26–7.
29. *Ibid.*, p. 29.
30. *Ibid.*, p. 32.
31. Geraghty, 'The Dublin and Drogheda Railway', p. 98.
32. *Ibid.*, p. 105.
33. *Ibid.*, p. 107.
34. Anon., *Journal of the Irish Railway Record Society* **9** (49) (1969), pp 26–7.
35. Geraghty, 'The Dublin and Drogheda Railway', p. 108.
36. Roseanne Dunne, 'No. 25 Fitzwilliam Place', *Dublin Historical Record* **49** (1) (1996), 59–61, p. 60.
37. Geraghty, 'The Dublin and Drogheda Railway', p. 109.
38. *Ibid.*, p. 111.
39. *Ibid.*, p. 110.
40. *Ibid.*, p. 112.
41. *Ibid.*, p. 113.
42. *Ibid.*, p. 116.
43. Proceedings of the Royal Dublin Society, vol. 63 (7 November 1844–26 June 1845), p. 82. RDS.
44. Thomas Cromwell, *The Irish tourist or excursions through Ireland, province of Leinster*, vol. 3 (Dublin, 1820), p. 27.
45. Pettigrew & Oulton's *Dublin Almanack and General Register of Ireland* (1840), advertisement.
46. Geraghty, 'The Dublin and Drogheda Railway', p. 119.
47. *Ibid.*, p. 116.
48. *Ibid.*, p. 117.

[49] C. Locock, *Suggestions on the present condition of Ireland and government aid for carrying out an efficient railway system* (London, 1852), p. 27.
[50] Francis J. Cullen, 'Local government and the management of urban space: a comparative study between Belfast and Dublin 1830–1922', unpublished Ph. D thesis, NUI Maynooth (2005), p. 90.
[51] Ann Mullin Burnham and Kevin Whelan, 'Roads', in R. Loeber, H. Campbell, L. Hurley, J. Montague and E. Rowley (eds), *Art and architecture of Ireland, vol. 4. Architecture 1600–2000* (Dublin, 2015), p. 143.
[52] John P. Clancy and John Montague, 'Railways', in R. Loeber, H. Campbell, L. Hurley, J. Montague and E. Rowley (eds), *Art and architecture of Ireland, vol. 4. Architecture 1600–2000* (Dublin, 2015), p. 160.
[53] Peter Hodgson, *The complete Revenue guide for imports and exports, the whole adapted to the use of merchants, Revenue officers, masters of ships and bankers in the united kingdom of Great Britain and Ireland and its dependencies* (London, 1809), pp 21–2.
[54] Clancy and Montague, 'Railways', p. 161.
[55] *Dublin Almanack* (1845), p. 837.
[56] *Ibid.*, p. 838.
[57] *Ibid.*, p. 509.
[58] *Ibid.*, pp 439–50.

Bibliography

Manuscripts

Anon., 'Diary of a tour in Ireland *c.* 1817'. NLI MS 194.

Anon., 'Notes of a tour in north Wales and Ireland 1788'. TCD MS 891, Rowland Hunt's Travel Journal.

Isaac Butler, 'Itinerary of a journey through the counties of Dublin, Meath and Louth, personal journal'. Armagh Public Library.

Isaac Butler, 'Weather diary 1716–1734', identified by Sam Smyth. No further information available.

Commissioners of the Ballast Board, 1846 (9 vols). Dublin Port Company archive, Damastown, Co. Dublin.

Charles Cosslett, six unpublished diaries (1793–4). Archive of St Malachy's College, Belfast.

Dublin Diocesan Archive, Holy Cross College, Clonliffe Road: Account Book, 1800–1916.

Dublin Diocesan Archive, Holy Cross College, Clonliffe Road: History of Dublin parishes, south city and RC chapels, 1749.

Christine Gordon, 'Miss Gordon's journal of a tour through Ireland, France and England from 1819–1820'. PRONI T2622.

Gormanston Papers, NLI MSS 44,448/1, 44,450/2, 44,450/3.

Grand Canal Company, minute-books of the Court of Directors, vol. 13. NAI.

Charles Grossett, 'Considerations on the silk trade in Ireland 1778, in a letter to John, Earl of Buckingham, Lord Lieutenant, and Governor General'. Royal Irish Academy.

P. Th. Hicks, 'Journal of a tour from Gloucester through Wales and Ireland 1818'. TCD MS 968.

Journal of the proceedings of the Corporation for Preserving and Improving the Port of Dublin, vol. 11 (3 December 1819–2 May 1823) and vol. 12 (9 May 1823–25 August 1826). NAI.

Letters, part of a series of boxes of letters from and to naval dockyards in England concerning all matters pertaining to fit and supply of shipping: ADM 106/879 (18 September 1741), 106/1044 (1747), 106/879 (1754), 106/1216 (24 July 1772). National Archives, Kew, London.

Dr Molyneux, 'Journal of Dr Molyneux'. TCD MS 883/2.

Monck papers, in MSS 26813–269746, Accession no. 1478, Collection List no. 4, Dublin City Council Archive.

'O'Connor's journal through the Kingdom of Ireland'. Irish tour Kilkenny to Dundalk, *c.* May, 1794..TCD MS 2568.

Benjamin Oakley's journal, including descriptions of three tours in Ireland (1819, 1825 and 1827). NLI MS 11,938.

Presentments of Dublin: County of Dublin, extract of presentments at Easter Term, 1815. Royal

Dublin Society Library, Ballsbridge.
Returns for the House of Commons by the Corporation, Dublin Port Accounts 1833–66, no. 5. NLI Ir 382 D5.
Charles Vallancey, letter and map (18 August 1777). NLI MS 13058.
Charles Vallancey, letter and report (18 August 1777). NLI MS 13060.

Maps
Jonathan Barker, Ringsend/Irishtown, 1762. NAI 16G 18 No. 6.
Thomas Bolton, original map, 1717. NAI M/7245.
Edward Cullen, map of Dodder, 1731. NAI 2011/2/8.
J. Cullen, map, 1692. NAI 2011/2/1.
J. Cullen, map, 1706. NAI 2011/2/6.
William Duncan, map of Dublin, 1821. Glucksman Library, TCD.
Thomas Matthews, Dublin survey map, 1778. NLI 16G 38.
Military map, 1815. NLI.
Fredrich Moll, map of Dublin, 1714. Marsh's Library, Dublin.
Arthur Neville, map, 1836. NAI 2011/2/1-36.
Alexander Nimmo, Dublin map, 1823. NLI 16G 33.
Pembroke estate map, NAI 2011/2/1/2.
John Roe, map, 1806. NAI 2011/25.
Sherrard Brassington Gale, map, 1836. NAI 2011/2/1-34.
Thomas Sherrard, survey of Annesley Bridge, 1797. NLI 16G (37).
Samuel Sproule, map, 1780. NAI 2011/2/1.
Gabriel Stokes, map of Dublin, 1725. Dublin Port Archive, Damastown, Dublin 15.
Major Alexander Taylor, Royal Engineers, map of Dublin, 1801–5. Glucksman Library, TCD.
John Taylor, 'Map of Dublin, dedicated to the Lord Lieutenant, the Earl of Whitworth, 1828'. Glucksman Library, TCD.

Pamphlets
A concise statement of the proceedings of the Ballast Corporation and the consequent state of the harbour (Dublin, 1833).
Concise statement of the Ballast Corporation and the subsequent state of the harbour, an inquiry into the promised and probable consequences to the trade and commerce of the proposed railway between Dublin and Kingstown, and an investigation into the project of constructing a ship canal connecting the asylum harbour at Kingstown with a floating dock in the river Anna Liffey (Dublin, 1833). NLI P1222 (5).
Considerations on the necessity and importance of an asylum port in the bay of Dublin and remarks on the harbour now erecting at Howth and that which is the object of various petitions proposed for Dunleary, by an ordinary seaman (Dublin, 1811). NLI P653 (5).
Facts and arguments respecting the great utility of an extensive plan of Inland Navigation in Ireland, with an appendix containing the report of William Jessop Esq., civil engineer, respecting the practicability and expense of making an artificial harbour for large vessels in the bay of Dublin, by a friend of National Industry (Dublin, 1800).
J.M., *Observations on the defects of the port of Dublin in which the former proposals for remedying them are considered, and new and comparatively cheap means of permanent improvement are suggested, addressed to the Rt Hon. and Hon. Directors of Inland Navigation in Ireland* (Dublin, 1804).
John McEvoy, *The gas question in six parts* (October 1872). NLI P1134.

The national importance of a great general harbour for the Irish Sea, accessible at all times to the largest vessels, proposed to be constructed at Douglas, Isle of Man (1836). NLI P1222 (6).

Remarks and observations on the intention of turning the course of the River Dodder in order to show the inexpedience of that measure (Dublin, 1787). (Courtesy of Dr David Dickson of Trinity College.)

Report and chart of Dublin Harbour: proposals upon the improvement of the Harbour of Dublin, made for His Excellency Philip, Earl of Hardwicke, Lord Lieutenant of Ireland (Dublin, 1804).

Peter Talbot, archbishop of Dublin and primate of Ireland, *A treatise of religion and government with reflections upon the cause and cure of England's late distempers and present dangers. Addressed to the Duke of Buckingham* (Dublin, 1670). NLI.

Secondary sources

Andrews, J.H. 2009 *New light on three 18th-century cartographers: Herman Moll, Thomas Moreland and Henry Pratt*. Dublin.

Anon. 1833 Rambles of a discontented gentleman: the bullet gatherers. *Irish Monthly Magazine, politics and literature* **2** (19) (May–December 1833), 417–20. Dublin. NLI.

Anon. 1961 *St Saviour's Church, Dublin, 1861–1961* (centenary book, generously lent to the author by Fr Crotty, acting prior).

Appleby, J.C. 1998 The defence of Ireland: a naval journal of 1627. *Analecta Hibernica* **37**, 237–48.

Archer, Lt. J. 1801 *Statistical survey of the County Dublin, with observations on the means of improvement, drawn up for the consideration and by order of the Dublin Society*. Dublin.

Baldwin, M. 1980 Review of *William Jessop, engineer* by Charles Hadfield and A.W. Skempton (London, 1979). *Technology and Culture* **21** (2), 246–50.

Barlow, P. 1817 *An essay on the stress and strength of timber of the Royal Military Academy founded on experiment*. London.

Barrie, D. 2014 *Sextant: a voyage guided by the stars and the men who mapped the world*. London.

Barrow, J. 1836 *A tour around Ireland through the sea counties in the autumn of 1835*. London.

Barrow, L. 1970 The use of money in mid-nineteenth-century Ireland. *Studies: An Irish Quarterly Review* **59** (233), 81–8.

Barrow, V. 1975 Dublin Custom House—the river heads. *Dublin Historical Record* **29** (1), 24–7.

Bigelow, A. 1821 *Leaves from a journal: Bigelow's sketches of rambles in some parts of north Britain and Ireland chiefly in the year 1817*. Boston.

Binns, J. 1837 *The miseries and beauties of Ireland* (2 vols). London.

Boxall, J. 1849 Raids on the Saltee Islands by French privateers: the petition of John Boxall. *The Wexford Independent*, 18 August 1849.

Brady, J. and Simms, A. (eds) 2001 *Dublin through space and time*. Dublin.

Brady, K., Moore, F. and Condit, T. 2007 Newhaven: a forgotten harbour in Fingal. *Archaeology Ireland* **21** (4), 8–11.

Briggs, A. 1961 Cholera and society in the nineteenth century. *Past and Present* **19**, 76–96.

Burke, N. 1972 Dublin 1600–1800: a study in morphogenesis. Unpublished Ph.D thesis, Trinity College Dublin.

Burnham, A.M. and Whelan, K. 2015 Roads. In R. Loeber, H. Campbell, L. Hurley, J. Montague and E. Rowley (eds), *Art and architecture of Ireland, vol. 4. Architecture 1600–2000*, 142–4. Dublin.

Cahalane, P. 1916 Social conditions in Ireland during the Napoleonic Wars. *Studies: An Irish Quarterly Review* **5** (18), 2010–25.

Campbell, T. 1777 *A philosophical survey of the south of Ireland in a series of letters to John Watkinson,*

MD. London.

Carlyle, T. 1882 *Reminiscences of my Irish journey in 1849*. New York.

Carr, J. 1806 *The stranger in Ireland; or a tour in the southern and western parts of that country in the year 1805*. London.

Carroll, J. 2014 7 Church Avenue, Irishtown. *Excavations.ie*, site no. 2014:060.

Carter, N.H. 1829 *Letters from Europe, comprising the journal of a tour through Ireland, England, Scotland, Italy and Switzerland in the years 1825, '26 and '27*. New York.

Cheer, K. 2008 Maritime trade in the eighteenth century: a study in patterns of trade, market structures and merchant communities. Unpublished MA thesis, University of Wellington, New Zealand.

Chetwood, W.R. 1766 *A tour through Ireland in several entertaining letters, wherein the present state of that kingdom is considered; and the most noted cities, towns, seats, rivers, buildings &c. are described; interspersed with observations on the manners, customs, antiquities, curiosities and natural history of that country; to which is prefixed a description of the road from London to Holy-Head*. Dublin.

Clancy, C. 1990 Gardiner St. employment exchange: the historical background and development. *Dublin Historical Record* **43** (1), 47–51.

Clancy, J.P. and Montague, J. 2015 Railways. In R. Loeber, H. Campbell, L. Hurley, J. Montague and E. Rowley (eds), *Art and architecture of Ireland, vol. 4. Architecture 1600–2000*, 159–62. Dublin.

Clarke, D.E. 1793 *A tour through the south of England, Wales and part of Ireland made during the summer of 1791*. London.

Clarke, P. 1992 *The Royal Canal: the complete story*. Dublin.

Clarke, P. 1993 The Royal Canal 1789–1791. *Dublin Historical Record* **46** (1), 46–52.

Collins, G. 1693 *Great Britain coasting pilot, being a new and exact survey of the sea coast of England 1693*. London.

Collins, J. 1913 *Life in old Dublin*. Dublin.

Comerford, P. 2014 Thorncastle Street Ringsend through the ages. *Dublin Historical Record* **67** (1), 29–41.

Cooney, D.L. 2011 Dinner in Sandymount. *Dublin Historical Record* **64** (2), 192–3.

Corcoran, M. 2015 Water, sanitation and electricity. In R. Loeber, H. Campbell, L. Hurley, J. Montague and E. Rowley (eds), *Art and architecture of Ireland, vol. 4. Architecture 1600–2000*, 164–6. Dublin.

Corry, G. 1969–70 The Dublin bar—the obstacle to the improvement of the Port of Dublin. *Dublin Historical Record* **23** (4), 137–52.

Cosgrove, D. 1904 Clonliffe. *Journal of the Royal Society of Antiquaries of Ireland* (5th ser.) **14**, 361–4.

Cosgrove, D. 1909 *North Dublin: city and environs*. Dublin.

Costello, V. 2007 Public spaces for recreation in Dublin 1660–1760. *Garden History* **35** (2), 160–79.

Craig, M. 1980 *Dublin 1660–1860*. Dublin.

Cromwell, T. 1820 *The Irish tourist or excursions through Ireland, province of Leinster*, vol. 3. Dublin.

Crossman, V. 2018 The growth of the state in nineteenth-century Ireland. In J. Kelly (ed.), *The Cambridge History of Ireland. Vol. 3: Ireland c. 1730–c. 1880*, 542–66. Cambridge.

Cullen, F.J. 2005 Local government and the management of urban space: a comparative study between Belfast and Dublin 1830–1922. Unpublished Ph.D thesis, NUI Maynooth.

Cullen, L.M. 1971 *Merchants, ships and trade, 1660–1830*. Dublin.

Cullen, L.M. 1972 *An economic history of Ireland since 1660*. Dublin.

Cullen, L.M. 1983 *Princes and pirates: the Dublin chamber of commerce 1783–1983*. Dublin.
Culliton, J. 1967 The Four Courts, Dublin. *Dublin Historical Record* **21** (4), 116–26, 131.
Cuming, G.F. 1921 James Gandon: his work in Ireland. *The Irish Monthly* **49** (578), 319–23.
Cunningham, J. 2011 *Conquest and land in Ireland: the 1641–1680 transplantation to Connaught*. Suffolk.
Daly, G.J. 1991 Captain William Bligh in Dublin, 1800–1801. *Dublin Historical Record* **44** (1), 20–33.
Daly, J.F. 1957 O'Connell Bridge and its environs. *Dublin Historical Record* **14** (3), 85–93.
D'Arcy, F. 1992 The Kingstown Races. *Dublin Historical Record* **45** (1), 55–64.
Dawson, J. 1819 *Canal extensions in Ireland recommended to the imperial legislature*. Dublin.
Dawson, T. 1973 Crane Lane to Ballybough. *Dublin Historical Record* **27** (4), 131–45.
Dawson, T. 1976 The road to Howth. *Dublin Historical Record* **29** (4), 122–32.
Dawson, W. 1805 *Plan for a complete harbour at Howth town for the use of His Majesty's packet boats; merchant ships, in case of storm; and fishing vessels to supply Dublin market*. Dublin. NLI JP 1486.
De Courcy, J.W. 1990 A bridge in its time: the River Liffey crossing at Church Street in Dublin. *Proceedings of the Royal Irish Academy* **90**C, 243–57.
De Courcy, J.W. 1996 *The Liffey in Dublin*. Dublin.
de Latocnaye, Chevalier 1984 *A Frenchman's walk through Ireland 1796–7, translated from the French of de Latocnaye by John Stevenson, 1917; with an introduction by John A. Gamble*. Belfast.
Deane, S. 2011 Montalembert letter on Catholicism in Ireland. *Field Day Review* **7**, 250–71.
Delany, R. 1986 *Ireland's inland waterways*. Belfast.
Dickson, D. 2000 *New foundations: Ireland 1660–1800*. Dublin.
Dickson, D. 2014 *Dublin: the making of a capital city*. London.
Dixon, F.E. 1953 Weather in old Dublin. *Dublin Historical Record* **13** (3–4), 94–107.
Doherty, N. 2006 *The complete list of the streets of Dublin*. Dublin.
Donnelly, N. (n.d.) *A short history of some Dublin parishes, Ringsend/Irishtown*. Dublin.
Dowling, N. 2002 *Mud Island: a history of Ballybough*. Dublin.
Duffy, P.J. 2007 *Exploring the history and heritage of Irish landscapes*. Dublin.
Dunne, J.T. 1990 The first Irish railway, by shriek and smoke to Kingstown. *Dublin Historical Record* **43** (1), 44–6.
Dunton, J. (ed. A. Carpenter) 2003 *Teague land; or A merry ramble to the wild Irish (1698)*. Dublin.
Dupin, Baron C. 1825 *The commercial power of Great Britain: a complete view of the public works of this country, streets, roads, canals, aqueducts, bridges, coasts, and maritime ports*. London.
Dutton, H. 1802 *Observations on Mr Archer's statistical survey of the county of Dublin*. Dublin.
Edwards, D. 2004 The construction of Dún Laoghaire harbour. *Dublin Historical Record* **57** (2), 204–10.
Egan, R. 2014 Denzeille St. Unpublished MA thesis, St Patrick's College, DCU.
Ellison, C.C. 1987 *The hopeful traveller: the life and times of Daniel Augustus Beaufort LLD, 1790–1821*. Kilkenny.
Elstob, M. 1779 *A trip to Kilkenny from Durham by way of Whitehaven and Dublin in the year 1776*. Dublin.
Evans, Revd J. 1812 Petition of the Protestants of Ireland in favour of Catholic Emancipation. *Belfast Monthly Magazine* **8** (45), 323–6.
Falkiner, C.L. (ed.) 1904 *Illustrations of Irish history and topography, mainly of the seventeenth century*. London.
Falkiner, C.L. 1909 *Essays relating to Ireland, biographical, historical and topographical, with a memoir of*

the author by Edward Dowden. London.

Falkus, M.E. 1982 The early development of the British gas industry, 1790–1815. *Economic History Review* (2nd ser.) **35** (2), 217–34.

Farmer, T. 2004 *Patients, potions and physicians: a social history of medicine in Ireland*. Dublin.

Fenning, H. 1988 A list of Dominicans in Ireland in 1832. *Collectanea Hibernica* **29**, 120.

Fenning, H. 2003 The cholera epidemic in Ireland, 1832–3: priests, ministers, doctors. *Archivium Hibernicum* **57**, 77–125.

Ferrar, J. 1807 *A view of ancient and modern Dublin*. Dublin.

Fisher, C.A. 1941 Evolution of an Irish railway system. *Economic Geography* **17** (3), 262–74.

Fitzpatrick, B. 1985 The municipal corporation of Dublin 1603–1640. Unpublished Ph.D thesis, Trinity College Dublin.

Fleetwood, J.F. 1983 *The history of medicine in Ireland*. Dublin.

Flood, D.T. 1978 Dublin Bay in the eighteenth century. *Dublin Historical Record* **31** (4), 129–41.

Gamble, J. 1818 *Sketches of history, politics and manners, taken in Dublin, and the north of Ireland*. London.

Gandon, J. 1846 *The life of James Gandon*. London.

Gaunt, Captain J. 1665 *Natural and political observations mentioned in the following index and made upon the Bills of Mortality*. London.

Geraghty, P.J. 2013 The Dublin and Drogheda Railway: the first great Irish speculation. *Dublin Historical Record* **66** (1/2), 83–132.

Geraghty, P.J. 2004 The battle of the Boyne: a Victorian engineering controversy. *Journal of the County Louth Archaeological and Historical Society* **25** (4), 400–25.

Giacometti, A. 2009 Pigeon House Fort, Ringsend, Dublin. *Excavations.ie*, site no. 2009:357.

Gibney, F. 1956 A civic achievement: Dublin 1760–1800. *Dublin Historical Record* **15** (1), 1–10.

Gilbert, J.T. et al. (eds) 1889–98 *Calendar of ancient records of Dublin, in the possession of the Municipal Corporation of that city* (19 vols). Dublin.

Gilligan, H. 1988 *A history of the port of Dublin*. Dublin.

Goggin, B.J. 2014 *The Royal under the railway: Ireland's Royal Canal 1830–1899*. Derby.

Goodbody, R. 2015 Bridges. In A. Carpenter, R. Loeber, H. Campbell, L. Hurley, J. Montague and E. Rowley (eds), *Art and architecture of Ireland, vol. 4. Architecture 1600–2000*, 145–8. Dublin.

Gough, J. 1818 *Account of two journeys southward in Ireland in 1817 … intended as a support to 'A tour in Ireland by an Englishman' lately published by John Gough*. Dublin.

Greer, D. and Nicholson, J. 2003 *The Factory Acts in Ireland 1802–1914*. Dublin.

Grimes, B. 2015 Patrons and architects and the creation of Roman Catholic church architecture in nineteenth-century Dublin. *Dublin Historical Record* **61** (1), 6–20.

Hall, Revd J. 1813 *Tour through Ireland, particularly the interior and least known parts, containing an accurate view of the parties, politics and improvements, in two volumes*, vol. 1. London.

Halliday, C. 1881 *The Scandinavian kingdom of Dublin*. Dublin.

Hammond, J.W. 1942–3 George's Quay and Rogerson's Quay in the eighteenth century. *Dublin Historical Record* **5** (2), 41–54.

Hardy, F. 1810 *Memoirs of the political and private life of James Caulfield, Earl of Charlemont*. Dublin.

Hardy, P.D. 1834 The Dublin and Kingstown Railway. *Dublin Penny Journal* **3** (113) (30 August 1834), 65–8.

Hartnell, Mr 1845 *Instructions for the housekeeper of the Custom House at Dublin*. Dublin. NLI 3A 5935.

Heard, R. 1977 Public works in Ireland, 1800–1831. Unpublished MLitt. thesis, Trinity College Dublin.

Hempton, D.N. 1980 The Methodist crusade in Ireland 1795–1845. *Irish Historical Studies* **22** (85), 3–48.

Hiney, D.J. 1997 5618 and all that: the Jewish cemetery, Fairview Strand. *Dublin Historical Record* **50** (2), 119–29.

Hitt, T. 1760 *A treatise of husbandry on the improvement of dry and barren lands*. Dublin.

Hoare, Sir R. 1807 *Journal of a tour in Ireland AD 1806*. London.

Hodgson, P. 1809 *The complete Revenue guide for imports and exports, the whole adapted to the use of merchants, Revenue officers, masters of ships and bankers in the united kingdom of Great Britain and Ireland and its dependencies*. London.

Horner, A. 2013 Dún Laoghaire's great harbour. *History Ireland* **21** (5), 24–7.

Hurley, L. and McKeown, J. 2015 Canals and inland navigation. In A. Carpenter, R. Loeber, H. Campbell, L. Hurley, J. Montague and E. Rowley (eds), *Art and architecture of Ireland, vol. 4. Architecture 1600–2000*, 148–50. Dublin.

Hurley, M.J. 2006 Baldoyle as a racecourse village. *Dublin Historical Record* **59** (1), 65–80.

Hutchison, K. 1985 The Royal Society and the foundation of the British gas industry. *Notes and Records of the Royal Society of London* **39** (2), 245–70.

Inglis, H.D. 1834 *Ireland in 1834: a journey throughout Ireland during the summer and autumn by Henry D. Inglis* (2 vols). London.

Johnston, T.J., Robinson, J.L. and Wyse Jackson, R. 1953 *A history of the Church of Ireland*. Dublin.

Jordan, T.E. 2008 Quality of life in seventeenth-century Dublin. *Dublin Historical Record* **61** (2), 136–54.

Joyce, St J.W. 1912 *The neighbourhood of Dublin, its topography, antiquities and historical associations*. Dublin.

Katsula, S. 2011 Conciliation, anti-Orange politics and the sectarian scare: Dublin politics of the early 1820s. *Dublin Historical Record* **64** (2), 142–59.

Kelleher Khan, H. 2011 Objects of raging detestation: the Charter schools. *History Ireland* **19** (2), 24–7.

Kemp, P. (ed.) 1976 *The Oxford companion to ships and the sea*. Oxford.

Kennedy, M. 2010 Dublin's coffee houses of the eighteenth century. *Dublin Historical Record* **63** (1), 29–38.

Kennedy, M. and Hardiman, P.N. (eds) 2000 *A directory of Dublin for 1738: compiled from the most authentic sources*. Dublin.

Keogh, D. 2006 Review of *The bible war in Ireland: the Second Reformation and the polarisation of Protestant–Catholic relations in Ireland 1800–1840* by Irene Whelan. *Irish Historical Studies* **35** (138), 251–2.

Kinahan, G.H. and McHenry, A. 1882 *A handy book on the reclamation of waste lands, Ireland*. Dublin.

King, P. 2005 The production and consumption of bar iron in early modern England and Wales. *Economic History Review* (new ser.) **58** (1), 1–33.

Klieneberger, H.R. 1960 Ireland through German eyes 1844–1957: the travel-diaries of Jakob Venedey and Heinrich Böll. *Studies: An Irish Quarterly Review* **49** (196), 373–88.

Leadbetter, G.T. 2010 *Privilege and poverty: the life and times of Irish painter and naturalist Alexander Williams*. Cork.

Leany, E. 2006 Vested interests: science and medicine in nineteenth-century Ireland. *Field Day*

Review **2**, 284–93.

Lennon, C. and Montague, J. 2008 *John Rocque's Dublin: a guide to the Georgian city*. Dublin.

Levistone Cooney, Revd D.A. 2003 Methodist schools in Dublin. *Dublin Historical Record* **56** (1), 41–52.

Levistone Cooney, Revd D.A. 2004 The Methodist chapels in Dublin. *Dublin Historical Record* **57** (2), 152–63.

Lewis, R. 1787 *The Dublin guide: a description of the city of Dublin, 1787*. Dublin.

Loeber, R. and Stouthamer-Loeber, M. (eds) 2002 Dublin and its vicinity in 1797. *Irish Geography* **35** (2), 133–55.

Long, M. and Murphy, B., *Difficulty with ground anchorages in hard rock in Dublin* (http:dx.doi.org/10.1023/A:1023584813392; acccessed 4 January 2016).

Lowth, C.F. 2000 Thomas Steele, patriot extraordinary. *Dublin Historical Record* **53** (2), 92–118.

Luckombe, P. 1780 *A tour through Ireland, wherein the present state of that kingdom is considered*. London.

Luckombe, P. 1788 *The compleat Irish traveller, containing a general description of the most noted cities, towns, seats, buildings, loughs &c. in the kingdom of Ireland, interspersed with observations on the manners, customs, antiquities, curiosities and natural history of that country*. London.

Lynch, P. 1977 A Dublin street—North Great George's Street. *Dublin Historical Record* **31** (1), 14–21.

Lyons, G. 2015 *Steaming to Kingstown and sucking up to Dalkey: the story of the Dublin and Kingstown railway*. Dublin.

McAdam, J.L. 1823 *Remarks on the present system of road making*. London.

McAuliffe, T.J. 1997 A study of travel writing in early Victorian Ireland. Unpublished MA thesis, NUI Galway.

McCabe, C. 1992 History of the town gas industry in Ireland 1823–1980. *Dublin Historical Record* **45** (1), 28–40.

McCullough, N. 1989 *Dublin: an urban history*. Dublin.

McGeery, L. 2004 *Medicine and chemistry in Ireland*. Dublin.

McHugh, N. 1998 *Drogheda before the Famine: urban poverty in the shadow of privilege, 1826–1845*. Dublin.

McKenna, F. 1976 Victorian railway workers. *History Workshop* **1**, 26–73.

McNamara, J. 2012 A case for the conservation of the graving dock. Unpublished MPhil. thesis, Trinity College Dublin.

McNeill, D.B. 1971 *Irish passenger steamship services, vol. 2: south of Ireland*. Devon.

McNeill, Sir J. 1846 *Report on the present state and proposed improvement of the Grand Canal Company's extensive floating and graving docks at Ringsend*. Dublin. NLI P1222 (6).

McParland, E. 1980 The early history of James Gandon's Four Courts. *The Burlington Magazine* **122** (932), 727–33, 735.

McQuade, M. 2010 George's Quay to Sir John Rogerson's Quay. *Excavations.ie*, site no. 2010:263.

McRedmond, L. 1991 *To the greater glory: a history of the Irish Jesuits*. Dublin.

Malcolm, E. and Jones, G. (eds) 1999 *Medicine, disease and the State in Ireland 1650–1940*. Cork.

Marchant, T.R. and Sevastopulo, G.D. 1980 The calp of the Dublin district. *Irish Journal of Earth Sciences* **3** (2), 195–203.

Marmion, A. 1856 *Marmion's history of the maritime ports of Ireland*. London.

Marsh, P. 2015 *The exploration of rail travel*. London.

Martin, J.H. 1973 Aspects of the social geography of Dublin city in the mid-nineteenth century. Unpublished MA thesis, University College Dublin.
Maxwell, C. 1954 *The stranger in Ireland, from the reign of Elizabeth to the Great Famine*. London.
Maxwell, C. 1994 *Dublin under the Georges*. London.
Meyler, Revd W. 1859 *Letter to the people of the parish of St Andrew*. Dublin.
Moody, T.W. and Vaughan, M.E. (eds) 1986 *A new history of Ireland, vol. iv: eighteenth-century Ireland 1691–1800*. Oxford.
Moore, D.F. 1961 The port of Dublin. *Dublin Historical Record* **16** (4), 131–43.
Moore, T. 1853 *Memoirs, journal and correspondence of Thomas Moore*, vol. 1. London.
Moorhouse, G. 2005 *Great Harry's navy: how Henry VIII gave England sea power*. London.
Morrissey, T.J. 2018 *The life and times of Daniel Murray, esteemed archbishop of Dublin 1823–1852*. Dublin.
Muendal, J. 1995 Review of *Power from wind: a history of windmill technology* by Richard L. Hills. *Technology and Culture* **36** (3), 692–4.
Mukerji, C. 2006 Tacit knowledge and classical technique in seventeenth-century France: hydraulic cement as a living practice among masons and military engineers. *Technology and Culture* **47** (4), 713–33.
Mulligan, F. 2015 William Dargan: an honourable life. *Studies: An Irish Quarterly Review* **104** (413), 40–50.
Mullin, A. and Whelan, K. 2015 Roads. In A. Carpenter, R. Loeber, H. Campbell, L. Hurley, J. Montague and E. Rowley (eds), *Art and architecture of Ireland, vol. 4. Architecture 1600–2000*, 142–4. Dublin.
Murphy, E. 2010 Atrocities at sea and the treatment of prisoners of war by the Parliamentary navy in Ireland 1641–1649. *Historical Journal* **53** (1), 21–37.
Murphy, J.H. 2003 *Ireland: a social, cultural and literary history, 1791–1891*. Dublin.
Murray, A. 1903 *A history of the commercial relations between England and Ireland from the period of the Restoration*. London.
Murray, K. 1938 Dublin's first railway. Part I—from the inception to the opening. *Dublin Historical Record* **1** (1), 19–26.
Murray, K. 1938 Dublin's first railway. Part II—the line in operation. *Dublin Historical Record* **1** (2), 33–40.
N.O.P.B. 1833 The Pidgeon House: a story of the last century. *Dublin Penny Journal* **2** (65) (28 September 1833), 99–101.
Neville, P. 1853 *Report to the lord mayor of the city of Dublin on the sewerage of the city and the general state of public works*. Dublin.
Ní Mhurchadha, M. 1999 *The customs and excise of Fingal 1684–1765*. Dublin.
Nicholas, S.J. and Nicholas, J.M. 1992 Male literacy, 'deskilling' and the Industrial Revolution. *Journal of Interdisciplinary History* **23** (1), 1–18.
Nimmo, A. 1825 *On the application of the science of geology to the practice of practical navigation*. Dublin.
Nimmo, A. 1832 *New piloting directions for St Georges's Channel and the coasts of Ireland*. Dublin.
Noel, B.W. 1837 *Notes of a short tour through the midland counties of Ireland in the summer of 1836, with observations on the condition of the peasantry*. London.
O'Boyle, A. 2001 Aldeborough House. *Irish Architectural and Decorative Studies: the journal of the Irish Georgian Society* **4**, 102–41.
O'Brien, A. 2007 The history of Nelson's Pillar. *Dublin Historical Record* **60** (1), 15–23.

O'Brien, G. and O'Kane, F. (eds) 2012 *Portraits of the city: Dublin and the wider world*. Dublin.
Ó Cionnaith, F. 2012 *Mapping, measurement and metropolis: how land surveyors changed eighteenth-century Dublin*. Dublin.
Ó Cionnaith, F. 2015 *Exercise of authority: surveyor Thomas Owen and the paving, cleansing and lighting of Georgian Dublin*. Dublin.
O'Donnell, E.E. 1999 *The Jesuits in Dublin*. Dublin.
O'Donoghue, P. 1972 Opposition to tithe payment in 1832–3. *Studia Hibernica* **12**, 77–108.
O'Flaherty, L. 2007 Drumcondra and the Tolka River. *Dublin Historical Record* **60** (1), 3–14.
O'Flaherty, L. 2011 The Tolka River. *Dublin Historical Record* **64** (2), 226–36.
O'Grada, C. 1991 Dublin demography in the early nineteenth century: evidence from the Rotunda. *Population Studies* **45** (1), 43–54.
Ó Gráda, D. 2015 *Georgian Dublin: the forces that shaped the city*. Cork.
O'K., F. 1939 John Rocque on Dublin and Dubliners, 1756. *Dublin Historical Record* **1** (4), 127–8.
O'Kelly, P. 1921 Road transport before the coming of the railways. Unpublished Ph.D thesis, London School of Economics.
O'Mahony, C. 1990 Iron rails and harbour walls: James Barton of Farndreg. *Journal of the County Louth Archaeological and Historical Society* **22** (2), 134–49.
O'Neill, T. 1973 Fever and public health in pre-famine Ireland. *Journal of the Royal Society of Antiquaries of Ireland* **103**, 1–34.
O'Neill, T. 1987 *Merchants and mariners in medieval Ireland*. Suffolk.
O'Shea, S. and McManus, R. 2012 Upper Buckingham Street: a microcosm of Dublin, 1788–2012. *Studia Hibernica* **38**, 141–80.
O'Sullivan, M. and Downey, L. 2012 Martello and signal towers. *Archaeology Ireland* **26** (2), 46–9.
Old Dublin Society 2008 Letters of John Rennie, and John Rennie Jnr, engineers on the building of Howth Harbour. *Dublin Historical Record* **61** (1), 2–4.
Otway, C. 1839 *A tour in Connaught*. London.
Page, Sir T. Hyde 1801 *Reports relative to Dublin Harbour and adjacent coasts made in consequence of orders from the Marquis Cornwallis, Lord Lieutenant of Ireland, in the year 1800*. NLI P 1077(19).
Park, T. 1808 *The Harleian miscellany: a collection of scarce, curious and entertaining pamphlets and tracts*. London.
Perry, Commander W. 1721 *An account of the stopping of the Dagenham Breach: with the accidents that have attended the same from the first undertaking, containing also proper rules for performing and the like work: and proposed for rendering the ports of Dover and Dublin (which the author has been employed to survey) commodious for entertaining large ships*. London.
Petty, Sir W. 1687 *Five essays in political arithmetic: an estimate of the people in London, Paris, Amsterdam, Venice, Rome, Dublin, Bristol and Rouen, with several observations upon the same, IV*. London.
Phillips, H. 1939 Early history of the Grand Canal. *Dublin Historical Record* **1** (4), 108–19.
Plumtre, A. 1817 *Narrative of a residence in Ireland during the summer of 1814 and that of 1815*. London.
Pool, R. and Cash, J. 1780 *Views of Dublin*. Dublin.
Price, J.S. 1997 Dublin 1750–1850: spatial distribution and organisation of economic activity. Unpublished MSc. thesis, Trinity College Dublin.
Prunty, J. 1998 Estate records. In W. Nolan and A. Simms (eds), *Irish towns: a guide to sources*. Dublin.
Prunty, J. 2004 *Maps and map-making in local history*. Dublin.
Purcell, M. 1982 Dublin Diocesan Archives: Murray papers. *Archivium Hibernicum* **37**, 29–121.

Quane, M. 1950 Pococke School, Kilkenny. *Journal of the Royal Society of Antiquaries of Ireland* **80** (1), 36–72.

Quane, M. 1964 The Feinaiglian Institution, Dublin. *Dublin Historical Record* **19** (2), 30–44.

Quane, M. 1964 Quaker schools in Dublin. *Journal of the Royal Society of Antiquaries of Ireland* **94** (1), 47–68.

Quane, M. 1967 The Hibernian Marine School, Dublin. *Dublin Historical Record* **21** (2), 67–78.

Quinquagenarian, A 1832 The Four Courts. *Dublin Penny Journal* **1** (18) (27 October 1832), 141–3.

Raumer, F. 1836 *England in 1835 volume 1, being a series of letters written to friends in Germany during a residence in London and excursions into the provinces by Friedrich Raumer, translated from the German by Sarah Austen and H.E. Lloyd, in three volumes*. London.

Reid, T. 1823 *Travels in Ireland in the year 1822, exhibiting brief sketches of the moral, physical and political state of the country with reflections on the best means of improving its condition*. London.

Rennie, Sir J. 1867 *An autobiography*. London.

Reynolds, T. 1994 Power from wind. *Science* (new ser.) **264** (5160), 745–90.

Rickard, K. 2017 Howth and its maritime past. *Dublin Historical Record* **70** (1), 19–35.

Rogers, T. 1805 *Observations on the reports laid before the Rt Hon. and Hon. Directors General of Inland Navigation in Ireland for the improvement of Dublin Harbour*. Dublin. NLI P1134 (16).

Ruddy, B. 2004 The Royal Charter School, Clontarf. *Dublin Historical Record* **57** (1), 64–80.

Ruddy, B. 2008 Mount Temple School, Clontarf. *Dublin Historical Record* **61** (2), 183–93.

Ruddy, B. 2012 The 1811 disturbance at Howth Harbour. *Dublin Historical Record* **65** (1–2), 47–52.

Ruddy, V. 2018 *Monster agitators: O'Connell's Repealers, 1843 Ireland*. Dublin.

Ryan, M. 1994 The Church of St Francis Xavier, Upper Gardiner Street, Dublin. Unpublished MA thesis, University College Dublin.

Scully, S. 1972 Ghosts of Moore Street. *Dublin Historical Record* **25** (2), 54–63.

Semple, G. 1776 *A treatise on building in water, in two parts*. Dublin.

Sharkey, J.U. 2004 St Anne's—the Guinness estate. *Dublin Historical Record* **57** (2), 132–45.

Shotton, E. 2015 Dublin's quays in the eighteenth and nineteenth centuries—a case study. In A. Carpenter, R. Loeber, H. Campbell, L. Hurley, J. Montague and E. Rowley (eds), *Art and architecture of Ireland, vol. 4. Architecture 1600–2000*, 155–7. Dublin.

Shotton, E. 2016 Augmented maritime histories: text, point, line. In L. Allen and L.C. Pearson (eds), *Drawing futures: speculations in contemporary drawing for art and architecture* (http://hdl.handle.net/10197/8115, accessed 13/01/2017).

Simms, J.G. 1965 Dublin in 1685. *Irish Historical Studies* **14** (55), 212–26.

Skempton, A.W. 1996 Embankments and cuttings on the early railways. *Construction History* **11** (1996), 33–49.

Smeaton, J. 1812–14 *Reports of the late John Smeaton, FRS, made on various occasions, in the course of his employment as a civil engineer* (4 vols). London.

Smiles, S. 1861 *Lives of the engineers, with an account of their principal works: comprising also a history of inland communication in Britain*. London.

Smith, F. 1961 *St Saviour's Church, Dublin, centenary 1861–1961*. Dublin.

Smyth, H. 1984 *The B & I*. Dublin.

Smyth, H. 1996 Some notes on Charles Wye Williams, his family, their life and times. *Dublin Historical Record* **49** (1), 64–9.

Steiner, F.H. 1981 Building with iron: a Napoleonic controversy. *Technology and Culture* **22** (4),

700–24.

Stephenson, J.B. 1969 *Irish Jesuits*, vol. 2. Dublin.

Stephenson, P.J. 1948 Seán McDermott Street. *Dublin Historical Record* **10** (3), 83–8.

Stevens, J. 1912 *The journal of John Stevens, containing a brief account of the war in Ireland, 1689–1691* (ed. R.H. Murray). Oxford.

Stokes, G.T. (ed.) 1891 *Richard Pococke's Tour in Ireland in 1752*. Dublin.

Storrie, M. 1969 William J. Bald FRSE, c. 1789–1857: surveyor, cartographer and civil engineer. *Transactions of the British Institute of Geographers* **47**, 205–31.

Swift, M. 1999 *Historical maps of Ireland*. London.

Tanel, F. 2013 *Trains: an illustrated history from steam locomotives to high-speed rail*. London.

TeBrake, W. 1981 Land reclamation and the agrarian frontier in the Dutch Rijnland 950–1350. *Environmental Review* **5** (1), 27–36.

Tonna, C.E. 1838 *Letters from Ireland, 1837*. London.

Tredgold, T. 1838 *Principles of warming and ventilating public buildings, hothouses & c*. London.

Trotter, J.B. 1819 *Walks through Ireland in the years 1812, 1814 and 1817*. London.

Tutty, M.J. 1959 Drumcondra. *Dublin Historical Record* **15** (3), 86–96.

Tutty, M.J. 1963 City of Dublin Steam Packet Company. *Dublin Historical Record* **18** (3), 80–90.

Tutty, M.J. 1971 Review of *History of the parish of Drumcondra, North Strand, St Barabbas*, by Arthur Garret. *Dublin Historical Record* **24** (2), 1–43.

Tutty, M.J. 1981 Bridges over the Liffey. *Dublin Historical Record* **35** (1), 23–33.

Twomey, B. 2005 *Smithfield, and the parish of St Paul, Dublin, 1698–1750*. Dublin.

Tyne, G. 1794 *The traveller's guide through Ireland, being an accurate companion to Captain Alexander Taylor's map of Ireland*. Dublin.

Veredker, H. 1846 *Letter to the Tidal Commission from the secretary of the Corporation for Preserving and Improving the Port of Dublin in answer to complaints by Captain Washington* [pamphlet]. Dublin.

Walsh, F. and McIlreavy, D. 2013 Dublin Waste to Energy Project, Poolbeg, Dublin 4. *Excavations.ie*, site no. 2013:282.

Warburton, J. and Whitelaw, J. 1818 *History of the city of Dublin* (2 vols). London.

Ward-Perkins, S. 1984 Bank of Ireland—old Parliament House. *Dublin Historical Record* **37** (2), 42–53.

White, R.A. 2014 *Charlemont's Marino: portrait of a landscape*. Dublin.

Wilkins, N.P. 2009 *Alexander Nimmo, master engineer, 1783–1832: public works and civil surveys*. Dublin.

Williams, M. 1970 The enclosure and reclamation of waste land in England and Wales in the 18th and 19th centuries. *Transactions of the Institute of British Geographers* **51**, 55–69.

Woods, C.J. 2009 *Travellers' accounts as source material for Irish historians*. Dublin.

Wright, G.N. 1821 *An historical guide to ancient and modern Dublin*. London.

Z.A. 1825 On railways. *The Belfast Magazine and Literary Journal* **1** (1) (February), 84–8.

Z.A. 1825 On railways. *The Belfast Magazine and Literary Journal* **1** (2) (March), 163–74.

Index

Note: Page numbers in *italics* represent illustrations.

A

Abbey Street, 6, *140*, 145, 199, 206, 294
Adelaide Road, 214
Aikenhead, Mother Mary, 202, 230, 231
Aird, John, 102, 247
Aird, William, 117
Aldeborough House, 62, 126, 144, 151, 152, 174–7, 178, 187, 194, 232
All Hallows, Drumcondra, 215, *215*, 291
America, 34, 39, 96, 195, 218
Amiens Street, 2, 3, 127, 173, 176, 212, 279, 280, 282, 285, 287
Amsterdam, 7, 8, 22, 26, 44, 102
Annesley, Arthur, 23
Annesley Bridge, 28, 62, 126, 151, 170–4, 177, 178, 186, 194, 277, 291, 292
Anthonisz, Cornelius, 44
Antrim, 11, 280
Appleby, Captain John, 15
Archer, Joseph, 65, 73, 142, 173, 176, 254
Ardgillan Castle, 288
Arigna Mines, 99
Arran Quay, 213
Artane, 223
Ashtown, 181
Aston Quay, 39
Aungier Street, 218
Avery, John, 98

B

Bachelor's Quay, 132
Bachelor's Walk, 163, 166
Baggot Street, 56, 212
Balbriggan, 17, 96, 121, 231, 232, 279, 285, 288, 292, 294
Bald, William, 102, 280
Baldoyle, 17, 228, 244, 245, 248, 249, 250, 252, 254, 287, 292
    inn at, *251*
    medical officers, 232
    port, 127
    post office, 294
    revenue station, 11
    St Peter's (Church of Ireland), 213

Baldoyle spit, 245, 247, 248
Baldoyle Station, *290*
Baldoyle Strand, *246*
Baldwin, Mark, 66
Ball, Mother Frances Teresa, 222
Ball, John, 232
Ballinasloe, 188
Ballsbridge, 41, 78, 79, 80, 85, 86, 87, 92, 114
Ballybough, 41, 128, 170, 173, 187
Ballybough Bridge, 6, 131, 142, 151, 170, 171, 173, 174, 187, 193, 223, 293
Ballybough Lane, 173
Ballybough River [the Tolka], 129–31
Ballybough Road, 277, 293
Ballymun, 216
Balscadden, 17, 247
Balscadden Ladies' Swimming Place, *250*
Baltimore, 11
Barker, Jonathan, 85–6
Barlow, James, 233
Barlow, Peter, 114
Barrack Bridge, Watling Street, 39
Barralet, Thomas, *79*, 86
Barrelet, John, 227
Barrow, John, 115, 116, 168, 197, 231
Barrow, Viola, 166
Barrow Street, 43, 107, 109, 121
Bath Street, 88
Beggar's Bush, 14, 76, 81, 83, 87, 90, 114
Beggar's Bush Barracks, 41, 81, 115, 117, 119, *119*, 122, 225
Belfast, 55, 60, 103, 105, 184, 271, 279, 280
Belfast Lough, 55
Bell, T., 154
Bellewstown Races, 288
Belvedere College, 202, 204, 222
Belvedere House, 204
Benson, Revd E., 222
Benson, Richard, 36
Beresford, Revd Charles, 120
Beresford, John, 80, 159, 164, 166, 173, 187
Beresford Place, 143, 161, 167, *169*, 206
Betham, Sir William, 233
Bethseda Chapel, Dorset Street (Lock Penitentiary),

214, 231
Bianconi, Charles, 99, 165, 291
Bigelow, Andrew, 40, 57, 165, 177
Bingham, Henry, 154
Binns, John, 182, 187
Binns, Jonathan, 116
Binn's Bridge, 187
Birkinshaw, John, 99
Bishop Street, 214
Black Church (St Mary's chapel of ease), Mountjoy Street, 212, *213*
Black Quarry, Clontarf, 223, 279
Blackhall Place, 109, 127, 154, 199
Blackrock, 83, 87, 101, 105, 110, 112, 113, 115, 116, 118, 132, 293, 294
Blackrock Road, 122
Blackrock Strand, 102
Blackwood, Hans, 232
Blacquiere, Sir John, 180
Blair, Thomas, 35, 47, *47*, 48
Blair's yard, 37
Blanchardstown, 185
Blessington Street, *146*, 173, 182, 188
Bligh, Captain William, 46, 57, 60, 88, 259, *260*, 261, 262, 263, 264, 265–6, 270
Blockhouse, *see* Pigeon House
Blood, Bindon, 175
Boate, Gerald, 16, 20, 79
Boland's Mills (Treasury Building), 117
Boles, George, 154
Bolger, James, 208
Bolton Street, 137, 138, 139, 140, 151, 154, *157*, 194, 222
Booker, Benjamin, 233
Booterstown, 55, 88, *113*, 233
Booth, Joseph, 144
Bow Street, 231
Bowen, Desmond, 196
Boyle, Richard, earl of Cork, 12
Boyne Navigation, 52
Braithwaite, John, 286
Bray, Co. Wicklow, 96, 232
Bray Head, 109
Brereton, Sir William, 16
Bridge Street, 121, 207
Brilge, Revd F., 232
Bristol, 24, 60, 101, 170, 247
Britain, *see* Great Britain
Britain Street, 207
Brixham, 279
Broadmeadow Estuary, 186
Broadstone, 114, 182, 185, 188, 194
Broadstone Harbour, *183*, 185, 188, 194
Broadstone Hill, 127
Broadstone Station, 291, *291*, 292

Brodigan, Thomas, 280, 286
Brooking, Charles, 14, 26, *30*, 32, 34
Brooking, Thomas, 31, 132
Brown Street, 230
Browne, John, 154
Brownrigg, John, 64, 180, 182
Brownrigg, Thomas, 137
Bruff, Peter, 282–3
Brunel, Sir Marc Isambard, 100, 109
Buckingham Street, 143, 144
Bull Island, 245, 270
Bull Wall, 294; *see also* North Bull Wall; South Bull Wall
Bullock, 53, 259, 265
Bullock Harbour, 56, 115, 269
Burdett, Sir Bagnell, 233
Burgh Quay, *33*, 122, 216, 266, 286
Burgoyne, Sir John, 286
Burke, Edmund, 3
Burke, John, 154
Burke, Luke, 35
Burke, Nuala, 6, 14, 136, 163
Burleigh, David, 36
Busáras, 127
Butler, Isaac, 11, 15, 17, 26, 34, 55, 77, 78, 145, 244
Butler, James, duke of Ormonde, 21, 158
Butler, John, 35
Butt, Sir Isaac, 154
Butterworth, Joseph, 196
Byrne, Michael, 293
Byrne, Patrick, 280
Byron, Samuel, 143

C
Cabinteely, 214
Caldbeck, William, 286
Campbell, Charles, 139
Canal Docks, 164; *see also* Grand Canal Docks
Cantisell, Thomas, 205
Capel, Arthur, earl of Essex, 127, 157
Capel Street, 6, 11, 127, 136, 137, 138, 151, 153, 154, 156, 158, 165, 193, 194, 226, 227
Capel Street Bridge, *see* Essex Bridge (Capel Street Bridge)
Cappagh Bog, 185
Cardiff shipyard, 36, 37
Carey, Fr James, 206
Carey Lane, Drumcondra, 41
Carlingford, 17, 145
Carlisle Bridge, 39, 40, 41, 62, 117, 126, 143, 151, 157–64, 166, 168, 177, 193, 249
Carlow, 202
Carlyle, Thomas, 254
Carolan, Edward, 120
Carrickfergus, 52, 55

INDEX

Castle Avenue, 45, 171, 213, 274
Castleknock, *183*, 294
Caulfield, James, earl of Charlemont, 115
Cavendish Row, Rutland Square, *141*, 142
Chancery Lane, 152, 201
Chapman, Edward, 66
Chapman, S., 154
Chapman, William, 265
Charlemont House, Marino, *147*
Charlemont Street, 175
Charles I, King, 7, 196
Charles II, King, 6, 7, 8
Chartre, John, 154
Cheer, Karen, 39
Chester, 14, 42, 46, 96, 144
Christ Church Cathedral, 1, 152, 213, 219
Church Street, 152, 194
Circular Road, 83, 232
City Quay, 21, 25, 28, 35
Clarendon, Thomas, 106
Clarke, John, 164
Clayton, John, 240
Clements, John, 269
Clinton, Clementine, 35
Clongowes Wood College, 222
Clonliffe College, Clonliffe Road, 215, *215*, 291
Clonliffe House, 187
Clonliffe Road, 127, 174, 277, 279, 291
Clonskeagh, 91
Clontarf, 11, 15, 116, 129, 136, 145, 173, 174, 187,
    194, 213, 270, 271, 274, 277, 279, 284, 293
    Charter School, 218, *219*, 223
    medical officers, 232
    Merchamp, 233
    Mount Temple School, 285
    Plumtre's description of, 179, 247
    post office, 294
    quarry, 2, 29, 223
    rail embankment, 291
    savings bank, 294
    the Sheds, 227, *272*
    sheds and an unfinished road, *138*
Clontarf Castle, 45, 132, *148*, 149, 247, 279
Clontarf Crescent, Howth Road, *148*
Clontarf Golf Club, 2, 29, 279
Clontarf Island, 1, 10, *10*, 11, 14, 128, 129, 131, 142,
    171, 173, 224, 263, 264, *273*, 277
Clontarf Road Crescent, *272*
Clontarf Station, 287
Clontarf Strand, 280
Clontarf Viaduct, *287*, *288*
Clonturk House, 159, *160*
Clyde and Forth Canal, 65
Clyncher, Giles, 21
Coalbrookdale, Shropshire, 164

Codling Rock, 101
Cole Alley, 65
Coleraine Street, 223
College Green, 23, 118, 120, 127, 157, 164, 195
Collins, Captain Grenville, 9, 12, *15*, 42, 51
Collins Barracks, 127
Colville, William, 248
Conciliation Hall, 216
Connolly Station, 2
Connolly Street, 287
Connor, Robert, 142
Conquer Hill, Clontarf, 53
Convent Avenue, 293
Convention Centre, North Quay, *4*
Conyingham, Gustavus, 55
Cooke Street, 207
Cooley, Thomas, 152
Coolock, 174, 194, 213, 216, 223, 227, 232
Coombe area, 11
Coombe Hospital, 230
Cooney, D.A. Levistone, 116, 222
Cooper, Austin, 233
Cork Gaol, 11, 224
Cork Street Fever Hospital, 228
Corn Exchange, Burgh Quay, 216
Corneille, Captain Daniel, 265
Cornwall, 247
Cornwallis, Lord, 180, 264
Corr Bridge, Howth, 2, 29, 223, 247
Corry, Geoffrey, 20, 23
Cosgrove, Dillon, 151–2, 271
Cosslett, Charles, 11, 38, 78, 81, 83, 88, 244, 252
Costello, Vandra, 126
Cowan, John, 83, 264
Cox, Watty, 186
Crab Lake, 45, 248
Cranfield's Baths, 58, 90
Creighton Street, 22–3, 26, 27, 121
Croke Park, 177, 179, 187
Croker, Edward, 139
Cromwell, Thomas, 116, 248, 288
Cromwell Harbour, 17
Cross Guns Bridge (Westmorland Bridge), 178, 181
Crosthwaite, Leland, 248, 265
Crow Street Theatre, 241
Cruise, James, 254
Cubitt, William, 271, 280, 281
Cugnot, Nicolas, 99
Cullen, Edward, 78
Cullen, Francis, 113, 271
Cullen, John, 42, 43, 46
Cullen, Louis, 18, 20, 41
Culross, 240
Cumberland Street, 142, 143
Custom House, 20, 21, 40, 41, 42, 49, 60, 63, 126,

311

151, 152, 153, 154, 161, 164, 165–70, 187, 193
  in the seventeenth century, 23
  Oakley's description of, 249
Custom House Quay, 20, 41, 49

D
Dalkey, 17, 29, 60, 65, 101, 105, 112, 247, 248, 265
Dalkey Island, 101
Dalkey Sound, 246
Dame Street, *118*, 120, 127
Dargan, William, 105, 271, 279
Darley, B.G., 232
Darley, Frederick, 206
Darling, George, 144
Davis, John, 64
Davis, Whitmore, 187
Dawson, T., 251
Dawson, William, 244, 246, 261
Dawson Street, 211
De Courcy, John, 127, 136, 163
de Gomme, Bernard, 12, 17, 64
de Joffroy, Claude, 100
de Phepo, Adam, 127
Delamere, Ida, 247
Delaney, Ruth, 64
Delmaine, Henry, 145
Denmark Street, 227
Denzille Street (Fenian Street), 117, 128
Despard, Philip, 219
Devon, 247
Dick, Samuel, 120
Dickson, David, 136, 167, 233
Dinelly, Thomas, *13*
Dispensary Lane, off Dorset Street, 232
Dobbs, Arthur, 34
Dodd, Martha, 161
Dodder Basin, 61, 74–92, *76*
Dodder River, 20, 22, 23, 26, 28, 32, 33, 61, 62–95, 131, 259
Dodds, Ralph, 99
D'Olier Street, 213
Dollymount, 293
Dominick Street, 136, 212
Donegal, 11, 224
Donnybrook, 33, 77, 91, 105
Donnybrook Quarries, 109
Donnybrook River, 77
Donnycarney, 29, 194, 223, 279
D'Orsay, Count Alfred, 138
Dorset Institute, 220
Dorset Street, 6, 127, 136, 137, 139, 140, 194, 212, 214, 226, 232, 277
Douglas, Isle of Man, 259
Douglas, Margaret, 121
Dove, Edward, 223

Downes, Thomas, 35
Dr Steevens's Hospital, 230
Draper, John, 38
Drennan, William, 232
Drogheda, 9, 11, 16, *17*, 52, 251, 271, 282, 285, 286
Drogheda Railway, *see* Dublin to Drogheda Railway
Drought, Mistress Hamilton, 223
Drumcondra, 127, 159, 173, 185, 215, 232, 294
Drumcondra Bridge, *139*, 187, 223
Drumcondra Lane (Bolton Street), 139
Drumcondra Road, 185, 187, 231, 279
Drummond, Thomas, 281
Dublin
  Ballast Office, 24
  to Belfast railway, 103
  Brooking's map of (1728), *30*
  Collins's map of (1686), *15*
  geological map (nineteenth century), *2*
  Moll's map of (1711), *24*
  Phillips's map of (1685), *14*
  Price's map of (1730), *31*
  Ricciardelli's painting (1750), *30*
  Rocque's map of (1756), *32*
  Wilson's map of (1798), *82*
Dublin Bay, 1, 2, 3, 15–18, 35, 51, 57, 132, 244, 264
Dublin Castle, 281
Dublin Port, 9, *34*, 131, 266
Dublin to Drogheda Railway, 113, 126, 174, 176, 254, 274, 277–96
Dublin to Kingstown Railway, 54, 96, 97, 104, 113
Duffy, Patrick, 7, 97
Duffy, P.J., 38
Duffy, Thomas, 185
Dún Laoghaire, 92, 126; *see also* Dunleary; Kingstown
Duncan, William, 112, 232
Duncannon, 9
Dunleary, 75, 96, 245, 247, 248, 249, 254, 256, 262, 265; *see also* Dún Laoghaire; Kingstown
Dunleary Harbour, 100, *101*, 102
Dunn, Christopher, 35
Dunton, John, 16
Dupin, Baron Charles, 91, 98, 100, 168, 241
Dutton, Hely, 142, 176

E
Earl Street, 127, 161, 208
East Link Bridge, 136
East Wall, 126, 127, 284
East Wall Road, 28, 136, 171, 263, 277
Eaton, B., 154
Eaton, Richard, 39
Eccles Street, 226
Eddystone Lighthouse, 65, 99
Eden Quay, 165, 170, 281

Edgar, Patrick, 72
Edgeworth, Richard, 138
Edward III, King, 17
Egan, Ray, 103, 128
Elizabeth I, Queen, 11, 45, 55
England, 7–8, 98, 179, 180, 186, 240, 244; *see also* Great Britain
English Channel, 90
Ennis, Richard, 139
Enniscorthy, 281
Enniskillen, 105, 280
Esmonde, Bartholomew, 161
Esmonde, John, 161
Essex Bridge (Capel Street Bridge), 3, 18, 20, *22*, 33, 39, 66, 127, *133*, 144, 157, 158, 159, 164, 166, 168, 225, 274, 292
Evans, Revd John, 196
Evans, Richard, 181
Eyre, Thomas, 96

F
Fagan, Revd A.J., 214
Fagan, Bryan, 87
Fagan, Elizabeth, 87
Fairview, 142, 170, 216, 279, 291, 293, 294
Fairview Park, 2, 171
Fairview Strand, 136, 171, 277
Farraday, Michael, 216
Farrell, Catherine, 252
Fawkes, Guy, 9
Fea, John, 232
Fenian Street (Denzille Street), 117, 128
Ferguson, Samuel, 154, 228
Ferrar, John, 68, 79
Ferrell, Revd D., 227
Finlay, John, 154
Finn, T., 176
Firth and Clyde Canal, 100
Fitzsimon, Thomas, 21
Fitzwilliam, Lord, 72, 77, 78, 79, 80, 83, 85, 87, 233
Fitzwilliam Estate, 116
Fitzwilliam Key, 43
Fitzwilliam Square, 87, 89, 233
Fitzwilliam Street, 212
Flynn, Henry, 92
Forbes, Edward, 120
Fortview Avenue, Clontarf, 252
Fossett, William, 232
Foster, Thomas Campbell, 224
Foster Place, 242
Four Courts, 126, 151, 152–7, *156*, 163, 193, 201
Four Courts Bridge, 127
France, 15, 26, 55, 88, 96, 100, 181, 197, 212, 218, 232, 240, 244
Francis Street, 65

Franklin, John, 154

G
Gaffney, John, 248
Galway, 251
Gamble, John, 41, 161, 168
Gandon, James, 152, 153, 166, 266
Gardiner, Charles, 138, 139
Gardiner, Luke, 36, 136, 137, 138, 142, 152, 159, 161
Gardiner estate, 6, 137
Gardiner Place, 232, 233
Gardiner Street, 127, *143*, 167, 176, 199, *201*, 202, 206, *206*, 214
Garzia, John, 201
Gaunt, John, 9
Gavin, John, 248
General Post Office (GPO), 161, 162, 165
George IV, King, 96, 102, 245, 251
George's Dock, 71, 266, 274
George's Hill, 201, 221
George's Lane, 226
George's Quay, 4, 28, 29
George's Street, 11, 224
Geraghty, P.J., 280
Gibney, Frank, 89
Gibson, George, 35
Giesebrecht, 3rd Count Amstel, 22
Giles, Francis, 265, 266, 267, *267*, 270
Gilligan, Harry, 80
Glasgow, 100, 102, 187
Glasnevin, 2, 178, 216, 220
Glasnevin Road, 6, 185
Glasthule, 101
Gloucester Place, 144
Gloucester Street (Seán McDermott Street), 142, *143*, 159, 176, *197*, 226, 232, 233
Goodwin Sands, 15
Gormanstown, Lord, 17
Gosson, John, 138
Gough, Edward, 14
Grainger, Revd J., 213
Grand Canal, 22, 61, 62, 64, 138, 181, 182, 185, 188, 226
Grand Canal Basin, 58, 62
Grand Canal Docks, 21, 33, 39, 54, 60, 61, 62–95, 103, 104, 117, 118, 184, 187, 242, 259, 261
Grand Canal Street, 73, 109
Grangegorman, 156, 231
Grangegorman Lane, 230, 231
Grantham, Captain Joseph, 268
Great Britain, 26, 96, 100, 111, 188, 240, 283; *see also* England
Great Britain Street (Parnell Street), 65, 136, 144, 225, 227, 232, 294
Great Brunswick Street (Pearse Street), 40, 54, 71–2,

103, 106, 119, 120, 121, 122, 223, 241, 242
Great Charles Street, *198*, 199, 232
Great Denmark Street, 137, 159, 212, 232
Great George's Street, 159
Great North Bull Wall, 25, 60, 126, 247, 259–76
Great South Bull Wall, 22, 29, 41–6, 55, 59, 60, 65, 74, 132, 158, 259, 266, 268
Green Street, 120
Gregg, John, 206
Gregory, William, 261
Grendon, Thomas, 285
Grenville Street, 232
Gresham, Thomas, 106
Gresham Hotel, Sackville Street, 106, 116, 250
Grossett, Charles, 22
Guinness, A.G., 232
Guinness, Arthur, 270
Guinness, W.J., 232
Guinness family, 271

H
Hadfield, Charles, 66
Hale, John, 247
Hale, Paul, 247
Hale, William, 247
Half Moon Battery, 232
Halfpenny Bridge, 114, *163*, 164
Hall, Revd James, 40, 57
Halpin, George, 39, 40, 41, 90, 134, 265, 266, 267, 268, 269, 270, 281, 284
Halpin, George Junior, 282
Hamilton, G.A., 286
Hamilton, James, 286
Hammond Lane, 203
Hanlon, Thomas, 119
Hanna, Hugh, 252
Hanover Street, 32, 208, 221
Hardwicke Street, 162, 199, 201, 222
Hardy, James, 196
Harold's Cross, 222
Hart, Alex, 100
Hawkins, William, 127
Hawkins Street, 33, 64, 117, 119, 213, *242*
Hayes, Edward, 114
Healy, Thomas, 173
Heard, Ruth, 245, 266
Hemans, George, 282, 284
Hempton, D.N., 196
Henrietta Street, 127, 136, 159, 219, 232
Henry, James, 222
Henry, William, 240
Henry IV, King, 17
Henry VIII, King, 21, 127
Henry Street, 127, 151, 232, 293
Hickey, John, 223

Hicks, P.Th., 232–3
Hill, John, 121
Hills, Richard L., 26
Hiney, Diarmuid, 170, 171
Hitt, Thomas, 88
Hogan, Edward, 252
Hogan, John, 207
Holland, 7–8, 22, 26, 63, 132, 181
Hollybrook Lodge, 252
Hollybrook Park, Clontarf, 219, 252
Hollybrook Road, Clontarf, 142, 171
Hollywood Park, 282
Holmes, George, 154
Holyhead, 96, 100, 144, 246, 250
Hore, James, *169*
House of Industry Hardwicke Hospital, 229
Howard, Frederick, earl of Carlisle, 159
Howard, John, 219
Howth, 17, 56, 92, 100, 121, 126, 139, 145, 178, 179, 194, 225, 228, 231, 232, 247, 254, 262, 265
  branch line to, 289
  Corr Bridge quarry, 2, 29
  pier between Ireland's Eye and, 101
  revenue station, 11
  Royal Hotel, 252
Howth Castle, 49, 233
Howth Harbour, 60, 96, 126, 244–58, 262
Howth Head, 245
Howth Lighthouse, *249*
Howth Road, *148*, 194, 213, 248, 274, 277, 279, 291, 293
Huddart, Captain Joseph, 265
Hutton family, Baldoyle, 254

I
Inglis, Henry, 102, 117, 168, 176, 226–7
Inn's Quay, 154, 163
Ireland's Eye, 101, 244, 246, 249, 256
Irishtown, 49, 57, 70, 74, 78, 80, 83, 86, 90, 91, 92, 118, 120, 259, 262, 293
  Barker survey map of, 85
  bridge, 77, 81
  development in the eighteenth century, 88
  houses constructed in, 89
  Pembroke estate maps of, 18, 42, 58, *84*
  plots, 87
  St Matthew's Church, *42*, 43
  watermill on the Dodder near, 75
Italy, 182

J
Jackson, Henry, 98
James II, King, 7
Jeffries, Nathaniel, 57
Jervis, Sir Humphrey, 11, 127

INDEX

Jervis, William, 6
Jervis Street, 2–3, 158, 176, 220, 221
Jessop, William, 64, 65, 66, 67, 181, 261, 264
Jones, Alfred, 203
Jones, John Paul, 55
Jones Road, 177, 187
Jordan, Thomas, 6
Joy, Arthur, *42*, *73*
Joyce, Weston, 78

K
Katsula, Shunsuke, 204
Kells, 289
Kelly, John, 219
Kenneddy, Charles, 214
Kennedy, Maire, 153, 161
Kenny, Mary, 137
Keogh, Daire, 196
Khan, Mirza Abu Taleb, 140
Kilbarrack, 246, 289
Kilcock, 184
Kilkenny, 202
Killarney Street, 143, 144
Killester, 252, 254, 279, 282, 291
Killiney, 99, 112, 247
Kilmacud, 116
Kilrock, 247
King Street, 182, 227
King's Inns, 151, 194
King's Inns Street, 223
Kingsbridge, 114, 164
Kingsbridge Station, *290*, 291
Kingstown, 56, 96, 112, 126, 214, 245, 279, 292; *see also* Dún Laoghaire; Dunleary
Kingstown Harbour, 60, 96, 99, 104, 113, 120
Kingstown Road, 110
Kinsale, 9
Kirwan, Richard, 2
Kirwan, Walter, 198
Kish Bank, 50, 264, 269

L
Lacy, Cecelia, 227
Laird, William, 117
Lamb, James, 35
Lambeth, 117
Landers, George, 250
Landy, Michael, 64
Langrishe Place, off Gardiner Street, 199
Lansdowne Road, 2, 122
Lazers Hill/Lazy Hill (Townsend Street), 17, 22, 25, 33, 35, 37, 40, 127, 137
Leavy, Richard, 119
Lebon, Philippe, 240
Lee, Joe, 280

Lees, Sir Harcourt, 106
Leeson Street, 72, 97, 228, 252
Lefroy, Baron, 286
Liffey, River
  embanking of, 21–4
  north bank, 126, 129–35
Liffey Basin, 1
Liffey Street, 151, 195, 207, 208
Lime Street, 32
Limerick, 71, 242
Lincoln Place, 91
Linen Hall, 145, *157*
Little Denmark Street, 207
Liverpool, 18, 23, 24, 46, 50, 60, 68, 100, 104, 231, 241
Lock Penitentiary, Dorset Street (the Bethseda), 214, 231
Lockome, Philip, 144
London, 9, 60, 67
Londonbridge Road, 69, 81, 90, 114
Love, Lee, 153
Lower Abbey Street, 145, 170, 199, 206, 214, 222
Lower Dominick Street, 207, 222, 232, 233
Lower Dorset Street, 187, 220, 232
Lower Drumcondra Road, 194
Lower Gardiner Street, 220
Lower Gloucester Street, 143, 144, 223, 231
Lower Mecklenburgh Street, 231
Lower Mount Street, 205
Lower Ormond Quay, 154
Lower Sackville Street, 161, 170, 227
Lowth, Cormac, 26
Lurgan, 9
Lurgan Street, 294
Lusk, 288
Lydon, William, 36
Lynch, Paula, 154

M
Mabbots Mills, 131
Macaile, Fr Betagh, 201
McAuley, Mother Catherine, 202, 231
McAuliffe, T.J., 228
McCann, John, 185
McCormack, William, 282
McCready, C.T., 142
McCullagh, Jane, 223
McCullough, Niall, 71, 104
McFarland, Edward, 116
McGeery, Laurence, 227
McGrane, Mary, 121
McIleary, David, 57
McKenna, Frank, 283
McKenna, Captain Michael, 270
McKenny, P., 251

315

McKenzie, Murdoch, *50*, 51, 264
McLoughlin, James, 140
McManus, Ruth, 88
McNeill, Sir John, 71, 262, 266, 281, 282, 284, 285, 286, 287, 289
McQuade, Melanie, 3–4, 26, 28
McRedmond, Louis, 201
Mahon, Hannah, 223
Malahide, 11, 17, 55, 174, 186, 187, 194, 206, 233, 244, 256, 282, 286, 287, 288, 292, 294
Malahide Castle, 244
Malahide Road, 29, 194, 213, 223, 233, 256, 274, 279, 293
Malahide Viaduct, *285*, 286
Malcolm, Captain Charles, 248
Mall, the, 151, 161, 225
Mallet, Robert, 91
Mallows, Charles, 139
Malta, 115
Malton, James, 33, 36, 37
Manchester, 187, 240, 242
Manor House, Raheny, 252
Mansion House, 242
Maquay, George, 265
Marino, *147*, 194, 233, 256, 277
Marlborough Green, 170
Marlborough Street, 142, 143, 152, 161, 162, 165, 176, 199, 204, 211, 214, 217, 230, 289
Marrot, William, 116
Marshall, William, 139
Martin, John, 217
Martin, Peter, 122
Mary Street, 142, 151
Maryann street, 43
Matthews, Thomas, 76, *76*, 79, 83, 86, 87
Maynooth, 186, 197, 216
Maynooth Harbour, *184*, 186
Mayo, 280
Mayor Street, 167, 179, 187
Meade, Mary Catherine, 202
Meath Street, 294
Mecklenburgh Street, 223, 233, 247
Medway River, 8
Meikle, Andrew, 98
Mercer, John, 36
Mercer's Dock, 29
Merchants Quay/Key, 21, 207
Merrion, 118
Merrion Gates, 81
Merrion Road, 101, 232
Merrion Square, 37, 38, 41, 74, 84, 87, 89, 103, 128, 233
Merrion Strand, 58, 102, 120, 293
Merrion Street, 87, 91
Meyler, Revd W., 208

Milford Haven, Wales, 9, 15
Military Road, 164
Milverton, 280
Mitchell, Margaret, 222
Moll, Heinrich, 23, *24*
Monkstown, 233
Montgomery, George, 254
Montgomery, Captain Thomas, 252
Montgomery Street, 140, 142
Moore, Howard, 35
Moore, James, 44
Moore, Thomas, 218
Moore Street, 127, 137, 139, 151, 225
Moorehouse, Geoffrey, 15
Morres, Redmond, 181
Morton, Robert, 121
Mosse's Hospital [the Rotunda], 144, 226
Mount Merrion, 207
Mount Street, 41, 103, 104
Mountjoy Fields, 202
Mountjoy Prison, 188
Mountjoy Square, 139, 162, 176, 177, 199, 201, 212, 226, 232, 233
Mountjoy Street, 222
Mountjoy Street Lower, 223
Mourny's Dock, 129
Mud Island, 128, 173, 174, 187, 279
Mulhuddart, 227
Mullingar, 185, 186
Murdock, William, 240
Murphy, Hugh, 54
Murphy, James, 155, 193
Murphy, William, 35
Murphy's Baths, 58, 90
Murray, Alice, 196
Murray, Terence, 41
Myles, Franc, 22, 26, 27

N
Napoleon, 96, 193, 195, 268
National Gallery of Ireland, 63
Nelson's Pillar, 165
Neville, Sir G., 211
New Haven, 17
Newcomen, Thomas, 99, 100
Newcomen, Sir William, 180
Newcomen Bridge, 178, *178*, 179, *179*, 181, 186, 187, 212, 277
Newcomen Terrace, 212
Newgate Prison, North King Street, 34, 154, 156
Newry, 145
Ni Mhurchadha, Maighread, 11
Nimmo, Alexander, 57–8, 92, 105, 250–1, 271, 281
North Brunswick Street, 231
North Bull, 15, 35, 132, 139, 261, 271

North Bull Sands, 259
North Bull Wall, 1, 57, 270, 271
North Circular Road, 151, 152, 176, 177, 199, 213, 220, 231, 232, 279
North Earl Street, 176, 288
North East Wall, 173
North Great George's Street, 154, 194, 204, 222, 233
North King Street, 127, 128, 222
North Lotts, 24, 26, 126, 129, *130*, 134, 136, 142, 145, 152, 170, 171, 174, 188, 193, 195, 233, 274, 279, 292
North Quay, *3*, 4, *4*
North Richmond Street, 153, 221, *221*
North Strand, 28, 127, 136, *140*, 145, 154, 159, 170, 173, 174, 176, 177, 179, 182, 212, 213, 242
North Strand Road, 223, 279
North Wall, 126, 127, 170, 182, 185, 187
North William Street, *200*, 202, 221
Nugent Street, 232

O
O'Brien, Gillian, 6, 80
O'Brien, Peter, 121
O Cionnaith, Fionnáin, 14
O'Connell, Daniel, 53, 58, 205, 212, 215, 216, 220, 221, 227, 242, 280, 286, 293
O'Connell Bridge, *see* Carlisle Bridge
O'Connell Street, 126; *see also* Sackville Street
O'Dwyer, F., 154
O'Kane, Finola, 6, 80
O'Kelly, Patrick, 158, 179, 180, 184
O'Reilly, John, 32
O'Reilly, Joseph, 119
O'Shea, Sinéad, 88, 128
Oakley, Benjamin, 60, 162, 166, 249, 250
Oriel Street, 204
Orkney Islands, 51
Ormond Quay, 132, 154
Otway, Caesar, 228
Overend, Thomas, 139
Owen, Robert, 35
Oxmantown, 6, 127

P
Page, Sir Thomas Hyde, 60, 101, 181, 182, 244, 259, *260*, 265, 268
Park, Thomas, 132
Park Gate, 144
Parliament Street, 63, 157
Parnell Square, 144, 162, 212, 230
Parnell Street, 137, 151, 162, 225
Paul, Revd Thomas, 142
Paul estate, 174
Payne, John, 42
Pearce, Matilda, 64

Pearse Square, 119
Pearse Street (Great Brunswick Street), 33, 40, 103, 128, 242
Pearson, Thomas, 20
Peel, Robert, 101
Pembroke estate, 18, 42, *58*, 72, 77, 78, 84, *84*, 87, 90, 205
Pembroke Street, 88, 121
Pepper, Charles, 252
Pepys, Sir Samuel, 9
Perry, Commander William, 28–9, 131, 259
Perry, John, 45
Peter Street, Westminster, 241
Petty, William, 127
Phibsborough, 188, 194
Philipsburg Avenue, 170, 171, 254
Phillips, Thomas, 12, *14*, 128
Phoenix Park, 40, 293
Phoenix Street, 65
Pigeon, John, 90
Pigeon House, 42, 47, 48, 52, 57, 59, 60, 75, 92, 96, 244, 245, 248
Pigeon House Fort, 56, 122, 232
Pigeon House Harbour, *54*, 56, 73, 74, 96, 262
Pill Lane, 174
Pim, James, 105
Pitts, Hivem, 98
Place, Francis, 14, 26
Plansante, Thomas, 6
Platt, Sir Hugh, 46
Plumtre, Ann, 28, 59, 73, 115, 139, 145, 162, 168, 179, 198, 245, 247, 248
Plymouth, 69
Pococke, Richard, 145, 219
Point Depot, 131, 136
Pollen, Hugh, 92
Pommoret, James, 121
Poolbeg, 45
Poolbeg Lighthouse, 42, 48, *49*, 52, 65, 262, 265, 268, 270
Port Tunnel, 1, 131
Portland Row, 143, 152, 174, 176, 177, 178
Portmarnock, 223, 244, 287
Portobello, 73, 182
Portrane, 17
Portsmouth, 32, 71, 88
Potters Alley, 176, 288–9
Preston, 241
Preston, Jenico, 205
Preston, William, 252
Price, Charles, 14, *31*, 33, 132, 145
Price, Jenny S., 144
Primates' Hill, 219
Prince Street, 33
Pro Cathedral, Marlborough Street, 165, 201, 203,

207, 208, *209*, 211
Prunty, Jacinta, 88–9
Prussia Street, 153

Q
Queen Street, 127, 128, 194
Queen Street Bridge, 144, 266
Queen's Square (Pearse Square), 122
Quested, John, 283
Quintan, Richard, 116

R
Raheny, 139, 174, 187, 223, 232, 246, 248, 254, 274, 282, 285, 287, 294
Ranelagh, 202, 293
Ranelagh, Lord, 53
Rathcormac, Co. Cork, 195
Rathfarnham, 77, 118
Rathgar, 293
Rathmines, 293
Rathmines Road, 97
Raumer, Friedrich, 71, 117, 204, 211
Razzell, Peter, 11
Reid, Elizabeth, 222
Reid, Thomas, 41, 57, 176, 220, 251
Rennie, Sir John, 115, 187, 246, 247, 259, 262, *263*, 265, 266, 268
Rialto Bridge, 22
Ricciardelli, Gabriele, 16, *17*, *30*, 31, 33
Richey, Benjamin, 248
Richmond Avenue, 293
Richmond Bridge, 163
Richmond Hospital, 229, *229*, *230*
Richmond Penitentiary, Grangegorman Lane, 230, 231
Richmond Road, 170, 174, 277, 291, 293
Rickard, Joseph, 245
Rickard, Kevin, 250
Ringsend, 9, *12*, 25, 28, 34, 43, 49, 53, 57, 67, *84*, *86*, 88, 89, 129, 268, 279
Ringsend Bridge, 39, 46, 54, 58, 69, 70, 74, 78, *79*, *81*, 83, 90, 118
Ringsend Docks, *69*
Ringsend Point, 46, 49, 74, 75, 131, 164
Ringsend Spit, 1, 12–15, 33, 62, 74, 84, 89, 120, 121, 142
Roberstown, 188
Robinson, William, 152
Robswall, Malahide, 17, 223
Rocque, John, 26, *32*, 33, 34, 35, 40, 71, 134, 136, 142
Rogers, Fred, 69
Rogers, Thomas, 92, 244, 261
Rogerson, Sir John, 24, 25, 26, 28, 83, 84, 142
Rogerson's Quay, *see* Sir John Rogerson's Quay

Rogerstown, 17, 288
Rome, 181, 202, 208
Rope Walk, 206 ; *see also* Gardiner Street
Rotterdam, 102
Rotunda Gardens, 136
Rotunda Hospital, 152, 162, 194, 205, 225, *226*
Royal Canal, 62, 126, 138, 151, 173, 175, 176, 177–88, 212, 225, 277, 281, *284*, 285, 286, 287, 288, 292
Royal Canal Dock, *180*
Royal Canal House, 185
Rush, 11, 17, 292, 294
Russell Place, 220, 232
Rutland Square (Parnell Square), 139, 177, 206, 226, 233, 242, 286
Rycut, Sir Paul, 12
Ryder, William, 195

S
Sackville Street (O'Connell Street), 106, 116, 139, 145, 151, 152, 157–64, 211, 225, 226, 249, 280, 293
  in 1803, 198
  Bitton Hotel, 231
  Dorset Institute, 220
  Moira Hotel, 249
Sadler, William, *49*, 55, *160*
Sadler, William, the younger, *156*
St Andrew's Church, Westland Row, 103, 106, *207*, 208
St Anne's estate, Clontarf, 223, 247, 270, 271
St Francis Xavier Church, 202
St George's Church, Hardwicke Place, *210*, 211
St George's Dispensary, 232
St George's Dock, 168
St George's Place, North Circular Road, 225
St George's Quay, 41
St John the Baptist Catholic Church, Clontarf Road, 213, 251
St John the Baptist Church (Church of Ireland), 213
St Joseph's Asylum, Portland Row, 231
St Laurence O'Toole Church, 214
St Lawrence, Lucy, 49
St Lawrence Road, 136
St Mary Magdelene's Asylum, Lower Gloucester Street, 231
St Mary's Abbey, 120, 127, 136, 138, 143, 152, 154, 158, 201, 214
St Mary's chapel of ease, Mountjoy Street (Black Church), 212, *213*
St Mary's Church, Donnybrook, 77
St Matthew's Church, Irishtown, *42*, 43
St Michael and St John Catholic Church, 213
St Michael's Hill, 122
St Michan's Church, 6, 142
St Nicholas of Myra Church, Kinsealy, 213
St Paul's Church, Arran Quay, 213

St Peter's Church, Baldoyle, 213
St Peter's Church, Drogheda, 286
St Peter's Church, North Circular Road, 213
St Stephen Church (Pepper Canister church), 205
St Stephen's Green, 84, 91, 230
St Stephen's Green West, 214
St Thomas Dispensary, 232
St Thomas's Church, Marlborough Street, 142, 152, 165, *209*, 211, 233
St Vincent's Hospital, St Stephen's Green, 230
Salisbury Place, 293
Sallins, 188
Saltee Islands, 11
Salthill, 110
Sandycove, 101, 269
Sandymount, 47, 57, 58, 78, 97, 112, 116, 202, 216, 230, 232, 259
Sandymount Strand, *58*
Santry, 294
Savary, Thomas, 99
Scalé, Bernard, 40
Schomberg, Sir Alexander, 70
Scotland, 145
Scott, Michael, 22
Seán McDermott Street (Gloucester Street), 128, 142, 143, 213
Seapoint, 118
Seaview Terrace, off North Strand, 213
Sedgrove, James, 14
Semple, George, 39–40, *43*, 55, 73, 80, 157, 158, 259, *260*, 268
Semple, John, 39, 46
Serpentine Avenue, 97, 109
Sheridan, Revd Bartholomew, 214
Sheriff Street, 167, *278*
Sherrard, Thomas, 137, 171, *172*, 173
Shotton, Elizabeth, 29, 39
Silvermines, Co. Tipperary, 9
Simmonscourt Fields, 107
Simms, J.G., 11
Sir John Rogerson's Quay, 25, 28, 29, 33, 34, 35, 36, 54, 65–6, 67, 74, 81, 86, 104, 114, 142, 242, 266
   in 1839, *38*
     diving bell museum, 22, 32
     excavations, 4
     Marine Hotel, 38
     Marine School, 35, *35*, *36*, 40, 58, 67
     ship construction at, 120
Sir John Rogerson's Wall, 75, 103
Sir Patrick Dun's Hospital, 115, 117, 121, 225, 230
Skempton, A.W., 66
Skempton, John, 107–8, 109
Skerries, 2, 11, 17, 96, 112, 280, 286, 292, 294
Skerries Islands, 51
Slane, 245

Smeaton, John, 22, 32, 64, 65, 99, 181, 217
Smith, Florence, 222
Smith, George, 173, 269
Smith, John, 50, 54
Smithfield, 128
Smyth, Edward, 121
Smyth, Revd John, 227
Sonmin, Digory, 32
South Bull, 25, 35, 42, 56
South Bull Wall, 39, 54, 61, 262, 270
South Great George's Street, 230
South Lotts, 24, 86, 126
South Wall, 35, 39, 50, 52, 55, 59, 66, 90, 232
Spatks, Michael, 265
Spear, Richard, 165
Speed, John, 126, 127
Spencer Dock, 3, 26
Sproule, Samuel, 80
Standon, Captain James, 50
Stanhope Street, 202, 231
Stanley, Edward, 217, 221
Steele, William, 32
Stephenson, George, 99, 108
Stephenson, P.J., 142, 143, 144
Stevens, John, 15
Steyn River, 21
Stone Bridge, Thorncastle Street, 69
Stoneybatter, 194, 227
Strand, the, 137, 143, 170, 173, 176
Strand Road, Clontarf, 248
Stratford, Edward, 174
Strongbow, 127
Summerhill, 4, 127, 136, *142*, 143, 154, 159, 176, 178, *186*, 187, 199, 227, 232
Sutton, 11, 46, 64, 92, 131, 178, 232, 251, 254, 268, 274, 282
Sutton Cross, 245
Sutton Strand, 55
Sweetman, Ellen, 251
Sweetman, John, 208
Swift, Jonathan, 49
Swords, 186, 187, 294
Sybil Hill, Raheny, 233
Sydney, Sir Henry, 11

T
Talbot, James, 79
Talbot, Lord, of Malahide, 170, 186, 286
Talbot family, 16
Talbot Street, 168, 199
Tandy, James, 144
Tanel, Franco, 99
Tarmonbarry, 186
Taylor, Alex, 101, 223
Taylor, Captain George, 246

Taylor, John, 101, 223
Teall, Henry, 121
TeBrake, William, 22
Telford, Thomas, 105, 248, 281
Temple Street, 176
Templeogue, 77, 79
Thomas, Philip, 219
Thomas Street, Ringsend, 27, 85, 86, 119, 122
Thorncastle Street, 43, 67, 69, 86, 87, 89
Tolka River, 20, 23, 28, 126, 128, 129, 136, 137, 174, 186, 277, 284, 293
Tomney, John, 211
Toutcher, Richard, 101, 102
Townsend Street (Lazers Hill/Lazy Hill), 17, 91, 115, 208, 225, 231
Tredgold, Thomas, 217
Trinitarian Church, North William Street, *200*
Trinity Church, Gardiner Street, *206*
Trinity College, 14, 17, 21, 103, 159, 161, 185
Trotter, John, 97, 118
Tullamore, 188
Tunstall, Francis, 39, 266
Twomey, Brendan, 128
Tyrone House, 152, 217

U
Upper Abbey Street, 232
Upper Buckingham Street, 88, 128
Upper Dominick Street, 182, 222
Upper Dorset Street, 222
Upper Gardiner Street, 232
Upper Gloucester Street, 143–4
Upper Liffey Street, 142
Upper Sackville Street, 212, 220
USA, *see* America

V
Vallancey, Charles, 51–2, 181, 245, 268
Vavasour, William, 83
Venedy, Jakob, 211, 231
Veredker, Henry, 266, 271, 272, 274
Vernon, John, 11, 45, 128, 132, 149, 218, 247, 279
Vernon Avenue, 45, 223, 279
Vernon estate, 270
Verschoyle, Barbara, 90, 212
Verschoyle, Richard, 87
Verschoyle, Robert, 101
Victoria, Queen, 99
Vignoles, Charles, 106, 111, 280
von Feinaigle, Professor, 175, 176

W
Wade, Patrick, 142
Wallace, William, 137
Walsh, Fintan, 57
Walsh, Matthew, 185
Walsh, William, 164
Waterfall Avenue, 293
Waterford, 16
Watling Street, 39
Watt, James, 99
Weeks, William, 281
Weller, Captain John, 56
Wellington Bridge, *see* Halfpenny Bridge
Wellington Quay, 49, 166
Wentworth, Thomas, 6
Wesley, John, 196, 198
Westland Row, 2, 97, 103, 109, 110, 111, 121, *207*, 208, 214, 233
Westland Row station, 21, *104*
Westminster, 241
Westmorland Bridge (Cross Guns Bridge), 178, 181
Westmorland Lock Hospital, Townsend Street, 115, 118, *118*, 168, 194, 225
Whately, Jane, 116
Whately, Richard, 116
Whitelaw, James, 56
Whitworth Bridge, 163
Whitworth Hospital, 187, 226, 229
Whitworth Road, 185
Whyte, Samuel, 218
Wicklow Head, 51
William of Orange, Prince, 7
Williams, Michael, 145, 146
Williams, Richard, 175
Williams, Thomas, 175
Williamstown, 101, 112
Wilson, William, *82*, 83
Windmill Lane, 22, 26, 27
Wood Quay, 1
Woodhouse, George, 280
Woodhouse, John, 11
Wright, R., 154
Wriothesley, Noel Baptist, 195

Y
Yarranton, Andrew, 12, *13*, 17, 64
Yew, Henry, 247
York Street, 208
Yorkshire, 110
Youghal, 9
Young, Arthur, 26, 145

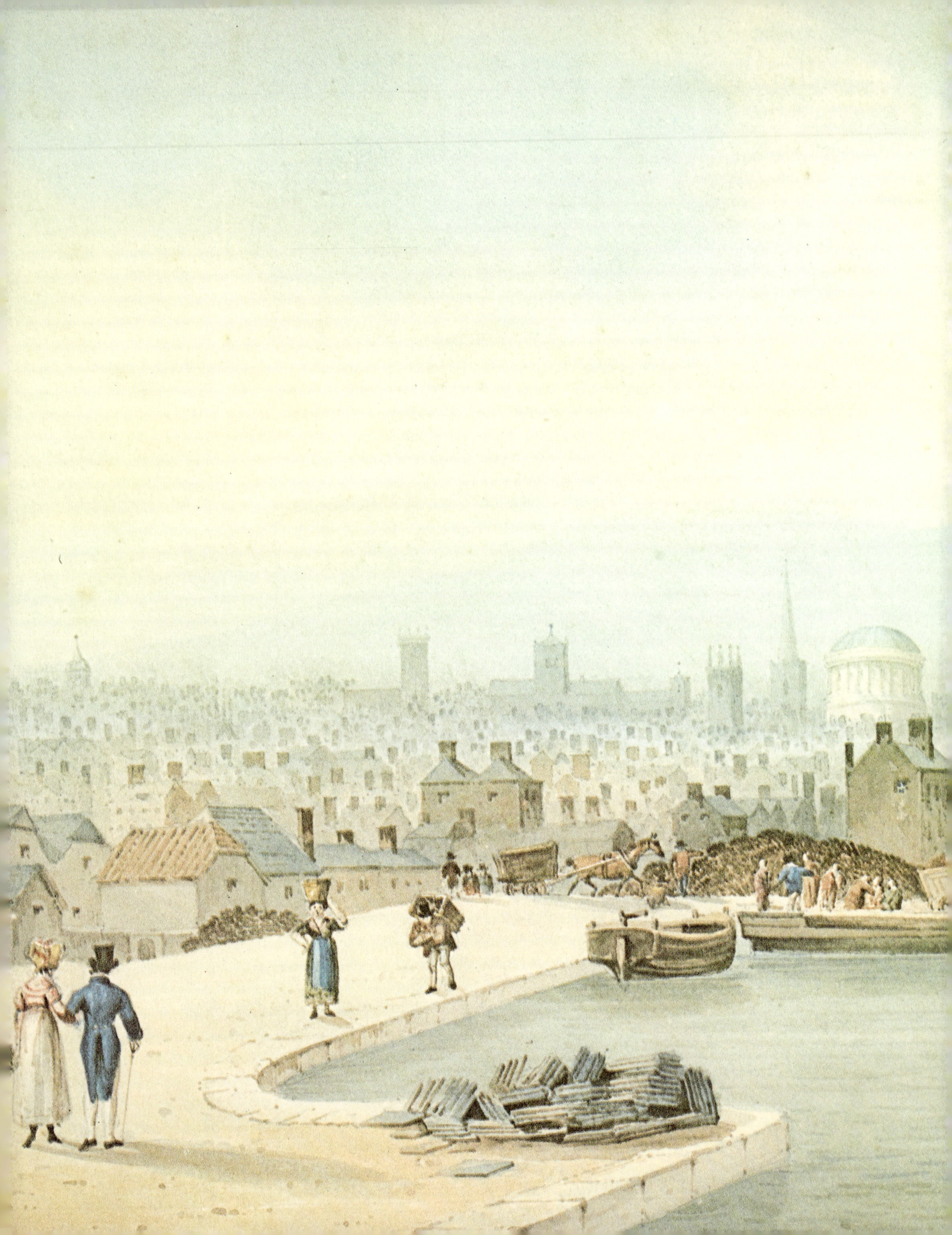